VOYAGES AND TRAVELS
INTO
BRAZIL AND THE EAST-INDIES
1640-1649

The Effigies of Mr. Jn. Vieuhoff.

VOYAGES AND TRAVELS
INTO
BRAZIL AND THE EAST-INDIES
1640-1649

CONTAINING

THE EXACT DESCRIPTION OF THE DUTCH BRAZIL
AND DIVERS PARTS OF THE EAST-INDIES
THEIR PROVINCES, CITIES, LIVING CREATURES AND PRODUCT;
THE MANNERS, CUSTOMS, HABITS AND RELIGION OF THE INHABITANTS

WITH

APARTICULAR ACCOUNT OF ALL THE REMARKABLE PASSAGES
THAT HAPPENED DURING THE AUTHOR'S STAY OF NINE
YEARS IN BRAZIL, ESPECIALLY IN RELATION TO THE
REVOLT OF THE PORTUGUESE AND THE INTESTINE WAR
CARRIED ON THERE FROM 1640 TO 1649

ALSO

AMOST AMPLE DESCRIPTION OF THE MOST
FAMOUS CITY OF BATAVIA IN THE EAST-INDIES
WITH COPPER PLATES

JOHN NIEUHOFF

GYAN

Published by

GYAN

Gyan Publishing House
5, Ansari Road
Daryaganj, New Delhi-110002
Phone: 011-47034999, 9811692060
E-mail: books@gyanbooks.com

Distribution Network
gyanbooks.com
India, USA, Canada, UK, Australia, France

ISBN : 978-81-212-4207-3 (PB)
First Published, London, 1732

2nd Impression 2020

Printed at: Gyan Press, Delhi.

A

COLLECTION

OF

Voyages and Travels,

SOME

Now firſt Printed from *Original Manuſcripts*,

OTHERS

Now firſt Publiſhed in ENGLISH.

In Six VOLUMES.

With a General PREFACE, giving an Account of the Progreſs of NAVIGATION, from its firſt Beginning.

Illuſtrated with a great Number of uſeful Maps and Cuts, Curiouſly Engraven.

VOL. II.

LONDON:

Printed by Aſſignment from Meſſrs. CHURCHILL,

For JOHN WALTHOE, over-againſt the *Royal-Exchange*, in *Cornhill*; THO. WOTTON, at the *Queen's-Head* and *Three Daggers* over-againſt St. *Dunſtan's* Church, in *Fleet-ſtreet*; SAMUEL BIRT, in *Ave-Mary-Lane*, *Ludgate ſtreet*; DANIEL BROWNE, at the *Black-Swan*, without *Temple-Bar*; THOMAS OSBORN, in *Gray's-Inn*; JOHN SHUCKBURGH, at the *Sun*, next the *Inner-Temple-Gate*, in *Fleetſtreet*; and HENRY LINTOT, at the *Croſs-Keys*, againſt St. *Dunſtan's* Church, in *Fleetſtreet*. M DCC XXXII.

Mr. John Nieuhoff's Remarkable
VOYAGES & TRAVELLS into ye
best Provinces of ye West and East Indies.
VOL. II.

A Brasilian

THE
CONTENTS
OF THE
SECOND VOLUME.

Pyrami-

The CONTENTS.

VOYAGES

VOYAGES
AND
TRAVELS
INTO
BRASIL
AND THE
EAST-INDIES.

CONTAINING,

An exact Description of the *DUTCH BRASIL*, and divers Parts of the *EAST-INDIES*; their PROVINCES, CITIES, LIVING CREATURES, and PRODUCTS; the MANNERS, CUSTOMS, HABITS, and RELIGION of the INHABITANTS:

WITH

A particular ACCOUNT of all the remarkable Passages that happened during the Author's stay of nine Years in *BRASIL*; especially in Relation to the REVOLT of the *Portuguese*, and the intestine War carried on there from 1640, to 1649.

AS ALSO

A most ample Description of the most famous City of *BATAVIA* in the *East-Indies*. By Mr. *JOHN NIEUHOFF.*

Both adorned with COPPER PLATES, done after the Life. Translated from the *Dutch* Original.

ADVERTISEMENT to the READER.

IT is about nineteen years since my brother, John Nieuhoff, *just before his second voyage into the* Indies, *presented me with his description of* China, *and certain draughts he had made during his embassy in that empire, which being afterwards published, were soon after translated into six several languages.*

My brother had, before that time, not only been in Brasil, *and several other places in those parts, but also since that time, has had the opportunity of travelling through a great part of* Asia, *till* 1671. *when returning into* Holland, *he brought along with him all his papers, observations, and draughts, he had collected during his voyages; which, though much coveted by all curious persons, yet, for some reasons best known to himself, he did not think fit to commit to publick view.*

But, after his decease, considering with myself, that such useful collections ought not to be buried in oblivion, I thought fit to publish them for the publick good.

As those things which he relates of the revolt of the Portuguese *in* Brasil, *are extracted* verbatim *out of the records kept during my brother's abode of nine years in* Brasil, *under the government of the lords,* Henry Hamel, Peter Bas, *and* Adrian Bullestrate, *and authentick letters; so the truth thereof admits not of the least doubt from unbiass'd persons.*

The vast countries through which my brother travell'd in his life-time, as Brasil, *part of* Persia, Malabar, Madura, Coromandel, Amboyna, Ceylon, Malacca, Sumatra, Java, Tagowan, *and part of* China, *besides many islands, could not in the least infect him with that disease, so incident to travellers, to relate fables instead of histories, it having been his constant practice, to adhere most religiously in all his treatises, to the naked truth, without the least disguise.*

His last voyage to the isle of Madagascar, *where he was lost, I have taken partly out of his own letters, partly out of the journal of captain* Reinard Claeson, *which he brought along with him from thence.*

As to his person, I will only add thus much. He was born at Ussen, *in the earldom of* Benthem, *(where his father, brother, and brother-in-law, were all three Burgomasters) of a good family, the* 22[d] *of* July 1618. *He was a comely person, of a good understanding, good humour'd, and agreeable in conversation; a great admirer of poesy, drawing, and musick: As he delighted in travelling, so he was thereby become master of divers languages: In what station he lived during his abode in* Brasil, *and the* East-Indies, *will best appear by the two following treatises.*

HENRY NIEUHOFF.

Mr. *JOHN NIEUHOFF*'s REMARKABLE VOYAGES AND TRAVELS TO *BRASIL.*

1640. IN the year 1640, I entred into the service of the *West-India* company, and on the 24th of *October*, went in the quality of merchant supercargo, aboard the ship called the *Roebuck*, of 28 guns and 130 men, commanded by *Nicholas Selles* of *Durkendam*. We set sail out of the *Texel* the same day, in company of several other vessels bound for *France*, *Spain* and the *Streights*; and pursued our voyage the 28th with a favourable gale through the channel betwixt *France* and *England*.

His departure out of Holland.

A violent storm.

On the 29th we were overtaken with a most violent tempest, which obliged us to take in all our great sails: It continued from morning to night, when the fury of the winds being somewhat allay'd, we found that we had escaped without any considerable damage; but the sea continued very turbulent all that night. The next day following our seamen catch'd a wood snipe, a wild pidgeon, and several other small birds; which were forc'd into the sea by the violence of the storm.

On the 31st we found ourselves under the 45th degree of northern latitude. The next morning being the first of *November*, some of our seamen catch'd a sea-hog by the means of a harpeon: It was so big, that four men could scarce lift it into the ship. It's taste was not very agreeable, but rankish, which was the reason our men did not catch any more of them, though they swam in vast numbers round about our vessel. By sun-set the wind beginning to encrease, we parted from the other ships, bound for *Spain* and the *Streights*, which were not separated from us in the last storm, steering our course south-west. The 2d and 3d it blew very hard, with thunder and lightning, so that we were forc'd to take in all our great sails, and the ship being very leaky ever since the last tempest, to ply the pump with all our might.

Another most violent storm.

The 4th we found ourselves under the 40 deg. 30 min. when about midnight the wind encreased with so much violence, that the air which surrounded us, appearing no otherwise than one continual fire, occasion'd by the lightning, which scarce ever ceas'd all that night. During this calamity we perceived certain small fires or lights fix'd to the mast: They are called *Peaceable's fires* by the seamen. These fires are suppos'd to be certain sulphureous vapours, forc'd by the violence of the winds from the shore into the sea, where being lightned by the violent agitation of the air, they burn till their oily substance be consumed. The seamen look upon them as a good omen, that the storm is going to abate; which prov'd true in effect, the fury of the winds beginning to allay from that

Wild-fire.

that time; and we had the good fortune to discover two leaks near our forecastle, which else might have prov'd of dangerous consequence.

They pass the Barrels.

The 5th we pass'd the *Barrels*, under the 39th degree; where according to an antient custom, every one, of what quality or degree soever, that has not passed there before, is obliged to be baptized, or redeem himself from it. He that is to be baptized, has a rope tied round his middle, wherewith he is drawn up to the very top of the bowsprit, and from thence three times successively tumbled into the water. There were some who look'd very blank upon the Matter, but others went cheerfully about it, and for a measure of *Spanish* wine, suffered themselves to be rebaptized for the master and the merchant. But this custom is abolished of late years, by special orders from the governors of the company, to avoid broils and quarrels, which used often to arise upon this occasion.

They discover two Turkish *vessels.*

Prepare for an engagement.

The 6th, as we were steering our course *S. S. W.* with a fresh gale, we descried two vessels, making all the sail they could towards us, whom we supposed to be *Turkish* pirates (as indeed they proved afterwards) it was resolved to defend us till the utmost extremity. Accordingly orders were given to clear every thing upon the deck, and to furnish the seamen with musquets, hangers, pikes, and other such like weapons. Every one having taken his station, we put up the bloody flag, and expected their coming under the sound of our trumpets. The master of the ship, being all that time very ill of some wounds he had received formerly, which were now broken up afresh; and the commissary *Francis Zweers*, not being in a condition, by reason of his great age, to remain upon deck, I was fain to undertake the whole management of the ship, and encouraged them to fight bravely for their lives and liberty, ordering them not to fire at all, till they were in their full reach, they being much better mann'd than we.

An engagement with two Turkish *rovers.*

About noon we saw the *Turks* make up towards us with orange-colour'd flags, which however they soon after changed for the bloody flags, and the biggest of them saluted us with two cannon shot out of his forecastle, without doing us the least harm, but the second time almost shot our foremast in pieces. In the mean while we were come so near to one another, that we sent them a good broadside into their ship, which the *Turks* repay'd us immediately; but it was not long before we observ'd the biggest of the two had received a shot betwixt wind and water, which made her keep at some farther distance, till she had repaired her damage, which gave me opportunity to encourage our people with words, and a good proportion of wine; which they mix'd with some gunpowder, and I, to please them, followed their example.

By this time they returned both to the charge, and saluted us so fiercely with their cannon and small shot, that they took away the roof of our great cabin, and did us some damage in our rigging. I then changed my scimeter for a musquet, and discharged continually upon the enemy, and I found myself sore several weeks after, by the hurt I received from a musquet of one that stood hard by me, which being by a cannon ball forced out of his hands against my body, I fell down stretch'd all along upon the deck, without sense or motion; but having after some time recovered myself, I returned to my post. I then perceived the captain of the biggest *Turkish* ship with a turbant on his head, in the stern, encouraging his men, which made me order those about me, to aim at him with their small shot, which, as I suppose, succeeded according to our hopes, it being not long before we lost sight of him. Notwithstanding this, the heat of the fight encreased on both sides, many broadsides passing betwixt us, accompanied with most dreadful outcries and lamentations of the wounded on both sides. However, the *Turks* durst not attempt to board us; whether it were that they thought us better mann'd than really we were, or that they feared we would set fire to the ship, which we threatned we would, shewing them a match ready for that purpose. They answered us in *Dutch*, that they would not part with us upon those terms; yet was it not long before we saw them make away from us, having received many shots thro' their ships; and we with a brisk gale, made all the sail we could to be rid of these unwelcome guests, steering a quite different course, which with the advantage of the darkness of the night, brought us quite out of sight of them by next morning.

The Turks *leave the fight.*

We gave thanks to God for his having delivered us from the danger of slavery, and crowning our endeavours with success against an enemy much stronger than us, the biggest of them carrying twenty-four guns, and the other two; whereas we had no more than eighteen, besides that they were much better mann'd than we. After having taken a view of our ship, and found it sound under water, we betook ourselves to repair the damage we had received during the fight; but whilst we were busy in this work, we were on the 7th surprized by so violent a storm, that we were forced to take

1640. take in all our sails. This put us to a great nonplus, but by good fortune the storm blew soon over, when orders were given to give an Allowance of three pounds and a half of bisket *per* week to the seamen, all our other bread being become musty by that time. The 10th we found ourselves under the 39th deg. and 30 min. about 20 leagues off of the *Canary Islands*; here we discovered the pike of *Tenariff*, being two leagues and a half high, and accounted the highest mountain in the world. It may be discovered at 60 leagues distance from the shore. Thus we continued our voyage till the 14th, without any memorable accident, when we passed the tropick of *Cancer*. About noon we were overtaken by another storm, which made us take in most of our great sails, for fear of the worst, but it lasted not long.

This tract of the sea is called by the *Dutch*, the *Kroos Sea*; by the *Portuguese*, *Mar del Aragaco* (or *Largaco*, or *Suargaco*) i. e. *The Sea of Ducks-meat*, because hereabouts, *viz.* from the 18th to the 30th degree, or as some will have it, from the 20th to the 22d and 23d degree of northern latitude, it is found in great quantity, and carried along with the stream: Its leaves are of a pale green colour, like that of parrots, small, thin and carved at the end. It bears berries of the same colour, about the bigness of a pepper corn, that are quite hollow, without any seed within or taste. It is sometimes so closely twisted together, that it stops a ship in its full course; tho' we had the good fortune to pass thro' it without much difficulty, being then about 400 leagues from the coast of *Africk*, where are no islands nor anchorage. It may be pickled with salt and pepper, and used like as we do capers, being accounted a good remedy against the gravel. It is generally found without roots, having only a few thin sprouts, which, as it is supposed, take root in the sandy grounds of the sea; tho' others are of opinion, that it is carried by the violence of the stream from the islands into the sea.

The 18th, one of our ships crew died, who was the next day thrown overboard, at which time I observed, what indeed I had heard often before, that the dead carcasses always float with their heads to the east at sea.

Travado, *what.* The 22d we were overtaken by another tempest, called *Travado*, which with horrible thunder and lightning surprizes the ships so suddenly, that they have scarce leisure to take in their sails, and sometimes returns three times in an hour. We catch'd here abundance of fish, such as *Bonytes* of ten foot long, and *Korets*, and a great lamprey, which we had enough to do to bring aboard; we only took out the brains, being look'd upon as a sovereign remedy against the stone in the bladder, the flesh being of an oily taste.

They catch abundance of fish.

The 24th we saw great quantities of small birds about our vessel, and catch'd one not unlike a crane, but somewhat smaller, it being a very fair day.

The 26th, being under the fifth degree, 47 minutes, we were so becalmed that we could not perceive the ship to move, and spent our time in catching of fish, of which we had such plenty, that we chose only the best for our eating; among the rest we met with a fish called the *king's-fish*: For by reason of the impenetrable depth of the sea in this place, the waters are so clear and transparent in still weather, that you may see the fish in vast numbers swimming near two feet deep; so that you need but fasten a crooked nail or any thing else like a hook to a string, and hanging it in the sea, you may catch as many fish as you please. This calm was followed by a most violent storm of rain.

The 30th we found ourselves under the fourth degree, 41 minutes, where we saw abundance of *flying fish*.

The 3d of *December* we came under the first degree, 30 minutes, where we met with millions of fish, and did catch as many as we thought fit: Some we put in salt, others we rubbed in the belly with pepper and salt, and hung them up by the tail in the sun.

The 4th, by break of day, being very clear weather, we saw the island of *St. Paulo*, as it is called by the *Portuguese*, which at a distance represents a sail, which as you approach nearer to it, proves five high rocks. About noon we found ourselves at 53 minutes of northern latitude, taking our course five leagues to the west. Here at several times we catch'd some sea-gulls; those birds make a shew as if they would bite you, but remain unmoveable in the place, till they are caught or kill'd.

They discover the island of St. Paulo.

The 5th, about eleven a clock we passed the equinoctial line, so that in the afternoon we found ourselves at five minutes southern latitude, where we had but little reason to complain of cold; it being often so calm here, that ships are forced to spend a considerable time in passing this tract. It is extreamly hot here, and great scarcity of good and sweet water, the rain water being not wholesome, but causing the scurvy, by reason of its being corrupted by the violent heat of sun.

About three years after my arrival in *Brasil*, a certan *Portuguese* ship was found adrift under the equinoctial line, without

1643.

They pass the Equinoctial Line.

any living creature in it, which according to the journal, had been six whole weeks under the line. We had a very good passage, and catched abundance of fish, and among the rest a certain fish called the *Blower*, which swallow a considerable quantity of water in their guts, and then at once spout it forth again. They will follow the ships for a long time.

The 8th we passed by the isle called *Ilha Ferdinando* of *Neronha*; it being very serene weather, we saw vast numbers of birds, and whole shoals of flying fish, which were followed by the *Bonytes* and *Korets*.

The Isle of Ferdinando.

The island of *Ferdinando* of *Neronha*, situate under the fourth degree of southern latitude, about fifty leagues from the coast of *Brasil*, was about the year 1630. inhabited by the *Dutch*, but by reason of the vast numbers of rats, which consumed all the fruits of the earth, deserted by them a few years after; it being otherwise a very fruitful island, and abounding with fish, the inhabitants of *Reeief* being used to send their fisherboats thither, which return commonly well freighted with fish. The council of *Brasil* did afterwards send a certain number of negroes thither, under the conduct of one *Gellis Vepant*, to cultivate the ground for their subsistence, who likewise stayed there for some time. About a year and a half after, the council of justice banished several malefactors into that island, who being furnished with necessary instruments for cultivating the ground, were forced to seek for their sustenance there.

The 11th at night we found ourselves under the seventh degree, over against the province of *Goyana*, about twenty leagues on this side of *Olinda*; with break of day we saw the shore of *Brasil*, but kept out at sea till it was broad day.

The 12th it was very foggy, and we kept our course with fair wind and water all along the coast, and arrived before noon safely near the *Recief*, where we cast our anchor at several fathoms depth, after we had spent seven weeks and one day in the voyage.

Their Arrival in Brasil.

After we had returned our thanks to God for his deliverance from the dangers of the sea, and slavery of the *Turks*; I went ashore the same night with the master and commissary in a boat, to notify our happy arrival, and to deliver a letter to count *Maurice*, and the governor of the council. I continued ashore that night, but returned aboard the next day. And,

The 15th the pilots conducted our vessel into the harbour of the *Recief*, where we found twenty-eight vessels and two yachts lying behind the *Water Castel*.

1643.

Towards the latter end of *August* 1643, I received orders from the council to sail with the yacht called the *Sea-Hog*, loaden with fullers-earth to the isle of St. *Thomas*, to exchange it for black sugar, this being the chief commodity transported from thence. My voyage proved fortunate enough, not meeting with any sinister accident, except with a violent tempest of thunder, lightning, and rains, and came the 9th of *September* at an anchor there; the cargoe did bear no good price, yet after a stay of fourteen days, I returned with a cargoe of black sugar to *Brasil*, where I arrived the 3d of *October* before the *Recief*, after a voyage of near three months. 1643.

The Island of St. Thomas.

The isle of St. *Thomas* is of a circular figure, about thirty-six leagues in compass; the high mountains in the midst of that island are always covered with snow, notwithstanding that in the low grounds, by reason of its situation under the line, it is excessive hot. It is very fertile in black sugar and ginger; the sugar-fields being continually moistned by the melted snow that falls down from the mountains. There were at that time above sixty sugar mills there, but the air is the most unwholsome in the world, no foreigner daring to stay so much as one night ashore, without running the hazard of his life; because by the heat of the sun beams such venomous vapours are drawn from the earth, as are unsupportable to strangers. This fog continues till about ten a clock in the morning, when the same is dispersed; and the air cleared, which made us always stay aboard till after that time. This mist is not observed at sea.

The air here is very hot and moist throughout the year, except in the summer about *June*, when the south-east and south-west winds abate much of the heat of the climate. The vapours drawn up by the sun, occasion certain epidemical intermittent fevers, which carry off the patient in a few days, with excessive pains in the head, and violent torments in the bowels; though some attribute it to the immoderate use of women, and of the juice of *Coco's*. Certain is it, that among a hundred foreigners, scarce ten escape with life, and those seldom live till fifty years of age; though some of the inhabitants, as likewise the negroes (who are all lousy here) live to a great age. Its first inhabitants were *Jews*, banished out of *Portugal*; they are of a very odd complexion. Among the mountains dwell abundance of negroes, who are run away from the *Portuguese*, and make sometimes excursions to the very gates of the city of *Pavaosa*. It is almost next to a miracle, that any people should inhabit so unwholsome a climate; but that the hopes of lucre makes all danger easy.

The city of *Pavaosa*, belonging to this island

Betwixt pag. 6, 7.

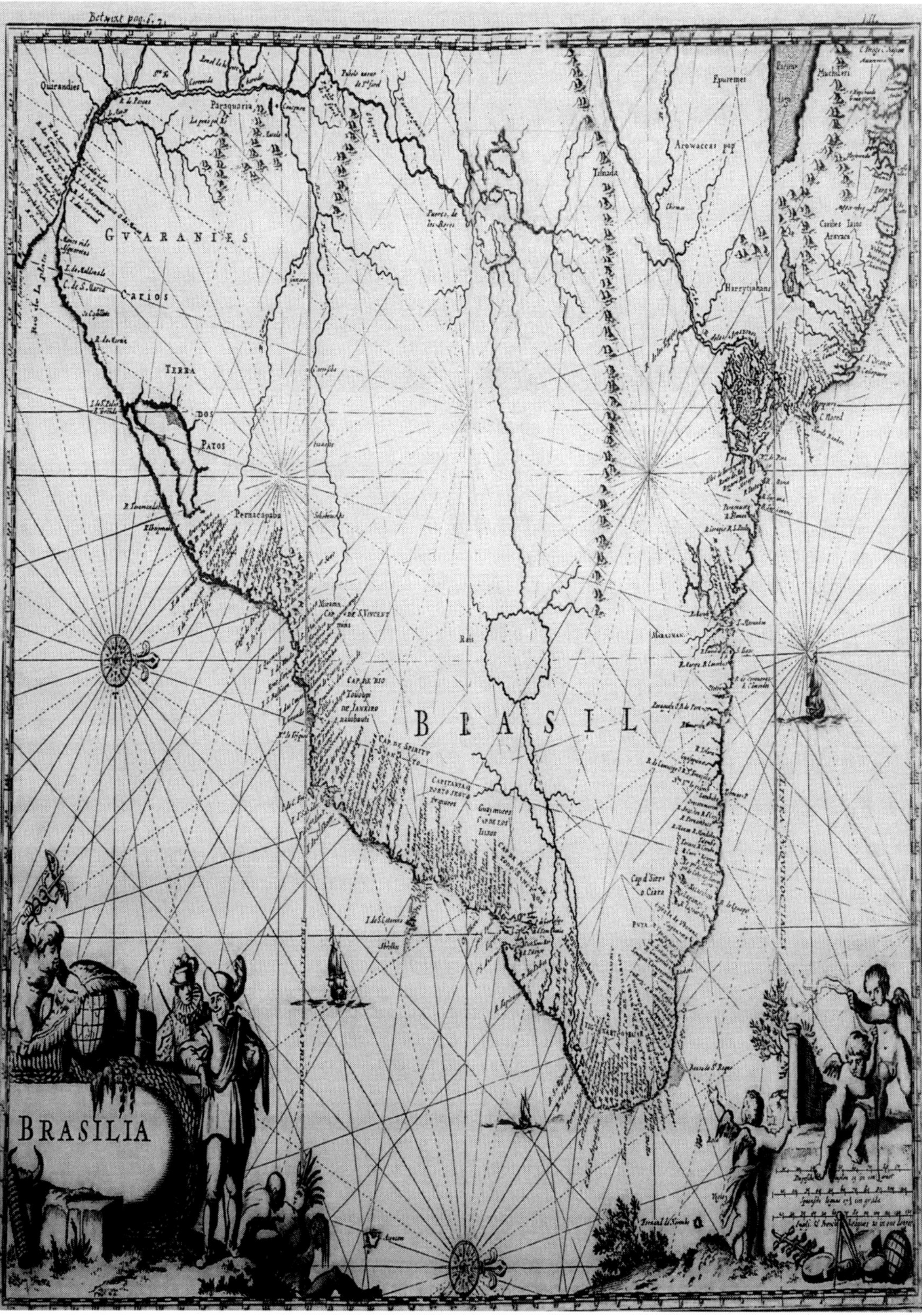

1643. island, is situate upon a rivulet; it contains about eight hundred houses, and three churches. This city, as well as the whole island, was 1641, *October* 16, conquered by the admiral *Cornelius Tol*, after a siege of forty days, without any considerable loss; but both he and his lieutenant, as well as several other commanders and many seamen, were swept away by this pestilential air; and of three hundred *Brasilians*, not above sixty escaped with life.

But, before I proceed to give you an account of all the remarkable passages that happened in *Brasil*, since the revolt of the *Portuguese*, and during my stay of eight years there; it will not be amiss to insert a short description of this countrey.

A description of Brasil.

America (or the *West-Indies*) is divided into the *northern* and *southern America*. *Brasil* is part of the last.

The *northern America* borders to the *North* upon the *Terra incognita*, or rather upon *Hudson's Streights*; to the *South* and *West* upon the *South-Sea*, and to the *East* upon the streights of *Panama*, the bay of *Mexico*, or *Nieu Spain*, and the *North-Sea*.

It comprehends the following provinces, *Estotiland* and *Labrador*, *Nieu France*, *Canada*, *Bakalaos*, *Nieu England*, *Virginia*, *Florida*, *Nieu Spain*, the provinces of *Mexico*, *Nieu Mexico*, *Tlaskalla*, *Guaxaka*, *Mechoakana*, *Zakatula*, *Kolim*, *Yukatan*, *Tabasko*, *Nieu Gallicia*, *Nieu Biscay*, *Chiametla*, *Kuliaka*, *Cimalon*, *Nieu Granada*, *Kalifornia*, *Anian*, *Quivira* or *Nieu Albion*, *Konibas*, *Guatemala*, *Sokonusko*, *Chiapa*, *Vera pas*, *Honduras*, *Nikaragua*, *Kostarika*, and *Veragua*.

The *southern America* is a demi-island in form of a pyramid; the basis of which lies to the *North*, the point extends to the streights of *Magellan*, under the 53^d degree of southern latitude; bordering to the east upon the *Atlantick Ocean*, or *North-Sea*, and to the west upon the *South-Sea*, its whole circuit being of about four thousand *Italian* or one thousand *German* miles. It contains the provinces of *Kastilla d'Or*, *Tierra fierma*, called by the *Portuguese*, *Paria*, *Kumana*, *Karibana*, *Brasil*, *Chika* to the east, to the west *Popayan*, *Peru*, *Chili*, besides several inland provinces.

First Discovery of Brasil. *Brasil* was first discovered by *Pedro Alvaro Kapralis*, a *Portuguese*, sometime before *Americus Vesputius*, viz. in the year 1500. He gave it the name of *Santa Cruz*, which was afterwards by the *Portuguese* changed into that of *Brasil*, from the wood of the same name, which is found there in great quantity, and from thence transported into all parts of *Europe*, for the use of the dyers. 1643.

It is situate in the midst of the *Torrid Zone*, extending to the *Tropick* of *Cancer* and the *Temperate Zone*. *Its Situation.*

Concerning its extent from *north to south*, there is no small difference among the geographers; but according to the best computations, its beginning may be fixed under the second degree and a half of northern latitude, near the river *Para*, and its end under the twenty-fourth degree and a half of southern latitude, to the river *Capibari*, two leagues above the city of St. *Vincent*; so that its whole extent from north to south, comprehends twenty-five degrees, or three hundred seventy-five leagues; some place *Brasil* betwixt the river of *Maranhaen* and *Rio de la Plata*. The extent of *Brasil* from the east (where it borders upon the *North-Sea*) to the west, is not determined hitherto, there being very few who have penetrated so deep into the countrey; tho' its bigness from east to west may be computed to be seven hundred forty-two leagues; there are however some who extend its limits farther to the east, and to the west as far as *Peru* or *Guiana*, which makes an addition of one hundred eighty-eight leagues. Some make the boundaries of *Brasil* to the north the river of the *Amazons*; to the south *Rio de la Plata*; to the east the *North-Sea*, and to the west the mountains of *Peru* or *Guiana*. *Extent.*

Brasil thus limited, is divided by the *Portuguese* into fourteen districts, called by them *Kapitanias*, or Captainships; *viz. Paria*, the first of all towards the north; *Maranhaon*, *Siara*, *Potigi* or *Rio Grande*, *Paraiba*, *Parnambuko*, *Tarmarika* or *Itamarika*, *Seregippo del Rey*, *Quirimune* or *Bahia dos todos los Santos*, *Nhoe-Kombe*, or *os Ilhos*, *Pakata*, or *Porto Securo*, *Rio de Janeiro* or *Nheteroya*, *St. Vincent* and *Espiritu St.* *Its Division.*

Whilst part of *Brasil* was in our possession, it might conveniently be divided into the *Dutch* and *Portuguese Brasil*. Each of these captainships is watered by some considerable river or other, besides several others of less note; most of these have very rapid currents in the rainy months, and overflow the adjacent countrey.

The river of St. *Francis*, the largest and most considerable in those parts, is the common boundary of the captainship of *Parnambuko* and *Bahia dos todos los Santos*, or the *Bay of all Saints*. In some places it is so broad, that a six-pounder can scarce reach over it, and its depth is eight, twelve, and sometimes fifteen yards; but it admits of no Ships of burthen, because its Entrance is choak'd up with sands. *The River of St. Francis.*

Its first spring is said to arise out of a certain

1643. certain lake, which being augmented by many rivelets out of the mountains of *Peru*, but especially by the rivers of *Rio de la Plata* and *Maranhaon* exonerates it self into the sea. Some of our people went in a shallop near forty leagues up the river, and found it of a good depth and pretty broad. If we may believe the *Portuguese*, there are about fifty leagues from the sea, certain impassable cataracts or water-falls, called by them *Kakocras*; beyond those the river winds to the north, 'till you come to its source in the lake, in which are many pleasant islands, inhabited by the barbarians; as is likewise the shore round about it. They find good store of gold-dust in this lake, but it is none of the best, being carried thither by the many rivulets, which wash the gold-bearing rocks of *Peru*; here is also most excellent salt-petre.

It is observable, that in the summer and and those winter months, when it rains but seldom, this river has more water than in the rain season: The reason alledged for it is, the vast distance from its first source, whether the rains that fall from the mountains must first be convey'd by many rivulets: All the other rivers near the *Receif*, are so empty of water during the summer season, that they are rendred quite unnavigable. But the ridges of mountains which lie not far from the sea-shore, exonerate their waters as well here as in *Peru*, backward to the west, and dividing themselves into two branches; the first runs into the north, and joins with the large and most rapid rivers of *Maranhaon*, and of the *Amazons*; the other with the rivers of St. *Francis de la Plata*, and *Janeiro*. The waters of these rivers being considerably encreased by many rivulets, they exonerate themselves with so much violence into the sea, that the seamen meet often with fresh water at a considerable distance at sea.

The increase of the waters in this river, during the dry season, may likewise be attributed to the vast quantity of snow among the mountains, which being melted by the heat of the sun, occasions the river to transgress its ordinary bounds; which in this point is quite different from other rivers, which commonly in the winter time over-flow their banks.

The Dutch Brasil.

Six of those *captainships* were under the jurisdiction of the *West-India* company, before the *Portuguese* revolted from the *Dutch*, which they had conquer'd with their Swords, *viz.* The *captainship*, (it begins on the south-side) *Seregippe del Rey* of *Parnambuko*, *Itamarika*, unto which belongs *Gauiana*, *Paraiba*, *Potigi* or *Rio Grande* and *Siara* or *Ciara*. The *captainship* of *Maranhaon* was 1644, by special command of the company, left by the *Dutch*. This part of *Brasil* used to be called by the *Portuguese*, the *Northern-Brasil*, as the other remaining in their possession went by the name of *South-Brasil*. 1643.

The six *Dutch captainships* did extend all along the sea coast from north to south, in length about a hundred and sixty or a hundred and eighty leagues; for from *Rio Grande*, to the northern border of *Seregippe del Rey*, is a hundred leagues: The two others, *viz.* that of *Siara* to the north, and *Seregippe del Rey* to the south, make up the rest. Each of these *captainships* contain several other lesser districts, call'd by the *Portuguese Fregesias*, and by us *Fregesien*; as for instance, in *Seregippe del Rey*, are *Pojuka*, *Kameragibi*, *Porto Calvo*, *Serinhaim*, and several others. *Fregasie*, comprehends a certract of ground, composed of divers villages, rivers, hills and vallies, betwixt each of which is commonly a tract of barren hills, of about three or four leagues in length. Most of the *Dutch captainships*, are but indifferently cultivated, because the *Portuguese* used not to manure the ground in those parts, beyond three or four, or at farthest, five leagues distant from the Sea.

Seregippe del Rey

The *captainship* of *Seregippe del Rey*, is likewise called *Carigi*, from a certain small lake of that name; it is situate in the southern part of *Brasil*, extending about thirty two leagues along the sea coast, bordering on the north side, upon the river of St. *Francis*, by which it is divided from *Parnambuko*; as on the south side it is separated by *Rio Real*, from *Bahia dos todos los Santos*. *Seregippe del Rey*, has among others, a certain *Fregasie*, called *Porto Calvo*, situated betwixt the 9th and the 10th degree of southern latitude; being encompassed on the north-west side by the *Fregasie* of *Serinhaim*, and the small river of *Pirasenunga*, extending to the south as far as the river *Parepuera*, by which it is divided from the *Fregasie* of *Alagoasi*, containing in all about twelve leagues in length near the sea shore, its bounds on the land side reaching to the unpassable woods.

The village of Bon Successo de Porto Cal

In this *Fregasie*, is a village call'd by the *Portuguese*, *Villa de bon successo de Porto Calo*, but was formerly called *Portocano Dos quatros Rios*, it being situate at the confluence of the four rivers, *Maleita*, *Tapamunde*, *Commentabunda* and *Monguaba*. It is built upon a rising ground, about four leagues from the sea shore, and by the *Dutch* strengthened with two forts; the biggest of which was called *Bon Successo*, being built all of stone, surrounded with a good counterscarp, with a large bason for fresh water within. The other fort was called by us, the *New-Church*, being created out of the ruins

1643. ruins of an old church, called by the *Portuguese*, *Nossa Senhora de Presentacao*. Betwixt both these forts, a third was ordered to be erected by count *Maurice*, upon the banks of the river, but it lying within the reach of musket-shot from the mountains, was not brought to perfection.

The village has two streets, the chief of which runs parallel with the river, from one fort to the other, and is call'd *St. Joseph's-street*; it contain'd no more than three houses of one story high, and about thirty six others cover'd with pantiles, being only built upon the ground. The *Portuguese* have in lieu of their churches, which are demolished, when the fortifications were erected, built themselves another on the other side of the river, where they sometimes hear mass. The village is situate in a most pleasant and wholesome air, being cooled by the continual breezes from the sea, which are not stopp'd by any hills, betwixt them and the shore. In the night time they enjoy the benefit of the land wind, which drives the cool vapours arising from the neighbouring rivers thither: Formerly there was a certain town called *Seregippe del Rey*, somewhat higher up the river, in a very barren place, of a considerable bigness, and well built, with three goodly churches, and a monastery belonging to the *Franciscans*, but without any fortifications. Above this town you see a chapel dedicated to St. *Christopher*, whether the *Roman Catholicks* come on pilgrimage.

This *captainship* was first of all reduced under the obedience of the *Portuguese* or *Spaniards*, by *Christovan de Barros*; who for this his good service, had all the lands betwixt the small lake of *Seregippe* and *St. Francisco*, granted to him, with full power to settle colonies there within a limited time. This drew many of the inhabitants of the *Bay of all Saints* thither; who within a few years after laid the foundations of this town, by erecting four sugar-mills, and building about a hundred houses, with four hundred stables for their cattle. But this town, with all the circumjacent houses, was 1637, the 24th of *December*, laid desolate by our people, the inhabitants retiring to the *Bay of all Saints*. For the *Spanish* general *Benjola* being, 1637, posted with a body of two thousand men near that place, did with ravaging and burning, considerable damage to our colonies, which oblig'd count *Maurice* to dislodge him from thence; but being then sick of an ague, he committed this expedition to the charge of colonel *Schoppe*; for which purpose having gather'd a body of two thousand three hundred men, besides four hundred *Brasilians*, and two hundred and fifty seamen out of the the adjacent Places, near the river of *St. Francis*, *Alagoas*, the *Cape of St. Austin*, out of the *Receif* and *Moribeka*, and given him for his assistant Mr. *John van Giesselen*, a member of the great council, he commanded the *Dutch* admiral *Lichthart*, to cruise with his fleet near the *Bay of all Saints*, thereby to draw the enemy out of his advantageous post to the sea-shoar. The *Spanish* general had no sooner notice of our passing the river, but fearing to be enclosed betwixt us and the fleet, march'd with his body to *Torre Garcie de Avila*, a place about fourteen leagues to the north of the city of *St. Salvador*. 1643.

The *Dutch* general *Schoppe*, hearing of his removal, immediately attack'd the place, which he laid desolate, and returned with incredible swiftness to the south side of the river of *St. Francis*.

Here he intrench'd himself, with an intention to annoy the enemy, by cutting off his provisions, and driving away his cattle; which succeeded so well, that we kill'd above three thousand of their horned beasts, besides what was carried away on the other side of the river; so that what was left by the soldiers, was by the inhabitants carried to the *Bay of all Saints*; from whence it is evident, what vast numbers of cattle this countrey did produce at that time.

The great council took once a resolution to re-people that part of the countrey, and agreed for this purpose with *Nunno Olferdi*, councellor of justice in the *Receif*, who found means to settle several families there: But the council of nineteen disapproving the matter, it was laid aside.

In the year 1641, count *Maurice* reduced this place under the obedience of the *West-India* company, erected a fort there, and surrounded the town *Seregippe del Rey* with a ditch. It lies upon a small river, betwixt *St. Francisco* and *Real*, which however at spring-tide has fourteen foot water or thereabouts. Within the jurisdiction of this *captainship*, is the mountain of *Tabayna*; from whence several sorts of valuable oar was presented to the council of nineteen; but upon proof was found not worth farther looking after.

The captainship *of* Parnambuko.

The *captainship* of *Parnambuko*, is one of the chiefest and biggest of the *Dutch-Brasil*. It extends above sixty leagues along the coast, betwixt the river of *St. Francis*, and the captainship of *Tamarika*. *Parnambuko* properly denotes the entrance of the harbour, which by reason of the many rocks and shelves hidden under water, was called by the *Portuguese*, *Inferno Bokko*, and

1643. broken *Parnambuko*, or the *Mouth of Hell*. It is subdivided into eleven lesser districts, inhabited by the *Portuguese*, viz. the city of *Olinda*, *Garazu*, *Receif*, *Moribeka*, *St. Anthony*, *Poyuka*, *Serinhaim*, *Consalvi d'Una*, *Porto Calvo*, the *Northern Alagoa*, and the *Southern Alagoa*. Among which *Olinda* and *Garazu* were the chiefest.

Eleven towns and villages of Parnambuko.

Garazu. The town, or rather the village of *Garazu*, lies at some distance from the shoar, over against the Island of *Tamarika*, upon a river of the same name, about five leagues from *Olinda*. It was formerly inhabited by *Portuguese* handicrafts men, but since our taking of *Olinda*, several rich Families settled there; we became masters of the place 1633, in *May*.

Moribeka. *Moribeka* lies deeper into the countrey, more to the south, about five leagues off of the *Receif*.

St. Anthony. *St. Anthony* is about seven or eight leagues distant from the *Receif* to the south, near the *Cape of St. Austin*.

Poyuka. The city of *St. Michael de Poyuka*, lies about ten leagues to the south of the *Receif* upon a river of the same name, which disembogues in the sea, on the south side of the *Cape of St. Austin*. It was formerly a very populous place; and had thirteen sugar-mills.

Serinhaim. The village *Serinhaim*, much about the same distance thence with the former, is a very pleasant place, has twelve sugar-mills, each of which produces six or seven hundred *Aroba's*, an *Aroba* making about twenty seven or twenty eight pound weight.

Gonsalvi d'Una. The village of *Gonsalvi d'Una*, lies twenty leagues from the *Receif*; it has five sugar-mills.

Porto Calvo. The village called *Porto Calvo*, is twenty leagues distant from the *Receif*; it has seven or eight sugar-mills. Here is the castle of *Porocano*, which was not conquer'd by us, till under the government of count *Maurice*.

The towns of the northern and southern *Alagoa's*, are forty leagues from the *Receif*.

Within the district of *Parnambuko*, are two woods, called by the *Portugueses* the *greater* and *lesser Palmairas*, or *Palmtree-Woods*.

The two Palmairas. The *Lesser Palmairas*, which is inhabited by six thousand negroes, lies about twenty leagues above the *Alagoas*, being enclosed with woods near the small lake of *Guagohuhi*, which exonerates it self into the great lake of *Parayba*, six leagues from thence to the north, about four leagues from the lake *Meridai*, to the south of the *Northern Alagoa*, being near that point of land commonly called *Jaragoa*. The village consists of three streets, each near half a league in length. Their huts are made of straw twisted together, one near another, their plantations being behind. They retain something of the religious worship of the *Portuguese*, but have their peculiar priests and judges. Their business is to rob the *Portuguese* of their slaves, who remain in slavery among them, 'till they have redeemed themselves by stealing another: But such slaves as run over to them, are as free as the rest. Their food is dates, beans, meal, barley, sugar-canes, tame-fowl, (of which they have great plenty) and fish, which the lake furnishes them withal. They have twice a year a harvest of barley, which being over, they make merry for a whole Week together. Before sowing time, they light great fires for fourteen days, which may be seen at a great distance. The shortest way from the *Receif* to this *Palmairas*, is along the lake of the *Northern Alago*. 1643.

The greater *Palmairas* is betwixt twenty and thirty leagues distant behind the village of St. *Amar*, near the mountain of *Bebe*, being surrounded with a double enclosure. About eight thousand Negroes are said to inhabit the Vallies near the mountains, besides many others, who dwell in lesser numbers of fifty or a hundred, in other places. Their houses lie straggling, they sow and reap among the woods, and have certain caves whither they retreat in case of necessity. They dress their victuals in the day time, and at night tell over their whole number, to see whether any be wanting; if not, they conclude the evening with dancing and beating the drum, which may be heard at a great distance. Then they go to sleep 'till nine or ten a clock the next day. During the dry season, they detach a certain number among them, to steal slaves from the *Portuguese*. The shortest cut to their habitations, is from the *Alagoas* through St. *Amar*, and so cross the plains of *Nhumahu* and *Kororipe*, towards the backside of the mountain of *Warrakaka*, 'till you come to the lake *Paraiba*; along which you pass 'till you reach the mountain *Bebe*, from whence you go directly into the vallies. Under the Government of Count *Maurice*, the negroes of this *Palmairas* did considerable mischief, especially to the country people about the *Alagoas*; to repress which, he sent three hundred firelocks, a hundred *Mamelukes*, and seven hundred *Brasilians*.

The Receif, Maurice's *town, and* Anthony Vaez.

The *Receif* is, by reason of its commodious and advantagious situation the strong- *The* Receif.

est

1643. eſt place of all *Braſil*; beſides that, it is ſtrengthened and defended by ſeveral adjacent Forts: But to give you the moſt commodious view both of the *Receif*, and the ſituation of *Maurice*'s town, it is to be obſerved, that the whole coaſt of *Braſil*, is from one end to the other ſurrounded with a long, thick, and flat ridge of rocks, which in ſome Places is twenty, and in others thirty paces broad: However, there are certain paſſages in this ridge, through which the ſhips approach the ſhoar, and ſome few places, where this ridge is not found at all. Thus a league on this ſide *Rio dolee*, two leagues on the northſide of the city of *Olinda*, there is nothing of this ridge to be found; but begins again near *Poumarelle* or *Soxamardo*, and extends to the iſle of *Itamarika*. Betwixt the ridge and the continent, you may paſs in boats at high water; for at low-tide moſt of thoſe rocks appear above water; tho' the tide never fails to cover the ſame. The rock overagainſt the *Receif* of *Parnambuko*, is between twenty and thirty paces broad, being not only at ſpring-tides, but at all other tides overflown by the ſea; it is there-abouts very flat, without any prominencies, and extends for a league from ſouth to north. On the north point is an open Paſſage for ſhips to approach the ſhoar, lying five hundred paces further to the north, than the *Receif* it ſelf. It is but narrow, and at ſpring-tide not above twenty two foot deep. 1643.

The ſtone ridge round the coaſt of Braſil.

Betwixt this rocky ridge and the continent, there is a ſandy ridge, or ſmall iſland extended to the ſouth from *Olinda*, a league in length, and about two hundred paces broad. This is by our people commonly called, *The Sandy Receif*, to diſtinguiſh it from *The Stony Receif*.

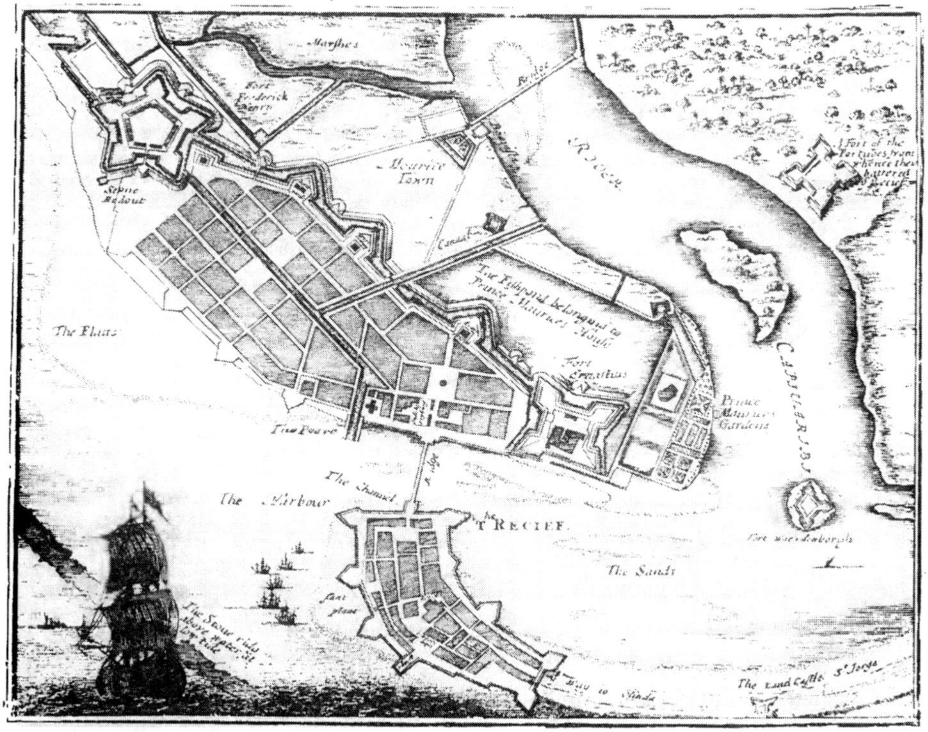

The ſandy Receif.

On the ſouthern point of this little iſland, a league off *Olinda*, the *Portugueſe* had built a village, called *Povoacano*, which ſignifies *peopling*, or elſe *Reciffo*; it was very populous for a conſiderable time, 'till the building of *Maurice*'s town, in the iſland of *Anthony Vaez*. For after *Olinda* was forſaken by its inhabitants, and deſtroy'd by us, many of them, but eſpecially the merchants, ſettled in this *Reciffo*, or the village of *Povoacano*, where they erected magnificent ſtructures. At our firſt arrival, we found no

1643. no more than two hundred houſes there, which were afterwards increaſed to above two thouſand, ſome of which are very goodly edifices. We ſurrounded it with Palliſadoes on the ſide of the river *Biberibi*, which at low-water is fordable; and for its better ſecurity fortified it with three bulwarks, one towards *Olinda*, the other to the harbour, and the third towards the *Salt River*; upon each of which was raiſed a good battery with three great cannon. This *Receif* is ſituate under the 8th degree 20 minutes ſouthern latitude.

The derivation of the word Receif. Some derive the word *Reciffo* from the *Latin*, *recipere* and *receptus* to receive, which after was turned into *Reciffo*, becauſe the ſhips uſed to be received betwixt the ſtony and ſandy *Receifs*, to load and unload their goods. Before the building of *Maurice*'s town, we kept here our factories, and all buſineſs both of peace and war, was tranſacted in this place. In the time of the *Portugueſe*, all the ſhips coming out of the ſea, did unload on the village of *Povoacano*, or the *Receif*, and the goods were from thence in boats and lighters conveyed up the river *Biberibi*, to the ſuburbs of *Olinda*.

Before the building of *Maurice*'s town, moſt of the traffick was in the *Receif*, where all the great merchants had their habitations, and from hence the Sugar was tranſported into *Holland*. To prevent the frauds in the cuſtoms, it was ſurrounded with palliſadoes, and a goodly hoſpital was erected for the conveniency of the ſick and wounded; and the education of orphans, under the tuition of four governors, and as many governeſſes.

Upon the uttermoſt point of the ſtony *Receif*, on the left ſide as you enter the harbour out of the ſea, is a ſtrong and large caſtle, built of free-ſtone, ſurrounded with a very high wall, upon which are mounted many heavy cannon, with ſuitable artillery and other proviſions. When we took the place, we found nine braſs, and twenty two iron pieces of cannon within it; ſo that it ſeems both by art and nature impregnable; there being no coming near it on foot, at high-water.

About five leagues higher, upon a branch of the great river, lies a ſmall town of little conſequence, called by our people, *The New City*; and upon another branch of the ſame river, oppoſite to the former, a village called *Atapuepe*.

The iſland of Anthony Vaez, *and* Maurice's Town.

The iſle of Anthony Vaez. To the ſouth of the *Receif*, oppoſite to it, lies the iſle of *Anthony Vaez*, ſo called by our People, from its ancient poſſeſſor. It is about half a league in circuit, being divided from the *Receif*, by the *Salt-River*, or *Biberibi*. 1643.

On the eaſt-ſide of this iſland, count *Maurice* laid the foundation of a city, which, after his own Name, he called *Maurice*'s town or city; the ruines of the churches or monaſteries of the city of *Olinda*, furniſh'd the materials for the building of it, which were from thence carried to the *Receif*, and ſo tranſported to this place. Maurice's Town.

On the weſt-ſide it is environ'd with a moraſs; and on the eaſt-ſide waſh'd by the ſea, which paſſes the ſtony ridge. Beſides which, it is on the land-ſide ſtrengthen'd with an earthen wall, four bulwarks and a large moat.

On that ſide where the fort of *Erneſtus* was, the town lay open, and the houſes took up a larger compaſs than thoſe in the *Receif*; but after the revolt of the *Portugueſe*, moſt of thoſe houſes were pulled down, and the place drawn into a more narrow compaſs, to render it more defenſible: Yet was the place well ſtocked with inhabitants, as well merchants as handicrafts men.

Maurice's town was on each ſide guarded by a fort. On the ſouth ſide by the fort called *Frederick Henry*, or the quinquangular fort, from its five bulwarks. This fort was beſides this, ſurrounded by a large ditch and palliſadoes, and ſtrengthened by two hornworks, ſo that it commanded the whole plain, which at ſpring-tides uſed to be overflown by the ſea. *The Fort* Frederick Henry.

The ſecond fort *Erneſtus*, thus called after *John Erneſt*, the brother of count *Maurice*, was four-ſquare, with four bulwarks, with a very large ditch; it commanded the river, the plains, and *Maurice*'s town. Near this laſt fort was the garden of count *Maurice*, ſtored with all ſorts of trees, brought thither from *Europe* and both the *Indies*. *The Fort* Erneſtus.

Upon the north point of the *Stony Receif*, juſt over againſt the *Sandy Receif*, lies the beforenamed fort, built all of ſtone, being about a hundred paces in circumference, provided with a good garriſon and twenty pieces of great cannon, though in ſtormy weather the water flies over it on all ſides. It commands the harbour, the land fort, the *Bruin Fort*, and the *Receif*. *The Fort of Stone.*

As the iſle of *Antony Vaez* was joined to the continent by a bridge, ſo it was thought neceſſary to join the *Receif* with another bridge to the ſaid iſland, for the conveniency of carriage; the ſugar cheſts being before that time never to be tranſported to the *Receif*, except at low water, unleſs the owners would run the hazard of expoſing them to the danger of the ſea in ſmall boats. Accordingly *The Bridge betwixt the* Receif *and the Iſland.*

1643. cordingly the great council, with consent of the governor count *Maurice*, agreed with a certain architect for the building of a bridge with stone arches, for the sum of two hundred fifty thousand florins. But after the architect had consumed a prodigious quantity of stone, and raised the structure near to the height of the banks of the river, finding that at low-water there was still eleven foot water, and despairing to be able to accomplish it, left it unfinished. But the council being unwilling to desist, renewed the work, which had already cost a hundred thousand florins; and by means of many trees of forty and fifty foot long, stopped the current till the bridge was brought to perfection, which was done in two months time, and a certain toll imposed upon all passengers, *viz.* for an inhabitant two pence, for a soldier and negroe one penny, for a horse four pence, and a waggon drawn by oxen seven pence.

The harbour. The space betwixt the *Sandy* and *Stony Receif*, is properly the harbour, which at high-water has about thirteen or fourteen foot depth, where the ships ride very safe, being defended from the sea by the stony *Receif*. The passage betwixt the *Sandy Receif* and the continent, is called the *Salt-River*, to distinguish it from the river *Kapivaribi*, which carries sweet water.

The river Kapivaribi. The river *Kapivaribi* has derived its name from a certain kind of river or sea hogs, which used to be found there, and were by the *Brasilians* called *Kapivaribi*. This river arises some leagues to the west, passing by the *Matta*, or the *Wood of Brasil*, *Masyasti*, St. *Lorenzo* and *Real*, where joining with the river *Affogados*, near another river of the same name, disembogues in the sea, near the *Receif*. The river *Kapivaribi* divides itself into two branches; one turns to the south, and passes by the fort *William*, and is called *Affogados*; the other running to the north, retains its former name, continuing its course betwixt the continent and *Maurice*'s town, or the isle of *Anthony Vaez* (into which you may pass over it by a bridge) and so to *Waerdenburgh*, where it joins with the river *Biberibi*, or *Salt-River*, both which are afterwards mixed with the sea. The two branches of this river, surround the river *Biberibi* on the west-side, and to the east the isle of *Anthony Vaez*. Upon that branch of the river called *Affogados*, are abundance of sugar-mills, from whence the *Portuguese* used to convey their sugar-chests, either in boats by the way of the river, or in carts to *Baretta*, and from thence in flat bottomed boats to the *Receif*, and to *Olinda*.

A league to the south of *Maurice*'s Town upon the branch called *Affogados*, is a four-square fort of the same name, otherwise called fort *William*; from whence you may pass along a dike to the fort *Frederick Henry*, or *Maurice*'s Town. It was a noble structure, surrounded with high and strong walls, a large ditch and pallisadoes, with six brass cannon: It defended the avenues to the plains. 1633. *The fort* William.

About half a league from thence, and at the same distance from the continent, lies another fort on the sea shore, called *Baretta*: This commands the avenues both by sea and land to the cape of *St. Austin*, and the *Receif*. *The fort* Baretta.

Upon that part of the island which lies betwixt the rivers *Kapivaribi*, and *Biberibi*, and betwixt the forts of *Ernestus* and the triangular fort of *Waerdenburg*, were the before mentioned gardens of count *Maurice*, stored with all kinds of trees, fruits, flowers and greens, which either *Europe*, *Africk*, or both the *Indies* could afford. There were near seven hundred cocoa-trees of all sizes, some of which were thirty, forty, and fifty foot high; which being transplanted thither, out of the circumjacent countries, bore abundance of fruit the very first year: Above fifty lemon-trees, and eighteen citron-trees, eighty pomgranate-trees, and sixty-six fig-trees, were also to be seen in these gardens. *The garden of count* Maurice.

In the midst of it stood the seat itself, called *Vryburgh*, a noble structure indeed, which as is reported, cost six hundred thousand florins: It had a most admirable prospect, both to the sea and land side, and its two towers were of such a height, that they might be seen six or seven leagues off at sea, and served the seamen for a beacon. In the front of the house was a battery of marble, rising by degrees from the river-side, upon which were mounted ten pieces of cannon for the defence of the river. About two or three rods from the river, were several large basons in the garden, containing very sweet water, notwithstanding the river all round about afforded nothing but salt-water; besides this, there were divers fish-ponds, stocked with all sorts of fish. *The palace of count* Maurice.

At the very foot of the bridge which is built over the river *Kapivaribi*, from *Maurice*'s town to the continent, count *Maurice* had built a very pleasant summer seat, called by the *Portuguese*, *Baavista*, i. e. *A fair Prospect*. It was not only surrounded with very pleasant gardens and fish-ponds, but served likewise as a fort for the defence of the isle of *Anthony Vaez*, and *Maurice*'s Town. *His summer seat.*

Upon the *Sandy Receif*, opposite to the *Sea*, or *Water Fort*, was a strong fort built of stone, called by the *Portuguese*, St. *Toris*, our people used to call it the *Land Fort*, to distinguish it from the beforementioned *Water Fort*; it defends the entrance of the harbour *The land fort.*

1643. bour with thirteen iron pieces of cannon.

About a musket shot thence to the north, lies upon the same sandy *Receif*, a small fort with four bastions, called the fort of *Bruin*; and about a musket shot further to the north, a redoubt, called *Madame de Bruin*: Both these forts were built by the *Dutch*.

The fort Bruin.

Near the continent, not far from the salt-pits, betwixt the *Sandy Receif*, and the isle of *Anthony Vaez*, was a triangular fort called *Waerdenburgh*. It was at first a four-square, but afterwards turned by the *Dutch* into a triangular fort, the fourth bulwark being not defensible, by reason of the ground: Those three bulwarks were afterwards changed into as many redoubts, and provided with some brass guns: At high tide it is surrounded on all sides with water.

The fort of Waerdenburgh.

The City of Olinda.

At a small distance from the *Receif*, or *Maurice*'s Town, to the north, is the ruinated city of *Olinda*, once a famous place among the *Portuguese*; the whole product of *Brasil*, being from thence transported by sea into *Europe*. The best part of the city was built upon divers hill; towards the sea, on the south side, these hills were pretty plain, extending to the sea-shore, which has a very white sand all along that coast: Towards the land side, or the north, those hills are more steep and craggy, full of thorn-bushes, intermixed with a few orange-trees. These hills are an additional strength to the place, which besides this, was guarded by several bastions to the land side, though by reason of the great variety of hills contained in its circuit, it was a difficult task to bring the fortifications into a regular form. There is a very fair prospect from the higher part of the town, both to the south and north, or to the sea and land side, by reason of the great quantity of circumjacent trees, which continue green all the year round. You may also from thence see the isle of *Anthony Vaez*, and *Maurice*'s town. The point of land near *Olinda*, is called *Tipo* by the inhabitants. 1643.

Olinda.

OLINDA p. 13

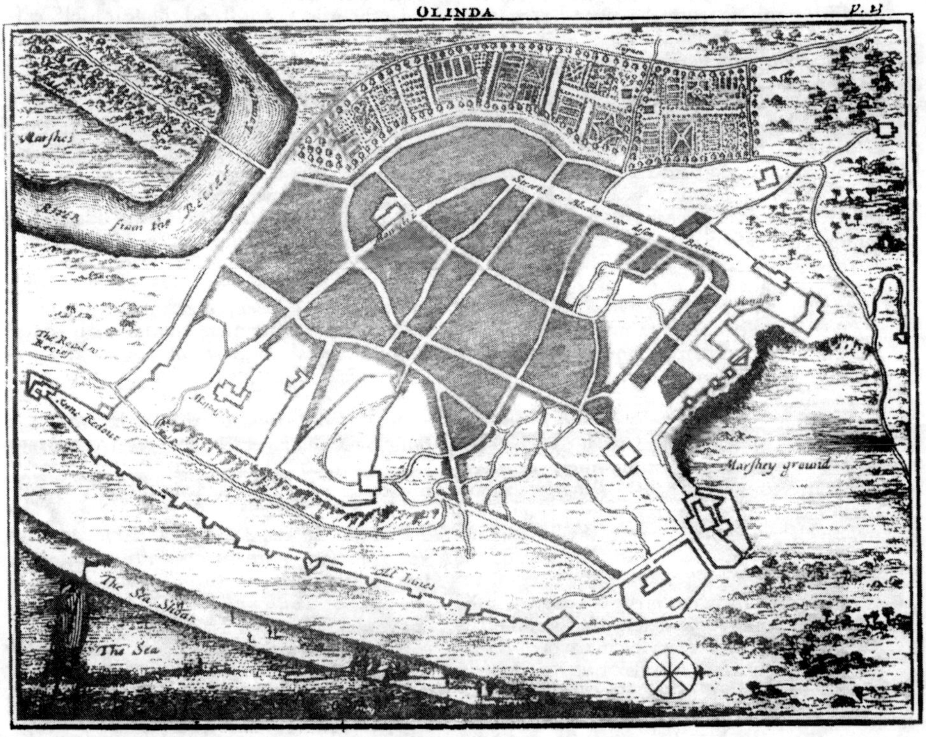

Upon

1643. Upon the higheſt hill within the place, ſtood formerly a convent belonging to the *Jeſuits*, being a magnificent ſtructure, founded by *Sebaſtian* king of *Portugal*, who endowed it with conſiderable revenues. It had a very fair proſpect, and might be ſeen at a good diſtance at ſea. Not far from thence was another Monaſtery belonging to the *Capucines*; and near the ſea-ſhore, another of the *Dominican* fryars: Beſides which, it had two churches, the one called St. *Salvador*, the other St. *Peter*.

It contained above two thouſand inhabitants, beſides the clergymen and ſlaves, among whom were two hundred that were accounted very rich. On the foot of the mountain upon which the city of *Olinda* was built, a ſtrong redoubt was erected, which in the year 1645, was by a ſerjeant betrayed to the *Portugueſe* for a ſum of money. About a league from the city, near the water-ſide, were the ſuburbs, well ſtored with inhabitants and packhouſes; but deſtitute of freſh water, which they were fain to fetch from beyond the river.

The whole diſtrict of *Parnambuko* abounds in divers kinds of fruits and cattle. The vallies afford good paſturage, and the lower grounds near the rivers, great ſtore of ſugar reeds, which are much cultivated hereabouts. The mountains produce richer minerals here, than in the other captainſhips. During the rainy ſeaſon the heat is more tolerable here in the day time than the cold nights.

The Cameleon, *or* Indian Salamander, *otherwiſe called* Gekko.

This creature, which is not only found in *Braſil*, but alſo in the iſle of *Java*, belonging to the *Eaſt-Indies*, and which, by our people is called *Gekko*, from its conſtant cry (like among us that of the *Cuckoe*) is properly an *Indian Salamander*. It is about a foot long, its ſkin of a pale or ſea-green colour, with red ſpots. The head is not unlike that of a tortoiſe, with a ſtreight mouth. The eyes are very large, ſtarting out of the head, with long and ſmall eye-apples. The tail is diſtinguiſhed by ſeveral white rings: Its teeth are ſo ſharp as to make an impreſſion even upon ſteel. Each of its four legs had five crooked claws armed on the end with nails. Its gait is very ſlow, but wherever it faſtens it is not eaſily removed. It dwells commonly upon rotten trees, or among the ruines of old houſes and churches; it oftentimes ſettles near the bedſteds, which makes ſometimes the moors pull down their huts.

Its conſtant cry is *Gekko*, but before it begins it makes a kind of hiſſing noiſe. The ſting of this creature is ſo venomous, that the wound proves mortal, unleſs it be immediately burnt with a red hot iron, or cut off. The blood is of a paliſh colour, reſembling poiſon itſelf. 1643.

The *Javaneſe* uſe to dip their arrows in the blood of this creature; and thoſe who deal in poiſons among them (an art much eſteemed in the iſland of *Java*, by both ſexes) hang it up with a ſtring tied to the tail on the cieling, by which means it being exaſperated to the higheſt pitch, ſends forth a yellow liquor out of its mouth, which they gather in ſmall pots ſet underneath, and afterwards coagulate into a body in the ſun. This they continue for ſeveral months together, by giving daily food to the creature. It is unqueſtionably the ſtrongeſt poiſon in the world; its urine being of ſo corroſive a quality, that it not only raiſes bliſters, wherever it touches the ſkin, but turns the fleſh black, and cauſes a gangrene. The inhabitants of the *Eaſt-Indies* ſay, that the beſt remedy againſt this poiſon is the *Curcumic* root. Such a *Gekko* was got within the body of the wall of the church in the *Receif*, which obliged us to have a great hole made in the ſaid wall, to diſlodge it from thence.

The ſtrongeſt poiſon in the World.

There are alſo ſeveral ſorts of *Serpents* in *Braſil*, ſuch as *Rattle Serpents*, *Double-headed Serpents*, and ſuch like; of which the *Braſilians* enumerate twenty-three, *viz.* *Boigvacu*, or *Liboya*, *Arabo*, *Bioby*, *Boicininga*, *Boitrapo*, *Boykupekanga*, *Bapoba*, *Kukuruku*, *Kaninana*, *Kurukaki tinga*, *Grinipaijaguara*, *Ibiara*, *Jakapekoaja* *Ibiboboca*, *Jararaka*, *Manima*, *Vona*, *Tarc*[illegible], *Kakaboya*, *Amorepinima*.

Serpents in Braſil.

We will give you an account of thoſe only that dwell in the houſes and woods of *Parnambuko*, paſſing by the reſt, as not ſo well known among us; and it is obſervable that though ſome of the *American* or *Braſilians* ſerpents exceed thoſe of *Europe* in bigneſs, they are nevertheleſs not ſo poiſonous.

The ſerpent of *Boicininga*, or *Boicinininga*, likewiſe called *Boiquira* by the *Braſilians*, is by the *Portugueſe* called *Kaſkeveda* and *Tangedor*, i. e. *a Rattle*, and by our people a *Rattle Serpent*, becauſe it makes a noiſe with its tail, not unlike a rattle: This ſerpent is found both upon the highway and in deſolate places; it moves with ſuch ſwiftneſs, as if it had wings, and is extremely venomous. In the midſt it is about the thickneſs of a man's arm near the elbow, but grows thinner by degrees towards the head and tail. The belly and head is flattiſh, the laſt being of the length and breadth of a finger and a half, with very ſmall eyes. It has four peculiar teeth longer than all the reſt, white and ſharp like a thorn, which it hides

The Rattle Serpent.

ſometimes

1643. ſometimes within the gums. The ſkin is covered with thick ſcales, thoſe upon the back being ſomewhat higher than the reſt, and of a pale yellowiſh colour, with black edges. The ſides of the body are likewiſe yellowiſh with black ſcales on each ſide; but thoſe upon the belly are larger, four-ſquare, and of a yellow colour. It is three, four, and ſometimes five foot long; has a round tongue ſplit in the middle, with long and ſharp teeth. The tail is compoſed of ſeveral looſe and bony joints, which make ſuch a noiſe that it may be heard at a diſtance. Or rather at the end of the tail, is a long piece conſiſting of ſeveral joints, joined within one another in a moſt peculiar manner, not unlike a chain. Every year there is an addition of one of theſe joints, ſo that you may know the exact age of the ſerpent by their number; nature ſeeming in this point to have favoured mankind, as a warning to avoid this poiſonous creature by this noiſe. One of theſe joints put in the fundament cauſes immediate death; but the ſting of this creature proceeds much ſlower in its operation, for in the beginning a bloody matter iſſues from the wound, afterwards the fleſh turns blue, and the ulcer corrodes the adjacent parts by degrees. 1643.

The moſt ſovereign remedy uſed by the *Braſilians* againſt the poiſon of this and other ſerpents, is the head of the ſame ſerpent that has given the wound, which they bruiſe in a mortar, and in form of a plaiſter apply it to the affected part. They mix it commonly with faſting ſpittle, wherewith they alſo frequently moiſten the wound. If they find the poiſon begins to ſeize the nobler parts, they uſe the *Tiproka* as a cordial, and afterwards give ſtrong ſudorificks. They alſo lay open the wound, and apply cupping-glaſſes, to draw the venom from thence. Or elſe they burn it with a red hot iron.

The ſerpent *Kukuruku* is of an aſh colour, with yellow ſpots within and black ſpeckles without, and has juſt ſuch ſcales as the *Rattle Serpent*. Kukuruku.

The ſerpent *Guaku*, or *Liboya*, is queſtionleſs the biggeſt of all ſerpents; ſome being 18, 24, nay 30 foot long, and of the thickneſs of a man in the middle. The *Portugueſe* call it *Kobre dehado*, or the *Roebuck*

1643. *Roebuck serpent*, because it will swallow a whole roebuck or any other deer it meets with; and this is performed by sucking it through the throat, which is pretty narrow, but the belly vastly big. After they have swallowed such a deer, they fall asleep, and so are catch'd. Such a one I saw near *Paraiba*, which was 30 foot long, and as big as a barrel. Some negroes saw it accidentally swallow a roebuck, whereupon thirteen musqueteers were sent out, who shot it, and cut the roebuck out of its belly. It was of a greyish colour, though others are inclining more to the brown. It is not so venomous as the other serpents. The *Negroes* and *Portuguese*, nay even some of the *Dutch* eat the flesh; neither are its stings look'd upon as very infectious, the wound healing often up without any application of remedies; so that it ought not to be reckoned among the number of poisonous serpents, no more than the *Kaninana*, *Mavina* and *Vocia*. This serpent being a very devouring creature, greedy of prey, leaps from amongst the hedges and woods, and standing upright upon its tail, wrestles both with men and wild beasts; sometimes it leaps from the trees upon the traveller, which it fastens upon, and beats the breath out of his body with its tail.

The Roebuck serpent.

Jararaka. The serpent *Jararaka* is short, seldom exceeding the length of an arm to the elbow. It has certain protuberant veins on the head like the adder, and makes much such a noise. The skin is covered with red and black spots, the rest being of an earth colour. The stings of this creature are as dangerous, and attended with the same symptoms, as those of other serpents. Its body, the head, tail and skin, being before taken away together with the entrails, boil'd in the water of the root of *Jurepeba*, with salt, dill, and such like, is look'd upon as a very good remedy.

Boitrapo. The serpent *Boitrapo*, call'd by the *Portugueze*, *Cobre de Cibo*, is about seven foot in length, of the thickness of a man's arm, feeds upon frogs, and is of an olive colour. It is very venomous, and when it stings, occasions the same symptoms as the serpent *Kukuruku*; nay, the wound is accounted past curing, unless you apply the hot iron.

Ibiara. The adder *Ibiara*, by the *Portuguese* called *Cobra Vega*, or *Cobra de das Cabecas*, i. e. *The Doubleheaded Serpent*, because it appears to have two heads, which however is not so. They are found in great numbers, lurking in holes under ground. They feed upon pismires, are of the thickness of the length of a finger, and a foot and a half long, of a silver colour; nothing is more poisonous than the stings of these creatures, tho' not beyond all hopes of cure, provided the before-mentioned remedies be applied in time. 1643.

The serpent by the *Brasilians* called *Ibiboboka*, the *Portuguese* call *Cobra de Corais*. It is very beautiful, of a snow white colour, speckled with black and red spots, and about two foot long: Its sting is mortal, but kills by degrees. Ibiboboka.

The serpent *Biobi*, called by the *Portuguese Cabro Verde*, or the *Green Serpent*, about three quarters of a yard long, and the thickness of a thumb; of a shining green colour. It lives among houses, and hurts no body, unless when provoked. Its sting is however full of poison, and scarce curable. A certain soldier being wounded by one of these creatures, which lay hidden in a hedge, in his thigh, did for want of proper remedies, die in few hours after: His body swell'd, and turn'd pale blue. Biobi.

The serpent *Kaninana* is yellow on the belly and green on the back; its length is about eight hands, and is look'd upon as the least venomous of all. It feeds upon eggs and birds, and the *Negroes* and *Brasilians* eat the body, after they have cut off the head and tail. Kaninana.

The serpent call'd by the *Brasilians Ibirakoa*, is of several colours, with white, black, and red spots. The sting of this creature is very poisonous, attended with the same symptom as that of *Kukuruku*; for it kills infallibly, unless proper remedies be applied immediately. If the poison has not seised the heart, they boil the flesh of the same serpent with certain roots, and give it the patient in wine. Ibirakoa.

The serpent *Tarciboya* and *Kakaboya*, are amphibious creatures. The first is of a blackish colour, very large, and stings when provoked, but is not very difficult to be cured. The *Kakaboya* is of a yellowish colour, six hands long, and feeds upon tame fowl.

Of the Senembi *or the* Leguan.

Not only in the *Captainship* of *Parnambuko*, but also all over *Brasil* and *America*; as likewise in the Isle of *Java* in the *East-Indies*, are a certain kind of *Land Crocodile*, call'd by the *Brasilians Senembi*, by our people *Leguan*: Some are larger than others, some being three, others four foot long, but seldom exceed five: They are all over covered with scales, which are somewhat bigger on the back, legs, and beginning of the tail, than on the other parts: The neck is about a finger and a half long, the eyes are black and bright, and the nostrils in the hindermost part of the head. Each jawbone is full of small, black,

1643. black, and ſhort teeth; the tongue is very thick: All along the back from the neck to the tail, are ſmall ſharp teeth of a greeniſh colour; they are biggeſt on the neck, and grow ſmaller and ſmaller towards the tail: Under the throat are likewiſe many of the ſame kind. The whole ſkin is of a delicate green, with black and white ſpots. It has four legs and feet, with five claws armed with very ſharp nails: It can live two or three months without food. Its fleſh is as white as that of a rabbit, and of as good a taſte as that of fowls or rabbits, if it be boil'd or well fry'd with butter. In the head of this creature are certain ſtones, which are an infallible remedy to break and drive the gravel out of the kidneys, given to the quantity of two drams at a time, or carried on ſome part of the body.

There are in *Brazil* lizards both great and ſmall; ſome are green, others greyiſh, and ſome four foot long, with ſparkling eyes. The *Negroes* feed upon ſome of them, whom they kill with blunt arrows; they broil them, after they have ſkin'd them, and eat them without the leaſt harm. Among all thoſe that are found among the thorns and briars, or the ruins of houſes, there is but one kind venomous, which is called *Bibora.* They are like the others, but leſſer, not exceeding the bigneſs of a thumb; they are of an aſh colour, inclining to white; the body and limbs thick and ſwell'd with the poiſon, but the tail ſhort and broad. The wounds given by them are full of a thin ſtinking matter, with blue ſwellings, with a pain near the heart, and in the bowels.

There are alſo certain creatures, called *Thouſand Legs*, as likewiſe *Hundred Legs*, by the natives called *Ambua*, who bend as they crawl along, and are accounted very poiſonous. The firſt are commonly found in the Houſes, and the laſt among the woods, where they not only ſpoil the fruits of the Earth, but alſo plague men and beaſts.

Scorpions. Scorpions, by the *Braſilians* called *Jaaciaüra*, are found here in great numbers, being in ſhape like the *European* ſcorpions, but not ſo peſtiferous, and conſequently the wounds given by them are eaſily cured. They lurk in houſes, behind old ſtools, benches and cheſts. They are exceeding big, no bigger being to be found in any other parts, ſome being five or ſix foot long, and of a conſiderable thickneſs.

There are ſuch prodigious quantities of piſmires in *Braſil*, that for this reaſon, they are called by the *Portugueſe*, *Rey de Braſil, i. e.* King of *Braſil.* They eat all *Piſmires.* that lights in their way, as fruit, fleſh, fiſh, and inſects without any harm. There 1643. is alſo a certain flying piſmire of a fingers length, with a triangular head, the body being ſeparated into two parts, and faſtned together by a ſmall ſtring. On the head are two ſmall and long horns, their eyes being very ſmall. On the foremoſt part of the body are ſix legs, three joints each, and four thin and tranſparent wings; to wit, two without, and two within; the hindermoſt part is of a bright colour and round, which is eaten by the *Negroes.* They dig into the ground like the moles, and conſume the ſeed.

There is another kind of great piſmires, reſembling a great fly; the whole body of which is about the length of half a finger, and ſeparated into three ſeveral parts. The laſt part reſembling in ſhape and bigneſs a barley corn; the middlemoſt of an oblong figure, with ſix legs, half a finger long, each of which has four joints: The foremoſt part, or the head, is pretty thick, in the ſhape of a heart, with two horns, and as many black crooked teeth: The white of the eyes is inclining to black, the whole compoſition of the head being the two eyes, placed oppoſite to one another, reſembling the figure of a heart. The fore and hindermoſt parts are of a bright red colour.

There is another kind of piſmire, of a bright black colour, with black and rough legs. It is about the length of a finger, with a large fourſquare head, ſtarting black eyes and teeth, and two horns, half a finger longer. The body is alſo ſeparated into three parts. The foremoſt of an oblong figure, not very thick, with ſix legs, each of the length of half a finger; the middlemoſt very ſmall and ſquare, not exceeding the bigneſs of a louſe; the hindermoſt is the biggeſt of the three, of an oval figure, and ſharp on the end. Theſe three parts are faſtned together with a ſingle ſtring, the *Braſilians* call it *Tapijai.*

There is beſides this another piſmire, call'd by the *Braſilians Kupia*, of a cheſnut brown colour; its head being as big as another piſmire, with black eyes, two horns, and two tuſks inſtead of teeth. The whole body is covered with hair; it is divided into two parts; The foremoſt with ſix legs, being ſomewhat leſs than the hindermoſt; at certain ſeaſons it gets four wings, the foremoſt being a little bigger than the hindermoſt, which it loſes again at a certain time.

The *Iron-pig* of *Braſil*, called by the *Braſilians Kuanda*; and by the *Portugueſe Ourico Kachiero*, is of the bigneſs of a large ape, its whole body being covered with ſharp

1643. ſharp ſpikes of three or four fingers long, without any hair. Towards the body thoſe ſpikes are halfways yellowiſh, the remaining part is black, except the points, which are whitiſh, and as ſharp as an awl. When they are vexed, they are able, by a certain contraction of the ſkin, to throw or dart them with ſuch violence, that they wound, nay, ſometimes kill men or beaſts. Their whole body to meaſure from the hindermoſt part of the head to the beginning of the tail, is a foot long, and the tail a foot and five inches in length, which likewiſe has always ſharp ſpikes, the reſt being covered with briſtles like other hogs. The eyes are round, ſtarting and gliſtering like a Carbuncle; about the mouth and noſe are hair of four fingers length, reſembling thoſe of our cats or hares: The feet are like thoſe of apes, but with four fingers only without a thumb, inſtead of which you ſee a place vacant, as if it had been cut away. The four legs are leſs than the hindermoſt, they are likewiſe armed with ſpikes, but not the feet. 1643.

This creature commonly ſleeps in the day time, and roves about by night; it breaths through the noſtrils, is a great lover of fowl, and climbs up the trees, tho' very ſlowly. The fleſh is of no ungrateful taſte, but roaſted and eaten by the Inhabitants. It makes a noiſe *Jii*, like the *Luyaert*.

That four-legg'd creature, by the *Braſilians* called *Ai*, by the *Portugueſe Priguiza*, and by the *Dutch Luyaert* (lazy-back) from its lazy and ſlow pace, becauſe in fifteen days time it ſcarce walks above a ſtones throw. It is about the bigneſs of a middle-ſized fox, its length being a little above a foot, to meaſure from the neck (which is ſcarce three fingers long) to the tail. The fore-legs are ſeven fingers long to the feet, but the hindermoſt about ſix; the head round of three fingers in length: its mouth, which never is without a foam, is round and ſmall, its teeth neither large nor ſharp. The noſe is black, high, and glib, and the eyes ſmall, black and heavy. The body is covered all over with aſh-coloured hair, about two fingers long; which are more inclining to the white towards the back. Round about the neck the

1643. the hair is ſomewhat longer than the reſt. It is a very lazy creature, unable to undergo any fatigues, by reaſon its legs are as it were disjointed in the middle; yet it keeps upon the trees, but moves, or rather creeps along very ſlowly. Its food is the leaves of the trees, it never drinks, and when it rains, hides itſelf. Wherever it faſtens with its paws, it is not eaſily removed; it makes, tho' ſeldom, a noiſe like our cats.

The *Piſmire-Eater*, is thus called, becauſe he feeds upon nothing but piſmires; there are two ſorts, the great and the ſmall: The *Braſilians* call the firſt *Tamanduaï*, and the laſt *Tamanduai-Guacu*. It is a four-legg'd creature, of the bigneſs of a dog, with a round head, long ſnout, ſmall mouth, and no teeth. The tongue is roundiſh, but ſometimes twenty-five inches, nay two foot and a half long. When it feeds, it ſtretches out its tongue upon the dunghills, till the piſmires have ſettled upon it, and then ſwallows them. It has round ears, and a rough tail; is not nimble, but may be taken with the hand in the field. The ſmall one, called *Tamanduai-Guacu*, is of the bigneſs of a *Braſilian* fox, about a foot in length. On the fore-feet it has four crooked claws, two big ones in the midſt, and the two leſſer on the ſides. The head is round, yet pointed at one end, a little bent below; with a little black mouth without teeth. The eyes are very ſmall, the ears ſtand upright about a fingers length. Two broad black liſts run along on both ſides of the back; the hairs on the tail are longer than thoſe on the back, the extremity of the tail is without hair, wherewith it faſtens to the branches of the trees. The hairs all over the body are of a pale yellow, hard and bright. Its tongue is round, and about eight fingers long. It is a very ſavage creature, graſps every thing with its paws, and if you hit it with a ſtick, ſits upright like a bear, and takes hold of it with its mouth. It ſleeps all day long, with its head and fore-feet under the neck, and roves about in the night time. As often as it drinks, the water ſpouts forth immediately through the noſtrils. 1643.

They have alſo a kind of ſerpents of about two fathoms long, without legs, with a ſkin of various colours, and four teeth. The tongue is ſplit in the middle, reſembling two arrows, and the poiſon is hid in a bladder in its tail.

The four legg'd creature, called by the *Braſilians*, *Tatu* and *Tatupera*, by the *Spaniards*, *Armadillo*, by the *Portugueſe*, *Encubèrto*, and by the *Dutch*, *Schilt-Verken*, (Shield-Hog) becauſe it is defended with ſcales like as with an armour, reſembles in bigneſs and ſhape our hogs; there are ſeveral ſorts of them. The uppermoſt part of the body, as well as the head and tail, is covered with bony ſhields, compoſed of very fine ſcales. It has on the back ſeven partitions, betwixt each of which appears a dark brown ſkin. The head is altogether like that of a hog, with a ſharp noſe, wherewith they grub under ground; ſmall eyes, which lie deep in the head; a little, but ſharp tongue; dark brown and ſhort ears, without hair or ſcales: The colour of the whole body inclining to red; the tail in its beginning is about four fingers thick, but grows by degrees ſharp and round to the end, like thoſe of our pigs: But the belly, the breaſt, and legs are without any ſcales; but covered with a ſkin not unlike that of a gooſe, and whitiſh hair of a fingers length. It is generally very bulky and fat, living upon maleons and roots, and does conſiderable miſchief in the plantations. It loves to rout under ground, eats rabbets, and the dead carcaſſes of birds, or any other carrion: It drinks much, lives for the moſt part upon the land, yet loves the water and marſhy places. Its fleſh is fit to be eaten. It is catch'd like the doe in *Holland* with the rabbits, by ſending a ſmall dog abroad, who by his barking, gives notice where it lurks under ground, and ſo by digging up the ground it is found and catch'd.

Shield-Hogs.

The

Batts. The batts in *Brasil*, called by the inhabitants *Andirika*, are of the bigness of our crows; they are very fierce, and bite most violently with their sharp teeth. They build their nests in hollow trees and holes.

Wild-geese. The bird called by the *Brasilians*, *Ipekati Apoa*, by the *Portuguese*, *Pata*, is no more than a goose; and for that reason by the *Dutch* called a wild goose. It is of the bigness of one of our geese of about nine months old, and in all other respects resembles them. The belly and under part of the tail, as likewise the neck, is covered with white feathers; but on the back to the neck, on the wings and head, the feathers are black intermixed with some green. There are also some black feathers intermixed with the white ones on the neck and belly. They differ from our geese in this, that they are somewhat bigger; their bills resemble rather those of our ducks, but are black, and turned at the end, and on the top of it grows a broad, round, and black piece of flesh, with white speckles. They are commonly found near the river-side, are very fleshy and well-tasted.

***The bird* Toukan.** The bird by the *Brasilians* called *Toukan*, or large bill, is about the bigness of a wood pigeon. It has a crop about the breast of three or four fingers in compass, of a saffron colour, with high red coloured feathers round the edges, which are yellow on the breast, but black on the back and all the other parts of the body. Its bill is very large, of the length of a palm of a hand, yellow without and red within. It is almost incredible how so small a bird is able to manage so large a bill, but that it is very thin and light.

***The bird* Kokoi.** The bird called by the *Brasilians*, *Kokoi*, is a kind of a crane, very pleasing to the sight, as big as our storks. Their bills are streight and sharp, about six fingers in length, of a yellowish colour inclining to green. The neck is fifteen fingers long, the body ten, the tail five: Their legs are half-ways covered with feathers, about eight fingers in length, the remaining part being six and an half. The neck and throat is white, both sides of the head black, mixt with ash-colour. On the far and undermost part of the neck are most delicious, white, long, and thin feathers, fit for plumes: The wings and tail are of an ash-colour, yet mixt with some white feathers. All along the back you see long and light feathers, like those on

1643. on the necks, but are of an ash-colour: Their flesh is very good, and of a grateful taste. There is another kind of these birds, which is somewhat bigger than a tame duck. Its bill is streight, and sharp at the end, of the length of four fingers and a half, with a double set of teeth both above and below: The head and neck (which is two foot long) resembles the crane, with black eyes enclosed in a gold coloured circle. The body is two foot and a half in length; the tail, which stands even with the extremity of the wings, four fingers. The bill is of an ash colour towards the head, the rest yellow, inclining to green. The head and upper part of the neck are covered with long pale yellowish feathers, intermixt with black. On the back and wings it hath ash coloured feathers inclining to yellow: but the legs and feet are dark grey: The flesh of this bird is eatable, and tastes like that of a crane.

Jabiru-guakú. The bird called by the *Brasilians*, *Jabiru Guaku*, and by the *Dutch*, *Schuur Vogel*, or barn-bird, has no tongue, but a very large bill, near seven foot and a half long; round and crooked towards the end, of a grey colour. On the top of the head is a crown of white and green feathers. The eyes are black, behind each of which are two great concavities instead of ears. The neck is ten fingers in length, one half part of which as well as the head, is not covered with feathers, but with an ash-coloured, whitish, rugged skin. This bird is of the bigness of a Stork, with a short black tail, which stands even with the extremities of the wings. The other part of the neck, and the whole body, is covered with white feathers, and those on the neck very long ones: The wings are likewise white, but mixt with some red. The flesh if boiled, after the skin is taken of, is good food, being very white, but somewhat dry.

Brasil produces incredible quantities of other wild fowl of all sorts, both great and small, some of which live among the woods, others in the water, but are very good food.

Of the best kind are the thrushes, called by them *Bamodi*; Pheasants of divers kinds, called by the *Barbarians*, *Magnagu*, *Jaku*, and *Arakua*.

Mouton is a bird of the bigness of a peacock, but has black feathers, the flesh is very good and tender. Because this countrey is full of fruit trees and woody places, it produces abundance of sparrow-hawks, and other hawks, called by the *Portuguese*, *Guavilon*, and by the *Brasilians*, *Teguata* and *Inage*, which are always at enmity with the chickens and pidgeons.

Among those that live both in the water and upon the land, the wild ducks claim the precedency; some of those are smaller than the *European* ducks, others much exceed them, being as big as a goose. They have also a sort of snipes, called *Jakana-miri* and *Jakana-guaku*. Besides these there are cranes, quails and ostridges, and many others of that kind; the flesh of which is eatable, but not very toothsome. 1643.

The rest of these birds are very greedy after the amber-greese, which is thrown ashore by the boisterous sea, which they devour before the inhabitants can come thither to gather it. They have also abundance of *Parrakets*, or small parrots, these never speak; but their parrots are extraordinary fine and large, some of which learn to speak as distinctly as a Man. I have seen some of these parrots express every thing what they heard cried in the streets very plainly; and among the rest I saw one, which if put in a basket upon the floor, would make a dog that belonged to the same house, sit up before the basket, crying out to him, sit up, sit up, you nasty toad. Neither did this parrot leave off calling and crying, till the dog came to sit up before the basket. It was afterwards presented to the queen of *Sweden*.

There is among the rest a certain small bird, no bigger than a joint of a finger, which notwithstanding this, makes a great noise, and is catched with the hands whilst it is sitting among the flowers, from whence it draws its nourishment. As often as you turn this bird, the feathers represent a different colour, which makes the *Brasilian* women fasten then with golden wires to their ears, as we do our-rings. The birds here are never destitute of food, which they always meet with either among the flowers or fruits of the trees, which are never spoiled here during the winter season.

The rivers and lakes of *Brasil*, as well as the neighbouring sea, furnishes them with great store of all sorts of fish, which are accounted so wholsome here, that they are even allowed for those that are troubled with agues. The standing waters near the sea-side, which sometimes are quite dried up, produce abundance of craw-fish, tortoises, shrimps, crabs, oysters, and divers others of this kind, which are all very good food. *Their fish*

There are abundance of fish in *Brasil*, common to the sea and rivers, especially during the rainy season; when a great quantity of the river water being conveyed into the sea, the sweetness of the water allures the fish into the rivers, where meeting with abundance of green weeds (the product of the bottom of the rivers) they never return to the sea.

Among the river fish the chiefest are, the *Duja*, *Prajuba*, and *Akara-Puku*, the last of

1643. of which resembles the best and largest of our perches.

Brasil produces also various kinds of insects, some of which are of four fingers length, and an inch thick. They have likewise silk worms, called by the *Brasilians*, *Isokuku*'s, and their silk, *Isokurenimbo*. There are also divers sorts of fire-flies, which are likewise found in the *East-Indies*, where we shall give you a further account of them. Besides these, there are many sorts of other flies, hornets, wasps, and bees: some of which produce honey, some none at all. 1643.

Spiders. Among other kinds of spiders there is one of a prodigious bigness, which is always found either in dunghills, or in the concavities of hollow trees: They call it *Nhanduguaka*. These creatures weave cobwebs like other spiders; the skin is rough and black, provided with sharp and long teeth. This creature if provoked wounds with its poisonous sting, which is so small as scarce to be visible, and raises a blueish tumour, which is very painful, and if care be not taken in time, occasions an inflammation, attended with such dangerous symptoms as prove afterwards incureable.

Ballar, *or* Kabitto. Near *Rio St. Francisco* are vast numbers of a certain small insect not unlike our crickets; I have been very curious to get sight of this creature, to satisfy myself as to its shape, and resemblance to others of this kind; but though it makes a very shrill noise, which resembles that of our crickets, I was never able to see any of them; for as soon as you approach they desist, so that you are at a loss which way to look. They sing sometimes for a quarter of an hour without intermission. In the island of *Java* in the *East-Indies* it is commonly heard in the months of *February* and *June*. At last I had the good fortune to get one of these creatures into my hands; by means of a certain *Chinese* woman, after I had often been in search of it, both within and without the city of *Batavia*. The *Javanese* set two of these little creatures a fighting together, and lay money on both sides, as we do at a cock-match.

There are also abundance of ravenous wild beasts in *Brasil*, such as tygers, leopards, &c. The tygers are extreamly savage here; they fall upon beasts, and sometimes

1643. times upon men, of whom ſeveral were killed by them in my time. A certain *Portugueſe* had a ſugar-mill very pleaſantly ſituated near a wood, whither we uſed to go to divert ourſelves ſometimes. The *Portugueſe* ſitting one time with four more of his friends in the houſe, with the windows drawn up for the conveniency of the land air, a dog belonging to the houſe, who had ventured too far into the adjacent wood, was purſued by a tyger, ſo that to ſave his life he leapt into the window to ſeek for ſhelter near his maſter; but the tyger cloſely purſuing him, leapt alſo through the window into the room, where the door being ſhut, he tore two of thoſe there preſent in pieces before the reſt could make their eſcape, and afterwards went his way.

There is another ſort of ſavage beaſt in thoſe parts, called by ſome of our people, *Jan-over-Zee*, or jack beyond ſea, which ſurpaſſes all others in nimbleneſs, and tears all to pieces it meets with.

Cattle. *Braſil* has alſo great plenty of cattle, but the fleſh will not keep above twenty-four hours after it is dreſs'd. The *Dutch* cut off the fat, and cut the lean in thin ſlices, and dry it in the ſun like fiſh. No butter is to be made here, becauſe the milk turns to curds immediately: the *Dutch* butter is drawn out of a veſſel like oil.

Hogs. Their hogs are ſmall and black, but very well taſted, and wholeſome; there is another kind of amphibious hogs, by the *Portugueſe* called *Kapiverres*, they are very near as black as the others, and good food.

There is another four legg'd creature in *Braſil*, called by the inhabitants *Taperete*, *Antes.* and by the *Portugueſe*, *Antes*; its fleſh has the taſte of beef, but ſomewhat finer. It is about the bigneſs of a calf, but ſhaped like a hog; it ſleeps all day among the woods, and ſeeks for belly-timber in the night: Its food is graſs, ſugar-reeds, cabbages, and ſuch like. They have likewiſe good ſtore of goats, called by them *Pakas*, and *Kotias*, and hares and rabbits, which don't give way in goodneſs to thoſe of *Europe*. There is alſo an excellent kind of lizards, called by the inhabitants, *Vuana* and *Teju*, which are accounted a dainty bit.

Fiſh. The fiſh in *Braſil* are no leſs conſiderable for the ſupply of our plantations, than the cattle, which are on the coaſts of *Braſil*, but eſpecially in *Parnambuko*, where they are found in ſuch plenty, that at one draught they catch ſometimes two or three thouſand fine fiſh, in the four or five ſummer months, for during the rainy ſeaſon, they catch but few. There are certain diſtricts along the ſea coaſt whither the fiſh moſt reſort; ſome of thoſe belong to the inhabitants, the reſt to the company, and are farmed at a certain rate *per annum*. The lakes as well as 1643. the bays, are ſtored with an incredible multitude of fiſh; the firſt are by the *Portugueſe* called *Alagoas*; and the beſt they produce are the *Sindia*, *Queba*, and *Noja*, all without ſcales. And though the fiſh which are catcht in the lakes are not ſo much eſteemed as the river-fiſh, nevertheleſs are they not much behind them in goodneſs, becauſe theſe lakes are not always ſtanding waters, but intermixt with ſeveral rivers. Some of theſe fiſh they dry in the ſun. The chiefeſt of this kind are thoſe called by the *Braſilians*, *Kurima Parati*, and by the *Dutch* inhabitants *Herders*. They abound no leſs in ſea-fiſh of all ſorts. The fiſh called by the *Braſilians*, *Karapantangele*, which is not unlike our perch, has the preference among them. And as the rivers furniſh infinite numbers of fiſh, ſo they are generally fatter and better taſted than the ſea-fiſh. Thoſe which are catcht in theſe fiſheries near the ſea-ſhore, are for the moſt part ſalted, and carried from thence into the countrey, for the uſe of the ſugar-mills, which cauſe great plenty among them.

The craw-fiſh, which are in great quantities near the rivers and in the marſhy grounds, ſerve likewiſe for food to *Braſilians* and negroes, and ſome of our people like them tolerably well.

It is further to be obſerved, that whereas a conſiderable number of cattle, during the war was run aſtray out of the parks into the foreſts and woods beyond the river of *St. Francis*, it was thought convenient by the great council of the company here, to agree with certain perſons to catch this cattle, and bring it to the *Receif*, in order to be killed for the uſe of the inhabitants. The time of the ſaid contract being expired, it was conſulted whether the ſame ſhould be renewed; but it being apparent that there were not enough left to quit coſt, the ſame was laid aſide, and this reſolution ſent to the council of nineteen. For in the mean while the inhabitants near *Rio St. Franciſco* and *Rio Grande*, having applied themſelves to the breeding of cattle, their parks were ſo well ſtockt by this time, that they not only furniſhed the inhabitants of the *Receif*, but alſo the ſugar-mills, with plenty of meat, which was bought at the rate of three and four pence *per* pound in the countrey; beſides that, they provided the garriſons with the ſame for a twelvemonth, after the ſtore-houſes of the *Receif* were emptied; and notwithſtanding this, the inhabitants of thoſe parts were not out of debt, when thoſe of *Parnambuko* and *Parayba*, were involved over head and ears; which ſhews what advantage they reapt from the breeding of cattle; and that if the

1643. the *Dutch Brasil* had continued in peace, those parks might have furnished all the garrisons with meat without impairing their stock for breeding; which, together with the great plenty of fish, are the two main pillars of the state of *Brasil*.

Notwithstanding all which, it is certain that the inhabitants of the *Dutch Brasil* cannot be provided with sufficient maintenance; without a yearly supply from *Europe*, as well eatables as other commodities; as has been found by experience, to the great detriment of the company; after our storehouses were exhausted by the several expeditions against *Angola*, *Meranhaon*, and other places.

Crocodiles. In the rivers and lakes here are also found crocodiles, by the *Brasilians* called *Jakare*, and in the *East-Indies*, *Kaymans*. They are like the *African* crocodiles, but not quite so big, seldom exceeding five foot in length: They lay twenty or thirty eggs bigger than geese eggs, which are eaten by the *Brasilians*, *Portuguese* and *Dutch*, as well as the flesh.

In the seas near the coast of *Brasil*, they meet also sometimes with great lampreys. Before the bridge from the *Receif* to *Maurice-town* was built, one of this kind of a considerable bigness did lurk near that passage, where the boats used to pass over from one side to the other, and snatcht all that fell in his way; both men and dogs that swam sometimes after the boat, into the water: But at a certain time, by the sudden falling of the tide; being got aground with the foremost part of the body, he was with much ado brought ashore.

The district of *Pernambuko* does also abound in various sorts of fruits, as well as all the other parts of *Brasil*, of which we shall say more hereafter.

Upon the captainship of *Pernambuko*, borders to the north the captainship of *Tamarika*, which owes its name to an island of the same name, being the chiefest part of this district, which however extends near thirty-five leagues along the sea coast on the continent.

The island of *Tamarika* lies two leagues to the north of *Pomerello*, in the sea; being parted from the continent by the river *Tamarika*, its most southern point lying under the 7th degree 58m southern latitude. It is from south to north about two leagues long, and its circuit near seven. To the jurisdiction of this isle did also belong *Goyana*, *Kapavaribi*, *Terukupa*, and *Abray* on the continent. Formerly it had but few inhabitants, and scarce any houses, though it is a very pleasant isle, and tolerably fertile, producing brasil-wood, coco nuts, cotton, sugar-reeds, melons, and such like; besides wood for firing, and fresh water for the conveniency of the *Receif*: It abounds likewise in wood both for building of houses and shipping. This island was much infested with wild beasts, which did great mischief to the sugar reeds: This moved *Peter Pas*, director of the captainship of *Itamarika*, to make his application to count *Maurice* and the great council in 1647, to know their pleasure, whether they should dispose of those beasts by contract, to such as would be at the charge of catching of them, or whether they should be taken and killed for the use of the garrisons; but this was rejected by the council, who enjoined the inhabitants not to kill those beasts in the open fields, unless they should break into their plantations, it being for the interest of the company to preserve them in case of a necessity: The damage which from thence might accrue to the sugar reeds, being to be prevented by surrounding their plantations with pales and stakes.

The consequence of this isle. The island is look'd upon as of the greatest consequence to us, it having been proposed by some to transfer the seat of the *Dutch-Brasil* from the *Receif* thither; but the directors of the company did not agree to it; considering that at that time this island was quite desolate; whereas upon the *Receif* were store-houses, magazines, ware-houses, and such like buildings ready to their hands; besides that the place was much more pleasant, fertile, and stronger; and the harbour much more convenient for ships: The river *Tamarika* on the other hand being not navigable, but for small vessels, by reason of the shallowness of the harbour, which was noted for shipwracks. The defect of fresh water in the *Receif*, in which this isle abounds, may be supplied from the river *Biberibi*; besides that, they had several basons with fresh water within the *Receif*, for their present use. During the war with the *Portuguese* we were sensible of the conveniencies we received from this island, by reason of its strength both by art and nature, which might serve as a safe retreat upon all emergencies; besides, that its preservation was absolutely necessary for the *Receif*, which was supplied from thence with fish, and several other other sorts of provisions.

Upon the banks of the river at the south entrance of the harbour, we had built a quadrangular fort, called *Orange*. It was provided with a goodly wall, but the ditch was not very deep, and for the most part without water, for which reason it was strenghten'd with pallisadoes. On the north-side we had a hornwork, but much decayed; within the body of the fort was a powder-vault, and other conveniencies for the bedding

bedding of ſoldiers. Several batteries were raiſed upon the walls, mounted upon ſix braſs and as many iron great guns. In the iſland near the entrance of the river, cloſe by a moraſs full of thorn-buſhes, was a ſmall town, moſt inhabited by ſoldiers, called by the *Portugueſe*, *Noſtra Senhora de la Conceptiano*. Upon a hanging rock, juſt by, was an old redoubt erected by the *Portugueſe*, called by the ſame Names, which together with the whole iſland, was taken by the *Dutch*, under the command of colonel *Schop* from the *Portugueſe*, and the place, after his name, called *Schop's Town*. This fort was afterwards by the *Dutch* cloſed up on the backſide towards the church, ſo that it afterwards ſerved both for the defence of the town and the harbour, as the *Blockhouſe* on the north-ſide cover'd the gates. There were then eleven pieces of cannon mounted upon it. At the north entrance of the harbour, was another redoubt, which defended that paſſage on that ſide, with three iron cannon. One Mr. *Dortmont*, governor of *Itamarika*, found under the before-mention'd rock, in 1645, as he was digging a well, a ſpring of freſh water, which proved very uſeful for the garriſon, becauſe it could not be cut off by the enemy.

Hanging-rock.

Somewhat higher up the river *Tamarika*, lies an iſland called *Magioppe*, where are found abundance of *Mandiboka* roots. You may go quite round this iſland in barks; it having a kind of a harbour on both ends, *viz.* to the ſouth and north, but the firſt is the beſt; becauſe there ariſes from the northern ſhore of the continent, a ſhelf, which reaches very cloſe to the iſland, the channel betwixt both not having above ten or twelve foot water. The only harbour fit for uſe thereabouts is the ſouth-entrance of the river, which makes *Tamarika* an iſland, where ſhips that drew fourteen or fifteen foot water, may paſs through; there is no convenient anchorage: That end, where the river returns into the ſea, is by the *Dutch* called the northern-entrance, and by the *Portugueſe Katuamma*.

The rivers Marafarinha *and* Garaſſou.

Betwixt *Pomerello* and the river *Tamarika*, a river comes from the continent, fit for barges, called *Marafarinba*; and half a league within the mouth of the river *Tamarika*, another falls likewiſe from the continent called *Garaſſou*, but is of little moment. From thence to the north, are ſeveral other rivers near the ſea-ſhore, which are navigable with barges, for the conveniency of the ſugar-mills, of which there are ſeveral thereabouts.

Punto Pedra.

A league and an half further to the north of the north-entrance of *Tamarika*, is a noted point of land called by the *Portugueſe*, *Punto Pedra*, ſurrounded with a *Receif*, betwixt which you may paſs with barges and yachts.

The river Goyana.

A league further to the north from this point, and three leagues to the north-weſt of *Tamarika*, is the ſmall river *Goyana*, under 7 deg. 46 min. which diſembogues in two branches in the bay; at the entrance lies a great rock, where is great ſtore of ſea-fowl. Before it lies a great *Receif*, but within are ſo many ſhelves that renders the paſſage very dangerous.

The river Auyay.

About two leagues and a half beyond the river *Goyana*, to the north, is a great river, called *Auyay*, but the entrance is ſo choak'd up with ſands, that there is ſcarce any paſſage for barges. This river ſends forth ſeveral branches into the country, upon one of which to the north, lies the village of *Maurice*, and upon the ſouthern branch the village *Auyay*.

Porto Franciſco.

Among others, *Porto Franciſco* lies in a creek three long leagues to the north of the river *Auyay*; and five leagues to the north-weſt of the ſame river, an unnavigable river called *Grammana*, beſides ſeveral other rivulets.

Parayba.

About a league and a half to the north-weſt of the river *Grammana*, is the *Cabo Blanco*, or *White Cape*, and three leagues from thence to the north-weſt, the cape of *Parayba*, being a long point of land, with a large adjacent bay. The whole coaſt from *Pomerello* to the cape of *Parayba*, is cover'd with receifs or rocks, which lying for the moſt part about half a league from the ſhore, and the water between them being generally very ſmooth, affords an eaſy paſſage to barges, even in tempeſtuous weather when it is almoſt impoſſible for ſhips to paſs without the rocks, by reaſon of the violence of the current from the northern and the ſouthern winds, which blow there continually.

The Town of Goyana.

Three leagues within the mouth of the river *Goyana* is a town of the ſame name, where is kept the court of judicature of this *captainſhip*. There are five or ſix ſugar-mills thereabouts, ſituated upon the banks of the river, for the more commodious tranſportation of ſugar in barges to *Pernambuko*. This countrey produces likewiſe braſil-wood, ginger, cotton, and *Indian* nuts; the people called *Petiguaves* inhabit here; tho' this whole tract of land, as far as *Cabo Blanco*, is not very populous, having only a few villages, inhabited by the *Braſilians*.

The iſle of *Tamarika* has ſeveral landing places on the river-ſide, the chiefeſt are: *Os Markos* and *Pedreiros*, where the river is narroweſt; *Tapaſima* and *Kamboa* of *Domingos Rebeyro*; the great *Makqueira* and

1643. and *Kamboa* of *Conrad Pauli*; in which places the enemy landed in that island. The pass near the north-entrance of *Topowa*, and the island *Taposoka*, where with one single ship you may defend the passage from the rivers *Tujukapape* and *Masserandaku*, as likewise from the sea. For the rest, the shore all along the river being very marshy and full of *Manga* trees, is of a very difficult access. The shore towards the sea-side is very flat, but woody, which together with the sands, that are at some distance in the sea, makes the approach of ships very dangerous on that side. Formerly the court of judicature of the *captainship* was kept in this island, but was afterwards transferred from thence, as we told you before, to the Town of *Goyana* and *Kapivaribi* on the continent, because these places were both more populous, and more sugar-mills were built thereabouts, the ground being much better here than in the Island. In my time there were five judges belonging to this court, three of which lived at *Goyana*, and the other two in the isle of *Itamarika*. However, this court was afterwards likewise removed from *Goyana*. In the year 1641, Mr. *Peter Pas* was director of the *captainship* of *Itamarika* for the *West-India* company, and captain *Sluiter* commander in chief over the soldiers.

Parayba. This *captainship* has derived its name from the capital city, which has borrow'd hers of the river *Parayba*, upon which it is situate. It is one of the most northerly *captainships*, about five leagues distant from the sea. It was formerly in the possession of the *French*, who were 1585, chased from thence and several other harbours, by the *Portuguese* general *Martin Leytan*.

The city Parayba. Five leagues upwards the river *Parayba*, is a city founded by the *Portuguese*, and after *Philip* king of *Spain*, called *Filippen* and *Nossa Senhora de nives*, otherwise *Parayba*, from the river *Parayba*; which name was by the *Dutch*, after they had in *November* 1633, conquered the whole *captainship*, changed into that of *Frederick's Town*, after *Frederick Henry* prince of *Orange*. This city had been but lately built by the *Portuguese*, and had several stately houses with marble pillars, the rest being only of stone. Here is kept the court of judicature of this *captainship*. Before the time of the rebellion of the *Portuguese*, this place was inhabited as well by the *Portuguese* as *Dutch*, being much frequented by the inhabitants of the circumjacent countrey, was used to exchange their sugar for what other commodities they stood in need of, which was afterwards from thence transported to other places.

Within the mouth of the river *Parayba*, were three very considerable forts. One on the south-point, by the *Portuguese* called *Catharine*, but by count *Maurice*, afterwards named *Margaret*, after his Sister. It was defended with five goodly bastions, and a hornwork without. 1643. *Fort* Margaret.

Fort St. Anthony. The fort called *St. Antonio*, by the *Portuguese*, was built upon a small island, which by a narrow breach was separated from the north-point. This is only the remainder of a large four square fort, formerly erected by the *Portuguese*, which was afterwards rased by the *Dutch*, part of it having been wash'd away by the river. It is surrounded with pallisadoes and a good ditch, supplied with water from the beforenamed branch of the river: The Walls are very strong, and upon a battery are mounted six iron pieces of cannon. It may be defended by the cannon both from the city of *Parayba*, and from the fort *Margaret*, lying just opposite to it on the south-side, which is the reason it was always but carelesly guarded by the *Portuguese*.

The third fort. The third fort lies upon a triangular island, called *Restinga*, not far from thence, more upwards the river. It was strengthened with pallisadoes, and upon the batteries were mounted five brass, and as many iron pieces of cannon.

The river Parayba. The *captainship* of *Parayba* is watered and divided by two considerable rivers, *viz.* the *Parayba* and *Mongoapa*, otherwise call'd *St. Domingo*. The great river of *Parayba* lies under the 6th deg. 24 min. four leagues to the north of *Cabo Blanco*, and discharges it-self in two branches into the Sea, being separated by a large sand-bank: One is called the northern, and the other the southern entrance. From the last extends a rocky-ridge as far *Cabo Blanco*, and within the river lies a sand-bank quite cross to the fort *Margaret*. This river is very shallow during the summer time, but in the winter season, the waters rise to that height that they overflow all the adjacent countrey, sometimes to the great loss of men and cattle.

Porto Lucena. Two leagues beyond this river to the north, is a bay which affords a very safe station to the largest ships. It is by the *Portuguese* called *Porto Lucena*, and by the *Dutch* the *Red-Land*, the grounds being red hereabouts. There is very good anchorage here at five and six fathom water, and the country near it affords very good fresh water; which is the reason why the *Dutch* ships bound for *Holland* from the *Receif*, used to stay for one anothers coming in this bay, and to provide themselves with fresh water.

Half

1643.

River Mongoapa. Half a league further to the north, under 6 deg. 34 min. the river *Mongoapa*, or *Mongoanawapy*, exonerates it self into the sea: This river is much larger towards its source than at the mouth; the banks on both sides being full of briers, bushes and *Manga* trees. Before its entrance lies a *Receif*, and at the very mouth two dangerous sand-banks; it has three fathom water at low tide.

About two small leagues to the north of the river *Mongoapa*, is a bay called by the *Portuguese Bahia de Treycano*, or *Treason*, where, at about a league distant from the shore, is eleven or twelve fathom water. Five leagues to the north of this bay, you meet with the river *Barra Conguon* or *Konayo*, which is scarce passable for Yatches. About a league and a half from thence is large bay of about two leagues in length, called *Pernambuko*; and five leagues beyond it to the north, the river *Jan de Sta*, or *Estau*.

The natives of *Parayba* inhabit about seven villages, the chiefest of which is call'd *Pinda Una*, which in 1634, contained about fifteen hundred inhabitants, where each of the others had scarce three hundred; each of these comprehending not above five or six very long buildings, with a great many doors, but very small ones.

The chief commodities of this *captainship* are sugar, brasil-wood, tobacco, hides, cotton, and such like. The sugar-reeds did bear extremely well, because they were transplanted into fresh grounds. Whilst the district of *Parayba* was under our jurisdiction, there were above one and twenty sugar-mills on both sides of the banks of the river, eighteen of which sent away every year four thousand chests of sugar. Near the river-side, the country is low and plain, but not far from thence rises by degrees, and affords a very agreeable variety of hills and vallies. The flat countrey, which is also the most fertile, is distinguish'd into several divisions, some of which have borrow'd their names from small rivers which run thro' them; as for instance, *Gramamma*, *Tapoa*, *Tibery*, *Ingeby*, *Monguappe*, *Increry*, *Kamaratuba*, and several more. All those countries are extremely fertile, occasion'd by the overflowing of the river *Parayba*. *Its fertility.* Their products are, sugar, barley, turky-wheat, potatoes, ananas, coco-nuts, melons, oranges, citrons, bananas, pakovas, markomas, cucumbers, and all other necessaries for the sustenance of men and beasts. They have here a kind of wild pears, called kajous, which are very juicy and well-tasted; within is a certain bean or small nut, the rind of which is bitter, but the kernel sweet, if roasted in the ashe. The pear is very cooling, but the nut has a contrary quality.

1643.

Towards the end of *November* 1634, the *Dutch* undertook the expedition against *Parayba*, their forces being embarked in thirty two ships under the command of colonel *Schoppe*, *Artisjoski*, *Hinderson*, *Stachouwer* and *Carpentier*. The whole fleet was divided into two squadrons, the first consisted of one and twenty ships, in which were nineteen hundred and forty five men, the other of eleven yachts, with four hundred and nine men. *Schoppe* was the first that landed six hundred men, and advanced towards the enemy, who betook themselves to their heels, leaving their arms and cloaths behind them; *Anthony Albuquerque* their general, himself scarce escaping their hands. In the mean while, the rest being likewise got a shore, three companies, under the conduct of *Gasper Ley*, marched directly to the fort of *Margaret*, and intrencht himself near the fort, whilst *Schoppe* kept all along the shore, and *Artisjoski*, posted himself on the right-side, in sight of the garrison: At the same time Mr. *Lichthart* attack'd the fort in the small island *Restinga*, which he took by force, and put the garrison to the sword. *The Dutch conquer Parayba.* By this time *Schoppe* had raised a battery against the fort, from whence he so sorely gall'd the besieged, that their commander *Simon d' Albukirque* surrendred the place. Hereupon the fort of *St. Antonio* was summoned to surrender, *Maglianes* the governor desired three days delay, which being denied, he march'd away secretly by night, leaving the place to *Lichthart*, who found there five great brass pieces, and nineteen iron pieces of cannon.

The same night our forces marched towards the city of *Parayba*, being sixteen hundred strong, and having pass'd a small branch of the river called *Tambra Grande*, made themselves masters of it without any opposition: The *Spanish* general *Banjola*, who commanded there with two hundred and fifty men only, having left the place before, and being retired to *Goyana*, after he had either sunk or nail'd up the cannon, set fire to three ships and two warehouses, in which were consumed three thousand chest with sugar. The fort of *St. Catharine* being much decay'd, was order'd by count *Maurice* to be repaired, and the ditch to be enlarged and deepen'd; giving it the name of *Margaret*, after his Sister. The fort of *St. Antonio* was rased, for the greatest part, there being only one bulwark left for the defence of the north-point of the river. The fort *Restingas* was order'd to be surrounded with new pallisadoes

1643. does, and the convent of *Parayba* fortified with a wall and outwork; and the command thereof given to *Elias Harkman*, together with the government of the whole *captainship*.

Potigi, *or* Rio Grande. The *captainship* of *Potigi*, or *Potingi* or *Poteingi*, is otherwise, by the *Portuguese*, called *Rio Grande*, from a river of the same Name: The *Dutch* call it *North-Brasil*, in respect of the more southern *captainships* of *Brasil*. It borders to the south upon *Parayba*, and to the north upon the *captainship* of *Siara*; tho' the *Portuguese* geographers extended its bounds as far as the island *Maranhaon*.

The *French* were once masters of this *captainship*, 'till 1597, they were chased from thence by the *Spanish* commander, *Feliciano Creça de Karvalasho*. It has four divisions, named after so many rivers, that run through them; *viz. Kunhao*, *Goyana*, *Mumpobu* and *Potegy*. And tho' this district has been much neglected by the *Portuguese*, yet does it produce plenty of wild-fowl and fish, which are so luscious, that they commonly eat them only with lemon-juice or vinegar, without oil. There is an incredible number of fish in the lake *Goraires*; besides which, abundance of *Farinha* is planted here. This part of the countrey stood us in good stead during the late rebellion of the *Portuguese*, our garrisons in *Parayba*, and other places, being supplied from thence with good store of flesh and fish.

River Rio Grande. Above the river *Rio Grande*, is a town of no great moment, call'd *Amsterdam*; the inhabitants live by planting *Farinha* and *Tobacco*, and fishing. Higher up in the countrey live some *Moradores* or husbandmen, who cultivate the grounds; but on the north-side of *Rio Grande* are but few inhabitants.

The river *Rio Grande*, *i. e.* the *Great-river*, is so called by the *Portuguese* from its bigness, but by the *Brasilians*, *Potigi* or *Poteingi*. The mouth of this river lies under 50 deg. 42 min. southern latitude, three leagues from *Punto Negro*, coming from the west-side of the continent. It disembogues four leagues above the fort *Keulen*, called by the *Portuguese*, *Tres Reyos*: It bears ships of great burthen; but the river *Kunhao* in the same *captainship* is only navigable with barges and yachts. The bays of this *captainship* are, *Bahia Formosa*, *Punto Negro*, *Ponto de Pipas*, and the *Bay of Martin Tüssen*. The *Bay of Ginapabo* lies beyond *Rio Grande* to the north; and beyond that a river call'd *Guasiavi*, upon which, near the mouth lies the village *Atape Wappa*. Near to the north you meet with the river *Siria Mixui*; and near the village of *Natal*, and the fort of *Tres Reyos*, passes a river called the *Cross-River*, which arises out of a small lake in *Rio Grande*. Over against the same fort, a fresh river falls into the great river, betwixt two land-banks, and not far from thence another salt-water river. 1643.

The fort Keulen. The fort *Keulen* was four-square, built upon a rock or point of a *Receif*, at some distance from the shore, at the mouth of the river *Receif*; being surrounded with water, as oft as it's flowing water, so that at high tide there is no coming at it but with boats. In the midst of this fort is a small chappel, where in 1645, and 1646, our people found a wall about a foot and a half wide on the top, but at the bottom three feet, cut within a rock, which brings fresh supplies of good and sweet water every tide; with an ordinary tide two hundred and twenty five, and at spring-tide about three hundred and fifty quarts; which is more than sufficient for the use of the garrison, in case of siege. The fort is built of a square stone; being towards the shore defended with two half bastions, in form of hornworks. In the year 1646, there was an artillery of twenty nine, as well brass as iron pieces of cannon in the place, and provided with a good under-vault, and convenient lodgments for the soldiers.

Its conquest by the Dutch. This fort was in 1633, taken by the *Dutch*, under the command of *Matthias van Keulen*, one o the governors of the company, who being assisted by several noted captains, *viz. Byma*, *Kloppenburg*, *Lichthart*, *Garstman* and *Mansfelt van Keulen*, set sail thither with eight hundred and eight men, embarked in four ships and seven yachts, and made himself master of it, and the whole captainship at the same time; since which it changed its name *Tres Reyos*, into that of *Keulen*, from the commander in chief of this expedition.

The *Tapoyers* (or mountaineers) use commonly twice a year, especially when the dry season puts them in want of fresh water, to make an inroad into this *captainship*; there being a constant enmity betwixt them and the *Portuguese*. It happen'd in *July* 1645, that these *Tapoyers* being advertised that the *Portuguese* intended to revolt from us, and had actually begun the same in *Pernambuko*, did, under the conduct of one of their leaders, called *Jacob Rabbi*, after several provocations given them by the *Portuguese*, make an incursion into *Kunhao*, where they killed thirty six Persons in a sugar-mill belonging to one *Gonsalvo d'Olivera*. From thence they march-ed to a certain place, where the *Portuguese* had cast up a line for their defence, which they made themselves masters of, and put

 the

1643.

the *Portuguese* to the sword. The *Brasillians* told us, that this had been done in requital of what had been done to some of those mountaineers by one *Andrew Vidal* in *Serinhaim*, after quarter given them before, of which we shall say more hereafter. Since which time, the *Portuguese* have laid this tract desolate, which the *Dutch* once had a mind to re-people, and to put it in the same condition as the *Portuguese* had possess'd it, but for want of people that design was fain to be laid aside.

Siara.

The *captainship* of *Siara* is one of the most northerly districts of *Brasil*, bordering upon *Maranhaon* to the north upon the river *Siara*. It is of no great extent, its whole compass being not above ten or twelve leagues.

The river Siara.

The river *Siara*, which rises deep in the continent, disembogues about seven leagues and a half to the north of the bay *Mangorypa*, under 3 deg. 40 min. southern latitude.

The native inhabitants of this *captainship*, according to the report of those that have frequently visited it, are very large of stature, with ugly features, long hair and black skin; except the space betwixt the eyes and mouth. They have holes in their ears, which hang downwards upon the shoulders; some make holes in their lips, some in their noses, in which they wear stones as an ornamen. Their food is *Farinha*, wild-fowls, fish and fruit. They drink most water, but make likewise a certain liquor out of *Farinha*; and of late began to be used to drink good store of brandy, tho' it was expresly forbidden to bring it into the villages, to keep them from the excessive use of strong liquors. The countrey produces sugar-reeds, chrystal, cotton, pearls, salt, and several other commodities. Ambergrease is also found on the sea-shore.

The inland part of the countrey was in 1630, governed by one of their own kings, call'd *Algodoi*; in some respect tributary to the *Portuguese*, who had built a fort upon the river *Siara*, and made themselves masters of the whole sea-coast thereabouts; notwithstanding which they were in continual broils with one another, 'till 1638, this fort and the whole countrey was taken by the *Dutch* from the *Portuguese*, in the following manner.

Siara conquered by the Dutch.

Count *Maurice* and the council, being sollicited by the natives of that country, to make themselves masters of the *Portuguese* fort on that side, and to deliver them from the oppression they lay under at that time, they offering their assistance, and and giving two young lads of their best families, as pledges of their Fidelity, this expedition was resolved upon. The chief command over the Troops design'd for this exploit, was conferr'd upon colonel *John Garstman*, a man of more than ordinary conduct in martial affairs, tho' as the case then stood, this enterprise was not likely to meet with any considerable difficulties; being assured of the assistance of the *Brasilians*, who bore an old hatred to the *Portuguese*, and were acquainted with the strength and condition both of their forces and places. *Garstman* being provided with ships, men, ammunition, and all other necessaries requisite for such an expedition, set sail towards the river *Siara*; where being met by the *Algodoi*, or king, with white ensigns in token of peace; and having landed his men, two hundred of the natives joined with them. With those he marched directly to the fort, which after a brave resistance from the *Portuguese*, who killed some of his men, he took by storm; and made most of the garrison prisoners, among whom were some commanders of note: They found good store of cannon and artillery in the place.

The fort Siara.

Since that time, the *Dutch* built a small fort upon the *Siara*, unto which they gave likewise the name of *Siara*, which was provided with a garrison of betwixt thirty and forty soldiers only; not so much for the defence of the countrey, as to maintain a good correspondency with the *Brasilians*, who being very numerous in those parts, might do us considerable service in time of war. It was upon this consideration, that the great council always commanded their officers, sent thither, to cultivate a good understanding with them; and at several times sent them some small presents, which, however proved ineffectual in the end, for in 1644, they attack'd and kill'd several of our men at *Komesay*, (a place about thirty leagues from *Siara*) as we shall hear anon.

For the *Brasilians* being, in 1641, increased to such a number in *Siara*, that the villages thereabouts were not able to contain them without great inconveniency, whereas the district of *Rio Grande* was almost destitute of inhabitants, and consequently not in a condition to oppose an enemy; one *Andrew Uliifs* proposed to the great council, to build a village in *Rio Grande*, for the use of such as intended to settle there out of *Siara*, desiring to be constituted chief of the said village. Count *Maurice* and the great council, being informed of the inclinations of those *Siara*, who were willing to settle in *Rio Grande*, their ancient place of abode, and considering the benefit that was likely to accrue to the company, from the settlement of those *Brasilians*, so near at hand, granted *Uliif*'s request, wishing him to bring thither

1643. thither as many of the *Brasilians* of *Siara* as he thought convenient, for the compass of a village of which he was made chief or captain. Things being thus settled, they chose, with the approbation of our directors, certain chiefs or heads out of the most ancient families of each division, called *Resídoor* by the *Portugueze*, and certain judges; as for instance in *Goyana*, *Domingoi*, *Fernandes*, and *Karapeva*; in *Parayba*, *Peter Potty*; and in *Rio Grande*, *Antonio Perapeva*. Notwithstanding all this, the *Brasilians* of *Siara* revolted against the *Dutch* in 1644. surprized the garrison in the fort, which they razed, and killed the commander in chief, *Gideon Morritz*, with the whole garrison, besides all the workmen belonging to the salt-pits near the river *Upanemma*, who were all cut in pieces by these *Barbarians*.

A certain master of a ship, with a captain, lieutenant, and some soldiers, who happened to come ashore in a boat to fetch some fresh provisions, being ignorant of their treachery, were also put to the slaughter, three seamen having the good fortune to escape with their lives into the wood.

Some laid the cause of this rebellion at the door of the *Portuguese* and *Brasilians* of *Maranhaon*, bordering upon them; but if we search into the true source of this evil, it must be attributed to the miscarriage of our own officers, who by their hard usage, had forced the inhabitants to revenge themselves for the injuries received at their hands.

Thus much concerning the *Captainships* of the *Dutch Brasil*; we will in the next place give you an account of all the memorable transactions that happened betwixt the *Dutch* and *Portuguese* in *Brasil* during our stay there; after I have represented to you the excellency and convenient situation of this country, together with the ecclesiastical estate of the *Dutch Brasil*.

The excellency of Brasil.

Brasil is a country excellently well qualified by nature for the producing of all things, which are generally found in the *West-Indies*, under or near the same climate; except, that hitherto no gold or silver mines have been discovered here worth taking notice of. But next to gold and silver, the sugar claims the precedency here before all other commodities. Among all the harbours and places of the *West-Indies*, there is not one that can compare with *Brasil*, either for the product, or conveniency of transportation of sugar; the whole coast of *Brasil* being full of small rivers, which flowing through the adjacent valleys, disembogues in the sea; from whence the sugar-mills built in the valleys reap the benefit of saving vast charges, which else must be bestowed upon labourers and carriages; whereas these rivers drive the mills, serve for the transportation of sugar to other places, and furnish them at an easy rate with what commodities they stand in need of; all which conveniencies, as they are not to be met with in any other place of the *West-Indies*; so, no sugar-mills could be erected there with any prospect of profit. The exportation of sugar from *Brasil* into *Europe* and *Africa*, is likewise performed with much more ease than from any other places in the *West-Indies*; for the situation of *Brasil*, (being the most eastern part of all *America*) is such, as could not be more conveniently contrived by human art or nature for the transportation of so general and agreeable a commodity as sugar, into all the other parts of the world; considering those two excellencies of *Brasil*, together with its vast extent, it is most certain, that, provided it were well peopled, it might command both the *North* and *Æthiopian* seas, and spread its commerce over all parts of the world; nay, it might extend its conquests both to the east and west, or at least establish factories there for the conveniency of traffick. To prove which, it is to be observed:

That all *East-India* ships, both going and coming, must pass by the coast of *Brasil*; and as those ships in their voyages thither, are often forced to touch upon this coast, so in their return, nothing could be more commodious for them, than to be supplied with fresh provisions here. From *Brasil* you may sail in fourteen days to the *Caribbee* islands, and in the same time, or a little longer, to *Sierra Leona* on the coast of *Guinea*. It is impossible to enter deep into the great south sea, (whereabouts a great part of the terrestrial globe remains as yet undiscovered) unless you take in fresh provisions and firing in *Brasil*, or expose yourself to the greatest hazards imaginable in so long a voyage, as is sufficiently evident from the journals of *Oliver Van North*, *Spilbergen*, *le Maire*, and *John l'Heremite*. And experience has taught us, since Mr. *Brewer's* voyage to *Chili*, how easy the passage is betwixt *Brasil* and the south sea; for he lost not so much as one ship out of four, and very few died in the whole voyage.

The wholesomeness of its climate.

Brasil enjoys likewise the advantage of a very wholsome climate; for tho' it lies betwixt the equinoctial line and the *Tropick of Capricorn*, and consequently is subject to burning heats, yet are the same much allayed by the winds, that blow out of the east from the sea, their free passage being

1643. being not interrupted by any mountains or islands; which is the reason, that in *Brasil* the same distempers are rarely to be met with which reign so frequently in *Angola*, *Guinea*, *St. Thomas*, and several other places, where the east winds cannot afford them the same advantage. A plague is a thing unknown in *Brasil*, in which it excels all other countries; tho' they are not free from continual putrid fevers, caused by the hot and moist air, and the excessive use of raw fruits.

Those that are bound for the coast of *Brasil* ought to have a special regard to the season of the year, which regulates the winds and stream thereabouts; and to be very careful to sail above the harbour whither they are bound; for if they miss and come below it, they lose their aim, and must stay till the next turn of the wind and stream. For it is observable, that on the coast of *Brasil*, the stream runs from *February* till past *July* constantly northernly, during which time there is no passing from the north to the south; but after those months are past the stream turns, and from the beginning of *September* to the latter end of *November*, runs as violently to the south as it did to the north before, and consequently there is no sailing from the north to the south, no more than before from the south to the north. The winds here turn with the stream; and at the beginning of *March* blow south-south-east, and south-east. And like as the stream changes its current till *September*, so the winds continue in the east, and blow till that time out of the east-south-east. For there are but two winds that reign along this coast, *viz.* the south-east and north-east winds; according to which ships must regulate their course here.

The ecclesiastical state of the Dutch Brasil.

The ecclesiastical state of the *Dutch Brasil* was in my time thus ordered:

Before the insurrection of the *Portuguese*, there were to the south of the *Receif* five protestant churches; *viz.* in *Rio* St. *Francisco*, *Porto Calvo*, *Serinhaim*, the Cape St. *Austin*, and St. *Anthony*; though these were seldom altogether provided with ministers, because that some or other of them returned into *Holland*, after their limited time was expired. In the isle *Tamarika* and fort *Orange*, was at that time a minister, one *John Offringo*, who lived formerly in the town of *Schop*, and at the same time preached in the church of *Igarassu*, which was afterwards left by the *Dutch* and possess'd by the *Portuguese*. In *Rio Grande* preached one *John Theodore Polheim*. In *Parayba* were formerly two ministers, whilst the town of *Frederica* was as yet under the *Dutch* jurisdiction, but after the revolt of the *Portuguese* the place was left by the inhabitants, and *Henry Harman* was the only minister in those parts. In the *Receif*, *Maurice*'s town, and the circumjacent forts, which contained about 400 protestants, *Dutch*, *French* and *English*, were three ministers, who preach'd in the *Dutch* tongue; *Nicholas Vogel*, *Peter Ongena*, and *Peter Grib*. Besides these there was a fourth called *Jodocus Astett*, who formerly had been minister of the Cape of *St. Austin*, but now was employed either aboard our fleet, or upon any land expedition. The *French* church here remained without a minister, after the departure of *Joachim Solaer*, so that they were forced to be contented with reading of certain chapters of the bible, and prayers every *Sunday* morning. The *English* minister was one *Samuel Batchelour*, who 1646 return'd likewise to *England*; about which time there were seven *Dutch* ministers in the *Dutch Brasil*. Our religious worship was both in its doctrine and practice regulated exactly according to the prescription of the synod of *Dort*, and peculiar care was taken for the education of the youth, for which purpose the catechism was every *Sunday* in the afternoon explained, both in the *Receif* and *Maurice*'s town. Four times in the year the holy sacrament was administred, those who desired to be partakers of it, being obliged to make their confession before the church-council, or the ministers, who entred their names in a book; and if they came from abroad, published their names to the congregation; and in all other respects the church discipline was carefully observed. The church-council was composed of six church-wardens, besides the minister, these met duly once a week, and if any business of moment happen'd, such as chusing a minister, *&c.* they called the deacons, who were likewise six in number, to their assistance. Out of the deacons were every month chosen two, who (besides their ordinary business) were to visit the sick and wounded, and to provide for them if necessity required. They also took care of the orphans, to have them instructed in reading and writing. In the same manner the other churches were regulated, with this difference only, that the number of church-wardens and deacons was less, in proportion to the number of their respective congregations. Thus much of the ecclesiastical state.

Their church-council.

Besides those living creatures we have given you a description of before, there are divers sorts of bees in *Brasil*, call'd *Eiruku*'s, which settle upon the trees in a most surprizing manner. They are not unlike

1643. unlike our bees, but ſomewhat ſmaller; and ſwarm chiefly among the woods. The *Braſilians* diſtinguiſh them into twelve different kinds; *viz. Amanakay-Miri*, *Amanakay-Veu*, *Aibu*, *Mumbuka*, *Pixuna*, *Urutuetra*, *Tubuna*, *Tujuba*, *Eiruku*, *Eixu*, *Kubiara* and *Kurupireira*; the laſt of which are in no eſteem among them.

The bees *Eiruku* are the largeſt of all, and produce a very good honey, though it is not commonly uſed. They make their combs within the hollowneſs of trees, which the *Braſilians* draw from thence by the means of a hollow pipe. The bees called *Eiku* and *Kopy* are ſmaller and of a blackiſh colour; they make holes from without, in the bark of the trees, in the nature of bee-hives; and the comb within is all of white wax; this is now counted the beſt thing, but is not gathered in the ſame quantity as the former; beſides that theſe bees ſting very furiouſly. The bees *Thanbuka* are likewiſe ſmall, of a yellowiſh colour; they fix their combs on the top of the higheſt trees, and afford the beſt honey, which is in great quantities tranſported from hence to *Europe*, where it is ſold very cheap. It is little inferior in goodneſs to the *European* honey, and of a good ſubſtance; tranſparent and of an agreeable ſcent. It is accounted very balſamick, corrects the ſharp humours in the inteſtines, and eſpecially in the kidneys, and provokes urine. They make of this honey metheglin, which is very ſtrong, and will keep a great while: You may alſo make meath with this honey without boiling, only mix'd with ſome ſpring water and expoſed to the weather.

Balſam. *Braſil* produces likewiſe ſeveral ſorts of balſams; the beſt of which is called by the *Braſilians Kopaiba*, from the trees from whence it comes. *Kopaiba* is a very high wild tree, with an aſh-coloured bark, which ſpreads at the top into many branches. The leaves are about half a foot long, ſometimes larger, ſometimes leſſer, which in the midſt of the branches ſtand oppoſite to one another, but on the end like other leaves. At the end of the great branches are abundance of leſſer ſprouts full of leaves, out of which comes forth the bloſſom, and afterwards berries, not unlike our laurel-berries. They are green at firſt, but as they ripen turn black and ſweet. Within is a round hard ſtone, the kernel of which is white, but mealy, and not fit to be eaten. The berries ripen in *June*, when the *Braſilians* ſuck the juice out of them, and throw away the ſtone and ſkin. The apes take great delight in this fruit.

The oily and odoriferous balſam, in which this tree abounds, drops every full moon, provided you cut a ſlit through the bark as deep as to the pith, in ſuch quantity, that in three hours time you may gather above twelve *Mengeln*. But if that does not drop immediately, the ſlit is made up with wax; and within fourteen days after, they are ſure the balſam will come in great quantity. This tree does not grow ſo plentifully in the captainſhip of *Pernambuko*, as in the iſle *Maranhaon*; from whence this balſam is tranſported into *Europe*. The balſam is hot in the ſecond degree, of a thick oleaginous and reſinous ſubſtance. It is very ſtomachic, and a good remedy againſt the cholick, occaſioned by cold, externally applied to the affected parts; ſome few drops taken inwardly ſtrengthen the bowels, and ſtop the overflowing in women, the looſeneſs and involuntary emiſſion of ſeed in men; againſt which diſtempers it likewiſe is uſed in clyſters or by ſyringing. Thus far concerning the ſole *Dutch Braſil*; we will now proceed to give you an account of what paſſed during our abode there. *A Mengeln is near thr quarts*

In the year 1640, Mr. *Henry Hamel*, one of the directors of the *Weſt-India* company for the chamber of *Amſterdam*, and Mr. *Dirck Kodde Vander Burgh* (both perſons excellently well qualified for the management of the *Dutch Braſil*, and of great experience in affairs of commerce) were at the requeſt of the council of nineteen, ſent to *Braſil*, and arrived there on the 8th of *Auguſt*, the two preceeding directors or councellors, *Matthias Van Keulen* and *John Güſeling*, reſigned their places to them, and with them the chief management of the *Dutch Braſil*, under the government of *John Maurice* count *Naſſau*. *New directors ſent to* Braſil.

At the time of their arrival in *Braſil*, there were under the juriſdiction of the ſtates the following *Captainſhips: Pernambuko*, *Itamarika* (unto which belongs *Goiana*) *Parayba*, *Rio Grande* and *Siara*, being the northern part of *Braſil*: The ſouthern part, which contained the *Captainſhips Bahia*, *Ileos*, *Porto ſecuro*, *Spirito Santo*, *Rio Janeiro* and *St. Vincent*, remained under the *Portugueſe*, who inhabited the country as far as *Rio de Plate*. Not many months after the iſland of *Maranhaon* was joined with the *Dutch Braſil*, but the charges we were fain to be at to defend it againſt the *Portugueſe*, thoſe of *Para* and the natives, which over-balancing the profit the company was likely to reap from thence, it was thought moſt expedient to quit the ſame; which was done accordingly in the year 1644, or rather to confeſs the truth, by the combination of the *Portugueſe*, thoſe of *Grand Para* and the natives, we were forced to abandon it. Dutch Braſil. Portugueſe Braſil.

1643. Before the arrival of those new directors a fleet had been sent to the *Bahia*, to land some men there, and to destroy all with fire and sword; which after they had put in execution, and returned to the *Receif*, the same fleet under the command of admiral *Jol* and *Cornelius Lichthart*, was by special command from the council of nineteen in *Holland* ordered to the *West-Indies*, to lay in wait for the *Spanish* plate fleet of *Terra firma* and new *Spain*; but they returned without doing any thing, 1640 in *December*, having lost four or five ships in this voyage. Colonel *Koin* was much about the same time sent with a body of soldiers into the captainship of *Rio Real*, to bridle the *Portuguese*, by making a diversion in their own territories; but those troops being but indifferently supplied with necessaries in an enemies countrey, and forced to undergo great fatigues; they were so much weakned that it was thought adviseable to recall them out of *Rio Real*, and to assign them quarters of refreshment in the garrisons. Major *Van Brande* had worse success than all the rest, for being sent abroad with a party to fetch in some cattle, was put to the rout, and he himself taken prisoner.

The Dutch *miscarry in their design upon the* Spanish *plate fleet.*

In the mean while that our whole fleet was waiting for the *Spanish* plate fleet on the coast of *America*, and we consequently were not in a condition to undertake any thing at sea; our directors had all the reason in the world to fear, that the *Portuguese* would take this opportunity to revenge their loss, by destroying our sugar-mills, which made them leave no stone unturned to secure the *Dutch Brasil* and its inhabitants, against the attempts of the enemy: And considering that a great part of our security depended on the good inclinations of the *Portuguese* living among us, it was thought convenient to call an assembly of the chiefest *Portuguese* inhabitants of the three captainships of *Pernambuko*, *Itimarika*, and *Parayba*, towards the latter end of *August*, to concert measures how to defend their sugar-mills and fields against the incursions of the enemy.

The most effectual means that could be pitched upon in this assembly were, to provide their forts with good garri sons on the borders, and to secure the sugar-mills, by putting a certain number of soldiers in or near them, for the security of the adjacent fields. This was put in execution accordingly, and the officers had strict charge to keep a watchful eye upon the least motion of the *Portuguese*, notwithstanding which it had not the desired effect; because those *Portuguese* who lived at a considerable distance from us, and near the enemies frontiers, durst not give timely notice of their approach; besides that many among them having a constant hatred to our nation, did favour the enterprizes of those parties that burnt the sugar-fields and plundered the mills, served them sometimes for guides, and had their share in the booty; which obliged our people to be at a constant charge of a strong guard to conduct their goods, and defend them against any sudden attempts. Such an incursion was not long after made by the *Portuguese* into our territories. For in *November* the viceroy, the marquis of *Montelvano* sent two barges full of soldiers to burn our sugar-reeds in the plains, which they effected, but durst not go too far, or attempt any thing against our mills, for fear of the soldiers quartered thereabouts; who could not prevent their burning in the fields, as being done in the night time. The *Dutch* were the greatest losers by it, because they had generally the greatest share in those fields and mills, besides that the *Portuguese* spared those of their own countrey-men; all which brought a great damp upon trade, every one being afraid to venture in any business, where he might lose all his substance in one night, and that perhaps by the hands of a single person, whereby the revenues of the company were greatly impaired, and their charges increased, being forced to maintain twenty or thirty soldiers for the defence of any considerable plantation or sugar-mills; which prevented them from bringing a sufficient body of men into the field, to make head against the enemy. This was the state of the *Dutch Brasil* towards the latter end of 1640. 1643.

The twenty-second of *December* in the same year, Mr. *Adrian van Bullestraete* arrived at the *Receif* from *Middleburgh*, in the quality of director of *Brasil*, so that now the great council being compleat, the best expedient to obviate all these difficulties, was judged to consist in our fleet; pursuant to this resolution, all our ships were ordered to the *Bahia*, to make the enemy sensible that we were in a condition to be even with them, and thereby to facilitate the negotiation that was in hand, for the surceasing of burning on both sides. The council of nineteen having also sent express orders to cruise with some ships before *Rio Janeiro*, from whence the *Spanish* ships used generally to return into *Spain*, about the month of *May* or *June*, some of the biggest ships were ordered that way to intercept if possible the *Flota*, the rest being left near the *Bahia*.

The Dutch *ships ordered to the* Bahia.

But whilst our commissioners were treating with the viceroy about the surceasing of burning and plundering, a certain *Portuguese*, *Paulo de Kunha* by name, committed

unheard

1643. unheard of cruelties, with murthering, plundering and burning, in the open countrey, which made count *Maurice* write the following letter to the viceroy.

Count Maurice'*s letter to the vice-roy.*

Count Maurice's letter to the viceroy.

THE *barbarities lately committed by* Paulo de Kunha, *with burning, murdering, and plundering in the open countrey, give me great reason to fear, that your last obliging letter was designed for a complement, without any reality. The confidence I had in your excellency's sincerity, made me recal our ships and forces from your territories, to take away all means of offence: But the long stay of our deputies affords great occasion of suspicion, that your intention is only to amuse us; which has obliged me to dispatch a vessel to let them know that in case the treaty is not brought to a conclusion, to return without delay; it being our intention that the said negotiation should not be continued longer. Your excellency will there dismiss them, together with our two hostages, as we are resolved to send back to you* Martin Feirera, *left with us as hostage from your excellency, his companion being dead of late.*

Hereupon, by the mediation of the clergy living under our jurisdiction, but especially by the indefatigable care of *Dirck Kodde Vander Burgh*, who was sent thither for that purpose, the treaty was brought to a happy conclusion in *February* 1641, by virtue of which, all destruction by burning and plundering were to surcease on both sides; which being published by proclamation, the *Portuguese* were ordered to quit our dominions, whereby we reapt this advantage, that now we might turn all our forces where we found it most expedient.

The treaty against burning concluded.

In *June* 1641, count *Maurice* and the great council received advice of the ten years truce concluded betwixt the states of *Holland* and the king of *Portugal*, with all the articles thereunto belonging, which were published by proclamation in all our captainships, and all acts of hostilities ceased on both sides; the *Dutch* living in good understanding with the inhabitants of the *Bahia*, giving them all the demonstrations of friendship, sufficient to convince the *Portuguese* that they had not the least reason to fear any infraction on their side.

The great council being willing to improve this interval of peace for the advancement of traffick, and the benefit of the company, gave all imaginable encouragement, in proportion to the circumstances of time and place, to all the inhabitants of what nation soever, for the cultivating the lands, which had this good effect, that the masters of the sugar-mills rebuilt their mills, and the husbandmen betook themselves with so much eagerness to the cultivating of their sugar-fields, that they borrowed considerable sums, upon a prospect of sure gain, which would over pay their debts; as without question it would have done in a short time, if by the treachery of the *Portuguese* they had not been disappointed in their hopes. The next thing to be taken in hand, was to make such wholesome laws as were thought most expedient for the establishment and increase of commerce, both in the *Receif* and other places, and to improve the domains and other revenues belonging to the company, during this time of truce. 1643.

Trade then began to flourish apace, so that some time after the truce, the merchants and factors sold more commodities than had ever been known either before or since. Many millions were dealt for in a little time, the merchants and factors being contented to sell to those who would pay some money in part, though there were buyers enough who would and could buy for ready cash.

The flourishing state of Brasil.

The finances of the company in *Brasil* were in so good a state by the extraordinary care of the great council, that 1640 and 1641, they bought considerable quantities of sugar upon the publick account, which they sent to *Holland*. In the *Receif* and *Maurice Town*, we saw several goodly structures erected by the inhabitants, who lived in great plenty and magnificence, every one looking upon his debts as secure, and having a fair prospect to increase his riches, by the flourishing state of commerce and improvement of the lands.

Its decay.

But this was of no long continuance, for in the beginning of 1643, things began to appear with a quite different face; for the magazines of the company being exhausted by several expeditions against *Angola*, &c. and having received no supplies in their stead out of *Holland*, as they used to do before, the great council was obliged to make use of what was due to the company, for the payment of the garrisons and other officers, and consequently to force their debtors to prompt payments.

For at the beginning of the government of the new directors, the company had a considerable naval force upon the coast of *Brasil*, their magazines were well provided with provision and ammunition, and they maintained a good number of soldiers. The great council of the *Dutch Brasil* relying upon their strength, did with consent of count *Maurice*, send in 1641, several fleets with soldiers to *Spirito Santo*, *Rio de Janeiro*, the isle of *Maranhaon*, *Angola*, *St. Thomas*, and other places thereabouts, to attack

1643. tack the same, which succeeded according to expectation; but their magazines were greatly exhausted by those expeditions. Besides this, the merchants in *Holland* began to call upon their servants and factors for considerable sums of money, in return of what they had received from them; who being obliged to send all the money they could bring together from their creditors, to their masters in *Holland*; this occasioned great scarcity of ready money, and consequently no small detriment in traffick, which continuing thus from time to time, there arose such a general scarcity of money, as is scarce to be imagined; many of the masters of the sugar-mills, that had no ready money to satisfy their debts at the appointed time, being forced to take up money upon credit, and to pay three or four *per cent per* month, which reduced many of them to such an extremity in a little time, that they were neither able to pay the principal nor interest.

The reason. Upon the arrival of the three new directors, or members of the great council in 1640, *viz. Henry Hamel, Kodde*, and *Bullestraete*, they found that the inhabitants, but especially the *Portuguese* of the *Dutch Brasil*, by buying of sugar-mills and plantations, as well as negroes and other commodities, had run themselves much in debt; having bought their negroes not only at three hundred pieces of eight *per* head, but also given most extravagant prices for all other sorts of commodities, and purchasing whole warehouses without making a just account how to be able to pay for them. This was done by the *Portuguese* in hopes of the good success of those great fleets they understood were equipping in *Spain*, to reduce *Brasil* under the king's obedience, which they supposed would free them from all their debts; which the factors not being aware of, and blinded with the prospect of vast profit, sold their goods to the *Portuguese* without reluctancy. But the design of the *Portuguese* vanishing into smoak for that time, they were forced to pay; but new supplies of all sorts of commodities being sent out of *Holland*, they bought on a-fresh, heaping debts upon debts, till failing in their payments, their credit began also to fail with the merchants, who now began to urge for satisfaction of their debts. For the countrey traders being urged by the factors and merchants, who received those commodities from their correspondents in *Holland*, was obliged to call to an account the *Portuguese* unto whom he had sold the goods. And because the *Portuguese* had not bought those commodities from the *Dutch*, but with an intention never to pay for them, the countrey trader who was obliged to pay the merchants in the *Receif*, saw himself reduced to ruin, the *Portuguese* having not wherewithal to satisfy their debts. 1643.

Great confusion in traffick. Thus through the unwariness and mismanagement of those factors, whom the merchants in *Holland* had intrusted with their goods, such a confusion was introduced, as tended to the great detriment of their correspondents in *Holland*. All the business at that time lay among the lawyers, and in the courts of judicature, which considering the chargeableness of law-suits in *Brasil*, tended to their farther ruin; for when they had obtained sentence and execution against the debtors, the greatest difficulty was, how and which way to lay the execution; most of the *Portuguese* sueing for protection from the regency, which if they could not obtain, they lived incognito; especially those who had no lands or effects, or if they had, it was no easy matter to find out where they were. Besides that, if the creditors executed their executions upon the lands, they were forced to be the buyers themselves, and to live in the countrey to manage the lands, a thing altogether inconvenient to the merchants, who had other business upon their hands in the *Receif*. Such as were cast into prison must be maintained there at the charge of the creditor, which in process of time amounted to such a sum, that they themselves were fain to solicite the releasement of their debtors, and to make the best composition with them they could.

Mortality among the negroes. Besides these inconveniences, there have happened of late several others, *viz.* a great mortality of the negroes and *Brasilians*, by a certain infectious distemper, incident to the natives, called *Bexigos*, resembling our small-pox in *Europe*. Most of these negroes were bought at the rate of three hundred pieces of eight, and consequently their loss drew after it the ruin of the planters, who also complained much of vermin, and several inundations that had done considerable damage to the sugar-fields. This confusion in traffick introduced no small broils among the inhabitants themselves, who in case of non-payment, threw one another in prison without mercy, and endeavoured to prevent one another by clandestine means, to get in their debts before the rest; offering considerable abatements and rewards to such as would underhand surrender or transport their effects; and those divisions were not a little fomented by some ill minded persons, to the prejudice of the government; many of those, who either by unwariness or other mismanagement lost their debts, laying the fault thereof at the door of the regency and of the courts of justice, vainly imagining that what they had lost by their own neglect

1643. lect or want of care, should be made good by the publick purse; especially if it happened so, that the same persons were indebted to the company as well as private persons, there arise great contests about the preference.

The debts of the company did also increase every day, which at last amounted to some millions: For the directors, which before the year 1640 had the management of affairs in *Brasil*, did sell most of the confiscated estates, sugar-mills, and merchandizes, as well as the negroes bought on account of the company in *Africk*, upon credit, so that their books were filled with debts, but their cash empty of money. The succeeding members of the great council, Mr. *Hamel*, *Bullestraet*, and *Kodde*, did leave no stone unturned to correct this custom, and to sell their commodities for ready money, or otherwise to exchange them for sugars, thereby to ease the company in the great charge they were forced to be at in their several expeditions; and it is certain, that in 1640, 1641, and 1642, they sent such vast cargoes of sugar to *Holland*, that the like had never been known before in *Brasil*. Notwithstanding which, by the vast numbers of negroes that were imported, after our conquest of *Angola*, the company fell more and more in debt, by reason their debtors were very dilatory in their payments. The council of nineteen sent express orders to remedy this evil, by selling the negroes for ready money, or exchanging them for sugar; but this could not be put in practice, because there was no body who would buy upon those conditions, so that the price of the negroes falling daily lower and lower, and these being a great burden to the company, and subject to distempers and mortality, this order was fain to be revoked, unless they would see the negroe trade dwindle away into nothing; for the inhabitants being for the most part such as had bestowed most part of their substance in their sugar-mills, plantations, and negroes, they could not pay ready money, but were forced to deal upon credit, till they could reap the benefit of their labour.

The members of the great council did therefore take all imaginable care to call upon their debtors exactly at the time of their sugar-harvest, and ordered their officers in the countrey to seize upon some of them on account of the company.

From hence arose nothing but law-suits, sentences, executions, and imprisonments: The members of the great council thinking it not below their station, to go sometimes in person into the countrey to promote the payment of the debts owing to the company. But this had a contrary effect, for the merchants and factors began to be extreamly dissatisfied, that the company should seize upon the sugar in the mills, without letting them who were creditors as well as they, have their share in them. This occasioned not only murmurings, but also threats, and complaints to the council of nineteen, where they misrepresented these transactions under the worst colours they could, hoping thereby to deter the officers of the company from doing their duty. The great council having taken the matter into mature deliberation, and fearing, not without reason, that in time it might occasion a general discontent, they left no stone unturned to satisfy the minds of the people; by finding out means to have their debts satisfied. It was proposed by several understanding persons, that the company should undertake to satisfy the debts of private persons, either by way of payment or exchange; in lieu of which the masters of the sugar-mills should surrender to the company every year, the whole product of these mills, till they had satisfied all their debts: And to make the same the more effectual, for the general benefit as well of the company and sugar-mills, as the merchants and factors, it was agreed, that certain articles should be agreed upon for that purpose; the greatest advantage the company pretended to reap by it being, that they should have a fair opportunity of recovering some of their debts, which were given over for lost. These agreements were wonderfully pleasing to the council of nineteen, who in the year 1645, on the 16th of *June*, sent their approbation of a second agreement made with one *George Homo Pinto* (which indeed was of as great consequence as all the other contracts together) to the great council as follows: 1643.

Approbation of the Agreement.

The approbation of the agreement.

Concerning the agreement by you (meaning the council) on the 14th of December *last, made with* George Homo Pinto, *we have had several debates, which we find to have been brought to a conclusion, with the previous advice and approbation of the councellors of justice and of the finances; so that both in respect of the same, and of the great benefit that is likely to accrue thereby to the company, we have thought fit to approve of the said Agreement; recommending to you the execution of it, with the same zeal as you have shewn your conduct and circumspection in the whole management of these contracts.*

That these agreements were by all people, that had any knowledge of those affairs, looked upon as greatly for the interest

1643. rest of the company, is most evident from hence, that several other merchants that were sensible of this advantage, made agreements with their debtors much upon the same terms as the company had done; which that it may be put beyond all doubt, we will give you a copy of one of those agreements, from whence it will plainly appear with how much circumspection the council proceeded in this matter, betwixt the company, the masters of the sugar-mills and their debtors.

The copy of an Agreement.

The copy of an agreement.

M*R.* Peter John Bas, *and* John van Ratsfield, *councellors of justice of* Brasil, *by special commission from the* West-India *company, and* John van Walbeeck, *assessor of the great council, did appear before us on one side; and* Manuel Fernando Cruz, *Sieur* de Ingenho Tapicura, *in behalf of himself and his heirs; as also* Benjamin de Pina *for ten thousand six hundred gilders;* Isaac de Costa *for thirteen thousand one hundred and eight;* Joseph Abenacar *for four hundred ninety;* Simon de Vale *for three hundred twenty-five;* Gasper Francisco *and* David Brandoa *for eleven hundred thirty-three;* Abraham de Tovaer *for one thousand;* John Parente *for three hundred and fifty;* John Mendonça de Moeribeca *for four thousand three hundred fifty;* James Gabay *for one thousand and fifty;* More de Leon *for six hundred;* Balthazar de Fonseca *for six hundred;* Simon Gomes de Lisboa *for five thousand nine hundred ten;* Bartholomew Rodrigues *for nine hundred; and* Daniel Cardosa *for nine hundred and ten gilders; the whole amounting to forty thousand five hundred twenty-six gilders, being all creditors of the said* Manuel Fernando Cruz, *and for the most part debtors to the company on the other side, who profess and declare to have agreed among themselves, that the beforementioned* Manuel Fernando Cruz, *shall pay to the company the full sum of sixty thousand seven hundred ninety five gilders,* viz. *nineteen thousand two hundred sixty nine gilders upon his own account, being by him owing to the said company, and the remaining sum on the account of his creditors, which proportionably to their respective debts, ought to be discounted for with him by the said company, upon the following conditions.*

I. *That the whole debt is to be satisfied in the three next following years, the first payment to begin in* January 1645, *and if it happen, that in one year a less share be paid than in the other, the whole is to be made good in the last year.*

II. *That no discounts shall be entred in the books of the company, 'till after the payment of the due proportion appointed for each respective term or time.* 1643.

III. *That the creditors of those with whom they have entred into articles of agreement, as well as the debtors of the company, shall not be discharged of their debts in the books of the company, but in case of failure or delay of payment, either of the whole sum or part thereof, all the respective appointed times, shall stand engaged and answerable, each for his respective debt, unless they give other security to the company; but those creditors who have no debts in the books of the company, shall have liberty to transfer other debts, or else to receive their share in two years time, either by assignments or in Negroes; but not in any commodities imported from abroad, or sugar to be exported; provided nevertheless that the articles of agreement be fulfilled, or otherwise the sum be put to their own account immediately, in which case they are to allow eighteen pound* per cent. *and nevertheless be liable to see the agreement put in execution.*

IV. *Those who are entred into articles of agreement shall be obliged to engage both their body and goods for the performance thereof, but especially to deliver an inventory of their personal estates, confirm'd by oath; besides which, they are to give such securities as shall be approved of by the great council; with renouncing the* beneficium ordinis, divisionis & excusationis, *as well for each respective payment at the appointed times, as the whole sum in general.*

V. *These before-mention'd securities are to be persons well-qualified, of good substance, not involv'd in debts, but especially in the company's; and shall be warranted by the magistrates of their respective places of abode.*

VI. *Publick notice is to be given to all persons, who have any bonds, bills, or accounts, or other engagements relating to the personal estates (which shall be named or specified) of such as are entred into those articles, that within the space of three weeks they are to produce the same, or else to be excluded from the benefit thereof, 'till after the expiration of the time mentioned and appointed in the said agreement.*

VII. *That he, who has engaged himself in such an agreement or contract, shall not be permitted to contract new debts, unless with the consent of the great council; otherwise the same to be void and null, of which publick notice shall be given. Neither shall he abalienate any sugars by land as remains, under the penalty of restitution to be made with full interest and charges.*

The

1643. *The creditors shall be obliged to surrender and renounce all their pretensions, engagements and actions to the company; neither shall they lay any claim upon that score of precedence or otherwise.*

Whenever it shall be judged requisite, by the great council, *to send a certain person to the* ingenho *of any person entred into such an agreement, for the better security of their debt, and the receiving and sending away the sugar, allotted to the company, he shall be obliged to find him with victuals and lodgings in his* ingenho; *but the company shall pay him for his pains.*

Pursuant to which, the before named Manuel Fernando Cruz, *with the advice and consent of his before-mentioned creditors, has obliged himself in general, and by these presents, obliges and engages his person and estate, both real and personal, without any reservation or exception; but especially the before-named* Ingenho Tapicura, *with all its appurtenances, according to the inventory thereunto affixed and confirmed by oath; which* Ingenho Tapicura, *he declares to be free from any pre-engagements, with all the grounds, sugar-fields, pasturages, woods, and other things thereunto belonging, viz. eight brass* calderns, *ten* tachoos *and ten* parvos, *besides several other copper vessels belonging to the said* ingenho; *twenty slaves belonging to the said* ingenho, *and* Manuel Ferdinando Cruz, *his house and sixty oxen. And for the better performance of this agreement,* Senhor John de Mendose *dwelling at* Moeribeca, *and* Manuel Gomes des Lisboa, *living in* Moquiaxe, *have, after certificates obtained from the magistrates of their respective dwelling-places, engaged themselves, and do by these presents engage themselves as securities for the whole debt, and as debtors for each and every part thereof, promising to indemnify the company of all actions, suits, or other pretensions which may be made against them on the account of any other creditors of the said* Manuel Fernando Cruz, *not mention'd or engaged in this agreement; as likewise, that no sugar shall be surreptitiously convey'd away or abalienated: That in case of non-payment, the company shall be hereby fully empowered to recover their damages with interest and charges, upon their persons and estates; they renouncing by these presents all exceptions,* ordinis, divisionis & excusationis, *as likewise all other pretensions of privileges tending to the invalidity of this contract. The before-named creditors also, in general, and every one of them in particular, declare that they have given in a true account of all their respective pretensions upon the said* Manuel Fernando Cruz, *neither that they do demand any other sum or sums of him, but what have been specified there under their respective names; promising to be well satisfied with what has been stipulated, and, if put in execution accordingly, to renounce all actions or private engagements, discontents or preference in favour of the company; and that in case of non-payment they will be obliged to make good and restore to the said company, not only each particular sum paid at certain limited times, but also the whole, in the same manner, as if the said agreement had never been made betwixt them; leaving it to the discretion of the company, whether they will lay their actions against* Manuel Fernando Cruz *and his securities, or against themselves and their estates; under the condition they were in before the conclusion of this agreement; the benefit of* actionem cessam *being allowed them against the said* Cruz *and his securities, for the recovery of their just debts. In witness and confirmation of which we have granted these our letters, as usual in such cases, sealed with the ordinary seal of the court of justice, and signed by the secretary of the council. Translated in the* Receif, 23[d] September 1644.

In the same manner all the other contracts were made and penn'd; the contents of which amounted in the whole to two million a hundred and twenty five thousand eight hundred and seven gilders, which were due from the farmers to the masters of the sugar-mills, and from those again to the company.

For what reason these agreements were made

The chief, if not the only reason, why these agreements were resolved upon, was, (as we said before) the intolerable vexations and exactions put upon the masters of the sugar-mills by their creditors, who, unless these masters paid them at the rate of two or three *per cent.* interest *per* month, made immediate seizure of their negroes, oxen, coppers, and other necessaries belonging to the sugar-mills; so that the masters of these sugar-mills being reduced to a necessity of paying such exorbitant exactions, or else to see themselves entirely ruined, began to defend their plantations and mills by force, so that things seemed to tend at that time to a general insurrection, if the same had not been prevented, by entring into those contracts; by which means the masters of the sugar-mills being freed from the oppressions of their creditors, and in lieu thereof now become debtors to the company, and time given them to employ their mills for the payment of their debts, at certain limited times, and that at the rate of one *per cent.* interest *per* month only, all pretensions and occasions of a revolt were thereby removed, at least for that time; the first term of payment being set out for a considerable time.

To

1643. To make this the more evident, these following heads deserve our particular observation: That the company and the merchants, being creditors of the masters of the sugar-mills, endeavouring at the same time to force them to the payment of their debts, by executions. This occasioned from the year 1647 to the time of the making of those contracts, such a confusion, as must needs have tended to the total destruction of the sugar-mills, and consequently of the merchants and company; which induced them to apply themselves to the great council, to find out some means, by way of discount, or otherwise, to put these debts into the company's hands.

The councellors of justice did not at first agree in all points to these proposals, but at their meeting on the 12th of *August* 1644, being better convinced of the matter, and that the company was sufficiently secured and benefited thereby, the next following day did not only approve of the same, but also were of opinion, that some things might be rather mitigated for the Advantage of the masters of mills and their creditors, than not to relieve them at this juncture; so that the conditions were the 10th of *November* 1644, agreed unto with the consent of the councellors of the court of justice and the finances.

Pursuant to these, the great council took care that publick notice should be given of these agreements made betwixt the company and certain private persons, by which every one was forewarned not to sell any thing upon credit to them, without the consent of the great council; and their creditors summoned to make good their debts within three weeks time, or else to be excluded from the benefit of the contract, 'till after the time therein limited was expired. From all which it is sufficiently demonstrable, with how little appearance of truth some have attempted to insinuate, that these contracts were prejudicial to the company, and had given no small occasion to the ensuing revolt of the *Portuguese*; when it is beyond all question, from what has been said before, that these were the only means to prevent those calamities, wherewith the masters of the sugar-mills, and the farmers or countrey planters, were over-whelmed all that time, who were forced to let their mills stand still, and leave the ground uncultivated; all which, as it tended to the utter destruction of the sugar-mills, so the company sustained an irreparable loss, *viz.* thirty eight pounds *per cent.* yearly in *Brasil*, and thirty seven pounds *per cent.* in *Holland*, which being seventy five pound *per cent.* did altogether arise from the use of the sugar-mills.

Besides this, there were not a few of those merchants that were creditors of the sugar-mills, that were considerably indebted to the company, who pleading insolvency, by reason of the non-payment of their debtors; the company would have been considerable losers by them, unless by this way of discounting they had found means to recover those desperate debts. All which moved the great council to make a virtue of necessity, and with the advice of the masters of the sugar-mills and their creditors, and the approbation of the council of nineteen, to enter upon those articles; which could not be in any wise detrimental to the company; tho' some malicious persons have objected against them, that (supposing there had been no revolt) these masters would not in twenty years, nay, perhaps never have been in a condition to wrong the company, what they had laid out upon their account; when it is sufficiently known that the great council never paid one farthing of ready money for them on the account of the company; besides that for the satisfaction of the company, twenty five sugar-mills were engaged, which one with another, affording from two hundred and thirty to two hundred and fifty chests of sugar yearly; if the company had drawn but a hundred and forty or a hundred and fifty chests from each, the same would have amounted to four hundred and twenty thousand gilders; from whence it is evident, that not to include the sugar-mills, their coppers, oxen, and other Instruments thereunto belonging, the sum of two millions one hundred and twenty five thousand eight and sixteen gilders, being the total sum of the debt owing to the company by vertue of these contracts, might have been satisfied without much hazard; the *Portuguese* masters of the sugar-mills, being by this expedient left in the quiet possession of their mills, and eased from the oppressions of their creditors, and our hopes were not a little increased by the industry of the inhabitants of the country, who finding themselves now at ease, applied themselves with so much assiduity to the improvement of their plantations, for the better satisfying of their debts, that in 1645 there was such a fair prospect of a plentiful harvest of sugar, as had not been known in many years before. 1643.

Reasons of the revolt of the Portuguese.

But it seems as if the *Portuguese* out of an in-born hatred to our nation, who had conquered them, were resolved not to rest satisfied, 'till by underhand practices and plots they had undermined our government. Add to this, that many of them having involved themselves over head and

1643. and ears in debt, and seeing no way to satisfy their creditors, were become desperate, and more forward to run the hazard of an open revolt (in hopes of assistance from *Portugal*) than to undergo the unavoidable necessities of poverty; which made some of them frankly tell our people afterwards, that in case they were disappointed in their hopes of succours from the *Bahia*, they would seek for aid in *Spain* or *Turkey*.

Towards the latter end of the year 1642, there were rumours spread abroad of a Plot contrived by the *Portuguese* against the state when they were disarmed, and their arms brought into the magazines, which however they got again under some pretence or other afterwards, they living very quietly among us, for fear, as I suppose, of our garrisons, and that they were not then sufficiently assured of succours from the *Bahia*. But it will not be amiss to trace the true origin of this revolt.

The 13th *December* 1642, one *John Fernandes Vieira*, alderman of *Maurice*'s-*Town*, appeared in the great council, count *Maurice* being present, where he told them, that he had been informed by certain *Jews*, how he and his father-in-law *Beringel* were suspected in *Holland*, of having sent letters by a son of the said *Beringel* to the king of *Portugal*, tending to the detriment of the state. He did not deny to have sent a letter by the said person to the king of *Portugal*, but containing no more than a recommendation of the said *Beringel*'s person, to help him him to some employment under the king: This he offer'd to prove by his copy, which being produced, there was found nothing material in it, but a congratulation to the king upon his accession to the crown, and a recommendation of the said *Beringel*; *Vieira* further proposed, that he thought it absolutely necessary, for the safety of his estate, to have the *Portuguese* disarmed, as likewise the captains *de Campo*, with those under their jurisdiction, the *Negroes*, *Brasilians*, *Mulatts* and *Mamalukes*.

Suspicion of treachery.

There was also a letter sent by the council of nineteen, dated 1 *June* 1642, to count *Maurice*, containing in substance, that one *John van North*, who had served for fourteen months in the quality of a cadee in *Brasil*, had declared to them at *Amsterdam*, that he had been a servant in a sugar-mill belonging to *John Fernandes Vieira*, where after a stay of two months, he was entreated by *Francisco Beringel Labrador*, to go with his son *Antonio Dandrado Beringel*, as an interpreter to *Holland*, and from thence to *Portugal*; which upon great promises he accepted of, and they set sail on board the Ship called the *Love* from *Brasil* for *Zeeland*, and afterwards from *Ulissingen* went to *Lisbon*. He said, that this *Antonio Dandrado Beringel*, after a familiar conversation of three weeks, had told him that he was sent with a letter sign'd by *John Fernandes Vieira*, *Francisco Beringel*, *Bernardin Karvailho*, *John Biserro* and *Lewis Bras Biserro*, in which they gave to understand to the king of *Portugal*, that they were well provided with men, money and arms, for the reducing *Brasil* under his obedience. The council added, that the king of *Portugal* had made the said *Beringel* a captain, for this piece of service, and that therefore they desired count *Maurice* and the great council to keep a watchful eye over them, being sensible what an aversion the *Portuguese* did bear to the *Dutch*. 1643.

At the meeting of the great council of *Brasil*, 16th *February* 1643, count *Maurice* assured them, that he had received intelligence, that some of the chiefest of the *Portuguese* had resolved to surprize our garrisons in the country, at *Moribeca*, *St. Anthony*, and some other places, and to put them to the sword, which was to be put in execution upon one of their saints days, when they used to meet in considerable Numbers. Those who had the chief management of this affair, had their dwelling-places in the *Vargea*, who had proposed to surprize likewise the *Receif*, not questioning that if they could make themselves masters of it, the other garrisons in the country would be easily reduced, and consequently the company not able to subsist long in *Brasil*, without soldiers and traffick.

Is encreased by letters from abroad.

Hereupon it was taken into deliberation, whether 'twere best to secure the heads of this rebellion immediately, or to delay it 'till a more convenient time, for fear of allarming the whole country by their Imprisonment: The last was resolved upon, because they did not think themselves as yet sufficiently assured of their designs, and did not question, but that by the secret intelligence count *Maurice* was to receive of their transactions, they might prevent them. It was however judged adviseable to draw the garrisons out of the country into the *Receif*, which was strengthened with new pallisadoes, and the old wooden battery repaired; a ship was also ordered with several great chaloops, the first on the sea-side, the others in the river, to defend the avenues of the *Receif* with their cannon. There were likewise divers letters sent by private persons, some without names, to count *Maurice* and the great council

What resolution taken thereupon.

1643.

council, confirming the traiterous designs of the *Portuguese*; among others, one Mr. *Van Els* sent a letter to count *Maurice*, dated at *Serinhaim* the 20th of *March* 1643, importing, that he had it from sure hands, that a certain *Mulat*, of the company of *Austin Hardoso*, being asked by certain inhabitants of that *Fregesie*, what business they had thereabouts, had told them, that they had been to carry letters to some persons living near the *Receif*, adding, that in a short time they would see that place taken without any effusion of blood, either of the *Dutch* or *Portuguese*.

In *December* 1643, *Don Michael de Krasto*, *Don Bastian Manduba de Sonho*, and *Don Antonio Ferdinandes*, three ambassadors from the count *Sonho* in *Angola*, arrived in the *Receif*, in the ship call'd the *Arms of Dort*; they had but one servant each, but brought along with them several negroes with golden collars, as a present to count *Maurice*, besides a great number of other Negroes for the company.

Ambassadors from the count of Sonho *admitted to audience.*

Being admitted to audience by count *Maurice* and the great council, they desired in the name of their Master, not to send any assistance to the king of *Congo*, whom they feared would attack them before long, notwithstanding they were at that time both engaged in a war against the *Portuguese*. They received for answer, that the council would write to Mr. *Niewland*, their director there, to interpose his authority and mediation, in order to maintain a good correspondency, and remove all occasion of contest betwixt the king of *Congo* and their master, they being both confederates of the States: The said Earl sent likewise a letter to count *Maurice*, in which he desired leave to buy a chair, a cloak, some ensigns of war, some apparel, and such like things. The great council writ also a letter, as well to the king of *Congo*, as to the count of *Sonho*, exhorting them to peace, and sent them the following presents in the name of the company.

To the King,

A long black velvet cloak, with silver galloons.
A scarf edged with silver lace.
A velvet coat.
And a castor-hat with a silver hatband.

To the Count,

A red velvet elbow-chair, with gold fringes.
A large velvet cloak, with gold and silver galloons.
A scarf with a gold and silver lace.
A velvet coat.
And a castor-hat with a gold and silver hatband.

They were entertained with all imaginable civility, during their stay here: They were very skillful in playing with the back-sword; in the management of which, they made most terrible postures and faces. They understood *latin* very well, and made several learned harangues in the same.

Fresh suspicion of a revolt.

The 13th of *October* 1644, a certain *Jew*, called *Gaspar Francisco de Kunha*, with two others of the chief of the same fraternity, gave notice to the great council, that they had been credibly informed by some *Jews*, who conversed and kept frequent correspondence in the country, that the *Portugueses* were plotting against the *Dutch-Brasil*, telling the council the reasons upon which they founded this suspicion. The council, after having returned thanks to these elders for their care, resolved to leave no stone unturn'd to discover the designs of the *Portuguese*; and having received certain intelligence, that they expected some arms and ammunition to be brought them by sea, they ordered the 12th of *October* 1644, the yacht called *Niewhouse*, with a galliot and a challoop, to cruise along the coast of *Dutch-Brasil*, to observe what vessels did approach the shore.

The 11th of *May* 1644, count *Maurice* left the *Receif*, in order to his return to *Holland*, after he had been eight years governor of the *Dutch-Brasil*. All the citizens and chief inhabitants, both of the *Receif* and *Maurice*'s town, appeared in arms, making a lane from the old town to the water-gate, of whom, as he pass'd by, he took his leave with all imaginable demonstration of kindness. At the gate he mounted on horse-back, and being accompanied by the great council, the councellors of justice and all the military officers, as far as *Olinda*, he there once more took his leave of them in particular, the Sieur *Bullestraet* remaining only with him, being deputed by the regency to conduct him on board the ships design'd for his transportation. They did not set sail from the *Red-Land* 'till the 22d of *May*, with a fleet of thirteen ships, on board of which were a good number of soldiers, leaving only eighteen companies for the defence of the *Dutch-Brasil*. Mr. *Bullestraet* return'd the 26th to the *Receif*.

On the 22d of *April*, not long before the departure of count *Maurice*, the commission from the governors of the *West-India* company, according to a resolution taken at their meeting the first of *July* 1642,

1643. 1642, concerning the government of *Dutch-Brasil*, and dated the 22^d of *May* 1643, was read in the great council, by which the members thereof were to have the administration of the government 'till further orders. Accordingly count *Maurice* having appointed a day to invest them with the administration of the government, he ordered (with the consent of the said council) an assembly to be called on the 6th of *May*, of the counsellors of justice, of the magistrates, the ecclesiastical council and ministers of *Maurice*'s *Town*; of the commanders in chief both by sea and land, the chief officers of the company, the officers of the militia, and the chief men among the *Jews*.

Count Maurice *abdicates the government.*

All these being at the appointed time met in the great hall of the *Stadthuis*, he told them, that since their high and mightinesses the states, his highness the prince of *Orange*, and the council of nineteen, had been pleased to grant him leave, after a stay of eight years among them, in the quality of governor of the *Dutch-Brasil*, to return into *Holland*, he had called them together, to return them thanks for the many services, each in his station, had done to the company; as likewise for the obedience, fidelity and respect they had always shewn to his person; telling them, that from this minute he resign'd the government into the hands of the great council, requiring and desiring them, in the name of the states, the prince of *Orange*, and the council of nineteen, to shew them the same obedience, fidelity and respect they had done before; whereupon count *Maurice* having congratulated the council, and the rest there present done the same, he took his leave of them in the hall, and immediately after in the council-chamber, of the members of the great council, giving them most hearty thanks for their faithful council and assistance upon all occasions, and for the respect and deference they had always shewn to his person; telling them, that since this would be the last time of his appearing in their assembly, he had drawn up a memorial, which might serve them as a guide, for the better administration of the government; and that, if they thought it convenient, he should be ready to discourse with them, and enlarge further upon that subject. The members of the great council returned him their unfeigned thanks, wishing him a happy voyage, and good success in all his undertakings, and recommended themselves and the whole *Dutch-Brasil* to his care hereafter. Before the breaking up of the assembly, it was debated in the presence of count *Maurice*, which of the members should have the precedency there as president, or whether the same should be taken by turns, the same being not determined in their commission: After several arguments *pro* and *con*, it was agreed, that things should remain, in respect of this point, in the same condition as had been usual before, in the absence of count *Maurice*, *viz.* for every one to keep his rank without any priority 'till further orders from the council of nineteen; to wit, first Mr. *Dirk Hamel*, then Mr. *Bullestraete*, Mr. *Kodde Vander Burgh*, &c. 1643.

Takes his leave.

The next thing the great council took in hand, was to inquire more narrowly into the designs of the *Portuguese* against the government; to effect which, it was resolved in *January* 1644, to send *Gilbert de Wit*, councellor of the court of justice, and captain *Dirk Hoogstrate*, then commander in chief in the *Cape of St. Austin*, to *Antonio Telles de Sylva*, then governor of the *Bahia*, with the following instructions, dated the 15th of the same month; to compliment the governor (after the delivery of their credentials) in the name of the great council, with a sincere promise and assurance of friendship, and good neighbourly correspondency. After this, they were to represent to him, that many of the subjects of the *Dutch-Brasil*, after having contracted considerable debts there, both with the company, and other inhabitants, did retire into the *Bahia*; wherefore they desired, that for the promoting of justice, they would either detain those bankrupts in prison, or at least give timely notice of their coming thither, to the *Dutch* government, whereby their subjects might be enabled to prosecute them at law: But their real errant was to be instructed underhand in the following points.

Envoys sent into the Portuguese-Brasil, *and their instructions.*

I. W*Hat forces the* Portuguese *had at that time in the* Bahia, *and the other southern provinces.*

II. *What number of ships.*

III. *What number of ships were expected there out of* Portugal.

IV. *How the negro's trade stood affected, and from what places they were brought thither.*

V. *Whether there was any commerce betwixt them and the inhabitants of* Bonas Aires.

VI. *In what condition their places were thereabouts; of all which they were to give the best account they were able to get, after their*

1643. *their return to the great council; they were also charged by word of mouth, to make diligent enquiry who were the persons that underhand encouraged the so much feared revolt of the* Portuguese *in the* Dutch Brasil, *and what aid or assistance they were to have from them; and to desire the governor not to permit for the future that such of the* Dutch *soldiers as deserted out of the* Receif, *and went by land to the* Bahia, *might from thence be transported into* Portugal, *but be stopt and sent back to the* Receif.

These envoys arrived safely the 8th of *February* 1644 in the *Bahia*, and dropt their anchor towards the evening near the city of *St. Salvador*, and the castle of *St. Antonio*, where two officers came on board them, to enquire from whence they came, and by whom, and to whom they were sent, in order to give an account thereof to the governor *Antonio Telles de Sylva*. The next following day they were complimented in the name of the governor by major *Domingo Delgados*, and captain *David Ventura*, who told them that he intended to send his chaloop with the first opportunity to fetch them ashore. About three a clock in the afternoon, the same officers with three or four more, came with the chaloop to fetch them; and they were no sooner landed but found several horses ready for them to mount upon, which they did, and were conducted up a high hill, all over covered with spectators, to the governor's palace. In the outward hall was a strong guard of soldiers, in the second several ensigns and other inferior officers, in the third apartment they met with nothing but captains and lieutenants, and in the fourth with colonels, general officers, some clergymen, and the governor himself; who after having received them at the door, desired them to sit down next to him, upon chairs set for that purpose. The envoys then begun their harangue, in which they told him, that they were extreamly glad to find him in good health at this time, when they were sent by the great council of the *Dutch Brasil*, to assure him of their good inclinations, to maintain a good correspondency and friendship with him, and of their hearty wishes for his majesty's, his own, and the government's prosperity; to preserve which, they were ready to contribute all that lay in their power. Then they told him that they had several things to propose to him, when he should think convenient to receive them; the rest of the discourse run upon mutual complements and news. After which, the envoys were again accompanied by the governor to the door of the apartment, where he ordered the beforementioned *Domingo Delgados* and *David Ventura*, to conduct them to a certain large house finely furnished, in *Bishops-street*, and to entertain them at his charge; which though the envoys refused, alledging it to be contrary to the intentions of their masters, yet were forced to accept of the same, and were very magnificently entertained at supper. 1643.

Their arrival at St. Salvador.

Are admitted to audience.

The next morning about eleven a clock they went again to the palace, and after having desired a second audience, were received in the same manner as before. Every one being ordered to withdraw, besides the secretary of the governor; the envoys made their propositions to the last, which they delivered to him in writing in *Portuguese*, recommending the same to his consideration, as tending towards the maintaining a good and firm correspondency betwixt them. To which the governor gave this general answer; *That he should always endeavour to cultivate a good understanding and correspondency with us, pursuant to the strict and reiterated orders he had received for that purpose from the king his master. And that concerning the propositions made by them to him, he would assemble his council of war and justice, and afterwards impart to them his answer.* Then they were by *Domingo Delgados* reconducted to his own house, where they were very well entertained the same day at dinner, and the next by the governor himself.

Their second audience.

The 17th they had another audience from the governor, who told them in very obliging terms, *that he had consulted the matter with his council, and could give them no other answer but what was contained in this letter*, which he delivered to them, and told them the contents thereof; whereupon our envoys told him, that since thereby a door was left open for rogues and vagabonds, they hoped he would at least order that the names of such as fled to the *Bahia* might be taken notice of, that the great council of the *Dutch Brasil* might not remain quite unsatisfied, whither they were fled; which he promised to do. After some further complements and mutual assurance of friendship, they parted for this time.

Their third audience.

The 22d they took their leave of the bishop, and several other persons of note, unto whom they owed any obligations, and last of all of the governor himself, being conducted thither by many persons of quality and officers; they returned him thanks for the civilities and respect he had been pleased to shew them, wishing both him and his *Portuguese* majesty a long and happy reign, and victory against the *Castilians*. The governor returned their complements, and conducted them out of the room, ordering several negroes to attend them down the precipice of the hill, upon which the city is built, with chairs; but the envoys choosing

1643. choosing rather to go on foot, they were in the same chaloop they came in ashore, carried back under the sound of musick on board their yacht. The *Portuguese* officers after having taken their leave, returned to the city, and ours made the best of their way to the *Receif*, where they arrived safely not long after.

Their return to the Receif.

The letter delivered to them by the governor, was as follows.

The Governour's Letter.

The governors letter.

GIlbert de Wit *councellor of your court of Justice, and* Dirk Hoogstraten *commander in chief on the* Cape of St. Austin, *your lordships deputies; whom I received according to their quality and merits, have delivered your letter to me, and proposed such other matters as they were impowered to treat with me about. Though I endeavour nothing so much as to cultivate and maintain in the strictest manner, our neighbourly good correspondency, yet am I constrained at this time frankly to acknowledge, that it is not in my power to give your lordships any more satisfactory answer than this, in hopes that the many proofs you have had of my sincere inclinations, will serve as a plea with your lordships, to assure you, that I shall always be ready in all points depending on my government, to give the same proofs both of obedience and fidelity to the king my master, whose pleasure is, that the truce should be observed inviolably; and of my sincere intentions, and the esteem I have for your lordships friendship, desiring nothing more than that you furnish me with an opportunity of giving real demonstrations of my readiness to serve you; whom I recommend to the protection of God almighty.*

Bahia, Feb. 14. 1645. Signed,

Antonio Telles da Silva.

Concerning the six points mentioned in their secret instructions, they made the following report to the great council.

Report of the envoys to the council.

I. T*HAT the* Portuguese *forces in those parts were generally esteemed to be less or more betwixt three and four thousand men, without the* Brasilians *and negroes. But that upon the most exact enquiry they could make, they had found them to be not above three thousand, including the* Brasilians *and negroes, and their garrisons both to the north and south, as far as* Rio Janeiro. *These consisted of five regiments, viz. three of* Portuguese, *under the colonels* John Darauge, Martin Soares, *and* N. N. *the fourth of* Brasilians, *under a* Brasilian *colonel,* Antonio Philippo Camarao; *and the fifth of negroes, under the command of negro* Henricio Dyas. *These two last regiments, amounting both not to above three hundred men, were divided in the garrisons to the north, about* Rio Real *on our frontiers; they being the scum and off-casts of all their territories; and consequently not to be quartered near the capital city, there having of late been some broils among them in the garrisons, whither officers were dispatched to compose them. The three* Portuguese *regiments consisting of about two thousand seven hundred men, kept garrison in* St. Salvador, *and the circumjacent forts, except two companies, one of which quartered about* Rio Real, *the other in the island* Morro St. Paulo; *and about one hundred fifty more, which were disposed in the captainships of* Os Ilheos, Porto Seguro *and* Spirito Sancto; *so that the garrisons of* St. Salvador *and the circumjacent forts, consisted in at least two thousand three hundred, each company consisting of one hundred men less or more, all chosen men and well cloathed; four companies mounted the guard every night, one at the palace, at each of the two gates one, and the fourth in the water-forts without the city.* 1643.

II. *Of their naval strength they gave a very slender account, being more considerable in number than force, as consisting only in fifty small vessels and yachts, not in the least fitted for war; neither could they observe the least shew of preparations tending that way; their aim being only to protect their ships bound to the* Portuguese *coasts, against the insults of the* Castilian *and* Denmark *privateers, and the* Turkish *rovers. It was, as they said, upon this account, that, during our stay there, two stout* Portuguese *ships fit for war, manned with six hundred men, and provided with good store of ammunition, arrived in the* Bahia, *under the command of* Salvador Correada-sa, *with orders to go directly from thence to* Rio de Janeiro, *and to fetch all ships ready loaden from thence to the* Bahia, *from whence they were to convoy these as well as such other vessels as they found ready there, to the coast of* Portugal; *for which reason also all the vessels which otherwise used to go according to their own conveniency, were ordered to stay for the said convoy. That news was brought by the said two ships, that the king of* Portugal *had forbid the building of* Caravels *and other such like small vessels, instead of which they were to build ships of better defence against the insults of an enemy at sea. From whence the envoys said they supposed would arise this inconveniency to the* Portuguese, *that the freights and convoy money paid for the commodities transported from* Portugal *to the* Portuguese Brasil, *and for the sugar transported from thence to* Portugal *must encrease, and consequently would not be able to sell the last at the same price the* Dutch *did, considering especially that they must be consi-*

1643. *considerable losers both in their interest and time, where they were forced to tarry for their convoys, whereas they used formerly to make the best of their way home.*

III. *They had observed, that though the inhabitants of the* Bahia *expected the coming of those ships at their first arrival, yet several vessels arrived there, both from the* Portuguese *coast and the islands before the rest.*

IV. *They concluded the negro trade to be very inconsiderable there, they having scarce ever heard it as much as mentioned; but because the price of a good negro did not at that time amount to above three hundred gilders, they supposed them pretty well stockt with them; those which were of late bought there being brought thither from* Cape Verde *and* Arder. *They further reported, that when on wednesday being the* 8th *of* February, *they entred the* Bahia, *they met two ships of good bulk, carrying about twenty guns each, and well mann'd going out, which upon enquiry were told them to be bound for* Portugal, *but could not learn to what harbour there, which together with some other reasons, made them suspect that they were intended another way, in which we found ourselves not deceived, when on the* 22d *of* February, *just as they were ready for their departure, they understood from* Mulat Juliana, *and of two monks, that these two ships were sent with men to* Angola, *for the security of the inhabitants of* Masagao, *who being but small in number, were sorely afraid to be set upon by the negroes of the countrey, and having desired the governor's assistance, who ordered those ships and the men to go in the night time, and to endeavour to reach* Masagao *unperceived by any, and without committing any hostilities against the* Dutch. *Whether and how far this might be true, time would shew, but they had all the reason in the world to believe, that it was upon their score of concealing this expedition, as well as some other matters from them, that immediately after arrival (though they were not informed of it till near the time of their departure) that no* Dutch *or* Germans *should appear, as much as in the sight of the envoys, much less discourse with them; which was observed with that strictness that they really imagined there had been no* Dutch *there; but found afterwards that they had been all (how many they knew not) carried on board the* Portuguese *vessels, to prevent their keeping any correspondency with us and our ships crew; to which end also, six centinels were placed in two boats lying near our yacht, during the time of our stay here, under pretence of protecting our vessel, but in effect to prevent any body from coming on board us, pursuant to the orders of the governor.*

V. *That the inhabitants of the* Bahia *and the other* Portuguese *captainships, had not the least commerce at this time with those of* Bonas Aires. *That immediately after the revolution in* Portugal, *those of the* Bahia *had attempted to go thither, but were treated as enemies by them; so that it was their opinion, the place would either soon, or was already totally ruined for want of commerce; all their livelihood consisting in the traffick from the coast of* Brasil *thither; which falling away, no silver could be transported thither from* Peru; *it being not probable that the* Spaniards *would run the hazard of passing along an enemy's coast, when they had a safer way to transport their treasures from the* West-Indies. 1643.

VI. *That they could not get the least certain information concerning the designs carried on betwixt some of the inhabitants of the* Bahia, *and those of the* Dutch Brasil *against the last; besides which they gave them a general relation of what they had been able to learn, concerning the condition of the city of* St. Salvador, *its inhabitants, governour, and some other matters relating to the countrey thereabouts.*

Another revolt of the Portuguese.

The rumours which in 1640 were noised about concerning the treacherous designs of the *Portuguese* inhabitants against us, being for that time vanished into smoak, the same was revived, and their designs began to be discovered in *February* 1645, *viz.* That confiding in the promised succours from *Bahia*, they intended to rise in arms against us, looking upon this juncture as the most favourable for their purpose, since count *Maurice* with the greatest part of our fleet, and a good number of soldiers were returned to *Holland*, from whence no fresh supplies were come of late into *Brasil*. The great council not being ignorant of this, were indefatigable in their care, to leave no stone unturned to find out the ring-leaders of this rebellion, so as to charge them effectually with this crime, and find out sufficient cause for their commitment. They sent out several of their officers into the countrey, as spies, to sound the inclinations of the people, and whether they could meet with any one who incited the rest to an insurrection. The like he did on the other side of the river of *St. Francis*, and in *Kamaron*'s camp, whither they had sent certain persons to investigate their designs, and to learn what preparations they made for war, and whether they were intended against *Pernambuko*, but were not able to find out any thing, upon which they could make any sure account. Being nevertheless sensible that those forewarnings were not altogether groundless, and knowing the *Portuguese*

1643. *tuguese* to be of so haughty a temper (besides the difference in religion) that they would scarce let any opportunity slip of withdrawing themselves from the obedience of their conquerors; they writ the 13th of *February* 1645 the following letter, concerning the designs of the *Portuguese* to the council of nineteen.

A letter from the great council to the West-India *company.*

Most noble and right honourable,

A letter from the great council to the West-India *company.*

D*Uring the government of his excellency count* Maurice, *there were already several of the inhabitants of this state entred into secret cabals to rise in mutiny against us, in hopes of assistance from the* Bahia; *their business was to insinuate into those that were well affected to them, after their good success in* Maranhaon, *that our forces being considerably weakned by the strong detachments sent to the garrisons of* Angola, St. Thomas, *and others, a fair opportunity was offered them, to withdraw themselves from our obedience, and to enjoy their former liberty under their own king. They were not a little encouraged in their design, imagining the same might be carried on without any great difficulty, when they found that of late we had received no supplies either of meat or other provisions, or of soldiers from* Holland, *whereby the storehouses of the company here being exhausted, the garrisons of the forts were forced to be supplied from time to time with farinha and fresh meats out of the countrey, they judged, if they could once be masters in the field, they must of necessity fall into their hands; as it happened in* 1640 *to the* Spanish *garrisons in* Portugal, *who for the same reason were not in a condition to hold out against the* Portuguese; *being besides that sensible that unless we would too much weaken our garrisons, we had no sufficient number of troops left to appear formidable in the field. These and other such like insinuations have been frequently spread among the* Portuguese, *by those, who finding themselves most uneasy under our government, hoped for a change of their affairs, by changing their masters; which however wrought no considerable effect, as long as his excellency continued in the government, partly because we being forewarned of their designs, kept a watchful eye over all their actions, partly because our sea and land forces being much more considerable at that time than they are now, they had but little prospect of succeeding in their enterprize, which therefore they judged most convenient to defer till after his excellency's departure, which as it was sufficiently known before hand, so they were sensible that thereby our forces both by sea and land must be considerably weakned, and consequently would furnish them with a fairer opportunity of putting their so long rejected design in execution; the more, because that many of the* Portuguese *who relying hitherto upon the authority of count* Maurice, *as the only means to keep the soldiers in awe, being now put in fear of the executions and exorbitancies likely to be committed by the covetous officers and rapacious soldiers, would be forced to join with them against us. After the departure of his excellency for* Holland, *those cabals have instead of divine things encreased every day; they have been very diligent in getting information concerning the strength of all our garrisons, with an intent to carry on their designs before we could be reinforced with supplies of men and provisions from* Holland; *to effect which, they have by messengers sent to the* Bahia, *sollicited for succours of men and arms, of which as it seems they have no small hopes. There is great reason to believe that the journey of* Andrew Vidal *from the* Bahia *hither, in* August *last, undertaken under pretence of taking his leave before his return to* Portugal, *in order to serve the king there, was founded upon no other motive than to inform himself most narrowly concerning the true state of affairs here, in order to give a verbal account thereof in the* Bahia *and afterwards in* Portugal; *as likewise to sound the inclinations of the inhabitants, and to animate such as he found well disposed for his interest, with hopes of speedy succours from the* Bahia; *we have since received secret intelligence that he has been present at several of these cabals. But though they were greatly encouraged with these hopes of good success, by reason of the diminution of our forces and scarcity of provisions, they were not very forward in venturing upon this enterprise, being sensible that their design having taken vent, we made all necessary preparations against them; besides that many of the* Portuguese *inhabitants, being beyond their expectation, well satisfied with the government of the great council, did rather chuse to live quietly and securely, than to engage in so dangerous an enterprise. So that things remained without any considerable alteration at present; and as matters stand now we are not able to find out sufficient cause to satisfy ourselves whether they proceed in the same design. Their chief design as we are credibly informed was laid against the* Receif, *which they intended to surprise, upon a certain day appointed for the sale of negroes, when the inhabitants of the countrey flocking thither in great numbers, they did not doubt but with the assistance of our own negroes, who are for the most part papists, to make themselves, masters of the place, not questioning but if this succeeded, the rest would soon be forced to yield. But in this they were prevented, by the strong guards we took care to post in the* Receif *on those fair days.* 1643.

The

1643. *The chief ringleaders, as they are specified to us, are* John Fernandes Vieira, *and his father-in-law* Francisco Beringel, *with several others, whom we would have committed to prison, if we could have had more certain information against them; but though we left no stone unturned to find out the truth, yet could we not meet with sufficient motives to induce us either to imprison them, or to proceed again to the general disarming of the inhabitants, we having received certain intelligence, that so soon as we should attempt it, we must expect no less than a general insurrection, which considering our own magazines and store-houses were so ill provided, and no sufficient force could be drawn out of the garrison to secure the open countrey, would have drawn after it very ill consequences for our nation, especially those living at some distance from our forts, who thereby, as we had reason to fear, might have been exposed to the danger of being massacred by the* Portuguese. *It is evident from the information given to your lordships in* Holland, *and transmitted to us, that the subjects of the king of* Portugal *themselves are encouraged and animated against us; wherefore it will be absolutely necessary to be very cautious, and to hasten the supplies we have so often requested at your hands. Upon the first information we received, that toward the south of the* Receif *the* Portuguese *intended to land some men or arms, we sent the* 13th *of* October *a yacht, the* Enckhuysen *with another galliot and chaloop to cruise thereabouts, but they returned after some time without being able to discover any such thing. The next intelligence we had was, that a fleet was equipping in the* Bahia, *to transport some forces, for the assistance of our rebellious subjects; to find out the bottom of this design, we thought we could pitch upon no better expedient than to send thither Mr.* Gilbert de Witt *and* Dirk Hoogstraten *with certain instructions; of which we have enlosed the copy, who set sail the* 22th *of the last month. Being further informed that a certain* Portuguese *captain with an ensign and three soldiers have been lately dispatched from the* Bahia *to our captainships, to endeavour to stir up our subjects to rebellion, with assurance of succours from thence; we have employed all necessary means to find them out and get them into our hands. We shall not be wanting in any thing, which according as occasion presents, may contribute to the preservation of this state.*

Receif 13th February, 1645.

The 4th the great council were informed by letter from *Isaac Rasiere* and captain *Blewbeck*, written at *Parayba*, that a rumour was spread thereabouts that *Kamaron* chief commander of the *Brasilians* in the *Bahia*, was on his march from *Sertao* to *Siara*, to join with the *Brasilians* inhabiting thereabouts, to attack with their united forces the inhabitants of the captainship of *Rio Grande*. Whereupon the council sent orders to *Hans Vogel*, governor of *Seregippo del Rey*, to get intelligence and send them speedy word whether *Kamaron* with his camp were still in *Rio Real*; and if not, whither he had taken his march, or whither he intended to take it. They also sent word to the inhabitants of *Parayba*, that they should be very diligent in enquiring after the cause of this rumour, and send them intelligence accordingly. The 15th of *May* they received an answer from *Hans Vogel*; dated the 25th of *April* at *Seregippo del Rey*, wherein he told them that pursuant to their orders he had sent a serjeant with some soldiers to *Kamaron*'s head quarters, about ten leagues from *Seregippo del Rey*, under pretence of looking for some deserters; who after their return reported, that his forces consisting of two hundred *Portuguese* and one thousand two hundred *Brasiians*, were still in the same place, busied for the most part in cultivating some plantations, *Kamaron* himself being then in the *Bahia*, to assist at the solemnity of their easter; from whence they conjectured, that the rumour concerning his march was only a fiction. But two days after the same rumour was renewed by two passengers coming from *Rio St. Francisco*, and being landed by one *John Hoen*, a master of a vessel near *Kandelaria*; but upon a more strict enquiry made by the council, the said master of the vessel declared, that on the eighth of the same month, when he left *Rio de Francisco*, there was no news of *Kamaron*'s march. 1643.

The 30th of *May* 1645, a letter without a name was delivered to the great council by one *Abraham Markado* a jew, subscribed only *plus ultra*. This letter being translated out of the *Portuguese* the same night, the contents thereof were, that three unknown persons gave them notice that a good body of troops were come from *Rio Real* into *Parayba*, with an intention to join with a discontented party there, and to surprize the *Dutch* forts; with advice to seize upon the person of *John Fernandes Vieira* their chief ringleader.

The letter is as follows,

A letter of intelligence to the council.

WE *stand amazed you are so secure, when it is reported that the* Matta *of* Parayba *is full of soldiers, come thither lately from* Rio Real, *who consisting in a good number of negroes, mulats, and* Portuguese, *with* Kamaron

1643. Kamaron *at the head of them, began their march in the month of* March, *expecting now to be joined by other troops, which hitherto were stopt by the overflowing of the rivers. Their aim is to encourage the inhabitants to take up arms, which done, they expect considerable succours from the* Bahia, *both by sea and land, wherewith they pretend to block you up in the* Receif, *intending to fix their camp either at* Olinda, *or in the* Vergea, *and quarter the soldiers in the* Fregesies *thereabouts. They boast that their forces are already considerably encreased by those who are indebted to the company, and other vagabonds, and threatned to massacre all such of your subjects as refuse to join with them. A certain person of note and reputation belonging to the same camp, has given us this information, in order to communicate it to your lordships to be upon your guard, which we do accordingly by these presents. The same person told us, that* John Fernandes Vieira *was the chief ringleader of this insurrection, who maintains the rebellious crew in the* Matta, *as they meet together, till a certain day appointed for their rendezvous, when they are with their joint forces to attack all the* Dutch *forts and out-guards at once. We were also told, that the said* Vieira *does not sleep in his house, and is always upon his guard; to try which, you have no more to do than to send some to take him, with his servants and factors; which if you could do they would be all amazed, and make an open confession, which may be done without the least hazard; for if you miscarry in the attempt, it will nevertheless not redound to your disadvantage. We conjure your lordships to take care of this poor nation, for fear they should be forced to join with the rebels against you. We judge it therefore absolutely necessary to undertake the business without delay, with all imaginable secresy; for if they find themselves discovered, they will begin the game immediately; so that strong guards ought to be put in the outworks, and in the harbours of* Kandelaria *and the* Receif. *We advise your lordships to oblige the inhabitants forthwith to surrender their arms, to order all the masters of the sugar-mills, with their planters, to appear in the* Receif, *especially those of the* Fregesies *of* Vergea, Garassu, St. Lorenzo, St. Amaro, Moribeca, de Cabo, Pojuka, *and* Serinhaim, *with assurance that they shall not be molested for any debts there; and when they are come, to detain them till they see what is further to be done, under pretence of securing them against the attempts of the rebels in the country, by which means you will both secure the government, and oblige many private persons. The same method ought to be used with those of* Parayba, *where they may be detained in the fort, as well as those of* Porto Calvo *in that place. Thus if you can get the chiefest into your hands, the design will dwindle away to nothing. We beseech you not to send away any more soldiers before you have made a full discovery of the rebellion, and provide your forts with good garrisons; whither we would also have all the* Dutch *inhabitants to retire for fear of being massacred. We three being faithful subjects of your lordships, have now satisfied our consciences in proposing your remedy, which consists in the taking of* Vieira, *which must be undertaken with great secrecy and foresight, he being, as it is said, continually upon his guard. Your lordships will be sensible without our advice how much it concerns them, not to divulge to any, from whom they have received this information; and we assure you, that we will not fail to give further intelligence of what we are able to learn by way of letters; and one time or other, we shall make no difficulty to let you know, who these three faithful subjects are. If we had been present, we could have declared no more than we have done in this letter. Your lordships must take effectual care against their attempts without delay, the approaching feast being the time appointed for the putting it in execution. We have sent you immediate notice after it came to our knowledge: We advise you likewise to seize upon* Francisco Beringel, Vieira's *father-in-law, and* Antonio Kavalkanti; *and in short, all the chiefest of the* Vergeas, *and other places.* Signed, 1643.

A. Verdade.

Plus Ultra.

Hereupon the great council called *Paul de Linge*, president of the council of justice, vice-admiral *Cornelius Lichthart*, and lieutenant colonel *Garstman*, into their assembly, to consult unanimously what were best to be done at this juncture for the preservation of the *Dutch Brasil*; when by this, as well as several other letters and intelligences, they were forewarned of the approaching danger; and notwithstanding they were much in doubt, whether they ought to make any certain account upon a letter written without a name; yet considering all the circumstances of this, as well as several other informations, it was judged absolutely necessary to provide for the safety of the *Dutch Brasil*, against any attempt of an enemy.

I. By providing all the forts with meal for two months.

II. By giving immediate notice to all commanders of forts to be constantly upon their guard.

III. To write to *John Listry*, chief commander

mander of the *Brasilians*, to keep his people in readiness with their arms in the villages, to be ready to march upon the first orders from the council, we being not in a condition to take the field without them.

IV. To send abroad their spies in all corners, even into the woods, to get intelligence whereabouts the enemies troops are, and to give timely notice of what they are able to learn to the council.

V. It was agreed, to summon *John Fernandes Vieira*, the chief ringleader of the intended rebellion, and his securities, *Francisco Beringel*, *Vieira*'s father-in-law, and *Bernardin Karvalho*, unto the *Receif*, under pretence of making a second agreement with him, which he earnestly desired; by which means they should secure his person, know the whole bottom of the *Portuguese* design, and consequently be the better able to prevent it. A certain broker called *Koin*, who sollicited this agreement for *Vieira*, was prevailed upon to undertake this task, which he might do without the least suspicion; but the *Whitsontide* holidays put some stop to it for the present. With the same care the great council employed all possible means to get the other persons of the *Vergea*, suspected to have a hand in this rebellious design, into their hands, under some pretence or other, they being not likely to be taken by force, because they did not lodge in their mills and houses in the night time, and by day were so strictly upon their guard, that they could not possibly be surprized.

The 31st of *May*, vice-admiral *Lichthart*, and *Henry Haus*, a lieutenant, offered to undertake the delivering of *John Fernandes Vieira* to the council, which they intended to effect, under pretence of giving him a visit, and going a fishing with him in the lake *Lewis Bras Biserra*.

Further advice concerning the insurrection.

The 9th of *July*, the great council received advice by a letter from Mr. *Koin*, governour of *Rio St. Francisco*, dated the 1st of *June*, that *Kamaron*, with a small body was passed the river *St. Francis*; therefore he desired some assistance of men, with suitable ammunition.

The same was confirmed by another letter, dated the 27th of *June*, with advice, that as yet no enemy had appeared within sight of the fort.

Frequent intelligence being likewise sent to the council, that in the *Matta* of *St. Lawrence*, and some other distant places, considerable numbers of soldiers from the *Bahia*, of Mulats and Negroes, were gathering in a body, they sent several small bodies thither, under command of such as were well acquainted with that country, who all unanimously reported, that they could meet with no soldiers, mulats, or any other vagabonds thereabouts. 1643.

The 12th of *June*, the director *Moucheron* sent further advice, that he had been credibly informed, by letters dated the 8th of the same month, from *Rio St. Francisco*, that *Kamaron* and *Henrico Dias*, with six companies of *Brasilians*, Mulats, and Negroes, were pass'd the said river; and that just as he was concluding his letter, two inhabitants of the *Algoas* had given him to understand, that some of them had been at their houses for some meal; the copies of which letters he sent to the council, who did now not in the least question, but that their aim was upon the *Dutch Brasil*, especially since they were forewarned by several letters from *St. Antonio*, that the inhabitants thereabouts seem'd to prepare for a revolt.

The Resolution of the council thereupon.

The council finding their project of taking *Vieira* by craft, not to succeed, because he and the securities of his father-in-law, *Francisco Beringel*, and *Bernardino Karvalho*, could not be cajoled into the *Receif*, under pretence of renewing their former contract, and looking upon him as the chief ringleader of this revolt, they ordered *Joachim Denniger*, a lieutenant, with a good number of soldiers, to the mill and house of the said *John Fernandes Vieira*, to bring his person from thence to the *Receif*. Accordingly *Denniger* advanced with his soldiers towards the evening near the mills, which he surrounded, and about midnight unexpectedly entred both the house and mills, making a most strict search throughout all the rooms and corners, but to no purpose. In the morning he withdrew at some distance, but return'd the next night, when after having made another search, but in vain, he was informed by one of his *Turkish* slaves, and some Negroes, that neither *Vieira*, nor his father-in-law *Beringel*, had slept in their houses these last three weeks; that sometimes they came thither on horseback, but after a very short stay went their ways again. *Denniger* likewise search'd the houses of *Antonio Kavalkanti* and *Antonio Biserra*, but to as little purpose as those of the former, being informed by their Negroes, that they had absconded for some weeks before.

In the mean while, the council sent divers parties abroad, under the command of *Hans Katner*, *Slodiniski*, and *Cunraed Hilt*, all which, after their return, agreed in this, that there were no enemies there as yet, especially not in the *Matta*, where they met with no body but those that

1643. that were employed in manuring the grounds.

The great council finding themselves altogether disappointed in their hopes of taking *Vieira*, resolved to secure immediately the persons of *Francisco Beringel*, *Vieira*'s father-in-law; *Bernardino Karvalho*, and his brother *Sebastian Karvalho*, *Lewis Bas*, *Amaro Lopez*, and *John Pessoa*, being persons suspected to have a hand in the conspiracy, inhabiting the *Vergea*. In the more distant provinces were ordered to be seized

In *St. Amaro*, *Antonio de Bulhous*.

In *St. Antonio*; *Amador d'Arouja*; *Pedro Marinho Falcao*; *Antonio del Rasto*.

In *Pojuka*; *Kornero de Morais*; father *Frey Lewis*; and *Francisco Dias del Gado*.

In *Serinhaim*; *John Albuquerq*, son-in-law of *Pero Lopez de Vera*.

In *Porto Calvo*; *Rodrigues de Barros Pimentel*.

In *Iguaraka*; *John Pimenta*.

In *Itamarika*; father *Lawrence d'Alkunha*.

And in *Rio Grande*; *John Lestan Navarro*.

Parayba *secured*. But it being most of all to be feared that the inhabitants of *Parayba*, who were much indebted, would revolt before all the rest, Mr. *Paul de Linge* was sent thither immediately in the quality of director, with full power to act both in that and the *Captainship* of *Rio Grande*, as he should find it most expedient for the company, with express orders to press 100 men out of the ships, with proportionable provisions, immediately after his arrival there, which were to be disposed in the fort of *St. Margaret*, both for its defence, and to keep the inhabitants in due obedience.

A small camp near St. Lawrence. And considering that the scarcity of provisions was one of the main obstacles to be surmounted on our side, which as the case then stood, would more and more increase, unless we could remain masters of the field, from whence we drew most of our provisions, and to over-awe the discontented inhabitants, it was judged requisite, to form a small camp near *S. Lawrence*; and accordingly the two lieutenants *Huykquesloot* and *Hamel* were order'd thither with 35 men each, the first from *Iguaraka*, the last from *Moribeka*, as likewise captain *Wiltschut*, with 50 men more from the *Receif*; *John Listry*, commander in chief of the *Brasilians*, was likewise ordered to join them with all possible speed, 300 *Brasilians* under their own commanders.

The same day (being the 12th) after a view was taken of the fortifications of *Moribeka* town, the same were ordered to be repaired, and news being brought, that *John Fernandes Vieira* had been seen in his mill the same night, the council endeavoured with all possible care to have secured his person, but in vain; it being certain, that (according to the depositions made by his steward of the mill, called *St. John*, before the publick notary *Indiik*, in the *Receif*, 21 *Jan.* 1647.) near six months before the breaking out of this insurrection, he had never slept one night in his house: And whenever he happened to be there in the day-time, he remained for the most part in a turret on the top of the house, from whence he could have a prospect at a great distance; if his business called him below, he put some body else there to keep the watch; who, if they saw but two or three persons come that way, gave immediate notice thereof to him; and if any *Dutch* in a body were discovered, he retired instantly into the adjacent woods. He had likewise placed some Negroes at a certain distance from the house, who were to give notice of the approach of any unknown persons that way.

The 13th *Sebastian Karvalho* and *Antonio de Bulhous*, were brought in prisoners to the *Receif*, the rest who were sensible of their guilt, having escaped their hands; the first being examined the same night by the assessor of the court of justice, Mr. *Walbeek*, concerning the intended conspiracy, gave him the following account by word of mouth. Sebastian Karvalho *brought in prisoner*.

His CONFESSION.

THAT he was one of those three, who a few days ago, had by way of letter given an account of an intended conspiracy in the Vergea, *to the great council, the ringleader thereof being* John Fernandes Vieira, *who, with the rest of his* Portuguese *accomplices, relied upon the succours promised them from the* Bahia; *with what he had judged most proper for obviating the same. That the whole design of this conspiracy was laid open to him by means of a certain writing, in form of an association, which was delivered to him by a* Portuguese servant *of the said* Vieira, *together with a letter, in which he desired him to subscribe the same, there being no more than two who had subscribed it at that time,* viz. John Fernandes Vieira, *and* Lewis da Costa Sepulpeda. *The contents of this association were, that they promised to rise in arms against this state, and to sacrifice their lives and estates for the recovery of the* Dutch Brasil, *under the obedience of the king of* Portugal. *That indeed he had signed the said association, but given immediate notice thereof to* Ferdinando Vale *and a third person besides; and that he, together with Mr.* Vale, *had* His confession.

1643. *had caused the beforemention'd letter, directed to the great council, to be delivered to* Merkado *the physician. That the insurrection was intended to extend all over* Dutch Brasil, *but that the inhabitants of the* Captainship *of* Parayba *were most to be feared, as being most indebted, and consequently bearing an ill-will to our government. That their main design was to surprize one of our forts, on or near the sea-side, whereby they might secure themselves a place to receive succours from the* Bahia; *from whence they expected to be assisted with two men of war, and three or four fregates. That he had signed this association barely out of fear of* Vieira, *who had threatned those that should refuse with no less than death, and had caused several to be murthered upon that account.*

His confession agreeing in all points with what *Ferdinando Vale* had deposed before, and being all that time sorely afflicted with the gravel, he was dispensed with from any further examination.

The council being by this deposition of *Karvalho* fully convinced of the treachery of *Vieira* and his adherents, it was resolved to attempt once more the taking of the said *Vieira*, if perhaps he might as yet lurk somewhere or other near the *Receif*, and of his factor *Mor Manuel de Sousa*, engaged in the same design; as likewise of *Antonio Bezerra* and *Amaro Lopez*, both inhabitants of the *Vergea*, but in vain. Those who were sent upon that errand, bringing back no other satisfaction, than that they were not to be met with thereabouts, and that besides that, *Antonio* and *Manuel Kavalkanti*, *Antonio Bezerra*, *John Pessoa*, and *Cosmo de Krasto*, were the same day retired out of the *Vergea* to the *Matta*. The same day captain *Wiltschut* was ordered to seize the publick notary, *Caspar Pereira*, dwelling in *St. Lawrence*, who was supposed to have drawn the beforementioned association; and it was resolved to send a pardon to *Antonio Kavalkanti*, and *John Pais Kaeral*, who having a great family at home, might thereby be prevailed upon to quit the party of the rebels, whereby we should both weaken that of the enemy, and get a further insight into their designs. *Antonio de Bulhous* being examined at the same time, ingenuously confessed that he had not the least knowledge of the conspiracy; *Sebastian Karvalho* being, notwithstanding his former confession, detained prisoner upon suspicion till the 4th of *August*, was, at his request, dismissed by the great council, after having given sufficient proof that he was one of the three who writ the letter concerning the intended conspiracy to the council.

Karvalho *discharged.*

The 14th of *June*, orders were given to all the inhabitants of the *Receif*, and those living upon the back of the river, to surround their dwelling places with pallisadoes, under forfeiture of 200 gilders. And to render the companies the more compleat, and expose our men to as little danger as might be of being surprised by the enemy, all the safeguards were commanded to be withdrawn by Mr. *Haus*, near the *Receif*, and in *Serinhaim* by captain *Fallo*, who was likewise ordered to remove the garrison of *Huna* to another place of more strength. The better to supply the scarcity of provisions in the forts, which for want thereof might be in danger of falling into the enemies hands, orders were dispatch'd to the chief commanders, to seize upon what quantity of *Farinha* (or meal) they stood in need of for the use of their respective garrisons among the inhabitants of the country, which they were to be paid for by the commissaries of the company. It was also thought necessary, that for the greater security of *Maurice*'s town, the ditches of the fort *Ernestus* should be made larger, as likewise the *Quinqueregular* fort, which was put in execution by *Haus*, as vice-admiral *Lichthart* took care to have two spy ships posted, one betwixt the *Quinqueangular* fort and the fort *Bruin*, the other beyond *Baretta*, to prevent any surprize on that side at low tide; it was also resolved not to let any ships or boats go out of the *Receif*, without a pass from the great council. The major of the city militia was ordered to keep the rest of his officers with the soldiery in readiness against the 17th, to pass the review, the same day being also appointed to the garrison for that purpose; several new commanders were also chosen for the militia, instead of those that were ready to return into *Holland*. The same day *Paul Linge* set out on his journey into *Parayba*, being furnished with fifteen hundred soldiers for necessary occasions; and *Bernardino Karvalho*, who had absconded for some time, had, at his request, leave granted him to come to the *Receif* to answer for himself. 1643.

The Receif *strengthened with pallisadoes.*

The fortifications of Maurice *town enlarged.*

The 15th *John Pessoa*, master of the sugar-mill *Pantello*, one of those that were ordered to be secured, desired leave also in a letter to the council, to appear before them, his flight being occasioned not by his guilt, but only fear, which was granted him, as well as the request of father *Lawrence Alkunha*, upon the same account.

On the 16th early in the morning, we received secret intelligence, that *Andrew Vidal*, at the head of 1000 *Portuguese*, and *Kamaron* with *d'Indeos Rondelas*, and *Henry*

1643. *ry Dias* with a body of arm'd Negroes, had posted themselves above *St. Anthony*, near the sugar-mill *Topekura*. The same day *John Karnero de Maris*, and *Francisco Dias del Gado*, both masters of sugar-mills in the district of *Pojuka*, ordered to be apprehended, were brought prisoners to the *Receif*, and *Amador da Rouje*, and *Pero Marinha Falkao*, inhabitants of *St. Anthony*, who had hitherto absconded, did ask permission to come to the *Receif* to answer for themselves, which was easily granted.

Our camp removed to Moribeka.

It was then taken into deliberation by the great council, whether, according to the last intelligences received of the enemies designs, it were not most expedient to remove our small camp from *St. Lawrence* to *Moribeka*, which after some debates, was agreed upon accordingly, thereby to secure the passage of the river *Sangea*, and consequently to remain masters of the country as far as the cape of *St. Austin*, from whence both the camp and the *Receif* might conveniently be supplied, both with *Farinha* and cattle; whereas on the contrary, if the enemy should be possessed of it, he might (as had been done in the former wars) cut off all supplies coming from the south to the *Receif*.

Pursuant to this resolution, orders were sent to captain *Wiltschut* to march immediately to *Moribeka*, to expect there the coming of the *Brasilians*, and some further succours: In the mean while, to post himself in the church, and to fortify the same against any sudden attack: And the aldermen of *Maurice*'s town were ordered to buy up the necessary provisions, both of *Farinha* and cattle about *Moribeka*, for their use. A proclamation was also issued, commanding all the inhabitants of *Serinhaim*, *Pojuka*, *St. Antonio*, and *Moribeka*, without any exception, to repair well armed, both horse and foot, with all possible speed to *St. Antonio*, there to list themselves for the defence of the open country, under the command of colonel *Gaspar Vander Ley*, and lieutenant colonel *John Heck*: Those that were not able to maintain themselves at their own charge, being to receive their provision from the company, like other soldiers: The said colonel and lieutenant colonel offering at the same time, to furnish fifteen hundred *Alquera*'s or measures of *Farinha*, for the use of our garrisons, for ready money.

The same day the great council received a letter from *Antonio Kavalkanti*, (unto whom they had lately sent his pardon) in which he protested, that neither he nor the rest of the inhabitants of the *Vergea* were concerned in any cabals against the state, their flight being occasioned only by fear of being imprisoned upon suspicion, raised against them by their enemies. The answer of the council was to this effect, That if he knew himself innocent, he should return to his mill, this being the only means to recover his former reputation. 1643.

The great council having great reason to suspect, that *Kamaron* would endeavour to bring the *Brasilians* under their jurisdiction over to his party, resolved, in order to secure them in their interest, to treat with *Listry*, their commander in chief, to persuade them, to send their wives and children into the isle of *Tamarika*, under pretence of securing them against any attempts of the enemy, to which they might in all probability be exposed in the open villages; but in effect, to keep them as pledges of their fidelity.

Number of those sent from Bahia *to the rebels.*

The same day the council received secret intelligence from *Antonio d'Olivera*, that the succours sent to the rebels from the *Bahia*, consisted in a considerable number of *Portuguese*, under the the command of the brother of *Kavalkanti*; of four hundred *Brasilians*, under the command of *Kamaron*; three hundred *Indeos Rondelas* from *Sertoa*; and fifty Negroes, under command of *Henry Dias*.

Ensign Slotenisky *sent abroad, and his account.*

On the same 16th of *June*, Mr. *Slotenisky*, ensign of the guards, was sent abroad to be at the campaigne, with eleven firelocks, and twelve *Brasilians*, who returning the 24th of *June*, gave the following account to the great council. That he took his way from the *Receif* directly to *St. Lawrence*, and from thence directly to the village of *St. Michael*; where being joined by his *Brasilians*, he marched thro' *St. Francisco* to *Kasura*, from thence to *Geyta*, and so further through the *Matta* to *St. Sebastian*, where all the inhabitants had left their houses. At *St. Sebastian* he passed the river *Topikura*, and coming to *John Fernandes Vieira*'s park, met there with good able horses. The Negroes told him, they had orders from their master to fly from before the *Dutch*, but to furnish the *Portuguese* with what they desired. From thence he marched to *Antonio*, and in his way thither did light upon a house belonging likewise to *John Fernandes Vieira*, where he found about fifty or sixty sheep, with good store of poultry, intended for the use of the sick belonging to those rebels, or those come to their assistance from the *Bahia*. They forewarned him not to advance too far, he being likely to meet some troops in the park belonging to the fathers of *St. Bento*; but coming thither found both the *Portuguese* and Negroes fled. From thence he marched to a house belonging to *Michael Fernandes*, who a-

1643. bove three months before had been ordered by *John Fernandes Vieira*, to provide a ſufficient quantity of *Farinha* for the uſe of the ſuccours expected from the *Bahia*; which he lately had tranſported from thence to *Pedro de Alkunha*, where was the rendezvous of two companies of the rebellious inhabitants, where the ſaid *Michael* expected a good ſtore of cattle, bought up by *Vieira* for their uſe, according to the information of a Negro, brought by *Slotcniſki* to the *Receif*. Near the park of *Don Pedro d'Alkunha*, he met with the ſame Mulat who had ſhot captain *Waldeck*, and with two *Hollanders* who had committed murther, and were never pardoned. *John Fernandes Vieira* had promiſed to be with them againſt *Midſummer* day. From thence *Sloteniſki* marched directly to *Vna*, and ſo further to *St. Luce*, but met with no body there except one monk, and ſo returned to the *Receif*.

On the 17th of *June* it was reſolved by the great council, with the conſent of the council of juſtice, to iſſue a proclamation for a general pardon, except ſome few ringleaders of the rebellion.

The proclamation was as follows.

A Proclamation *for a general pardon.*

THE great council of Braſil *makes known to every body, whom it may concern, that they being ſenſible, to their grief, how many of their ſubjects, having been miſled by ſome of the ringleaders of the rebellion, have left their mills, wives and children for fear, as has been inſinuated to them, of being diſturbed, plundered, and killed by our ſtragling parties: We being willing to provide againſt it, and to contribute as much as in us lies, to the proſperity of our ſubjects, and their eſtates, have thought fit to publiſh their intention, to be, to defend and protect the inhabitants of the open country, againſt all evil intention'd perſons to the utmoſt of their power. And to reduce thoſe who have left their habitations, to obedience, and prevent their utter deſtruction, we promiſe our pardon to all ſuch as ſhall within five days after ſight of this our proclamation, make their perſonal appearance in the* Receif, *not excepting thoſe who have been actually engaged in the ſaid rebellion (unleſs they are among the number of the chief ringleaders) provided they leave the rebellious party, and return to their former obedience; and that they ſhall enjoy the quiet poſſeſſion of their mills and lands as before, under our protection; under condition however, that they ſhall be obliged to take a new oath of allegiance to the ſtate. Thoſe on the contrary, who ſhall perſiſt in their rebellion, or ſhall aſſiſt the rebels under what pretence ſoever, are hereby declared enemies of the ſtate, who have forfeited their lives and eſtates, whoſe perſons and eſtates ſhall be liable to be proſecuted with fire and ſword,* &c. 1643.

This proclamation being immediately tranſlated into the *Portugueſe* tongue, was ſent in the morning to *St. Antonio* and the *Vergea* to be publiſhed there; ſeveral copies were alſo diſtributed among the friars, in order to publiſh them from the pulpits, and cauſe them to be affixed to the church doors.

The 18th, good ſtore of proviſion and ammunition was ſent to the fort *Keulen*, and *Rio Grande*, and the garriſons of both theſe places forewarned to keep upon their guard. At the ſame time the proclamation of pardon was ſent thither to be publiſhed; and *Antonio Parayba*, chief of the *Braſilians* in thoſe parts, was ſummon'd to keep his *Braſilians* in readineſs with their arms, whenever they ſhould be commanded to give proofs of their fidelity to the company.

The 19th of *June*, two inhabitants of *Porto Calvo*, that were landed but the ſame morning in a ſmall boat on the *Receif*, brought news to the great council, that *Kamaron*, at the head of the *Braſilians*, and *Henry Dias*, with his armed Negroes, conſiſting in ſeven companies, had poſted themſelves in the *Alegoas*, near the ſugar-mill *Velho*; that their number was increaſed ſince to four or five thouſand men, by the conjunction of thoſe who were paſſed the river *St. Franciſco* through the *Matta*, and that they had begun to commit open hoſtilities; ſo that now the council had not the leaſt reaſon to doubt any further of the deſign of the *Portugueſe*. The commander of *Porto Calvo* ſent word much to the ſame purpoſe, and that he prepared for a vigorous defence. The firſt effects of this inſurrection broke out in the diſtrict of *Pojuka*, and conſidering that our whole force there conſiſted only in 30 men, under *Jacob Flemming*, a lieutenant, orders were ſent him to retreat to *St. Antonio*, there to defend themſelves with their joint-forces. The firſt beginning of hoſtilities was made by thoſe of the *Pojuka*, by ſeizing upon two boats, all the paſſengers of which they took priſoners, and ſlew them afterwards, except one ſeaman, who had the good fortune to eſcape. This done, the inhabitants both of the village and the open country, choſe for their head *Tabatinga Amador d'Arravio*, whereby they cut off all communication with the cape *Auſtin* by land, and all about to the ſouth, beſides that, the fort on the ſaid cape could

Open rebellion begun in Pojuka.

1643. could not, but with great difficulty, be ſupplied with water from the river.

The 20th of *June*, a *Braſilian* arrived very early in the morning in the *Receif*; his errant to the council was, that he being ſent by *John Blaar*, from *Porto Calvo*, with letters to the great council, was ſet upon by thoſe of *Pojuka*, near *Kamboa*, who took from him the ſaid letters, and kill'd his companion. For the reſt he told them, that *Kamaron* was poſted in the diſtrict of *Porto Calvo*, and that captain *John Blaar* was in the fort. A council being called to conſider of the beſt means to ſecure the *Dutch-Braſil* againſt any attempts of the enemy, the firſt thing that fell in debate was, whether, according to the general advice of thoſe of the inhabitants, who wiſh'd well to our government, it were not moſt expedient for our defence, to form a camp to make head againſt the enemy in the field; who, if once maſter of the open country, would force the inhabitants to join with him, and cut off our proviſions, without which we could not ſubſiſt long. The next thing to be taken into conſideration was, where to find forces for this camp, the garriſons being ſo weakly manned, as not to be able to ſpare any, and the body under captain *Wiltſchut* conſiſting only of one hundred and twenty men, beſides the three hundred *Braſilians*, to be joined with him. Conſidering therefore that the whole force in the *Allegoas*, conſiſted only of two companies under the command of *Mucheron*, a number not any ways proportionable to the extent of ſo large a tract of ground; it was judg'd moſt convenient to make a virtue of neceſſity, and to draw them from thence to the *Receif*, as indeed they had been ordered before. But their way by land being cut off by the rebels of *Pojuka*, a veſſel, which lay ready to go out a cruſing, was ordered to *Porto Franciſco*, with orders to *Mucheron*, to embark forthwith thoſe forces aboard her, without having any regard to the baggage; but the reſt, which could not be put aboard the veſſel, ſhould be ſent by land to *Rio Franciſco*, to reinforce captain *Koin*, for the better defence of that place. Captain *Fallo* was likewiſe ordered to march with the garriſon of *Serinhaim* to *St. Antonio*, it being not likely that the troops in *Serinhaim* ſhould be able to make head there, after the coming of *Kamaron* into *Porto Calvo*, it being an inland country.

A reinforcement ſent to Tamarika. The ſame day forty new-liſted ſoldiers were ſent to *Tamarika*, under command of captain *Peter Seuliin*, maſter of the ſugar-mill *Harlem*; becauſe this iſland was of the greateſt conſequence to us; and the garriſons of the fort *Orange*, and the town of *Schop*, conſiſting each of one company, were very weak, and the armed inhabitants did not amount to above one company more. 1643.

The ſame day Mr. *Bas* and Mr. *Van de Voerde*, counſellors of the court of juſtice, were ordered to examine *Gaſpar Pereira* the publick notary, concerning his drawing of the inſtrument of aſſociation; as likewiſe *John Kariero de Maris*, *Franciſco Dias Delgado* maſters of ſugar-mills, in the diſtrict of *Pojuka*, and *Sebaſtian Karvalho*, concerning what they knew of the intended conſpiracy.

Karvalho declared a ſecond time, at the houſe of lieutenant colonel *Haus*, that ſome days ago (he could not remember exactly which) a certain *Portugueſe* ſervant, whom he knew not, did come to him in the name of *John Fernandes Vieira*, with a letter, in which the ſaid *Vieira* deſired him to ſign the encloſed writing drawn in form of an aſſociation, to take up arms againſt the government, as ſoon as they ſhould receive any ſuccours from the *Bahia*; which at that time was ſubſcribed only by *John Fernandes Vieira* and *Lewis da Coſta Sepulpeda*; but, as he ſuppoſed, was to be carried to moſt of the inhabitants. He further declared, that he refuſed to ſign the ſaid writing upon the bare letter of *John Fernandes Vieira*, and the hand-writing being unknown to him, he ſent both the letter and inſtrument of aſſociation back by the ſame lad that brought it, with his anſwer by way of mouth, that he could not ſubſcribe it. Having more maturely weighed the matter, he ſent the ſame evening to his friend *Fernando Vale*, to deſire him to give him a meeting the next morning upon the hills of *Garapes*; which being done accordingly, it was agreed among them to give notice of this conſpiracy to the great council, in a letter without a name. This letter, with the ſubſcription of *plus ultra*, was writ by *Vale*, and about ten days after given him to read in a bakers houſe in the *Pont-ſtreet*, and afterwards given to *Abraham Merkado* the phyſician, who delivered it to the great council. *Second confeſſion of* Karvalho.

The ſame day, the 20th of *June*, the great council received a letter from Mr. *Ley* and *Hoek*, dated at *St. Antonio*, importing, that the whole *Fregeſie* had taken up arms, and made ſixteen or eighteen *Dutch* inhabitants priſoners; that they had fortified the church againſt thoſe of *Pojuka*, whom they did not queſtion to force from thence, provided they received any ſuccours from the *Receif*. The council having taken the whole matter into ſerious deliberation, and conſidering with themſelves,

1643.

selves, that, as the case then stood, they had no great reason to fear any rebellion in the north, in *Parayba* and *Rio Grande*, as long as our fleet remained near the *Red-Land*, and judging it highly necessary to bring the rebels in *Pojuka* to reason, and by their punishment to deter the rest from attempting the like; they ordered lieutenant colonel *Haus*, with a detachment of a hundred men, to march the next morning to *Moribeka*, there to join with captain *Wiltschut* and the *Brasilians*, and so continue their march to *St. Antonio*; from whence they were with their joint forces to go directly against the Rebels of *Pojuka*, to reduce them to obedience; it being otherwise to be feared that they would cut off all communication betwixt the *Receif* and the garrisons to the south. This expedition proved so successful, that the rebels were put to flight, and lieutenant colonel *Haus* made himself master both of the town and convent, forcing them to quit all the passes thereabouts; and forty prisoners were released, whom they had loaded with irons in the said monastery. But having received intelligence of the approach of *Kamaron* with his whole Body against him, he desired further succours from the great council to keep the field; but the garrison of the *Receif* being too much weakened already, they could send him no other reinforcement 'till the expected succours should arrive from *Holland*.

Succours sent to Pojuka.

A fast.

The 21st, it was resolved by the great council, to proclaim a general fast all over *Dutch-Brasil*, to be kept the 28th of *June*, to return thanks to God Almighty for the great mercy shewn to them on several occasions, but especially of late, in the timely discovery of the treacherous designs of their enemies, who intended to have surprised them when they were least aware of them.

Scheme of the Portuguese *Plot.*

The design of this conspiracy was laid thus by the *Portuguese*: They intended in the *Whitsuntide* holidays to make solemn rejoycings, with feasting, tournaments, and such like, on occasion of several weddings appointed for that purpose, unto which were to be invited all the chief men of *Dutch-Brasil*, both civil and military; whom, after they were flushed with wine, they intended to murther, in imitation of the *Sicilian vespers*, or the noted *Parisian wedding*; not questioning but that, when the heads of the *Dutch-Brasil* were cut off, the rest, when attack'd at once in divers places, would fall an easy prey into their hands. But being prevented in this bloody design for that time, *Midsummer-day* was pitcht upon, as most proper for the execution of it, when the ships were departed out of the harbour of the *Receif*. For the *Portuguese* were not ignorant, that we having received no fresh supplies, especially of gun-powder, for a considerable time out of *Holland*, our magazines were but very indifferently supplied both with ammunition and provisions; and that consequently we must soon be reduced to great extremity, if they were masters of the field: They knew also, that all our ships, except two, were ready to sail with the first fair wind, being already fallen down to the *Red-Land*; thus being sensible of our weakness, the *Portuguese* proposed to themselves no less than the conquest of the whole *Dutch-Brasil* at one stroke. But the whole design being discovered before *Midsummer-day*, it vanish'd into smoke, both sides betaking themselves to decide the matter by arms.

1643.

Pretences of the Portuguese.

The *Portuguese* pretended not so much the Allegiance due to their king, as liberty of conscience; notwithstanding which, we have all the reason in the world to imagine, that this insurrection was undertaken not only with the knowledge, but also at the instigation of the court of *Portugal*, and of those of the *Bahia*; it being very improbable, that *Kamaron*, *Henry Dias*, and the rest of the ring-leaders, should without the approbation of the king of *Portugal*, have attempted to attack us by open force. Besides this, *Mucheron* declares to have read in a *Portuguese* commission these words: *This revolt and war undertaken for the honour of God, the propagating of the roman catholick faith, for the service of the king and common liberty:* He further adds, that he has heard several *Portuguese* say, that if they miscarried in their design of chasing us out of *Brasil*, to destroy all with fire and sword, thereby to bereave us of all future prospect of receiving any benefit from those lands; which done, they would retire with their wives and children to the *Bahia*, or settle in some more remote place; where they might be secure against any attempts of the *Dutch*. There have indeed been some, who, considering the unsettled estate of the king of *Portugal*, and the odd fancy of his reign, have thought it very improbable, he should involve himself in a war with us, or have given his consent to this insinuation, but the event has sufficiently contradicted that opinion.

A letter from the heads of the rebels to the council.

The 22d of *June* a letter was delivered to the *great council*, signed by *John Fernandes Vieira*, *Antonio Kavalkanti*, *John Pescoa*, *Manuel Kavalkanti*, *Antonio Bezerra* and *Cosmo de Crasto Pasos* in which they complained, that they being a considerable time ago accused by the *Jews* of a treacherous

1643. rous design against the government, had been great sufferers upon that score; that now they being informed by the same *Jews* that they were in danger of losing all their mills and lands, to be given to certain *Hollanders*, who were sent for, for that purpose, they desired that the time of five days appointed in the last pardon might be prolonged, as being too short for a business of such moment, and that the said pardon might be granted without exception; which they refusing to grant, they did hereby protest before God and all the *Roman* catholic princes, that they thought themselves innocent, and not in the least guilty of all those miseries which might ensue from this refusal hereafter.

The council debates the matter. The 23[d] in the morning the council was assembled, to consider of the said letter; where after several harangues upon the present state of our affairs and the enemy's design against us, they were divided in their opinions, some being for granting a general pardon, without the least exception, as the case stood with us at present, when we were destitute of sufficient provision, ammunition and men; others maintained, that a letter which contained so many notorious untruths deserved not the least answer; others were of another opinion. Whilst they were thus debating the matter, letters were brought to the council, written by lieutenant colonel *Haus* from *St. Antonio*, that he was ready to attack the rebels of *Pojuka* the next day, not without hopes of good success, so that the council considering of what moment the event of this action was to their affairs, resolv'd to adjourn the said debate 'till the next day, when they hoped to know the issue of the whole enterprise.

The 28th of *June*, *Mucheron* arrived with his two companies in the *Receif*, from the *Allegoas*, where it was resolved to dispose his own company in the *Quinqueregular* fort, of which, as a place of great consequence, he was made commander in chief; the other of captain *William Lambert* was put in the fort *Ernestus*.

Good news out of Parayba. By letters from *Paul Linge*, governor of *Parayba*, dated the 25th of *June*, we received advice, that the inhabitants thereabouts offered to give him fresh assurance of their fidelity, by taking a new oath of allegiance, and that he did not observe the least motion towards an insurrection.

Jacob Dassine master of the sugar-mill *Supapema*, who had been abroad with a good party, made his report to the council, that he had been at several sugar-mills, where he had met with about two hundred of the enemies troops divided into divers small bodies, composed of *Portuguese*, mulatts and negroes, under the command of *Amador de Araouje*, *Antonio de Crasto*, one *Taborda* and *Henry Dias*. 1643.

The 29th of *June*, by special commission from the council, *Balthasar Vander Voerden* examined *Antonio d'Oliveira*, concerning the design of the *Portuguese* form'd against our government. He declared, that about the beginning of this present *June*, being then at the house of *Sebastian de Karvalho*, together with *Francisco d'Oliveira*, *Bernardin Karvalho*, and the before-named *Sebastian de Karvalho*, a certain *Portuguese* very well known to them all, delivered to him a letter, directed to all the persons there present, with another piece of writing unsealed, which he began to read; but finding the contents to be, that the underwritten persons promised to be, and declare themselves faithful subjects of the king of *Portugal*, and that *John Fernandes Vieira*, *Francisco Beringel*, *Antonio de Sylva*, and several more, whose names he would not look upon, had signed the same, he returned the said writing, and refused to subscribe the same, telling his son at the same time, *You ought rather to suffer your hand to be cut off, than sign this paper*; and so went his way immediately, not any one of all there present having subscribed their names at that time: He protested he knew not the hand-writing. After a more serious consideration, he thought it requisite to make a discovery of it, which he did accordingly within two days after, to *Matthew Reex*, desiring him to give an account of it to the great council; he declared further that the said writing was signed by above one hundred of the inhabitants. *Before-named examination and confession of* Antonio Oliveira.

The 30th of *June* one *Digos Lopes Leyte*, who was not long ago taken prisoner by the *Brasilians*, was examined by Mr. *Bullestrate*, *Dortmont* and some other military officers. His confession was, that at the first beginning of the design of the *Portuguese* against this state, they had sent a letter to the governor of the *Babia*, *Antonio Telles de Silva*, to crave assistance from him, which if he refused, they would seek for aid in *Spain*; and if they did not succeed there, they would rather surrender themselves to the *Turks*, than endure any longer the ill treatment they met with from the *Hollanders*. That nevertheless he had heard many dire imprecations made against *John Fernandes Vieira*; that he deserv'd no less than the gallows, he having raised this rebellion for no other end, than thereby to free himself from the vast debts he owed to the company. Digos Lopes Leyte *examined.*

The same day it was agreed to send abroad a party of twelve soldiers and eight *Brasilians*, to fetch a good quantity of *Fa-*

1643. *rinha* from *St. Lawrence*, who were put to the rout near that place, so that very few escaped. At the same time the council received the unwelcome news, that some of the inhabitants of *Iguarasu* had taken up arms against them.

In the beginning of *July* it was resolved to draw the fortifications of *Maurice*'s *Town* into a narrower compass, and to add a new line with a breast-work. This task was performed by the negroes belonging to the inhabitants of *Maurice*'s *Town* and the *Receif*, under the conduct of vice-admiral *Lichthart*, who took care to have the same perfected, according to the model drawn by the engineer.

The same day advice was brought, that *John Lawrence Frances*, and *John Dias Leyte*, inhabitants of *Iguarasu*, made it their business to incite the inhabitants to an insurrection. Captain *Sluyter* sent also word from *Tamarika*, that about eighty men, and one hundred ten women and children, all *Brasilians* of the villages of *St. Michael* and *Nassau*, were come into that island for shelter, and that the *Brasilians* of *Otta* intended to do the like. The magistrates and chief *Portuguese* of *Goyana*, gave the council fresh assurances of their fidelity, provided they might in case of necessity be allowed to retire into the said island, which was granted, and thanks given them for their loyalty. The magistrates of *Iguarasu* advised, that *Vieira* had caused a declaration to be affixed in the sugar-mills of *Gonsalvo Novo de Lira*, which they had order'd to be torn down, and sent a copy of it to the council, assuring them, that they would take all possible care to keep the Inhabitants thereabouts under obedience, tho' they found some of them much inclined to a revolt.

Fernandes Vale *examined.*

At the same time *Fernandes Vale* was examined by Mr. *Vander Voerde* and Mr. *Bas*; he declared, that having received a letter from *Sebastian de Karvalho*, to meet him the next morning upon the hills *Garapes*, because he had something to communicate to him, concerning no less than their estates, lives and honour; he without mentioning any thing of it to his wife or brother, went thither on horse-back, accompanied only by a boy; notwithstanding he happened at that time to be afflicted with the gravel; there he met *Sebastian Karvalho*, with one boy only, who told him, that he having received a letter, with another writing, containing a project of an insurrection to be undertaken against the government, he thought it absolutely necessary, to give notice thereof to the great council; and that he desired him to write a letter accordingly to the council; he being pretty well versed in the *Dutch* Tongue. 1643. That *Vale* ask'd him, whether any body besides himself knew of the matter, unto which he answered, that his Brother *Bernardin* did, whose opinion was likewise to disclose it to the council; hereupon they returning each to their respective homes, *Vale* writ a letter in *Portuguese*, pursuant to the instructions he had received from *Karvalho*, for whom the said letter was left to peruse in a baker's house, on a publick fair-day for the sale of negroes; after which he had sent the said letter inclosed in another, to Dr. *Markado*, desiring him to see the same carefully dispatch'd to the great council, without mentioning the contents thereof.

The council recal their Ships from the Red-Land.

The great council receiving frequent intelligence, that the *Portuguese* from the *Bahia* intended to send a fleet to the assistance of the rebels, it was resolved to send orders to the four ships, the *Amsterdam*, the *Blackmore*, the *North-Holland*, and *Groningen*, then at anchor near the *Red-Land*, in order to their return to *Holland*, to return forthwith to the *Receif*; the government standing in great need of their assistance, to prevent the conjuction of the forces from the *Bahia* with the rebels. They received also letters from lieutenant colonel *Haus*, dated at *Pojuka* the 26th of *June*, assuring them, that he had granted passes to above two hundred persons that were returned to their duty; that two or three of the ring-leaders, excepted in the last pardon, sued for the same favour, and that he had caused one *Franko Godinho*, one of the chief of the rebels, taken by his people, to be hanged on the gallows he had erected himself; that *Amador d'Araouje* being gone from thence with a hundred and fifty men to the *Vergea*, to join with *Vieira*, he expected their orders whether he should follow him, he looking upon it as a faint to draw him from thence. He further told them, that with the *Brasilians* and their wives and children, he was above five hundred strong, and that unless they were soon supplied with provisions from the *Receif*, they should consume all the cattle thereabouts.

The great council sent an answer the same night to lieutenant colonel *Haus*, requiring him to grant free pardon to all who should desire it, not excepting the ringleaders themselves, thereby to weaken *Amador d'Araouje* and his party. That with what forces he could spare in *Pojuka*, (after sufficient provision made for the defence of the garrisons, according to their own discretion) he should march to the *Receif*, in order to attack *Vieira*, where they need not fear but to be able to subsist upon what the said *Vieira* had laid up for the use of the

expected

1643. expected ſuccours from the *Bahia*, and the cattle belonging to the rebels.

But whilſt lieutenant colonel *Haus* was employed in ſecuring *Pojuka* againſt their attempts, thoſe of the *Vergea* ſtrengthned themſelves with all poſſible diligence; to further which, *John Fernandes Vieira* and *Antonio Kavalkanti*, who ſtiled themſelves the heads of this war, did not only affix their declarations round about *Maurice's Town*, and in *Iguaraſu*, inciting the inhabitants to rebellion, by promiſing them conſiderable ſuccours from the *Bahia*, but their parties alſo, which they ſent frequently abroad, forced thoſe of the open country to take up arms, killing ſuch as refuſed. The ſame was practiſed by *Amador d'Araouje* in *Pojuka*; ſo, that what with proviſions, what with threats and force they got together a conſiderable body in the *Vergea*, we being not in a capacity to prevent it, becauſe what forces we had were in *Pojuka*.

But judging it abſolutely for our intereſt to ſtop as much as poſſible theſe proceedings, it was reſolved to arm ſome of the luſty young fellows with firelocks, which they were furniſhed withal by the citizens, (there being none in magazines) and to join with them a detachment of the garriſon, beſides a hundred *Braſilians*, that were lately arrived under *Peter Potti*.

Captain Blaar *ſent abroad with ſome troops.*

Purſuant to this reſolution, captain *John Blaar* received orders to put himſelf at the head of three hundred men, with whom he was to march with all imaginable ſecreſy from the *Receif*; and by lying in ambuſh near the paſſes, to endeavour to intercept ſome of the enemies Troops, not queſtioning, but that out of the Priſoners, they ſhould be able to learn where *Vieira* was poſted with his main body, and of what ſtrength both he and the ſuccours from the *Bahia* was reputed to be among them. He had ſtrict orders not to moleſt any of the inhabitants, who were not in arms, but to protect them and their eſtates, and to receive thoſe who ſought for mercy, and bring them into the *Receif.* Orders were alſo ſent to lieutenant colonel *Haus* to march with what forces could poſſibly be ſpared out of the garriſons to the ſouth, to the *Vergea*, in order to join with captain *Blaar*, and endeavour to attack the heads of the rebels, which if they could once put to the rout, might be a means to quench the whole fire of rebellion, and to reſtore peace to the *Dutch-Braſil.*

The firſt of *July* it was debated in council, whether all ſuch perſons as were ſuſpected to have a hand in the conſpiracy, ought not to be granted to all that deſired it, without exception. The laſt was reſolved upon as conducing moſt to the quieting of the ſubjects minds.

The 2d in the evening, the council received advice from captain *Blaar*, that he was poſted at *Mongioppe*, with an intention to attack the enemy, wherever he met them. 1643.

The 3d he marched to *Iguaraſu.*

The 4th they received letters from lieutenant colonel *Haus*, from *St. Antonio*, importing, that after having left a garriſon in *Pojuka* under lieutenant *Flemming*, and one hundred *Braſilians* in *St. Antonio*, he was ready to march to the ſugar-mill *Velbo*, and from thence to *Moribeka*; where he would expect their further orders.

At the ſame time the inhabitants of *Goyana* having fortified themſelves in a certain houſe, belonging to *Liſtry* their chief magiſtrate, they deſired the council to furniſh them with forty muſquets, for the uſe of ſuch among them as were unprovided with arms. Their requeſt was granted, and poſitive orders ſent at the ſame time to *Servaes Karpentier*, to take this opportunity to diſarm all the *Portugueſe*, either by fair or foul means; to effect which, he ſhould keep the *Dutch* together in a body as much as poſſibly he could; his anſwer was, *he would endeavour to diſarm the* Portugueſe *by fair means, he wanting power to do it by force.* Beſides which, he gave notice in his letter dated the 11th of *July*, that every thing remained quiet hitherto in *Goyana*, but that the *Braſilians*, (contrary to his expreſs orders) claiming a prerogative to be commanded by none but their own officers, purſuant to a decree of the council of nineteen, had in their paſſages to *Tamarika* plundered ſeveral of the *Portugueſe* inhabitants. *The condition of* Goyana.

Moſt of the rebellious *Portugueſe* had left their wives and children in their houſes and mills, which as it tended to their no ſmall conveniency, ſo ſome of the faithful *Portugueſe* inhabitants did propoſe on the 3d of *July* to the great council, whether it would not be for our intereſt to oblige thoſe wives and children to quit their houſes and mills, and to ſend them after their huſbands. Several reaſons were alledged for it.

I. Becauſe the rebels being encumbred with their families, muſt of neceſſity make greater conſumption of *Farinba*, and other proviſions, which would oblige them the ſooner to alter their meaſures, and to change their places.

II. That thereby they would be much diſheartened, for fear of a vigorous attack.

III. That they would not be able to march or to change their camp ſo conveniently as before, or to lurk in unhabitable places.

IV. That by the removal of theſe women, who ſerved them as ſpies by the help of

1643. of their negroes, we should take away all opportunity from them, to be informed of our designs.

All which reasons being well weighed, the following proclamation was published.

A Proclamation *for the removal of the rebels wives and children.*

THE *great council of* Brasil, *by the authority of the states general of the* united provinces, *his highness the prince of* Orange, *and the* West-India *company, make known unto every body, that whereas many of those, who have sided with the three head rebels,* John Fernandes Vieira, Antonio Kavalkanti, *and* Amador d'Araouje, *against this state, have left behind them their wives, children and families, which hitherto continue in their former dwelling places; we do by these presents strictly command all the wives and children, whether male or female, whose husbands and fathers are engaged with the rebels, to leave their respective houses within six days after the publication of this proclamation; and to repair to their respective husbands and fathers, or else to incur the penalties due to rebels; it being our resolution not to take the same into our protection; nay, to take away our safe-guards from all such of our subjects as shall be found to harbour or conceal these beforesaid wives, children, and their effects, unless the husbands and fathers of these wives and children shall within the limited time of six days, return to their dwelling-places, and sue for pardon to the council.*

Thus decreed in the assembly of the great council of *Brasil.*

About this time near one thousand *Brasilians*, among whom were three hundred and sixty nine men, the rest women and children, being retired to the isle *Tamarika*, to shelter themselves against the rebellious *Portuguese*, Mr. *Dormont* counsellor of the finances, was sent thither in the beginning of *July*, as supreme director of the territory of *Iguarasu*, to secure that island, which was of so great consequence to the state, in our interest.

The 5th of *July*, a proclamation was issued against the three chief rebels, *John Fernandes Vieira*, *Antonio Kavalkanti*, and *Amador d'Araouje*, declaring their lives and estates to be forfeited, offering a reward for the apprehending of them, as follows.

A proclamation for apprehending the three head rebels.

THE *great council of* Brasil, *by authority of the states general of the* United Provinces, *his highness the prince of* Orange, *and the* West-India *company, send greeting: Be it known by all, that whereas we are fully satisfied that* John Fernandes Vieira, Antonio Kavalkanti, *and* Amador d'Araouje, *setting aside their allegiance, have a considerable time ago entered into a conspiracy against the state, sending their letters throughout several Fregesies of our jurisdiction, to excite our subjects to a revolt; that they have gathered and still are gathering forces to maintain their treacherous designs against this state, forcing our faithful subjects to join with them, threatning with death such as refuse to enter into this rebellion; nay, having caused several, as well* Hollanders *as* Brasilians, *to be murdered upon that score: That they have affixed and published declarations in several places, tending to the disquieting and disturbing the minds of the subjects of this state, with the name and title of governours of this war (whereas they ought to have stiled themselves faithless traitors) covering their villainous designs under the name of the divine majesty, besides many other misdemeanours, whereby they have rendered themselves guilty of high treason. It is for these reasons that we thought it our duty to declare the above named* John Fernandes Vieira, Antonio Kavalkanti, *and* Amador d'Araouje, *and by these presents do declare them enemies of this state, disturbers of the publick peace and our good subjects, rebels and traitors against their lawful magistrates; and to have forfeited all their privileges, rights, lives, and estates; and as such, we grant not only free leave to every one to apprehend or to kill the said* John Fernandes Vieira, Antonio Kavalkanti, Amador d'Araouje, *but also promise a reward of one thousand* Charles's *gilders, to such or such persons as shall do so signal a piece of service to the company, as to apprehend either of those persons, so as they may be brought to justice; and the like reward to any person who shall kill either of the said traitors, besides his pardon for any offence he may have committed before; and if he be a slave, his liberty, together with the reward. We also strictly command by these presents, all the inhabitants of this state, of what quality, degree or nation soever, that they shall not presume to assist the said rebels with arms, provisions, money, men, and ammunition, or harbour, conceal, or advise them in any respect, or keep the least correspondence with them, under pain of being declared traitors, and to be punished as such with the utmost rigour,* &c.

Whilst the great council were thus endeavouring to quench the flame of rebellion, they received frequent intelligence, that besides the succours already come to the rebels from the *Bahia* by land, by way of *Rio St. Francisco*, they expected a considerable fleet from thence; it was resolved to

1643. to send once more some deputies to the governor *Antonio Telles da Silva*, to represent to him that *Kamaron* and *Henry Dias* being under his jurisdiction, their entring in an hostile manner into the *Dutch Brasil*, could not be interpreted otherwise than a breach of the truce concluded betwixt the king of *Portugal* and their high and mightinesses the states general.

Deputies sent to the governor of the Bahia. The persons pitched upon for this purpose were *Balthasar Vander Voerde*, councellor of the court of justice, and *Dirk Hoogstrate*, then commander in chief to the cape of *St. Austin*, who being looked upon at that time as a very loyal person, was sent for the 4th of *July*, leaving *Barent Van Tichlenborgh* to command in his absence. *Francis Krynen Springapple* was appointed their secretary, and *Gerrard Dirk Laet*, *Alexander Sylve*, and *Jacob Swearts*, to attend them as gentlemen.

Their instructions. Their instructions were, to lay open to the governor the true reason and occasion of this insurrection, and the ringleaders thereof, who would never have dared to attempt it without the hopes of succours, which were sent them by land through *Rio St. Francisco:* They were to search into his intentions as near as possibly they could, and to desire him to recal *Kamaron* and *Henry Dias* with their troops out of the *Dutch Brasil*, and to punish them according to their deserts. If they found the governor not inclined to give them due satisfaction, by recalling those troops either by publick proclamation, or sending some person of authority to bring them back, or by giving them some other real demonstrations of his sincere intention before their departure, they were to protest to, and to declare themselves innocent of all the damages, murders, and rapines as well against the *Hollanders*, as *Portuguese* and *Brasilians*, already committed or to be committed by those forces. They were to declare to the governor, that they would look upon it as an open breach of peace and act of hostility, of which they must give an account to their masters, who, without question would know how to make themselves amends for the damages sustained; and to protest once more, that the *Dutch* declared themselves innocent of all the miseries which must ensue from their taking up arms for their own defence, after their so reasonable request had been rejected.

Arrive in the Bahia. Accordingly they set sail the 9th of *July* 1645, from the *Receif*, in the ship called the *Roebuck*, and coming to an anchor the 17th in the *Bahia*, were in the name of the governor *Antonio Telles da Silva*, complimented aboard their ships by several *Portuguese* gentlemen, from whom they asked leave to come ashore, having several matters of moment to propose to him in the name of the great council of *Brasil*. 1643.

Are admitted to audience. The next day being the 18th of *July*, about noon, lieutenant colonel *Andrew Vidal*, and captain *Pedro Kavalkanti*, with some other officers, came in a brigantine to fetch them to the palace; where, after the first complements, they delivered their credentials, telling the governor, that out of those he would understand that they were sent to treat with him of certain points, which they were ready to propose either now or whenever he should be disposed to receive them. The governor, after the usual return of complements and perusal of the credentials, told them, that he was ready to hear them whenever they pleased; whereupon they proposed,

Their propositions. That some *Portuguese* subjects of their high and mightinesses the states general of the *United Provinces*, have entred into a cabal, in order to take up arms and attack *Pernambuko*; to effect which, they have by certain letters solicited their fellow subjects to enter into a rebellion, and provided themselves with arms, in hopes of succours from abroad. That in the beginning of *May*, *Kamaron* and *Henry Dias* with their *Brasilians* and negroes, and some *Portuguese*, being on their march in an hostile manner to *Pernambuko*; *John Fernandes Vieira*, *Antonio Kavalkanti*, and *Amador d'Araouje*, with other *Portnguese* their accomplices had no sooner notice of their coming, but they absconded from their houses, gathered what forces they could, some by force, some otherwise, published their declarations, styling themselves governors of this war for the public liberty; all which they undertook upon hopes of being backt by foreign troops. That through God's mercy their masters did not want power to protect their faithful subjects, and to punish the rebels according to their deserts: But as they could not comprehend what it was that could induce these foreign troops to enter their territories in time of peace, in order to aid their rebellious subjects against them, so they were at a stand how to deal with them. That the great council as well as all the rest of the inhabitants, being too well acquainted with his excellency's extraction, exquisite knowledge in state affairs, and the good neighbourly correspondency he had always cultivated with our government, than to harbour the least thought that he should give the least encouragement to any of his subjects, to aid rebellious subjects against their sovereigns: That they were sensible he would use all possible

1643. possible means to prevent it. It was for this reason that they were sent by the great council to give his excellency notice of the hostilities committed by *Kamaron* and *Henry Dias*, desiring that he would be pleased not only to command them not to assist the rebels with their troops, but also to retire out of *Pernambuko* and the other captainships under the *Dutch* jurisdiction; that so the rebels being disappointed of their assistance, might be sooner reduced to their former obedience, and our subjects enjoy the benefit of the truces stipulated betwixt his present majesty of *Portugal*, Don *John* IV. and their high and mightinesses the states general. All which, the great council of *Brasil*, highly recommended to his excellency's consideration, in a letter which was then delivered by the deputies to the governor, which is as follows.

A letter from the great council to the governor of the Bahia.

IT is sufficiently known to your excellency with what strictness the truce betwixt his majesty of Portugal *and the high and mighty the states general of the* United Provinces, *has been observed in all its circumstances by the inhabitants of the* Dutch Brasil, *even according to the constitution of those of the* Bahia *and other places, who have of late passed through our captainships; neither have we ever received the least complaints upon that account, either from the king your master, or from your excellency; all which gave us sufficient reason to believe that you would not in the least consent that your subjects should attempt any thing contrary to the said truce. And though some of the* Portuguese *inhabitants, subjects of the states, laying aside their allegiance, have taken up arms and are risen in rebellion against this state, as soon as* Kamaron *and* Henry Dias *at the head of their* Brasilians *and negroes, besides some* Portuguese, *did without licence or the least encouragement from us, enter our territories, contrary to the law of nations, and joining with the rebels, exercised open hostilities against our subjects, not like soldiers but robbers and thieves; yet can we not be persuaded that those troops should have made this attempt by order or consent of his majesty of* Portugal *or your excellency, against us your confederates.*

Thanks be to God we don't want means to bring our revolted subjects to reason, and to destroy those foreign troops; but to shew to all the world how ready we are to fulfil the reiterated command of our masters, to maintain inviolably the truce betwixt his majesty and them; and to remove all sinister interpretations which might be made in foreign courts upon this head, as also to give sufficient opportunity to his majesty of Portugal *and your excellency, to convince the world that you have neither consented to nor abetted this conspiracy; we in the name of their high and mightinesses the states general, his highness the prince of* Orange, *and the governors of the* West-India *company, have sent Mr.* Balthasar Van Voerden, *councellor of the court of justice, and* Dirk Hoogstrate, *commander in chief on the cape of* St. Austin, *as our deputies to you, with full power to propose these points to you, and to desire you forthwith to recall the said* Kamaron, Henry Dias, *and other leaders, with their troops, within a limited time out of our territories, either by publick proclamation, or such other means as your excellency shall think most forcible or expedient, and to punish them according to their deserts; and if they refuse to obey, to declare them open enemies to his majesty; it being impossible for us to conceive, how due satisfaction can be given without it to their high and mightinesses, to the prince of* Orange, *and the* West-India *company, which nevertheless we ought and do expect from your excellency.*

Subscribed, *Your excellency's Well-meaning friends,*

On the side stood, Henry Hamel,
A. Van Bullestraten,
From the Receif, P. J. Bas,
July 7, 1640. J. Van Walbeck,
and
Henry de Mucheron.

The governor gave immediate answer to the deputies propositions, that he was so far from sending any succours to the rebels that he had not had the least knowledge of it. That the *Brasilians* and negroes were disbanded by his majesty's order, and that these as well as the *Portuguese* among them, that were come to the assistance of the rebels, could be in no great numbers, consisting (as he supposed) in some vagabonds, or others, who having committed misdemeanours in the *Bahia*, had taken this opportunity to shelter themselves, and flee from punishment, as it frequently happened that such like persons did come to the *Bahia* from *Pernambuko*, which nevertheless had given him not the least suspicion of the councils sincerity. He told them that he was extremely glad to understand the good confidence their masters reposed in him, of maintaining the truce concluded betwixt his majesty of *Portugal* and their high and mightinesses the states general, assuring them

The governor's answer to the deputies.

1643. them that he never should be prevailed upon to act contrary to it, for fear of hazarding his life. And that if he had any such intention, he did not want means to attempt it by the assistance of the *Brasilians*. But that he had never had any thoughts that way, notwithstanding he had been provoked to it by the *Dutch*, who since the truce had taken a *Portuguese* ship and carried it to the *Receif*, which by the bravery of the *Portuguese* was delivered from the *Hollanders*, and they and the ship brought to the *Bahia*; the *Dutch* mariners being dismissed without any punishment. He told them further, that he was not insensible what an opinion their masters entertained of his sincerity; and that he had reason to believe, that they had at this time as they had done before, sent their deputies chiefly to feel his pulse, to enquire into his strengrh, and to dive into his designs. That however, he would communicate the letter to his council, and give them a speedy answer, in order to their return home, pursuant to the request of their masters. Then the governor arising from his seat, the deputies took their leave and returned aboard.

Their second audience. The 19th in the morning they were sent for a shore by a lieutenant, and brought to the house of lieutenant colonel *Pedro Korea de Gama*, where they dined in company of *Andrew Vidal* and *Paulo de Kunha*. Towards the evening they were again conducted to the palace, where the secretary desired them to tarry a minute, because his excellency was busy with closing his letters; after some stay they were introduced to the governor, who told them, that he had understood the contents of the letter, which he found altogether agreeable to the propositions made to him the day before by way of mouth by them, which consisted chiefly in two points.

The governor's second answer. First, the good opinion their masters had of his sincere intention, in maintaining a good correspondency with them, in order to maintain the truce betwixt his majesty and the states general, and the confidence they had of his not being concerned in the rebellion, either by encouraging or assisting the same. Wherefore he desired they would continue in the same sentiments, because he never had made the least infraction of the said truce, neither ever thought of any thing like it, nor suffered any of his subjects to act contrary to it; notwithstanding, said he, the *Hollanders* have broke the same in several respects, *viz.* in their expeditions against *Angola*, *St. Thomas*, and *Marinho*; by the plundering of *Pedro Cesar Mines*, who had been basely used during his imprisonment, not like a man of quality, being forced to shelter himself among the woods after his escape. They had also taken a *Portuguese* ship in his own harbour. Neither did the inhabitants of *Pernambuko* want reasons of complaint as well as the other captainships; he had understood out of several letters from thence, how the *Jews* were always busy in forging accusations against them, which were taken for truth; and when the *Portuguese* had thereupon absconded themselves out of fear, the *Tapoyers* or mountaineers were armed against them, among the rest they had caused a poor hermit to be hanged. The great council had always given him sufficient proofs of their suspicion, the last embassy being intended to no other purpose (as captain *Hoogstrate* could testify) than to dive into his designs and strength. Thus it was reported and believed, that *Andrew Vidal* and *Paulo Kunha*, with several other officers, were sent by him into *Pernambuko*, though they saw them here before their eyes. 1643.

Upon the second point, concerning the troops said to be sent to *Pernambuko*, he gave for answer, that they must be some *Brasilians* and negroes lately disbanded, who were of little account, as we were sensible ourselves: That if a few *Portuguese* were among them, they must be supposed to be criminals who were fled from justice; that he was not unwilling to call them back by proclamation, but feared that he should be but slenderly obeyed, by a sort of people who could not be kept in obedience within his own jurisdiction. That to satisfy our request, and to remove all reasons of complaint, he intended to send his deputies shortly to *Pernambuko*; all which he had more clearly exprest in his letter to the great council, wherewith he would, according to the request of our masters, dispatch us with all imaginable speed.

The deputies replied, that their masters had never entertained any suspicion of his excellency, neither had they given any orders to dive into his designs; but always had a favourable opinion of his firm adherence to the truce, as might be evidenced by Mr. *Andrew Vidal*, who during his stay with them, had liberty to go where he pleased, without any attendance but his own. That what he objected concerning the accusations of the *Jews* was of no moment, the same being never hearkned to, the intended insurrection being discovered by persons of unquestionable credit. That *John Fernandes Vieira*, *Antonio Kavalkanti*, and others their adherents, had always been protected *A reply of the deputies.*

1643. protected against any false accusations, and had free access to all the counsellors of the court of justice, and those of other colonies, as well as the chiefest among the *Dutch*, so that they had no reason to abscond out of fear for the *Tapoyers*, who never were intended to be employed against them. That they did not know of any hermit that was hanged by them, but remember'd that in an engagement with *Amador d' Araouje*, such a one was shot by the *Brasilians* as he was ringing the bell to give the alarum.

They further told him, that tho' they had no orders to treat with his excellency upon any other points than those that concern the rebellion, they could easily make it out before all the world, that *Angola* and the other places were conquered according to the rules of war, without the least infraction of the truce, it having been expresly stipulated, that the war should continue in those parts till the same was published there. The *Brasilians*, Negroes and *Portuguese* were come in considerable numbers into our territories, not like disbanded soldiers, but well armed, and their coming was not unexpected, but well known to the rebels; but the council was not so much concerned for their number, as to be satisfied under whose authority they had taken up arms against them, that they might deal with them accordingly. But however it was, they desired his excellency to believe, that their masters would be extremely glad to understand his good inclinations, that thereby the effusion of humane blood might be saved; intreating him to send his deputies forthwith with the necessary instructions.

The governor promised to send his deputies soon after their return to *Pernambuko*, telling them, that as he thought himself secure of the good neighbourly correspondency of their masters, so he was resolved to continue in the same on his side. What he had proposed for the rest, had been only by way of discourse, not with an intention to enter into a dispute concerning the legality or illegality of it; tho' it appear'd very odd to him, that they should assist his master at home, and at the same time wage war with him in other parts, under pretence that the peace was not published there; and what had passed with *Pedro Cæsar de Mines* was a thing not justifiable in his understanding.

After the usual compliments he arose from his seat, telling them, that he would send the letter directed to the council to them aboard the next day, and so our deputies returned aboard their ship. The 20th in the morning the secretary of the governour came aboard our vessel, with the governors letter to the council, which he delivered to the deputies, requesting in his master's name, to send him a translation of the letter from the council to the governour out of the *Dutch* into the *Portuguese*, subscribed with their own hands; which they did, and having delivered the same to the secretary, he took his leave and returned ashore. 1643.

They take their leave.

Their return to the Receif.

Our people set sail the same day about noon from the *Bahia* to *Pernambuko*, where they arrived the 28th in the afternoon before the *Receif*, and gave an account the same day of their negotiation to the great council, unto whom they also delivered the letter written by *Antonio Telles da Silva*, and directed to them. The contents of which are as follows.

The governours letter to the council.

The governors letter to the council.

MR. Balthasar Vander Voerden, *counsellor of justice, and captain* Dirk Van Hoogstrate, *commander in chief on the Cape of* St. Austin, *your lordships deputies have delivered your letter to me, in which you are pleased to give me notice of the revolt of some of your subjects against you. I received this news as I ought to do, and should not have been able to receive it without the greatest surprize and discomposure of mind, if I had not been assured in my conscience, that your lordships did not in the least imagine, that this insurrection could derive its source from our government; and, tho' I could upon this occasion enter upon a long recital of the proceedings of my government, tending from its beginning till now, to a sufficient justification, in the eyes of all the world, and of the greatest kings and princes of christendom, that the said good correspondency has been maintained as strictly on our side, as the same is promised in your lordship's letter: But rather than give the least occasion of disgust or difference, by enlarging myself upon those heads, in which your subjects have expresly and manifestly violated the truce concluded and ratified betwixt the king my Master, and the States General of the United Provinces, I will sacrifice the same to the interest of our common neighbourhood, rather than to enter upon a particular account of these miscarriages, in the expedition of* Angolà, *at a time when the States General did assist the crown of* Portugal *with their naval force, when our ambassadors residing in the* Receif, *were told, that these troops were not intended to be employed against any of his majesty's harbours, but in the* West-Indies, *tho' at the same time they were embarked for the conquest of* Angola. *The same may be said of the taking of the isle of* St. Thomas, *and the city* Luy de Mapanha, *and the seizing of a* Portuguese

1643. guese *ship upon our coast, loaden with sugar from* Spiritu Sancto. *The commissary* Greening *was dispatch'd hither, under a pretext of buying of* Farinha, *but in effect to sound my inclinations, as he himself confesses, when he says in a certain letter of his,* I was sent thither with this commission, but rather to feel his pulse and try his friendship, than that we were in want. *The unfaithful dealings of the directors of* Angola *in the capitulation with the governor* Pedro Cesar de Mines; *the razing of our fort* Araval *in* Bengo; *the base treatment put upon the said governor, being a person of quality, and a general of his majesty's, are matters altogether inconsistent with the rules of war, nay, with humanity itself, and contrary to the practice not only of the more civilized nations of* Europe, *but also the* Barbarians *themselves. Of the same stamp was the answer given by your council to our ambassador, who urging a cessation of arms in the kingdom of* Angola, *was answered, that the same had no dependency on our jurisdiction, quite contrary to the sincere intentions always observed by me in all our transactions with you; for no sooner did your lordships make complaints to me against one captain* Augustino Condago, *and one* Domingo de Rocha, *who having carried away a barge with sugar, had brought her into the harbour of our city, I sent back the said vessel immediately, and put the captain in prison till he was sent over to his majesty. And that time being informed, that two soldiers living under my jurisdiction, whose names were* John de Campos, *and* Domingo Velho Sigismundo, *had committed some insolencies in your captainship of* Pernambuko, *I caused them to be hanged immediately, looking upon it as a duty not to be dispensed with by me, for the maintaining of our mutual good correspondency: All these beforementioned infractions having never been able to make me forgetful of the reiterated orders of his majesty,* viz. *To improve the effects of the peace and alliances made betwixt him and the States General, to our both sides satisfaction: I must at the same time confess, that looking upon myself as a soldier, (abstracted from the consideration of the interest of the state, and the duty of a subject) I thought I ought not to take tamely so many affronts, and to let slip so many fair opportunities of doing myself justice; much beyond what can be supposed to arise from the conjunction of a few unarmed* Portuguese, *a few discontented Negros, and some rebels, whose protection cannot, as I said before, come in any competition with the several opportunities and provocations pass'd by on our side before, for the common interest; and that consequently our government cannot as much as be conceived to be the hidden cause of this rebellion, as your lordships themselves are pleased to confess; neither would I have entred upon a recital of those particularities, if I had not thought my self obliged both in duty and affection, to give this satisfaction to you. To give you the true account of the absence of* Henry Dias, *you must know, that one night he left his guard in* Rio Reael, *and passed over to your side;* Don Antonio Philippo Kamaron, *captain of the* Brasilians, *being sent after him, and not returning, I judged that they were gone towards* Mocambo, *to attack the* Palmairas *of* Rio St. Francisco, *which made me (to avoid all suspicion of being concerned in any thing that might tend to the breach of peace) send two jesuits to persuade them to return, but in vain, they refusing to obey, either for fear of punishment, or that they were already engaged with the rebels, (as I now am apt to believe they were) so that I have heard nothing from them since, except what I have understood out of your lordships letter. The* Portuguese *under your jurisdiction have sent to me the reasons which moved them to this insurrection, imploring my assistance, as subjects of the king my master; they told me, that they stood in fear of being sacrificed to the fury of four hundred* Tapoyers, *sent for that purpose from* Rio Grande; *to avoid which, and dreading your lordships anger, awakened against them by the false accusations of the* Jews, *(the most perfidious and irreconcileable enemies of* Christendom) *had rather chosen to expose themselves to a most miserable flight, leaving behind them their wives and children, than to endure the hardships of a tedious imprisonment. I could scarce have imagin'd, that you could be so far misled by the fictions of a people so much despised by all other nations, as to be persuaded by them, that certain persons were sent from hence into your territories, who have been seen here by your deputies. And tho' I am apt to persuade myself, that some of the* Portuguese *would, as the case now stands, be glad to embrace our protection, it being much more natural to be oppressed by ones own king or prince, than by foreigners: Yet when I seriously reflect upon your lordships proposals made by your deputies,* viz. *to oblige captain* Kamaron *and* Henry Dias, *to return to the* Bahia, *and to use all other proper means to bring the revolted* Portuguese *to reason; when I say, I seriously reflect upon the publick calamities on one side, and how destitute I am of suitable means at present to satisfy your desires, I cannot but be infinitely concerned thereat; being sensible that these captains will not be brought over by persuasions; and wanting means to reduce them to obedience, who have now settled themselves at so great a distance among the woods and forests. But as I am ready to conform* 1643.

1643. *myself in all respects to your lordships desires, to convince you of the sincerity of the* Portuguese *nation, which is such, that no opportunity, tho' never so great of promoting their own interest, does ever stand in competition with what they think they owe to their confederates: I am willing to take upon me the office of a mediator, in order to endeavour to appease these troubles by my authority; for which end I intend to send to you with all possible speed, certain persons of known ability, with sufficient instructions and power, to the rebellious to return to their duty; which, if they decline, such measures may be taken as will force them to it; which, as I hope, may serve as the most effectual means to restore tranquillity to your dominions, and to cultivate the good opinion and correspondency betwixt us; which I wish God Almighty will be pleased to continue betwixt these two nations, by a perpetual tye of amity.*

Bahia, July 19, 1645. Signed,

Antonio Telles da Silva.

Mr. *Hoogstrate* at the same time gave a secret verbal account to the great council, that soon after their arrival there, *Andrew Vidal*, captain *Paulo Kunha*, and *John de Sousa* came to them, the last of whom sat himself down near him, (Mr. *Hoogstraten)* enquiring secretly after his uncle *Philip Pays Baretto*, whether he was among the mutineers; to whom he gave for answer, that he was still in his mill. After which, the table-cloth being laid, *Sousa* was invited to stay at dinner with them, which he refused; because, as he said, he was upon the guard: Before dinner was ended *Sousa* came back, and after the table-cloth was taken away, invited Mr. *Hoogstrate* and *Kunha* to smoke a pipe with him in a back room, whither they went, but were followed by the secretary, Mr. *Springapple*. As they passed through a gallery, *Paulo de Kunha* took *Springapple* a little on one side; and in the mean while, *Sousa* told *Hoogstrate* with a loud voice, that he was surprized to hear that his uncle *Philip Pays* had not sided with the rest: Unto which *Hoogstrate* answered, *That he thought he did very wisely to keep himself quiet, because it was likely to turn to no account. That is your opinion*, reply'd *Sousa*, *but have a little patience; and, because I know you to have always been a friend to the* Portuguese, *I can assure you it will turn to a considerable account. And it is upon this score, I advise you, like a friend, to provide for your own safety and your family. You may rest assured, that if you will engage to do a piece of good service to the king my master, and to the governor, you shall want neither money, sugar-mills, places, nor preferments.* 1643.

Hoogstrate *it tempted by the* Portuguese Sousa.

Mr. *Hoogstrate* appearing somewhat discomposed at this discourse, told him, *That though he was not unwilling to do the king and governor what service he could, he did not know what sort of service he meant.* Unto which, *Sousa* replied, *I am sure you are able to do good service to the king; but then*, says *Hoogstrate*, *you must tell me how: That I will*, answered *Sousa*; *are you not governor on the cape of* St. Austin? Unto which Mr. *Hoogstrate* said, *Yes, I am; then*, replied *Sousa*, *all that is required of you, is, to surrender the said fort, with all its works, into the king's hands, that we may land our men thereabouts: If you will promise to do it, you shall have a very ample reward, and be made commander in chief of our forces.* Mr. *Hoogstrate* gave for answer, *that these were things of such a nature, as were not consistent with his oath and honour.* Their discourse being interrupted at that time by the coming of another person into the gallery, *John Sousa* and *Paulo Kunha* went out another way. Mr. *Hoogstrate* told his secretary, Mr. *Springapple*, with a discomposed look, *What is the meaning of these dogs, do they take me for a traitor?* He was going on to say more, when *Sousa* and *Kunha* returning into the gallery, took him aside, and told him, *That he might be sure every thing should be performed that had been promised him; that if he wanted any money he should have it immediately; and for the rest, they would introduce him alone to the governor, to receive the confirmation of it from his own mouth.* Mr. *Hoogstrate* reply'd, *What you desire is not in my power to perform, if I would never so fain; because I am promised to have a commission of mayor immediately after my return, and then I shall certainly be employed in another place.* During this parley, Mr *Vander Voerde* entred the gallery in company with Mr. *Andrew Vidal*, who entertained him all the while the others were talking together, till *Hoogstrate* taking his opportunity as they were walking together, whispered Mr. *Vander Voerde* in the ear, *I wish I was well rid of them, to talk with you in private, for I know not what their design is; I am afraid they will either kill or detain me here.* Mr. *Vander Voerde* would willingly have made a reply, but could not, by reason *Sousa* and *Kunha*, and *Piedro Korre de Gama*, (the last of which understood *Dutch)* were so near them; so that he thought it the safest way to dissemble, and to pretend as if they had been talking about some indifferent matter. Mr. *Hoogstrate* then told *Sousa*, that he had a great mind to pay a visit to *Donna Katharine de Melo*, mother-in-law

1643. law of *Philip Pays Sousa*; he answered him, that he would ask the governor, who having given his consent, *Hoogstrate* went thitherward with *Sousa*, and at his going out of the gallery, whispered *Vander Voerde* again in the ear, *They have catch'd a mackrel, for I intend to act the hypocrite to the life.* As they were walking along the street to madam *de Melo*'s house, *Sousa* and *Kunha* repeated their former discourse, endeavouring to encourage Mr. *Hoogstrate*, by hopes and promises of great reward, both from the king and governor, with whom they said he should confer in private concerning the point in hand, and that in the following manner.

After their return from madam *de Melo*'s, to the house of *Piedro Korre de Gama*, where *Vander Voerde* expected their coming, *Kunha* was to go privately to the governor, to agree with him, that when Mr. *Vander Voerde*, *Hoogstrate*, *Sousa*, and *Kunha*, should come to speak with him, he should by his secretary, desire them to stay a little while. In the mean while, *Sousa* was to ask Mr. *Hoogstrate* to take a glass of wine with him, and under that pretence bring him to the chamber of the confessor of the governor, where they were to have this private interview. Accordingly, *Paulo de Kunha* went to the governor, whilst *Hoogstrate* and *Sousa* were returning to *Piedro Corre de Gama*'s house; when *Sousa* entertained him with nothing else, but the probability of succeeding in their enterprize against the *Dutch Brasil*, telling him, that the governor stay'd only for the coming of *Salvador Korrea de Saa* and *Benevides*, who were expected with four galleons from *Rio Janeiro*, besides some other ships; and that twenty five hundred men were designed for this expedition, besides those already in arms in *Pernambuko*, who were to be sent from the *Bahia*, and to be landed on the Cape of *St. Austin*; *This is*, said *Sousa*, *the governor's request to you.*

Scarce were they returned to the house of *Piedro Korrea de Gama*, when *Andrew Vidal* came and told them, that the governor was ready to receive them; so they went to the palace, where they were no sooner come within the anti-chamber, but the governor's secretary came to desire them to tarry a little, the governor being busy with closing some letters. So whilst some *Portuguese* were entertaining Mr. *Vander Voerde* near the window, says *Sousa* to Mr. *Hoogstrate*, *Come, shall you and I take a glass of wine in the mean while?* Which Mr. *Springapple*, secretary of the embassy understanding, told him, that he would go along with them; but *Paulo de Kunha*, and some other *Portuguese* taking him aside, kept him in discourse, whilst Mr. *Hoogstrate* was conducted by *Sousa* into the confessor's chamber. 1643.

Within a few minutes after, the governor *Antonio Telles da Silva*, entring the room, saluted Mr. *Hoogstrate* very courteously, and setting himself in a chair near him, order'd the chamber to be lock'd, no body being present besides themselves but *Sousa*. The governor then told Mr. *Hoogstrate*, that he had always taken a particular notice of his character, of his being a friend to the *Portuguese*, that he hoped he would continue in the same opinion, and would not refuse the offer made him by *Don John de Sousa*, in the king's and his name; their intention being not to enter into a war with the *Dutch*, but only to repossess themselves of what of right belonged to the present king of *Portugal*, *Don John* IV. and that if count *Maurice* of *Nassau* had stay'd any longer in this country, he himself would have been instrumental in bringing this matter about. Mr. *Hoogstrate* answered the governor, that he should be glad to understand what it was he could serve him in; *You have*, says he, *understood that from Mr.* Sousa, *and I desire you to turn absolute* Portuguese. Mr. *Hoogstrate* told him it was beyond his power, because immediately after his return, he should be provided with a majors commission, and consequently not be employed in the same place: Unto which the governor reply'd, *You need not question any place of honour or profit among us, but it will perhaps not be convenient to discourse together upon this point at present, for fear Mr.* Vander Voerde *should suspect us: But I intend to send two ambassadors, (of which Mr.* Paulo de Kunha *is to be one) to your government, who shall be empowered to treat with you further upon this account. And*, says he, *giving his hand to Mr.* Hoogstrate, *rest assured in the name of the king my master, that whatever Mr.* Paulo de Kunha *shall promise you will be punctually observed and performed.*

Mr. Hoogstrate's private interview with the governor.

Then the governor took his leave, telling him that he would not detain him any longer, for fear of creating a suspicion in his collegue, and so retired into his own apartment. But Mr. *Hoogstrate* and *John de Sousa* were no sooner return'd from thence, but the governor sent for the said Mr. *Hoogstrate* and his collegue Mr. *Vander Voerden*, to confer with them, concerning their proposals, made in the name of the council of *Dutch Brasil*: As they were walking thither, Mr. *John de Sousa* told again to Mr. *Hoogstrate*, with a low voice, and why are you obliged to accept of the

majors

1643.

majors commiſſion? It is an eaſy matter for you to tell them, that you would rather continue governor of the place where you now are; and be ſatisfy'd that when you come among us, that you will not want any employment fit for a good ſoldier as you are. Mr. *Hoogſtrate* being not a little moved with this diſcourſe, was more deſirous to get aboard their veſſel, as ſoon as poſſible he might, to get an opportunity of communicating the whole matter to Mr. *Vander Voerde*; which he did accordingly, as ſoon as they were entered the cabin, the door of which he ordered to be lock'd immediately.

The Dutch *debate, whether to employ the* Tapoyers.

In the mean while, *viz.* the 5th of *July*, it was debated in the council of the *Dutch-Braſil*, whether for the ſecurity of the country, they ſhould not want the aſſiſtance of the *Tapoyers*, under their king *John Duwy*, dwelling in *Rio Grande*; who for that purpoſe had gathered a good body near *Kunhau*, eſpecially ſince the *Portugueſe* committed all manner of barbarities againſt the *Dutch*, and had ſummon'd the *barbarians* called *Rondelas*, from the *Bahia*.

But conſidering the devaſtations which muſt needs enſue upon the march of thoſe barbarous people in the flat countrey, it was thought convenient not to come to any certain reſolution upon this point, 'till they had adviſed with lieutenant colonel *Haus*, to whom a letter was diſpatched, immediately upon that account.

On the 7th of *July*, the ſaid Mr. *Haus* ſent word to the council, that he intended to march the ſame day from *Moribeka*, and after being joined with captain *John Blaar*, to attack the enemy at *St. Lawrence*; but by another letter of the 16th, written by captain *Blaar*, they were informed that the rebels continued very ſtrong at *St. Lawrence*, expecting a certain reinforcement from the *Matta*, where they had forced the people to take up arms for them; deſiring a ſuccour of fifty men, to drive them from thence. Hereupon the council diſpatched meſſengers both to *Blaar* and *Haus*, ordering them to join their troops, and to rout the rebels near *St. Lawrence*, on which in a great meaſure depended the preſervation of the *Dutch-Braſil*.

Haus *and* Blaar *ordered to join.*

The 7th of the ſame month the council received alſo a letter from lieutenant *Flemming*, dated at *Pojuka*, in which he advertiſed them, that he had received certain intelligence, that *Kamaron* was marching againſt him, and that two companies were already come to the ſugar-mill of *Pikdora*. Hereupon orders were ſent him, that if he found himſelf not in a condition to keep the monaſtery for want of proviſions, he ſhould at the approach of *Kamaron*'s troops retire to *St. Antonio*, the better to make head againſt the enemy. The ſame day enſign *Hartſtin* marched with a detachment of ninety ſoldiers and thirty *Braſilians*, of the garriſons of the *Receif* and *Itamarika*, to *Ajama* and *Jegoaribi*, in queſt of the rebels, but meeting with none returned about noon, and the ſame evening directed his march towards *Haus*.

Lieutenant Flemming *ordered to retire to* St. Antonio.

1643.

The 8th of *July* the council having received advice from *Haus* that they intended the ſame day to march from the ſugar-mill of *St. John Ferdinando Vieira* to attack the rebels at *St. Lawrence*, if they would abide his coming, it was reſolved to ſend as many forces as poſſibly they could ſpare to his relief, conſidering that the preſervation of the whole *Dutch-Braſil* depended on the ſucceſs of this expedition; and accordingly two companies of foot, of *Mucheron* and *Blaar* were ordered to march thither, not queſtioning but that before their arrival *Haus* would be join'd by captain *John Blaar*; and in effect the next following day they received advice from Mr. *Haus*, that he was ready to join with the ſaid *Blaar*.

The council ſends ſuccours to Haus.

The 10th of *July*, the council gave an account by letters to *Haus*, what intelligence they had received concerning the poſture of affairs in *St. Antonio* and *Pojuka*, with orders to ſend as many firelocks and *Braſilians* as he could poſſibly ſpare to their relief, to keep the paſſage from *St. Antonio* to *Pojuka* and *Serenhaim* open; without which all communication betwixt them and the *Receif* would be cut off by the enemy. Two letters of *John Fernando Vieira* and *Antonio Kavalkanti* were the ſame day read in council, in which they complained of the ſeverity of the two laſt proclamations, but were not thought fit to be anſwered; eſpecially ſince *Amador d'Araouje* had about the ſame time retired from the paſs of *Pinderama*.

Haus *ordered to ſend relief to* St. Antonio.

Two days before, *viz.* that the council had received letters from Mr. *Hoek*, dated the 25th of *June*, at *Rio Grande*, intimating that hitherto there had not happened any commotions in thoſe parts, that however he had diſarmed the *Portugueſe*, and that the *Tapoyers* appeared to be well inclined to the government: Orders were ſent him to cultivate a good underſtanding with the *Tapoyers*, for which purpoſe they ſent ſome preſents to *John Duwy* their king, and that the council approved his diſarming of the *Portugueſe*. On the ſame day father *Imanuel*, *Lewis Bras*, *Imanuel Ferdinand de Sa*, *Kaſpar de Mendoza*, *Furtado* and *Jeronymo de Rocha*, all *Portugueſe* inhabitants of the *Dutch-Braſil* delivered their

1643. their petition to the council, requesting, that the time of six days appointed by the last proclamation, for the wives and children of the revolted *Portuguese*, to leave the countrey, being expired, they might be allowed to stay in their habitations at least, 'till the ways, which at that time were rendred unpassable, by the overflowing of the rivers, were somewhat mended. But considering that the *Portuguese* rebels forced the inhabitants by threats and other unusual methods to take up arms against the government, their request was not granted.

The petition of the Portuguese *refused.*

The 13th of *July* the council were advertised by letters from *Haus*, dated the 12th, that he had passed the river *Kapivaribi*, and marching thro' the *Matta* to the sugar-mills of *Arnao d'Ollanda*, had met with four hundred rebels, who at the approach of his troops were fled to *Moribeka*, with the loss of some of their men, from whence they might without any opposition march to the *Matta* of *Brasil*, and that he was ready to march directly to *St. Lawrence*, where he would expect the further orders of the council. They immediately dispatched their orders to him, to pursue and rout the flying rebels with all possible speed, before they could make head again, which done, he should fix his head quarters, in such a place where he was sure he might be supplied with provisions out of the adjacent countrey; their magazines being so exhausted, as not to be in a condition to supply his troops. *Haus* had already in some measure taken effectual care of this point, having in the mean while sent a reinforcement of one hundred foot, and a company of *Brasilians*, under the command of captain *Tallo*, to Mr. *Ley* governor of *Moribeka* and *St. Antonio*. The council also ordered the governor of the *Cape of St. Austin* to strengthen the fort with pallisadoes; and at the same time received Advice from Mr. *Ley* from *St. Antonio*, that the rebels under *Amador d'Araouje*, and *Pedro Marinha Falkao*, had posted themselves within sight of them, in the new sugar-mill, but as soon as he received the expected succours, he did not question to chase them from thence, *Amador d'Araouje* having in vain attempted to force those of *Pojuka*, to take up arms against the government.

The rebels flee before Haus.

Revolt in Pojuka.

He received also intelligence from Mr. *Carpentier* out of *Goyana*, that things remained in quiet there as yet: But whilst *Haus* was busy in making head against the rebels in the *Vergea*, *Petro Marinho Falkao* having declared himself head of the rebels of *Pojuka*, had gathered a body sufficient to block up the garrison of *St. Antonio*, who had no other supplies of provision, but what they received from the circumjacent countrey; so that the council being sensible of the danger, sent immediately orders to *Haus*, to hasten to the relief of that place; who, accordingly directed his march the same night to the sugar-mill of *Lewis Bras*, leaving captain *Wiltschut* with a company of soldiers, and all the sick, behind at *St. Lawrence*. 1643.

The council received also advice by letters from *Paul de Linge*, dated the 12th of *July* at *Parayba*, that things were as yet quiet thereabouts, but that with much ado he had hitherto kept the *Brasilians*, inhabiting the villages, from plundering the *Portuguese* inhabitants, who were extremely dissatisfied, because some of the *Brasilians* and *Tapoyers*, that had done them considerable mischief, were discharged out of custody. They ordered him to take all possible care to keep both the *Brasilians* and *Dutch* inhabitants, who were both for plundering the *Portuguese*, from doing any mischief to them; for which reason the council sent the following proclamation to be publish'd there.

A PROCLAMATION.

WE the members of the great council, having received frequent complaints, that many of the faithful inhabitants of the countrey, who lately have taken a new oath of allegiance to the government, are plundred and robb'd by the soldiers and volunteers; and being resolved to maintain them in the possession of their estates and goods, have for that reason granted them safeguards, and taken them into our peculiar protection; do hereby forbid all our officers and soldiers, as well as the other inhabitants under our Jurisdiction, to attempt to plunder any of the inhabitants, provided with such safeguards, or to endamage them any otherwise, either in their goods or persons, upon pain of corporeal punishment.

The 15th of *July* in the evening, the council was advertised by Mr. *Ley*, that the rebels had kill'd some soldiers of the garrison of *St. Antonio*, that were sent abroad to fetch some cattle from the sugar-mill *Gurapou*, and had so closely block'd up the place, that no provision could be brought thither; and as they were not provided with necessaries for above a few days longer, they were in the utmost danger of being lost. Lieutenant colonel *Haus* being expected the same evening with his troops at *St. Lawrence*, orders were dispatch'd thither for him to go either in person, or at least to send as many able soldiers as he could bring together, under the

1643.

the command of captain *John Blaar*, to the relief of *St. Antonio*, the council being of opinion, that the safety of the *Cape of St. Austin*, and of all the southern provinces, depended on the preservation of this place; for which reason, they also ordered captain *Falbo*, who was expected about the same time with a company of soldiers, and as many *Brasilians* at *Moribeka*, to march directly to *St. Antonio*, and to stay there 'till further orders; of all which they sent advice to Mr. *Ley*, and Mr. *Heck*. *Haus* having, pursuant to these orders, directed his march to *St. Antonio*, (notwithstanding the weariness of his soldiers tired by a tedious march) *Pedro Marinho Falkao* had no sooner notice of his approach, but he raised the blockade of *St. Antonio*, and with his body of rebels gathered out of the three districts of *St. Antonio*, *Pojuka* and *Moribeka*, to the number of six hundred, joined with the rebels in the *Vergea* of *Moribeka*.

The blockade of St. Antonio *raised.*

The 17th of *July* the council were advertised by *Haus* in a letter dated at *Moribeka*, that having received a message from Mr. *Ley* and Mr. *Heck* out of *St. Antonio*, with advice, that in *Puerto de Gallinas*, two boats with ammunition were landed by *Pedro de Kunba*, he had sent thither captain *John Blaar*, and ensign *Hartstein*, with a good Body of his ablest soldiers and *Brasilians*, he himself not being in a condition to follow with the rest, disabled by their late marches; for which reason he had put them into quarters of refreshment in *Moribeka*, where he would expect their further orders, as not judging his presence necessary at the *Receif*, now the enemies were fled before him.

Orders sent J. Haus *by the council.*

Orders were thereupon dispatch'd to him by the council the 19th of *July*, to keep his head quarters in *Moribeka*, the better to keep a watchful eye over the rebels that were retired into the woods; and to be the nearer at hand to succour either *St. Antonio* or *Pojuka*, for which *Moribeka* lay very convenient; but if the enemy should become too strong for him, he should retreat towards the *Receif*. Advice also was sent him, That *Amador d'Araouje*, *Pedro Marinho Falkao*, *John Pais*, and *Kabral*, were with the rebels they had gathered in *St. Antonio* and *Pojuka*, march'd the day before in the morning from *d'Ingenio Moreno Gardo*, to join their troops with those of *John Fernandes Vieira*.

The council likewise received several letters from *John Hoek*, *Rudolph Baro*, and *James Rabbi*, dated the 5th, 6th and 7th of *July*, concerning the present state of affairs in *Rio Grande*, and that they being threatned with an invasion by *Kamaron* on the south side, and by the *Brasilians* of *Siara* and *Maranhaon* from the north, they had disarmed all the *Portuguese* and laid up their arms in the fort of *Keulen*. They had also by the advice of king *John Duwy*, taken into custody a certain *Portuguese* called *Antonio Vetello*, with his son, being accused by the said king *Duwy* of having had a hand in the murther committed upon the *Dutch* in *Siara*, and in the conspiracy of the rebels. They further complained of the ill practices of the *Portuguese*, who sought by all means possible to oppress the *Dutch* thereabouts; adding withal, that king *Duwy* was ready with his *Tapoyers* to fall upon the *Portuguese*, as soon as he received orders for that purpose, which had made many of the *Portuguese* fly out of *Parayba*.

1643.

About the same time, near one thousand *Brasilians*, *viz.* three hundred and sixty nine men, the rest women and children, being fled for shelter into the isle of *Itamarika*, where they were maintained out of the magazines, it was resolved the 21st of *July* by the council, to send thither Mr. *Listry*, to take effectual care, to ease the company of that burthen, that they might be engaged to provide themselves out of their respective *Aldeas*. Things were as yet quiet about that time in *Itamarika*, *Goyana* and *Parayba*, by the good conduct of Mr. *Paul Vander Linge*, governor of the last. For as soon as the fire of rebellion began to break out in the *Vergea*, *Pojuka*, and in *Olinda*, the council being advertised that they ought to keep a watchful eye over those of *Parayba*, where several were suspected of being conscious of the design, they sent the 13th of *July*, *Paul de Linge*, one of the Assessors in the court of Justice thither, with an ample commission, to endeavour to keep the inhabitants in obedience, and to act for that purpose, as he should find it most conducing to the publick security. He was no sooner arrived there, but he made it his chiefest care to provide the forts with sufficient garrisons, ammunition and provisions, which he took from the ships then lying in the road, behind the *Red-Land*: He further took care to secure all the suspected persons, and summoned the rest to take a new oath of allegiance to the government, which they did accordingly.

The council used the same precaution in the district of *Pojuka*, in the *Vergea*, *Garassu* and *Goyana*, where they obliged such of the inhabitants as had not left their dwelling-places to take a new oath of obedience. But the late succours sent thither from the *Babia* frustrated all these endeavours.

On the 24th of *July*, Mr. *Ley* came with credentials from *St. Antonio* to the council, unto

Propositions made by Mr. Ley *to the council.*

1643. unto whom he made the following propositions.

I. That whereas several young and able men, living near *St. Antonio*, had not listed themselves pursuant to the proclamation issued for that purpose, they desired orders might be sent for all those living in the jurisdiction of *Maurice*'s *Town* and *St: Antonio* in the open countrey, to be obliged to take up arms for the defence of the country.

II. To oblige all such young men as were not able to serve as volunteers, at their own charge, to list themselves for soldiers, and to instruct them in martial discipline.

III. That perhaps it might not be unadviseable to draw the garrison out of *Porto Calvo*, to appear the more formidable in the field.

IV. To divide our land forces into two bodies, the better to maintain themselves in the open countrey; whereas now upon the least motion of the enemy, our whole force was obliged to follow them; and that the garrison of *St. Antonio* should be reinforced with such a number, as to be able to send abroad a good party, for the conveniency of fetching the necessary provisions out of the countrey.

After mature deliberation, the council was of opinion as to the

Their resolutions. I. That the young inhabitants of *St. Antonio*, *Pojuka*, and *Moribeka*, ought not to be forced to serve in the fort *St. Antonio*.

II. That they would empower Mr. *Ley* and *Heck*, to take as many of the young men as voluntarily offered themselves into the service for four months, at nine gilders *per* month, and one months advance money.

III. They were absolutely against the leaving of the fort *Porto Calvo*, but that ought to be defended to the utmost.

IV. What concern'd the dividing of their land forces in two bodies, they would advise with colonel *Haus*, but they approved of the proposed reinforcement of the garrison of *St. Antonio*, for reasons by them alledged.

Lieutenant *Haus Vogel*, by his letters dated the 18th and 27th of *July*, at *Seregippo del Rey* advised the council, that he had sent a detachment towards *Kamaron*, who could not get sight either of any *Portuguese* or *Brasilians*, but that they had taken a single *Portuguese*, who was charged with letters to be carried to *Rio St. Francisco*: He told them, that *Kamaron* with some troops was march'd through *Rio St. Francisco* into the captainship of *Seregippo del Rey*; and that three or four small vessels or *caravans*, with some troops under the command of *Andrew Vidal*, were sail'd from the *Bahia* to *Maranhaon* and *Siara*. He likewise sent the letters found upon the said *Portuguese* to the council, by which it appear'd, that the first foundation of this revolt had been laid among those of the *Bahia*; or at least that they had been made privy to it, and that they had provided these succours. For among others, there was a letter from the bishop of that place, to a certain friar of the *Receif*, in which he told him, that he hoped to be with him before long; whereupon the *Fiscal* was ordered to examine the matter, in order to find out the bottom of this correspondency betwixt these two clergymen. *Certain letters seized and communicated to the council.*

In the mean while the *Tapoyers* of *Rio Grande* (according to Mr. *Linge*'s letter of the 19th of *July*) had murther'd thirty five *Portuguese* in the sugar-mills of *Kunha*, who being of the number of those that had surrendred their arms, pursuant to the proclamation, this caused no small terror among the rest of the *Portuguese* thereabouts, and especially in *Parayba*, where they left their habitations; so that it being to be fear'd they would associate with the rebels, under pretence of self-defence, Mr. *Linge* desired a reinforcement of soldiers to keep the *Tapoyers* in awe. The council therefore commanded Mr. *Astellen* and captain *William Lambert* with his company of foot, besides twenty fusileers, and a detachment of fifty men out of the garrisons of *Parayba* and *Rio Grande*, to take care of the *Tapoyers*, and to conduct them to the *Receif*, *Jacob Rabbi* their commander was ordered to march along with them, and *Rudolph Baro* appointed to provide them quarters upon the road. *The Tapoyers murther thirty five Portuguese.*

Haus having by this time sufficiently refresh'd his troops, writ a letter dated the first of *August* to the council, in which he desired their orders to go in quest of the rebels, and to attack them before they could be reinforced with their expected succours; which being granted him, he attack'd them in *d'Ingenio* of *Balthasar Moreno*, with such success, that he beat them from place to place; 'till on the 3d of *August* they retired to their entrenchment upon a high steep hill, accessible only in one place. Notwithstanding which, he relying upon the bravery of his soldiers, and hoping thereby to put an end to the war, attack'd them vigorously in this advantagious post; but the rebels being superiour to him both in number and in the strength of their camp, his forces were repulsed with the loss of one hundred men, (some say five hundred) among whom was captain *Lor*. After this defeat, *Haus* being sensible that the enemy expected daily a fresh *Haus engages the rebels.* *Is worsted and retires to the Receif.*

1643. a fresh reinforcement from the *Bahia*, retired to the *Receif*, where he knew his troops were absolutely necessary for the defence of the place.

Two Portuguese condemned to death.

On the first of *August Gonsalvo Kabral de Kalkos*, was by the court of justice condemned to death, having at the instigation of *John Fernandes Vieira*, undertaken to head the rebels in the captainship of *Goyana*. The same fate attending one *Thomas Pais*, an inhabitant of *Tienpio*, who had endeavoured to raise some troops for the said *John Fernandes Vieira*. The same day the great council received advice out of *Serinheim*, (the letters being sent privately in the night time in a small boat down the river to the sea-side) that the rebels began to be very numerous thereabouts, that they were masters of the river, had staved all the boats, and plundred *d' Ingeneo Formosa*, where they carried away the negroes, and kill'd the beasts belonging to the *Dutch*, but spared those of the *Portuguese*. The council being sensible that nothing but force would be able to reduce these rebels to their duty, and that they were from time to time reinforced from the *Bahia*, whereas the *Dutch* troops diminish'd daily, they resolved the first of *August*, to send Mr. *Balthasar Vander Voerden* councellor of justice to *Holland*, to represent to the council of nineteen there, the true state of the affairs of the *Dutch-Brasil*, and to sollicit prompt succours. Accordingly the said Mr. *Vander Voerden* having taken his leave of the council, set sail the next day, with the rest of the ships that lay ready to sail for *Holland*, being instructed with sufficient power and credentials from the council; as follows.

Rebellion in Serinhaim.

Mr. Vander Voerden *sent with a credential into* Holland.

Most noble, honourable, and most prudent lords.

Notwithstanding the rebels make not the least use of the royal authority, but cover their revolt with the cloak of godly liberty, we were always of opinion, that this rebellion of our Portuguese *inhabitants has not only been undertaken with the consent of the king of* Portugal, *or at least of his governor of the* Bahia, *but also encouraged and fomented by his authority and conduct. For how can it be supposed that* Kamaron, Henry Dias, *and the other ringleaders, should have dared to attempt to attack us by force of arms without his approbation? It was likewise our constant opinion, (considering the present unsettled state of* Portugal, *and the alliance betwixt that King and the states of* Holland *against* Spain*) that he would be sure never to acknowledge the transactions of the heads of the rebellion, and the succours sent them, to have been done by his authority, lest the breach of faith and all its ill consequences might be one time or other laid at his door, 'till he thought himself sure in the entire conquest of the* Dutch Brasil. *Our guess has since proved more than too true, for* Antonio Telles de la Silva, *governor of the* Bahia *(as is evident from his answer to our letters here inclosed) denies to have had the least knowledge, much less any hand in the contrivance or the conduct of this conspiracy; laying the blame of this insurrection upon their ring-leaders, who refused to obey his orders; and offering to send certain commissioners to appease the fury of the rebels; and in case they should refuse to comply, to force them by the kings authority to lay down their arms. But how little agreeable this offer of putting an end to this rebellion, is to his real intention, is apparent out of the report made by Mr.* Vander Voerden *and captain* Dieterick Hoogstrate, *under-written by their own hands; in which you will find these express words of the governor:* That the *Brasilians* and negroes were disbanded by his majesty of *Portugal*'s particular order. *The abstracts of the several enclosed letters sent from the* Bahia, *and taken from the messenger by our forces in* Seregippo, *will put it beyond all doubt, that several inhabitants of the* Bahia, *and among them the Bishop himself, had already in* May *last some knowledge of the intentions of* John Fernandes Vieira, *and his accomplices; add to this the depositions of captain* Dieterick Hoogstrate *subscribed by himself, concerning the propositions made to him in private, whilst he was managing the company's business there, in the quality of one of our deputies; which as it directly contradicts the governors answer to us, so it unravels the whole secret of his real intentions. And for as much as all these things are sufficient forewarnings to us, that the rebels will be constantly supplied from the* Bahia, *whereas we on the contrary must expect to be weaken'd more and more in every respect, we judged it absolutely necessary and requisite for the service of our state, to send to you the members of the council of nineteen, Mr.* Balthasar Vander Voerden, *councellor in our court of justice, to give you a verbal account of the deplorable state of our affairs here, in a more ample manner, than the same may be express'd in writing, not questioning, but your lordships will thereby be encouraged to send us a speedy and sufficient succour, to re-establish our affairs here, and to deliver your faithful subjects from the imminent dadger that threatens no less than the ruin and loss of their lives and estates, and desiring you to give a favourable reception to the said Mr.* Balthasar Vander Voerden.

Receif *the 2d of* Aug. 1645.

Immediate-

1643.

The Portuguese prepare for the Invasion of the Dutch-Brasil.

Immediately after the departure of the two beforementioned envoys, Mr. *Vander Voerden* and captain *Hoogstrate* out of the *Bahia*, being the 20th of *July*, the governor *Antonio Telles de Silva*, ordered all the sea and land men that could be got together in haste, to be embark'd in twelve ships ready fitted out for that purpose; with necessary ammunition, arms and provision, for the intended invasion. *Hieronymo Serrao de Payva* had the supreme command over the fleet, as the colonel *Martin, Soares Moreno*, and *Andrew Vidal de Nigreiros* had over the land forces, both officers in the service of the king of *Portugal*. The orders given to the admiral by the governor, dated the 20th *July*, contained in substance, that the great council of the *Dutch-Brasil* having notified to him the insurrection of the *Portuguese* inhabitants of *Pernambuko*, he had judged it expedient to equip his fleet, in order to put a speedy stop to those disorders; because he was willing to comply with the said councils request, in respect of the sincere friendship and correspondency betwixt the crown of *Portugal* and them, which he had strict orders from his majesty to observe; whereas it is evident, that the great council of the *Dutch-Brasil* in their letter to *Salvador Korrea de Saa Benavides*, of the 13th of *August* expresly declare, never to have desired any assistance from the governor of the *Bahia*, against the rebellious *Portuguese* inhabitants.

Pretences for this invasion.

Instructions of the Portuguese *Admiral.*

The further Instructions given to the said admiral *Payva* were, that he should directly steer his course from the *Bahia* to *Pernambuko*, keeping about twenty or thirty leagues distance at sea, from the shore; that coming to the tenth degree he should approach the shore, and if he found the wind to blow hard from the south, before he came to the before mentioned height, he should be very careful not to pass beyond the lands point in the night time. After having taken a view of the country, he should, with the advice of his best pilots, endeavour to land his men in the most secure place he could meet with thereabouts, either at *Una*, *Lagamar* or *Tamandare*; being three leagues to the south of the isle of *Alexo*. But if they could not make any of these harbours, they should enter at *Porto Dosser*, *Nambous* or *Lagamar* of *Marakaipe*, lying two leagues to the north of *Alexo*. But if notwithstanding all their endeavours, they also should miss their aim in those places, to make themselves masters of *Porto de Gallinhas*, and to land their men betwixt that place and *Barra Grande*. After they had landed their men, with the necessary ammunition and provisions, he should set sail to the bay of *Pernambuko*, in order to deliver with his own hands the governors letter to the lords of the great council.

1643.

The Portuguese *set sail from the* Bahia.

Accordingly the said fleet set sail towards the latter end of *July* from the *Bahia*, and in few days after arrived in the Bay of *Tamandare*, betwixt the rivers *Olna* and *Formosa*, about four or five leagues beyond *Alevo* and *Serinhaim*. They were no sooner come to an anchor there, but the colonel *Martin Soares Moreno*, and *Andrew Vidal de Nigreiros* landed the 28th of *July* one thousand eight hundred or two thousand landmen, among whom were many reformed officers well appointed, and great store of arms, ammunition, and other necessaries.

Land their men.

The first of *August*, towards evening, three ships with five small vessels appeared in sight of the *Receif*, steering their course to the north, whereupon the council dispatch'd their immediate orders to the two ships, the *Zoutlandia* and the *Zealandia*, to make all the sail they could after them, to observe what course they steer'd, and to prevent their landing of men. About the same time an adviceboat arrived from admiral *Lichthart*, with letters to the council, intimating, that he had seen the said ships, and that he supposed their intent to be, to land some men on the south of the cape of *St. Austin*, for which reason he desired them to send him some ships, and grant him leave to take as many of the garrison of *St. Antonio* as he should judge necessary to attack the enemy; of all which immediate notice was given to the northern parts, to be upon their guard against any sudden surprise.

A false alarum upon the Receif.

But the next following day those ships being got out of sight, several masters of small vessels, that had been near them at sea, reported, that they were heavy freighted ships, which by the strong north winds were forced near the shore, so that it was concluded that they had steered their course towards *Portugal*.

The Portuguese *Fleet sail to* Pernambuko.

Immediately after admiral *Payva* set sail from the bay of *Tamandare*, and meeting with the fleet under the command of admiral *Salvador Korrea de Saa de Benavides*, which was latterly sailed out of the port of *Rio Janeiro*, he returned with him into the said harbour, and on *St. Lawrence*'s day with their joint forces sailed from thence towards the bay of *Pernambuko*.

The first news the council received of it was on the 11th of *August*, by a master of a small vessel called, *John Hoen*, bound for *Seregippo del Rey*, and by commissary *John Barentz*, with advice that they had seen a fleet of twenty eight or thirty ships off of *Una*;

1643. *Una*, or *Rio Formosa*, and that three of them had pursued them, and discharged some of their guns upon them. Much about the same time they received letters from major *Hoogstrate*, from the *Cape of St. Austin*, and the fort *Vander Dussen*, intimating, that *Andrew Vidal*, *Henry Dias* and *Paul de Kunha* were landed at *Una*, and marching to *Serinhaim*, had made themselves masters of the place, where they had given quarter to the *Dutch*, but cut to pieces all the *Brasilians*. The council hereupon took immediate care to send some ammunition and provisions to the said cape, having already, for the better security of that place, ordered Mr. *Ley* and Mr. *Hoek*, two days before, to leave the fort of *St. Antonio*, and to retire with the garrison to the cape of *St. Austin*, before they were enclosed by the enemy. That two ships, the *Deventer* and the *Elias*, which were in the harbour unlading their goods and provisions brought along with them for the service of the company, were ordered to be equipped immediately, in order to join with the other five ships that lay at anchor in the road, *viz.* the *Utrecht*, the *Zealandia*, *Ser Veer*, the *Zoutlandia*, and the *Golden-Doe*. The same Night advice of all what pass'd was sent to colonel *Haus*, with orders to be upon his guard, and to retire with his troops to the sugar-mill belonging to Mr. *Hoek*, or any other convenient place, from whence he might be able to maintain a communication with the *Receif*. Letters were also dispatch'd to Mr. *Dortmont* in *Itamarika*, to Mr. *Carpentier* in *Goyana*, and Mr. *de Linge* in *Parayba*, to advertise them of the enemies arrival.

The council advised the Receif.

They equip some ships.

To supply the want of sea men, many labourers were imprest aboard the ships, as were likewise thirty-five land soldiers of *Moucheron*'s company, who had spoiled their fleet by their last long march; and out of the ship *Elias* were a thousand pounds of gunpowder, and out of the *Douchter* six hundred, sent a shore for the use of the garrison.

Not long after dinner time the enemies fleet, consisting of twenty-eight or thirty ships, appeared in sight of the *Receif*, where they cast anchor to the north of four of our ships and a yacht, which lay in that road; so that the next following night was spent in ballasting the two ships, the *Elias* and *Deventer*, and in fitting them for the sea. The next morning with break of day the *Portuguese* admiral who carried the white flag, sent *Martinho de Rebeira* and *Balthasar de Castilho*, as his deputies aboard the *Dutch* admiral *Cornelius Lichthart*, who brought four letters, *viz.* two from the governor of the *Bahia*, *Antonio Telles de Silva*, the first dated the 21st, and the second the 22d of *July*, the third from the *Portuguese* admiral, *Salvador Korrea de Saa Benavides*, and the fourth from *Jeronymo Sarrao de Pavia*, dated the 12th of *August*; besides another letter from the before-mentioned governor, directed to *John Fernando Vieira*, *Anthony Kavalkanti*, and the other heads of the *Portuguese* rebels. 1643.

Letters sent to the council.

Admiral *Lichthart* carried the said deputies ashore, in order to deliver the letters to the council; which being translated, were read at the meeting of the council the 14th of *August*, as well those of the governor from the 21st, 22d, and 24th of *July*; as from *Salvador Korrea de Saa Benavides*, commodore of the *Portuguese* fleets, and *Jeronymo Sarrao de Pavia*, who had landed *Andrew Vidal* with his men near *Rio Formosa*.

The first letter was as follows.

The first letter.

Pursuant to your lordships letter, and the propositions made in your behalf by your deputies, Mr. Balthasar Vander Voerden *councellor of justice, and* Dieterick Hoogstrate *governour of the* Cape of St. Austin, *in which you requested the recalling of the troops under* Henry Dias; *I being desirous to fulfil my promise, sent to you in my answer by the most effectual means that I could possibly think of, have sent you the two colonels* Martin Soares Moreno, *and* Andrew Vidal de Negreiros *(both persons of unquestionable conduct and prudence) to the captainship of* Pernambuko, *with full power and instructions, to reduce the revolted* Portuguese *to their due obedience, for which reason also I have sent a letter to the said rebels, to exhort them to the remembrance of their duty, and to lay down their arms. Which that it might prove the more effectual, I have sent thither suffitient force, which may be serviceable to your lordships, to reduce those that remain obstinate to reason, and to chase the rebellious troops out of your dominions. I hope that with God's assistance this may prove an effectual means to quench the fire of rebellion, to restore the peace of* Brasil, *and to encrease the good understanding and friendship which has been established betwixt both these nations. We recommend you to God's protection, remaining,*

Bahia, July 21, 1645.

Your lordships affectionate servant,
Antonio Telles de Sylva.

The second letter of the said governor to the council runs thus,

The

The second letter.

I *Have dispatched my orders to colonel* Jeronymo Sarrao de Pavia, *captain-major of our fleet (which I have sent to your assistance) to deliver these presents to you, immediately after the landing of the forces aboard the said fleet, and to offer in my name all the assistance he is able to give you, pursuant to my command and your lordships request. I am very ready to embrace this opportunity to give you these marks of my zeal for your welfare, especially in contributing what in me lies to the reducing of your revolted subjects to their obedience. Neither do I in the least question, but that by this expedient the flames of an intestine war will be quenched, beyond all hopes of being ever rekindled hereafter; and that I shall have the satisfaction of having been instrumental to answer the expectation of your lordships, pursuant to the proposals made to me upon that account in your behalf. So recommending you to God's protection, I rest*

Your lordships

Bahia, July 22, 1645. *affectionate servant,* Antonio Telles de Sylva.

Besides these he sent another letter by *Don Salvador Korrea de Saa Benavides*, admiral of the *Portuguese* fleet, directed to the council of *Dutch Brasil*, as follows,

The third letter.

W*Hilst I was endeavouring to satisfy the request made to me by your ambassadours, and busied in embarking the forces designed for your service, under the command of the two colonels* Martin Soares Moreno *and* Andrew Vidal de Nigreiros, *together with colonel* Jeronymo de Payva, *captain-major of the forces,* Salvador Korrea de Saa Benavides *admiral of this state, and a member of the council of transmarine affairs, established by authority of the king my master, happened to arrive by God's peculiar direction, with his fleet from* Rio de Janeiro, *in the* Bahia, *in order to conduct them to* Portugal. *But being desirous to redouble my efforts, as well in the conduct of his person as in the strength of his fleet, to render the whole the more serviceable to your lordships, I thought convenient to send the said admiral with the fleet under his command, in conjunction with the rest, to the revolted captainship, not questioning but that by his prudent conduct and authority, he will be very instrumental in restoring the peace in your dominions, according to our utmost wishes; and I live in hopes, that this may serve as real demonstrations of the good understanding and friendship I am willing to cultivate betwixt these two states, both as a just friend and good neighbour. I recommend you to God's protection.*

Bahia, July 25, 1645. *Your affectionate servant,* Antonio Telles de Sylva.

The chief contents of these letters tended to persuade the great council of the *Dutch Brasil*, that the governor of the *Bahia* had, pursuant to the request made by the deputies of the said council to him, sent certain land forces under the command of the two colonels *Martin Soares Moreno*, and *Andrew Vidal de Nigreiros*, aboard the fleet commanded by *Jeronymo Sarrao de Payva*, in conjunction with the whole fleet of *Rio de Janeiro*, under the conduct of admiral *Korrea*, to assist them both by sea and land, as is evident from the words of the preceding letters: He also requested by his deputies, *viz.* captain *Martinho de Rebeira*, and auditor-general *Balthasar de Kastilho*, that the great council would be pleased to acquaint the king his master with it, in a particular letter from them to his majesty. *The contents of these letters.*

What deserves our particular observation in his letter to *John Fernandes Vieira*, and the rest of the rebels is, that he calls them *the king's subjects, unto whom he has sent this succour for their defence*; yet with this restriction, in order to reduce them by all gentle means to their former obedience to the *Dutch* government. It being evident that the propositions made by our deputies to the governour *Telles* tended to no other purpose than to engage him to recall *Kamaron* and *Dias*, and such others as were come to join with the rebellious *Portuguese*, out of the *Dutch Brasil*, and in case of refusal to declare them rebels and enemies to the king of *Portugal*; but he directly contrary to the intention and request of the said council; had instead of recalling them, sent these forces to their succours; and instead of leaving them to the disposal of the council, had caused them to be landed in a remote place, where the said *Kamaron* and *Dias* were with their forces at that time. Neither was the council ignorant of their intention, in sending a fleet into the road of the *Receif* at this juncture; tending to no other end than to back the revolted rebels in their design, and to encourage the rest to take up arms against them.

The council was fully satisfied as to this point, when they received advice from the cape of *St. Austin*, that the garrison of *Serinhaim* had been forced to surrender to *Andrew Vidal* after his landing thereabouts.

Their

1643. Their chief debate then turned upon this point, by what means this fleet might be removed from the road of the *Receif* and our coasts; considering that the whole naval force of the *Dutch* then ready to sail, consisted only in five ships, *viz.* the *Utrecht*, *Zelandia*, *Ter Veere*, *Zoutlandia*, and the *Golden Doe*, not very well manned, and but indifferently provided with ammunition, especially with gunpowder, and few soldiers could be drawn out of the neighbouring garrisons; whereas the *Portuguese* fleet consisted at least in eight or ten stout ships, the admiral being a two-deckt ship, resembling at a distance one of their large galeons, so that the attacking of them appeared to be a hazardous enterprize. After mature deliberation it was unanimously resolved in the said council, to return thanks to the admiral *Salvador Korrea de Saa Benavides*, for the offered succours against the rebels, and to tell him the reasons that obliged us to desire him to retire with his fleet out of our road, as will more at large appear out of the following letter: It was thought convenient to dispatch the said letter immediately, and whilst we staid for his answer, to use all possible diligence in equipping the two beforementioned ships, the *Deventer* and *Elias*; that if the *Portuguese* refused to comply with the councils request, we might be in a condition to attack them, and to drive their fleet from our coast, without which we saw but little probability to make our party good against the rebels, as long as they were backed by constant supplies from the *Bahia*. It was also taken into consideration whether it were not expedient to detain one of the *Portuguese* deputies till such time that *Jeronymo Sarrao de Payva*, should according to the request of the council, come ashore in the *Receif*; but this proposition was rejected, for fear of furnishing the *Portuguese* with a new pretence of staying in our road: Mr. *Gilbert de Wit* and *Henry Moucheron*, both members of the council of justice, being ordered to carry the said letter, they went aboard the *Portuguese* admiral the same evening, unto whom they delivered the following letter to *Salvador Korrea de Saa Benavides.*

A letter from the council to the Portuguese *admiral.*

WE understand both out of your lordship's letter and those of the governor Antonio Telles de Sylva, *delivered to us by captain* Martin de Rebeira, *and the auditor-general* Balthasar de Castilho, *as also by the verbal assurances given to us by them in your behalf, that your coming with the fleet into our road is with no other design than to assist us with your authority and council in bringing the rebels to reason, for all which we return our hearty thanks to your lordship. But at the same time we cannot forbear to represent to you, that the coming with so considerable a fleet in this juncture, gives us no small cause of jealousy, not only because we never requested any such assistance, but also by reason that instead of recalling* Kamaron *and* Henry Dias *with their troops, the two colonels* Andrew Vidal *and* Martin Soares Moreno, *have under pretence of reducing the rebels to obedience, landed their men and ammunition without our knowledge, in a far distant place, and consequently for the defence of the revolted* Portuguese; *whereas (pursuant to his excellency the governour's promise to us) this reduction might have been much better obtained by a severe proclamation, to oblige them to return to the* Bahia; *or at least the before-mentioned colonels ought to have made their first addresses to us. These proceedings have, contrary to your lordship's intention, drawn this ill consequence after them, that many of the inhabitants imagining no otherwise than this fleet was intended for the assistance of the revolted* Portuguese, *have also begun to take up arms, in order to join with them; which obliges us to return our thanks to your lordship for the offered succours, desiring you would be pleased with all possible speed to retire with the fleet out of the road; which, as it will undeceive the inhabitants concerning the sinister interpretations of your lordship's intentions, so it will serve as an effectual means to keep them in quiet, which at this juncture will work upon us a singular obligation. What relates to your lordships request to take in fresh water and fuel here, being ill provided with both by reason of your sudden departure from the* Bahia, *we should be very ready to comply with it, were it not for the before alledged reasons, and the badness of the season, which would make it very tedious, which obliges us to beg your excuse for this time upon that account. His excellency* Antonio Telles de Sylva *having told us in his letter that he had ordered* Jeronymo Sarrao de Paiva, *immediately after the landing of the infantry under* Martin Soares Moreno *and* Andrew Vidal, *to give us in person a full account with what power he was instructed by his excellency, we desire your lordship to send the said* Jeronymo Sarrao de Paiva *without delay to us, to confer with him concerning the instruction he has received from his excellency, in relation to the sending and landing of these officers and land forces. For the rest, we refer ourselves to our deputies, councellours in our court of justice here, unto whom we desire your lordship* 1643.

ſhip to give full credit, proportionable to their own merits and the truſt we have repoſed in them. God protect your lordſhip.

Signed by
Henry Hamel,
A. Van Bulleſtrate,
P. J. Bas,
J. Van Walbeck,
G. de Wit,
Receif, Aug. 13, 1645. J. Albrecht,
Henry de Moucheron,
J. Van Raeſvelt,
and
J. Lichthart.

This letter was pitched upon by the before-mentioned great council, as the beſt expedient at this juncture, till by the conjunction of the *Deventer* and *Elias*, we might be put in a probability of diſlodging them by force, if they refuſed to retire at the council's requeſt.

The Portugueſe *fleet leave the road.*

The 14th by break of day we ſaw the whole *Portugueſe* fleet under ſail, and for the moſt part out of ſight; and conſidering that the boats, which carried both ours and the two *Portugueſe* deputies, would ſcarce be able to overtake them, and that our deputies in their return were to give an account to our admiral on board his ſhip, whether, purſuant to the council's letter, the *Portugueſe* admiral had conſented to ſend *Jeronymo Sarrao de Paiva* to the *Receif*, in order to open his inſtructions to the great council, which they had now all the reaſon to believe he would not, they diſpatched immediate orders to our admiral *Lichthart*, to make all the ſail he could with the ſhips under his command after the *Portugueſe*, to obſerve their motions, and to endeavour to come up with the flag ſhip, on board of which was the ſaid *Jeronymo Sarrao*, to deſire him to return with his ſhips to the road of the *Receif*, in order to confer with the council in perſon, concerning his inſtructions. But after mature deliberation, the whole proceedings of the *Portugueſe*, and the letters of the governour of the *Bahia* concerning the pretended reduction of the rebels, being looked upon as meer amuſements, orders were ſent to our admiral *Lichthart*, to oblige all the *Portugueſe* ſhips he could meet with to ſtrike, and to treat them for the future like enemies.

A letter to the council from Rio Grande.

The 28th of *Auguſt* the council was advertiſed by letters dated the 20th, at the fort of *St. Magaret* in *Rio Grande*, from the governour *de Linge*, that twelve of the enemies ſhips, after having landed ſome forces near *Tamandare*, were come into the bay of *Traikona*; and that according to the depoſition of a certain *Portugueſe* priſoner from on board the ſaid fleet, they intended to land likewiſe ſome men thereabouts, provided they might be joined by the rebels from the *Matta*; but if they failed to come, they would return to the *Bahia*. Whereupon orders were ſent to Mr. *de Linge*, to bring what forces he was able together, either of ſoldiers, *Tapoyers*, or *Braſilians*, to prevent their landing, and their conjunction with the rebels in that captainſhip.

The next thing under debate was, whether it were not convenient to ſend ſome ſhips under the command of admiral *Lichthart* that way, to attack the *Portugueſe*; after various conſultations, it was agreed to ſtay till all the ſhips might be got ready for that ſervice, to ſupply the want of ſeamen by good able labourers from the *Receif*, and ſo to render ourſelves as formidable at ſea as poſſible could be.

The Dutch *admiral ſets ſail from the* Receif.

In the mean while the ſaid admiral *Lichthart* ſet ſail the 1st of *September* with four ſhips and a yacht only, he himſelf being in the *Utrecht*, but was forced by ſtreſs of weather (in which the *Zelandia* loſt a maſt) and for fear of the rocks, to come to an anchor not far from the *Portugueſe*, who endeavoured to gain the wind of him. Mr. *de Wit* and *Moucheron* returned alſo with their boat, having not been able, by reaſon of the violent winds to overtake the *Portugueſe*, but had put their deputies on board a ſmall veſſel to ſail after their fleet.

The ſame day the council received letters from Mr. *Hoogſtrate*, *Ley*, and *Heck*, from the cape of *St. Auſtin*, that the enemies had poſted themſelves in the ſugar-mills *Salgado*, *Surhague*, and other places thereabouts; and becauſe the *Portugueſe* fleet, which had been ſeen off of the bay of *Traikona*, appeared again in ſight of the *Receif* the ſame evening, it was thought expedient to order admiral *Lichthart* immediately to go on board the *Utrecht*, and with that and the ſhip *Ter Veere* and two ſmaller veſſels, to keep a watchful eye over the *Portugueſe*: Care was alſo taken to get the ſhip the *Overyſſel* ready againſt next day, not queſtioning that when joined by this and the *Zoutlandia* and *Golden Doe*, which were ſent abroad for intelligence, they ſhould be able to cope with the *Portugueſe*, or at leaſt to force them out of the road. The next morning early the *Portugueſe* fleet might be plainly diſcovered from the *Receif*, but our admiral was not able to ſtir by reaſon of the contrary winds; nevertheleſs the *Zoutlandia* and the *Ter Veere*, which came from the ſouth a cruiſing, made all the ſail they could to eſcape

1643. escape the *Portuguese*, which they did, being much the nimbler sailors, and joined our fleet.

The 4th of *September* major *Bayert* and Mr. *Volbergen*, complained to the council, that Mr. *Vierbergen* count *Maurice*'s steward, had made it his business to give it out, that they being impowered to cut down certain trees, and some part of the stabling and gardens, for the better fortifying of the fort *Ernestus*, had transgressed their commission, in cutting down many of the great trees, with an intention, as he said, to ruin the whole plantation; whereas they declared, that they had been very careful in preserving as much as possible could be, all the largest cocoa-trees that stood not in their way; that by these rumours the rage of the populace had been raised to that pitch that they had much ado to appease them, they being for the cutting down not only of all the trees, but also for the pulling down of the whole palace of count *Maurice*; all which they desired to be registered in the publick records, to serve them for a legal defence in due time and place.

In the mean time our admiral *Lichthart* being gone out in pursuit of the *Portuguese* fleet, met with them in the bay of *Tamandare*, consisting of seven ships, three smaller vessels, and four barks, the rest being sent loaden with sugar to *Portugal*. He was not as yet joined by all the ships from the *Receif*; but being resolved not to let slip this opportunity of attacking the enemy, sent the 7th of *September* advice to the great council, that being come in sight of the enemies fleet near the bay of *Tamandare*, consisting in all of eleven vessels, he was resolved to attack them there, desiring them to send as many ships as possible they could immediately. Hereupon it was resolved to join the two ships the *Deventer* and *Elias*, with the *Unicorn* and *Leyden*, then lying ready in the road and bound for *Holland*, and such tenders as were at hand, and to send them forthwith to the admiral *Lichthart*. Pursuant to these resolutions, the whole next following night was spent in manning the said ships, but were the next morning detained for some time by the contrary winds.

The same day orders were given to all the soldiers and inhabitants of the isle called *Antonio Vaez*, to provide themselves with baskets filled with earth; and pallisadoes were planted from the point of the *Receif* next to the river, to the utmost point near the sea-side, and five great guns were planted upon a certain wreck, from whence they could command the sea-shore as far as to the fort of five bastions. 1643.

The Dutch fight and worst the Portuguese fleet.

The 8th of *September*, the *Dutch* admiral having ordered the red flag to be put up, boarded the *Portuguese* admiral carrying sixty guns and three hundred men: He behaved himself very valiantly, having posted himself at the entrance of his cabin with a flaming sword in his hand, wherewith he killed three or four, but having received several wounds, was at last forced to yield. The rest of the ships following the example of their admiral, had likewise boarded the *Portuguese* ships; but these seeing the flag taken down from the admiral (a dismal signal of her misfortune) they lost all hopes, and threw themselves headlong into the sea, to escape the fury of the fire and sword; whither being pursued by the *Dutch* in their boats, many perished before they could reach the shore. Above seven hundred *Portuguese* were killed in this action, besides a great number of prisoners, among whom was the admiral himself: Three ships were taken and sent to the *Receif*, the rest were set on fire, being not in a condition to be carried off, because they had cut their cables and were run ashore, where the *Portuguese* had planted some cannon upon batteries, which so annoyed our people, that fearing they might run aground within the reach of the enemies cannon, they set fire to them, and with much ado got their ships clear from among the shelves. After this engagement I returned to the *Receif* to take care of my affairs there, and the admiral sent an express in a fisher-boat, with the following letter to the council of the *Dutch Brasil*.

A letter from the Dutch *admiral to the council.*

No sooner were the ships Leyden, *the yacht and the* Doe, *arrived last night, near the point of* Tamandare, *but pursuant to the result of the council of war, it was resolved to enter the next morning within the bar, which was performed in the following order: First the ship* Utrecht *admiral, second the* Ter Veere, *third the* Zelandia, *fourth the* Overyssel, *fifth the* Zoutlandia, *followed by the* Doe *and* Leyden, *and the yacht, the* Unicorn, *the tenders being ordered to be at hand as occasion should require. Being come within the bar, we found the enemy seven sail strong, besides three small vessels and four barks; and that they had planted several pieces of cannon upon two batteries on the sea shore. We received a very warm salute both from their ships and batteries, and several vollies of small shot; notwithstanding which, the ship the* Utrecht *couragiously laid the* Portuguese *admiral on board*

1643. *board, after a ſhort but ſharp diſpute took the ſhip and the admiral's flag: To be ſhort, the reſt of our ſhips behaved themſelves ſo well, that ſoon after they forced the* Portugueſe *to quit their ſhips; God be praiſed for this victory.* Jeronymo Sarrao de Paiva *the* Portugueſe *admiral is our priſoner, and at preſent in my ſhip, being ſorely wounded, whom I intend to deliver up to your lordſhips ſo ſoon as I ſhall come to the* Receif; *in the mean while, I intend to ſend back the* Leyden *and the* Unicorn *to morrow morning, according to your lordſhips directions. And foraſmuch as there is likely to be no more action hereabouts, the enemy having ſtrengthened themſelves near the ſea-ſhore, I will with the firſt opportunity return to the* Receif, *where I hope to give in perſon a more ample account of the whole action; I recommend your lordſhips to God's protection. In haſte,*

From the ſhip the Utrecht, *within the bay of* Tamandare, September 9, 1645.

Your lordſhips ſervant,

Cornelius Lichthart.

The *Portugueſe* admiral *Sarrao de Paiva* in his letter dated the 18th of *September*, gave the following account of his engagement to the two colonels *Martin Soares Moreno* and *Andrew Vidal Negreiros.*

The Portugueſe *admiral's letter to* Andrew Vidal.

It being the general diſcourſe here in the Receif, *which is likewiſe come to my ears, that it is reported by you there, how the* Dutch *admiral* John Cornelius Lichthart, *did before the beginning of the laſt engagement enter the bay with a white flag, thus ſurprizing our people, killed many of them in cool blood. I thought myſelf obliged to acquaint you, that indeed two days before the ſaid engagement, a yacht and a bark with white flags, appeared at the entrance of the bay, at which one of our ſmall veſſels and a bark ſhot three cannon ſhot. But that day when the admiral entred the ſaid bay, he had put up both the* Dutch *and red flags. Neither is it true what had been ſaid of their killing our men in cool blood, there being not one man ſlain aboard my ſhip, but during the heat of the engagement, five or ſix that had hid themſelves below deck having received quarter, and a ſoldier ſorely wounded ordered immediately to be looked after with all care imaginable. Neither was there a ſtroke given after the yielding of the ſhip, but every body treated and provided for according to his quality and preſent neceſſity.* 1643. *The reaſon why ſo few had quarter given them was, becauſe moſt leapt over-board, the ſea men firſt, and then the ſoldiers; I being not able with ſword in hand to keep them from chuſing rather to periſh in the ſea than to ſtand it out aboard the ſhip. Two or three perſons of note ſeeing me ſorely wounded, freely gave me quarter, without knowing either my perſon, or being aſked it by me; a convincing argument that they would not have refuſed the ſame to all the reſt that would have begged quarter. I muſt confeſs myſelf ſo much obliged to the humanity and generoſity of the admiral, that it is not to be expreſt in writing. Beſides that it is unqueſtionable that we firſt ſhot at them, both from our ſhips and batteries near the ſea-ſhore. I have given you a true account of the whole matter, of which as I have been an eye witneſs myſelf, ſo I don't queſtion you will give an entire credit to what I have written to you on this account. God protect you for many years.*

Receif, Sept. 18, 1645. *Jeronymo Sarrao da Paiva.*

Andrew Vidal ſent a Letter in anſwer to this by one of our drummers (ſent to the enemy upon ſome errand) dated the 20th of *September* as follows:

His anſwer to the admiral's letter.

We are ſufficiently ſatisfied by your lordſhips letter, that inſtead of being entertained according to your merits, you receive the ſame ill treatment with the reſt of our countreymen; though conſidering that your caſe is different from the reſt, you ought to have been treated in another manner, your lordſhip being come without the leaſt intention of waging war againſt them (which they ought to have made due reflection upon) but only as you were going to convoy ſome ſhips homeward, did at their own requeſt, land our forces in that captainſhip; conſidering the ill uſage and tyrannies our ſubjects have received at their hands, we are afraid we cannot promiſe your lordſhip a much better entertainment; of all which murders committed in cool blood, we have taken ſo circumſtantial an account, that we are ſure we ſhall be able to juſtify our cauſe and ourſelves, both to the ſtates of the United Netherlands *and the reſt of our allies; for we have fiſhed up many of our* Portugueſe *with bullets and ſtones tied to their legs and necks, ſome had the good fortune to be ſaved as they were ſwimming aſhore, but many were burnt alive in the wrecks of the ſhips, the intention of theſe gentlemen being without queſtion*

1645. *question, by making so general a slaughter among their fellow christians, to cut off from us all hopes of returning home: of all which they will be obliged to give one day a severe account, both to God almighty and those who shall require satisfaction for it at their hands, it being our constant opinion, that they never will be able to justify their cruelties, and the mischief done to our people, either before God or the king our master. We hope your lordship will rest satisfied in this present condition, and put your trust in God and our king, who are still alive to demand a severe satisfaction from them. God protect your lordship.*

From our quarters at St. John *in the* Vergea, Sept. 29, 1645.
signed
Andrew Vidal de Negreiros.

A certain lieutenant belonging to the enemy, called *Francisco Guomes*, came along with the same drummer, with a letter from the said *Andrew Vidal* directed to the great council, the contents of which were as follows.

Andrew Vidal de Negreiros's *letter to the great council.*

I *Received your lordships letter at* Iguaracu, *wherein you seem to be extremely disgusted at the killing of some* Brasilians, *with their wives, by our soldiers; under pretence that the absolute command over them belongs only to you, which I cannot but be much surprized at, when I consider that your lordships in your proclamation, wherein you command not to give quarter to any* Portuguese *inhabitants (though natural subjects of the king my master) you alledge among other reasons, because they had received their birth and education in this captainship (which however was first conquered by the* Portuguese *kings at the expence of many of their subjects) whereas now you would impose this hardship upon the same inhabitants, to give quarter to those* Brasilians, *who not long ago have been maintained and instructed in the catholick faith, as being their vassals, and consequently not yours, but the king my master's subjects. Your lordships ought to remember, that you are not in possession of this countrey by right of succession, or any other legal pretension, but basely by force of arms. We desire your lordships to take effectual measures concerning the methods to be observed in the carrying on of this war, which we hope will be managed so by your prudence, as that quarter may be allowed to the inhabitants of our nation; if not, I shall be obliged to act as I find it most consistent with my honour, to take satisfaction for these injuries. We desire also to put a stop to the murdering of the women, children, and ancient people, in cool blood, as has been done lately at* Tihicupapo, Rio Grande *and* Parayba. *God protect your lordships.* 1645.

From our quarters at St. John, September 29, 1645.
signed,
Andrew Vidal de Negreiros.

The great council returned with the consent of the members of the court of justice, and colonel *Garsman*, an immediate answer to the said letter, wherewith they sent the said lieutenant in company of the drummer, back the same evening.

An account of their proceeding since their landing.

But we must look back to their proceedings: After *Andrew Vidal de Negreiros* and *Martin Soares Moreno* had landed their men, to the number of eighteen hundred or two thousand, the 28th of *July* 1645, with good store of arms and ammunition, near *Tamandare*, betwixt *Olna* and *Formosa*, they were soon after joined, not only by four companies which had taken their way by land from the *Bahia*, but also by the troops under the command of *Kamaron* and *Henry Dias*, who had hitherto kept *Porto Calvo* blocked up by their forces. From thence they directed their march to the city of *Serinhaim*, and laid siege to the fort in which there was only a garrison of eighty *Dutch* soldiers and sixty *Brasilians*, commanded by *Samuel Lambert* and *Cosmo de Moucheron*. Two days after their arrival near *Serinhaim*, the enemy posted themselves in the d' *Ingenio* of *Daniel Hohn*; about which time *Henry Dias* was seen in *Serinhaim*, notwithstanding the *Portuguese* commanders *Andrew Vidal* and *Moreno* disowned to have any correspondence with them at that time: The said commanders had also sent the captain major *Paulo de Kunha* before to summon the said fort, which he did accordingly by his letter dated the 2d of *August* at the sugar-mill of *James Peres*, and directed to *Samuel Lambert*.

The summons sent to the fort of Serinhaim.

I *Am come to this sugar-mill by special orders from* Martin Soares Moreno *and* Andrew Vidal de Negreiros *our governors, they being very busy at present in landing their men; they have sent me before to prevent all mischief that otherwise might happen betwixt you and us; and if in the mean while you will join your forces with ours, or retire with them to some other place, you may safely do it, I being ready to furnish you with passes for that purpose, the before-mentioned governours* being

1645. *being come with an intention to put a stop to the present insurrection. God protect you.*

From the sugar-mill in St. Antonio, August 2, 1645.

Paulo de Kunha.

Two days after the before-mentioned commanders in chief sent another letter to *Samuel Lambert*, very little different from this.

A second summons from the Portuguese *commanders.*

WE *suppose you not to be acquainted with the intention of our coming, which makes us to be the less surprized at your standing upon your defence. The great council of the* Dutch Brasil *have sent an embassy to our governor general by sea and land,* Antonio Telles da Sylva, *to desire his excellency to make use of his authority and forces to appease the insurrection in this captainship, which request being readily granted, in order to be serviceable to the council, and to free the* Portuguese *from the outrages they suffered in their houses and families, we were sent to land our forces near these sugar-mills of* Rio Formosa; *which having been done accordingly, and ready to march further into the countrey, we thought fit to acquaint you with our intentions, which in all probability may have reacht your ears, the same having been published in several places by our proclamations, of which we send you one, desiring it may be affixed on the church of* Serinhaim. *We desire you therefore to lay by your arms to remove all suspicion; not questioning but that we shall meet with a favourable reception on your side, as we on the other hand shall make it our main endeavours to restore tranquillity among the revolted* Portuguese *by all gentle means that possibly may be used; assuring you at the same time, that in case you refuse to concur with us in this design, you will cause no small displeasure to the great council of the* Dutch Brasil. *God protect you.*

From the sugar-mill of Formosa, August 4, 1645.

Martin Soares Moreno,
Andrew Vidal de Negreiros.

The next following day *Paulo de Kunha* came in person before the place with a body of soldiers and boors, provided with arms from on board the fleet, and after having invested the place, cut off the water of the fountains and rivers from the besieged. In the mean while *Rowland Carpenter* and *Daniel Hohn* had been sent away with passes by the commanders of the *Portuguese* forces, who embarked their heavy cannon on board *Carpenter*'s vessel, in order to carry it up the river *Formosa*. Within five days of the arrival of *Paulo da Kunha*, the whole force of the enemy appeared in sight of *Serinhaim* in battle array, and closely blockt up the fort. The *Dutch* garrison was inconsiderable in proportion of the enemies strength, who had so well guarded all the avenues leading to the place, that they were soon reduced to want all manner of necessaries, especially water. Besides this, many of the circumjacent inhabitants and volunteers went daily over to the enemy, who gave them an account of the condition of the fort; and notwithstanding they had sent several messengers to the *Receif*, they had heard nothing from the council for two months last past; so that being without all hopes of maintaining their post, they judged it more for the interest of the company to preserve the garrison, which might be serviceable in other places, where there was sufficient want of good soldiers, than rashly to expose themselves to the fury of the enemies sword: Accordingly *Samuel Lambert*, *Cosmo de Moucheron*, and *La Montagny*, who commanded in the fort, upon the second summons made by the enemy, entred the 6th of *August* into a capitulation with the *Portuguese*, of which *Moucheron* gave an account in person the 15th of *August* to the council, and delivered it the 20th of *August* to them in writing. *The fort of* Serinhaim *blocked up by, and surrendred to the* Portuguese.

"WE the *Portuguese* commanders make "known to every body that we "were sent into this countrey at the re- "quest of the great council of the *Dutch* "*Brasil*, to appease the revolt and trou- "bles arisen among the *Portuguese* inhabi- "tants. But at our landing here, being "informed that notwithstanding this re- "quest and our good intention, the *Dutch* "had murdered many *Portuguese* in cool "blood (it being evident that they had "cut to pieces several *Portuguese*, who "were inticed into a church for that pur- "pose) and that they had formed a camp "to oppose us, which ought to be a cau- "tion to us, not to leave any strong holds "behind us, whilst we are marching to- "wards the *Receif*, we have thought it "necessary to enter into this capitulation, "till such time that we may have the oppor- "tunity of concerting new measures with "the great council, of which the articles "are as follows:

I. The commanders *Samuel Lambert* and *Cosmo de Moucheron* shall have leave to march out of the fort and castle, with the garrison, with ensigns displayed, all their arms, matches burning, &c.

II. They

1645.

II. They shall be permitted to march along the road with their ensigns, and swords drawn, and shall be safely conducted by one or more captains, who also shall be obliged to provide them carriages and boats, for the transportation of their persons and goods to the *Receif.*

III. The *Portuguese* oblige themselves to restore to *Moucheron* all what has been taken from him, and belonged to him before the siege.

IV. They also oblige themselves to engage the inhabitants of the city as well as those of *Kamara*, to pass by all past injuries either by word or deed; and that such of the *Dutch* as are willing to continue there, shall be maintained in their possessions in the same manner as the *Portuguese* are; and shall enjoy the same privileges, and their own religion, provided they do not preach in publick, and pay due reverence to consecrated places. They shall be at liberty to traffick with the *Portuguese*, and call in their debts as before, neither shall they be obliged to take up arms against the states of the *United Provinces.*

V. The *Dutch* officers shall restore to the *Portuguese* all their *Brasilians*, with their wives and children, as being subjects of king *John* IV. whom God preserve; and what relates to their reception and entertainment, is to be left to the discretion of the chief commanders of the *Portuguese.*

Upon these conditions they shall be obliged to surrender the fort, with every thing thereunto belonging, this afternoon, but are permitted to provide themselves with necessaries for their journey, which they shall have liberty to perform at their own leisure.

signed,
Andrew Vidal de Negreiros,
Alvaro Fregosa d'Albuquerque,
Diogno de Silveira,
Lopes Laurenzo,
Fereiro Betenkor,
Suppolito Abuko de Verkosa,
and
Sebastian de Guimares.

Evasions of the Portuguese.

Immediately after the surrender of the fort, *Moucheron* entred into a long discourse with the *Portuguese* commanders, about their proceeding, which he told them were far different from what the governor pretended in his letters, to wit, the appeasing of the revolt of the *Portuguese* inhabitants, according to the request of the *great council.* They answered him with tergiversations, telling him that they would be very careful not to act contrary to the peace establish'd betwixt the king his master and the states general. But it was not long before they began to lord it over the country, by taking such as were in the least suspected to them into custody, and taking an account of those of the *Dutch* that had married *Portuguese* women; nay they erected a court of Justice of their own, and forced *Moucheron* to sell his slaves for the fourth part of what they were worth. They had so little regard to the late articles, that they caused thirty *Brasilians*, part of that garrison, to be tied to the Palisadoes, where they were strangled; the *Portuguese* alledged in their behalf, that they had suffered death for certain crimes they had confessed themselves, tho' it is more probable they were made sacrifices to the discontented *Portuguese* inhabitants, that had made heavy complaints at the *Brasilians.* However, about thirty of them were spared, and bestowed upon the officers to carry their baggage, and their wives given to the inhabitants. The *Portuguese* made *Alvaro Fregoso d'Albuquerque* governor of the city and fort, and made one *Francis de la Tour*, a *French* deserter, captain over forty deserters, who had taken service among them.

The Porteguese *play the Master.*

They also raised three companies out of the *Portuguese* boors, or inhabitants, commanded by *Pedro Fregoso*, *Ignatius Ferrere* and *Immanuel de Mello*, which were put into *Serinhaim* for the defence of that place, where they also caused two *Jews* to be baptized, called *Jacquo Franco* and *Isaac Navare.* Most of the *Dutch* who had any possessions or sugar-mills thereabouts had safe-guards allow'd them, so that none, except two, who came to the *Receif*, left that captainship, of which they had sufficient reason to repent afterwards, being very ill treated by the *Portuguese*, as shall be shewn more at large hereafter.

The 15th of *August* in the afternoon, the garrison of *Serinhaim*, consisting of thirty two men (the rest having staid behind) arrived in a bark at the *Receif*; and their commander in chief appear'd the same day before the council, where he gave an account of the reasons that moved him to surrender the place, notwithstanding which he was ordered to be examined by a court-marshal, to answer the same: The ensign who had conducted the garrison to the *Receif*, delivered the same day a letter to the said council, from *Martin Soares Moreno*, and *Andrew Vidal*, dated the 8th of *August*, intimating that they were come into the *Dutch-Brasil*, by special command from the governor of the *Bahia*, and exaspera-

ting

1645. ting the outrages, they said were committed by the *Hollanders* against the *Portuguese*. This letter had another enclosed from the said governor, dated the 30th of *July*, with a proclamation, to be publish'd in the captainship of *Pernambuko*, whereby all the inhabitants were summon'd to appear peremptorily before them, within the space of eight days, to receive their directions for restoring tranquility among them. The letter from *Martin Soares Moreno* and *Andrew Vidal* was as follows.

A Letter from the Portuguese *Commanders to the council.*

WHEN your lordships found your selves entangled by a dangerous conspiracy among the Portuguese *inhabitants of this captainship, you made your applications to* Antonio Telles da Sylva, *governor general of* Brasil, *desiring him to make use of the most effectual means he could to appease this rebellion. About the same time the inhabitants of this countrey by one unanimous voice implored his aid and protection against those many affronts, plunderings, murthers and ravishments of women they groaned under; being resolved with joint consent to arm themselves with sticks (the use of arms being taken away from them by their tyrannical governors) against those oppressions, and to defend their honour to the last gasp; not questioning but that God Almighty would take vengeance for the blood of so many innocent people. They represented to his excellency, that he was obliged by his station to assist them in this extremity, as they were his countrymen; but, if that should not be prevailing enough, reasons of state would induce him, not to force them to despair by denying them his aid; which if he did, it should be at the peril of his head, and that he must give a severe account of it before God Almighty, and others, if they should be constrained to beg that from a foreign power, which they could not obtain from their countrymen. The governor having taken all these pressing reasons into mature consideration, and in respect both of your lordships request, and the heavy complaints of the* Portuguese, *made it his chief care to find out the most effectual means (which your lordships seem'd to leave to his discretion) to appease this revolt. Being sensible that the revolt of the* Portuguese *inhabitants had taken deep root among them, and was likely to prove more universal against your government, he judged it most expedient, to send hither certain persons with such forces as he thought might either by their prudence, and, if that fail'd, by force of arms, restore the so much desired tranquility. It is upon this account, my lords, we are come to this place, in order to employ all our force and assistance, according to your request, pursuant to the peace established betwixt these two nations, in regard of which we value not the expences we have been put to upon this occasion. But we scarce had set foot ashore, when our ears and hearts were struck with the doleful outcries of forty innocent catholick* Portuguese, *murthered in the church of* Rio Formoso, *whither they were enticed for that purpose, by those that were in your service, without the least respect of age or sex, the very babes being by the natives barbarously murthered, as they were lying on their mothers breasts. Neither have the sighs and groans of many noble maids escaped our ears, that were ravish'd in the* Vergea *and* St. Lawrence, *by the* Brasilians, *not to mention here what barbarities have been committed in* Pojuka, *where is the sight of many a hermit and innocent babe who were slaughter'd in a cave. Neither have they abstained from holy and consecrated places; they have cut to pieces the images of the saints, and stripp'd the queen of heaven, the virgin* Mary, *our blessed lady, of all her apparel; things so enormous, and never heard of before, enough to create horror and astonishment in a generous heart. And notwithstanding your lordships had desired the governor general to interpose his authority, you did form a camp, which continues in the field to this day; and we being obliged by our orders to come to you upon the* Receif, *we judged it not convenient to leave any armed power behind us, which in time might prove the occasion of great inconveniences to us; we shall endeavour to shew all due respect and kindness to your subjects, and carry the garrison of* Serinhaim *along with us, 'till matters may be concerted betwixt your lordship and us, for the service of god and the state. In the mean while, we most earnestly desire a stop may be put to the outrages committed by your soldiers hitherto, to avoid all occasion of a rupture on your side; we protest on the other hand, in the name of God and* John IV. *the king our master, whom God preserve, as also in the name of the states general, whose power God encrease, that we desire nothing so much, as the continuation of the late established peace, which shall be the guide of all our actions; of which we have brought along with us an authentick copy, to serve us as a sufficient justification by all the princes of* Europe. *And that your lordships may be satisfied in the reality of it, we have sent you enclosed a copy of the proclamation published by us, at our landing in in this captainship.* 1645.

God preserve your lordships.

Serinhaim, Aug. 8, 1645. Martin Soares Moreno, Andrew Vidal de Negreiros.

The before-mentioned proclamation runs thus:

Their

1645.

Their PROCLAMATION.

WE the commanders in chief of the Portuguese *forces,* Martin Soares Moreno, *and* Andrew Vidal de Negreiros, *make known to all persons and inhabitants of the captainship of* Pernambuko *that the* great council *of the* Dutch-Brasil, *having by a letter sent to the governor and captain general of* Brasil, *given advice of the revolt arisen among the* Portuguese *of this place; desiring to endeavour the appeasing of this rebellion by his assistance; for which purpose the said governor now having sent us with a sufficent force into this captainship, we command all the* Portuguese, *of what condition and quality soever, to appear peremptorily within eight days after the publication of these presents before us, in order to restore tranquility among them, pursuant to the request of the lords of the council of the* Dutch-Brasil. *We also hereby intreat the said lords, in the most friendly manner that can be, pursuant to the tenour of the strict alliance there is betwixt both these nations, to stop the further persecution of the* Portuguese, *or any other warlike executions; and that if any of their soldiers presume to act contrary to it, they may, upon complaint made thereof to them, be severely punished.*

I Alexes Antunes *have penned this proclamation, and I* Franco Bravo Desembarquador *have approv'd it.*

Martin Soares Moreno,
Andrew Vidal de Negreiros.

The great council resolved to give a short answer to the said letter, and to refute the proclamation by another; and considering, that the origin and cause of all those troubles and misdeameanours were laid at the door of the council, they ordered the two councellors of the court of justice *De Witt* and *Moucheron*, in conjunction with Mr. *Walbeek* assessor in the same court, to answer the same, and thereby to represent to the council of nineteen in *Holland*, that they were occasioned by the rebels and their adherents.

In the month of *August* the troops lately come from the *Bahia* marched from *Serinhaim* to *Pojuka*, and so to the *Cape of St. Austin*, where being join'd by the forces under the command of *Kamaron* and *Dias*, and the inhabitants, they resolved (after our men had quitted *Pojuka* and the city *St. Antonio de Cabo*) to attack the fort *Vander Dussen* on the *Cape of St. Austin* from the land side; pursuant to which resolution they posted their troops all along both sides the river.

The Portuguese *besiege the* Cape of St. Austin.

2

1645.

The council in the mean while being forewarned of the enemies design, had ordered the 2^d^ of *August*, Mr. *Adrian Bullestrate*, one of their own members, and admiral *Lichthart*, to go thither with all speed, and to take effectual care that nothing might be wanting for the defence of the place. They were for that end to take a full view of the fort *Vander Dussen* and all its outworks, and to consider whether the redoubt upon the hill call'd *Nazareth*, and the battery at the entrance of the harbour might be repaired for the better defence of the fort. Accordingly Mr. *Bullestrate* and admiral *Lichthart* left the *Receif* the 5th of *August*, and arrived the same evening in the fort *Vander Dussen*, where having executed their commission, Mr. *Bullestrate* returned the 9th of *August* to the *Receif*, where he gave the following account to the council.

Mr. Bullestrate *and admiral* Lichthart *sent to the* Cape of St. Austin.

That he left the *Receif* the 5th of *August*, in the morning about nine a clock, and came the same evening to the fort *Vander Dussen* on the *Cape of St. Austin*.

That the 6th of *August*, after forenoon sermon was ended he rid with the admiral, and some other officers, to the hill of the *Cape of St. Austin*; where having taken a view of the harbour, he found the stone-redoubt in a condition to be repaired, without any great charge, the cannon upon the batteries nail'd up, but the works towards the seaside in pretty good order.

An account of their transactions.

That he had ordered a draught to be made, to surround the redoubt with pallisadoes, to raise a battery within it, to build a guard-house, and to widen the ditches: He also had ordered a stone breast-work, (for want of wood) to be made on the backside of the battery, with a row of Pallisadoes, and a guard-house; and that with the first fair weather, they should set on fire all the bushes and brambles on the said hill, and clear the ground round about the church *Nazareth*.

Upon view of the fort *Vander Dussen*, he had commanded the major *Hoogstrate* with all possible speed to put it in a good posture of defence, the admiral having already taken care to have it surrounded with pallisadoes. That on the 7th of *August*, having paid off the garrison, and those belonging to the artillery, he passed through very difficult ways to *St. Antonio*, where he likewise paid off the soldiery, visited the retrenchment, and put every thing in the best order he could.

That he had bargained with certain persons to repair the said redoubt on the hill called *Nazareth*, and the stone breast-work, the building of two guardhouses, and surrounding both the works with pallisadoes

1643. lisadoes, according to his draught, for nine hundred gilders, the whole to be compleated within three weeks time. Here it was he had the first notice of the landing of some forces from the *Bahia*, near *Rio Formosa*, by the same fleet which the week before was seen off of the *Receif:* But not being able to get any sure intelligence, he had sent a messenger to lieutenant *Montangie*, then commander in *Serinhaim*, to give him a true account of the matter, and in what condition he and his garrison were at that time; encouraging him by fair promises, all communication by land being already cut off betwixt them. Here he also listed thirty eight volunteers that offered their service.

That the 8th of *August* he left the said place, and notwithstanding the badness of the weather, rid cross the hills of *Hegendos* to the sea-shore, where meeting with the admiral, they went together up the river *Sangado* with the tide, as far as *Calandaria*, where they staid for some time, and received the news, that in the last encounter betwixt colonel *Haus* and the rebels near that hill, above two hundred of the last, among whom were some officers, were slain, and about forty or fifty on our side. One *Melchior Alvares* came on purpose to tell them, that about three hundred of the revolted inhabitants were inclined to accept of a pardon, which he referred to the council.

That being ready to take horse in order to his return to the *Receif*, a certain soldier of our troops, that had been left behind, complained that he had been stripp'd stark naked by the servants of the ferryman of the river *Sangada*, who had wounded and beat him miserably. *Melchior Alvares* was ordered to take care of his wounds, and captain *Pistor* to go with twenty of his men in quest of these villains; who, coming to the ferry, beset the house, took the ferryman and his three sons prisoners, but the *Mulat*, who had committed the fact, escaped their hands.

That he pursued his journey on horseback towards the *Receif*, notwithstanding the violent rains, and not without great danger pass'd the river the same night near the fort *Æmilia*.

That on the 9th of *August*, he was advertised by some negroes belonging to *Moses Navarre*, whom he had sent with letters to *d'Ingenio Surfacque*, that an ambush had been laid for them near *Candelaria*, but the enemy durst not attack them, their negroes being all such as were taken prisoners, and afterwards made their escape to us.

Major *Hoogstrate* sent advice by his letters on the 13th of *August*, to the council, that the garrison and volunteers of *St. Antonio* being safely arrived on the *Cape of St. Austin*, they were now about two hundred and eighty strong, *viz.* two hundred and seventeen soldiers and gunners, and sixty three volunteers. That immediately after our garrison had left *St. Antonio*, *Kamaron* and *Henry Dias* had posted themselves with their troops in the sugar-mill *Algodais*, near that place, where they expected to be join'd by *Martin Soares* and *Andrew Vidal*'s forces, safely arrived from the *Bahia*. That he expected every day to be besieged, and fear'd nothing so much as want of fresh water, the spring being cut off by the enemy. Hereupon immediate orders were given by the council to send thither thirty barrels of water, some ammunition and provision, and what else should be requisite for a vigorous defence of the place, which was sufficiently provided before with soldiers. The next following day they received intelligence from Major *Hoogstrate*, Mr. *Ley*, and Mr. *Heck*, that the enemies troops had taken post in the sugar-mill *Salgado Zuvisiaque* and other circumjacent places. The council rely'd much upon the bravery and fidelity of the offices within the fort, from whom they promised themselves a very vigorous defence, they being all persons who had advanced themselves in their services, and were in expectation of better preferments, *viz.* Major *Hoogstrate*, *Caspar Vander Ley*, formerly a captain of horse, *John Hick*, and *Albert Gerritson Wedda*, an old captain belonging to the company: But their unfaithfulness and covetous temper over-balanced all these considerations; for the said major *Hoogstrate*, commander in chief, with the consent of *Casper Vander Ley*, and *Albert Gerritson Wedda*, treacherously and villanously sold and surrendred the said fort to the *Portuguese* the 23d of *August* for the sum of eighteen thousand gilders, besides some other rewards promised them upon that account. They went over with the whole garrison to the enemy, who made *Hoogstrate* colonel of a *Dutch* regiment, raised out of these and other soldiers of several nations, that had deserted our service. Thus this strong hold was betray'd to the *Portuguese*, by a person who owed his whole fortune to our company. 1645. *Advice from the* Cape of St. Austin.

Martin Soares Moreno gave the following account of the surrender of this fort to the governor *Antonio Telles da Sylva*, in his letter dated from the hill of *Nazareth*, *Aug.* 26, 1645.

1645.

A letter to the governor of the Bahia, *concerning the taking of the* Cape of Puntael.

SUnday the 23ᵈ of this month God Almighty, through his mercy, was put us into the possession of the fort of the cape of Puntael, which was besieged by Andrew Vidal de Negreiros: The next day we were rejoyced with the money sent to us by your lordship, and the wine presented to me in particular, part of which I have bestowed upon entertaining some of our friends, who are merry with me at this time.*

We have made an excellent bargain; for besides the importance of the place, and its artillery, we have got the very flower of their soldiers; besides that, this will be like a signal to the rest to follow their footsteps.

John Fernand Vieira *has raised on saturday last the sum of four thousand ducats for our use, though not without force, but it was very welcome to us at this time, when we were upon striking up the bargain for the better fortifying of this place, the harbour of which is not inferiour to that of the* Receif: *But I will not trouble your lordship any longer with this point.*

Not long after the surrender of the fort, a bark appeared in sight, sent to its relief from the Receif. *We sent captain* Barreiros *with a well arm'd bark out against her, who took her with thirty five men, and good store of gunpowder and bullets, all which will prove very serviceable to us.*

I kindly desire your lordship, that in case you send a messenger with this news to his majesty, captain Damian de Lankois *may be employed upon that errand, it being very probable, that the king, besides a good present, will reward him with some honourable employment.*

Last night we received advice, that the fleet under Jeronymo de Paiva *was entred the bay of* Tamandare; *I am sorely afraid they will be attack'd by the ships sent thither from the* Receif, *notwithstanding we have desired him several times to come into our road.*

Kapivara *is gone from that place by land to the* Bahia, *perhaps he has given him notice that we are masters of the cape; if he thinks fit to bring his fleet to this place, he is safe, if not, it lies at his door. 'Tis discoursed here, that the ship the* Bishop *is missing, perhaps he has a fancy to convoy* Salvador Korrea *some part of the way.*

I cannot forbear to let your lordship know how much you stand indebted to major Dieterick Hoogstrate, *and the rest of the commanders of the fort. We have promised to the first a commandery of Christ. I beg of your lordship to make my promise good to him in his majesty's name, as soon as possible may be, he being a person who will be ready to do*

us all the further service he can. We have for the present engaged him with some presents of less moment, of which we shall give an account to you hereafter. Captain Vander Ley *has likewise deserved well of us, and so have all the rest that had married* Portuguese *women: It is reported here that he is a person of note in his country: We have likewise promised to him a commandery of Christ, and a yearly pension for one of his sons: We hope your lordship will not refuse to make good our promise, because his sons are born of a* Portuguese *woman: The name of the eldest being* John, *and the youngest* Caspar Vander Ley. *The rest are at present at their habitations, as soon as they return we must engage them with some promises, of which we will give an account to your lordship. They are all of consequence to us, having married* Portuguese *women. I hope your lordship will be well satisfied with this piece of service, for* John Fernand Vieira *sometimes brings us more money in an hour, than the conquest of the cape costs us. He is at present in the* Vargea *among the* Barbarians, *and we in the fort on the cape, till we have got every thing in readiness.* Kapivara *is about three days ago gone by land, possibly he may be with you before the bark which carries this letter; I wish it may arrive in safety, and to your lordship a long life for the defence of this state.* Signed

Martin Soares Moreno.

Martin Soares Moreno, and *Andrew Vidal de Negreiros*, had in the mean while sent seven or eight letters from the cape of *St. Austin*, dated the 23ᵈ, 30ᵗʰ, and 31ˢᵗ of *August*, and the 2ᵈ and 6ᵗʰ of *September*, in which they advertised the admiral *Paiva*, that they were in possession of that cape, desiring him by all means to come with his fleet into that harbour. The first of the two last letters was thus written.

Letter from the Portuguese *commanders to admiral* Paiva.

My lord,

WE are got now into the possession of the harbour of Nazareth, *and that, as the saying is, without casting an anchor; which is the reason we intreat you likewise to come with your fleet hither, where you may careen your ships, and provide yourselves with fresh provisions, men, ammunition, and all other necessaries, till such time we shall mutually agree in what is further to be undertaken for the service of God and his majesty. The enemy has hitherto but one ship of strength at sea, the rest being of no consequence; neither are they for engaging with you at this time, but endeavour to cut off your communication with the sea coast. My lord, you have*

1645. *have given so many proofs of your courage before this time, that this retreat will not abate any thing from the fame of your victories: On the other hand, you have to consider, that you are answerable for so many thousand lives of those that are in your fleet; wherefore we desire you once more to come hither with the fleet, and such officers as are under your command, where you will meet with a very kind and comfortable reception. But being sensible that it would be a gross error in us, to urge a matter so evident in itself, any further, to so great a commander as you, we live in hopes of your coming; where we intend, in the house of* Nazareth, *to receive the blessed sacrament, which name we have given to the fort, having among other things found a mass book here, which is of no small service to us.*

God preserve your lordship.

Puntael, *the* 2[d] *of* Sept. 1645. *Martin Soares Moreno*, and *Andrew Vidal de Negreiros.*

The contents of the second letter to the same admiral, are as follows:

Y*OUR lordship being already acquainted with our being masters of the* Puntael *(cape) we hope you will take the first opportunity of coming to us; the enemies having two squadrons of ships at sea, with one fireship, to force you from this coast, which has been discovered to us by a letter writ at the* Receif, *and directed to the governor, and taken by us in a bark design'd for the relief of that place, of which we thought fit to give you immediate notice, that you might take your measures according to your wonted prudence. These* Dutch *gentlemen have, by their treacherous dealings, obliged us to have recourse to open force, and we desire your lordship to repay them in their own coin, with fire and sword, as they do to us. If you design to come hither, it must be done speedily, all delay being dangerous at this time. We have a true copy of this letter in our journal to serve for our justification hereafter.*

God preserve your lordship.

Dated in the *Puntael* of the blessed sacrament, *September* the 6th, 1645.

Martin Soares Moreno, and *Andrew Vidal de Negreiros.*

An account of the surrender of the cape of *St. Austin*, and of the further transactions betwixt us and the *Portuguese*, was sent in a letter by *Caspar da Costa d'Abreu*, from the said cape to his friend *Domingos da Kosta*, an inhabitant of the *Bahia*, which runs thus:

I *Wish this letter may find you in good health, as I who am your faithful comrade desire; I am in a tolerable good condition in the* Puntael *of* Nazareth, *which after a siege of twenty days was surrendred to us at an easy rate, because those who commanded within the fort had* Portuguese *wives, and their estates thereabouts. The captain of horse was the most forward of all in surrendering the place they have obtained what conditions they demanded, and a gratuity of four thousand ducats besides. We found in the fort three hundred* Dutch, *of their best troops, and twelve brass pieces of cannon, four of which were four and twenty pounders, and provisions for three months; so that if they had not come with us to a composition, it would have cost us abundance of men, whereas now we have gain'd the place with the loss of one single man, who was kill'd by a random cannon shot. We made ourselves masters of a bark, firing from the* Puntael, *before its surrender, in which was a gentleman with several hundred men that were going to the* Receif. *This gentleman and another of* Serinhaim *(being both magistrates in their respective places) we delivered up to the inhabitants, who soon kill'd them, notwithstanding one was married with a* Portuguese *woman; for they having been heard to say, that they hoped to wash their hands in the blood of the* Portuguese, *the women were so much exasperated against them, that they soon dispatch'd them, according to their desires. The prisoners are for the most part detained at* St. Anthony, *in order to be sent to the* Bahia; *but many among them have taken service with us. We suppose the number of the dead and* Dutch *prisoners amount to near thirteen hundred: We have not seen the squadron under* Salvador Korrea de Saa; *we are afraid some misfortune has befallen him; some of our ships were cruising hereabouts, but within these three or four days none of them have appear'd on this coast. The* Dutch *have a fleet of twelve ships at sea, it is well if they don't venture a brush with us. The* Receif *with all its forts are invested,* Lawrence Karneiro *is at* Porto Calvo; *the* Jews *report, that orders are come to take all the* Dutch *forces out of* Rio Grande, Paraiba *and* St. Francis, *in order to transport them to the* Receif. *There is no great harmony betwixt the* Jews *and* Dutch, *the first pretending that the others intend to sell the country. Four of their head officers, which are our prisoners, are ordered to be sent to the* Bahia, *and among them their master of the artillery. The same day that we were become masters of* Puntael, *a bark arrived there from the* Receif *with orders to keep it to the last extremity; we took the bark with good store of ammunition and provision, worth in all about fifteen hundred ducats.* 1645.

Sept. *the* 5th, 1645. *Caspar da Costa d'Abreu.*

From

1645. From this and the following letters, it is apparent, that major *Hoogstrate* had laid the foundation of his treacherous design of betraying the cape of *St. Austin* to the *Portuguese*, long before; to wit, ever since he with Mr. *Balthasar Vander Voorde* was sent to the governor of the *Babia Antonio Telles de Sylva*. Thus a certain serjeant sold a redoubt near the city of *Olinda* to the enemy for three hundred gilders.

At the beginning of the siege of the cape of *St. Austin*, *Andrew Vidal de Negreiros* sent two letters to major *Hoogstrate*, *Ley* and *Hick*, by one *John Guomes de Mello*, dated the thirteenth of *August*; in the first of which the said *Vidal* complains of the ill treatment and murthers committed upon the *Portuguese* by the *Dutch*; in the second he requests them to declare, pursuant to the promises made by *Hoogstrate* in the *Babia*, for the king of *Portugal*, and to deliver the fort into their hands.

Two letters from Vidal *to* Hoogstrate.

The first was as follows:

I *Am come this morning to the village of* St. Antonio de Cabo, *in hopes of receiving news from you and captain* Ley. *I give by these presents notice to you, that we are sent hither by order from the governor* Antonio Telles de Sylva, *with no other intention than to appease the troubles lately arisen in this country, pursuant to the request of the council; of which you are a sufficient witness. No sooner were we arrived at* Tamandare, *but we received many informations directly contrary to what we expected to meet with here; viz. That in* Rio Grande *thirty seven inhabitants had been murthered, many virgins deflower'd, and the image of the virgin* Mary *grosly misused by the* Dutch; *things so abominable in themselves, that it is scarce to be imagined so brave a nation should be guilty of such enormities. Whilst I am writing this letter, news is brought me, that the* Dutch *have caused many of the inhabitants of* Goyana *to be murthered, tho' I can scarce give credit to it; for supposing this to be true, we could not avoid giving assistance to these miserable people, tho' they were the most despiseable of all nations, considering they crave our help, and are not only christians, but also subjects of the king our master, whom God preserve. Whilst the council was in expectation of the issues of the intended accommodation, they have surprized and killed many of the inhabitants, which obliges us, to require you in the name of God, of his majesty, his highness and the states general, not to give any occasion for a rupture, but to maintain the late concluded peace to the utmost of your power, as we are ready on our side, to concert all possible measures with the commander in chief of this place, which may tend to the tranquillity of both parties. The bearers hereof are captain* John Guomes de Mello, *and lieutenant* Francis Guomes, *who we desire may be dispatched back with all possible speed.* 1645.

God preserve you for many years.

August 13, 1645. *Andrew Vidal.*

The second letter was written thus:

The second letter.

Y*OUR promise made to us in the* Bahia, *and what has since been told by captain* Ley *to* John Fernandes Vieira, *and captain* John Guomes de Mello, *encourages us to proceed in our former design, not questioning but that both you and captain* Ley *will not in the least recede from the engagement you have been pleased to oblige us with, and to tie us to your service. We are come into this country at the head of three thousand chosen men, back'd by two squadrons of men of war well equip'd, one of which has not as yet appear'd on this coast, the other you have seen yourself pass by the other day. I hope this may serve as a means to set the poor miserable inhabitants at liberty; and as both they and we wish for nothing more than to see you embrace our side, that we may not want an opportunity to give you more evident proofs of our respect and affection towards you, so we desire you not to entertain the least sinister suspicion of us; we being ready (for the performance of which we by these presents give you our words) to accomplish in every point, what has been promised to you, by* John Fernandes Vieira, *and* John Guomes de Mello. *And I for my part assure you, that I will not fail to perform and agree to whatever you shall further demand upon this occasion.*

The inhabitants of the place shall be provided with passports, and protected by us, in the same manner as the commander of Serinhaim, Carpenter, *and some others were; and we expect the same at your hand. And that you may be sure whom to treat with upon this account, we have sent to you* John Guomes de Mello, *who is intrusted with the whole matter; which if you refuse to do, we must take such measures as we shall judge most expedient for us.* In the mean while God preserve you for many years.

St. Antonio de Cabo, Aug. 13, 1645. Your affectionate friend

and servant,

Andrew Vidal de Negreiros.

Major *Hoogstrate*, Mr. *Hick* and *Ley*, sent an answer to this letter immediately, containing

1645. containing in substance, that they were not in the least concerned in the outrages committed by the *Tapoyers* against the *Portuguese*, and seemingly refused to treat with *de Mello*. It runs thus:

His answer to them.

WE *have received your letter sent by* John Guomes de Mello, *out of which we understand, that you are come to* St. Antonio. *We are extremely well satisfied, that the governor* Antonio Telles da Sylva *has undertaken to appease the tumults arisen in these parts, and don't question but that your presence will contribute much towards the accomplishment of it. The affronts and outrages you speak of by the* Tapoyers *and* Dutch *soldiers put upon the inhabitants, as they were committed sorely against our will, so I can assure you, that no body, not so much as the least child, has been suffer'd to be misused upon our accounts, so that these complaints must not be made to us, but ought to be referr'd to the council. The treaty you propose with captain* John Guomes de Mello, *and lieutenant* Francis Guomes, *is beyond our province and power, so that we earnestly desire you not to use any further sollicitations to us upon that account. So we kiss your hands, recommending you to God's protection.* We rest

Your servants and good friends,

Caspar Vander Ley,
D. Van Hoogstrate.
John Hick.

Hoogstrate *discovers these letters.* Major *Hoogstrate* took care to send these two letters, together with their answer to the council, with repeated assurances of their constant fidelity; whereupon the great council confirm'd *Hoogstrate* in his government, and exhorted *Ley* and *Hick* to persevere in their brave resolution, which they would in due time take care to reward with better preferments. This discovery of the enemies letters being look'd upon as an undeniable proof of Mr. *Hoogstrate*'s sincere intentions, had such an influence upon the generality of the people, that there was scarce any body but what thought himself secure of his fidelity and duty. Nevertheless, as these temptations could not but raise some jealousy in the minds of the council, they thought fit to send colonel *Haus* to the *Receif*, to order him to the Cape of *St. Austin*.

The council in the mean while, being by *Vidal*'s letters to *Hoogstrate* sufficiently convinced, that the intended recalling of the rebellious troops were nothing but amusements, sent immediate orders to their admiral *Lichthart*, that for the future he should treat all the *Portuguese* ships he could meet with as enemies. 1645.

Consultations about drawing all the forces into the Receif. The 15th of *August*, colonel *Haus* being come to the *Receif*, proposed to the council, that he judged it absolutely necessary for the service of the state, that since by the succours come from the *Bahia* to the assistance of the rebels under *Martin Soares Moreno* and *Andrew Vidal*, they were grown very strong and numerous, the troops encamped in the field should be drawn into the *Receif*, because they being besides the *Brasilians*, not above three hundred strong, they might easily be cut off in a place where they could not be seconded from the *Receif*, where they were wanting for the defence of that place, which being the capital of the whole *Dutch Brasil*, would in all likelihood be attack'd with the utmost vigour by the enemy.

Against this opinion many reasons were alledged too.

I. By so doing they must quit all the open country from whence they were now supplied with cattle and meal, which they stood highly in need of, till such time that they could receive new supplies from *Holland*, and that in such a case they must expect the enemy immediately at their gates.

II. That thereby the number of the enemy would be encreased, the inhabitants of the country being freed from the dread of our troops, would join with them against us.

III. That by so doing we must leave the *Tapoyers*, that had taken up arms at our request, and were to be joined by our troops near *Machiape* or *St. Antonio*, to the enemies mercy. To this it was answer'd,

1. That as to the supplies of cattle and meal from the country, they should be in a much better condition to be furnished withal, when their forces could be sent abroad into all circumjacent parts of the country, whereas now they were forced to remain in one certain place. Besides that, we being masters at sea, might embark at any time a certain number of men, and land them where we found it most convenient, which would oblige the enemy, instead of besieging the *Receif*, to divide his forces for the defence of the country. What related to the increase of the enemies forces, by the accession of the *Portuguese* inhabitants of the country, was to be look'd upon as of no great consequence against us; it being more for our interest to see them appear as declared enemies than dissembling friends; it being generally known, that their inclinations were bent for their countrymen, and that notwithstanding all their

1645.

their specious pretences, they miss'd no opportunity of giving intelligence to the enemy of what passed among us; whereas, if they were once declared enemies of the states, we should have a fair opportunity of seizing upon their cattle, provisions, and other moveables, for the use of the *Receif*; which being thus provided, would discourage the enemy from attempting to reduce it by famine.

What was alledged concerning the danger of the *Tapoyers*, was acknowledged to be of no small moment; but considering they had received no news as yet of their motion, it was not judged of such vast consequence as to be put in balance with the welfare of the whole *Dutch Brasil*, which depended in a great measure on the safety of these troops.

After mature deliberation of the whole matter, it was resolved, on the 15th of *August*, by the council, with the approbation of the members of the court of justice, that considering the danger the troops were exposed to, and that on their safety depended the preservation of the *Receif*, they should with all possible speed march thither, and that only fifty men should be left in the house of *de Wit*, under captain *Wiltschut*, in order to command some part of the circumjacent country, and to serve as a retreat for our parties that should be sent abroad to fetch in cattle, and *Farinha*, or meal.

Pursuant to this resolution, colonel *Haus* went thither on horseback the same day, to put it in execution the same evening, if possible he could, or at furthest the next morning. But it seems colonel *Haus* was so neglectful, as to delay the march of these troops not only that afternoon, but also the whole next following day; and instead of retreating towards the *Receif*, tarried in the same sugar-mill, without having the least intelligence of the enemies approach; so that on the 17th of *August*, being surprized by the troops of *Andrew Vidal*, much more numerous than his, before they could betake themselves to their arms they were put to the rout. The council being advertised, that colonel *Haus* with his troops were attacked by the enemy in the sugar-mill of Mr. *de Wit*, they call'd the city militia to their arms, Mr. *Bullestrate* and *de Bas* went to the house *Bavista*; from whence, as being near at hand, they might give the necessary orders, according as they should receive advice from *Haus*: And twelve firelocks were posted in this house for the better security of the bridge cross the river. *Dieterick Hamel*, and the counsellors of justice, took care to look after the *Receif*. Immediately after, word being brought to the council that colonel *Haus* had been overthrown, and was retired to the house of *de Wit* belonging to the sugar-mill, it was consulted, whether by any means they might be able to relieve him; and, tho' by reason of the weakness of the garrison, it was no easy matter to do it; nevertheless, it was resolved, with one hundred volunteers of the inhabitants, and one hundred and fifty soldiers, to attempt his relief. But before this could be put in execution, a certain *Brasilian* that had been present at the whole action, and having, by changing his clothes with a *Portuguese*, found means to escape to the *Receif*, brought the unwelcome news, that colonel *Haus*, with the forces under his command, had surrendred the house belonging to the sugar-mill, and themselves, upon promise of quarters, at discretion.

Colonel Haus *put to the rout.*

Colonel Haus *surrenders at discretion.*

It was generally believed, that this misfortune was chiefly occasioned by colonel *Haus*'s own neglect, who did not, till it was too late, put the soldiers into a posture of defence, which was afterwards confirmed by the deposition of *William Jacobson*, late captain lieutenant of colonel *Haus*'s own company, made before the great council the 6th of *July*, 1646.

A further account of the defeat of colonel Haus *by captain* Jacobson.

It was not till the night before our defeat, that colonel *Haus* received the first intelligences from a prisoner, a *Negro*, that the enemy with a strong body were broken up from *Moribeka*. The next morning, one of our safe-guards brought word to the colonel, that the enemy was passing the river; and soon after, the colonel's groom, who had been to water his master's horse in the said river, came in a full gallop, telling him likewise, that the rebels were passing the river, so that we soon after heard them fire upon our advanced guard, who retired immediately to the main body. Colonel *Haus* did not call the soldiers to their arms, or caused the alarum to be given, until the enemy came within sight of us, and charged our out-guard, when we first began to skirmish with them: But they charging us with their more numerous forces in the front, whilst *Kamaron* with his troops endeavoured to cut off our retreat to the *Receif*, which we were not able to prevent, by reason of the smallness of our number, *Haus* ask'd captain *Wiltschut*, *Blaer* and *Listry*, *What was best to be done? Wiltschut* answered, *You never ask'd our advice before, do what you think best.* Whereupon *Haus* ordered to retreat to the house of Mr. *de Wit*: Captain *Blaer*, who expected no quarter, being on the other hand for fighting our way through to the *Receif*. The house was bravely defended for four

1645. four hours, but at last powder and ball beginning to fail, because half a barrel of gunpowder (which was all they had left) blew up by accident, they surrendred at discretion to *Andrew Vidal*, under condition to have their lives saved, as well for themselves as the *Brasilians* among them; which agreement being signed by *Vidal*, and two or three more of the chief commanders of the *Portuguese*, was delivered to colonel *Haus*. Notwithstanding which, the *Brasilians* were cut to pieces by the inhabitants, with the consent of the *Portuguese* commanders, as soon as we had quitted our post in the house. The *Brasilian* women seeing their husbands murthered before their faces, dash'd most of their childrens brains against the walls, for fear they should fall alive into the hands of the *Portuguese*. All the *Dutch*, about two hundred and fifty strong, among whom were colonel *Haus*, captain *Blaer* and *Listry*, were made prisoners of war, and were for the first four or five days kept in the sugar-mill of *Hacq*, when *John Fernandes Vieira*, and many of the inhabitants sollicited *Andrew Vidal*, to deliver the said prisoners up into their hands, with an intention to kill them, but *Vidal* refused to grant their request, and caused them forthwith to be sent by land to the *Bahia*: They were indifferently well treated in their journey thither; but such as either by reason of sickness, or any other accident, were left behind, fell into the inhabitants hands, who cut them to pieces, and would have done the same with all the rest, had it not been for their convoy. After their arrival in the *Bahia*, an account being taken of their names, they had certain quarters assigned them, and thirty-one pence halfpenny *per* week for their pay, and a measure of meal for every ten days.

They had liberty to walk up and down within the city where they pleased, except colonel *Haus*, captain *Wiltschut*, and *Listry*, who were confined to their lodgings, and durst not, without special leave, talk with any body. Colonel *Haus* was at last sent to *Portugal*, and *Wiltschut* and *Listry*, in *June* 1647, put on board a ship, with two hundred and thirty *Dutch* prisoners; about sixty of our men took service among them there, but they refused the natives of *Holland*.

The enemies being greatly encouraged by these successes, and their strength encreasing daily by the great concourse of the *Portuguese* inhabitants, who in the captainships of *Parayba* and *Goyana*, which hitherto had remained in quiet, and engaged themselves to the government by a new oath of allegiance, now also took up arms against us; so that it was thought 1645.
convenient to recal our garrisons out of those parts.

What became of the garrison of the cape of St. Austin.

But to return to the cape of *St. Austin*, after the surrender of which the garrison was carried to *St. Antonio*, where they were forced to deliver up their arms. Among the rest of our prisoners there was *Isaac Zweers* afterwards vice-admiral of *Holland* and *Westfriseland*, *Abraham Van Millingen*, and *John Broeckhusen*, both still living in *Holland*. Major *Hoogstrate* address'd himself to them, endeavouring to bring them over to the *Portuguese* side, by the allurements of captain, lieutenant, and ensign's places, telling them, that it would now be in his power to promote them to much higher employments; but when he saw them refuse his offer, he swore they should repent it. At the same time he preferr'd three *Dutch* men, to wit, *Winsel Smith*, formerly his lieutenant; *Alexander Boucholt*, and *Claes Claesen*, a native of *Amsterdam*, to captains places; the last of these three being an intimate friend of *Zweers* and *Broekhusen*, told them, and confirmed it by many oaths, that he had taken service among them for no other end, than to get an opportunity of returning to us. They had also liberty given them to walk abroad, but not without a guard to keep a watchful eye over all their actions.

Not long after, the *Portuguese* provider *Mor* sent for *John Broekhusen*, and after the first complements were pass'd, told him, that if he would serve the king of *Portugal* in the quality of commissary-general, he should go along with him to the camp, where he should receive one hundred gilders *per* month, and be welcome to his table besides; and that if he refused his offer, and stay'd behind, he would be in danger of being murthered by the inhabitants. He reply'd, that being engaged by his oath to the company, he could not break it, though with the hazard of his life. *And* (said the providor) *will you chuse rather to serve a company of mob than a king? We are just now upon the point of executing a design which is infallible, and then you will begin to see that the king's cause is the justest, and will be crown'd with success for ever.* Then he gave him a cup with brandy, of which after Mr. *Broekhusen* had taken a good draught, he took his leave, and return'd to his comrades, unto whom he gave an account of what had pass'd betwixt them.

These had in the mean while been inform'd by some *Portuguese*, that this design was upon the isle *Itamarika*, and being certain that the council did not foresee

1645. see this danger, they were contriving all possible means to give them notice of it, but could not pitch upon any person fitly qualified for this undertaking. At last, *Isaac Zweers*, by vast promises of reward, prevailed so far upon a *Dutch* trumpeter, call'd *Martin Stomp*, that he undertook to carry this piece of news in person to the council, and at the same time to request the releasing of the *Dutch* prisoner still remaining at *St. Antonio*. Every thing being agreed upon betwixt them, the trumpeter took his leave of Mr. *Zweers*, and set out on his journey to the *Receif* about midnight, leaving his wife and children behind him. Mr. *Zweers* and Mr. *Broekhusen* appear'd very well satisfied, but nevertheless were in their hearts not a little concerned for the issue of this enterprize.

A Dutch *trumpeter discovers the enemies design upon* Itamarika *to the council.*

They would often call upon the trumpeter's wife to enjoin her silence, and ordered her, that if any enquired after him, to tell them that he was run away from her, in order to take service in the camp in the *Vergea*.

Some days after they met with one *Peter Ritsau*, formerly baker to the garrison of the cape of *St. Austin*; *Broekhusen* having a mind to feel his pulse, and finding him not averse to such a task, he at last with fair words prevail'd upon him to undertake the same journey the trumpeter had done before; that in case he should miscarry, which they much feared he might, the council might nevertheless be advertised of the enemies intended expedition against *Itamarika*. The baker having desired a certificate from them, testifying, that he never had taken service among the *Portuguese*, prepared himself for his journey, which he intended to begin with the first dark night.

A baker sent upon the same errand.

The same night they were forewarn'd of a design against their lives, by a certain *Italian* call'd *Jacomo da Perugalho*, so that *Zweers* and *Broekhusen* guessing, not without reason, that some of the *Portugueze* had got scent of their sending away the trumpeter and baker, thought it not adviseable to stay longer in this place, but to ask leave from colonel *Pedro Marinha Falkaho*, to go to the *Algodais*, where they could not want conveniency to go along with the rest of the prisoners, that were intended to be sent to the *Bahia*, which was readily granted.

In the mean while, the baker having taken the first opportunity to set out on his journey, was met by two *Portuguese* in the sugar-mill *Trapicha*, who having found the beforementioned certificate about him, carried him prisoner to *St. Antonio de Cabo*, where being put to the torture, it made such a noise among the inhabitants, that they all rise up in arms, protesting, they would not be satisfied till they had fetch'd *Zweers* and *Broekhusen* from the *Algodais*, and cut them to pieces; for which purpose they also obtained seven soldiers from *Pedro Marinha*, and had certainly put it in execution if captain *Ley* had not opposed it; for as good luck would have it, they happened at that time to be in his sugar-mill, and the baker had stood it out bravely, without discovering the matter. The next morning captain *Ley* gave them a visit, telling them what had happened, and says he, to *Broekhusen*, *What is your meaning by this?* but he having no great confidence in *Ley*, denied every thing to the utmost. 1645.

Is seized.

But the 2^d of *October* the whole design was likely to have been discovered by the imprudence of the beforementioned trumpeter's wife, who being got drunk, told some of her acquaintance, that her husband was gone to the *Receif*. She was carried a prisoner to the cape of *St. Austin*, where she was miserably tortured, but being a resolute woman, would not confess any thing: It was however major *Hoogstrate*'s advice, that the *Portuguese* ought not to keep the *Dutch* any longer in *Pernambuko*, but that all such as refused to take service among them, ought to be sent to the *Bahia*. Accordingly all the *Dutch* prisoners then about the cape and *St. Anthony*, were sent to the *Algodais*, where every one was ask'd by colonel *Pedro Marinha*, whether they would take service under the king of *Portugal*, and such as would not, should be sent forthwith by land to the *Bahia*, a tedious journey; besides, that they ran the hazard of being murthered by the way. Many took service for fear, but *Zweers* and *Broekhusen* being ask'd again, whether they were not willing to serve the king, they answered, they would rather die than bear arms against their own nation.

The trumpeters journey discovered.

The 5th of *October*, all the prisoners under a convoy, both of soldiers and boors, were carried from the *Algodais* to *Pojuka*. But scarce were they come thither, when *Zweers* was ordered to be sent back to the cape of *St. Austin*, where he was put to the rack, to extort from him a confession concerning the trumpeter's journey to the *Receif*, who, as they supposed, had discovered their design upon *Itamarika*; but not being able to bring him to make the least discovery, they sent him, after an imprisonment of five weeks, to the *Bahia*.

Zweers *tortured.*

In the mean while Mr. *Broekhusen*, with the rest of the *Dutch* prisoners, had been forced to travel day and night till the 28th of *November* 1645, when they came to a castle call'd *Tapuao*, on the sea-shore of the *Bahia*,

The Dutch *prisoners come to the* Bahia.

1645. *Bahia*, about half a league from the city of *St. Salvador*, after a dangerous journey: They were carried in ten boats to the city, on that side where it is best fortified, the *Portuguese* being not willing to let them have a sight of the fortifications on the land side, Mr. *Broekhusen* was by order from the governor *Antonio Telles da Sylva*, made a prisoner in a citizen's house, and the soldiers disposed into quarters. The next day they heard the drums beat up for volunteers, every one being invited to serve the king of *Portugal*, of what nation soever, except the *Dutch*.

1646. The next following year, on the 18th of *January* 1646, *Zweers* and *Broekhusen* intercepted a letter writ by *Hoogstrate* to *Hondius*, concerning several transactions to be communicated to the governor, of which captain *Ley* having got scent, gave immediate notice thereof to the governour the first of *February*, who threatned them with no less than the gallows, sent them to a loathsome prison; with strict orders that no body should be permitted to speak with them, nor that pen, ink, or paper, should be allowed them; nay, whilst the clerk was setting down their names, a captain came and told them from the governor, that they were the traitors who kept correspondence with the *Dutch* in the *Receif*; and ordered that a centinel should be set at the prison door, to keep the inhabitants from laying violent hands upon them; for as they were carrying to prison, they made a horrible noise, crying, *To the gallows with these impostors and traitors.* They remained five whole days in this prison, without any victuals or drink, till being almost spent with hunger and thirst, they got leave to write to the governor, representing to him their deplorable condition; who gave immediate orders that victuals should be given them for the future: The *Portuguese* keeper being afraid, that if they should give them plenty of victuals at first, it might turn to the danger of their lives, was so cautious, as to send them no more than each a piece of bread well dipt in wine at first, and after some hours, such another, but something bigger, till by degrees their stomachs were restored to their former digestive faculty.

A letter intercepted by Zweers *and* Broekhusen.

Are committed to prison.

Suffer for want of victuals.

Are provided with victuals.

The last day of *February* the governour gave publick audience (which is done three times every year) for the releasing of those that are prisoners on the king's account. Upon this occasion a free access was likewise granted to our people to the governor. They passed thro' the anti-chamber, lined on both sides with his guards, into the room of audience, adorned with damask hangings of divers colours: Here they found the governor sitting in an elbow chair, on the right-side of which stood the royal throne, raised four steps higher from the ground than the governor's seat, which was surrounded upon the floor with very fine tapestry: Just behind him stood his secretary, and some halbardiers; on both sides sat several councellours and lawyers, their heads covered. and behind them the officers of the army, all uncovered. The governor, as soon as he saw our prisoners, gave them a sign to come nearer, which they having done accordingly, Mr. *Broekhusen* upon his knees, spoke to him thus: *We suppose your lordship not to be ignorant, that now for a whole month we have been detained in a miserable prison; without being conscious of any crime committed against you, unless it were, that we have detained the letter your lordship knows of; if in this we have committed a fault we beg your lordship's pardon.*

Have audience of the governour.

1646.

And (replied the governour) supposing you had done such a thing in Holland? Upon which *Broekhusen* answered, *That his lordship would be pleased to remember that it was no more than a private letter, and not directed to his lordship*; the governour after having paused for a little while, gave immediate order for their discharge; from that time they had liberty given them of walking abroad, but were fain to carry themselves very swimmingly, for fear of the inhabitants, who kept a watchful eye over them.

Are discharged.

The 7th of *May*, *Isaac Zweers* and *John Broekhusen* were carried on board a yacht called the *St. Francis*, in order to be conveyed to the isle of *Terceira*; and as they were the first *Dutch* prisoners that were sent to that island, every body looked upon it no otherwise than a pretence to throw them over board after they were come at sea. Here they met with worse treatment than before, being forced to stand to the pump during the whole voyage, and yet were ready to be starved, notwithstanding the sea-men catched more fish than they could consume. At last the 28th being arrived in the road near *Terceira*, they saw within an hour after a *Dutch* ship coming to anchor near them; they called to the ship till the master sent some of his people aboard them, unto whom they made their complaints, and understanding that the master was a native of *Niewendam* called *Martin Peter Honing*, they began to be a little chearful, tho' the *Portuguese* would not allow them to go aboard the *Dutch* ship. But the 29th being left alone with the steer-man and only one boy in the vessel, they found means to go in spight of their keepers, aboard *Martin Peter Honing*, who promised to see them delivered. The same afternoon *Moor* the governour of this

Are sent to Terceira.

1646. this and the adjacent islands, residing in *Terceira* sent for *Zweers* and *Broekhusen*, and told them that he had received a letter from the governour *Antonio Telles da Sylva*, in which he desired him to detain them prisoners in the castle for a twelve month; but that he did not think himself obliged to follow his directions, he having no other dependance but on the king, who being not concerned in this war, his orders were to send all the prisoners brought thither to *Portugal*; that they might rely upon it, and for their present sustenance, till a ship should be ready to go, ordered them nine rix dollars.

And from thence to Portugal.

The 13th of *June* they met with a master of a *French* vessel, who offered to carry them without any reward to *Portugal*, which they willingly accepted of: Here they met with many of their fellow prisoners, who had imagined no otherwise but that the *Portuguese* had thrown them over board. They continued here till the 10th of *September*, when Mr. *Zweers* and *Broekhusen* embarked themselves at *Lisbon* aboard a man of war called the *Prince Henry*, and at last, the 4th of *December*, after a thousand dangers and miseries, which they had sustained since their departure from the *Dutch Brasil*, arrived safely in the *Maese*.

Arrive safely in Holland.

But we must return towards the *Receif*. The unexpected defeat of colonel *Haus*, put all the inhabitants of the *Receif* under a great consternation; but the council left no stone unturned to put the place with all the adjacent forts, in a condition to make a vigorous defence, in case it should be attacked by the enemy; and that every thing might be performed with the best order that could be, *Peter Bas* was constituted commander in chief in the *Receif*. Admiral *Lichthart* was to take care of the batteries, and artillery thereunto belonging; *Henry Moucheron* was made commander in *Maurice's town*; all their thoughts being now bent upon the defence of these places, which before they judged out of danger.

Preparations in the Receif.

The stables and out-houses for the use of the negroes, as likewise the walks and gardens belonging to count *Maurice*'s house being no small impediment to the fort *Ernestus*; it being to be feared that under favour of these houses and trees, the enemy might unexpectedly surprize the fort and *Maurice's town*, and the inhabitants earnestly requested the pulling down of those stables, out-houses and trees, and what else might prove dangerous to the place; orders were given to Mr. *Valbergen* and major *Bayert*; commanding in the fort *Ernestus*, to see the same put in execution, with as little damage to the house as possibly could be. The houses near the fort *Bruin* were likewise ordered to be pulled down, and the horn-work belonging to it, to be levelled at the request of the citizens. Many negroes were also employed under the conduct of major *Beck* and the captain of the city militia, to break down all the houses in *Maurice's town*, which lay too near the new retrenchments. All *Portuguese* prisoners were ordered to be distributed in the ships, and several volunteers who had committed many outrages in the countrey, and were detained in custody, were taken into service for three months. A rumour being spread abroad that 18 of the enemy were come into the *Affagados*, a company of citizens were got in readiness to assist them, but it proved not true. 1646.

The same day the ship called the *Orange-tree* arrived near the *Receif*, being come out of the *Maese* the 21st of *May* with thirty-five soldiers for recruits. The watches were so disposed, that in *Maurice's town* Mr. *de Wit* and *Raetfield* (besides the ordinary offices) and in the *Receif* Mr. *Aldrich* and *Valbergen* should go the rounds.

The ship the Orange tree *comes from* Holland.

Balthasar Dortmund, governour of *Itamarika* sent advice to the council the 17th of *August* that *Kavalkanti* was with some troops come to *Iguaraku*, and had summoned the *Brasilians* to join with him in four days, under forfeiture of their lives.

The 19th the citizens presented a petition, shewing the necessity of having the house of count *Maurice* pulled down, as hindring the prospect from the fort *Ernestus*, and if once possessed by the enemy, they might from thence annoy both the fort and the *Receif* itself with their cannon. But the council having advised with Mr. *Walbeck*, admiral *Lichthart*, *Aldrick de Wit*, *Raetfield*, *Moucheron* and *Valbergen*, thought fit not to agree to it for that time, being in hopes that it might be made useful for their defence. Mr. *de Wit* and *Hamel* were commanded to go from hence to each house in *Maurice's town*, and to take an exact account of what negroes were able to bear arms, and to furnish them with musquets and pikes; the same charge was given to admiral *Lichthart*, and captain *Bartholomew Van Collen*, for the *Receif*. All the sick that were in a state of reconvalescency in the castle were likewise ordered to be armed for its defence.

The citizens petition for the pulling down of Maurice's *house.*

Negroes armed.

At the same time an answer was sent to Mr. *Dortmund*, with orders to draw as many *Brasilians* as possibly he could into the isle of *Itamarika*, and to provide himself with as much cattle and meal (farinha) as he was able to get out of the adjacent places; but that if he found himself not in a condition to maintain the whole island, or

Orders sent to Mr. Dortmund.

1646. or the city of *Schop*, he should retire into the fort *Orange*, where he might be supplied by sea, and consequently make a vigorous defence. Mr. *Carpenter* was likewise forewarned to be upon his guard, and to retire in time into the isle of *Itamarika*, with his soldiers and *Brasilians*, if he found the inhabitants ready to take up arms against him.

The 19th at night a party went abroad to get intelligence, but met with no enemy. Some negroes were also sent towards the enemies quarters to know their strength. The same evening the council received a letter by lieutenant *Francis Meades* from *Andrew Vidal*, in which he testified his readiness still to maintain the peace, complaining at the same time of outrages committed by our soldiers, as may be seen out of the following letter.

A letter from Vidal *to the council.*

WE have sent you advice before by lieutenant Manuel Antonio, *of our arrival in this captainship, by orders from the governor* Antonio Telles da Sylva, *and at your own request, in order to restore tranquillity here by the most effectual means we could devise. We also did represent to your lordships the many innovations and unaccountable proceedings which had reached our ears, by the lamentable cries of several noble ravished virgins, and the doleful complaints of the inhabitants of* Rio Grande, *where forty persons of note together with a priest, and the other day two more in the* Salinas *were murdered in cool blood. I can scarce mention without horror (and the respect every one ought to have to sacred places forbids me to particularize) the outrages committed against the Images of saints, and especially that of the mother of God, and sacrileges committed by your soldiers: All which considerations, together with that we found you in a warlike condition, with your troops in the field, natural right of self defence established by the constant custom of war did teach us, not to leave an armed power behind our backs, which upon occasion might have proved fatal to us, before we could come to a resolution in conjunction with your lordships, what measures were best to be taken for the re-establishment of that tranquillity which was the only aim of our coming into these parts; according to which we have regulated ourselves in our march towards the* Receif, *till we come to the town of* St. Antonio de Cabo; *where having caused* John Fernandes Vieira *to be taken into custody, under a guard of twelve soldiers, we were surprized at the vast numbers of inhabitants, children, women, and religious men, who to shelter themselves from the outrages and robberies committed against them by captain* Blaer *in the* Vergea, *came to seek for shelter among us. They gave us an account how that the said captain not satisfied with having plundered their houses, had carried away three of the noblest ladies of the countrey, after they had been grievously disgraced before; the inhabitants being exasperated by those violences, did (against our will) leave our camp so suddenly, that whatever haste we made to march after them, we could not overtake them before they were engaged with some of your troops, in the sugar-mill of* Isabel Gonsalves, *which they intended to have set on fire, had it not been for our men, who were forced to interpose betwixt them and your soldiers, to their no small danger and our loss, as being exposed to the vollies of your small shot, which consisted for the most part of bullets cut in pieces and made four square. As the hostilities committed daily against our troops, afford fresh occasions of revolt among the inhabitants, so we cannot but lay before your lordships the late proclamation and ratification of peace betwixt us, protesting now and for ever in the name of God,* John IV. *our king, as also in the name of the states general and all our allies, that your lordships will not let things come to a rupture, and not give us new cause of acting offensively, or to declare war against you. We cannot longer dissemble our opinion, that the reiterated complaints of the inhabitants, may at least in some measure serve for an excuse, if not a justification of the proceedings of* John Fernandes Vieira, *concerning whom we are sufficiently satisfied that his first intentions were only to afford protection to some innocent persons threatned with destruction; which though it was in his power to do, yet did he retire from place to place with his forces, in hopes of avoiding any engagement, till forced thereunto by necessity, he was constrained to repel force by force. We beg of your lordships to take this letter into serious consideration, being of so much consequence, to our both sides safeties; for it seems as if heaven itself were offended at our proceedings. God preserve your lordships.* 1646.

Andrew Vidal de Negreiros.

From de Ingenio of St. John Baptist de Venies, Aug. 19, 1645.

An answer from the council was sent the next following day by the same lieutenant.

The council's answer.

OUT of our answer to your letter dated at Serinhaim *the* 8th *of august, you may sufficiently see that the protestations made both by the governour* Antonio Telles da Sylva, *and by yourself, concerning the maintaining of the*

1646. the peace betwixt his majesty of Portugal and the states general of the United Provinces, were never looked upon by us as sincere, or to be relied upon, since your actions did in no wise agree with your words. The treacherous proposals made to one of our deputies, to betray one of our best strong holds into your hands; the landing of so formidable a force in our territories without any knowledge, under pretence of a misinterpreted sense of our letter to his excellency; the coming with a strong fleet into our road; the taking of the fort of Serinhaim; the slaughter of so many Brasilians our subjects in cool blood; the summons sent to the cape of St. Austin for a surrender, nay the attacking and surprising of our troops, who were forced to keep in the field, for the bridling of our rebellious inhabitants; all these, we say, cannot by any unbiass'd persons be looked upon otherwise, than manifest infractions of the said treaty, and open hostilities. We on our side can without the least contradiction to truth positively declare, that our armament was not in the least intended against his majesty of Portugal, but against the rebels and their adherents; which we were compelled to, when we saw many armed troops to penetrate into our territories cross the river St. Francisco. The surprising of some of our barks in the Salgados; the taking of the house Marecape, and making our safeguards prisoners there, as well as at Cambao, and several other places; the gallows that were erected on purpose to terrify our inhabitants into a compliance with the revolted party; the killing of three of the said inhabitants of Pojuka in cool blood, and the surprising of several of our soldiers and Brasilians sent to St. Lawrence to fetch farinha; the plundering of the houses and shops of several tradesmen in the countrey, with many such like violences committed by the revolted party; and what is the worst, before ever we appeared in arms, but endeavoured by proclamations of pardon and of maintaining them in their possessions, to divert the danger; all these actions, we say, will not admit of any other interpretation but of open hostilities.

How can it be supposed that in the station we are, we could after all those provocations and slights of our kind offers, desist any longer from drawing the sword? Whatever in the mean time has been transacted contrary to the custom of war, has been done without our knowledge and intention, being occasioned by the treacherous dealings of the rebels, and consequently to be looked upon as deserved punishments, rather than the consequences of a just war; besides, that neither his excellency Antonio Telles da Sylva, neither you nor any body else, has any legal power to call us to an account concerning the government or punishment of the subjects of the states general, no more than the king of Portugal is answerable to us for what is transacted upon 1646.
that account in his kingdom or other dominions.

Notwithstanding which we would have you not in the least lay the before-mentioned crimes and violencies at our door, we are so far from having encouraged or commanded the Tapoyers to kill the Portuguese inhabitants in Kunhao, that for these several years last past we have endeavoured to prevent it; for having, by the ill treatment they had received from the Portuguese, been exasperated against them, they were for killing most of the inhabitants of that captainship, and had actually put it in execution, had we not interposed our authority, and ordered our garrisons to take them into their particular protection. What you say of ravishing of women, is not only beyond our knowledge, but even beyond whatever we heard of before, having taken all imaginable care to prevent such violences by our proclamation, published for that purpose. It is known to all the world that we afforded our peculiar protection to the women of de Ingenio, of St. Arnout d'Orlanda, and what concerns the taking of the ladies by captain John Blaer, was, as we are informed, done with no other intention, than to exchange them for his wife, or at least to keep them as hostages for her, he having received intelligence that she was very ill treated by you at Serinhaim. The rebels themselves made the first step towards those robberies and rapines that have been committed by our soldiers since; which however cannot come into balance with those cheats, frauds and rapines, wherewith those rebels have defrauded and robbed their creditors of their debts and goods; notwithstanding which we have by granting safeguards and otherwise done all what in us lay to prevent the same.

The late murder upon the person of the Salinhas was committed the 17th of August, without our knowledge, to our great dissatisfaction by the flying Brasilians, who being enraged at the killing of their men, women and children at Serinhaim, without any distinction of age or sex, took this opportunity of revenging themselves. You may easily guess that the papers dispersed by Antonio Kavalkanti at Iguaracu, have also contributed a little to this enterprize.

Of the bullets mentioned by you to have been used in the last encounter, we have more reason to complain than you, it being our constant order not to recede from what is the custom of war in these cases.

The courtesy shewed in saving and receiving our soldiers, we are ready to acknowledge, and to return upon the like occasion, desiring you would send us back your resolution upon this point by the same drummer.

It being evident from what has been alledged, that all the past misfortunes ought to be

1645. *be imputed to the rebels, unto whom we endeavoured by all requisite means to restore tranquillity and peace; but they persisting in their rebellious designs, deserve rather condign punishment than the least excuse at your hands. For which reason it is that we protest before God and the whole world, against the proceedings of his excellency* Antonio Telles da Sylva, *and what else has been committed by yourself contrary to the treaty concluded betwixt his majesty of* Portugal *and the states general of the* United Provinces; *not questioning but that upon the receipt of these presents, you will retire with your forces to the* Bahia, *and thereby put an end to the further violation of the said treaty. Thus expecting your answer, we rest, sir,*

Receif. Aug. 20, 1645. *Yours, &c.*

Preparations against the Enemies coming to the Receif.

The same night word being brought that some of the enemies troops were advanced to *Olinda*, notice was given to all the circumjacent forts, to prepare for a vigorous defence, and two batteries ordered to be raised on the back-side of the dwelling-place of the negroes, from whence they might command the avenues to the *Receif* along the river-side. Several volunteers lately come from the flat country, were incorporated into one company under the command of secretary *Hamel*, as captain, and *Jeronymo Holman* their lieutenant: Two advanced guards were placed, one betwixt the fort *Bruin* and the triangular fort; the second betwixt the last and count *Maurice*'s plantation: Part of the bridge of *Boavista* was broken down, to hinder the enemies passage that way; and considering the importance of the triangular fort, a detachment of twenty six soldiers out of several companies was ordered to reinforce the garrison there. The same care was taken for the security of *Maurice*'s *Town*, *Antonio Vaez*, the fort *Ernestus*, the quinquangular fort, and all the rest.

In Maurice's Town *and other forts.*

Major *Bayert* was ordered to have the remaining walls of count *Maurice*'s stables pull'd down, because they hindred the prospect from the fort *Ernestus*; and *Henry Vermeulen* was commanded to employ thirty negroes in clearing the plantation of count *Maurice* and the ditches from all rubbish; and the before-mention'd *Bayert*, ordered to remove the pallisadoes from the said gardens, and to put them round his fort. The engineer *Pisteor* had orders given him to set a row of pallisadoes on that side of the fort of *Ernestus*, where it fronts the before-mention'd gardens, and to extend them five rods into the river. And this fort being not sufficiently stored with heavy cannon, commissary *Sticht* was to carry thither two great pieces, then planted at the bridge-root, and instead of them to place there two culverins; likewise the entrance of the channel of *Maurice*'s *Town* was stopt by a double row of pallisadoes. The members of the council, in conjunction with those of the court of justice, took another view of the suburbs of *Maurice*'s *Town*, to consult whether it were best to maintain or to desert that post, but the resolution thereof was deferr'd 'till the next day. Two great cannons were planted in the *Quinquangular-Fort*, to command the river-side; and in consideration that the hornworks belonging to that fort, required a considerable number of men for their defence, the governor of the fort was ordered to have the same levell'd by his *Brasilians* and soldiers, and one hundred negroes; and the woods betwixt the said fort and the *Afagados*, were ordered to be cut down by the *Brasilians* belonging to the fort, when it was also resolved to draw the fortifications of *Maurice*'s *Town* into a narrower compass, and to repair the walls round the *Receif*; so that by the indefatigable care of the council, all the fortifications both of the *Receif* and the other adjacent places, were put into such a good posture of defence, that the enemy, tho' very strong, durst not attempt any thing thereabouts for that time. Mr. *Dortmund* had drawn near 1400 persons into *Itamarika*, 700 of which being women and children, he desired some supplies of provisions, but for the rest, had put the island in a good posture.

Mr. *Linge*, by his letter dated in *Parayba* the 22[d] of *August*, sent advice to the council, that after notice given him of the defeat of colonel *Haus*, he had judged it most convenient to remove the garrison and inhabitants of *Fredericia* into the forts; that however the *Portuguese* were pretty quiet as yet, notwithstanding his whole force consisted not in above four hundred soldiers, one hundred inhabitants, and fifty *Brasilians*, among whom were a good number of sick and maimed men; and that the *Tapoyers* had slain about twelve or fourteen labouring countrymen. Major *Hoogstrate*, *Ley* and *Heck*, had not long before given notice to the council, that they had burnt all the houses, but especially the magazine and church without the fort, for its better defence, and that the enemy had posted themselves on the hill of the cape, and on the southern island. 1645.

Letters to the council out of Parayba.

On the 25th of *August*, upon another review of the fortifications of *Maurice*'s *Town*, the same were ordered to be brought forthwith to perfection.

The same day the council received letters from Mr. *Linge*, by the way of *Itamarika*, dated

1645. dated the 18th and 19th of *August*, in *Parayba*, that *William Barents* had sent him advice from *Kunhao* the 14th of *August*, that he and *Rudolph Bawn* had a troop of *Tapoyers* ready for our service, every thing being very quiet thereabouts; but that the said *Tapoyers* had carried away all the cattle belonging to *Peter Farcharson*, which had occasioned no small scarcity of fresh flesh thereabouts.

It was also judged absolutely necessary by the council, to take into their serious consideration the present condition of the forts in *Rio St. Francisco* and *Seregippo del Rey*, which being provided but with slender garrisons, and all communication cut off betwixt them and the *Receif*, and in great danger of being lost; it was judged absolutely necessary, after the defeat of colonel *Haus*, to endeavour the preservation of them, and consequently of the whole *Dutch-Brasil*, by removing them from thence to the *Receif*.

Consultations about removing several garrisons to the Receif.

To accomplish this with all imaginable security, Mr. *Walbeck* was deputed by the great council to the council of war, to know their opinion, by what means these garrisons, as well as that of *Porto Calvo*, might be with safety brought to the *Receif*, or whether, considering that they would be forced to leave their cannon behind them, they should be ordered to defend themselves to the last extremity, in hopes of receiving speedy succours from *Holland* for their relief.

The council of war, having well weighed the whole matter, unanimously agreed upon the following resolution.

The resolution of the council of war.

THAT it was their opinion, considering the capital city was in danger for want of a sufficient garrison, the garrisons of the before-mention'd forts, which in all probability could not make any long resistance, ought to be taken from thence with as much ammunition and cannon as could be done, and carried to the Receif. *But in regard that the fort of* Porto Calvo *lay pretty deep into countrey, where the river was very narrow and shallow, the garrisons of* Rio St. Francisco, *and* Seregippo del Rey, *were to pass that way in order to join them, and that they should bury or break their cannon.*

By order from the council of war, *Aug.* 24, 1645.

Signed,

Kornelis Bayer,	Henry Advocaet.
Albertus Oosterman,	Frederick Pistoor.
L. Van. Harkema,	*capt.* Haelmeister.
John Denning,	Rene de Mouchy.
Samuel Lambartz.	

Accordingly two barks, with the ship *Zelandia*, were ordered for the execution of this enterprize, to *Rio St. Francisco*. 1645.

The last day of *August*, one of the captains of these two barks return'd, and gave an account, that he being advanced into the river of *Rio St. Francisco*, within a league of the said fort, he received so warm a salute of small shot from a *Portuguese* vessel full of firelocks, that he was forced to return, without being able to penetrate any further up the river; that the other bark being discouraged thereat, durst not venture to go to *Seregippo*, but that they thought fit to retreat back with the ship *Zelandia*; he further added, that it would be very difficult to put this design in execution, unless they were provided with some galliots and yachts well armed.

Pursuant to this advice, the council ordered the yacht called the *Sprew*, with three other barks thither, to join with the ship *Zelandia*, for the more effectual execution of this design.

They set sail from the *Receif* the 2d of *September*, captain *William Lambartz* commodore. He return'd with the said yacht, and the *Zelandia*, the first of *October*, to the *Receif*, where he gave the following account of his expedition to the council.

Some ships sent to Rio St. Francisco *under* William Lambartz.

We came the 22d of *September* within a half league of the fort of *St. Maurice*, where we met with a bark, which at the discharge of one of our cannon, sail'd away before us up the river. As we were in pursuit of her, we espied another small vessel, in company of the bark belonging to *John Hoek*, both full of soldiers: We saw the first of these two run ashore, and the soldiers landing, who skirmished with an opsite party for the defence of the vessel: Our yacht under favour of our cannon, boarded the said vessel, with an intention to set it on fire; but finding it loaden with the baggage of our soldiers, fell to plundering first; and soon after espied a boat with a white flag, making all the sail they could towards them: Major *Pappenheim*, late commander of the fort of *Rio St. Francisco*, and Mr. *Hoek*, were in this Boat, being sent by the enemy to let us know, that if we set fire to the vessel, he would cut all the prisoners with their wives and children to pieces, so that we desisted from it. They gave us an account, that the said fort had been forced to surrender three days before, for want of wood and provisions, after a siege of twenty six days: That the *Portuguese* having taken a serjeant with four soldiers of the garrison of *Seregippo*, had killed the soldiers, and sent the serjeant back with a convoy of two hundred men, to fetch the garrison of *Seregippo*, which had

He gives an account of his expedition.

1645. had not above four days provision left, from thence. That about eight days before the surrender of the fort, colonel *Haus*, captain *Listry*, and captain *Wiltschut* pass'd by that way in their journey to the *Bahia*, whither they, pursuant to their capitulation, were to be carried with the rest of the prisoners, and from thence to *Portugal*, and so further to *Holland*, without any other loss except their baggage, being for the rest indifferently well treated. They further added, that the *Portuguese* not long ago detach'd two hundred men to the island of *Melchior Alvares*, in hopes to cut off the retreat of our men, and to prevent their excursions, but came too late, our people being retired before. That the enemy had likewise made themselves masters of the fort *dos Affagados*; where Mr. *Bullestraete* being made a prisoner, was now on his way to the *Bahia*. Captain *Lambartz* hearing this account, thought it his best way to retreat towards the mouth of the river, where having spent two days in refitting his ships, he returned the first of *October* to the *Receif*.

The garrisons of the three forts forced to surrender. The same ill success attended us at *Seregippo* and *Porto Calvo*; for the council having sent a bark with provisions to their relief, the same, contrary to her orders, came to anchor before *Rio St. Francisco*, where being seized by the enemy, the garrison of *Seregippo* being thereby disappointed in their hopes, were forced to surrender after they had spent all their provisions. After this misfortune, there was not the least probability left of saving the garrison of *Porto Calvo*, which lying deep into the countrey, the river was not navigable thereabouts by reason of its narrowness, and that the enemy was master of the field on both sides, so that they were likewise obliged to surrender for want of necessaries. *Are carried to the Bahia.* The garrisons of these three forts, were contrary to their capitulation, (by virtue of which they were to be conducted to the *Receif*) carried prisoners to the *Bahia*; but those that could not follow the rest, by reason of sickness, or otherwise, were cut to pieces by the *Portuguese*.

Many of the soldiers belonging to these as well as other garrisons, and of the troops under colonel *Haus*, dreading the danger of the land-journey to the *Bahia*, did take service among the *Portuguese*; but captain *Nicholas Nicholson* being sent with sixty four of these *Dutch* to prepare an ambush for some of our forces, took this opportunity to join with us, *The Portuguese kill all the Dutch in their service.* which exasperated the enemy to that degree, that they disarmed all the *Dutch* that had taken service there, and murthered them in cool blood; the like they did with the *Dutch* inhabitants that had staid behind in the country. 1645.

In the mean while the captainship of *Parayba*, through the good conduct of their governor *Paul de Linge*, remained in obedience, at least in outward appearance, 'till the 25th of *August* 1645, when the inhabitants, having received intelligence of the defeat of colonel *Haus*, and the surrender of the *Cape of St. Austin*, and being at the same time encouraged by the succours of five companies, and good store of arms, sent to them by *Vidal* from *Pernambuko*, they began also to take up arms, with an intention to cut off the communication betwixt the garrison in the Monastery of *St. Francisco*, as the inhabitants of *Fredericia*, (a place of no strength) and the forts near the sea shore; but Mr. *Linge* shrewdly suspecting their design, *Revolt in Parayba.* did with consent of the rest of the officers there, order all the citizens with their effects, and the before-mention'd garrison to withdraw within these forts, to prevent their being surprised by the *Portuguese*, and to serve as an additional strength for the defence of the forts; for which reason also the *Brasilians* inhabiting with their families in those parts, were commanded to intrench themselves under the cannon, which served for outworks to them. The enemy finding themselves by the conjunction of these forces, disappointed in their design of making themselves masters of *Parayba* by force, had recourse to their wonted artifice, not questioning, but they might have the same success in purchasing the forts of *Parayba*, as they had had at the *Cape of St. Austin*. To encompass which, they sent in *September* 1645, one *Ferdinand Rodrigo de Bulhaus*, clerk of the court of justice of *Parayba*, with a letter directed to the commander in chief, *Paul Vander Linge*, offering him the sum of 19000 gilders, if he would surrender the said fort into their hands. But this message had not the desired effect, the messenger being by order from Mr. *de Linge* taken into custody and hanged the next day; *Their messenger hanged.* of which he sent notice to the council the 16th of *September*. In the mean while, (according to Mr. *de Linge*'s letter from the 6th of *September*) five companies more of the enemies troops, making in all about three hundred Men, were arrived in *Parayba*, which being join'd by the ablest of the inhabitants, had posted themselves near *Tibery*, where they had published by proclamation, for every one to repair to his sugar-mill, under pain of forfeiting the same.

The Passage betwixt the *Affagados* and the *Quinquangular-Fort*, where the cattle belonging to the *Receif* were kept at pasture, being much infested by the enemies parties, one of which had taken good part of

1645. of it, a small wooden fort was ordered to be erected in the most convenient post, for the security of the meadows thereabouts.

Sometime before, *viz.* the 26th of *July*, orders were sent from the council to *Servaes Carpenter*, to disarm the inhabitants of *Goyana*, who thereupon petitioned the said council to be excused from surrendering their Arms, considering that thirty seven *Portuguese* of *Kunhao*, who had been disarmed, were murthered by the *Tapoyers*, and that they were daily in fear of the same treatment, 'till they were further removed from their borders. The council answered, that the murther committed upon these *Portuguese* had been done without their knowledge, and contrary to their orders; that in case they persisted in their allegiance, they had nothing to fear from the *Tapoyers*, whilst they were under their protection; neither ought they to imagind that the disarming of them, was done with an intention to leave them a prey to the *Tapoyers*, but for our own security, and to furnish them with a plausible excuse not to join with the rebels, whenever they should be prompted thereunto by them. At the same time they repeated their orders to Mr. *Carpenter*, not to desist from disarming those of *Goyana*, notwithstanding their petition to the contrary, but that he should be very careful, that neither the soldiers, nor *Brasilians* of *Marni* might be burthensome to them. The council also deputed Mr. *Astelle* and captain *William Lambartz*, with letters to *John Duwy* and *Karakara*, the first king, and the second commander in chief of a troop of the *Tapoyers*, with presents to all the rest of their commanders, in order to engage them to join with us, they having complained of their not having been presented, like as *John Duwy* was before; accordingly the said Mr. *Astelle* and captain *William Lambratz* having taken their leave the 28th of *August* of the council, took shipping for *Parayba*, in order to go from thence to *Kunhao* to treat with the *Tapoyers*.

Deputies sent the Tapoyers

The Members of the Court of Justice and the council of war, in conjunction with the magistrates, having represented to the *great council* the absolute necessity of having the houses in *Maurice's Town* pull'd down and laid level with the ground; an order of the said council was publish'd the 29th of *August* by beat of drum, enjoining the inhabitants to pull down such houses, within the space of two days, and in case of failure, every body to be at liberty to break down the same for his use; the house of Mr. *Rechteren* only excepted, which was to be converted into a redoubt, for the defence of the adjacent plain. The same day *John Denninger*, lately lieutenant to colonel *Haus*, succeeded captain *Blaar*, now a prisoner with the enemy, in his command; and many negroes offered to serve the company under a captain of their own choosing. 1645.

The 30th of *August*, captain *William Lambartz*, with part of his forces return'd to the *Receif* from *Parayba*, where he gave the council an account of his negotiation: That not without a great deal of trouble they at last obtained two hundred *Tapoyers* from their king *John Duwy*, who pretended that he dreaded an incursion from one of his neighbours, who in the absence of his troops might perhaps kill him with all his family, and demanded at the same time, that all the *Portuguese* might be killed in *Parayba*. That he marching with these *Tapoyers* into the said captainship of *Parayba*, they actually slew all the *Portuguese* they met with in their way, to the number of one hundred persons, and plunder'd their houses; and as soon as they found him prepared to appease them, one half of them, with what negroes and other booty they had got, returned home; but continuing his march with the rest thro' *Goyana* towards the *Receif*, the *Tapoyers* did no sooner understand, that they were likely to meet with some opposition by the way, but they followed the footsteps of the rest homewards; so that he was forced to retire with all speed to the fort of *St. Margaret* in *Parayba*, from whence he returned by sea to the *Receif*. Hereupon the council dispatched some letters the 16th of *September* for *Rio Grande*, directed to king *John Duwy*, *Jacob Rabbi* and *Rudolf Baro*, exhorting them to join their arms with ours, for our mutual defence, and to chase the *Portuguese* that were on their march thither, from thence.

The successes of their negotiation.

The Tapoyers desert.

The 13th of *September* 1645, *Jeronymo Serrao da Paiva*, late admiral of the *Portuguse* fleet, (made prisoners in the late sea engagement in the bay of *Tamandare*) appeared before the council, where being examined concerning the designs of the governor of the *Bahia* in sending a fleet, and landing his forces in the Bay of *Tamandare*, as likewise concerning the fleet under the command of *Salvador Korrea de Saa*, he refused to give any other answer, or to make the least confession, except that he was sent with the said fleet and forces to offer his assistance to appease the revolt arisen among us. He desired also leave to send a letter by a drummer to the colonels *Martin Soares Moreno* and *Andrew Vidal*, about the exchanging of his person, and some other *Portuguese* Prisoners, which was granted.

The captive Portuguese *admiral examined.*

1645. Some of the citizens having conceived a jealousy, as if their pressing circumstances and the need they stood in of present relief, had not been sufficiently represented to the council of nineteen in *Holland*, it was thought fit by the council to communicate the contents of the two last letters to them for their satisfaction.

The 19th of *September*, about noon, our whole fleet retired from the bay of *Tamandare* into the road of the *Receif*, with two men of war, and two small vessels taken from the enemy; where I was arrived long before, having left them, immediately after the engagement. The same night *Servaes Carpenter* who died the day before, was interr'd. The same day the yacht call'd the *Doe*, and one of the small vessels taken from the enemy, and call'd by us the *Receif*, were sent out a crusing to the *Cape of St. Austin*, to prevent the enemies receiving any supplies by sea thereabouts.

The council being sensible that the enemy made it their chiefest endeavour to drive away their cattle, and to prevent them, by strong parties from fetching of wood and fishing, a company of fusileers was order'd to be erected out of other companies, who were to be commanded by captain *Renbagh*, and to serve as a constant guard against the enemy's flying parties. The 21st of *September*, the following proclamation of pardon for such as had taken service with the enemy, was publish'd.

Company of fusileers erected.

A PARDON *publish'd.*

THE great council of the Dutch-Brasil *being made sensible, that many of their subjects being fallen into the enemies hands, have either for fear of being killed or transported, and out of other considerations, taken service among the enemies troops, and considering that most of them have been inveigled by their commanders, and perhaps are in a fair way of repenting of their error, have thought fit, by these presents to grant our pardon to all such as shall return to our service, for all past offences; with our promise, that they shall receive the advantage of the same station they were possess'd of among us before; and such as are willing to return to their native countrey, shall have passports granted them for that purpose; from the benefit of which pardon, are however excepted* Dirck Hoogstrate, *and the other traytors, who being commanders of forts, have treacherously delivered up the same to the enemy.*

By this time the enemy had block'd up all the avenues by land, leading to the *Receif*, in hopes to reduce us by famine, having posted both all the *Portuguese* forces sent to their aid from the *Bahia*, and the rebellious troops, from the city of *Olinda* to the *Barctta*, in the form of a half-moon; 1645. and made about half a league from the fort of *Affagados* an entrenchment provided with six pieces of heavy cannon, brought hither from *Porto Calvo*; but durst not attack us by force, knowing we were prepared for their reception.

Mr. *Dortmund* having by his letters represented to the council, the necessity there was of sending one of their members to provide for the security of *Itamarika*, and to keep the *Brasilians*, (consisting of 1500 men, women and children) by his authority in their duty against the solicitations of *Kamaron*, who left no stone unturn'd to bring them over to his side; they desired Mr. *Bullestrate* to take upon him this province; who accordingly the 23d of *September*, set sail thither in the ship the *Deventer*, and returning the 29th of *September* to the *Receif*, gave the following account to the council.

Mr Bullestrate *sent to* Itamarika.

He arrived about noon at the entrance of the river *Maria Farinha*, where being informed by *John Vos*, master of a bark, that the enemy had twice attack'd the city of *Shoppe*, and continued before it still, he went into a challop, with five or six seamen to the fort *Orange*, but was no sooner espied by the garrison, but they desired him not to come nearer, they being still smartly engaged with the enemy upon the hill, and doubtful of success: Whereupon he sent two seamen, with a letter to Mr. *Dortmund*, who being encouraged by the reward of two reals, brought an answer from him the same night, intimating that the enemy, had been forced to retire.

An account of his proceedings.

The 25th of *August*, by break of day, he went in a challop to the city of *Shoppe*, and finding that the enemy, what with the brave resistance made by the garrison, what with fear of this ship, had abandon'd not only the city, but also the whole island, he ordered the fortifications to be forthwith repaired, and to be put into a good posture of defence.

For the enemy perceiving that it was in vain to attack us upon the *Receif*, sent great part of their forces, embark'd in 8 boats and a bark against *Itamarika*, the 20th of *September*; where having surprized, and vigorously attack'd our forces posted on the hill near the city, (our deserters making the first attack) that they the third time made themselves masters of it, forcing our troops to retreat into their entrenchment of the church.

The Portuguese attack Itamarika.

About three days after, *viz.* the 23d, Mr. *Bullestrate*, as we told you, arrived in the ship *Deventer*, to give the necessary orders for the defence of the place; and to keep the *Brasilians* in awe, he brought along with him

1645. him some volunteers chosen from among the citizens, the garrison of the *Receif* being so weak as not to be rendred useless by any further detachments; besides that there were 400 *Brasilians* capable of bearing arms at *Itamarika*. He was charged by the great council, and the members of the council of war, to watch above all things for the defence of the fort *Orange*, which was to be maintained to the last, if they were not able to keep the whole island on the hill.

Mr. *Bullestrate*, after his arrival there, found it absolutely necessary to preserve likewise the city of *Shoppe*, from whence the said fort must be supplied with wood, its situation being such, as that so long as we were masters at sea, we could maintain a correspondence betwixt the said fort and city; for which purpose also, the yacht call'd the *Golden-Doe*, had her station appointed betwixt the fort *Orange* and the hill, to maintain the passage of the river between both. But to return to the siege of the city: The enemy made three vigorous attacks upon the entrenchment on the hill, but was repulsed with the loss of 150 kill'd; tho' a barber, who after the fight deserted them, made their loss amount to 450. *Kamaron* and *Hoogstrate* were wounded, and we had only 15 kill'd and 16 wounded. The *Brasilians* lately transported thither, from the villages of *Goyana*, *Iguaracu*, and other places, behaved themselves to a miracle upon this occasion, tho' it must be allow'd, that the arrival of Mr. *Bullestrate* did not a little cool their courage, which made them abandon the island in the night, betwixt sunday and monday.

Abandon it again.

Further consultations about the safety of Itamarika.

The 2[d] of *October* the great council entred upon a second debate concerning the preservation of *Itamarika*, they having received certain intelligence, that the enemy had undertaken the last expedition against that island, upon hopes of being seconded therein by certain persons of our party, with whom they kept a secret correspondency; and tho' they were in the dark upon whom in particular to fix the intended treachery, yet did they think it conducing to the safety of that so important place, to remove captain *Sluyter* with his company from thence, and in their stead to send thither the company commanded by captain *William Lambartz*, and to entrust him with the supreme command of all their forces there, which was put in execution accordingly the next day. The entrenchment round the church and the fort *Orange*, were also ordered to be strengthen'd with pallisadoes; and the first, pursuant to the advice of *Garstman* and *Dortmund*, I ordered to be surrounded with a counterscarp, within the compass of which a company of *Brasilians* were lodged, with their wives and children, and the rest to be employed in the defence of the fort *Orange*; so the redoubt which commanded the place, from which the fort was supplied with water, was ordered to be repaired against a sudden attack, without which the fort could not long subsist, or hold out against an enemy. 1645.

Letters were about the same time delivered to the council, dated the 5th of *October*, by Major *Austin de Magethaes*, sent by *Andrew Vidal*, to treat about the exchange of prisoners; he told them, that since admiral *Serrao de Paiva*, had by two several letters sollicited his releasement, he desired that the same might be exchanged for other soldiers, or be ransomed by *Antonio Telles da Sylva*, governor of the *Bahia*. He desired also that a cartel might be agreed upon for the exchange of the soldiers; and that in the mean while such of the *Portuguese* inhabitants, as were prisoners with us, might be released for reasonable ransom, which was not accepted of by the council.

Vidal *sollicits the exchange of prisoners.*

In the mean while, (pursuant to the letters from the commander in chief of *Rio Grande*, and *John Hoek* of the 6th of *October*) *Jacob Rabbi*, with a small troop of *Tapoyers* and *Brasilians*, in conjunction with 30 *Dutch* inhabitants, made themselves masters of the seat of *John Lestan*, with the slaughter of 15 *Portuguese*. But they had not the same success at *Fernandes Menda*'s house in *Potigi*, which being defended by 50 *Portuguese*, they were repulsed with some loss.

Fifteen Portuguese *killed by the* Tapoyers.

The enemies finding themselves disappointed in their design of gaining *Parayba* by treachery, did again apply all their care to block up all the avenues leading to the *Receif*, in hopes of reducing it by famine. This occasioned many skirmishes, in which the *Brasilians*, who got the greatest part of their provision out of the countrey, did a considerable mischief to the *Portuguese*; who for their greater security built a fort in *Pernambuko* (as they likewise did in the *Vargea* of *Parayba*) near the sugar-mill of *George Huomo Pinto*, but slightly fortified, and not able to hold out against any vigorous attack. In *Rio Grande* the *Tapoyers* plaid the masters over the *Portuguese*; for as we told you before, that according to their custom they entred the said captainship in *July* 1645, when being informed of the rebellion of the *Portuguese* in *Pernambuko*, they out of an inborn hatred to that nation, attacked the 16th of *July* some of them in the sugar-mill of *Kunhao*, and killed every soul of them, the *Dutch* inhabitants thereabouts not being strong enough to prevent it. From thence the *Tapoyers* marched to *Monpobu*, *Goyana*, and

1645. and *Potosi*, places belonging likewise to *Rio Grande*, where finding a body of *Portuguese* entrenched with pallisadoes in the nature of a *Palanka*, they forced them in conjunction with some *Brasilians*, to surrender, under condition that their lives should be saved, provided they did not give any further occasion of disturbance. But some of the *Portuguese* flying afterwards into *Parayba*, the *Tapoyers* looking upon this as a breach of the late treaty, did with the beforementioned *Brasilians* agree to put the rest to the sword wherever they met with them, which they did accordingly, the *Brasilians* exclaiming against the tyranny committed upon thirty or forty of their comrades, who by *Andrew Vidal*'s order, were tied to pallisadoes in *Serinhaim* and strangled, which had this good effect, that *Rio Grande* for that time was entirely purged of the rebellious crew, except some few who escaped their hands. Their estates and cattle were afterwards dispos'd for the benefit of the company, and others their creditors, which furnished the publick magazines with good store of flesh, at a very seasonable time. The *Portuguese* being sensible that we drew considerable supplies of provisions from that countrey, endeavoured to prevent it by sending several bodies of their troops thither, but were always forced to retire to *Parayba*, whither they carried as much cattle along with them as they could.

The Tapoyers *clear* Rio Grande *of the* Portuguese.

An account of the enemies forces.

According to the deposition of captain *Nicholas Nicholson* (who came over to us the 12th of *November*, as we shall see anon) the four companies of *Dutch* quartered in the *Vargea*, were as follows.

The company of *Nicholas Nicholson*, 63 men, and among them 23 musquets.

The company of *Alexander Buchhalt*, of 43 men, among whom 36 musquets.

The company of captain *Anthony*, who was mortally wounded in a late engagement, consisting of 36 men, and among them 32 musquets.

The company of *John de Witt*, of 40 men, but miserable wretches, and among them only 12 musquets.

Besides these they had two other *Dutch* companies in *Goyana*, one commanded by *George Peterson* of 17 men, all pikes, the other by *La Cour* of 19 men, likewise most pikes. They had also two more in *Parayba*, one under the command of captain *Peter Gendre* of 19 men, most pikes; the second by *Edward Versman* of 20 men, among whom was but one musqueteer: So that the whole number of these eight companies, amounted to no more than 257 men; their colonel was *Hoogstrate*, and *Francis la Tour* late alderman of *Serinhaim*, major, a profest enemy to the *Hollanders*. Most of the 1645 *Dutch* prisoners were put under a necessity of taking service with the enemy, being otherwise in danger of being murdered in their way to the *Bahia*, as it happened to 42 prisoners taken at the cape of *St. Austin*, who were all slain in the sugar-mill *Konjau*, near *Serinhaim*. He further declared, that the enemies forces in the *Vergea*, consisted of about 700 men sent from the *Bahia*, divided into nine companies, well armed with musquets and firelocks. That besides these, they had about 100 men, gathered from among the *Portuguese* inhabitants, they having forced all the young men from the south of *Huma*, as far as *St. Lawrence* to take up arms; some being armed with firelocks, others with musquets they had taken from us; they were for the most part mulats, and an undisciplined rabble, commanded by *John Fernand Vieira* as colonel, and *Anthony Dias* (who came from the *Bahia*) their major. Their captains most in esteem among them were, *Simon Mendes*, *Domingos Fagundos*, and *John d'Albuquerque*. *Kamaron* commanded 100 *Brasilians* armed with blunderbusses, and *Dias* 200 negroes (among whom 50 were ours) provided with very good guns; besides some *Tapoyers*. Each soldier had for his daily allowance, a pound of meat, and about a pint of farinha or meal, and 12 gilders *per* month; a captain 120 gilders, an ensign 42, a serjeant 21, and a corporal 15 gilders *per* month. But they only paid the *Dutch* troops with ready money, the account with the *Portuguese* from the *Bahia* being made up but once a year. They were at that time busy in raising of a fort with four small bastions and a powder house, betwixt *Bierbrom*'s sugar-mill and *Casa de Sabrodo*, upon each of which were to be mounted three pieces of cannon, eight pieces having been brought for that purpose from *Porto Calvo*, among which were five of metal. Round about this fort the soldiers from the *Bahia* had their quarters assigned them, except the company commanded by *John de Magehais*, which was quartered in the *Baretta*, with four *Dutch* companies, *viz.* the *Dutch* that were in the sugar-mill of *Bierbrom*; and those commanded by captain *Peter Kavalkanti*, and *Anthony Jaconio*, and two or three companies of the *Portuguese* come from the *Bahia*, in the sugar-mill *Brito*; the rest being *Portuguese*, *Mulats*, and other idle fellows they had forced to follow them from the south. These were armed for the most part with firelocks and musquets, the rest with pikes, *Andrew Vidal*, *John Fernand Vieira*, and major *Hoogstrate*, were at that time in the *Casa de Sabrodo*; all these consisted not in

1645. in above 600 men. About the sugar-mill of *John de Mendonce* were quartered three companies, two at the house of *Sebastian Karvalho*, and two more in the sugar-mill of *Mengao*. The rest were posted in the *Salines*, *Baretta*, and the city of *Olinda*. Some of *Kamaron*'s troops were in the sugar-mill of *Van Scholl*, and in the house of *John Kordero de Mendoje*, upon the bank of the river, being their advanced guard; *Henry Dias* with his troops had his post in the house of Mr. *Luffelen*. The redoubts belonging to the city of *Olinda*, were manned only with 17 soldiers.

In *November* the great council received intelligence, both by letters from *Paulo de Linge* out of *Parayba*, as also by several deserters, that the enemy had sent 400 men, 200 of which were soldiers, the rest inhabitants, from *Rio Grande* into *Parayba*, to make themselves masters of the open countrey, or at least to drive away the cattle; whereupon it was resolved, with consent of colonel *Garsman*, to endeavour to hinder the execution of the enemies design.

Captain Nicholas Nicholson *deserts the enemy.*

The 12th of *November*, captain *Nicholas Nicholson*, a native of *Amsterdam*, came, as we told you before, over to us to the *Receif*. He was among other prisoners of the cape of *St. Austin*, carried from thence to *St. Antonio*, where he took service among the *Portuguese*, but with no other intention than to desert them upon the first opportunity; he being intrusted with a captain's commission, to command a company of *Dutch* soldiers forced to list themselves from among the prisoners they had taken, was ordered, at the recommendation of *Hoogstrate*, and *Albert Geuitz Weddo*, with the approbation of *Vidal* and *John Vieira*, to lye in ambush for some of our people in the *Salines*, with a detachment of 60 men, out of the four *Dutch* companies in their service; and four more companies were ordered for a reserve, to assist him upon all occasions. The supreme command of the whole body being committed to him, he approached as near as he could with his *Dutch* to the fort *Bruin*, where he took the opportunity to pass the river by break of day, and to go with them (they being all willing to follow) over to us to the said fort. Captain *Nicholas Nicholson* had the command over the said company confirmed to him by the council, they being all willing to enter into their service: But the enemy had no sooner notice of it, but they disarmed all the *Dutch*, and under pretence of sending them to the *Bahia*, caused them to be murdered by the way, with their wives and children.

The 2[d] of *November*, the council had received advice from Mr. *Linge* from *Parayba*, that *Andrew Vidal* had entred that captainship with 200 men, and that *Kamaron* had by letters strongly sollicited *Peter Potty*, to desert our service with his *Brasilians*, but had received a smart refusal; the council sent him two pieces of fine linnen cloth as a reward of his fidelity. For it ought to be observed, that the *Portuguese* when they first began to take up arms against the government, did with letters and great promises, tempt the *Regidors* or commanders of the *Brasilians* to join with them, but they were so far from hearkening to them, that they sent all the letters written upon that account, both by *Kamaron* and the rest of the rebellious ringleaders, without opening to the council, thereby to avoid all suspicion of keeping any correspondence with the enemy, *Peter Potty* being a near kinsman of *Kamaron*; and ever since that time they have behaved themselves so well upon all occasions, and have done such considerable mischiefs to the *Portuguese*, by plundering and killing them, wherever they could meet with them, that we had not the least reason to mistrust the sincerity of their intentions. 1645.

The Dutch *defeat the* Portuguese.

The said Mr. *Linge* did also send word *November* the 4th, that the enemy had attempted nothing as yet; and from *November* 14, that a party of 300 of our people being joined by some *Brasilians* of *Parayba*, had engaged 800 of the enemies troops, whom after a smart engagement they put to the rout, with the slaughter of a good number of their men. The *Brasilians* being encouraged by this success, did over-run all the flat countrey, and meeting with a good number of *Portuguese*, who were merry-making upon *St. Martin*'s eve in the sugar mill of *Andrew Dias de Tigeireda*, they attackt them so furiously, that after a slender resistance they put them all to the sword, even the son of the said *Tigeireda* himself, and a priest, without giving quarter to any body, except to a very beautiful maiden; who though almost distracted at the death of her father, and some of her other relations, that lay wallowing in their own blood, had such a powerful influence upon the hearts of these *Barbarians*, that they brought her a prisoner safely to the fort of *Parayba*.

The Tapoyers *kill many* Portuguese.

The Dutch *attack the* Portuguese *near* Kunhao *without success.*

The 21st of *November* towards the evening, 360 soldiers (20 of whom were taken from the *Receif*) set sail in small boats to the bay of *Traican*, and continued their march the same night, under the command of lieutenant *Berge*, justice *Hoek*, and the receiver-general of *Pernambuko*, towards *Kunhao*, in order to attack the enemy that were lately come into *Rio Grande* from *Parayba*; but these enemies having got some intel-

1645. intelligence of our designs, were retired from *Kunhao* to a retrenchment among the bogs, which being accessible but in one place, they so warmly saluted our forces that would have forced them from thence, with their shot, that they were obliged to retreat with the loss of some dead and wounded, to the castle of *Keulen*, partly to refresh their men, partly to prevent their penetrating deeper into the council.

The 4th of *December* it was resolved to send the ship the *Overyssel*, and the yacht called the *Sprew*, towards the *Babia* a cruising, to get intelligence of their naval strength thereabouts, and to endeavour to take some prizes. The 5th of *December* the great council sent for all the commanders of the *Brasilians*, to inform them, that they had received considerable supplies of powder, ball, and all other sorts of ammunition, by the ship called the *Swan*, with letters from *Holland*, that they were equipping a considerable fleet for their relief; at which the *Brasilians* were extremely rejoyced; the *Portuguese* commanders having made it their business to persuade them, that no such thing was expected from *Holland*.

The Brasilian *commanders summoned.*

The same evening a *Brasilian* deserter declared, that all the *Dutch* were killed by the rebellious inhabitants, and their wives and children made slaves. The same thing was confirmed by a negro deserter, concerning captain *Bockholt*; who having taken service with the enemy, and being afterwards suspected by them, had caused him to be murdered, as they had done with all the rest of the *Dutch* in their service, who were slain in their way to the *Babia*.

Advice that all the Dutch *were killed by the* Portuguese.

The 7th of *December* it was resolved in council, to erect four companies of fusiliers, the same being found by experience to be more serviceable at this juncture, for which purpose the companies of colonel *Garsman*, captain *Jurian Remberger*, captain *Nicholas Nicholson*, and captain *John Taylor*, were pitched upon before all the rest.

Four companies of fusiliers erected.

In the same month of *December*, a certain *Portuguese*, *Gasper Gonsalves*, was taken by the *Brasilians* in the island of *Itamarika*, sent on purpose to persuade the *Brasilians*, that the *Dutch* intended to deliver them up to the *Portuguese* for a certain sum of money, and they to retire with their effects into *Holland*, which caused no small commotion among the *Brasilians*, who began to give credit to the relation. And because *Gonsalves* had spread this rumour abroad some time before the arrival of *Caspar Honyhouse* (who the 28th of *August* was appointed commander in chief of the *Brasilians* of *Itamarika* instead of *Listry* taken prisoner by the enemy) he was hardly put to it how to remove this jealousy from among them. 1645.

Jacob Rabbi, pursuant to his letters of the 11th of *December*, was about the same time preparing to enter 80 leagues further into the countrey towards the *Tapoyers*, to sollicit their assistance: He at last came to *Oyepe*, son-in-law of king *Duwy*, who promised, in case those of *Siara* would send their troops to us, he would endeavour to raise as many of his vassals as he could; but king *Duwy* excused himself under pretence that many of his troops died by sickness in the *Sartan*.

The night before the 27th of *December*, the enemy had by means of a boat, fastned two puppets with fire-works to the ship called the *Swan*; but being discovered as soon as it took fire, was soon quencht without doing any damage to the vessel; which made the ships to be constantly upon their guard for the future.

The 30th of *December* two such puppets found by two soldiers in a small boat near the fort *Bruin*, were presented to the council. This boat, which questionless was sent on purpose to fasten these puppets to some ship or other, being discovered by the centinels, the men quitted the boat, leaving the said puppets behind them.

The Portuguese *endeavour to fire the* Dutch *ships.*

Mr. *de Linge*, by his letters dated the 30th of *December* from the fort *St. Margaret* in *Parayba*, advised, that a certain negro who had deserted the enemies quarter of *St. Andrew* had declared, that the enemy had built two large barks in order to transport 300 men in each, in order to attack *Peter Potty* commander of the *Brasilians* in his entrenchments. That *Kamaron* had been near three weeks in *Parayba*, the enemies troops consisting thereabouts in 16 companies; but that they had many sick among them for want of provisions, and that they had drawn all their forces out of *Rio Grande*.

The 6th of *January* 1646, *Peter Bas* one of the members of the great council, did by order from the said council, set sail with the two ships the *Lichthart* and the *Receif* and a bark called the *Blue-Boar*, towards the captainships of *Parayba* and *Rio Grande*. His instructions were, to consult with Mr. *Linge* commander in chief in *Parayba*, and the rest of the officers there, how to put the intrenchments and other works of the *Brasilians* into a posture of defence. From thence he was to go to *Rio Grande*, there to take an exact account both of the real estates and chattels of such *Portuguese*, as by reason of their being engaged with the rebels, were forfeited to the company; he was also to use his endeavours to have those goods which were upon that account concealed or embezzled, restored for the benefit of the said company. He was also ordered

Mr. Bas's *commission.*

1645. ordered to act in all other respects, but especially in providing for the security of the captainship and the fort, as he found it most consistent with our present interest, and to exhort the inhabitants to remain stedfast in their duty, and not to neglect the cultivating of the grounds and breeding of cattle.

The 12th of *January*, *Peter Dunkerke* arrived from *Parayba*, where he had been a cruising before the *Receif* in the ship *Hamel*; he brought a letter from Mr. *Linge*, dated in the fort *St. Margaret*, the 11th of *January*, who sent also one Mr. *Steinhuisen* to the council, he having deserted the enemy when they began to kill the *Dutch* in their service. This *Steenhuisen* brought advice to the council, that *Kamaron* with 500 well-appointed soldiers, was marched out of *Parayba* into *Rio Grande* to be master of the field there; and consequently to keep our garrisons from being supplied with cattle and farinha from thence. He further added, that the enemy were in want of meat, oil, and other necessaries; but that the inhabitants flattered themselves, that for want of provisions, we should shortly be obliged to surrender our forts into the hands of the *Portuguese*. This being likewise confirmed by Mr. *Linge*'s letter dated the 10th of *January*, a council was called against the 13th of *January*, *Dirk Hamel*, and Mr. *Bullestrate* being present, both members of the great council, besides the assessor *Walbeck*, as likewise lieutenant colonel *Garsman*, Mr. *Raetsfield*, Mr. *de Witt*, *Alrich*, *Volbergen*, and *Sams*, in order to deliberate concerning the present exigency, considering, that in case we should, by the enemies being masters of the field, be bereaved of the supplies of cattle and farinha of *Rio Grande*, at a juncture when *Itamarika* and *Parayba* are closely beset by their troops, it would be next to an impossibility to maintain our selves in the possession of the *Dutch Brasil*, till the arrival of the expected succours from *Hollland*. It was therefore taken into consideration, whether this captainship might be best secured by a powerful diversion, or by endeavouring to drive him from thence. But being sensible that the enemy were so powerful near the *Receif*, *Parayba*, and *Itamarika*, as not to be attack'd in any of these places, without exposing the whole *Dutch Brasil* to an imminent danger, it was resolved, that in order to attempt the relief of the captainship of *Rio Grande*, Mr. *Dortmund* should be ordered to send 60 soldiers under the command of captain *Welling*, and 100 *Brasilians*, in the barks sent him for that purpose, from *Itamarika* to *Rio Grande*: At the same time orders were dispacht to Mr. *Linge*, commander in the fort *St. Margaret* in *Parayba*, to send the same number of soldiers under lieutenant *Bresman*, and of *Brasilians* to *Rio Grande*, to join with the rest that were to rendezvous there. These forces consisting of 120 soldiers and 200 *Brasilians*, set sail the 19th of *January* for *Rio Grande*, and were thought sufficient to oppose the enemies designs on that side. 1645.

An account of the enemies designs.

Consultations held hereupon.

Their resolution.

Mr. *Dortmont* and *William Lambartz*, by a letter dated the 15th of *January*, gave notice to the council, that they had sent a body of 60 soldiers and 100 *Brasilians* abroad, as far in the *Aldea* by *Oubus*, and from thence to the sugar-mill *Arraripe*, but did not meet with any enemies in that part of the countrey, tho' they had several guns discharged at them from among the woods; so that they return'd to *Itamarika* by the way of *Tapasima*.

Mr. *Linge* not long after sent advice by his letter dated the 22d of *January*, at the fort of *St. Margaret* in *Parayba* to the council, that *Peter Potty* with 150 *Brasilians* had attack'd the enemy 400 strong in the *Aldea* of *Magrebbe*, and put them to flight with the loss of 20 killed, and many wounded, whereas they lost but one *Brasilian*.

The Portuguese defeated.

The 29th of *January* it was resolved in council, to bring the ships the *Elias*, *Orange-Tree*, *Deventer*, *Omlandia* and the *Swan*, into the road of the *Receif*, to be ready upon all occasions, in case the enemy should again appear at sea.

Mr. *Bas*, pursuant to his letter from the castle of *Keulen* in *Rio Grande*, dated the 23d of *January*, could not, by reason of a tempest, land his forces at *Kunhao*, in order to join them with those under captain *Rhineburgh*; but was forced to land his forces the 14th and 15th near *Peringi*. In the mean while *Kamaron* having found means to break in through the *Matta*, had surprised many of the inhabitants in their *Fazendas*, and kill'd them without distinction of age or sex: He had since posted himself with his forces, consisting of 400 soldiers, as many *Brasilians*, and 80 *Tapoyars*, under the command of *Antonio Jacomo Beserro*, at a house of *Henry Hamme* in *Mompabou*, to cut off the provisions from us. Our forces consisting of about 1000 soldiers, *Brasilians* and *Tapoyars*, march'd the 23d of *January* to a house of *John Lestan Navarre*, to attack the enemy, and to force them to quit the captainship of *Rio Grande*. Besides these *Jacob Rabbi* and the sons of king *Duwy*, were the 19th past, by the fort *Keulen*, at the head of 60 *Tapoyers*, and were daily follow'd by others, that came to our assistance. Mr. *Bas* sollicited also some supplies of provisions, of which they stood in great want, there being above 1500 *Brasilians*

Mr. Bas gives an account of his proceedings.

1643. *Consultations held thereupon.* *silians*, men, women and children, lodged under the castle. He desired also some money, ammunition, linen and silks to present to the *Brasilians* and *Tapoyers*; all which, together with some pieces of redcloth, was sent him by the council.

According to this advice, it being much to be feared the enemy would scarce stand the brunt in *Rio Grande*, but retire into *Parayba*, it was taken into serious consideration the 29th of *January*, whether it would be adviseable, in case the enemy should be forced by our troops, or voluntarily retreat into *Parayba*, to pursue them thither, and thereby endeavour the recovery likewise of that captainship: But considering that by reason of the weakness of our garrisons, we were not in a condition to send any further succours from the *Receif*, *Itamarika* or *Parayba*, without running a manifest hazard to our troops there; whereas, on the contrary, the enemies did not want opportunity to relieve theirs from the adjacent places of *Parayba*, and that we *Their result.* lived in daily hopes of succours from *Holland*, it was judged the best way, that the welfare of the whole *Dutch-Brasil* ought not to be put to the hazard by such an enterprize as this.

Accordingly orders were sent to Mr. *Bas* and the rest of the commanders of our troops there, to act with all imaginable caution, and rather than expose our men, in following the enemy into *Parayba*, to be contented with the recovery of the captainship of *Rio Grande*.

Colonel Garsman *sent to* Rio Grande. The 30th of *March*, colonel *Garsman* was by special order from the council sent a second time with some Troops to the captainship of *Rio Grande*, to inform himself, whether any troops of the enemy were posted in that captainship, and in what number; his instructions were, that so soon as he had received intelligence of the enemy, he should, with what forces he was able to bring together, endeavour to stop their progress. But if he found himself not strong enough to oppose them, he should send speedy advice thereof to the council, that they might send him speedy succours, and that he was to take all imaginable care not to engage the enemy, before the arrival of the said succours. But if he found the enemy already so strongly entrench'd as to be master of the countrey, without any hopes of forcing them from thence, the defence of the fort *Keulen* should be his chiefest care, as likewise of the *Brasilians*, with their wives and children, and since, in case the said fort of *Keulen* should be in danger of being attack'd by the enemy, it would be of ill consequence, to have these women and children enclosed within the fortifications, for fear of want of provisions, he was strictly ordered to transpo t them in time, to some place of security, such as *Siara*, or the like, where they might be able to subsist, and be secure against any attempt from the enemy. He was ordered also in his return to the *Receif*, to take *en passant* (if it could be done without inconveniency) a view of the fortifications of *Itamarika* and *Parayba*, in order to give an account of their condition to the council. 1645.

But to return to Mr. *Bas*: According to his letters dated the 30th of *January* from the fort *Keulen*, captain *Rhinebergh* had with his body made six several attacks upon the enemy, who was retired from *Mompabou* and *Kunbao* into a bog, without being able to force their entrenchments; we lost about 100 kill'd and wounded in this action, and retreated to the house of *John Leytan* with order to get some cattle, which was very scarce thereabouts, our forces feeding most upon fishes, which they caught by the help of two large nets; 28 of our wounded men were brought to the *Receif*, with advice that notwithstanding this unsuccessful attack on our side, the enemy were retreated into *Parayba*. Mr. *Bas* also sollicited some fresh supplies of men and Ammunition, in order to pursue them into *Parayba*, but the resolution upon this head was deferr'd 'till they should hear further from Mr. *Bas*. The 7th of *February* it was resolved by the council with the approbation of admiral *Lichthart* to equip the *Hollandia* and the *Swan* together with the yachts, the *Flight*, the *Hamel*, *Bullestrate* and *Lichthart* for cruising. By letters from Mr. *Linge*, dated the 11th of *February* at the fort *Margaret* in *Parayba*, the council was advised, how that, according to the deposition of a negro deserter, *Kamaron* was come with all his troops into the city of *Parayba*, with an intention to attack our forts on that side; an answer, with what was thought necessary for this present purpose, was immediately sent back in a bark by the council. By another bark sent by Mr. *Bas* from *Rio Grande*, they were advertised, that he lay still encamped with his troops near the house of *John Lestan*, where with much ado he could get provisions for them, the enemy being still posted at *Momguappe*, and guarding all the avenues into the countrey; that he had sent several spies abroad, to get intelligence concerning the present posture of the enemy. The 17th of *February* the ship the *Swan* and the yacht call'd *Bullestrate* were ordered to go out a cruising; the 18th the yacht the *Flight*, and the 20th the ship *Hollandia* set sail for the same purpose. The ship the *Overyssel* was also

The Dutch *attack the enemy, without success.*

Advice from Mr. Linge.

1645. also ordered to go out, to serve for a spie ship on the coast of *Parayba.*

The 21st of *February* the council received a letter from Mr. *de Linge*, dated the 18th, in the fort of *St. Margaret*, intimating that he had heard nothing since of the enemy. Yet that he wish'd the forces he had sent to *Rio grande* might be returned with all convenient speed, to make use of them for the defence of his forts, in case of an attack. The 24th of *February* a party under command of captain *Killion Taylor* and captain *Nicholas Nicholson*, were sent abroad towards the island of the *Barette* to get some prisoners, but they return'd the 20th to the *Receif*, having met with no body except with a man, at a considerable distance. Another party which had taken their way towards *Olinda* and *Bracco de St. Jago*, but with the same success, the enemy having only shewn himself at a distance, as they were returning to the fort *Bruin*. The 27th of *February* the enemy appeared with a strong body in the *Salinas*, but being saluted by some cannon-shot from the fort *Bruin*, retired without attempting any thing.

Parties sent abroad without success.

News from Parayba.

In the mean while, according to Mr. *Linge*'s letter, from the 2d of *March*, three barks with soldiers were arrived in *Parayba* from *Rio Grande*, so that the rest, under the command of Mr. *Bas*, being 500 in number, might be hourly expected at the *Receif*. He further advised, that he had seen no enemy of late, but being informed that a considerable body lay encamp'd in a valley near the village of *Magarebbe*, he had ordered thither 120 soldiers, and 100 *Brasilians*, to beat up their Quarters, and to get some prisoners. In effect the 4th of *March*, he, with his troops consisting in 500 Men, arrived from *Rio Grande* at the *Receif*, and the 5th of *March* gave the council an account of his expedition.

Several skirmishes.

The 9th of *March* in the night, the enemy appeared in three bodies near the fort *Prince William*, and gave us several volleys of small shot, but being answered with our cannon retired immediately. The same day a party of 50 men were sent abroad under lieutenant *Mos* to get intelligence; being met by two companies of the enemy, a sharp encounter ensued, our forces retiring without any considerable loss, under the fort *Wardenburgh*, and the enemy retreated at the discharge of some of our cannon. By letters from Mr. *Linge*, dated the 8th of *March* at fort *St. Margaret* in *Parayba*, the council received the unwelcome news that the enemy in *Rio Grande* had by a pretended flight drawn the 5th of *March* lieutenant *John de Vael* with 48 soldiers, who were too eager in the pursuit of them, into an ambush, where they had kill'd 30 of them, tho', according to the report of some deserters that were present at the engagement, not without considerable loss also on their side; *Kamaron*, *Andrew Vidal* and some other *Portuguese* officers of note were also present. About the same time 15 *Brasilians* surprised five men, six women and eight children, in an entrenchment seven leagues above *Iguaracu*, called *Papeku*. 1645.

In the mean while the *Tapoyers*, who according to their custom, come once a year, about midsummer, from among the mountains, some hundreds strong, into the captainship of *Rio Grande*, were, after they had carried away all the horses and mares they could light on, retired to the hills; a thing very fortunate for us, for without it our garrisons would not have been able to subsist there. Provisions growing every day scarcer in the *Receif*, it was agreed the 6th of *March* by the council, to send the *Brasilians* raised in *Rio Grande* with a company of fusileers to *Itamarika*, to ease our magazines of that burthen, whilst they might provide themselves with *farinha* roots in that island. Much about the same time the two majors *Bayert* and *Pistoor*, appear'd before the council, intimating, that being informed that the citizens began to murmur at their staying at home, pretending that they were sufficient to guard the forts; for which purpose, as it was reported admiral *Lichthart* had offered 300 men, they were come on purpose to offer their service, and were ready to take the field with those few forces they had left in the garrison; tho' they at the same time protested, that they were of the same opinion, which had been approved some days before, to wit, that this undertaking, by reason of their small number, would be full of danger, and yet not answer the end of bringing provisions into the *Receif*. Admiral *Lichthart* being thereupon ask'd whether he had made any such offer, he declared not to have spoken any thing like it, his ships being so ill mann'd, that he could spare no men for any other service.

Propositions about the taking of the field.

The night before the 13th of *March*, the enemy appear'd both on the other side of the river and the dike leading to the fort *Bruin*, discharging their musquets and blunderbusses at our centinels, but upon the first salute from the cannon of the fort retired. The same they did near the fort of *Affagados*. The same evening betwixt nine and ten a clock they made an attack upon the wooden fort, built betwixt the *Affagados* and the *Quinquangular-Fort*, for the defence of the plain, which they continued 'till one a clock, cutting down some palisadoes, and bringing great store of dry reeds, in order to set it on fire, but in vain, being

The Portuguese *attack a wooden fort near the* Receif.

1645. being forced to retreat with the loss of some of their Men; on our side two were kill'd, and four or five wounded, among the last was lieutenant *Casper Ferdinand van Grol*, who received two dangerous wounds. The next morning the broken palisadoes were repaired, and another row ordered to be set beyond the first, and footangles to be laid betwixt both. The 17th of *March* the bark call'd the *Parayba* coming from *Siara*, brought advice, that the *Brasilians* were gone from *Siara* to *Komesi*, having refused to return to *Rio Grande*, for fear they should be call'd to a severe account there for the murther of several inhabitants, committed by them before.

By the same bark Mr. *Linge* sent advice from the 14th of *March*, that the enemy had appeared of late in a considerable body near the northern fort, but was retired now, but whether to *Rio Grande* or *St. Andre*, he was not able to tell. They had spoil'd all the *farinha-root* fields in the *Aldeas Magarebbe*, and thereabouts; so that the *Brasilians* being for the future to be furnished with provisions out of the magazines, he desired a supply of wine and oil: Immediately advice hereof was sent to *Dortmund* commander in chief of *Itamarika*, and some ammunition, besides 1000 gilders in ready money. The same sum was transmitted to Mr. *Linge* in *Parayba*, and a barrel with oatmeal, a pipe of wine, a hogshead with oil, and another fill'd with dry pease, besides good store of ammunition. He was also ordered to send the *Brasilians* back to *Rio Grande* for defence of that captainship, and to get intelligence whether the enemy had directed his march thither, in order to oppose his designs.

In the mean while admiral *Lichthart* (pursuant to his letter of the 21st of *March* to the council) had embark'd some soldiers and *Brasilians* in *Itamarika*, and taking his course to the north-entrance of the river, was got up as far as to the isle of *Tapesco*, from whence they had brought back a great quantity of *farinha* roots, for the use of the *Brasilians* in *Itamarika*, and of the magazines there.

Good store of farinha *roots brought to* Itamarika.

The 30th of *March* it was resolved, with the approbation of admiral *Lichthart*, to send the following ships a cruising before the *Bahia*; the *Ulissingen*, the *Ter Veer*, and the yachts, the *Greyhound*, the *Heemstede*, *Sprew* and *Bullestrate*; and on the 6th of *April* the *Swan*, the *Zouteland*, the *Flight*, and the yacht the *Lichthart*, were ordered to go a cruising before the *Cape of St. Austin*, and set sail the 10th of *April* accordingly.

Ships sent out a cruising.

The 31st letters were brought to the council, dated the 25th of *March* in *Rio Grande*, intimating, that *Paulo de Kunha* and *Kamaron* were entred *Kunhao* with 800 men, among whom were 300 musqueteers, to carry away the cattle from thence to *Parayba*. 1645.

But, according to colonel *Garsman*'s letters to the council, upon his arrival, which was the 4th of *April*, the enemy were already retired out of *Rio Grande*, without undertaking any thing against our people, who consisting only in 400 soldiers and 300 *Brasilians* lay encamp'd near the house of *John Lestan*, yet they carried off some cattle.

News from colonel Garsman.

About the same time they received letters from Mr. *Linge*, that the enemy had made several false alarms near the forts, without attempting any thing. And in effect in *June*, they did not appear any more thereabouts.

In the year 1646, the 5th of *April* in the night, *Jacob Rabbi* was at the instigation of lieutenant colonel *Garsman*, near *Potosi*, about three leagues distant from the castle of the same name, villainously shot with two bullets, as he was going home from one *John Miller*'s house, where he had been entertained that evening in company with colonel *Garsman*. *Rabbi* had a considerable time before (as he had declared to his friends) suspected the treachery of *Garsman*, and was for that reason just upon his departure out of *Rio Grande*, in order to shelter himself among the *Tapoyers*. The council resented this villainy to the highest degree, since, considering that this *Jacob Rabbi* was in great esteem among the *Tapoyers*, and his wife a *Brasilian*, it was to be feared, that this would exasperate both the *Tapoyers* and *Brasilians* against us. So that *Garsman* returning the 19th of *March* to the *Receif*, after he had given an account of his expedition to the council, was by their particular order, the 24th of *March*, taken into custody, and sent on board the *Hollandia*, major *Bayert* being ordered in the mean time to supply his place. This *Jacob Rabbi* a native of *Germany*, had been employ'd by authority of the states general, his highness the prince of *Orange*, and the company, to engage and keep the *Tapoyers* in the interest of our government; in which commission he had acquitted himself so well, that he brought these *Tapoyers* several times, out of the mountains (their habitations) to our assistance. His dwelling-place was in the fort *Keulen* in *Rio Grande*, where he had married a *Brasilian* woman. *Gasper Honyhouse*, commander of the *Brasilians* in *Itamarika*, being slain in the last engagement in that island, Mr. *Vincent van Drillenbergh*, was, at their request, constituted their commander by the council. 1646.

Jacob Rabbi *treacherously killed.*

Garsman *secured.*

1646. The 17th of *April*, some papers were delivered to the council, which had been dispersed by the enemy, to debauch our soldiery; in return of which, they sent abroad their summons, upbrailing such of their subjects as were in the enemy's service, with treachery, and exhorting them to return to their duty. It was also agreed to publish a copy of a letter delivered by the *Portuguese* ambassador at the *Hague* to the states general from the king his master; with the answer of the states to the said letter: For since the king of *Portugal* in this letter did disown the war, and the proceedings of *Antonio Telles da Silva*, and his sending of his troops into the *Dutch-Brasil*, they did not question but by this means to open the eyes of the *Portuguese* inhabitants, not to flatter themselves with vain hopes of assistance from *Portugal*; besides, that we were in hopes thereby to sow the seeds of mistrust betwixt them and the *Portuguese* commanders from the *Bahia*.

The 24th of *April*, two *Portuguese* companies commanded by captain *Lawrence Karnero* and *Peter Kavalkanti*, consisting of about 40 men each, marched from the *Vargea* and the city of *Olinda* to *Iguarasu*.

They were headed by *Vidal* and *Hoogstrate* in person, who having got intelligence that admiral *Lichthart* and *John Nicholson* were gone to *Itamarika*, to get some *farinha* roots. The 25th of *April*, as they were marching from *Iguarasu*, a certain *German* chirurgeon, named *Christopher Mars*, who was formerly taken prisoner by them, happening to stay somewhat behind, whilst he was pissing, was surprized by one of our parties near *Tapasino*. Upon examination by Mr. *Walbeck*, he declared, that not long ago there were nine companies of the enemies forces quarter'd in the *Baretta*, the city of *Olinda*, and in the mills of *Bierboom* and *Brito*; each company consisting of betwixt 40 or 50 men. That there were five companies more, much of the same strength, posted in the *Salinas*, and *Henry Dias* with 200 mulats and negroes in *Gaspar Cox*'s house, but they had then no forces in the *Vargea*.

One Mars *taken prisoner.*

His depositions.

That after *Nicholas Nicholson* was come over to us with his troops, *Martin Soares Moreno* had caused 260 *Dutch*, both soldiers and inhabitants, (among whom were six women and two children) to be killed by a company of the country militia, in the woods of *Tabatinga*, betwixt *Sibero* and *Deriba*, in their way to the *Bahia*, besides those killed by his order in other places, amounting in all to 300.

By this time there began to be great scarcity of meat in the *Receif*, notwithstanding which, the garrisons in the outworks, as well as the *Brasilians* in *Itamarika*, with their wives and children, were to be supplied from thence; and the *farinha* roots being either all taken up before by our own people, or else destroy'd by the enemy, in the island *Itamarika*: To supply this pressing necessity, it was resolved by the great council, to send a detachment of 400 men in barks to *St. Lawrence de Praja* or *Tujukapa*, to fetch *mandinka* or farinha-roots from thence. This detachment was composed out of these following troops. 1646.

The Dutch *go out for some* farinha *without success.*

Out of captain *Nicholas Nicholson*'s company 9 men.

From the *Quinquangular-fort* 25.

From the *Affagados* 25.

Out of the company of captain *William Lambartz* 50.

Volunteers from *Itamarika* 30.

Brasilians 150.

The 29th of *April* the council was, by letters from *Itamarika*, advertised, that our forces being sent abroad to fetch some *farinha*, had chased the enemy out of two or three entrenchments; but they retiring into another, surrounded with a deep ditch, they were there also with more courage than conduct attack'd by our troops, being forced to retire with the loss of 16 kill'd and 26 wounded, among whom was captain *William Lambartz*: The enemy had likewise not a few kill'd on their side. Mr. *Dortmund*, commander in chief of *Itamarika*, therefore desiring to be supplied with meal, his magazines being quite exhausted, the council sent thither the first of *May*, 20 barrels with meal, two with oatmeal, two with dry pease, besides a pipe of wine and brandy, and 1000 gilders in money, for the use of the *Brasilians*.

The 3d of *May* the council received advice by a letter dated the 2d of *May* from Mr. *Dortmund*, that the enemy had carried away ten Negroes, four belonging to the company, the rest to one Mr. *Seulin*, and four other men from *Itamarika*; and that the *Brasilians* there had been so far debauched by their intreagues, that they retired into a wood, and being twice summon'd to rejoin our troops, had refused so to do. That at last, Mr. *Apprisius*, (Minister of the *Brasilians*) having been sent to reduce them to their duty, either by persuasions or threats, his arguments were so prevailing, that they return'd quietly, alledging for their excuse, that they were forced to fly thither for want of subsistance. Hereupon *Dortmund* desired fresh supplies for his magazines, that a person of authority might be sent thither, and that another company might be put in place of that of captain *Vosterman*, his men being ready to revolt.

Mutiny of the Brasilians *appeased.*

1646. *Mr.* Bullestrate *sent to* Itamarika. To remove all these obstacles, it was resolved immediately to dispatch thither Mr. *Bullestrate*, a member of the great council, who was to agree with certain private persons, to provide our garrisons with fish, and to act in every thing there, as he should find it most expedient for the service of the company.

Accordingly Mr. *Bullestrate* set sail the 4th of *May*, in the yacht the *Greyhound*, and arrived the same day in the afternoon in *Itamarika*, where having executed his commission, he return'd the 10th of *May* to the *Receif*, and gave the following account to the council: *An account of his proceedings.* That he had taken a view of the city of *Schoppe*, and the fort *Orange*, both which he had ordered to be strengthned; as also, to fortify the old brickhouse, formerly the *Stadthouse*, with pallisadoes, against any sudden attempt; that he having call'd before him all the commanders of the *Brasilians*, had represented to them that we were in daily expectation of a powerful succour from *Holland*, exhorting them to remain stedfast in their duty, and to keep their soldiers under the best discipline they could; he had also presented their commander with cloth for a suit of clothes, and the rest with some wine and money, which they very thankfully accepted: He had *En Passant* taken a view of the plantations of *Conradt Pauli*, where he had found about 160 cocoa-trees cut down by the *Brasilians*, being forced by famine to feed upon the fruit; the like they had done in several other places; that he had endeavoured to treat with several private persons for a certain quantity of fish to be delivered at the *Receif*, but could meet with none that would accept his offers; they alledging, that most of their negroes being either run away or taken by the enemy, they did catch no more fish but what they could readily sell in the island, without the charge of salt and transportation; that he had likewise proposed to the commander in chief of the *Brasilians*, to give them for the future money instead of meal; and that they were to be furnished with three nets to catch fish for their own use; that the commander promised to propose it to the rest, and gave him some hopes that they would accept of the said offer.

To supply the present want of provisions, which began to be scarcer and scarcer every day in *Itamarika*, *Parayba*, *Rio Grande*, and the *Receif*, by reason that the expected supplies from *Holland* were not as yet arrived, and we were closely block'd up by land; it was thought fit to give all imaginable encouragement to the fishing trade, for which purpose the two members of the great council, Mr. *Hamel* and Mr. *Bas*, ordered the 7th of *May*, to buy up as much yarn as possible could be got to make fishing nets of, which afterwards stood us in good stead. *Fishery encouraged.*

A certain *Portuguese*, who had committed manslaughter in *Angola*, and was fled from thence to the *Receif*, having accused *John Vieira d Allegoas*, he was by order from the council taken into custody. John Vieira *accused of treason.*

This *Portuguese* declared, that the said *Vieira* had delivered to him a certain piece of parchment, written in characters, and a box, wherein were several other papers, in order to carry them to the enemy, which parchment and box he produced in the presence of the members of the council. *John Vieira* denying the matter, was put to the rack, but continued resolute in his denial; till at last, the key of these characters being found among his papers, and a certain *Jew* having unciphered these letters, it appear'd, that he had given an account of the whole posture of our affairs to the enemy, with directions how to make themselves masters of the *Receif*: so that finding himself discovered, he confest that he had written and delivered these cyphered papers to the *Portuguese*, and was executed the 29th of *May*. *Is executed.*

The magazines being by this time almost exhausted, there being scarce provisions left for a few weeks, it was proposed by the council to the majors, *Beyert* and *Pistoor*, that considering it was not adviseable to exasperate the soldiery at this juncture, by retrenching their allowance of bread and other eatables, whether instead of a pound of meat, they might not be prevailed upon to take six-pence, by this means to preserve that small store of flesh they had left, which these two majors undertook to propose to the soldiers, not without hopes of succeeding in their project, and that nobody might be excepted from bearing his share in the publick calamity, it was ordered that the loaves which used before to weigh a pound and half, should be reduced to one pound weight, and that each citizen and others depending on the company, nay the members of the great council themselves, should have an allowance only of two loaves *per* week; the same was to be given to all seamen, captains, lieutenants and ensigns; but the rest, from the serjeant to the common soldier, should have three pounds of bread allow'd them *per* week. *Orders concerning the allowance of bread.*

Mr. *Linge* advised from the 1st of *May*, out of *Paraiba*, that the enemy had not attempted any thing against the forts, and that a party of *Brasilians* was gone abroad towards *Tapoa*, in hopes to take some prisoners. Much about the same time the council received advice, that colonel *Garsman*,

1646. *man*, without orders from the council, had endeavoured by some presents, to draw the *Tapoyers* into *Rio Grande*, under pretence of keeping them at hand, to enter into a confederacy with the new members of the great council that were expected from *Holland*. The council being not a little surprized at this undertaking, since by the coming of the *Tapoyers* into that captainship, they should be disappointed of a considerable part of those supplies they received from thence; they sent word to *Rudolph Barro* to leave no stone unturned to draw the *Tapoyers* by fair means back to their habitations, but that if they would send some of their commanders to the *Receif*, all imaginable satisfaction should be given them concerning the murther of *Jacob Rabbi*; and the more to engage *Barro* to do his utmost, a present of wine, brandy, and some toys, was ordered to be sent him. For as the case then stood, it was absolutely necessary for us to remain masters of *Rio Grande*, till the arrival of the succours from *Holland*; the vast numbers of *Brasilians* that were fled to *Itamarika*, having consumed all sorts of provisions there to that degree, that that island could not only not send any supplies to the *Receif*, but most of the women and children of the *Brasilians* must be supplied out of the magazines there; so that *Rio Grande* was the only place left from whence they received a considerable quantity of *Farinha* and cattle, which in some measure abated the scarcity of provisions in the *Receif*, and by the prudent conduct of the council, was the chief means that the place continued in tolerable good health till the arrival of the succours, which without it, it would in all humane probability have been impossible to be done; and no question but this captainship might for a considerable time after, have furnished the garrisons to the south with necessaries, had it not been for the following accident.

Garsman *summons the* Tapoyers *without orders.*

The consequence of Rio Grande *to the* Dutch.

The expected succours from *Holland* being detained by the winter season and contrary winds, the *Brasilians* of *Gojana*, who with their wives and children had sheltred themselves in *Itamarika*, were reduced to the greatest extremity for want of food; for after they had consumed all what the island could afford for their subsistance, and all the avenues by land being block'd up by the enemy, they had no other supplies but what they received from our magazines: These being now exhausted to such a degree, that each citizen had but one pound of bread allowed him *per* week (which however at that rate would not hold out above fourteen days longer) the council was under an absolute necessity to have it proposed to the *Brasilians*, to retire with their wives and children (in all about 1200) to *Rio Grande*, where they might subsist some time upon what the country afforded. Accordingly they writ to Mr. *Dortmund* the 1st of *May*, and sent Mr. *Walbeck* thither in person, to persuade the *Brasilians* to send at least 500 women and children, with a certain number of their men, to *Siara* and *Rio Grande*, there being at that time in all near 1500 *Brasilians*, men, women and children in that island, among whom were only 500 fit to bear arms, under the command of *Caspar Honyhouse*, who had each scarce a pound of bread allow'd them *per* week. 1646.

Provisions, as I told you before, growing daily scarcer and scarcer, by reason the succours from *Holland* were detained beyond all expectation, by contrary winds; a general council was call'd, where the three numbers of the great council Mr. *Hamel*, Mr. *Bullestrate* and Mr. *Bas*, being present, as likewise admiral *Lichthart*, and the two majors *Beyert* and *Pistoor*, the following points were taken into debate.

Consultations about the scarcity of provisions.

First of all, the sending of the *Brasilians* from *Itamarika* to *Rio Grande*, being look'd upon as unavoidable, immediate orders were given to get the necessary transport vessels ready for that purpose. It was also taken into consideration, whether it were not feasible to gather a sufficient force out of the forts, who in conjunction with the *Brasilians*, might attack some place or other, from whence to provide ourselves with *Farinha*; but to this it was objected by the majors *Beyert* and *Pistoor*, that the garrisons of the forts could not be weakned by any detachment, without running a great hazard; besides that it was a hard matter to pitch upon any place where there was any store of *Farinha*, the enemy having either consumed, spoiled or carried it away before; so that we must expose our men to an apparent danger, without a sure prospect of interest; for, supposing we should be successful, the quantity that might be got, would not be sufficient to maintain our garrisons for any considerable time. It was however agreed to take an exact account of all the garrisons, to see whether upon an occasion something might be undertaken for the service of the state. Accordingly these two majors, *Beyert* and *Pistoor*, having presented a list of these forces the next day to the council, it was concluded that no troops could be spared out of the forts, except it were out of the *Assagados*, but they were but few in number. At the same time it was resolved to send captain *Niger* with his company of *Brasilians* to *Rio Grande*, and the *Omlandia* and *Greyhound* yacht were ordered forthwith to

I sail

1646. sail to *Itamarika*, to transport the *Brasilians* to *Rio Grande*.

Further debates about the attacking of the enemy.

The 30th of *May* the council, the admiral, and two majors, entred into a second debate, whether it were possible to attack the enemy, and in what place: Against which it was alledged, that their chiefest force was at present in the *Vergea*; but supposing it was not, no *Farinha* was to be got there, because they were supply'd with it themselves from far distant places. That the *Farinha* fields nearest to the *Receif* were about *St. Lawrence*, at least five leagues from thence; that the nearest *Farinha* fields to the south were about *St. Antonio* and *Moribeka*, where by reason of the strength of the enemy, and the great distance from us, there was no probability of encompassing our design; and that the *Farinha* fields to the north were likewise at such a distance from the sea-side, as could not in any likelyhood answer our expectation. It was farther taken into consideration, whether some forces might not be spared in *Itamarika*, but it was carried in the negative, because since the *Brasilians* were ready to depart for *Rio Grande*, it was not adviseable to expose the rest of our troops there to a hazard. After serious deliberation, what forces possibly could be raised out of the forts, (their places being in the mean while to be supplied by the inhabitants) it was found that the *Affagados* could furnish about 70 or 80 men, the quinquangular fort, and *Maurice*'s town the same number, and that of *St. Antonio Vaez* about 50. But, considering that the city militia of the *Receif* consisted only of six companies of 70, or at the most 80 men each, and that they were obliged to be upon the guard every night there (the place being without a garrison) if a considerable number of them should be employed in the forts, this must needs expose the capital place, which the enemy chiefly aimed at, to an imminent danger. The seamen being not above 250 in all, could likewise not be employed in that service, unless we could leave our ships quite unmann'd and useless. So that after many arguments on both sides, it was agreed to chuse the securest way, and according to the orders of the council of XIX in *Holland*, to expect the succours from thence with patience, and in the mean while to provide for the security of our forts.

The same day the council received letters from Mr. *Walbeck*, that some of the *Brasilians* of *Itamarika* had deserted, a rumour being spread among them, that we intended to leave them to the mercy of the *Portuguese*, which had put all the rest into a great consternation, but that Mr. *Dortmund* had convinced them to the contrary. 1646. Mr. *Walbeck* and *Dortmund* had in the mean while represented to the *Brasilians*, that they being many in number, and consequently very ill provided for at this juncture, whether it were not best for them to go for some time to *Rio Grande*. They were at first averse to his proposals, for fear of being deserted by us, nevertheless the urgent necessity of providing for their sustenance, and to shew their compliance with the governments orders, were so reconciled with them, as to resolve to go to *Rio Grande*, provided they might be furnished with convenient transport-ships, provisions, and some ammunition for their defence, and fifty men of regular troops. Mr. *Dortmund* having again sollicited for provisions, some were sent (sufficient for fourteen days) immediately, with some gunpowder, bullets, and other ammunition.

The Brasilians *resolve to leave* Itamarika.

Accordingly above 1200 *Brasilians*, most women and children, whose husbands and fathers had been slain in our service, embark'd aboard the *Omlandia* and some yachts, a pound of salt-cod fish being allow'd to each for the whole voyage without bread. At their arrival in *Rio Grande* they were so emaciated by famine, that they appear'd more like dead carcasses than living bodies, and laid hold of every thing they could meet with to satisfy their greedy stomachs, so that in a little time they consumed all the *Farinha* that was left there.

Mr. *Linge*, by his letters from the 25th of *June* sent advice to the council, that there appear'd no enemy at that time in *Parayba*, but that ten *Tapoyers*, vassals of king *John Duwy*, being come into *Rio Grande*, had shewn themselves extremely dissatisfied at the murther of *Jacob Rabbi*, whereupon it was resolved to reconcile that king to our interest by the following presents:

Presents sent to king John Duwy.

200 gilders in ready money.
1000 Ells of *Osnabrugh* linnen cloth.
100 gallons of *Spanish* wine.
Two casks of brandy.
40 gallons of oil, and a barrel with powdered beef.

The Brasilians *depart from the forts near the* Receif.

The *Brasilians* in garrison in the fort, the *Bruin*, the *Quinquangnlar*, and some other forts, being dissatisfied at their being detained there for eight months last past, petitioned the council the 12th of *June*, to be sent back into *Rio Grande*.

The opinion of the two majors being ask'd thereupon, they advised, that considering they did no extraordinary service there they might well be spared; so that it was resolved the 14th of *June* in council, to pay them their arrears, and to send them back

1646. back to *Parayba* and *Rio Grande*, to inhabit their villages as before.

In the *Quinquangular* fort, the company of *Immanuel Barros* was order'd to keep guard instead of the *Brasilians*, who were commanded to depart the 20th of *June*. The 11th, 12th, 13th and 14th of *June*, the enemy shot in the night-time very fiercely against the fort *de Affagados*, a redoubt call'd *Kirk*, and the house *Boavista*.

The 15th of *June* it was proposed to the council by admiral *Lichthart*, and the two majors, *Beyert* and *Pistoor*, to beat up the enemies quarters in the house of *Immanuel Kavalkanti*, and in the *Baretta*, with the following troops.

The company of captain *Killian Taylor*, 40 men.

The company of captain *Nicholas Nicholson*, of 70 men, which were to be joined by captain *de Niger* with 30 men out of the fort *Frederick*, with lieutenant *Mos* from the fort *Ernestus* with 10 men, and lieutenant *Katnar* from the fort *Prince William* with 20 men.

In all 200 men.

A project to beat up the enemies quarters. About 100 volunteers were supposed to be raised from among the citizens, under the colonel *Walbeck*, and *Immanuel Baros* with his Negroes, consisting in 50 men, these joined with the other 200, would make up a body of 350 men, to be commanded in chief by major *Pistoor*, and to be conducted by sea by admiral *Lichthart* to their landing place, *viz.* the regular troops to the south of the *Baretta*, and the Negroes upon the island on the north-side, from whence they might break thro' the marshes to the *Affagados*, and so further to the house cross the river, where they were to make a false attack, whilst the troops landed at the *Baretta*, assaulted them from before; the admiral, with his transport vessels, to lay ready all this while to receive them, and to secure their retreat upon all occasions. This proposition being approved of by the council, partly to animate our soldiers, partly to get at least some provisions for the sick, it was resolved to be put in execution the next day, but the wind proving contrary, and afterwards the tides being unseasonable for the convenient landing of our men, this project was laid aside, *Is laid aside.* especially when instead of 100 volunteers, scarce 25 offered themselves for this service, notwithstanding the council gave them all imaginable encouragement, by promising them to receive the same treatment as the other servants of the company had, in case they should be wounded or come to some other misfortune.

In the mean while, the enemy having been informed by some of our deserters, that by the departure of the *Brasilians* from *Itamarika*, the garrisons there were much weakned, they thought fit to lay hold of this opportunity, to land such a force there, as should be beyond our power to drive from thence. The 15th of *June*, with the break of day they surprized our spy ship there, call'd the *Sprew*, with several barks and boats at the entrance call'd *Passoos*, (*Markers*) they got three prisoners, the rest escaping with the loss of two of their comrades kill'd.

The ship before *Tapasima* was set on fire by our own people, leaving the galliot, that lay hard by, to the enemy, after they had taken out all her men, who went aboard the yacht call'd the *Golden Doe*, lying before the north entrance. They landed with about 2000 men in chalops and other transport vessels, and *Andrew Vidal* and *John Ferdinand Vieira*, writ the same night the following letter to Mr. *Dortmund*, commander in chief of *Itamarika*, which they sent by a boy they had taken prisoner in the *Sprew*. *The Portuguese land on Itamarika.*

Their letter to Mr. Dortmund.

Most honourable and most brave,

YOU are doubtless not unacquainted with the resolution of the inhabitants of this country to retrieve their former liberty; to effect which they neither want power nor any other means; but their chief aim being to encompass their design without effusion of blood, we thought fit to let you know that we are ready to attack you in this island with all our forces, unless you will prevent it by a treaty. For being sensible that you are pass'd all hopes of relief, we were willing to advise you to treat with us, according to the custom of war, used in such cases; that, in case hereafter things should fall out contrary to your expectation by the fury of the conquering sword, you may not lay the fault thereof at our doors; for which reason it is, that we offer to you and the rest of the commanders there, all their arrears due to them from the company. Whereupon we expect your answer to-morrow.

From our head quarter, *June* 15, 1646. *Andrew Vidal de Negreiros.*
John Ferdinand Vieira.

The 17th of *June* the council received advice from Mr. *Dortmund* of their landing, desiring prompt succours, without which he would not be in a condition to maintain the island against them. It was therefore taken into debate, whether it were possible for us to bring together such a force, as without much hazard might be able to force the enemy from thence, but 'twas carried in the negative.

For

1646.

Consultations about the relief of Itamarika.

For it was alledged, that without manifest danger, not above 200 soldiers could be taken out of the forts of the *Receif*, which number was not sufficient to attack the enemy, who had already entrench'd himself there, with hopes of success: And, considering that these forces must be transported thither by sea, we wanted ships (there being at that time not above two barks at the *Receif*) both to convoy them thither, and to cut off the communication with the continent to the enemy. Besides, that at least fourteen days provisions were required for this expedition, in case the enemy should stand his ground, which at this juncture was not to be done, unless we would leave the magazines of the *Receif* quite empty; there being then no possibility of attempting its relief, the next thing under consideration was, whether the entrenchments on the hill might be defended or not? Against the maintaining of it was objected; that without fresh supplies of provisions this fort could not hold out a week, especially since the enemy, by cutting off the pipes of the spring that furnished them with fresh water, would soon put them under a necessity of coming to surrender; when it was evident, that they might post themselves betwixt the fort of *Orange* and this hill, and consequently prevent their receiving any supplies from thence.

Whether the fort on the hill was to be defended.

Besides that the hill being of a considerable compass, was the more difficult to be mention'd by our forces, the fort itself being irregular, and but slightly fortified on that side, especially where the old church-wall, making up part of the courtain, would not be proof against the enemies cannon, and consequently expose the whole fort, with the garrison, to the mercy of the enemy: So that it being beyond all dispute in the enemies power to cut off all communication with the fort *Orange*, it was unanimously resolved and ordered, to leave the said entrenchments, and to retire with the garrison, and what provisions and ammunition they had, into the fort *Orange*, before their retreat was stopt by the enemies troops; it being past all doubt, that in case they could maintain themselves in that fort, they could at all times, if they were masters of the field, recover the hill and the whole island.

The council were the more forward in coming to this resolution, because they had received certain information, that the enemy, who knew the importance of the fort *Orange*, had gain'd some of the gunners and volunteers of the fort by presents, who had engaged to assign them a place where it was easiest to be attack'd, whereabouts they were to charge the cannon with gunpowder only, to facilitate their attack: Two of the gunners were hang'd the 23d of *June* for this treachery, the rest made their escape to the enemy. For the better preservation therefore of this fort, our people left the entrenchments upon the hill the 21st of *June*, where the enemy posted a strong body of their troops immediately after. The council likewise ordered the yacht the *Heemstede*, to cruise in conjunction with the *Golden Doe*, before the north entrance of the island, to keep open free communication for us with our garrison, and to prevent the enemy from receiving any succours that way; and at the same time some provisions were sent thither for the use of the garrison.

Some gunners turn'd traitors.

1646.

Were hanged.

But whilst things were thus transacting with various fortune, tho' for the most part to our disadvantage, and the so long expected succours from *Holland* not arriving, the want of necessaries encreased more and more every day in the *Receif*, to such a degree, that whatever was found fit for sustenance, either in the publick magazines, or with private persons, was apply'd to the common use; which however amounting to no more than one pound of bread a week for each single person, many died for hunger; their legs beginning to swell first, which was the forerunner of certain death: Cats and dogs, of which we had great quantities, were look'd upon as dainties at that time; and you might see the Negroes digging the half-rotten bones of dead horses out of the ground, and to gnaw them with incredible eagerness; neither was the want of fresh water less insupportable, by reason of the heat of the climate, and the constant use of salt meats, all springs that were dug being brackish. The poor slaves, who had the least share of what was left, look'd so gashly and wild with their eyes and jaws sunk, as appear'd terrible to the most undaunted of men. At last (notwithstanding all the care taken by the council) things came to that pass, that the allowance of one pound of bread *per* week was fain to be taken away from the inhabitants, and allotted the soldiers; who, by the enticements of the *Portuguese* beginning to desert apace, had two pound of bread allow'd them, as long as there was any left; but when all was spent, and no remedy was to be found against this lingring evil, it was proposed by the council, and unanimously resolved, rather to die bravely than to starve, and to fight their way through the enemy. The soldiers were to lead the van, the women, children, sick, and other unable people to keep in the middle, and the members of the great council, with the inhabitants to defend the rear: The *Jews* were

Great famine in the Receif.

1646. were above all the rest in a desperate condition, and therefore resolved rather to die with sword in hand than be burnt alive, which is their doom in *Portugal*.

But when we were just reduced to the last gasp, all horses, cats, dogs, and rats being consumed, and a few quarterns of *Farinha* sold at the rate of betwixt 80 or 90 gilders *per* quartern, which however could not suffice for above two days longer, on the 22[d] of *June*, (a day never to be forgotten) we saw two vessels with *Dutch* colours making all the sail they could towards the *Receif:* They had no sooner cast there anchors, and giving us the signal by the discharge of three guns each, that they came from *Holland*; but you might have read in all our faces the sudden joy we conceived at this relief in our last extremity: There was no body that could stand upon his legs for want of bread, but did crawl to the harbour, where you might hear the cries of the people weeping for joy at a great distance. These two ships, call'd the *Falcon* and *Elizabeth*, were freighted for the chamber of *Amsterdam*, and had left the *Texel* the 26th of *April*; they brought us the welcome news, that we might hourly expect the whole convoy. The captain of the *Elizabeth* told me himself, that having a very fair wind one day, he said to his crew, *I am sure they are in great extremity at the* Receif, *God send us fair wind and weather to relieve them in time*, which happened thus accordingly. The captains were each presented with a golden medal, with the following inscription; *The Falcon and Elizabeth did relieve the* Relief.

The Receif *releived.*

The 23[d] of *June*, Mr. *Bas*, a member of the council was sent to *Itamarika*, to assist in the defence of the fort; by his letters of the 28th he advised, that the enemy continued still in his post on the hill, and that he had sent abroad some spies to get intelligence. The 7th of *July*, the said Mr. *Bas* return'd to the *Receif* with the companies commanded by captain *Blewcock* and *Cunrad Held*, leaving the two companies of *Reinard Sikkema* and *Dignus Bysterman* there in garrison. The enemy had some days before, after having blown up the fort on the hill, and set fire to their camp, left the island, carrying along with them all the cannon, and among them two brass ones. For when they saw that we were reinforced with several ships from *Holland*, they did not think fit to abide there till we should stop their passage back by our vessels; neither were they insensible, that without being masters of the fort *Orange*, they could not promise themselves the possession of the island, the south entrance being commanded by the said fort, and the north passage by our yachts. 1646.

Mr. Bas *sent to* Itamarika.

The Portuguese *leave* Itamarika.

The 29th of *June*, the council received advice from our head quarter at the house of *John Lestan*, in *Rio Grande*, that two sons of king *John Duwy*, with 23 *Tapoyers*, were sent thither by their father, to assure our people of his good inclination and service; but they refused to come into the fort *Keulen*, before they had spoken with *Rudolph Baro*, who had been sent for upon that account. About this time several merchants set out some privateers, but as this could not be done without great charge, and there were but few ships at sea of the *Portuguese*, this turn'd to no great account, and consequently continued not long. A very odd accident happened to me much at the same time: For some of the labourers, who were employed to unload a vessel belonging to the company, were got so drunk, that they had kill'd a man, and hurt several others, by letting a pipe of wine fall upon them: I went thither to prevent any further disorder, but was no sooner entred the ship, when on a sudden I found the silver galoons upon my coat turn black, and myself bereaved of my sight, which however I recovered by degrees in a few days after, the cause of which I attributed to the strong exhalations of the wine, that had been closed up for a considerable time before. Much about the same time a difference arose betwixt the officers of the army and the city militia, about the chief command of the head guard in the *Receif*, which the city officers laid claim to.

An accident happens to the author.

But to return to our so long expected succours.

The reiterated letters from the council of the *Dutch Brasil* to the states general, and the directors of our company, wherein they presented their dangerous condition to them, had had such an influence upon the first, that they advised the directors of the company, to send us a reinforcement of 5 or 6000 men, and a good fleet; for which purpose they sent them 25 companies of their regular troops, and gave leave for the raising as many more, as in all mounted to 4000 land soldiers, besides seamen and volunteers.

This fleet consisting of a good number of brave ships, was ready to set sail in *November* 1645, but by reason of a sudden and hard frost, were detained in the road of *Ulyssingen*, till *February* 1646. One Mr. *Bankert*, admiral of *Zealand*, had the chief command of this fleet, and at the same time the following five gentlemen, who were appointed members of the great council of the *Dutch Brasil*, and were to relieve the old ones, were sent to their stations there; to

A fleet equipt in Holland *for the relief of* Brasil.

1646. to wit *Walter Schonenburgh* president, *Michael Van Goch* Pensionary of *Vlyssingen*, *Simon Van Beaumont* fiscal of the city of *Dort*, *Henry Hacks*, and Mr. *Trowens*, two great merchants of *Amsterdam*, and Mr. *Heremite* a lawyer of *Dort*, their secretary. One *Sigismund Shoppe*, formerly under count *Maurice*, and who had commanded the land forces of *DutchBrasil*, was now sent in the quality of commander in chief of these forces; he was a most experienced captain, and who always kept a strict discipline among the soldiers.

Never did any fleet sent from *Holland* to *Brasil* meet with so many unfortunate accidents as this, during the six months they were at sea. For within two days after they had left the *Dutch* coast, they were forced to cast anchor in the *Downs* opposite to *Newport*, where they lost two of their ships by stress of weather. After a stay of three days, the winds being somewhat allayed, the squadron under Mr. *Van Goch* set sail again, but was two days after again forced into *St. Helens* in the isle of *Wight*: Three days before their arrival a rich *Dutch* ship, valued at two millions of livres, then lately come from *Brasil*, was lost among the rocks, so that of 300 persons, no more than 30 were saved. Here they were detained by foul weather and contrary winds seven weeks, when another *Dutch* ship coming from *Brasil*, chanced to cast anchor near them, and told them, that their countreymen in the *Receif* were drove to the last extremity; nay, that perhaps the place was surrendered by this time, they having no more than two months provisions left at the time of his departure. Hereupon it was resolved to continue their voyage with the whole fleet, notwithstanding the winds were against them; but on the coast near *Portland* were again overtaken by a violent storm, in which they saw a *Scotch* ship with 200 persons in her perish. The fleet under Mr. *Van Goch* came with much ado to an anchor behind a rock, where they staid till the fierceness of the tempest being allayed, they prosecuted their voyage. But scarce were they got through the channel, just as they were entring the *Spanish* sea, but a difference arose betwixt Mr. *Van Goch* and Mr. *Beaumont* about the flag, the *Zelanders* (in a council of war held for that purpose) allotting the precedency to Mr. *Van Goch*; whereas the *Hollanders* pretended the same to belong to Mr. *Beaumont*; but Mr. *Van Goch* persisting notwithstanding to claim the precedency, Mr. *Beaumont* gave a signal to the *Holland* ships to follow him, and so bid adieu to Mr. *Van Goch*, who after a troublesome and tedious voyage, in which he lost many of his men by sickness, and especially by the scurvy, he arrived the 14th of *July* with his ship in the road of the *Receif*, being the first of the five new lords of the council that arrived in the *Dutch Brasil*. The 31st of *July* 1646, the ship the *Bluecock*, and the *Vlyssingen* of *Zealand*, came likewise to an anchor there; in the first came Mr. *Trowens*, and in the last colonel *Sigismund Shoppe*. 1646.

Some ships arrive from Holland, *at the* Receif.

The 6th of *August* the said colonel gave an account to the members of the council, how pursuant to their orders, he was advanced with 450 men as far as the fort of *Olinda*, to discover the countenance of the enemy, and to take some prisoners; that they had made a shew of attacking us, but after some slight skirmishes retired, and with a body of their troops marched thro' *Bracer de St. Jago*, to cut off our retreat; but our people forced them to retreat again with the loss of several of their men killed and wounded; whereas we had but one wounded during the whole action, besides colonel *Shoppe* himself, who received a slight hurt on his leg.

The 8th of *August* the *Arms of Dort*, and in it Mr. *Beaumont*, arrived before the *Receif*, he was conducted the next day with all imaginable respect to the *Receif*.

The 12th late in the evening Mr. *Walter Schonenbergh*, president of the new council, and *Henry Hacks*, arrived in a bark from the north in the *Receif*, where they were received by all the citizens and soldiers in arms; they had been forced to leave their ship called the *Middleburgh*, before the north entrance of *Itamarika*, as likewise the *Dolphin*, loaden with provisions on account of the chamber of *Zealand*, both which were seen the 30th of *July* off of *Olinda*, but being forced back by contrary winds, the last of these two did not come to an anchor near the *Receif* till the 13th of *August*.

More ships arrive from Holland.

The same day a certain negro deserter coming to the *Receif*, brought information that the enemy intended to erect a fort on the pass of the *Baretta*, to prevent our excursions into the open countrey; whereupon it was resolved, with unanimous consent of Mr. *Schonenbergh* and the whole council, as likewise with the approbation of colonel *Shoppe* and admiral *Lichthart*, to prevent the enemies design by fortifying and maintaining the said pass, as being the only inlett we had left for the recovery of the whole *Dutch Brasil*, all the other passes being so strongly fortified by the enemy, as not to be attempted without great hazard.

Accordingly the said colonel *Shoppe* marched the same night with all the forces he could bring together, ordering the boats laden with materials for the intended fortifications, to follow him the next tide.

Colonel Shoppe *marches to the* Baretta.

1646. The colonel at his arrival having soon chased the enemy from thence, and possessed himself of the house of the *Baretta*, sent for immediate orders the council, to know whether he should continue in that post all night; who, with the approbation of the new president *Schonenbergh*, dispatcht Mr. *Bullestrate* thither immediately to take a view of it, and to make his report accordingly; he returned the 14th against night, and reported to the council, that he had found the work there very far advanced already, and the fortifications in such a state, that they would soon be in a posture of defence against any attempts from the enemy.

The 13th of *August Rudolph Baro*, who, as we told you, was sent with some presents to *John Duwy* king of the *Tapoyers*, brought a letter from the said king dated the first of *July*, to the council, wherein he thanked them for their presents, and desired they would be pleased to send him some iron weapons, he being then in war with the *Pojuku*'s, and that after he had humbled them, he would march with all his forces against the *Portuguese*.

By this time the president *Walter Schonenbergh*, and the other members of the new great council being arrived at the *Receif*, and having delivered their commissions from their high and mightinesses the states-general, his highness the prince of *Orange*, and the council of XIX. constituting them joint governours of the *Dutch Brasil*, the late members of the said council, to wit, *Henry Hamel*, *Bullestrate*, and *Peter Bas*, ordered all the colleges and other persons of note to be called together, to be present at the installment of the future lords of the council.

Accordingly all the members of the court of justice, and of the finances, next the magistrates and commissaries of *Maurice's town*, then the ministers and church council, together with the sea and land officers, the heads of the *Jews*, and last of all the factors and book-keepers of the company, being assembled, Mr. *Walbeck* told them in the name of the council, that Mr. *Henry Hamel*, Mr. *Bullestrate*, and *Peter Bas*, had called them together, to lay down in their presence the reins of the government, and to surrender the same to Mr. *Schonenburgh* and the rest of the lords appointed by their high and mightinesses, by his highness the prince of *Orange*, and the council of XIX. for the supreme management of the government of the *Dutch Brasil*; returning them their hearty thanks for the services each in his respective station had done to the government, and for their constant fidelity during these intestine commotions, exhorting them to persevere in the same obedience to the new council; whereupon the new president and other members, having received the congratulations, first of the old council, and then of the other colleges, they from thence forward transacted every thing by their own authority, tho' they in all affairs of moment took the advice of the said members of the old council, during their stay in *Brasil*; for which purpose they desired them the 20th of *August*, to appear every day at eight a-clock at their assembly, and to assist them with their counsel for the better management of the affairs of the company. The 19th of *August* Mr. *Trowens* died late at night.

The members of the old council surrender the government.

The 3d of *September* was appointed for a general muster of all the forces in garrison in the forts near the *Receif*. Mr. *Heck* and commissary *Zweers*, were ordered to take a review of those in the fort *Ernestus*, *Wardenburgh* and *Boavista*. Mr. *Beaumont* and *Moucheron* in the fort of *Anthony Vaez* and *Maurice's Town*, Mr. *Van Goch*, *Hamel*, and *Alrich* at the *Receif*, and of those belonging to the artillery. Mr, *Raetsfield* and *Crowvanger* at the *Baretta* and adjacent quarters. Mr. *Volbergin* and commissary *Stricht* in the forts *William* and *Frederick Henry*. Mr. *Bullestrate* and *de Witt* in the fort *Bruin* and the land and sea fort.

A general review.

The 4th of *September*, a pardon being agreed upon by joint consent of the old and new council, the same was the 6th day sent by a drummer to the enemy, with a letter to the *Portuguese* commanders from the *Bahia*, desiring them to withdraw their forces.

The 10th of *September* being appointed for a review of the militia of the *Receif* and *Maurice's Town*, the same was found to consist of 700 men; they received the thanks of the old council for their faithful services during the present intestine war, and then returned their thanks to them for their prudent management of the government.

The 13th of *September* the letters written by the *Portuguese* colonel the 11th of *September*, in answer to ours of the 6th, were read in the great council, filled with untruths and fictions of their own invention. They pretended that they were prevented by the inhabitants from retiring to the *Bahia*, besides that they wanted transport vessels, their ships being detained in the bay of *Tamandare*, and that they must expect the king's orders for that purpose.

They took also a great deal of pains to magnify their strength. The 12th and 13th of *September* several letters were dispersed abroad by the *Portuguese*, directed to justice *Daems*, to *Matthew Bek*, *Balthasar de Fonseca*, *Duarte Sarayva*, *Caspar Francis da Costa*,

1646. *sta*, being all merchants, and written by *John Fernand Vieira*; in which they again exaggerated their own number, and spoke very despisably of ours, threatening, that in case they should be forced to quit the countrey, they would destroy all with fire and sword, as they had already done in some parts of *Parayba*. The contents of these letters were as follows.

A letter from Vieira *to some merchants in the* Dutch-Brasil.

Experience has without question convinced you sufficiently of the reasons that moved us to undertake this war, and the success we have met with is an ample testimony that God was pleased to inflict this punishment upon our enemies, for the many outrages committed against the inhabitants of this countrey. This is however in a great measure to be attributed to the general consent of the said inhabitants, who having now forced themselves from the tyrannical yoke of their oppressors, ought to expect from me, who, tho' unworthy, am appointed the chief manager of this war, to be back'd in so brave a resolution. I would not have you be ignorant of our strength, which, in comparison of yours, exceeds all that can be said upon that head; I will only tell you that as by our quitting the captainships of Parayba *and* Goyana, *we are considerably encreased in number, so it is most evident from thence, that the inhabitants chose rather to lose their possessions, than to endure any longer the indignities that were put upon them, which was the true cause of their insurrection, and not (as it is given out among you) because they were unable to satisfy their creditors; because they left more than what would have paid their debts. But if it should happen so, that the said inhabitants should not be able to maintain themselves by force of arms, they are resolved to lay all the other captainships desolate in the same manner.*

Having therefore well weighed the reasons which seem to promise us a good issue of this war, I thought myself obliged as a friend, to advise you that that party is back'd by reason and the unanimous resolution of many thousands; for, I can assure you, we are at least 14000 strong besides the negroes and Tapoyers, *dispersed in several places from* Rio Grande *as far as* Rio St. Francisco. Kamaron *commands 600 musqueteers,* Henry Dias *800 negroes, 200* Minos *and 700* Tapoyers; *and those of the* Sertan *are at our devotion, whenever we are pleased to call for them; but above all the rest we have God on our side. We are not ignorant, that before the arrival of Mr.* Sigismund Shoppe *your whole force consisted not in above 600 men, and that the succours come along with him do not amount to above 1200 more, most of which are boys, and the rest either dead or sick. You see I am well acquainted with your strength, having kill'd and taken prisoners about 2600 of your best soldiers, and 500* Brasilians, *besides the wounded that were carried to the* Receif; *when our troops had no other arms than pointed sticks and clubs. These are blessings from heaven, for if we were able to perform these things without powder and ball, what may not be expected from our forces, now they are strengthened with good troops, and provided with sufficient arms and ammunition? All which I confirm to you upon my word, to be nothing but the real truth, and had it not been in respect of those colonels sent from the* Bahia, *and of his majesty of* Portugal, *I had by this time been master of the* Receif, *or some of the forts, or at least I might have done much greater mischeif:* But if matters are not brought to a happy conclusion, I am resolved to act like a desperate man, and not to leave any sugar-mills, cattle or negroes in the countrey, but will rather turn all to ruin and destruction, before we will be compelled to submit again to your obedience. 1645.

As these presents may serve as a warning to you, so, I hope you, and the rest of the merchants will not delay to enter with us into such articles of agreement, as may be most conducing to the preservation of your Possessions; for I would have you call to mind that there are many Ingenios (mills) *reduced at present to such a state, as not to be likely to be in a condition to be used these ten years next to come. The* Vargea *is in no better condition than* Parayba *and* Goyana, *and the cattle (without which the mills cannot subsist) destroy'd in most places.*

Colonel Sigismund Shoppe, *I suppose, pretends to keep the field against us, as he did in the last war, but he will find himself egregiously mistaken, because the inhabitants will not be of his side, for if I should hear of one that was, I would cause him to be hanged immediately. You alledge that we are vassals of the company, but when was ever any conquered nation treated thus as we were, worse than the vilest slaves, of which you are sensible as well as we; so that being forced to break our chains, we don't owe you any further obedience. If we had not been in hopes of this opportunity, we would long before have implored the assistance of the king of* Spain *or* France; *and if those had fail'd us, to have had recourse to the* Turks *and* Moors. *I desire you not to throw away this letter, because experience will convince you of the truth of it; and that we shall pursue the same methods here, as we have done in other places; wherefore I would have you not give credit to any body, except to those that come in person from those places; I having told them nothing but the bare truth, which you*

1646. *you will find in effect thus: In the prosecution of this war, I hope you will consider, what is most for your interest, in which I am ready to serve you; for tho' your governors don't direct their letters to me, 'tis I that have the chief management of this war, and under my command the power of the colonels came from the* Bahia, *extending no further, than over those troops they have brought along with them.* A Reyal de bon Jesus September 11 1646.

On the 10th of this Month, the before-mentioned colonels having sent an answer to a letter directed to them from your council, by one of our captains; several ensnaring questions were ask'd him concerning the present war, which he perhaps not answering according to their expectation, they replied more like drunken cowards than soldiers; if they will be pleased to come out and tell me these things, I will try whether their swords are as nimble as their tongues are, and teach them what respect is due to the messengers of those persons who have the supreme command here.' This I write to you at present, but shall not fail in due time to make my words good by the sword, of which your people feel the daily effects as often as they dare to come out of their forts. Pray be not deceived, for Brasil *is not allotted to you; not questioning but that God will bless our arms, and if we happen to die, we shall lose our lives in the defence of our holy religion and liberty; and all those that have refused to accept of our offers, will pay for it with the loss of their lives, possessions and debts.*

A Reyal, Sept. 12, 1646.

Signed,

John Fernand Vieira.

The 14th of *September* a man of war, call'd the *Ter Veer*, equipped by the chamber of *Zealand*, (aboard of which was colonel *Hinderson*) arrived before the *Receif*, after a voyage of 14 weeks. The 24th of *September* the enemy caused some pamphlets to be dispersed, promising in very haughty terms a general pardon, and a composition of their debts, in case we would leave the island. The 27th of *September* colonel *Shoppe* returned with some troops from *Goyana*, by the way of *Itamarika*; I had not met with any enemy, but had found all the sugar-mills burnt in the first place, but the sugar-reed and farinha fields in a pretty good condition; we received afterwards further information, that the sugar-mills of *Goyana*, were not quite burnt down. The 27th of *October* a conference was held betwixt the old council and Mr. *Van Goch*, unto whom they imparted their advice concerning several matters relating to the state of the *Dutch-Brasil*, and especially to the planting of the *mandioka* or *farinha* roots,

Colonel Shoppe *returns from* Goyana.

A conference betwixt the old council and Mr. Goch.

and the killing of cattle, which they advised to be done with great circumspection, *Brasil* being not able to subsist without a considerable number of oxen, which were continually employed in carrying of sugar-reeds, wood and other necessaries to the mills. 1646.

For the planting of *farinha* roots they proposed *Itamarika*, *Rio Grande* and *Parayba*, which countries were thought sufficient to supply their present occasions; provided it were done before the season was elapsed.

In the mean while colonel *Shoppe* having made several, but for the most part, unsuccessful attempts upon the enemy; our forces were thereby so diminished, that we were not in condition to made head against the *Portuguese* near the *Receif*; which made our council take a resolution to endeavour the recovery of *Rio St. Francisco*, the execution of which being committed to the management of colonel *Hinderson*, proved more fortunate for us, he meeting with little resistance thereabouts.

The Dutch *attempt the recovery of* Rio St. Francisco.

Accordingly the 24th of *October* the following ships; count *Eano* admiral, *Loanda* vice-admiral, the *Arms of Dort* rear-admiral, the *Bluecock*, the *Watchful-Dog*, the *Greyhound*, *Eagle*, the *Star*, *Heemstede* and the *Flight*, with eight barks, set sail under the command of admiral *Lichthart*, and colonel *Hinderson* to the south. The 17th of *November* the council received advice, that our troops under colonel *Hinderson* were safely landed at *Korasippa*, and marching from thence to *Rio St. Francisco* and the fort *St. Maurice* had met with no opposition from the enemy, who had begun to raise the said fort. That they had been seconded by the small vessels, which had followed them up the river, which our forces had passed, and were marched to *Seregippe del Rey*, having left some behind to repair the fort; and that four *Portuguese* had requested their pardon, which was promised them. Whilst our forces were employed thereabouts, I was ordered thither to take care of the necessary provisions (of which there was great plenty) for our troops; having accordingly caused my cargo to be embarked aboard a ship call'd the *Brownfish*, *Francis Frantz* master.

Mr. Nieuhoff *ordered thither.*

I set sail the 24th of *November*. We were carried with a brisk gale as far as the mountains call'd by our people the *Saddlehills* from their shape, the coast all thereabouts being white sand downs. About half an hour after sun-set we saw our selves off of the Bay of *Tamandare*, and from thence continued our course with a fair wind, which in two days after brought us happily to the entrance of that great river, which is

1646. is so broad at the beginning that a six-pounder can scarce reach cross it; it falls with a very soft current into the sea, its waters being low in the winter, but encrease in the summer; perhaps by reason of the snows that are melted by the heat of the sun. About 50 leagues from its mouth is a great cataract or water-fall, surrounded by a great many islands; the sea at its entrance meeting in tempestuous weather with the current, are so boistrous, that they strike terror into the stoutest mariners, and carry away great pieces of the continent along with them. We entered the said river, but were forced to cast anchor immediately after sun-set, for want of an east wind to carry us higher up, which commonly begins to blow thereabouts at three in the morning. The countrey appeared very pleasant on both sides, and we saw abundance of wild beasts near the river-side, and several huts made of straw. We were detained near 24 hours upon a sand-bank, which after we had passed, we came at last to the village called *Penedos*, situate upon a high hill; here we landed with our boats, and found a few houses which were rebuilt by our people, the rest being burnt by the enemy before their flight. In the fort was formerly (in the time of the *Portuguese*) a church, which we turn'd into a magazine; it was surrounded with a goodly wall, the river passing by it on the north-side, where the hill is very steep.

Admiral Lichthart *dies.*

The 30th of *November* admiral *Lichthart* was seized with a sudden and violent illness, occasion'd by his drinking too much cold water, after he had over-heated himself before; he was carried into a boat with three soldiers under the command of an officer, lower down the river, but soon after lost his senses, and in my presence expired. The next day his corps being put in a coffin was carried aboard the *Golden-Star*, being conducted by the chief officers there present, and four companies of soldiers to the river-side, who gave three salvo's with their musquets, as did the cannon from the fort and ships, in order to his interment at the *Receif*.

Mr. Nieuhoff *in danger of being drowned.*

Towards evening as I was going aboard our ship the boat overturned by the swiftness of the current, and had I not been a good swimmer, I had infallibly been drowned; the master threw out a great cable over-board, by the help of which, and God's mercy I got safely into the ship. The soldiers in the mean while scower'd the countrey, and brought 700 oxen, (of which there was great plenty) and 300 calves into our quarters, having been at pasture in one of the adjacent Islands of the river, under the guard of some soldiers; they were not extraordinary fat, but tolerable good meat.

A fire in the soldiers quarters.

The soldiers huts were for the most part planted on the north-side of the hill, which being composed of branches and leaves of trees took fire accidentally the 3d of *December*, with such fury, that in a quarter of an hour the whole quarter was in a flame, notwithstanding that the alarum was given immediately, by the beating of drums and the sounding of trumpets; some soldiers that were then swimming in the river, lost all their cloaths by this accident. It was well it happened by day; for if it had been in the night it would have put us under a great consternation, it being generally reported, that it had been done by treachery. 1646.

There was at that time a plentiful crop of tobacco upon the circumjacent fields, but was not quite fit for reaping, which must be done at a certain season, before the low grounds overflow'd. The colonel desired me to provide those who had lost all, with new cloaths, and to deduct it out of their pay; but I told him, that I being only a factor, could not do it without special order from the council, some having but little pay due to them. The 25th of *December* we received intelligence that the enemy began to appear in a considerable body, whereupon the companies of captain *Cousin*, *Schut*, *Gyseling*, *la Montayne*, and of a *Brasilian* captain, call'd *Tomee*, were sent in quest of them, with orders to set their stables on fire, and bring the cattle to our quarters. The next following *Monday* word was brought us, that our troops were so narrowly enclosed by the enemy, that it was feared scarce one of them would escape with life. Whilst we were in a great consternation, not knowing what resolution to take, a *Brasilian* brought us the unwelcome news, that our whole body was routed and dispersed, and captain *Schut*, *Cousin* and *La Montayne*, kill'd upon the spot. He had scarce finish'd his doleful relation before a *German* soldier, who had escaped the fight, by his bleeding wounds and his words gave us a confirmation of what had been told us before, with this addition, that captain *Gyseling*'s lieutenant, *La Montayne*'s ensign, and one *Kilmet*, belonging to captain *Schut*, had fought their way through the enemy, with about 30 soldiers, and would soon be here. This mishap was chiefly attributed to the fool-hardiness of our troops, who contrary to colonel *Hinderson*'s command, having at once discharged all their musquets against the enemy, fell in pell-mell, without any regular order, with sword in hand upon the enemy, which the enemy perceiving, retreated back and drew them into an ambush. Towards night we saw several soldiers miserably wounded with darts come to our quarters, some who had

1646.

The Dutch *defeated in* Rio St. Francisco.

thrown away their arms, were forced to cast lots for their lives, the misfortune of which fell upon a *Dutchman* and a *Brasilian*, who being tied to a stake to be shot to death, were however pardon'd by the colonel. Captain *Gyseling*'s lieutenant, who came without his arms to the fort, was sent immediately to the *Receif*, where his sword was broke over his head, and he declared incapable of serving the company for the future, notwithstanding he had done them faithful service for seven years last past.

By this time I was sent for to the *Receif*, so that after having taken my leave of the colonel and Mr. *Dames*, I embarked on board the *Bat* the 16th of *December*, and we were the same evening with a fair wind and stream carried to the mouth of the river. It being a fine moon-light night we catch'd abundance of *Zaggers* as we call them, a fish of a very good taste, and continued our course with a brisk gale: Not far from the rivers mouth we met with four of our ships, who told us they were to fetch provisions, but in case they could not, were to return forthwith to the *Receif*. The 18th we advanced but little, the ships being not out of sight of us, near the rivers mouth, but did catch more fish than we were able to eat. The 20th we were likewise becalmed, and we perceived the moon to be half eclipsed for the space of two hours. The next following day we sailed so near to *St. Antonio*, that we could see them walking along the sea-shore. Towards night we discovered *Porto Calvo*, about 30 leagues from *Rio St. Francisco*. We were often becalmed, but catched abundance of *King's-fish* and *Codds*, and saw fires in many places along the coast. The 24th of *December* we came so near to the cape of *St. Austin* that we discovered five ships and seven row-barges in the harbour; we might have reached some of those that went ashore with our shot, had it not been for the sand-bank which hindred our nearer approach. About noon we came before the *Receif*, but it was so foggy that we could scarce discover the water fort, nevertheless we ventured in, and I got ashore immediately, with an intention to give an account of the state of affairs in *Rio St. Francisco* to Mr. *Schonenburgh*, being conducted thither by colonel *Shoppe*, who happened to meet me immediately after my landing.

Mr. Nieuhoff*'s return to the* Receif.

The enemy lay an ambush.

The 27th of *October* the enemy had laid two ambushes in the way to the fort *Prince William*, beyond the redoubt *Kiik*. They did not stir till towards noon, when perceiving a company of our soldiers marching along the dike, they fired so briskly upon them, that they killed 11, wounded 12, and took three prisoners; yet notwithout the loss of some on their side.

1646.

The Tapoyers *leave our party.*

In the mean while the *Tapoyers* being much exasperated at the murder of the before-mentioned *Jacob Rabbi* their commander, had left our party; the council did what they could to appease them, imprisoned and banished *Garsman* the author of it, and confiscated his estate, notwithstanding which, the *Tapoyers* could not be prevailed upou to join with us as before.

Debate concerning an enterprise against the enemy.

The 18th of *November* Mr. *Van Goch* entred into a conference with the members of the old council, whether it might not be feasible to embark what forces we were able to spare on board our great ships, and to attempt to make a powerful diversion to the enemy by attacking them in some place or other. But those of the old council having represented to him the danger of this enterprize if it should miscarry, whilst they were blockt up in the *Receif*, the further debate thereof was deferred till the next day. It was then proposed, upon second thoughts, that in case we could bring all our forces together, something of moment might be undertaken without manifest hazard, whereby to oblige the enemy to withdraw his forces from the *Receif*; but Mr. *Van Goch* apprehending no small danger in case we miscarried, they came to no resolution for that time.

Another about refusing of quarter.

It being found by experience that all our promises of pardon had proved ineffectual, it was proposed by Mr. *Van Goch* the first of *December*, whether it were not most expedient to give no quarter for the future; unto which it was answered, that very seldom quarter had been given by us, and few prisoners were taken, and that the enemy had likewise killed most of our people that were fallen into their hands, but they judged it not convenient to refuse quarter to all without distinction, which would induce such of the inhabitants as had remained quiet hitherto, to betake themselves likewise to their arms.

The 23d of *November* we laid an ambush for the enemy near the fort of *Affagados*, who being by some few sent out for that purpose, engaged in a skirmish, and pursuing our men with great eagerness under the cannon of the fort, were set upon by those lying in ambush, who killed and wounded many of them.

The 12th of *December* the corps of the late admiral *Lichthart* was interr'd, one company of the city militia, and two of soldiers appearing in arms upon that occasion, gave him three salvoes with their musquets.

News from Rio St. Francisco.

The 30th of *December* the *Eagle* yacht brought letters to the council, dated in *Rio St. Francisco* the 4th of *December*, intimating, that in an island a little above the fort

1646. fort, one colonel *Rebellia* was arrived with 200 men from the *Bahia*; and that they expected another reinforcement; as well from thence as from the *Vargea*; that our people being sent higher up the river, had attackt some of the enemies troops; but they made their escape to the other side, leaving their arms and clothes behind them.

1647. The 2[d] of *January* 1647, colonel *Shoppe* who had been with 300 fusileers in *Goiana*, returned to the *Receif*, giving an account that he had taken a view of all the rivers thereabouts, but met with noenemy.

Shoppe returns from Goiana. The 5th of *January* the council received an account of the beforementioned action in *Rio St. Francisco, viz.* Five companies of our forces being sent to *Orambou*, to beat up the enemies quarters; they met with a body of 100 men; whom they attackt and put to flight; but soon after our forces were attackt by a much stronger body; who put them to the rout, with the loss of 150 men; of our officers one captain was killed; and five taken prisoners, *viz.* captain *Samuel Lambart*, *La Montagne*, *Gerrit Schut*; *Kilian Taylor*, *Daniel Koin*, and three lieutenants, *Joost Koyman*, *Anthony Baliart*, *Jeronymus Hellemen*, and one ensign.

Consultations concerning the state of Parayba. The 8th of *January* Mr. *Van Goch*, in the name of the new council, advised with those of the old, that it being resolved among them to send for a considerable number of their forces out of *Parayba*, in order to gather a body of troops for some important design, they desired to be informed concerning the present condition of the said captainship; and whether the city of *Parayba* and *St. Andrew* might be defended by a small garrison; whereupon those of the old council replied, that the town of *Fredericia* had no fresh water but what they must fetch at a miles distance, and consequently might be cut off by the enemy; the same thing might be done at the passage leading to the river-side; besides, that there was no fortifications belonging to the place but the monastery; which was of no great consequence, and the *Guarte Domaiges* church, which had been fortified by the enemy in this war. As to *St. Andrew* it was no more than a sugar-mill about four hours distant from the city of *Parayba*, situate upon the bank of the river; that the communication of this place with the fort of *St. Margaret* might easily be cut off by the enemy, as being likewise about four leagues from thence, but it might be relieved from the water-side, and yet not without great difficulty. Mr. *Van Goch* told them he would make his report thereof to the council.

The 12th of *January* the council received advice, that the enemy were with a strong body of troops entred *Parayba*, and advancing very near to the sugar-mill of *St. Andrews*, had in the night time surprised some *Dutch* and *Brasilians*, to the number of 50 men; women and children, of which they had killed some; and ript up the womens bellies. 1647.

The 13th of *January* some pamphlets were again dispersed by the enemy, containing in substance, that since the inhabitants of the *Receif* were now beyond all hopes of further relief, it would be their surest way to come to an accommodation; for they resolved to venture all before they would lay aside their design; but if all failed they would destroy the whole countrey, and so leave it: They exhorted them not to be deceived by the insinuations of those who belonged to the company, and called them rebels; they being no more to be stiled so than the *Dutch* themselves, who had asserted their liberty against *Spain*.

The 17th of *January* four negroes belonging to one *Isaac de Rassier*, who had been taken prisoners some days before in *Parayba*, came over to us into the *Receif*, and brought advice, that the enemy, after having tarried but a little time in that captainship, where they had killed five *Dutch* men and some *Brasilians*, were retired from thence. *Advice from* Parayba.

The 22[d] of *January* early in the morning, the enemy began to batter the wooden fort near the *Baretta*, from a battery on the bank of the south side of the river which he continued the whole day; but desisted at night; the garrison having been reinforced about noon with five companies of soldiers, and some provisions; because Mr. *Hamel*, one of the members of the old council, did represent to Mr. *Van Goch*, that tho' the fort itself was so inconsiderable, as scarce to be worth the trouble of defending it by a good garrison, yet at this juncture, when the enemy had made his first attempt upon it, it would not be adviseable to desert it, for fear of giving encouragement to the enemy to attack the other forts; but that on the contrary, as long as they did meet with a brave resistance here, they would not be so forward to attempt others; especially since we had the conveniency of relieving them with boats at high-water, with low-tide by land by the way of the sandridge; and that we might annoy the enemy with the cannon from our yachts in his trenches, as we had done that day. About the same time a map was ordered to be made, shewing the true situation of the *Receif*, with the turnings and windings of the adjacent rivers and marshes, as far as the *Baretta*, for the better instruction of the council. *The wooden fort battered.*

The 24th of *January* in the morning, news was brought that the enemy had raised the siege *Raise the siege.*

1647. siege of the fort of the *Baretta* the night before, and carried off all their cannon, being sensible that as long as they could be annoyed from the sea-side, and we be able to reinforce them daily with fresh troops, they could promise themselves but slender success: But besides that our people were to struggle against the enemy and famine, they were frequently troubled with desertions, many of our soldiers, nay even to the sergeants and other officers, who begun to despair of our ease, running over to the enemy, even at that time when the before-mentioned ships the *Faulcon* and *Elizabeth* were in sight of the *Receif*.

Now the members of the old council began to prepare in good earnest for their return to *Holland*, they had already in *December* 1646, sollicited Mr. *Schonenburgh* president of the new council, to order some ships to be got ready to transport them thither, and the *Vlyssingen* had been appointed for that purpose; but the same being not as yet returned from crusing, they applied themselves the 25th of *January* 1647, to Mr. *Van Goch*, and told him, that whereas according to their commission, one of them should return after the expiration of three years, they had continued in *Brasil* these six years, Mr. *Kodde* having indeed been ordered to return about that time, but his place not being supplied by another, he died before his departure: That they had for these three years last past, sollicited their return, and had two years ago received promises of being relieved by others; which had not been performed till within these few months, to the great prejudice of themselves and their families: Mr. *Van Goch* promised them to take effectual care to have the ships got ready, and to send for the ship the *Vlyssingen*, in order to their return home. At the time of the accession of the new council to the government, and the departure of *Henry Hamel*, *Adrian Bullestrate*, and *Peter Bas*, late members of the great council, the following forts remained still in the possession of our *West-India* company.

The members of the old council sollicit their return.

A catalogue of the forts in the hands of the Dutch.

The fort *Keulen* at the mouth of *Rio Grande*, provided with 28 brass and one iron cannon.

The redoubt of *St. Antonio*, on the north-side of the river of *Parayba*, with six iron pieces of cannon.

The fort *Restangues* in an island of the same name within the river *Parayba*, with four brass and five iron pieces of cannon.

The fort *Margaret* on the south side of the river *Parayba*, with 14 brass and 24 iron pieces of cannon.

The fort *Orange* in the isle of *Itamarika*, with 6 brass and 7 iron pieces of cannon.

Nossa Senhora de Conceptiano, an old battery upon the hill of *Itamarika*, with two brass and eight iron pieces of cannon. 1647.

The redoubt called *Madame de Bruin*, three iron pieces of cannon.

The fort *Wardenburgh*, alias the *Triangular Fort*, betwixt the *Bruin* and the *Receif*; the first provided with four brass and five iron pieces of cannon; the last with 14 brass guns.

The *Land Fort*, alias *St. John*'s, with 11 iron guns.

The *Water Fort*, at the mouth of the river of the *Receif*, with seven brass guns.

The fort *Ernestus*, with 5 brass and 3 iron pieces of cannon, and the battery with five brass and two iron pieces of cannon.

The *Receif*.

Maurice's Town upon the island of *Anthony Vaez*.

The fort *Frederick Henry*, alias the *Quinquangular Fort*.

The redoubt of stone near this fort.

The redoubt *Kiik*, betwixt the fort *Frederick Henry* and the fort *Prince William*.

The fort *Prince William* upon the river *Affagados*.

The forts then in possession of the *Portuguese*, and taken by them from the *Dutch*, are these;

Forts in the hands of the Portuguese.

Seregippo del Rey, *Rio St. Francisco*, and *Porto Calvo*, being reduced by famine, were rased by the *Portuguese*, being sensible that our people could not maintain themselves there without erecting of new ones, which was not to be done without a vast charge. Near the point of *Tamandare*, the place where the *Portuguese* from the *Bahia* first of all landed their men; and where afterwards their fleet was beaten by ours, the enemy laid the foundation of a fort for the security of that harbour, where ships of great burden might safely ride at anchor.

A conference about Rio. St. Francisco.

The 23d of *January*, Mr. *Beaumont* was sent by the new council to confer with the late members concerning the present condition of *Rio St. Francisco*, and what was best to be done there: They answered him as before, that the fort as it was now, could do but little service, and that therefore it would be worth our consideration, whether the proposals made by them in writing, might not now be put in practice. The said Mr. *Beaumont* further proposed, whether it would not be requisite to erect an earthen redoubt for the defence of the *Baretta*; unto which those of the old council replied, that considering the vast charge and the small benefit which could be expected from it, the same might be more conveniently built in some place or other, to facilitate our passage into the open countrey. *Beaumont* was of opinion, that thereby

And the Baretta.

1647. by the enemy would be prevented from advancing to the fort *Frederick Henry*; but the old members told him, that notwithstanding we had now a fort on the *Baretta*, we could not hinder the enemies coming upon that island near the fort, unless we would keep a considerable force there for that purpose; that we need not fear their transporting any cannon thither, because their retreat might be cut off at high tide; neither could they from thence do any mischief to the *Receif*, it being evident, that the shot of our biggest cannon in the fort *Frederick William* could not reach the said island. The same evening Mr. *Van Goch* and *Hack*, came to tell the members of the old council, that the *Hollandia* and *Ulyssingen* would be ready in a little time, in order to conduct them to *Holland*, the *Ulyssingen* being ordered forthwith to return from the *Bahia*, whither she was sent a cruizing.

The Receif *closely blockt up.* By this time the enemy had block'd us up so closely in the *Receif*, that on the land side we durst scarce look without the gates; and a certain *Portuguese* had prepared us a worse entertainment, having invited all our chief commanders abroad to his daughters wedding, during which time the enemy were to have surprized the city; but this design being timely discovered by some *Portuguese* and *Jews*, miscarried.

The Portuguese *rebuild a fort.* About the 15th of *October*, the *Portuguese* began to rebuild the fort *Bon Jesus*, as it is call'd by them, but by us *Altena*, on the other side of the river. We had some notice of it by deserters, but could not discover the truth of it, because they kept us from advancing that way by their cannon, and the place was surrounded on all sides with woods; but as soon as they had caused them to be cut down, we discovered it both by sight and the roaring of their cannon, which thundring incessantly against the city, caused such a consternation, as is not easy to be express'd, most people sheltring themselves in vaults, to avoid the fury of the enemies cannon. Of this I saw *A miserable spectacle.* a most miserable spectacle in a certain young lady, a niece of the late admiral *Lichthart*, who being come to visit one of her acquaintance, lately married, had both her legs shot off by a cannon bullet, which at the same time kill'd the new married woman upon the spot. At the outcry of these miserable wretches, I ran thither instantly, my house being just by, where I was an eye-witness of their misery, the poor young lady grasping my legs with such an agony, that she could scarce be pull'd off with all the strength I had; it being a most doleful spectacle for me to see the floor covered with the legs and arms of these miserable wretches; the poor young lady died likewise within three days after. It was not long after that I narrowly escap'd the same misfortune; for whilst I was talking with some of the inhabitants of the city, as I was going the rounds, two of them were kill'd by a cannon bullet, and another had both his hands shot off as he was lighting his pipe. Nay we were forced to remove all the ships out of the harbour for fear of being sunk. Colonel *Shoppe*, in the mean while, had made himself master of and destroyed *Taperika*, 2000 *Portuguese* only having saved themselves by flight; but by the many unsuccessful encounters we had with the *Portuguese*, our forces decreasing daily, whereas theirs encreased, colonel *Shoppe* was ordered to command colonel *Hinderson* to leave *Rio St. Francisco*, and to join him in *Taperika*; but this stood us but in little stead, being not long after obliged to leave likewise *Taperika* for the relief of the *Receif*. All our force consisting of about 1800 men, being now come to the *Receif*, (where they had not provisions for above seven months left) it was several times taken into consideration, what was best to be done at this juncture. Colonel *Shoppe*, with some other officers, were of opinion not to hazard an engagement, our forces being so much inferior to the enemy, but to stay for a more favourable opportunity; but it was carried by the majority to venture a general salley for the relief of the *Receif*, the chief command thereof being given to colonel *Brink*, because colonel *Shoppe* was not as yet cured of his wounds he had received in a late encounter. *A general salley made by the* Dutch. Our forces marched towards evening as far as *Guerapes*, a place fatal to us the year before by the defeat of our people, the fields thereabouts being as yet covered with their bones. The *Portuguese* no sooner perceived us to be upon the march, but they left the fort *Altena*, of which we having got notice, possess'd ourselves of it immediately, and thus drew the thorn out of our foot. But the 16th of *May* prov'd the most fatal of all we had seen for many years before in *Brasil*. For though our forces attack'd the enemy with bravery, and maintained the fight with great obstinacy for some time, yet the enemy, flush'd with their number and late success, with 2500 of their best men, at last forced our men to give way, and afterwards to fly, being pursued by 150 *Portuguese* horse; so that both in the fight and flight, we lost above 1100 men, among whom were colonel *Brink*, and *Are routed.* almost all the rest of our commanders: We lost also 19 colours, and all our cannon and ammunition we had carried along with us. It was not till five days after before leave could be obtained to bury our dead, which

1647. which began to corrupt and ſtink moſt nauſeouſly, by reaſon of the burning heat of the ſun. This was the laſt effort we were likely to make in the field; all our future care being for the preſervation and defence of the *Receif*, unleſs we ſhould be ſupplied with freſh ſuccours from *Holland*; but the ſame arriving but ſlowly, moſt people began to fear, that in caſe God Almighty did not ſend us ſome unexpected relief, we ſhould be at laſt forced to leave that place likewiſe to the mercy of the enemy: The great council laying the fault of our late misfortunes upon the council of war, and theſe again upon them, alledging, that the ſoldiers were ill provided for, and wanted their pay. As for myſelf, being ſenſible that things would be worſe and worſe every day, I thought it the ſafeſt way for me alſo, to deſire a paſſport for my return to *Holland*, which at laſt, with much ado I obtained, and ſo prepared every thing for my voyage. But before I leave *Braſil*, I ought to give you a ſhort account of the products of the ſaid country. 1647.

The captainſhip of *Pernambuko* and *Braſil* in general, being not only well ſtored with cattle, but alſo with ſeveral ſorts of herbs, trees and fruits, we will give you a ſhort view of them, and begin with the *Mandiiba*, and its root, call'd *Mandioka*, unto which the *Braſilians* ſtand chiefly in- Mandioka root.

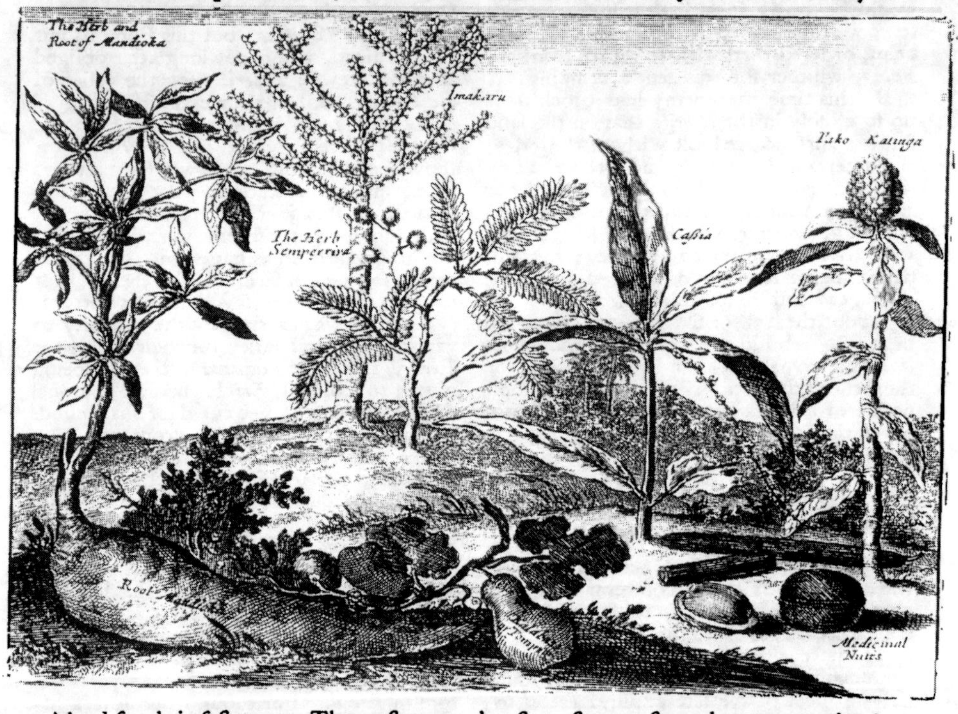

debted for their ſuſtenance. The moſt parts of *America* are ignorant hitherto of wheat or any other grain, inſtead of which nature has furniſhed them with a certain ſhrub, the root of which dried and powdered, and afterwards boil'd and bak'd as we do our bread, is the common food of the inhabitants of *America*. This ſhrub grows in vaſt plenty every where, being by the *Braſilians* called *Maniiba* and *Mandiiba*, and its root *Mandioka*. There are divers kinds of it, diſtinguiſhed by the *Braſilians* by different names, but the root is in general called *Mandioka*. Their leaves are ſmall, green and long, pointed at the end, which grow upon large ſtalks or branches, each of which has five, ſix, or ſeven leaves, growing in a cluſter, reſembling a ſtar, call'd by the *Braſilians Manikoba*. The ſtock or ſtem is diſtinguiſhed by certain knots, not above an inch thick, but generally ſix, ſometimes ſeven foot high, from whence ſprout forth ſeveral branches, which producing again leſſer ſtalks, bear the before-mentioned leaves: It bears a ſmall flower of a pale yellow colour, and of five leaves only, with ſmall ſtalks within, which at laſt turn to ſeed. The root *Mandioka* reſembles our parſnip in ſhape, being two or three foot long, and about a man's arm thick, but grows thinner towards the bottom. Its outward rind reſembles that of a haſel-tree, but

1647. but its substance is white, affording a milky sharp juice, which is pernicious to beasts. This shrub grows in dry, barren and sandy ground, its nature being so averse to moisture, that they are obliged to plant it only in the summer months, where it is most exposed to the sun. For this purpose it is, that the inhabitants cut down the woods on the hills and in the plains, which they burn, and so prepare the ground for the production of this root: These fields are by the *Brasilians* called *Ko*, by the *Portuguese Roza*, or *Chokas*, and by our people *Rossen*. These fields are turn'd up into small round hills like mole-hills; the *Portuguese* call them *Montes de Terra Cavada*, or *Hollowed Hills*; the *Brasilians Kujo*. These hills they make about two foot and a half asunder, each being about three foot in circumference, and half a foot high, that the rain-water may be carried off with the more ease. In each of these hills they commonly plant three small taks of this shrub, of about nine, ten inches, or a foot long, without leaves, notwithstanding which they grow and soon bear fresh leaves, and in time produce new roots, which cannot be transplanted, because no sooner are they taken out of the ground, but they begin to putrify and stink. After these taks have been about ten days in the ground, they begin to bud and produce as many fresh taks as they have knots; each of these taks is about a finger long, from whence sprout forth many lesser ones of a purple colour. The fields must be three or four times a year cleared of the weeds, which grow in great plenty amongst it, and choak it up before it comes to its full growth. The small taks and leaves of these shrubs are mightily infested by the *Pismires*, and likewise coveted by the wild-goats, oxen, horses and sheep, for which reason they are very careful to fence these plantations with stalks and branches of trees: The bees, coneys, and some other *Brasilian* creatures are mighty fond of the root, which takes no harm, tho' the shrub be stript of all the leaves, provided the root itself be not touch'd. This root does not come to its full perfection till a year after the planting of the taks, tho' in case of necessity they may be drawn in six months, but afford but little *Farinha*. Each shrub produces two, three, four, nay sometimes twenty roots, according to the goodness of the ground, and after they are come to full maturity, will keep two or three years under ground; but it is much more safe to take them up at the years end, for else many of them will rot; nay, if the season happens to prove very wet, they must of necessity be drawn tho' they are but half ripe. The root, after it is taken out of the ground, will not keep above three days, but stinks, take what care you can; for which reason they seldom draw more at a time than they can make immediately into *Farinha* or meal. That kind of *Mandioka*, commonly called *Mandibuka*, grows faster and ripens sooner than any other, and affords the best *Farinha*; it thrives best in sandy and hot grounds. But that kind which is most generally used is called *Mandiikparata*, and grows indifferently in all grounds. The *Farinha* is prepared thus: The root after it is taken out of the ground is purged from its outward rind by a knife, and wash'd in fair water: Then the end of the root is held close to a wheel of about four or five foot diameter, which being covered round the edges with a copper or tin plate full of sharp small holes, not unlike a nutmeg-grater, and the wheel being turn'd round continually, grates the said root into small particles, which fall into a trough underneath. The wheel is by the *Brasilians* called *Ibecem Babaca*, and by the *Portuguese Roda de Farinha*, or the flower wheel; the trough the *Brasilians* call *Mukaba*, and the *Portuguese Kothe de rater Mandiboka*. But the poorer sort are fain to be contented with a hand-grater, called *Tapiti*. The root thus grated is put into a bag, made of the rinds of trees, about four inches wide, called by the *Portuguese Espremendouro de Mandiboka*. This bag with the root is put into a press, and all the juice prest out, (it having a venomous quality) which is by the *Brasilians* called *Maipoera*, or *Munipuera*, and by the *Portuguese Agoa de Mandioka*, i. e. *The water of Mandioka*. The next thing to be done is to beat the root through a sieve, called by the *Brasilians Urupema*; and then to lay it upon a copper plate, or earthen pan, over the fire, and to stir it continually with a wooden spoon or spattle till it be quite dry. This pan or vessel the *Brasilians* call *Vimovipaba*, and the slice *Vipucuitaba*. The *Farinha*, before it is quite dry, is called by the *Brasilians Vitinga*, and by the *Portuguese Farinha Relada*; but when it is compleatly dried and fit for keeping, the *Brasilians* call it *Viata* or *Viccia*, and the *Portuguese Farinha Seca*, or dry meal; or *Farinha de Guerra*, war-meal, because it is most used in time of war. For the more it is dried the better it keeps, but never keeps good above a year, the least moisture being apt to taint it; which is the reason, that both the *Portuguese* and we, in imitation of the *Brasilians*, bake biskets of it upon a grate iron, with hot coals underneath, for the magazines. 1647.

How the Farinha *is prepared.*

The juice *Manipuera*, which is press'd out

1647. out of the root *Mandioka*, put into a vessel, gets in two hours time a white settlement at the bottom, call'd by the *Brasilians Tipioja*, *Tipiaka*, and *Tipiabika*: This dried, affords a very white meal, called *Tipiocui*; which bak'd into cakes as before, call'd by them *Tipiacika*, taste as well as wheaten bread. This juice is also boil'd to pap, and eaten, and serves likewise instead of starch or paste. The *Portuguese* take this pap, mix it with sugar, rice, and orange flower-water, which they make into a conserve of a delicious taste; they call it *Marmelada de Mandihoka*. The juice *Mandigo* or *Manipuera*, is of a sweetish taste, which is the reason the beasts covet it, but commonly die soon after they have drunk of it, it being pernicious, nay mortal, both to man and beast. If the juice be kept twice 24 hours it produces worms, called by the *Brasilians Tapucu*; yet it has been found by experience, that this juice loses its pernicious quality after it has stood 24 hours, there being many of *Brasilians* who boil and drink it without any harm. The root *Mandioka* is likewise immediately after it is taken out of the ground, sliced in pieces, and laid in fresh water for four or five days, when it begins to be soft, it is called *Puba*, or *Mandiopuba* and *Mandiopubo*. This the wild *Brasilians*, inhabiting the deserts and woods, roast in the ashes and eat; because it is done without much trouble. The same *Mandiopuba*, toasted before the fire, is called *Kaarima*, which being afterwards beat to powder with a wooden pestel in a mortar, they call *Kaarimaciu*; of this they make a pap with boiling water, which seasoned with some *Brasilian* pepper, or *Nhambi* flowers, affords a very good dish, especially with the addition of some fish or meat, when it is called *Minguipitinga* by the *Brasilians*, who look upon it as one of their best dainties. It is also very wholsome, for this *Kaarima*, and the flower *Tipiaka*, boil'd in orange-flower-water, and sugar, to the consistency of a syrup, affords a very good antidote. They make also a kind of starch of the flower called *Kaarima*, which they call *Minguapomonga*; as likewise very fine cakes, by mixing it with water, butter, and sugar. There is a kind of meal prepared from the dregs of the *Mandioka*, or *Mandiopubo* root, thus steept in water, call'd by the *Brasilians Vipuba*; and *Viabiruru*, and by the *Portuguese Farinha Fresca*, or fresh flower, and *Farinha d'Agoa*, or water flower. It is very well tasted; but will not keep above 24 hours. But if you make it up with water into balls or rolls, and let them dry in the sun, they will keep good for a considerable time: These they call *Viapua* and *Miapetika*. The *Tapoyers*, and almost all the other *Brasilians* prepare it thus, and afterwards mix it with another meal, called *Viata*; which affords it a more agreeable taste. 1647.

The *Mandioka* root is likewise prepared thus: After it has been cleansed and cut in thin slices, they beat it with a wooden pestel, and squeeze the juice of it out with their hands only, which being dried, they call *Tina* and *Mixakuruba*; another way of preparing the *Mandioka* root is, to cut it into pieces, of about two fingers long, and two inches thick, which without being squeezed, is exposed to the sun, and afterwards beat to powder in a wooden mortar, call'd by the *Brasilians Tipirati*, by the *Portuguese Farinha de Mandioka crua*, or the flower of raw *Mandioka*: The pieces before they are beaten to powder are very white, and may be used instead of chalk. Out of this flower they make very good white bread and biskets, call'd *Miapeta*, the last of which are chiefly used in the camp, because they will keep a great while.

Out of the root *Aipimakaxera*, the *Brasilians* boil a certain pleasant liquor not unlike our whey, call'd by them *Kavimakaxera*. The same root, chaw'd and mixed with water, furnishes them with another liquor they call *Kaon Karazu*. The cakes made from the flower of this root, laid in a cask with water, till it ferments together, affords them likewise a sort of strong and very good beer.

All these different kinds of *Mandioka* roots, if they be eaten fresh prove mortal to mankind, except that call'd *Aipiamakaxera*, which roasted, may be eaten without danger, and is of a good taste. But all sorts of beasts, both wild and tame ones, don't only feed upon the said roots and leaves, without the least hurt, but also grow fat with them, notwithstanding that the juice of both is mortiferous as well to men as beasts. The Negroes and *Brasilians* bruise the leaves of the *Mandiiba* in a wooden mortar, which being boil'd, they put oil or butter over it, and eat it like as we do our spinage; this is sometimes done by the *Portuguese*, likewise and the *Dutch*, who make a kind of sallet of the same leaves. The *Brasilians* prefer the bread made of the *Mandioka* root before ours, but it is not so natural to the *Europeans*, it being, if used in a great quantity, pernicious to the nerves and stomach, and corrupts the blood. About three bushels of this meal, (at the rate of two gilders *per* bushel) will suffice a strong labouring man for a whole month, and a piece of ground planted with this root, produces four times the quantity, as if it had been sown with wheat. There is a certain kind of *Mandioka* root call'd *Pitinga*,

1647. *tinga* by the *Brasilians*, the flower of which cleanses and heals old ulcers. This root is likewise found in the isle of *St. Thomas*, and in those of *Hispaniola*, *Cuba*, and others thereabouts, and in most parts of the continent of *America*; the inhabitants of which call it *Yuka* and *Kassave*, and those of *Mexico Quauhkamoth*, and the bread which is made of the flower, *Kazabis*, *Kazabi*, or *Kakavi*. The *Mandioka* root is originally the natural product of *Brasil*, and from thence transplanted into other parts of *America* and *Africk*. Its flower furnishes all the inhabitants of *Brasil*, as well the *Portuguese* and *Dutch*, as the natives and negroes with bread, which next to wheat is the best of all, so that our soldiers would rather chuse to have their allowance in *Farinha*, than wheaten bread out of the magazines. Since the war in 1645, the price of the *Farinha* was risen to three or four gilders *per* bushel, which, as it tended to the utter destruction of the sugar-mills, so by special orders from the great council of the *Dutch Brasil*, all the inhabitants of the open country were enjoined, under a severe penalty, to plant a certain quantity of *Mandioka* yearly, in proportion to their abilities, by which means the price of the *Farinha* was so considerably abated, that three bushels were sold for two shillings ready money, at the *Receif*, and for less in the country.

Kaaeo *or* Herba viva.

Brasil produces a certain herb call'd *Kaaeo* by the *Brasilians*, by the *Europeans* in Latin, *Herba viva*, because it seems to shrink when you touch it, and so it does likewise about sun-set; its seed has been transmitted into *Europe*, where it grows to its full perfection.

Kalabasses.

The *Kalabasses* are a kind of pompions, their rind, if dried, being so thick and strong, as to serve for materials for cups, porringers, and such like utensils. But what is most surprizing is, that they always grow of a different shape, some being long, others round, others oval, some thick before, others at the end. They blossom and bear fruit once a month, the blossom being yellow, mix'd with green; the pulp is white at first, but turns to a violet colour; they are of a tolerable pleasant taste, but very unwholesome, by reason they are too astringent.

The tree Imaraku.

The tree call'd *Imaraku* by the *Brasilians*, is of a middle size, its trunk round, and its bark grey, covered with small thistles of the same colour. Its branches sprout forth on the top, with broad leaves of an oval figure, edged likewise with small thistles or thorns. There is also another kind of *Imaraku*, much larger than the former, call'd *Kakabu* by the *Brasilians*, and *Kardon* by the *Portuguese*. This sprouts forth first of all in the form of a large octangular leaf, upon which grow crosswise many thorns; this produces other leaves of the same kind, each being three, nay sometimes six foot long, and of the thickness of a man's arm. By degrees the first leaf turns into a woody substance, of a greenish colour, but somewhat spungy; those leaves that grow next to this stem are instead of branches, which produce other leaves. The stem bears only one large white flower, the fruit of which is of an oval figure, and of about twice the bigness of a hens-egg, of a dark brown colour, and fit for use. This tree grows to a great height. There is also another kind of *Imaraku*, being altogether the same with the former in respect of its largeness, blossom and fruit, except that its leaves are of a triangular figure. 1647.

Pako Kaatinga.

What the *Brasilians* call *Pako Kaatinga*, the *Portuguese* commonly call *Canodo Mato*, or wild reed or canes. The stem or stalk is like that of other canes, about an inch thick, containing a white marrow or pith, of a sweetish taste, on which grow leaves of eight or nine inches long, and three inches broad, shaped like a tongue, smooth and pale green on one, and covered with a white woolly substance on the other side. The fruit of which is not unlike a pine-apple, about ten inches long, growing on the top of the stem; it is divided into several partitions, which opening by degrees, a pale grey flower appears betwixt each, containing underneath twenty or more grains of a black shining seed. The stalk chew'd draws the rheum from the head, and breaks the stone in the bladder. It is look'd upon as an excellent remedy against the involuntary emission of the seed throughout *Brasil*, and cures it in eight days time.

The tree and fruit Kasjou.

All over *Brasil*, but especially in the isle of *Itamarika*, grows a certain tree call'd *Kasjui* or *Kasjou*, bearing a fruit of the same name. Its leaves are dark green, broad and round, interspersed with many small veins. It bears two different blossoms and fruits. The white blossom which appears in the lower branches, produces a juicy spungy fruit like an apple, of a very cooling and astringent quality: But the red blossom on the top a kind of chesnut. The *Brasilians* draw no small advantage from this tree; out of the apples they make a very good cyder, call'd by them *Kasjouwy*, which is sourish, but if mix'd with sugar, makes it as pleasant as *Rhenish* wine, and has this excellency, that tho' it soon seizes the head, yet it passes off without any harm. The other fruit they eat like as we do our chesnuts.

Among the products of the *West* and *East*-

1647. *East-Indies* is a tree call'd *Papay*, by the *Javaneses* and *Dutch*, and *Pinoguacu* or *Mamoeira* by the *Americans*; and sometimes intitled with the name of the *Melontree* by our people, by reason of the resemblance of its fruit to our melons. This tree is of two different kinds, to wit, the male and female. It grows and perishes again in a short time; its trunk being so spungy that it may be cut as easy as a cabbage stalk; the leaves it bears are very large and broad, not unlike our vine leaves, growing on long stalks round the top of the tree, and covering the fruit, which hangs in a knot, and is green at the first, but turns yellow at last, resembling in shape a pear, but of the bigness of our small melons, unto which its pulp resembles both in colour and taste, when come to maturity, but whilst they are green, they are boil'd with meat, and give it a tart taste.

Pinoguacu or Papay.

Chili Lada or Brasil *pepper*.

The red pepper, known by the name of *Brasil pepper*, and call'd *Chili Lada* by the *Brasilians*, grows on knotty stalks of about five or six foot high; the rind being a dark green, distinguished with white rings, from whence shoot forth small crooked branches of a hands breadth in length, bearing a small white flower, which produces a green husk, and turns red by degrees as it ripens, with a certain seed within it, being as hot and biting upon the tongue as the common brown pepper, and so does the husk. In the *East-Indies* they preserve it, and call it *Aetzar*, and use it raw in their fish sauces. In *Brasil* they cut two or three of these husks whilst they are green in slices, and mix them with oil and vinegar, or some limon juice, to acuate their appetite, but it is too hot for those that are not used to it, which is allayed by a good quantity of salt. This kind of pepper grows likewise in the *East-Indies*, in the island of *Java*, in *Bengala*, and several other places. I have seen it also in some of our gardens in *Holland*. There is another shrub which grows frequently in the *East-Indies*, not unlike this in shape and bigness, which bears a yellow flower; it is call'd *Halika Kabus* by the *Arabians* or *Alkekengi*, and sufficiently known in these parts. The flower produces a small bladder which contains the fruit and seed, they are not so big as ours. The *Indians* and *Chinese* mix it with a certain fruit call'd by them *Poma d'Oro*, *Tamatas* by the *Portuguese*, and *Melansana* by the *Italians*; they also eat it with *Chili Lada* or *Brasilian* pepper. The *Portuguese* cut the *Poma d'Oro* and the husk of the *Brasilian* pepper in thin slices, which being mix'd with oil and vinegar, they eat as a sallat, and look upon it as a proper remedy to cut the rough flegm of the stomach, a distemper very common in those parts. The *Brasilians*, as well as the *Dutch*, chaw this pepper for the same purpose, but it is very burning upon the tongue. 1647.

The sugar canes or reeds, call'd by the *Brasilians Viba*, are the product both of the *West* and *East-Indies*, but grow in great plenty throughout all *Brasil*, but especially in the captainship of *Pernambuko*. They are of two different kinds, one bearing small, the other larger leaves. The last, which is accounted the best, sprouts up into a long stem of the thickness of a child's arm, the leaves growing all on the top in a cluster, being of an oval figure, and a dark blue colour. The rind is distinguished by certain joints or knots; the other kind bears small leaves from the top to the bottom. The sugar-canes are propagated from their small sprouts, which being put in the ground like our vines, grow up to the height of twelve foot, if they are planted in good soil, and are kept free from weeds. Six months after they have been planted, a brown seed appears on the top, then it is fit to be cut; for if they stand longer in the ground their juice diminishes, dries up, and turns sour. The juice, if taken immediately after it is drawn, causes a looseness. The low grounds are much more convenient for the planting of sugar-reeds than the hills, especially near the river side, where the banks are often over-flown by the stream. There are a certain kind of winged worms, call'd *Guirapeakoka* by the *Brasilians*, and *Pao de Galinha* by the *Portuguese*, which are great enemies to the sugar-canes, especially in moist grounds, where they gnaw and consume the roots. The sugar, which is the product of these canes, is not procured without a great deal of toil and labour, in which for the most part are employed slaves, under the tuition of certain overseers, appointed by the masters of the sugar-mills, who were for the most part *Portuguese*, the *Dutch* being hitherto not arrived to the utmost perfection in that art. In the captainship of *Pernambuko*, many fine *Ingenho*'s or sugar-mills, with their adjacent plantations were erected for this purpose, amounting in all to above 100 in number, and the labourers, negroes, and other *African* slaves thereunto belonging, to near 40000. The whole yearly product of sugar of the *Dutch Brasil*, is computed to be betwixt 200000 and 250000 chests.

Sugar-canes or reeds.

In the year 1642, one *Gillin Vonant* brought some indigo seed from the *American* islands into *Brasil*, who having certain lands assigned him near the small river *Mercera*, and being provided with all other conveniencies by the special command of the

Indigo.

Sugar reeds
Sugar reeds
Pagaven
Indigo
Brasil Pepper
Fruit of Palalas

1647. the great council, erected several plantations for the producing of *Aniel* or *Indigo:* But it being found by experience, that the pismires consumed most of the leaves, the said Mr. *Venant*, by employing many labourers and negroes, to destroy these pismires with burning and digging, at last so well cleared the ground, that the *Indigo* came to its full perfection, several patterns of which were sent into *Holland*. Mr. *Venant* having made an agreement with Mr. *Christopher Eyershettel* to instruct him in the most necessary points relating to the coagulating the indigo, he was treating with the great council concerning certain grounds for the planting of indigo, so that there was a fair prospect of bringing this design to a considerable perfection here, if the same had not been prevented by the intestine war.

The wild *Aniel*, which grows in *Brasil* in great plenty, has a great resemblance to the true indigo in outward appearance, but affords no good colours. Some pretend to have seen also a kind of wild cochenille in *Brasil*, and the ground would produce good store of cotton, but that the inhabitants draw much more profit from the sugar-plantations.

Drugs. Some ginger is likewise planted in *Brasil*, but not in such quantities as to be transported into other parts, no more than the *Mechoaconna*, *China* and some other medicinal roots; and the *Herba de Cubra* or *Herba de Nossa Senhora*, which is look'd upon as an infallible remedy against the gravel; and the root called *Paquoquanha*, which is the universal medicine of the *Brasilians*. There are also many transplanted hither from other parts, as ginger, tobacco, rice, cotton, turkey-wheat, *Aniel*, or indigo, and the sugar-reeds were first of all transported by the *Portuguese* from the *Canary Islands*. The fruits in daily use among the inhabitants, are *Ananas*, *Bananas*, *Mangaba*, *Akaju*, *Arakou* great and small, *Guajaba*, divers kinds of *Murukuja*, *Ibapiranga*, *Mazaxanduba*, *Akaja*, *Araliku*, *Guitakori*, *Biringela*, *Mamaon*, *Coco-nuts*, and several sorts of *Indian* figs. The roots chiefly in use, are the *Batatas*, *Nhambi* and *Umbi*, and the *Indian* acorns, call'd *Tembi*, which are of a delicious taste.

Fertility of Brasil. The whole country of *Brasil* is extremely fertile and pleasant, being watered by many rivers and standing waters, most of which arise from the hills, and pass through spacious plains, the last of which are clayey and marshy grounds, (call'd *Vargea*'s by the *Portuguese*) which produce all sorts of fruit: but especially sugar-canes in great plenty. Their meadows and pasture grounds do not appear so pleasant in the summer as in the rainy season, when they are very green; wheat and rye grow soon rank here, which is occasion'd partly by the nature of the soil, partly by the heat of the sun; to prevent which they never let their grounds lie fallow, and manure them with sand instead of dung. The same must be observed with all other foreign seeds here, that require to be kept a considerable time under ground. In *February* and *March* (which is the rainy and winter-season of this climate) they sow their seeds, and that towards evening, not by day time, or about midnight. They take great care not to plant any thing too deep under ground; for whatever is planted beyond the sun-beams, seldom produces any fruit, which our people have learned to their cost. There is a remarkable difference betwixt the seeds and fruits which are produced on the hills, and those of the marshy grounds, as to their time of ripening; tho' the coco and palm-trees are transplanted here without the least regard to their age, bigness, or the season, and grow very well. Most of their own trees and shrubs bear flowers and fruits throughout the whole year, so that at one and the same time, you enjoy the benefit of the spring, summer and winter; the like is observable in the vines, citron, limon, and other trees, brought by the *Portuguese* from *Angola* into *Brasil*, and in several roots pot-herbs, and other fruits, transplanted thither by the *Dutch*. Those who covet ripe-grapes throughout the whole year, do only prune their vines at divers times, which produce a fine grape, and a wine as sweet as molosses. The worst is, that they are much infested by the pismires, which suck all the juice, and leave nothing but the husks to the owners; several other sorts of trees have been transplanted thither from *Holland*, which thrive extremely, and bear very good fruit.

The standing waters of *Brasil* are for the most part covered on the surface with green shrubs and herbs, that they appear rather like land than water, and feed both land and water fowl. At the entrance of most of their rivers, (where you meet with vast quantities of oisters and crabs) the countrey is so overstock'd with a certain kind of a tree call'd *Guaparaba* or *Mangle* by the *Brasilians*, that they render it impassable for travellers. In short, the whole *Brasil* is well stored with trees, shrubs and useful woods, there being scarce a place, either in the vallies or rising grounds, which are clayey, or among the hills, which don't produce something that is useful, and that in such plenty, that the *Portuguese* after their first arrival here, were forced to cut their way through these trees with incredi-

ble

1647. ble pains and charge. The hills furnish also great store of wood, which is of a very good scent, and is used by dyers; as for instance the *Brasil* wood, which is from hence transported into *Europe*.

Brasil wood.

The stem or trunk of this tree is knotty, of a very agreeable scent, and sometimes two or three fathoms thick: Its leaves are dark-green, and small, thorny at the end, and grow on small stalks; the bark, which is about three inches thick, is generally taken from the trunk, before it is fitted for sale: It sprouts from its own root, and produces neither blossom nor fruit. Most of these trees grow about 10 or 12 leagues from the sea-side, where they cut them down, take off the bark, and carry them upon waggons to the sea-shore, from whence they are transported into *Europe* for the use of the dyers chiefly; the *Brasilians* call this tree for its excellency's sake, *Ibirapitanga*. After the *Dutch* had conquered part of *Brasil*, they found great store of this wood ready cut and fitted for use by the *Portuguese*, who sold it to the *Dutch* company; since which time it was cut down promiscuously by the *Portuguese* as well as the *Dutch*, and such vast quantities of it were transported in 1646, and 1647, that the members of the great council of the *Dutch-Brasil*, Mr. *Henry Hamel*, *Bullestrate* and *Codd*, being made sensible of the destructive methods that were made use of in cutting this wood, which must in time have tended to the utter extirpation of these trees, did by their proclamation regulate these abuses. They have another kind of very fine wood in *Brasil*, called by the *Portuguese*, *Pao Santo*, as likewise those call'd *Gitayba*, *Vio Wood*, *Massaranduba*, cedar, and divers others woods fit for cabinet-work. The tree call'd *Tataiba* by the *Portuguese*, the wood of which the *Portuguese* call *Pao Amaretto*, affords a yellow colour for the Dyers. The bark of the tree *Araiba* is of an ash-colour, but boil'd in water gives a red tincture. The tree *Jakauranda*, or *Jaturiba*, or the white-cedar, as well as several other Trees, furnish the inhabitants with materials for building, being very hard and durable. The *Brasilians* make also matches and a kind of hemp out of the bark of some trees.

The Timbo *or* Tipo.

The most barren places of *Brasil* do produce a certain kind of trees without leaves, which they call *Timbo* or *Tibo*; out of these they make hoops, by reason of their flexibility, and the bark serves the ship-carpenters instead of hemp.

Their fuel.

The *Brasilians* light their fires by striking two pieces of wood, of the trees *Karaguata Guacu* and *Imbaiba* together, as we do with our flint-stones and iron. The first is a tree of an admirable nature: Its stem grows 14 or 15 foot high, which being come to its full perfection, bears yellow flowers on the top, and abundance of large long and thick leaves. Out of the stem they make sticks to hang their mattresses on, the leaves afford the fishermen stuff for yarn to make nets of; and out of the leaves issues a certain unctuous liquor, which serves instead of soap. The trees and woods of *Brasil* are never seen to be covered all over with leaves at a time; but whilst some cast their leaves, you see others bring forth new ones; nay, sometimes one tree is half covered with leaves, and bare on the other side. *Brasil* likewise abounds in shrubs and reeds, some of which creep along the grounds, whilst others twist themselves up to the top of the highest trees, which affords a very agreeable spectacle at a distance, and a pleasing shadow to men and beasts, tired with the heat, hunting, or any other exercise. 1647.

Oranges.

Among other fruits, *Brasil* produces very fine oranges of divers kinds; the other vegetables, which besides the *Mandioka* root, serve for the sustenance of the inhabitants, are rice, millet, *Patatas*, *Ananas*, *Bananas*, melons, pompions, water-melons, cucumbers, beans, figs, *Bakovas*, *Marakuja*, *Mangavas*, *Arataku*, *Ape*, cabbages, radish, lettuce, purslain, parsley, chervel, carrots, &c.

The Akaju.

Nothing is so much in request among the *Brasilians*, as the *Akaju*, a kind of wild apple, which furnishes them both with food and drink, being very juicy; so that this tree seems by kind nature to have been planted here for the peculiar comfort of the inhabitants: It spreads its branches round about in a great compass, but does not grow to that height as many other trees in this countrey: Its wood, which is very solid, is very fit for the building of ships, from whence issues a very clear gum in the summer-season. Its leaves, which are red, resemble those of our walnut-trees, especially when they first sprout forth in the spring, but are of a much finer scent, which they never lose but by being distill'd. The blossom is a flower consisting of five small leaves, which grow to the number of about a hundred in one cluster; each of these flowers has a stalk, with a small head in the middle. At their first coming out, which is in *September*, they are very white, but turn soon after to a rose colour; they are very odoriferous, and fill all the circumjacent grounds with their agreeable smell. This tree bears a double fruit, *viz.* an apple, and a chesnut: The apple is of an oval figure, very juicy; its pulp spungy, full of kernels, and of a tartish taste. The juice taints linen with a

 certain

1674. certain colour, such as we call iron-molds; which is never to be taken out, but returns as often as these trees stand in blossoms; it is of a whitish colour after it is first prest out, and tartish, but changes both its colour and taste by fermentation, and becomes very strong. The rind of the apple, which is very thin, is white mixt with red. The chesnut, which grows on the top of the apple in the shape of a lambs kidney, is covered with a thin skin, over which grows a thick ash-colour'd shell, full of a hot, sharp and burning oil, which bites the tongue; To correct which, they roast the chesnut in the ashes, break the shell with a hammer, and eat the pith or kernel, which tastes better than a common chesnut, and will keep good for several years. The *Brasilians* are so fond of this fruit, that they often fight for it; then they encamp among these trees, and remove not 'till they have consumed all thereabouts, unless they are forced thereunto by the enemy. They number the years of their ages by this tree, because it bears fruit but once a year, which ripens towards the latter end of *December* or in *January*, there being none to be found on the trees after *February* in *Pernambubo*. About the time the sun returns back from the tropick of *Capricorn*, it commonly rains in *Brasil*, which the inhabitants call the *rains of Akaju*, for, if the same happens to be moderate, they promise themselves great plenty of this fruit. The chesnuts are hot in the second degree; if eaten raw with wine and salt, they taste like walnuts, but if roasted or preserved with sugar, they are of a delicious taste. The oil which is taken out of the shell, is an excellent remedy against the hair-worm; it is hot in the third and fourth degree, and frequently applied to cancers and other malignant ulcers. The gum, powdered and taken in a convenient vehicle, opens the obstructions of the womb. The juice of the apple furnishes them with good cyder.

Palm-trees. There are many sorts of palm-trees to be met with in *Brasil*, some of which grow wild, some are planted and cultivated by the inhabitants. Among the first the palm-tree call'd *Pindava* by the *Brasilians*, which grows very tall, claims the preference, of which there are whole woods to be seen in the open Countrey. In the more remote and unfrequented places, grows a certain palm-tree called *Karanatham* and *Anabekairi* by the *Brasilians*, and by an *Arabick* word among the *Portuguese*, *Tamar*, or date, which this fruit resembles. The tree grows as high as a common date-tree, its wood is red and very solid, but of no great use. The bark is grey, which from the ground upwards to a certain part of the tree is distinguish'd by many scales, which are largest at the bottom, and small by degrees, 'till about the middle of the tree they quite disappear; these scales being nothing else but the remnants of the branches, which fall off by degrees, as the tree grows higher; and continue only towards the top, spread round about the stem, like the *African* date-tree, but much finer. Each of these branches is about two or three foot long, flat on two sides, and cover'd with small thorns, they grow to a vast thickness. At the end of each branch grows one single leaf, which is very large and green, pleated like a fan, and about the middle divided into several other leaves, like those of the common date tree; each of these last is about two foot long. Betwixt those branches, on which grow the leaves, spring forth other branches of four or five foot in length, and these again are full of other white sprouts, which bear flowers, with three pale yellow leaves; these produce a fruit of the bigness of an olive, which is green, bitter and not eatable, but turn black when they ripen, which is in *February*. The *Brasilians* call this fruit *Tirade*, and eat it raw; but our people never took any fancy to it. With the leaves they cover their huts, and make baskets of them. The palm-tree call'd *Pindava* by the *Brasilians*, has instead of the bark a white and rough wooden substance. which contains a spungy sulphurous substance, out of which the *Brasilians* prepare a strong lee. This tree is for the rest but of small use, being rather esteemed for ornaments sake, by reason of its height and fine spreading branches, which however furnish the inhabitants with leaves to cover their hutts, and to make baskets of; the *Portuguese* plant them near their walks and arbours, and round their churches. The leaves of this tree do not hang downwards like those of the coco-tree, but stand upright. Just by these leaves sprout forth certain branches, on which hang bunches of flowers, which produce the fruit, resembling in shape and bigness one of our largest hen-eggs, being sharp at the end, and fasten'd to the bunch on the other like the pine-apple. The outside is of a green yellow colour, inclining to a chesnut; being composed of a hairy substance like that of the coco-nuts, but not near so thick, scarce exceeding in thickness two egg-shells. Under this shell is an insipid saffron yellow pulp, which however is used by the negroes, who eat it with *Farinha*. Within this pulp is a hard nut, of an oval figure, not unlike the coco-nut, of the same thickness, but without holes; it contains a pith or kernel, as white and big as a walnut, but is not near so sweet as the coco-nut; they are eaten both by the natives and strangers, who are furnished with

1647. with them throughout the whole year, and call'd by the *Brasilians Inajamira, i. e.* the small coco-nut. The kernels of these nuts furnish them likewise with a white cooling oil, which is used instead of our oil of roses, and when fresh drawn mix'd among their sallets, but when decay'd, in their lamps. The shell affords an oil of the same nature, but not altogether so cooling. Out of the top of the tree flows a fine and odoriferous gum, used here instead of *Gum Arabick*; they also pick a certain pith or marrow out of the top, which has a taste like our walnuts, and when eaten with bread and salt is accounted very nourishing.

Coco-trees. There also grow coco-trees in *Brasil*, call'd by the natives *Inajaguacuiba*, and the fruit *Inajaguacu*. They are very different from the just now mentioned *Pindava* tree, their trunk or stem being seldom straight, but commonly crooked, sometimes from 7 to 14 foot thick, and 50 foot high; it is without branches, having only 15 or 20 leaves round the top, each of 15 foot long. They have also good store of the common date-trees both male and female. The vast quantity of pismires wherewith *Brasil* abounds, are great enemies to all the products of their grounds, which they endeavour to destroy by fire and water; it is farther to be observed, that some fruits as well as creatures, which are accounted venomous in *Europe*, are commonly eaten in *Brasil*, as on the other hand certain things are poisonous there, which are not in *Europe*. For they have a kind of froggs and some fishes which are extremely poisonous; whereas a certain sort of great pismires and adders, toads, worms and wild rats are eaten by the natives, without any harm.

The food of the Brasilians. The most universal food of the *Brasilians*, is the flour made of the *Mandioka* root, called by them *Vi*, and *Farinha de Mandioka* by the *Portuguese*, as has been shewn more at large before. They feed also upon the flesh of several wild beasts and birds, crabs, craw-fishes, fruits, herbage; their meat whether boiled or roasted they eat half raw. They boil in earthen pots called *Kamu*, which they make themselves. Their flesh they roast thus; they dig a hole in the ground, the bottom of which they cover with leaves of trees, and upon them lay the meat to be roasted, which being covered with the same leaves, they throw sand or earth upon them. Upon this they light a good fire, which they continue till they think it sufficiently roasted. If they hit it right it eats very well, exceeding in goodness all other roasted meats, they call it *Biaribi*. Their fishes whether roasted or boiled they eat with *Inquitaya*, that is, salt and pepper. They boil their crabs or craw-fishes without salt, and eat them with *Inquitaya*. Small fishes they wrap in leaves, and roast them in the ashes. They take the flour of the *Mandioka* root with their 3 hindermost fingers of the right hand, and so throw it into the mouth; in the same manner they do with beans and such like things; they eat often both day and night, they having no set times for their meals, without the least noise, or any drink, which they reserve till after they have done. They seldom use any spoons, but instead of that their fingers, or some oyster-shell or other serves their turn. The flesh of several wild beasts is much in esteem among the *Brasilians*; as for instance, that of the greater and lesser wild-boars; they have a bunch like a camel on their backs, and are very good food, as well as the flesh of the river pigs, called *Kapiverres* by the *Portuguese*, which is of a very agreeable taste, 1647.

Their drink. The most general and most wholesome liquor used among the *Brasilians*, is their river or fountain water, which by reason of its coolness is a great refreshment to such as are tired by the heat, or the fatigues of other exercises; this is chiefly to be understood of their spring-water, which, though used here in great quantities, never causes any griping in the guts, or other inconveniencies in the bowels, but on the contrary occasions a good appetite, and is soon evacuated by sweating.

The waters of the rivers *Paray* and *Paratybi*, are accounted a good remedy against the stone and gout, which is the reason that many arrive to the age of above 100 years, who drink nothing but those waters, and are never troubled with any of those distempers; for those who are advanced in age are as nice in the different tastes of those waters, as the *Europeans* in their wines; and they look upon those as indiscreet who use the waters without distinction. For, since most of their springs arise among the high eastern hills, they receive no addition either from the snows or any metallic bodies, and being well digested and purged from their dregs by the heat of the sun-beams, they are very clear and wholsome; tho' it must be confess'd that in the winter months some waters, by reason of the rains, are not fine and cool as during the summer-season. The negroes make sometimes a nasty mixture of black sugar and water only, without the least fermentation, which they call *Garapa*; this as it is very cheap, so both men and women sit at it for 24 hours together, spending their time in drinking, singing and dancing, but seldom quarrel, unless they have conceived some jealousy of one another. Sometimes they add to it some leaves of the *Akaju*-tree, which by rea-

1647. son of their hot quality make it the more heady. The *Portuguese* and *Dutch* frequently made a kind of sorbette of water, sugar and lemons. Others pour water upon certain herbs, others put a lemon only in water. But besides these, the *Brasilians* know how to make wines or cyder out of several roots and fruits, which they drink at their merry meetings; especially of the *Bakovas*, *Ananas*, *Mangaba*, *Janipaba*, *Karaguata*,&c. For tho' the vines here bear grapes 3 times a year, neverthelefs are they not sufficient to furnish them with wine. They make a kind of cyder, called by them *Kooi*, of the apple *Akaju*; these they stamp in a wooden mortar and squeeze the juice out with their hands, which after it is settled they strain; it appears at first like milk, but turns to a pale colour in a few days; its taste is tartish, and apt to seise the head if drunk in any quantity; after some time it turns sour, and makes very good vinegar. The wine or liquor called by the *Brasilians* *Apy*, is made two different ways: First, the slices of the root *Aipimakakara*, a kind of *Mandioka*, are chewed by old women till they are as fluid as a pap, which they call *Karaku*; this they put into a pot, and boil it with a good quantity of water, stirring it continually till they think it fit for expression, which done, they call it *Kaviaraku*, and drink it luke-warm. Or else they take the same root purged and sliced in thin pieces, which they stamp and boil with water as before, which produces a whitish liquor, not unlike our butter-milk or whey; they drink it likewise warm, its taste being agreeable enough; they call it *Kacimakaxera*, tho' both kinds are generally comprehended under the name of *Aipy*. The liquor called *Pakoby* is made out of the fruit of the tree *Pakobete*. What the *Portuguese* call *Vinho da Millo*, is a liquor called *Abaty* by the *Brasilians*, and made of barley or *Turkey* wheat, called *Maiz* by the *Indians*; the liquor *Nandi* has also derived its name from that excellent fruit called *Nana* of *Ananas*, being the strongest of all their wines or cyders. There is another sort of liquor called *Vinho da Batatas* by the *Portuguese* because it is made of the root *Batatas*: The natives call it *Jetici*. Thus the liquors called *Beeutingui* and *Tipiaci* are both made out of the *Farinha* of the *Mandioka* root, *viz.* of the *Beju* and *Tepioja*.

The *Brasilians* are also great admirers of *French* or *Rhenish* brandy, called by them *Kacitata*, and swallow it very greedily as often as they can come at it. They are no less fond of tobacco, the herb of which they call *Petima*, and the leaves *Petimaoba*. After they have dried the leaves in the air, they lay them before the fire, to render them the more fit for cutting. They smoke 1647.
in pipes made of the shell of the nut *Pindoba*, or of the *Urukuruiba*, *Jocara*, *Aqua*, or such like; to wit, they cut a hole in one end of the shell, take out the kernel, and after they have polished them, put a wooden pipe or a piece of reed in the hole. The *Tapoyers* use very large pipes made of stone, wood or clay, the holes of which are so big that they contain a handful of tobacco at a time. Sometimes the *Brasilians* make use of our *European* pipes, called by them *Amrupetunbuaba*, and *Broken Katunbaba* by the *Portuguese*, and *Katgebouw* by the *Dutch*. Whenever the *Tapoyers*, especially those inhabiting the villages, descended from the *Tapoyers* called *Kariri*, prepare the liquors *Akavi* and *Aipy*, it is done at the same time; then a day being appointed for a general merry meeting, they meet early in the morning at the first house in the village they belong to, where they consume most of the liquor, and make themselves merry with dancing; this done they go to the next house, where they play the same game, and so from house to house, till nothing be left or they can drink no longer. When they find themselves overcharged with liquor, they spew and fall to drinking again, and thus he who can spew and drink most, is accounted the bravest fellow of the company.

On the coast of *Brasil*.

On the north-west coast of *Brasil* are several considerable salt-pits: That near the *Salt-pits.*
house called the *Desert*, is about three or four leagues distant from the river *Aguarama*, of which one branch extends to the east, and discharges its water in this salt-pit with a spring-tide, which is here commonly with the new-moon. It is about 550 paces from the sea-shore, and receives no other water but from the river *Aguarama*. There is no bay or harbour near it, but only a flat sandy bottom for about half a league distance from the shore, where you may anchor at three fathom deep. The land-wind which constantly blows on this coast, commonly ceases towards evening, so that the vessels take the opportunity of the night to load salt. This salt-pit produces every month a certain quantity of salt, provided they be careful to shut their sluices as soon as the same is filled with water, for else they are in danger of losing what they had got before, by the next high-tide. To the east of this salt-pit are the famous rocks called *Baxos*, which at low-water may be seen from thence; they extend about three leagues deep in the sea, but don't begin till about a league from the shore, betwixt which and the rocks there is a passage, where you have ten foot depth at low-water. It ebbs here with the lowest tide about eight foot, and a west-

1647. a west-south-west-wind raises the water to the highest. 1647

About five or six leagues to the west of the house called the *Desert*, is the great salt-pit *Karwaratama*, which receiving its water from the sea, and being detained by sluices, produces very good salt in three weeks time. Five leagues further to the west is the river *Maritouva*, the second in rank in those western parts, but has not above twelve foot water at high-tide. On its east point, not above half a league within the mouth, is a very convenient salt-pit: These salt-pits are computed to be manageable with the assistance only of 10 or 12 negroes, 10 christians, and about 30 *Brasilians*, and to afford 2000 tuns of salt *per annum*, which may be transported from thence into the other parts of the *Dutch Brasil* in small barks, during the summer season. About half way betwixt *Rio Grande* and *Siara*, as likewise in *Siara*, near the river *Wapanien*, are likewise several *Salina*'s or salt-pits.

Traffick of Brasil.

The chief traffick of *Brasil* consists in sugar, brasil-wood, and such like; as also in tobacco, hides, preserves, ginger, and cotton, which grows wild here, some indigo was likewise planted there before my departure; but among these, the sugar and brasil-wood are staple commodities. For since the tobacco began to be transported into *Holland* from the *American* islands, the planting of it was neglected in *Brasil*, where labourers wages being excessive high, they could draw much more profit from the sugar, of which, according to computation, betwixt 20000 and 25000 chests were yearly made only in the sugar-mills of the *Dutch Brasil*, if the harvest proves very good.

The peopling of Brasil.

The inhabitants of *Brasil* may at present be divided into free-born subjects and slaves; and these again consist of divers nations, both natives and foreigners. The free inhabitants of *Brasil* were the *Dutch*, *Portuguese*, and *Brasilians*, the last the natives of the countrey. But the *Portuguese* did not only surpass all the rest, at least ten to one in number, during my abode in *Brasil*, but also were in possession of all the sugar-mills and lands, except what was possess'd by a very few *Dutch*, who had applied themselves to sugar-planting, but were for the most part ruined by the intestine war, being forced to leave all behind them in the country:

Free inhabitants of Brasil.

Besides those of the free inhabitants, who made it their business to manure the grounds, there were many merchants, factors, and handicrafts men: The merchants sold their commodities generally with vast profit, and would have questionless been rich men, had they not vented their goods upon credit to the *Portuguese*, who were resolved never to pay them, as the event has sufficiently shewn. The handicrafts men were able to get three, four, five, nay six gilders a day, so that many returned very rich to *Holland*. Those that kept publick houses and chandlers shops were likewise great gainers here, and carried off abundance of ready money. The officers in the company's service whether civil or military, were likewise punctually paid, which made many who had lived in the countrey before the beginning of the civil war, and had served the company before, take service again, who were all entertained according to their respective qualities and former stations.

The Jews.

Among the free inhabitants of *Brasil* that were not in the company's service, the *Jews* were the most considerable in number, who had transplanted themselves thither from *Holland*. They had a vast traffick beyond all the rest, they purchased sugar-mills and built stately houses in the *Receif*. They were all traders, which would have been of great consequence to the *Dutch Brasil*, had they kept themselves within the due bounds of traffick,

The slaves of Brasil.

The slaves of *Dutch Brasil* were either negroes or natives of the countrey; the last of which were either bought in *Maranhaon* being prisoners of war, or from the *Tapoyers*, who likewise had made them captives, and otherwise, according to their custom, would have put them to death. For it being resolved immediately, at the first entrance of the *Dutch* in *Brasil*, that none of the natives should be made slaves (except they were either bought from the *Tapoyers* or brought from *Maranhaon*) the *Brasilians* were settled in certain villages to enjoy their own liberty under certain limitations, and permission was given them to assist the *Portuguese* in the management of their mills and grounds, for certain wages appointed for that purpose; by which means many *Alicas* or villages were filled with *Brasilians* in *Parayba* and *Rio Grande*, who during the time of our government enjoyed the sweets of a perfect liberty.

Negroes.

Vast numbers of negroes of divers nations were entertained in the *Receif*, and the open countrey, for the manureing of the ground, and working in the sugar-mills of the *Portuguese*, which could not be done without them, by reason of the extremity of the heat of the climate, and the incredible toils they are fain to undergo; so that in my time near 40000 negroes were employed in the sugar-mills betwixt *Rio Grande* and *St. Francisco*. Most of these negroes are brought hither from the kingdoms of *Congo*, *Angola*, and *Guinea*; a black shining skin, flat nose, thick lips, and short curled hair, is their chief beauty. The lustiest and most

Negros Playing upon Kalabasses

1647. most laborious used in time of good trade, to be sold in *Brasil* for 70, 80, or 100 pieces of eight, nay sometimes for 1400 or 1500 gilders, but these understood something more than ordinary: But when trade began to decay, they were sold for 40 pieces of eight. There was scarce a *Hollander* of any substance but what had several of these slaves. They are most miserably and beastly treated by the *Portuguese*, though at the same time it must be confess'd that it is absolutely necessary they should be kept under a strict discipline; for they are full of rogueries, superstitious to the highest degree, and sorcerers: They would often pretend to tell us what ships were at sea from *Holland* for *Brasil*, tho' they were yet on the other side of the line, and how to recover stolen goods. I remember I happened once to be at a friend's house of mine, when I saw an old negro enter the kitchen, who came thither to cure a negro slave of his illness, which he told us was occasioned by witchcraft. He made the patient rise from his chair, and taking a piece of wood from the fire-hearth, he ordered him to lick three times with his tongue that end which was burning hot with the glowing coals. The same end of the wood he afterwards extinguish'd in a bason of water, and rubb'd the coals in it, till it turn'd as black as ink. This he ordered the sick negro to drink off at a draught, which he did accordingly, and was immediately seized with a slight griping in the guts. This done he rubbed both his sides, and taking hold with his hand of a piece of flesh and fat above the hip, he made an incision there with a knife he pull'd out of his pocket, of two inches deep, out of which he drew a bundle of hair and rags, with a little of the black water that was left he washed the wound, which soon after was healed, and the patient cured. They are very dextrous at swimming and diving, and will fetch a single piece of eight from the bottom of the sea, where it is very deep. They are also excellent fishermen, and get a great deal of money by it. They tie three or four great pieces of wood together, this they manage with one oar, and upon it go a good way into the sea, where they catch great quantities of fish with their hooks, and so return. It happened in my time, that a certain negro, who was very expert in fishing, was sold three times in a little while; this he took so much to heart, that the next time he went thus out a fishing, he tied a stone to his leg and drowned himself. Another negro having conceived a hatred against his master cut his throat, cut out his tongue, and made a house-of-office of his mouth, according to his own confession; he was broke alive upon the wheel, which he endured with an incredible obstinacy. A negro woman was brought to bed in my time of a child, the hair and skin of which were not black, but red. I saw also a young lad born from negro parents, whose skin was white, and his hair and eye-brows the like, but curl'd, with a flat nose like the other negroes. Sometimes I have seen old negroes with long grey beards and hair, which looks very fine. 1647.

The Brasilians. The natives of *Brasil* consist of divers nations, distinguished by their proper names, to wit, the *Tubinambos*, *Tobàjaras*, *Petiguaras* and *Tapuijas*, or *Tapuyers*, or *Tapoyers*. The three first use one and the same language, and differ only in the dialect; but the last are subdivided into several nations, differing both in manners and tongue. The *Brasilian* men, which lived among us and the *Portuguese*, are middle-sized, strong and well made, with broad shoulders. They have black eyes, a wide mouth, with black curl'd hair, and a flat nose; the last of which is not natural to them, but the parents, looking upon it as a great beauty, squeeze their childrens noses flat, whilst they are very young. They paint their bodies, and some likewise their faces with divers colours; they have generally no hair about the mouth, tho' some have black beards. Their women are likewise of a middle stature, well limb'd, and not ill-featur'd; they have likewise a black hair, but are not born black, but by the heat of the sun-beams, acquire by degrees a yellow brown colour. The *Brasilians* come soon to maturity, and arrive to a great age, and that without distempers; they also seldom become grey, which is likewise observable in many *European* inhabitants here, who come to the age of 100 or 120 years. This must be chiefly attributed to the temperature of the climate, which is such, that in former times many *Spaniards* that laboured under some lingring distemper, whether in *Spain* or the *East-Indies*, used to come to *Brasil* to partake of the benefit of that excellent air and water; 'tis true, most of the children of foreigners are troubled with lingring sicknesses, so that scarce one in three arrives to a state of manhood; but this must not be attributed to the air, but rather to the bad nourishment. Few cripples or crooked people are to be met with among the *Brasilians*, they being generally very strait and nimble, which is the more admirable, because they never do their children up in swathing cloths, except their feet, looking upon it as unwholsome.

Before the *Dutch* got footing in *Brasil*, the *Portuguese* had made all the natives their slaves, and look'd upon it as the greatest piece

1647. piece of policy quite to extirpate them, which they did so effectually, that whereas about 100 years ago, the captainships of *Rio Grande* alone could raise 100000 fighting men, scarce 300 were to be met with in 1645 and 1646, which had created a mortal hatred in the *Brasilians* against the *Portuguese*; tho' it must also be confess'd, that the late war and some epidemical distempers did sweep away many of the natives. The remainders of them liv'd in certain *Aldens* or villages assigned them for that purpose, where they had their plantations; besides which they served the *Portuguese* in their sugar-mills for a certain monthly pay, which furnished them with clothes and other necessaries. Their huts are made only of wooden stalks, covered with palm-tree leaves. They can't endure the yoke of slavery, nor any toil, especially the *Tapoyers*; they live very quietly among one another, unless they get drunk, when they sometimes sing and dance day and night. Drunkenness is a vice belonging to both sexes here, of which they are so fond, as to be past remedy, tho' this occasions often quarrels and other enormous vices among them. They are likewise much addicted to dancing, which they call *Guau*; they have several ways of dancing, one of which is call'd *Urukapi*; they commonly sing whilst they are dancing. The children divert themselves with divers sorts of games, one is call'd *Kurupirara*, another *Gualbipaie*, and a third *Guaibiquaibibuku*. They will sleep sometimes a whole day and night, and would not stir then if they did not want victuals. Near their hammocks they keep a fire day and night, in the day to dress their victuals, in the night to allay the rawness of the air, which here is colder than in most parts of *Europe*, because day and night is almost of an equal length here throughout the year. 1647.

Their clothing. The inland *Brasilians* of both sexes, go quite naked without the least covering. But those inhabiting nearer to the sea-shore, who converse with the *Dutch* and *Portuguese*, wear only a shirt of linnen or callicoe; tho' in my time, some of the chiefest among them began to take a pride to cloth themselves after the *European* manner. The wife

The habit of ye inland Braziliáns

constantly follows her husband whereever he goes, even in the war. He carries nothing but his arms, but the poor woman is loaden like a mule or sumpter-horse. For besides a great basket which is tied to her back, (call'd by them *Patigua)* she has another upon her head, with all the houshold stuff in it, or a great basket with flower; besides which several other smaller vessels hang on both sides, wherewith they take up water for their drinking. The child is carried in a piece of callicoe, which is fastned

1647. to her, and hangs down from her right shoulder. It lies there with its legs wide open, one being stretch'd cross the mother's belly, the other over her shoulder. After all this, she carries a parrot or ape in one hand, and leads a dog in a string with the other. Thus they proceed on their journey, without any farther provision except a small quantity of *Farinha*; the hedge or open fields serve instead of inns, which furnish them with necessary food, as the rivers and springs with drink; and so does the tree call'd *Karageata*, which contains always some rain-water within the hollowness of its leaves, to the great relief of travellers, who in some barren places, do often not meet with a river or spring for 12 leagues together. Towards night they hang their hammocks on trees, or else fasten them to stalks neatly; they make a fire to dress their victuals, and against the rain defend themselves with palm-tree leaves. When they are at home, the husband goes commonly in the morning abroad with his bow and arrow, to shoot some wild beast, or catch birds, or else to the sea-side, or next river a fishing, whilst the women are employed in the plantations; some women go abroad with their husbands and carry home the prey. The wild beasts are caught by them in a different manner; some they kill with arrows, others they catch in pits dug for that purpose, and covered with the leaves of trees, under which is hidden some carrion, the scent of which draws them to the pit; this they call *Petaku*. They make also certain wooden traps, and use divers other ways of catching the wild beasts, each of which they distinguish by their proper names. To catch birds they use three sorts of snares or nets, call'd by them *Jukana*; the first sort catches the birds by the feet, this they call *Jukanabiprara*; the second entangles them by the neck, which they call *Jukanajuprara*; the third ensnares their bodies, call'd by them *Jukanapitereba*. They kill the fishes with arrows, or catch them with fishing hooks, their baits being commonly worms, crabs, or some small fishes. They bait the water where they intend to fish, with the leaves of *Japikai*, or with *Timpotiana*, *Tinguy*, or with *Tinguiri*; sometimes with the fruit call'd *Kururuape*, the root *Magui*, or the bark of the tree *Anda*, which make the fish swim on the surface of the water like dead, when they take them with a kind of a sieve, call'd by them *Urupema*, made of cane or reed, which they call *Uruguiboandipia*. Their sea-fish they catch with iron hooks, the bait being some carrion; they go a good way into the sea, only upon three pieces of wood fastened together, which they call *Igapeda*, and the *Portuguese Jangada*; the wood is commonly of the tree *Apiba*. 1647.

Their houshold stuff. The *Brasilians* are not burthened with much houshold-stuff, their hammocks being their chiefest care in this kind; they call them *Ini*, are wrought of cotton like net-work, of about six or seven foot long, and four broad. When they are going to sleep, they fasten them either to two beams of their huts, or else in the open air to two trees, and some distance from the ground, for fear of some obnoxious creatures, and to avoid the pestiferous exhalations of the earth. The *Tapoyers*, call'd *Kariri*, have very large hammocks, of 12 or 14 foot long, which contain four persons at a time. The *Portuguese* women make some very fine hammocks, wrought with divers figures in them. In lieu of dishes and cups they use the *Kalabassek*, cut in the middle, which are painted without with a certain red colour, call'd *Uruku*, and within with black. Their cans, cups and mugs, are likewise *Kalabasses* of divers kinds, call'd *Kuite*, *Jaroba*, and *Kribuka*. One of the biggest of these *Kalabasses* hold 30 or 35 quarts; this the *Brasilians* call *Kuyaba*, but when cut thro' the middle it is called *Kuipeba*. The poorer sort make certain knives they call *Ituque*, of stone, as also of cane, which they call *Taquoaquia*, but the better sort use *Dutch* knives. Their baskets they make of palm-tree leaves, they call them *Patigua*; they have also some made of reed or cane, these are with one general name call'd *Karamemoa*. They make also large broad baskets of reeds and branches twisted together: These they call *Panaku*, and are chiefly used for the carrying of the *Mandioka* root. In their journeys they always make use of the *Patigua*, but the *Panaku* is used by the slaves and negroes in the *Receif* for the conveniency of carriage.

Their weapons. The arms of the *Brasilians* are only bows, arrows, and wooden clubs. Their bows, which they call *Guirapara* and *Virapara*, are made of very hard wood, called *Guirapariba* and *Viraparibia*: The bow-strings are made of cotton twisted, and by them call'd *Guirapakuma*; the darts they call *Uba*, and are made of wild cane. The points of these darts are either of wood hardned, or of fish teeth call'd *Jacru*, or of bones or cane well sharpned; some have several points, others but one.

Their way of accounting their age. Being not in the least acquainted with arithmetick, they compute the number of their years and age by the chesnuts which grow on the fruit *Akaju*, which chesnuts they call *Akaguakaya*, as likewise *Akajuti* and *Itamabara*, of which they lay one by every year, this tree producing fruit but once each season, *viz.* in *December* and *January*;

1647. *nuary.* They begin the computation of their years with the rise of a certain star, call'd by them *Taku*, or the *Rain-star*, which is always there in *May*; they also call the year by the same name.

Their religion. The most barbarous of the *Brasilians* inhabiting the inland countries, scarce know any thing of religion, or an almighty being. They have some knowledge remaining of a general deluge, it being their opinion, that the whole race of mankind were extirpated by a general deluge, except one man and his own sister, who being with child before, they by degrees re-peopled the world. They know not what God is, nay, they have no word expressing the same, unless it be *Tuba*, which signifies as much as something most excellent above the rest; thus they call the thunder *Tubakununga*, *i. e.* a noise made by the supreme excellency, for *Akununga* implies as much as a noise. They are unacquainted with heaven or hell, tho' they have a tradition among them, that the souls don't die with the bodies, but that they are either transplanted into devils or spirits, or else enjoy a great deal of pleasure with dancing and singing in some pleasant fields, which they say are behind the mountains. These fields are enjoyed by all the brave men and women, who have kill'd and eaten many of their enemies; but such as have been idle, and never did any thing of moment, are tortured by the devil, unto whom they give many names, *viz. Anhanga, Jurupari, Kurupari, Taguaiba, Temoti, Taubimama.* They have however some sort of priests among them whose business is to sacrifice, and to foretel things to come; these are especially consulted when they are to undertake a war or journey; they call them *Paye* and *Pey*. They dread spirits to the highest degree; they call them *Kuripira, Taguai, Macachara, Anhanga, Jurupari*, and *Marangigona*, tho' under different significations: For *Kuripari* implies as much as the God of the mind or heart. *Macachara* the God or patron of travellers; *Jurupari* and *Anhanga* signify the devil; *Marangigona* implies as much as the *Manes* or remainders of the soul after death, which are so much dreaded by the *Brasilians*, that some of them upon an imaginary apparition of them, have been struck with sudden death. They don't perform any worship or ceremony to those spirits, except that some pretend to appease their wrath by certain presents they fasten to certain stakes fix'd in the ground for that purpose. Some of the *Brasilians* acknowledge the thunder for the supreme being, others the *Lesser Bear* in the firmament, others some other stars. The *Potiguaras*, a nation among the *Brasilians*, are accounted such sorcerers, that they bewitch their enemies even to death: They call this manner of witchcraft *Anbamombikoab*. The *Brasilians* that lived among the *Portuguese* and *Dutch*, did in some measure follow the christian doctrine, but so coldly, that few, when they come to an advanced age, shew much zeal for it; because the fundamental articles of our faith are not easily imprinted in them, unless in their tender years, and when they are remote from their parents. However several of the *Dutch* ministers, *viz.* Mr. *Doreslaer*, and after him Mr. *Thomas Kemp*, have had good success in converting many of the *Brasilians* in the *Aldeas* or villages where they preached, the last of these two being well versed in the *Brasilian* tongue. Neither were *Dionysius Biscareta*, an honest old *Castilian*, and *Johannes Apricius*, less remiss in performing their duty to instruct these infidels. There were likewise three *Dutch* schoolmasters among them, who taught their young people to read and to write, but these were forced to leave their *Aldeas* or villages during the last intestine commotions raised by the *Portuguese*. 1647.

Many distempers which are common in *Europe* are unknown in *Brasil*: They use nothing but simple remedies, and laugh at our compositions. They are very dextrous in applying their remedies, especially their antidotes: They draw blood by suction with horn cups, by scarification, or opening a vein; instead of a lancet they use the tooth of a lamprey, call'd by them *Kakaon*, without which no body stirs abroad. So soon as any one of their acquaintance is fallen ill, they all meet, each offering his remedy, which he has found good by his own experience: Then they begin to cut and slice the most musculous parts of the body, either with the thorns of the tree *Karnaiba*, or with fishes teeth, till they have drawn as much blood as they think fit, and for that purpose suck the wounds with their mouths, by which means they pretend to draw all ill humours from the affected part. Vomiting they procure by means of the leaves *Karnaiba*, which being twisted together, they force down the patients throat. When all these pretended remedies prove ineffectual, they proceed to no others; but after some consultation, quite despairing of his recovery, knock him on the head with their clubs, looking upon it more glorious to be thus bravely delivered from their misery, than to expect death till their last gasp. They exercise as much barbarity upon the dead carcasses of their friends as of their enemies; upon the first out of love, against the last out of revenge; for they tear them to pieces with *Their distempers and remedies.*

1647. their teeth, and eat the flesh like a dainty bit.

Their child-bearing. The *Brasilian* women are extremely fruitful, have very easy labours, and rarely miscarry: For no sooner is a woman delivered, but up she gets to the next river, and without any farther help washes herself there: In the mean while the husband keeps the bed for the first 24 hours, and is made as much of as if he had been lately brought to bed. The mothers lament the death of their infants with howling and crying for three or four days.

How they welcome their friends. They receive their friends after a long journey with open arms and tears, and beating their foreheads against their breasts, in remembrance of the misfortunes they have undergone during their absence. Tho' the *Brasilians* were always supposed to be descended from the race of men-eaters, yet by their conversation with us and other nations, many of them have laid aside their barbarity, and are become as affable and civilized as most of the *European* nations.

The Tapoyers. The *Tapoyers* inhabit the inland country of *Brasil* to the west of these countries in the possession of the *Portuguese* and *Dutch*, betwixt *Rio Grande* and the river *Siara*, as far as *Rio St. Francisco*. They are divided into several nations, distinguished both by their language and names: For the *Tapoyers* bordering upon the utmost confines of *Pernambuko*, are called *Kariri*, under their king *Cerioukejou*; the next to them the *Karirivasu*, whose king was *Karapoto*; then the *Kariryou*, and so farther the *Tararyou*; the last of which were best known unto us, *Janduy* or *John Duwy* being their king; tho' some of them lived under the jurisdiction of one *Karakara*. Divers were govern'd by other kings, *viz. Prityaba, Arigpaygn, Wahasewajug, Tsering*, and *Dremenge*. Those under king *John Duwy* inhabit to the west beyond *Rio Grande*, but change their habitations pretty often: About *November, December*, and *January*, when the fruit *Kajou* begins to ripen, they come towards the sea-side, because little of it is to be met with in the inland countries. The *Tapoyers* are very tall and strong of body, exceeding both the *Brasilians* and *Dutch* both in strength and tallness by the head and shoulders. They are of a dark brown colour, black hair, which hangs all over their shoulders, they only shaving it on the forehead as far as to the ears. Some are shaved according to the *European* fashion; the rest of their bodies they keep without hair, even without eye-brows. Their kings and great men are distinguished from the vulgar by the hair of their heads and their nails; the first their kings wear shaved in the shape of a crown, and have very long nails on their thumbs; but the king's relations or other officers of note, wear long nails on all their fingers, except their thumbs; for long nails is accounted a peculiar ornament among them. The *Tapoyers* are very strong; prince *Maurice* being one time in a humour to try their strength and skill in fighting with a wild bull, caused one to be brought within his outward court, which was surrounded with pallisadoes, in order to engage two *Tapoyers* appointed for that purpose. There was a great concourse of people to see this spectacle, when on a sudden two *Tapoyers* (the rest with their wives being only spectators) came in stark naked, without any other arms but their bows and arrows. The bull saw them no sooner enter, but he made towards them, who being extremely nimble, avoided the strokes he made at them with great dexterity, and in the mean while so gall'd his flanks with their arrows, that the beast roar'd most terribly, and being all in a foam, set upon them with all his vigour, which they avoided by retiring every foot behind a tree that stood in the middle of the court, and from thence continued to pierce his sides with their darts, till finding the beast begin to languish by the loss of blood, one of the *Tapoyers* got upon his back, and laying hold of his horns, threw him upon the ground, and being seconded by his comrade, they both kill'd the bull, roasted him under ground, with a fire above it, according to their custom, and feasted upon the meat, with the other *Tapoyers* there present.

The *Tapoyers* of both sexes, from the king to the common fellow, go quite naked, only that the men hide their privities, by tying the yard in a little bag or net made of the bark of trees; this they close up with a small ribbon call'd *Takoaynhaa*; when they want to piss they unty it, and are more cautious in exposing their privities, than some of the *Europeans*: In the same manner do the rest of the *Brasilians* inhabiting the inland countries. The women of the *Tapoyers* cover their privities only with a handful of herbs, or a small branch of a tree, with the leaves on them: This they thrust barely under a small cord or rope which is fastned round their middle like girdles: In the same manner they cover their backsides; but so carelesly, that both before and behind, great part of both is exposed to view; they change it every day. The men wear also a kind of garland made of the feathers of the bird *Guara* or *Kaninde*, upon their heads, from which certain feathers of the tail of the bird *Arara*, or *Kamud*, hang down behind upon the back; some only *Their clothing.* 1647.

tie a cotton ſtring round their hands, in which ſome red or blue feathers are faſtned behind; this they call *Akanbuaçaba.* They have alſo cloaks made of cotton-thread, and woven like a net; in each of the holes they ſtick a red feather of the bird *Guara*, and intermix them with black, green, and yellow feathers of the birds *Aakukaru*, *Kazinda*, and *Arara*, which lie as cloſe together as fiſh ſcales: There is a kind of cap on the inſide of this cloak, which with the reſt covers the head, ſhoulders, and the body, ſomewhat below the middle, ſo that it is worn both for ornament and conveniencies ſake, it being proof againſt the rain; they call theſe cloaks in their tongue *Guara Abuku.* They alſo faſten certain combs of birds with wild honey to their foreheads, theſe they call *Aguana.*

If their fathers or mothers die, they pull every hair out of their heads; they have holes in their ears ſo big, that you may thruſt a finger into them; in this they wear either a bone of an ape call'd *Nambipaya*, or elſe a piece of wood, wrapt up in cotton-thread. The men have holes in their under lips, in which they wear either a cryſtal, ſmaragd or jaſper, of the bigneſs of a haſel-nut: This ſtone they call *Metara*, and if it be green or blue, *Metarobi*; but they are moſt fond of the green ones: They have alſo holes in their cheeks on each ſide of the mouth; in theſe the married men wear a piece of wood of the bigneſs and thickneſs of a good gooſe-quill: Sometimes they wear a ſtone in it call'd *Tembekoareta:* In the holes of their noſtrils, ſome have alſo ſuch like ſticks of wood, which they call *Apiyati:* Their bodies are all over painted with a certain juice of brown colour, ſqueezed out of the apple *Janipapa*; this is even uſed among the women and children. Beſides this, they ſtick feathers of divers colours with wild-honey or maſtick to the ſkin of their bodies, which make them appear at a diſtance like large birds; this they call *Akamongui.* Thus they adorn their arms with garlands made of red and yellow feathers of ſeveral birds, call'd *Aguamiranga*; ſometimes they mix corals among them, which they call *Arakoaya.* They make alſo a kind of bracelets of the rind of the fruit *Aguay*; theſe they wear round their legs, and make a noiſe when they are dancing. Their ſhoes are made of the bark *Kuragua*, and call them *Miapakabas.* Some nations of the *Tapoyers* uſe no bows or arrows, but throw their darts with their hands, but the *Kariri* have bows. Their clubs are made of very hard wood, are broad on the top, and full of teeth or bones, well ſharpned

at

1647. at the end. Round the handle they wind a piece of callicoe, or ſome other ſtuff, and at the end a buſh of feathers of the tail of the bird *Arara*; ſuch another buſh is faſtned round the middle; they call them *Atirabebe* and *Jatirabebe*. Their trumpets which they call *Kanguenka*, are made of mens bones; but thoſe called *Nhumbugaku*, which are much larger, are of horn; they have alſo another ſort made of cane, called *Meumbrapara*. The *Tapoyers* are not ſo good ſoldiers as the reſt of the *Braſilians*, for upon any ſmart encounter they truſt to their feet, and run away with incredible ſwiftneſs. They neither ſow nor plant, not as much as the *Mandioka* root, their common food being fruits, roots, herbs, and wild beaſts, and ſometimes wild honey, which they take out of the hollow trees. Among all other roots they are extremely fond of a certain kind of wild *Mandioka* root, which riſes up to the height of a ſmall tree. Its ſtem and leaves reſemble the other *Mandioka* root, but it is not near ſo good; the inland *Braſilians* call it *Cuguaçuremia*, but thoſe inhabiting near the ſea-ſhore *Cuaçumandiiba*.

They eat alſo mens fleſh; for if a woman happens to miſcarry they eat the child immediately, alledging, that they cannot beſtow a better grave upon it than the belly, from whence it came. The *Tapoyers* lead a kind of vagabond life, like ſome of the *Arabians*, though they always remain within their certain bounds, within the compaſs of which they change their habitations according to the different ſeaſons of the year; they dwell for the moſt part among the woods, and live upon hunting, in which perhaps they excel all other nations; for they will ſhoot a bird flying with their arrows. So ſoon as a woman has conceived, ſhe abſtains from her husband; after ſhe is brought to bed, ſhe goes into the next wood, where ſhe cuts the child's navel-ſtring, with a ſhell, boils it afterwards with the after-burthen, and eats them both. She waſhes her ſelf and the child every morning and evening, neither does her huſband keep her company, as long as ſhe gives ſuck, unleſs he has but one wife. If a woman be diſcovered to have had an unlawful commerce with another man, her huſband turns her away, but if they are catch'd in the act, he may kill them both. The mothers take extraordinary care that the nuptials of their daughters are not conſummated 'till after they have had their monthly times, which they give notice of to their phyſicians, and theſe to the king, who then gives them licenſe to go to bed with the bridegroom, who pays his acknowledgment to her mother, for the care ſhe has taken of her daughter. 1647. If a young maiden be marriageable, and yet not courted by any, the mother paints her with ſome red colour about the eyes, and thus carries her to the king, who orders her to ſit down near him upon a carpet, and blows the ſmoak of tobacco in her face. After which he thruſts his yard into the woman's privities, and if any blood comes forth, he licks it up, which is eſteem'd a ſingular honour among them. For the reſt of the *Tapoyers*, are the worſt of all the other *Braſilians*, being ignorant of any thing that relates to God or religion; neither will they receive any inſtruction of that kind. They have certain prieſts or rather forcerers, who pretend to foretel things to come, and to raiſe ſpirits, which they ſay appear to them in the ſhape of a fly, or any ſuch like inſect: When theſe ſpirits diſappear, the women make moſt horrible cries and lamentations, in which conſiſts the main point of their devotion. They avoid night journies, for fear of ſerpents and other venomous creatures, neither will they ſet on a journey 'till the dew be dried up by the ſun-beams. Several nations of the *Tapoyers*, eſpecially thoſe under king *John Duwy*, liv'd always in a good correſpondence with the *Dutch*, unto whom they afforded at divers times conſiderable aſſiſtance; tho' they did not ſubmit to their juriſdiction, but were governed by their own kings. King *John Duwy* had 60 children by 50 wives, tho' ſometimes he had not above 14 wives at a time; theſe *Tapoyers* having a mortal hatred to the *Portugueſe*, uſed to kill them wherever they could meet with them. And thus much may ſuffice concerning the manners, way of living, cloaths, *&c.* of the natives of *Braſil*; I will now proceed to give you an account of my voyage back into *Holland*.

The author's return to Holland.

Being ſenſible, as I told you before, that 1649. things grew worſe and worſe every day with us here, I with much ado got leave to depart, and accordingly the 23[d] of *July* 1649 I went aboard the ſhip call'd the *Union*, mann'd with 80 ſailors, under the command of captain *Albert Jants*, a native of *Groningen*. We ſet ſail the ſame day in company of the *Blue-Eagle*, and a yacht call'd the *Braſilian*. We left the city of *Olinda* to the ſouth-weſt in the evening; the 25th we were under 3 degrees 6 min. with a north-north-eaſt courſe, we ſail'd that day about 28 leagues. The next day we paſs'd the line, with very fair weather and wind; we continued our courſe without any remarkable accident 'till the 1[ſt] of *Auguſt*, when about noon we found our ſelves under 9 deg. 46 min. having ſail'd 29 Leagues in the laſt 24 hours. The ſame evening we

1649. we ſaw the firſt time the north-pole ſtar, after we had paſs'd the line. The 2[d] of *Auguſt* we ſail'd 23 leagues with a freſh gale, and found our ſelves under the 11th deg. 13 min. We continued this our courſe with a fair wind, 'till the 16th of *Auguſt* when we were becalmed, we did not advance above 60 leagues that day, being under the 26 deg. we found it exceeding hot. The 20th of *Auguſt* we had but a ſlender ſouth-eaſt wind, we found our ſelves under 29 deg. 45 min. we were much troubled with heat, for want of the cool winds, that the knives in the cabin were ſo hot, that nobody could hold them in his bare hands, nor any one could touch the deck of the ſhip with his hands or feet. We continued our courſe thus 'till the 29th, when being under 38 deg. 46 min. we made about eight leagues that day. The 3[d] of *September* being under the 40th deg. 18 min. we eſpied a ſail which we found to be a veſſel bound for *Virginia*. Towards evening we were forced to ſtay ſometime for the *Braſilian* yacht, ſhe having loſt one of her maſts. The next following day in the morning we diſcover'd the iſland of *Corfu*, whither we directed our courſe.

The Flemming *iſlands.* *Corfu* and *Floris* are two of the nine iſlands, the *Dutch* commonly call the *Flemming Iſlands*. The biggeſt is *Tercera*, being about 16 leagues in compaſs. It is very rocky, but fruitful, producing a conſiderable quantity of oxen, and abounding in canary and other birds. Here is a ſpring that turns wood into ſtone, and ſeveral hot-ſprings, in which you may boil an egg. The ground ſeems to be full of concavities, which is the reaſon of the many earthquakes here, which over-turn and deſtroy houſes, men and beaſts. The iſland call'd the *Peake* has a rock which reaches to the very clouds, and which as ſome ſuppoſe, may be parallel'd for its height to the peake of the *Canary Iſland* itſelf. Betwixt the coaſt of *Braſil* and the ſaid Iſlands, the compaſs bears due ſouth and north. We were gone eight degrees farther to the weſt, than we intended. About noon we found our ſelves under 40 deg. and 34 min. We continu'd our courſe without any remarkable accident, 'till the 16th of *Sept.* when we ſuppoſed our ſelves to be not far from land, which we diſcovered the ſame evening to the north north-eaſt of us. The 17th we were becalm'd, and catch'd more fiſh than we were able to eat. The 18th we diſcover'd the *Iſle of White* to the north of us, whereabouts one of our ſhips was ſeparated from us; not long after we ſaw the point of *Dover*. The 19th we paſs'd by *Dunkirk* and *Oſtend* with a briſk gale, and about noon ſafely arrived in the road of *Fluſſingen*. I got immediately aſhore, and after having refreſhed my ſelf for five days, I went to *Middleburgh*, where I likewiſe continued five days. From thence I continued my journey over *Dort*, *Rotterdam*, *Delft* and *Harlem* to the famous city of *Amſterdam*, from whence I undertook this *Weſt-India* voyage 1640. From *Amſterdam* I went to *Zwell*, the birth-place of my father *John Nieuhoff*, and ſo to *Benthem*, my native countrey, where I met with my parents in good health, after ſo many fatigues of a tedious voyage; whilſt I was at *Benthem* my father died 1651, the 15th of *May*, in the 85th year of his age, being lamented by all, by reaſon of his good qualifications. 1649.

The author arrives at Fluſſingen.

He arrives at Benthem.

Some troubleſome people laid the loſs of the *Dutch-Braſil* at the door of the members of the great council, *viz. Henry Hamel*, *Adrian Bulleſtrate* and *Peter Jande Bas*, who left *Braſil* 1647. It was alledged that the before-mentioned contracts made with the *Portugueſe* had given them great opportunity of a revolt; for which it was ſaid the ſaid members had received great ſums of money; but it being evident that the ſucceeding members of the great council having taken cogniſance of that affair before their departure, *Nov.* 6, 1646, and in *March* 1647, they were fully cleared of theſe accuſations, the ſame having been tranſacted by ſpecial orders of the council of XIX. in *Holland*; beſides, that the revolts which were about the ſame time in agitation in *Angola*, *Africa*, and the iſland of *Ceylon* in the *Eaſt-Indies*, where no ſuch contracts were made, do ſufficiently teſtify that the foundation of this inteſtine war was laid in *Portugal*, long before the contracts were ſet on foot. What is more ſurpriſing is, how the *Portugueſe*, conſidering we were pretty well provided with forts and garriſons, durſt think of ſuch an attempt; but the reaſon is plain, for what they wanted in ſtrenghth or otherwiſe, they were ſupplied with from the *Bahia*.

What induced the Portugueſe *to rebel.* The motives that induced the *Portugueſe* to this revolt, were the recovery of their liberty, the difference of their language and manners from ours; but eſpecially of religion, which our people endeavoured to eſtabliſh in *Braſil*; theſe with ſome other concurring circumſtances, ſuch as our preſent weakneſs and the diſpoſition the ſtates were in at that time, to be fairly rid of *Braſil*, gave them ſufficient encouragement for this attempt. It has been the opinion of ſome, that the firſt ſparks of this rebellion might ſoon have been quench'd by ſeiſing ſome of the heads of the *Portugueſe* faction; but it being apparent from the records, that nothing was left unattempted upon that account, tho' without

1649. any considerable success, the same cannot be imputed to the neglect of the government; the true reasons of the loss of *Brasil* were the slender garrison, and the inconsiderable number of *Dutch* inhabiting there; nothing being more obvious, than that a conquered country must be maintained, either by a sufficient military force, or strong colonies; the last of which was the constant practice of the ancient *Romans*, who besides this back'd them with good armies to keep the conquered nations in obedience. Another way of establishing themselves in a conquered country, tho' a very barbarous one, was introduced by the *Spaniards* and *Portuguese* in *America*, who by destroying the ancient inhabitants, and planting colonies of their own, saved themselves the charge of keeping many forts and garrisons for their defence. Neither of these was sufficiently observed by the *Dutch*, after their conquest of the *Dutch-Brasil*; for according to their agreement made with the *Portuguese*, the last were left in the entire and quiet possession of all the sugar-mills, plantations, and grounds thereunto belonging, whereby the *Dutch* subjects were in a manner excluded from getting any considerable footing in the open countrey, especially, since such of the sugar-mills as happened to fall into the companies hands, by forfeiture or otherwise, were sold promiscuously to both nations, and commonly at such excessive rates, that the *Dutch* durst seldom venture upon them; the taxes laid upon every thing belonging to the sugar-mills, and upon the sugar itself, being so great, that little profit was to be reap'd from thence, unless the sugar sold at a very dear rate; whereas on the contrary, we ought after the example of the *Spaniards*, to have endeavoured to draw our subjects into *Brasil*, by the granting of considerable immunities of honour and other advantages. The military force of the *Dutch* in *Brasil*, was likewise not duely regarded; for whereas according to a just estimate made in 1641, by count *Maurice*, 7076 men were absolutely requisite to maintain the *Dutch* garrisons there, the states of *Holland* instead of following his directions, did after the conclusion of the ten years truce with *Portugal*, order the great council of the *Dutch-Brasil*, to reduce their forces there to 18 companies of 150 men each; and tho' several remonstrances were made upon that head to the contrary, the truth of which was verified by the event; yet the succours sent from *Holland* arrived so slowly, that after my departure things grew worse and worse every day, and the *Dutch* had lost all their strong holds 1654. For the *Portuguese* began to blow up the *Receif* by sea, with 16 ships, and to besiege it by land 1653, in *December*, with such success, that our people being constrain'd by hunger, and the garrison refusing to fight, were forced to surrender the place with all its circumjacent forts to the enemy; since which time the *Portuguese* have remained in the entire possession of *Brasil*; the same being confirmed to them by the peace made the 6th of *Aug*. 1660, betwixt *Portugal* and the states of the united provinces, in which, among others these following points were agreed upon. 1649.

Reasons why Brasil *was not sufficiently peopled by the* Dutch.

Their want of forces.

Lose all Brasil.

That the crown of *Portugal* shall be obliged to pay to the states the sum of 80 tuns of gold, either in ready money or sugar, tobacco or salt, or else assign the said money upon the *Portuguese* customs.

That the places taken on each side should remain to those, who were then in possession of them.

And that a free trade should be allowed to the *Dutch* in *Portugal*, *Africa* and *Brasil*; without paying any more customs than the native *Portuguese*.

Mr. JOHN NIEUHOFF's REMARKABLE VOYAGES AND TRAVELS TO THE EAST-INDIES.

1653.

AFTER a short stay in my native country, I resolved to take a view of the *East-Indies*, and accordingly embarked at *Amsterdam*, on board the ship call'd the *Calf*, carrying 24 guns, under the command of *Cornelius Just*. The 23[d] of *August* 1653, we set sail from the *Texel*, in company of four ships more, *viz.* the *Peace*, the *Lamb*, the *Golden Drake*, and the *Naerden*, steering our course towards the north of *Ireland*, not thinking it safe to pass thro' the channel of *England*. The 24th we steer'd our course north by west, under 54 deg. 46 min. toward evening we cast anchor at 13, and in the night found 17 fathom water. We continued the same course the 25th, under 55 deg. 59 min. 23 fathoms water, and from thence farther till the 29th, under 28 deg. 24 min. Then we took a north-east course with a brisk gale. The 30th, with break of day we discovered at about 6 leagues distance *Hetland*, lying at the northern point of *Scotland*, and found ourselves about noon under 60 deg. 3 min. latitude, and 18 deg. 49 min. longitude. The 1st of *September* we were under the latitude of 62 deg. 40 min. and 19 deg. 2 min. longitude: We steer'd our course with a brisk gale to south-west by west, betwixt the *Fairo* islands and *Hetland*. The 4th, being overtaken by a violent storm, we lost sight of one of our ships call'd the *Lamb*, under 60 deg. 11 min. We continued the same course till next day, when about noon we discovered the isle of *Kilda*, under 59 deg. at 6 leagues distance to the south-west of us, the island lying to the west of *Scotland*. Thus we pursued our voyage for the most part with stormy weather till the 13th, when we lost our small sail at the prow of the ship: We found ourselves about noon under 50 deg. 1 min. the weather continuing very stormy, but on the 17th, under 46 deg. 27 min. all our rigging was torn to pieces by a violent storm, in which we got out of sight of all our company. The 19th we descried two sail which we guess'd to be our own, as one of them prov'd afterwards to be the *Lamb*. The 20th we continued our course with a brisk wind to the south-west, and under 43 deg. 25 min. discovered the *Cabo Finis terræ*, or the point of the lands end of *Spain*, at about 5 leagues distance as we supposed. The same evening we met with the ship the *Lamb*, which as the master informs us, had lost sight of the ship the *Peace*, in the last storm, and had her main-mast and all her sails brought by the board. Thus we sailed forward with a strong gale till the 30th, when we found ourselves under the 30 deg. 20 min. and discovered the *African* coast about five leagues to the south-west of us, with a variable wind. The 2[d] of

The author's departure to the East-Indies.

1653.

The isle of Kilda.

1653. of *October*, we continued the same course under the 28 deg. 51 min. of latitude, and 57 deg. of longitude; all along the isle of *Lancerotta*, one of the canary islands, we descried a ship, but were not near enough to see what she was. The next day we found ourselves about 40 leagues to the north north-east of the islands *Fretevanture* or *Forterentum*, under 27 deg. 45 min. and sail'd thus in 24 hours, 40 leagues among the *Canary* islands. The 7th a brisk north wind carried us near 20 leagues forwards to the 19 deg. 14 min. In the evening we found but 14 fathoms water, and a small bird settled upon our ship, tho' we judged our selves above 100 leagues from land. The 9th we were under 17 deg. 41 min. and towards evening saw land to the south-west

The isle of St Vincent. of us. The 10th with break of day we discover'd the isle of *St. Vincent*, one of the salt islands, about five leagues to the south-west; we steering our course south-west, betwixt this island and that of *St. Anthony*. About noon we cast anchor in the bay of *St. Vincent* at four fathom water, in a sandy bottom, and provided ourselves the same day with a whole boat full of fresh water and seven goats; I went in another boat to the isle of *St. Anthony*, to fetch some fresh provisions; but could get none. The 15th our ships crew catch'd 10 tortoises, and those of the *Drake* as many. The 18th I was sent ashore to complement the governor of *St. Vincent*, who received us very kindly, and furnish'd us with an ass to carry us back to the harbour. All this while we catch'd abundance of fish; and the 20th sent some on shoar with some toys, which they exchanged with the inhabitants of *St. Vincent*, for oranges, limons, bekoras and pompions. The same day the ship the *Rose*, bound for *Brasil*, came to an anchor in the same bay. Mr. *Wiltschut* the elder, commander in chief of the land-forces, came on board us, being much surprised to meet with me there. Being by this time provided with as many necessaries as we were able to get, we were ready to set sail, but were detained by contrary winds 'till the 25th. The isle of *St. Vincent* is a rocky and barren island, affording nothing but a little grass for the sustenance of wild goats. It is about five leagues in circuit, under the command of a *Portuguese* governor, who was then a *Mulat*, one born of a christian father and a negro mother.

The inhabitants here are negroes, transplanted hither from several parts to catch wild goats, the skins of which they send to *Portugal*, and the flesh they can't consume they

1653. they throw away. They lead a wretched life without women. All their water is brakish, and of a taste like salt-peter, except what they gather at the foot of the highest rock in bags of goat-skins, which being always covered with clouds on the top, sends a considerable quantity of rain water down to the bottom by small natural channels. The governor's residence is on the other side of the great rock, not far from the sea-shore, near 3 leagues from the harbour. His officers live in hutts cover'd with tortoise-shells, among trees, the shadow of which defends them against the excessive heat of the sun-beams: I went in company of some belonging to our ship, up to the top of the highest rock to take a view of the countrey; my companions stay'd about half way, but I with much a-do got to the top, where I had a full prospect of the island, but lost my hat by the violence of the wind, and was forced to lay upon my belly, for fear of tumbling down the precipice. The inhabitants relate a ridiculous story of a king's daughter turn'd into a serpent here. As I was coming down and met with the rest of my companions in the place where I left them, we saw at some distance a great number of crows, which made us hasten thither, and found them busy in picking the flesh of a living tortoise which was turn'd upon her back; we found above 300 eggs within her, which one of our company kept for his own use, but the flesh was carried on board for the use of the sick.

The island of St. Antony.

The island of *St. Antony* lies at about 3 leagues distance, just opposite to *St. Vincent*. On the foot of the east-point of this island, is a small sandy bay, fit for small vessels only, call'd by the *Portuguese*, *Et Pracaden Siniao*, whereabouts are about 30 hutts inhabited by *Portuguese* and negroes, who sustain themselves most by fruit; of which they had no great store formerly, but of late years they have great plenty, which were transplanted thither by the industry of the *Portuguese*; the isle being full of high barren rocks. The vines bear here twice a year, as well as most other fruit-trees; they abound in wild-fowl of all sorts, but especially in wild-goats. We found the heat so excessive about noon, that it was insupportable: At our first arrival, they refused to supply us with refreshments, but after some time they began to be more pliable, and furnish'd us with what fruits we wanted.

The salt islands.

These islands commonly call'd the *Salt Islands*, being ten in number, are thus call'd from the great quantity of salt they produce, and lies about 160 leagues from the *African* coast, being first discovered by the *Portuguese* 1572, who inhabit there to this day.

We set sail again the 26th with a moderate north-north east wind, and pass'd by the *Ilha Blanco* or *White-island*; so call'd from its *white colour*, being the last of the ten, under 15 deg. 11 min. At first we had a brisk gale, but were soon becalm'd, and advanced very little that day and night. The next following day we had a more prosperous wind, and discovered land the next morning, at about 10 leagues distance, under 14 deg. 16 min. The 3d of *November*, we advanc'd no more than 3 leagues, because the wind slacken'd under the 8 deg. 11 min. Thus we continued our course, but very slowly till the 18th, when we found our selves under 5 deg. being forced much farther to the east than we expected: We were continually afflicted with calms till the 1st of *December*; so that oftentimes we did not make above 3, 4 or 6 leagues a day, and without meeting with any thing remarkable, found our selves under 2 deg. 15 min. The 8th in the morning we pass'd the line, and the next day were under 50 min. southern latitude, and under 359 deg. 10 min. longitude: Here we were overtaken by a violent *Travado* from the east, with violent storms and rains, which much endamaged some of our small sails, being about noon under 1 deg. 37 min. We often saw small black clouds, which in an instant increased prodigiously, and were the certain fore-runners of tempests. For the rest we had favourable wind and weather all this month, and found our selves under 33 deg. 52 min. of southern latitude, and under 358 deg. 36 min. longitude, the sun setting 14 deg. 3 min. north-east; in the mean while our ship's crew began to be much afflicted with the scurvy for want of fresh water. The 1st of *January* we sail'd with a moderate gale under 34 deg. 58. min. about 39 leagues in 24 hours. The 3d we pursued our course east to the north, under 35 deg. 38 min. latitude, and 6 deg. 29 min. longitude: The 6th we continued the same course with a very brisk gale under 35 deg. 4 min. till the 22d, with strong winds and tempestuous weather; when in the morning under 31 deg. 36 min. we discovered land at about 3 leagues distance, to our no small satisfaction; we found 58 fathoms water and a rocky bottom; and in the afternoon 55 fathom sandy ground; we were forced to return deeper in sea, and in the afternoon approached nearer the shoar, but were forc'd to turn back again into the main. The next day about 7 or 8 leagues from the continent, we found a sandy bottom at 80 fathoms depth, and saw abundance of birds; we had very misty weather for some time, during which we lost the *Drake*. The 25th towards evening we got sight again of the *Drake*

St. Anthony

St. Vincent

1653. *Drake* about 7 or 8 leagues from the shore, under 32 deg. 38 min. without being able to fathom the bottom of the sea. We continued this sailing to and from the shoar till the 28th, but could not make the *Cape of good Hope*, tho' we advanced within a league of the land among the rocks, not without great danger, being then under 32 deg. 58 min. we were therefore oblig'd to choose the main again, to our great dissatisfaction, being so disabled by sickness, and especially the scurvy, that we had scarce hands enough left to manage our ship: Our surgeon was a *German* by birth, a very able person, but never used to the sea before, was so much surprised at it, that he confess'd he never had seen the like, and that few of them would recover; but I told him, that in case we could make the cape, he would find a remarkable alteration in a weeks time, as soon as they touch'd the land, and receiv'd suitable refreshment, which accordingly proved true. The 29th and 30th it was very tempestuous weather, when we lost sight again of the *Drake*; we were forced to keep the open sea 'till the 2d of *February*, when we found our selves under 34 deg. 39 min. southern latitude, and 36 deg. 32 min. longitude. The 3d being overtaken by a storm from the south-east, we were forced to leave the shore again, which continued the next day with such violence that we lost our main-sail. The 4th we pursued our course with a brisk gale under 33 deg. 40 min. when we again discovered land at about 6 or 7 leagues distance. Towards evening we came within a league of *Dassen (Doe Island)* at 60 fathoms depth, but were forced to put to sea again, the shore being all along very rocky here: Thus we made to and from the shore 'till the 8th, when we saw the *Table Mountain* about 9 leagues to the south-west of us, and the isle of *Dassen* 2 or 3 leagues to the N. W. we found hereabouts 30, 36 and 40 fathoms water, about half a league from the shore in a sandy bottom; we did all we could to make the *Robben Island (Rabbet Island)* but being becalm'd, were fain to put to sea again. The 9th we were not above 2 or 3 leagues from the *Table Mountain*, and about noon being favour'd with a brisk S. W. wind got happily into the *Table Bay*, where we cast anchor at five fathoms depth in a sandy bottom. Here we met with the galliot the *Fox*, *John Zymentz* master. Mr. *Rietbeck*, *Dutch* governor of the *Cape of good Hope*, sent us immediately a chaloop with fish on board, and a pilot to conduct us into the harbour. We had lost 8 of our ships crew in this voyage, and had about 40 sick, besides which the rest were so much afflicted with the scurvy, that unless we had received some seasonable refreshments, we could scarce have held it out much longer. I went immediately a-shore in company of the captain *Cornelius Just*; and brought back good store of mustard-leaves which were dress'd for the ship's crew. Much about the same time the fiscal came a-board us, to forbid all commerce with the *Hottentotes* or natives, and to carry a shore, without special leave from the governor; we were also supply'd with more fresh water, which is very good and easy to be got thereabouts. The 12th we saw the ship the *Drake* making the bay, but was forced to cast anchor behind the *Robben Island*, by reason of the violence of the wind; we were then busy in fishing, but the wind blowing hard from the land side, could catch none. The 14th the tempest being somewhat allay'd, we approach'd as near the shore as we could; when we got sight of the top of the *Table Mountain*, which is very often covered with small clouds, a certain presage of tempestuous weather. The same day we went to our former employment of fishing, and catch'd as much in one draught as the chaloop was able to carry, the governor having 14 wheelbarrows full for his share. They were for the most part mullets, which swim in shoals along the shore of this bay. It was not 'till then the *Drake* came into the harbour, having lost 20 of her crew and 50 sick, and the rest being so much disabled by the scurvy, that according to their own confession, if it had lasted thus 14 days longer, they must have left the ship to the mercy of the wind and sea: We were all this while very busy in fishing as often as the weather would permit; but the 19th it blew so hard, that we were forced to make use of all our Anchors. The 22d we spent in providing ourselves with fresh water and fuel, the last of which our carpenters cut down near the banks of the *Salt-River*. The 23d I, in company of some others, went cross the mountain as far as the *Fresh-River*, to see whether we could meet with some wild-fowl, we saw some negroes with about 300 head of cattle, but at the first sight of us they retired. The fields hereabouts were all covered with white lilies and tulips; we saw also abundance of partridges. Being informed that a *Rhinoceros* was fallen into the boggs, the governor *Rietbeck* sent some fusileers thither to kill him, but the musquet ball not being able to penetrate his thick hide, they were forced to cut a hole in it first, and so to shoot it to death; the horn is preserved there to this day, and sometimes used instead of a cup. The 1st of *March* we had very fair weather, notwithstanding which, few of our ship's crew were fond to go on shoar, every

Violent scurvy.

They arrive in the Table Bay.

The ship the Drake *enters the bay.*

They take a view of the country.

A Rhinoceros *kill'd.*

1653. every thing being there at an excessive rate; as for instance, a quartern of *Arack* was sold for six-pence; of brandy for twelve-pence; a water-melon about the bigness of a coco-nut for half a crown. The next day being informed that a whale was got on shoar in the *Salt-River*, the governor and his lady, our master of the ship and I, went thither to see it, it was a very large one; we got upon the back of it, whilst the trumpet sounded merrily, and the negroes were busied in cutting great pieces of the flesh which they buried in the sand in order to eat them. The 6th the governor sent some of his soldiers to the *Hottentots*, to endeavour to exchange some of their cattle for copper, tobacco-pipes and such like baubles, but they retired at first sight. The 9th it was very calm and fair weather, which made most of our crew go on shore to wash their linen, having received orders to be ready to sail the next day; for which reason also good store of cabbage and two sheep were brought a board, a slender provision for such a number of men, but it was impossible to get more for that time. During our stay here, we fetch'd daily two sacks full of cabbage and mustard-leaves, which being boiled with bacon, was served twice a day, this being the best refreshment we were able to get. The *Cape of Good Hope* is situate under 34 deg. 20 min. southern latitude, which jetts out into the sea like a demi-island being to the north joined to the continent by a strait neck of land, with a bay on each side, very convenient for anchorage. The *Table Bay*, which has borrow'd its name from the *Table Mountain*, is about 4 leagues in compass, so that a whole fleet of ships may safely enter, or go out with any wind, except the north-west wind. Near the shore of this bay, upon the banks of the *Fresh-River*, the *Dutch East-India* company has erected a quadrangular fort, call'd the *Good Hope*, well provided with artillery and a good garrison, in which, at this time, Mr. *Rietbeck* was commander in chief; and had his habitation there, with a well-planted garden of about 15 acres round about it. Upon the banks of the *Salt-River* is likewise a small redoubt. Behind the fort of *Good-Hope*, all along the banks of the river, are many fine plantations or gardens, which produce cabbages and such-like herbages, being cultivated by certain *Hollanders* who have settled there, and pay only a small annual acknowledgment to the governor for the use of their grounds, which are for the most part clay, and consequently fruitful, tho' in some parts they are likewise rocky and sandy. Near the sea-shore is great store of small wood, tho' the natives assure us, that deeper in the countrey they have trees of a vast bigness. Their gardens produce likewise olives, oranges, apricocks and peaches; the fields grass and some herbs and flowers; nay, they would bear very good wheat, rye, rice, and barly, were they manur'd as they ought to be. Their field herbs are great and small, some with knotty roots, housleek and some other pot-herbs, besides tulips and white-lilies, *&c.* They have also here a certain root which the *Hottentots* roast and eat instead of bread, and sometimes make flour of them; some taste like our potatoes or chesnuts, tho' they have others that are much sweeter, not unlike our anniseed. The *Dutch* have planted many thousands of vines on a hill adjacent to the fort, they bear very plentifully, but the wine is of a crab-like tast. The worst of all is, that the winds which arise from the clouds in the mountains, blow in the summer, especially about *July*, with such violence, that they tear up all by the roots, at which time it is very dangerous landing at the cape. For the rest the air is very wholesome here, being always clear, and neither too hot nor too cold. Their winter is in *June* and *July*, when it freezes sometimes, that you may see Ice of the thickness of the back of a large knife. In *October*, *November*, and *December*, there blows always a south wind, which produces a cool air, as the north wind does in *Holland*; and in this season they are troubled with violent rains, which however render their ground very fruitful. 1653.

The Cape of Good Hope.

Table Bay.

The fort.

This countrey likewise abounds in all sorts of wild and tame creatures: They have here birds they call *Pinguwyns*, *Flamingos*, *Antenayas*, *Alkatraces*, *Faysons*, *Gavoytoyns*, *Garagians*, &c. The *Pinguwyns* are short-legged, and may soon be taken, but are not to be forced from their nest without a good stick, because they will bite and defend themselves there to the utmost. They abound also in partridges and pheasants, geese, quails, crows, sparrows of divers kinds, rock-ducks with yellow necks, teal, wood and water snipes, and a kind of demi-ducks; there is also a sort of black birds here of the bigness of a small goose or large duck, call'd by us cormorants, wild peacocks, blue, white and black cranes. The white ones are indifferently large, the black ones of the bigness of our sea-gulls, living for the most part in the marshes; they have a kind of reed-birds with red necks and legs, monkeys, hawks of divers kinds, ravens, magpies and very large ostriches, which can reach with their long necks a man on horse-back. They are gray, and run with their wings spread as swift as a horse; they live upon herbs, but sometimes devour likewise stones, copper and iron. They have

What creatures are at the Cape.

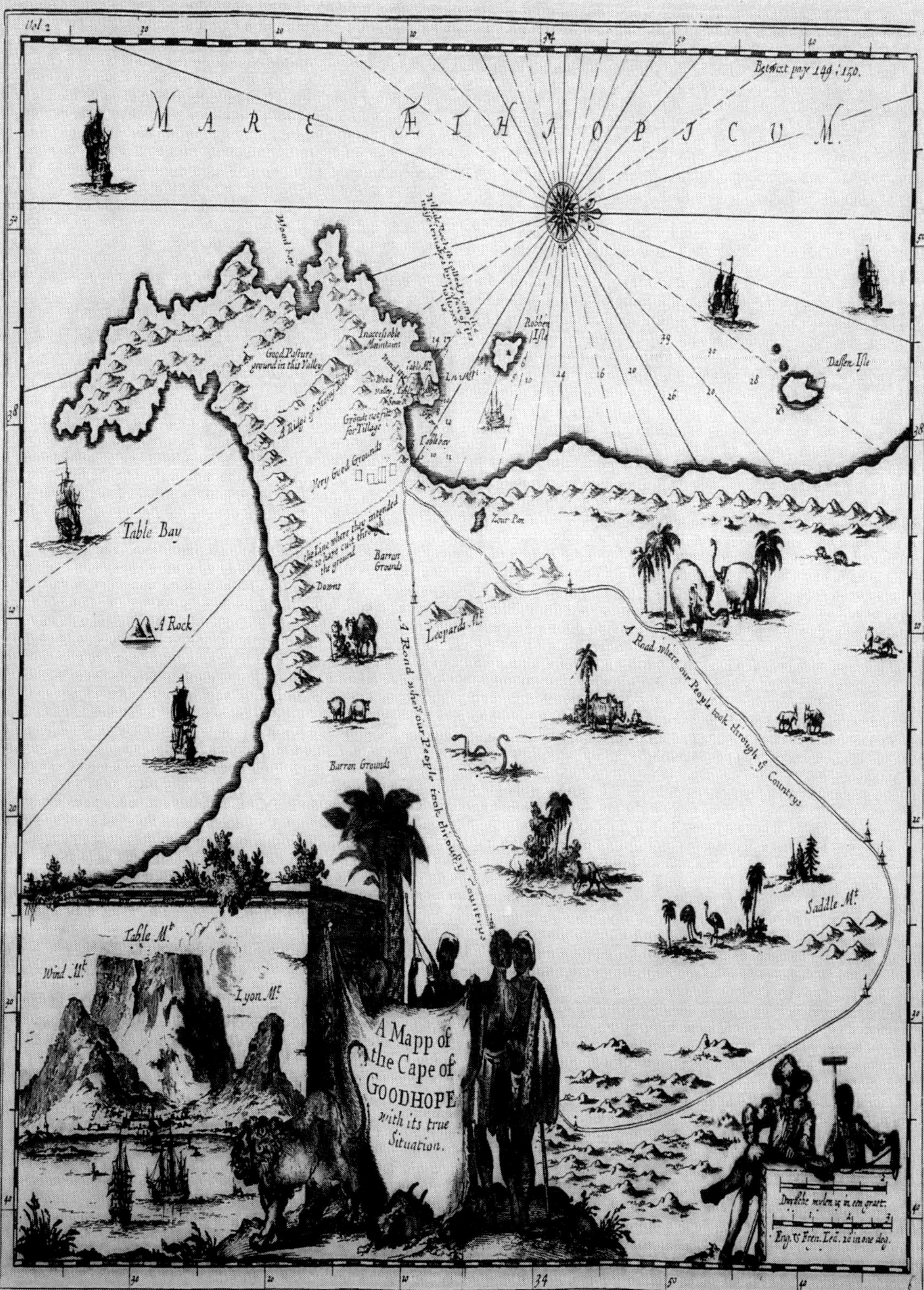

Betwixt page 149 & 150.
MARE ÆTHIOPICUM
Inaccessible Mountains
Good Pasture ground in this Valley
Table Mt.
Robben Isle
Dassen Isle
Ground not fit for Tillage
Table bay
Very Good Grounds
Zout Pan
Table Bay
Barren Grounds
Downs
A Rock
Leopards Mt.
A Road where our People took through ye Countrys
A Road where our People took through ye Countrys
Barren Grounds
Saddle Mt.
Table Mt.
Wind Mt.
Lyon Mt.
A Mapp of the Cape of GOODHOPE with its true Situation.
Eng. & Fren. Leg. 20 in one deg.

1653. have likewise certain birds not unlike our geese, which lay eggs without yolks, as big as a common goose egg. They are so full, and taste so much like fish, that they are not eatable. Another kind of geese they have somewhat less than ours, tho' their legs are larger, with grey spots all over their bodies; they are not to be tam'd, because they kill any other bird that comes within their reach.

The Pinguwyns. Formerly the sea-shore used to abound with certain birds call'd *Pinguwyns*, both black and white; their skin is very hard, and are of the bigness of an ordinary goose. They live both upon land and in the water; they have a fin on each foot, which makes them swim very swiftly after their prey the small fish, which is the reason their flesh is of a rank taste, and scarce eatable, unless it be seven times boil'd in fresh water, and afterwards fry'd with butter; they make their nest, and lay their legs in hollow places in the sand.

The Flamingos. The *Flamingos* is a very fine bird, resembling a crane, but with a crooked bill. They are pale red, tho' some of their feathers are half white and half black, but the uppermost feathers which cover the rest, are of a rosy colour.

Their oxen are very fat and thick set, with long crooked horns, tho' some have their horns bent back close to the neck; others have no horns at all, they are generally a foot and a half taller than our oxen. Among other creatures they have here those they call *Sea Cows*, being much bulkier than an *European* ox. They are without horns, but have long ears and round eyes, with a short tail, thick legs and feet like an elephant. They have no hair upon their bodies, but prodigious large teeth. They feed upon grass, which they find in the marshes near the lakes, where they duck under water as long as they please, so that they are seldom to be seen or catch'd. The flesh is like other beef, but somewhat coarser; when it is salted, it appears and keeps like the ordinary *Dutch* salted beef. *Sea Cows.*

They have likewise here what they commonly call *Iron Pigs*, with long spikes, which by drawing the skin together, can shoot at those that come too near them with such force, as to wound them mortally. A dead lion was once found here, with such a spike sticking in the breast, which had questionless caused his death. The skin is hung up, and to be seen in the fort to this day. They abound also in hares, wild goats and rabbits; and deeper in the country they have tygers, lions, wolves, leopards, *Rhinoceros*'s, deer, cows, calves and rock-does. They have plenty of sheep, which the inhabitants exchange for copper, tobacco, tobacco-pipes, and such like baubles. They bear no wool, but hair like our goats; their legs are long, and the tail consists of one long and thick piece of fat, which weighs sometimes 20 pound and above. 1653.

On this cape is also a certain creature call'd a *Jackal*, being betwixt a fox and a dog, with grey hair; it roars frightfully in the night time, being very greedy after men's flesh, so that it will dig sometimes ten foot deep to come at a dead carcass: It is said to be the most quick-scented of all creatures, and by its scent to discover any carrion that is near at hand to the lion. Among others, they have likewise a certain wild beast in shape and bigness like an elephant, but with two horns on the top of the nose; its tail is likewise like that of an elephant, but has a bush of black hair on the head where it joins to the neck, with two strait and round horns, with short mouse-coloured hair all over the body. On the top of the *Lions Mountain*, (so call'd from its resemblance to a sleeping lion) are great numbers of baboons, which are so unlucky, that they will sometimes with stones, force those who ascend the mountain to turn back. However, most of your ravenous beasts, such as lions, leopards, wolves, jackals and tigers, are but rarely to be met with near the sea-shore, where they are almost rooted out by the inhabitants; a certain reward being set for every one that kills any of these beasts, of which several skins hang up in a gallery of the fort. They have also sea and land tortoises in great quantities, and the woods furnish them with plenty of honey, which the bees hide in the deepest hollowness of the trees. Neither are they without dogs, which are commonly of a red colour, and have short tails. *The Jackals.*

There is here a certain kind of fish call'd by the *Dutch* the *Hottentots* fish, because the *Hottentots* are very dextrous in taking them. They are very fine fishes, and taste like our cods. Formerly they used to catch abundance of seols, but now most of their fishes are unknown to us. In the *Table Bay* are also whales in abundance, but they are too lean to afford any considerable quantity of oil. Near the sea-shore you meet with the fish call'd by *Latines Torpedo*, by the *Greeks* in the same sense *Naroe*, by the *Spaniards Hugia*, and by the *Dutch Krack Fish* or *Lazy Fish*, not because of its laziness in swimming, but of its hidden qualities, which as is reported, consists in this, that when it finds itself in distress, it sends forth a certain juice, which seizes the fishermen with a cramp in all their limbs. The inhabitants here are call'd *Hottentots* by the *Dutch*, by reason of their stammering. *The* Hottentots *fish.* *The fish* Torpedo.

The men here appear for the most part naked, *The* Hottentots *and their habits.*

1653. naked, having only a kind of a cloak made of doe, sheep, or rabbit skins sowed together, hanging from their shoulders down to their buttocks, fastned under the chin with a ribband, with the rough side outward in the summer, and the same turn'd inside in the winter. When they are travelling they wear over this another cloak with the rough side outwards. Their shoes are made of *Rhinoceros* skin without any heels, tied together on the middle of the feet with two leathern straps. In the night time, or in rainy weather, they wear caps of lamb skins with the woolly side inwards. Their privities they cover with a piece of tiger's skin or such like, which is tied behind with two leather strings. In their hair, which is shaved in some places of the head, they twist small copper plates, horns, and pieces of coral. The women wear cloaks of lamb skins like the men, with the rough side inwards, tho' somewhat longer; besides which they cover their bellies and buttocks, as also their privities, with another four-square skin. On their heads they wear caps of doe, sheep, and rabbit skins, tied round about with a broad sheep-skin strap. Their shoes are the same with the men. Such men or women as are rich in cattle, grease not only their bodies and faces, but likewise their cloaks and caps with suet, but the poor wear no cloaks at all; so that greasiness is among them both an ornament and a token of riches. In both ears they wear strings of coral, each weighing commonly four ounces; about their necks copper beads, round the arms they wear an ivory ring, and a strait copper ring about their wrists. When the women go abroad, they commonly have an empty leathern bag hanging down from their shoulders, in which are only some baubles, but if they have a young child it is carried in this bag. They wear stinking guts twisted twice or thrice round their legs for an ornament, or else dried guts, which serve them as a defence against pricking of thorns, and make a rattling noise when they are dancing and merry making. The men wear them likewise about the neck, and hang their tobacco-pipes and other toys in them.

Their arms. The arms chiefly used among the *Hottentots* are javelins, being sticks of 3, 4, or 5 foot long, pointed at the end with a sharp broad piece of iron; these they make themselves, and use them with great dexterity. They have also some bows and arrows, but are as yet quite ignorant of the use of fire arms. When they go abroad they carry this javelin, call'd by them *Assagaye* in one, and an ostrich feather, or a small stick with a wild cat's tail on the end, in the other hand, wherewith they defend themselves against the gnats and other insects.

The *Hottentots* are very nasty and aukward in eating, for they are ignorant of any thing that relates to cookery, but devour raw pieces of flesh or carrion, as greedy as dogs. The guts themselves they swallow down without washing or dressing, after they have only squeezed them a little. For want of carrion they eat dead stinking fish, such as they meet with near the sea-side, mussels and such like. They kill no cattle except it be rendered useless by sickness or age, except it be a sheep against a wedding dinner. The flesh of sea-dogs or rabbits is a dainty with them, which they devour either quite raw without cleansing, or sometimes broil it a little upon coals. They cut and eat the bacon of dead whales which happen to be cast ashore with great eagerness; nay they drink the oil which is drawn from thence by the heat of the sun, like water. Some bury pieces of this bacon in the sand for their future use. However their best and daily food are certain roots, not unlike our large potatoes, which the women dig up near the rivers and in some other places, those they eat either broil'd or boil'd. They are very eager after our wheat or rice bread which is baked there, and willingly exchange it for cattle. 1653. *Their food.*

Their drink. Their chief drink is water, or milk which their cattle affords them. 'Tis incredible how fond they are of brandy or *Spanish* wine, but a small quantity makes them drunk, when they baul out fearfully, and are very unruly.

Their complection. Those inhabitants near the cape are of a brown olive colour, like the *Mulats*, which however is not their natural complection, but acquired by art, for they broil certain herbs with grease, wherewith they besmear their bodies and faces to make them swarthy, it having been found by experience, that a girl, which was carried into the fort immediately after she was born and brought up there, proved of the same complection with the best of our *European* women. They are of opinion, that in case they don't frequently besmear themselves thus from that time of their birth, they shall be subject to the dropsy, a distemper to which many of the *Africans* are most subject, as the *Abyssines* have one thigh swell'd twice as thick as the other. Upon the arrival of our ships on the cape, they get into the cook's room, and with the fat and black of the kettle, besmear their hair and faces to make them shine the better; this being look'd upon as a great piece of beauty among them, tho' it makes them smell very rank, especially if they put grease into the gashes which they make in their skin for that purpose, when you may smell them at 100 yards distance.

Their constitution and habit of body. They are generally lean, short and ugly, yet

1653. yet they have black quick eyes, and very good white teeth. Their noses are somewhat flat, tho' not always, and the lips, especially the uppermost, very thick. Their foreheads are broad but wrinkled, and the hair of the men is curl'd and short like lambs wool, but very nasty and greasy. The women have thicker hair than the men, the last of which pull out all their hair upon their chin. The men have very well made legs, but slender calves, and are so nimble as to be able to out-run a strong bull, and stop him in his full career. The women especially have very fine and small feet, with flat bellies and round buttocks; their hands are very well shaped, but their fingers and nails very long. The mens privities or yards are very large, but have only one stone; for so soon as a male child is born, the mother cuts out the right stone to make it the more fit for running, and afterwards gives it some sea-water and tobacco. The women, especially those that are married, have long breasts which are always bare, and when they are suckling their infants, hang backwards over their shoulders. The inside of the womens privities are so relaxed that they hang out. Their chiefest riches consist in their cattle, which they never kill but when forced thereunto, either by sickness or age of the beast.

Their tongue. They stammer much in their speech, and bluster out their words like a turky-cock; they make use of no letters, neither do they know what writing and reading is; some however have been taught to speak, read and write *Dutch*, which shews them to be apprehensive enough. For the rest of the *Hottentots* are so very stupid, that they are not able to form to themselves the least idea of attacking or defending a strong hold; a house of brick, such as is proof against fire, being as profitable against them as the best fort, for if you enclose them in a house, and only shut their doors and windows fast, they are as safe here as in the strongest prison, having not the least sense to open them for their deliverance, in which they are inferior to beasts, which commonly endeavour to deliver themselves from bondage. Notwithstanding the *Hottentots* are so stupid, and in my judgment, the most wretched nation upon earth, there are some among them that want not cunning, especially if they are brought up to it; an instance of which we saw in our time in two young fellows, who were carried from hence to *Batavia*, where they were instructed in speaking, reading and writing of *Dutch*. One of them was employed as a servant by the general director, *John Maet Zuicker*, and after some time was sent back to the cape to serve as an interpreter there. I met with him at my first return from the *East-Indies*, among the *Hottentots*, and ask'd him whether he would not rather be with us where he lived much better? he told me, he would rather be with his own countrymen. I understood afterwards, that this fellow had proved the occasion of great mischief and differences among the *Hottentots*, and that several had been kill'd in the quarrel on both sides. At last he fell again into the hands of the commander of the cape, who banish'd him to the *Robben Island*, where he died. Theft they punish with a bastinado, and so they do murther, not out of any regard to God Almighty, but for custom's sake. They talk of one *Hunumma*, who has the disposal of rain and fair weather, but they pay no adoration to him.

Their stupidity.

1653.

Their marriage. Marriage is in pretty good esteem among them, tho' a man marries as many wives as he pleases. The maid, as soon as she is betrothed, performs the oath of fidelity in the following manner: The mother cuts of the first joint of her daughters little finger, which is tied to her future husband's finger, this they bury, and afterwards kill a cow for their wedding dinner. The maids are distinguish'd from the married women by green twigs which are twisted round their legs; these are taken off at the wedding day, and instead of them the dried guts of the cow kill'd for the wedding dinner put on; these when they dance make a noise, which seems very agreeable to them.

They have something of religion. 'Tis true the *Hottentots* are the most barbarous upon earth; notwithstanding which, I can't agree with those that will not allow of any religious worship among them; it being the opinion of all learned men, that no nation is so barbarous but what has something of religion, be it true or false. For they adore the moon with unusual outcries; and it is not improbable but that they pay the same devotion to the sun, because they follow its course as much as is possible, by changing the pasture of their cattle; for when the sun comes to the tropick of *Capricorn*, it has been observed that they feed their cattle on the south-east side of the rivulet, but when the sun returns to the tropick of *Cancer*, they go to the north-side; if it happens to rain very hard, they shelter themselves in their huts, seem to be fearful, and don't creep out till it be fair weather. Then they begin to be very merry, lifting up their heads and eyes to heaven, which is interpreted by us as a kind of thanksgiving; for when they are asked why they hide themselves during the rain, they answer, that the *Great Captain* being incensed against them, does punish them with this element, which he knows to be contrary to their nature. By this *Great Captain* they questionless

leſs underſtand the ſupreme Being; for if you ſpeak to them of God, they are unwilling to hear it, and puniſh ſuch among them as make uſe of it; alledging that it is not ſufficient to expreſs the glory of the ſupreme Being. If you talk of the devil they point to the ground Concerning the reſurrection, they are of opinion, that thoſe that die near the cape, ſhall ariſe again behind the mountains: But perhaps all this they may have learned from the *Portugueſe* and *Dutch*. They frequently ſkirmiſh with one another, commonly for the conveniency of paſtorage, ſo that ſometimes ſix or ſeven are left dead upon the ſpot.

Divers nations of the Hottentots.

The *Hottentots* are divided into ſeveral nations, known by different names. Thoſe inhabiting near our fort are by the *Dutch* call'd *Capemen*, but in their own tongue *Chouriequa*; they are the moſt cunning of all the reſt, by their frequent commerce with the *Dutch* and other *Europeans*; they live for the moſt part upon roots, fiſh and muſſels. Somewhat deeper in the country live thoſe commonly call'd *Tobacco Thieves*, becauſe they uſed to ſteal the tobacco out of the fields, which is the reaſon the *Dutch* plant no more tobacco there; in their own tongue they are call'd *Korrochaukon*. There is another ſort call'd *Chemakwa*, much more potent and richer than the *Capemen*, yet don't approach in power to the *Cochukwas*, who living ſtill deeper in the country, are accounted many thouſand ſtrong, and have vaſt herds of cows and ſheep; they were then under the juriſdiction of two captains, the firſt call'd *Odoſoy*, the other *Monomana*. The firſt of theſe two had married the ſiſter of our interpreter's wife in the fort, and being invited thither by Mr. *Rietbeck*, the governor, he at laſt, after much enquiry concerning his quality, for fear of demeaning himſelf, gave him a viſit. They rid out together a hunting, when *Odoſoy* had the misfortune to be ſet upon by a fierce lion, who certainly would have torn him to pieces, had not his followers kill'd the lion with their javelins; however he did not eſcape without being ſorely wounded on the neck, the fleſh was all torn from one of his ſhoulder blades, and his face all miſerably maul'd: Being judged paſt recovery, the governor offered him his own ſurgeon, but he would not accept of him, truſting more to thoſe of his own nation; tho' the ſkill of theſe ſurgeons among the *Hottentots* reaches no farther than to cure a green wound, which they ſcarce ever perform without leaving a great dent or ſeam. They carry their remedies about them, and commonly have a parrot or ſome ſuch creature (not unlike our mountebanks) along with them. Their herbs they keep in tortoiſe ſhells, but the roots, claws, teeth, and horns of beaſts (theſe b eing the ingredients of their phyſical prepa ations) are faſtned to a ſtring, which they n the ſame manner as our tooth-drawers hang about the neck.

There is another nation of the *Hottentots* call'd by the *Dutch Sardiniamen* or *Saldanhas* (from a bay of that name) the natives call them *Krijegoekwa*. Some of the *Hottentots* relate, that to the north-eaſt of thoſe call'd *Kochukas*, there is a potent nation dwelling in ſtone-houſes, that they are not black, and governed by the ſame laws as we are. Some ſuppoſe them to be a people inhabiting the mountains of the moon, but conſidering they are ſaid to underſtand gold and ſilver, and to agree in many other things with the *Europeans*; our people judge them to be a colony of the *Portugueſe* that have tranſplanted themſelves thither from *Mozambique*. The *Dutch* have ſeveral times attempted to find out a paſſage thither by land, but without ſucceſs, having always been forc'd to turn back for want of water. They alſo talk much of two other nations call'd *Heukumqua* and *Grocman*. The *Hottentots* or inhabitants here are not ſubject to one head, and what reverence they pay to their captains, is more out of cuſtom than any ſenſe of duty; they have no fix'd habitations, but lead a vagabond life like the antient *Scytes* and *Arabians*, carrying their wives and children along with them. They are not very deſirous of gold and ſilver, unleſs ſome few that converſe with the *Dutch*, and know the conveniency of buying from them what they ſtand in need of; for otherwiſe copper is in the greateſt eſteem with them. Boats they have none, being extremely fearful of water, and therefore venture ſeldom farther than to their knees. They are of a very lazy temper; moſt of their traffick conſiſts in cows and ſheep, which they exchange for copper and corals; but after the bargain is ſtruck, they expect an additional preſent of tobacco, pipes and brandy, which has been introduced among them by foreigners. The ſeamen do alſo ſometimes ſwap with them for oſtrich feathers, and ſmall tortoiſe ſhells call'd *Harego*. It is to be admired how they ſhould make ſo much account of copper, which they daily tread under their feet, it being certain that very good copper mines are to be found hereabouts. The *Dutch* have at divers times attempted ſeveral land journeys into the country; as for inſtance, in the year 1660, when they diſcovered two nations, *viz.* the *Illunha* and *Namakkawa*; they ſuppoſed to have not been very far from the *Portugueſe*, becauſe they thought to have heard a cannon ſhot at a diſtance. The inland country ſwarms with wild fowl, ſuch as wild geeſe, ducks and teal, but they are ſo ſhy as not

1647. to come within reach of a gun, which is the reason that the governor's huntsman sets up small huts of green boughs, from whence he shoots them, this being the only way to come at them. Among the mountains are abundance of rocks, and some of them contain fresh water in their concavities. Several of our people as they were going one day up the mountains to take a view of the circumjacent country, found a certain rockstone of four fathom long, and one and a half broad, being hollow in the middle, of the depth of a quarter of a yard, where they met with good store of fine fresh water. Here are ostriches of an extraordinary bigness; they are so swift as to outrun a horse when they set up their wings, and thus by the help of the wind are forced forward, no otherwise than a ship under sail. Their large legs and feet are a great addition to them, by the help of which they trot on with such a force and nimbleness that like a horse running down a hill, they are scarce to be stopt. The same way of setting up their wings has been observed in the tame swans. But before we leave this cape, I will give you a short account of the *Lions Mountain*, the *Table Mountain* and *Table Bay*, as likewise of the *Robben Isle*.

The Table Mountain. There are two very high mountains near this cape, *viz.* the *Table Moutain* and the *Lions Mountain.* The first is so call'd from its flatness on the top like a table, being about two leagues high, but small in circumference, and for that reason of very difficult access. It is divided from another adjacent mountain, call'd the *Devil's Mountain* by a vast cliff. Towards the sea-side it is bare, without any grass or trees, but on the land-side you see very agreeable woods, with many tall strait trees fit for building; and towards the foot abundance of lesser trees for fuel. Among the rest are a great store of wild almond-trees, but the fruit is very bitter; and if we may believe the *Hottentots*, poisonous; wild pine-trees are here likewise in abundance, they grow very tall, but bear nothing but a husk.

Table Bay. The *Table Bay* is situate under 34 deg. and some min. about 5 leagues more to north, this being the most southern point of *Afrita*. It is a very fine bay, tho' on the south-side of the *Robben Island* are some rocks call'd the *Whale*; a large ship may anchor in this bay, from 9 to 7 fathom water, but yachts at 4 or 5 fathom in a good sandy ground. There is however no trusting to a single anchor, by reason of the blustring south-east winds which blow often here.

Robben Island. At the entrance of the *Table Bay* you see the *Robben Island*, thus call'd from the vast quantity of *Sea Robben (Sea Rabbits)* which are found here. It is not very high, and about two leagues in circumference. In the towns some rabbits have been put by the inhabitants which thrive very well. The ground produces a certain herb in great plenty; it has yellow leaves almost like cowslips, which fatten the sheep exceedingly. 1653.

To the north-east of the *Robben Island* lies the *Dassen Island*, under 34 deg. 33 min. It has got its name from the vast numbers of *Dassen (Does)* which formerly were found there, but are of late years much diminish'd. It is about a league in compass, and produces likewise many sea rabbits and *Pinguwyns*. It is inhabited by four families only with their slaves, whose chief employment it is to breed pigs and poultry, and to draw oil from the sea-rabbits, which they sell to the inhabitants living in and near the fort. Before the bay of *Saldanba* are several small islands, where those of the *Dassen Island* have their liberty of fishing and hunting; they catch vast quantities of partridges, mullets and other fish. The two chief rivers of this cape are the *Salt* and *Fresh Rivers*. Besides these there is another rivulet, which arising from among a neighbouring wood, exonerates itself in the *Salt River*. It is not above 12 or 14 foot broad, but very deep. Not far from the source of this, arises another rivulet among the marshes near the *Wood Bay*. It runs south-east thro' the downs, (which extend as far as *Cabo falso*) and disembogues itself into the sea. Dassen Island.

No place in the world is more subject to storms than the *Cape of Good Hope*, so that it would be impossible for ships to abide here, had not nature provided against these inconveniencies by the several commodious bays that are here. Among those the bay of *Saldanba*, commonly call'd *Sardinia*, is none of the least consequence, where ships may ride safely at anchor without the least danger, and were it not for the want of fresh water, it might claim the preference before the *Table Bay* itself. The winds blow generally throughout the year very hard here, but especially the south-east wind, which blows from *October* to *April* (call'd the *South-East Monzon)* and tears so terribly thro' the clift, (betwixt the *Table* and the *Devil's Mountain)* that except the country and ground were very smooth and hard here, it would be impossible for any ship to ride it out; from *April* until *October*, the north-west wind blows with not much less violence, (call'd the *North-West Monzon)* but yet not altogether so fierce as the south-east wind, there its violence is more observable on the land-side of the clift. The main difference betwixt these two winds here is, that the south-east wind always produces dry weather, whereas the north-west wind brings rains, *The Cape subject to storms.*

1653. rains, which are very pernicious to the fruit.

By what signs to discover the nearness of the cape.

So soon as you come near the sight of the cape, under the 34 deg. of southern latitude, you meet with certain signs and tokens, by which you may discover whether you are far from land or not. I don't much wonder that some of the ancient authors who have given us an account of the *Indies*, affirm, that when they were at a loss to find out whether they were near land or not, they used to let fly some birds, and according to their flight, to direct their course. Tho' this is out of date now, yet certain it is, that the birds are the best guide as to those who sail to the *East-Indies:* For at a great distance from the cape, whilst you are yet in the open sea, you meet with a peculiar kind of small sea-gulls, which foretel you your approach to this cape. But as these come abroad sometimes above 100 leagues or more at sea, they are but uncertain forerunners, but when you see another kind of large spotted sea-gulls appear, by those that are acquainted in these seas call'd *Cape-Birds*, with speckled wings, you may hope to see land in a very short time, and if you meet with some turtle doves, this puts it beyond all doubt. If you find anchorage at 40 or 50 fathoms depth, in a white sandy ground mix'd with red, you may conclude yourself to be upon the sandridge of the cape *d'Aguillas*, tho' you see no land. If you come to the west of the *Cape of good Hope*, you will find, besides the aforementioned *Cape-Birds*, certain hollow roots growing among the rocks in the sea, the leaves of which swim upon the water; the *Portuguese* call them *Trombas*, and they are to be met with in vast quantities in the *Table Bay*, just under the fort, which the chaloops and boats are very careful to avoid, they being so entangled together, that there is no breaking thro' them with oars: It is likewise found in the seas of *Japan*, and in great esteem among the inhabitants, who make pickles of these leaves, and use them as the *Europeans* do cucumbers, or the *Indians* their *Actsjar*.

The *Hottentots*, a barbarous generation, were so ill-natur'd at that time, that they would not exchange an ox or any other sort of fresh provisions with us, nay they made the spring or places where we used to fetch our fresh water, muddy; we fell rough upon some of them, but they being much stronger than we, pelted us with stones and made us retire; I was at that time with a gun upon the *Table Mountain*, but could not come time enough to their assistance; but the next day several of us went well arm'd to give them another visit, and to fire at them in case they pretended to make any opposition, but they no sooner discovered our arms, but fled with wife, children, and their cattle. 1653.

Their departure from the cape.

After we had stay'd there about three days ashore, we set sail the 13th of *March* from the cape, steering our course westward, in hopes to get sight of the ship the *Drake*; but not meeting with her, we chose the open sea, and advanced about 60 leagues from the *Table Bay*, under 34 deg. 20 min. southern latitude. We contiuued our voyage with pretty good success till the 18th, when about noon we found ourselves under 38 deg. 26 min. southern latitude, and 33 deg. 27 min. longitude. The compass shew'd due south and north. The two next following days proved very rainy and blustring, and the 27th it thundred and lightned very hard, with strong winds and much rain, which ending at last in a violent storm, oblig'd us to take in all our sails, under 39 deg. 20 min. southern latitude. The 1st of *April* we found ourselves far to the north, being forced by the stream, and the weather continued windy and rainy, as it had been ever since the 27th of *March*; we found ourselves then under 39 deg. 21 min. of latitude, and 95 deg. 30 min. of longitude, and had sail'd 36 leagues in the last 24 hours. The same night the winds began to rise to that degree, that we were fain to take in our main sail, which continued to the 3d, when the compass was changed to 15 deg. N. W. The 7th we sail'd 44 leagues with a moderate gale, under 38 deg. 13 min. The rains and strong winds continued till the 13th in the morning, when it began to clear up, and sail'd that day and night 46 leagues under 36 deg. 30 min. latitude, and 98 deg. 42 min. longitude. Then it began to be blustery weather again. The 15th we found the rising of the sun at 24 deg. N. W. this being the first time since the 4th of the last month, by reason of the strong weather. About noon we were under 35 deg. 14 min. of latitude, and 104 deg. 40 min. longitude; having sailed 34 leagues in 24 hours. Towards evening it began to be calm, but continued not long, the winds and rains infesting us by turns, till the 1st of *May*, when we found ourselves under 12 deg. 18 min. latitude, and 124 deg. 46 min. longitude: We then proceeded in our voyage with a good brisk gale till the 3d, when in the night we were overtaken with a violent *Travado* with thunder and lightning, which continued till the next following day. The 6th of *May*, early in the morning, we descried the coast of the isle of *Sumatra*, about 4 or 5 leagues from us, and to the leeward a sail under 5 deg. 22 min. In the night the wind blowing from the land-side, we were forced to take

They get sight of Sumatra.

1653. take our course to the south. By the 9th we had not advanc'd above 6 or 7 leagues along the coast of Sumatra, being continually pestred with Travadoes, thunder and lightning; all our endeavours were to get above the flat point of the streights of Sunda. The 12th we had pretty fair wind and weather, and about noon found ourselves under 6 deg. 5 min. In the afternoon we sail'd forward with a moderate gale, within a league and half of the forementioned point to the N. N. E. of us, where we found 16 fathom water. The next day we found ourselves about three leagues from the said point. The 14th we saw the *Imperial Island*, at about three leagues distance, and the next following day discovered to the south-east to east, about 5 or 6 leagues from us the *Princes Islands*, under 60 deg. 45 min. where we were becalm'd all the rest of the day. The 17th we found ourselves under 17 deg. 10 min. about two leagues from these islands, and toward the evening saw the utmost point of land of the isle of *Java*, at 4 or 5 leagues from us; the 18th we were becalm'd again, and the following day advanc'd within two leagues of the point of *Java*; and 2 or 3 leagues of the *Princes Islands*. We endeavoured to have pass'd betwixt them, but were prevented by a *Travado* from the east. The 20th being under 60 deg. 41 min. we were at 6 leagues distance from the said islands, and kept in sight of them the 21st and 22d, with an intent to pass by them on the 23d, but being becalm'd came to an anchor the same night at 30 fathoms depth; the stream did run here very strong to the S. W. The 24th we were directly opposite N. N. E. to the isle of *Java*, and the same evening, a boat with all sorts of refreshments came aboard us from thence, which was very welcome to us, after so tedious a voyage: We came soon after to an anchor at 30 fathoms water, the stream running so strong here, that we were forc'd to remain here this and the next following day; during which time, several other boats with fresh provisions came aboard us. The 26th we set sail again, but by reason of the violence of the stream could not advance far, so that we were forced to cast anchor again, at 25 fathoms depth, where we continued all the next day. The 28th we set up our sails again, but were forced soon after to cast anchor, having the *Iulo* (the isle) *Baly* to the N. E. Great *Pulo modi* to the E. and the lesser *Pulo modi* to the S. of us. Towards evening we set sail again, but whatever we did could not reach the road of the so long wish'd-for city of *Batavia*, being forced to come to an anchor about half a league from the isle of *Rotterdam* at 11 fathoms water. The 30th we put up our sails once more, but with no better success, being oblig'd to cast anchor again, which put us in mind of what befel us lately on the *Cape of good Hope*, where we met with the same ill success before we could double the cape. However, the wind turning fair in the afternoon, we arrived the same afternoon about four a clock, (after a very tedious voyage, in which we had many sick) before the city of *Batavia*, where we cast anchor at four fathoms and a half depth. The next day I went ashore, and took up my lodgings in that famous city, at one Mr. *Gerard Utsens*, till further orders. In the mean time I was very curious in taking an exact view of this city and the circumjacent country: Whilst I tarried at *Batavia*, an embassy was sent from the general director *John Maetzuicker* and the other directors of the *East-India* company, to the *Cham of Tartary*, who some few years before had conquered the most potent empire of *China*, to treat about a free commerce betwixt the two nations, which had several times before been attempted and sought for by the *Dutch*, but was as often refused by the *Chinese*. *Jacob de Keisar* and *Peter de Goyer* being appointed ambassadors, two yachts, *viz.* the *Kaukerk* and *Bloemendael*, man'd with 90 men, and provided with several fine presents for the emperor were got ready for their transport, and I was ordered to go aboard the *Bloemendael* in the quality of steward.

The Imperial Island.

The Princes Islands.

They arrive at Batavia.

The ambassadors embark'd the 14th of *July* 1655, and set sail the same day from the road of *Batavia*. The 4th of *September* they arrived in the city of *Kanton*, and the 4th of *May* 1656, in the city of *Nanking*, and the 16th of *July* at *Peking*. After some stay there, they returned the 21st of *November* to *Nanking*, to *Kanton* the 28th of *February* 1657, and came into the road of *Batavia* the 21st of *March*, where they gave an account of their negotiation to the *Dutch* council of the *Indies*: Of all which I have given you an ample account in my *Chinese* voyage, publish'd first in *Low Dutch*, and since translated into several other languages, and printed at *Amsterdam* for *Jacob Meurs*, with many cuts and draughts of places, living creatures, fruits and other remarkable things.

Mr. Nieuhoff sent to China.

After my return from thence, eight ships were ordered to be equip'd and loaden for *Holland*. viz. the *Pearl*, *Prince William*, the *Orange*, the *Crowned Lion*, *Achilles*, *Malacca*, the *Ulysses* and *Hector*. The command in chief of this fleet was conferred upon Mr. *Koenes*, then first director of the council of the *Indies*, who embark'd aboard the *Pearl* of 700 tuns, man'd with 180 men, and provided with 26 guns. At his 1658.

1658.

He returns from Batavia *towards* Holland. *Arrival at* St.Helens.

request I went aboard along with him in the *Pearl*, which carried the flag, in order to my return into *Holland*, tho' my appointed time was not expired here. We set sail the 22d of *December*, and the last day of *March* 1658, arrived safely without any remarkable accident, (except that we met with some *Travados*, which soundly tost our ship) at the isle of *St. Helens.*

The isle of *St. Helens*, is situate under 16 deg. 15 min. of southern latitude, at a great distance from the continent, lying at least 350 leagues from *Augusta*, the next place of all. It is very surprising to conceive so small an island at so vast a distance at sea, round about which there is scarce any anchorage, by reason of the vast depth of the seas. It is about seven leagues in circum- 1658.

The isle of St.Helens.

ference, covered all over with rocky hills, which in a clear day may be seen 14 leagues at sea; the valleys being stor'd with all sorts of trees: So that tho' this island is not very large in its compass, yet it comprehends a large tract of ground by reason of those hills. It has many fine valleys, among which the *Church-Valley* and the *Apple-Valley* are the most remarkable. In the *Church-Valley*, you see to this day the ruins of a chapel, formerly belonging to the *Portuguese*; the whole valleys are planted with lemons, oranges, and pomegranate-trees. At that time the island was destitute of inhabitants, but since the *English* have made a settlement there. After the *Portuguese* left it, a certain hermit, under pretence of devotion, used to kill great numbers of wild goats here, and sell their skins, which the *Portuguese* having got notice of, they removed him from thence. At another time certain negroes with two female slaves were got into the mountains, where they encreased to the number 20, till they at last were likewise forc'd from thence. The valleys are excessive hot, but on the hills it is cool enough: tho' the heat is much tempered by the winds and frequent rain showers, which fall sometimes several times in a day; which, with the heat of the sun-beams, renders the soil very fruitful. It abounds in fine and cool springs, which fall down from the tops of the hills, the water being as clear as crystal, and exonerating itself at last into the sea, it is very pleasant to behold the seamen at their arrival here, to drink, wash and bath themselves in these spring waters. Most of the fruits and beasts which are produced here in great plenty, have been first brought hither by the *Portuguese*;

1658. *tuguese*; as for instarce, orange-trees, (of which you may see whole woods) pomegranate-trees and others, which bear fruit throughout he whole year. Here are likewise, mustard-leaves, parsly, sorrel, purslin, wintercresses and other such-like herbs, which are very good against the scurvy; neither is this island destitute of trees, but such as are not fit for timber, but only for fuel. It abounds likewise in beasts; wild goats are here in vast numbers, but very difficult to be taken, by reason of the many rocks. Tame hogs were brought hither by the *Portuguese*, which have multiply'd to admiration, but are degenerated into wild ones, and are not easy to be kill'd for the aforemention'd reason. Thus it is with the partridges, wild pigeons and peacocks, which are here in vast plenty, but are so shy, that so soon as they see any one approach, they fly from one hill to another cross the valleys, so that you must be an hour before you can come at them again, which when you have done, you are in danger of losing your labour, for they return commonly from whence they came. The only way to catch them, is to go abroad with a good company. It produces no ravenous or poisonous creatures, except large spiders and flies. All about the island you see vast multitudes of sea-gulls, which feed on the fishes in which the sea abounds. Here you meet likewise with several colours fit for dyers, especially with a most excellent red colour, and with very fine white salt, made out of the sea-water by the heat of the sun-beams. By reason of its great distance from the continent, the seas hereabouts are covered with fishes, such as mackarel, carps, &c. They are not to be catch'd with nets by reason of the vast depth, but with a hook, or only an iron nail bent, you may catch as many as you please; craw-fish, crabs, oysters and mussels are likewise to be found in vast quantities near the sea-shore. After we had sufficiently refresh'd our selves here, and provided what necessaries we thought fit, or could get, we left this island the last day of *May*; We continued our former course, and without any remarkable accident, came in sight of *Holland*, and the 6th of *July* 1658 arrived happily at *Amsterdam*. I took up my lodgings at my brother *Henry Nieuhoff*'s, whom as well as most of my other friends, I had the good fortune to find in good health. Many of the most curious persons of that place came daily to see me, to take a view of the *Chinese* characters, and other draughts I had brought along with me.

They depart from St. Helens.

Arrive in Holland.

After I had tarried for three months in *Holland*, and dispatch'd my business both here and in *Zeland*, I delivered the journal of my late voyage into *China* to my brother, in order to have it review'd and printed, at the request of several persons of quality; with an intention to take a second voyage to the *East-Indies*, with the first fair opportunity, which was soon after offered me by the directors of the *East-India* company. 5 ships lay then ready for the *East-Indies* under the command of Mr. *Adrian Aelmonde*, *viz.* the *Arnheim*, burthen 500 tuns, with 40 guns and 430 men, *John Tymensz* master; the second the *Pearl* and three yachts; I was ordered aboard the first. We set sail all together from the *Ulic* the 22d of *Dec.* 1658. The ship the *Arnheim* at her entrance into the sea, struck upon the sands and was in some danger of being stav'd, and another ship run foul upon her, by which she lost part of her gallery; but by God's singular mercy, we got clear again the next high tide, and continued our voyage with the rest.

Nieuhoff's *second voyage to the* East-Indies.

1659. The 16th of *March* 1659, we arrived safely at the *Cape of Good Hope*, where we cast our anchor. The 22d, the *Pearl* with the other three yachts came likewise to anchor in the same bay. The first thing we did was to take care of our sick, of which we had not very many, but 12 died in the voyage; we went every day ashore to fetch fresh water, fuel, and what provisions we were able to get; sometimes we catch'd good store of fishes. One day several of us went ashore to shoot some wild fowl; but advancing pretty high up the *Table Mountain*, we unawares espy'd a sleeping lion, at no great distance from us, which made me soon retreat, telling my companions it was dangerous to awake a sleeping lyon, who were glad as well as I, to make the best of their way backwards.

Arrives at the Cape *of* Good-Hope.

After a stay of 14 days at the cape, we set sail again, and with a much more prosperous gale, than I had in my last voyage, arrived safely on the coast of *St. Java*, where just as we got sight of that island, Mr. *Adrian Aelmonde* died, to our great grief; his corps was carried to *Batavia*, where it was honourably interr'd.

He leaves the Cape.

The 18th of *July* 1659, we came to an anchor before the city of *Batavia*, after a voyage of about 7 months; during which, there happen'd scarce any thing worth taking notice of. After I had delivered up the merchandises under my charge, and my accounts: I took a turn to the western coast of *Sumatra*, *viz.* to *Jambe* and *Padane*, which produce abundance of pepper, some gold and salt-peter, and returned the 10th of *December* to *Batavia*.

His arrival at Batavia.

Not long after I was ordered on board the ship *Henrietta Lowisa* bound for *Amboyna*, *Gerard Gerardson* a native of *Flussigen* master,

1659. master, laden with rice and provisions. We set sail from *Batavia* the 23d of *Dec.* 1659, and in a month after got among the rocks near the point of *Bimaer*, being forced thither by a whirlpool, which turn'd our ship within the compass of three times the length of the ship, as swift as the nimblest horse could run; we were within a few yards of having been struck against a rock, but had the good fortune to escape without much damage, and after some *Travadoes* at last got into the road of *Amboyna*, not without great difficulty, by reason of the swiftness of the stream there, and cast anchor at 36 fathoms depth. We were very kindly received by Mr. *Jacob Hustard* the governor of *Amboyna*, a man of singular probity and conduct. After the ship was unladen, and I had delivered my cargo, the governor and I resolved to take a tour in the small circumjacent islands. Among the rest we visited the island of *Buero*, where the inhabitants made us heartily welcome after their way, and drank to us merrily in cups made of the leaves of trees.

Goes to Amboyna.

The isle of Bouro or Buero.

The isle of *Bouro* or *Buero*, is situate about 24 leagues off *Amboyna*, being near 30 leagues in compass. The sea, especially on the south side, of a vast depth, from whence the shore rises by degrees, and surrounds the whole island like a steep wall. The south wind produces both high and low water here. In the island of *Buero* are mountains which reach to the very skies: Near the bay of *Tamahoo* are high mountains of the same name, the blue tops of which penetrate thro' the clouds, and may be seen at 28 leagues distance at sea; tho' it be very difficult to distinguish them from the clouds. The bay of *Tamahoo* is surrounded with these mountains. Hereabouts you see neither houses, huts, nor inhabitants, but only woods and wildernesses. A certain river exonerates itself into this bay, the banks of which are on both sides full of green trees. On the north-east side of the isle *Buero*, in another bay, called the bay of *Kayelle*, which in some places is two leagues broad. The sea-shore of this bay is very pleasant, by reason of the many woods and wildernesses. Here you see great store of green ebony wood-trees, but the wood is somewhat knotty. Within the marshy grounds, adjacent to the middle of the bay, is a whole wood of trees as hard as iron, and of a reddish colour; the *Dutch* call them *Lary* trees. 1657.

The Bay of Kayelle.

The constitution of this island.

The island *Buero* is very fertile and abounding in trees near the sea-shore. It produces *Coco* and *Bananas* trees, *Pynany*, green ebony wood-trees, potatoes, beans, *Katjang* (a certain kind of pease) millet or indian-wheat, tobacco, lime-trees, and divers

1659. vers sorts of herbs. In the mountains are civet-cats, and the inhabitants have a peculiar easy way of taking the civet from them, which they sell very cheap. In short, the whole countrey is full of fertile grounds and pleasant woods, and is watered with many fresh water rivers; the worst of all is, that it is much subject to earthquakes.

In the isle of *Buero* lives, among other beasts, a certain strange creature, which by the *Indians* is counted among the number of monsters. It is of the bigness of a large dog, or of a roe-buck, of a dark brown and gray colour, the hair like our gray-hounds; the head and mouth like a hog, with small eyes and ears, the tail curls twice or thrice, and the legs and claws like those of a roe-buck. The flesh is both by the inhabitants and strangers look'd upon as a dainty, and as good as venison. The circumference of its mouth and jaws is as big as a large calf's head, with very strong jaw-bones; on both sides backwards to the throat, are about 12 teeth, but in the fore-part of the undermost jaw-bone, 6 teeth and 2 large ones in the upper part, which are covered by the mouth. From the middle part of the undermost jaw-bone issue forth two large teeth which pierce the mouth. They are a foot long each, about an inch thick, and somewhat crooked like those of the wild boar. Out of the upper jaw-bones spring forth two horns, on each side one, of an inch thick, a quarter of a yard long, smooth like teeth, and turn'd like a hook at the end, which makes it appear at first sight as if it were armed with 4 horns.

On the north-east of the isle of *Buero* are the following villages, *Waiselonga*, *Fogi*, *Wainite*, *Tamahou*, *Palmatte*, *Hokonima*, *Bara*, *Liciela*, *Waisamma*, *Ilat*, and *Romaite*; The eight first of these villages were in 1653, burn'd to the ground by the *Dutch*, with all their boats, the inhabitants having revolted against them. This island is under the jurisdiction of the king of *Tarnate*. In the year 1660, the *Dutch* built a fort with four small bastions, provided with convenient habitations for the use of the garrison in this island, to keep out those of *Makassar*. It was nam'd *Mandarshaa*, after the then king of *Tarnate*. The natives of *Buero* are pursuant to their capitulation made with the *Dutch*, obliged to inhabit round about the bay of *Kayelle*, where they are possess'd of about 14 villages under the *Dutch* protection: Their houses are neatly built of cane, and some have convenient appartments; and for the improvement of the adjacent grounds, are obliged to cut down and burn the trees and woods, and to turn them into fields, gardens and orchards. Before that time, they lived only in wretched huts built along the sea-shore among the woods. They 1659. are very black, and like most of the inhabitants of the other neighbouring islands, almost naked both men and women, having only a piece of stuff to cover their nakedness from the waste down to the knees; but girls and boys till they are twelve years old, go quite naked. A young fellow that has a mind to marry a certain maid, may soon obtain her, by making a small present of eatables, or any other thing of no value to her parents. As soon as a woman is brought to bed, she goes streight to the next river, where she washes both her self and the child, and so returns to her usual employments, in the mean while the husband is attended and made much of in the wife's stead. They bemoan their dead neighbours and friends with lamentable out-crys, but after the corps is buried, they dance, sing, feast and make merry. Their graves are made of brick-work, with stones and clay, to preserve them against the wild-beasts. The common food of the natives is *Zagow*, millet, rice and dry'd fish. They are for the most part mahometans, tho' some retain much of paganism, and adore the crocodiles. In the year 1650, one *Madira* governor for the king of *Ternate* in the isle of *Amboyna*, having taken up arms against the *Dutch* in *Amboyna*, the inhabitants of *Buero*, as well those under the king's as *Dutch* subjection, join'd with *Madira* with so much obstinacy, that they chose rather to die than to leave *Madira*; and in 1652 kill'd four sea men belonging to a vessel call'd the *Goose*, who ventured too far into the woods. Mr. *Arnold Flaming van Outshorn* being, 1652, sent with a strong squadron of ships to *Batavia*, and from thence to *Amboyna* and *Buero*, to bring the inhabitants to reason; having understood their barbarous proceedings, burn'd all their boats, and the before-mention'd villages. The king *Mandarshaa* came along with him in person, having before concluded a peace with the *East-India* company at *Batavia*.

After we had taken a full view of this island, we returned to *Amboyna*, where the governor gave a splendid entertainment to the chiefest officers of the company, and some of the courtiers belonging to the kings of *Amboyna*. After dinner we play'd together, and they seem'd so well satisfied, that it might easily be seen there was a good correspondence betwixt them and the company at that time. In the mean while my ship having been loaden with 16 tuns of cloves and some other commodities, I took my leave from Mr. *Hustard* the governor, and the 3d of *May* directed my course back towards *Batavia*. Under the government of this Mr. *Hustard* were at that time all the

The author's departure from Amboyna.

1659. *Molucco* islands, whose business it is to keep a strict eye over them, for fear they should export cloves. But before I quite leave the isle of *Amboyna*, I will give you a description of its situation, and what else is worth our observation there.

The isle of Amboyna. The Isle of *Amboyna* or *Amboyno* is by some numbred among the *Molucco* islands, because it produces great store of cloves like the *Molucco* islands. It is situate under 3 deg. southern latitude, about 24 leagues from the isle of *Banda*, and consequently nearer the coast of *Malacca*, than any of the *Molucco* islands. It is 24 leagues in circumference, being divided almost in two parts, by a vast bay or rather gulph. It has a very fine bay where ships may ride safely at anchor near the shore; about two leagues within this bay, is the *Dutch* fort called *Victoria*. It appears like two islands joined together by a neck of land. About 60 or 70 years ago, there were 57 goodly villages or great plantations, inhabited by *Indians* and christians, (some of which were of good strength,) but many of them have been laid desolate, or at least are much decay'd by the intestine wars.

The village Way. Among the rest *Way* was a very fine plantation on the north-side of the island, half a league from the sea-shore, built upon a rock, and defended by a good breast-work; notwithstanding which, it was 1630 surprised by one *Kimelaha*, the inhabitants were christians. Near this village are abundance of clove and *Zague* trees, and all along the sea-shore are several other plantations of less note, all well provided with clove and *Zague* trees. The village of *Way* has this conveniency, that it is well provided with fresh springs, a thing of the utmost consequence in those hot countries.

Noussanive. The village *Noussanive* was situate upon a river on the west-side under the cannon of the fort *Victoria*, being divided into three plantations. The countrey thereabouts abounds in clove-trees; the plantations of which extend as far as to the utmost point of the western cape, and on the other side, as far as *Ayer Kabouba*: The king or captain of this district used to be formerly president of the council of *Amboyna*.

Hittoe. The village of *Hittoe* is very ancient, and built near the sea-side, under the redoubt belonging to the *Dutch* company, being the capital of the whole district of *Hittoe*.

Wawami. *Wawami*, the head village of all, lies above a league from the sea-shore, upon a hill near an *English* mile high, unto which leads but one passage, which in the midst is defended by strong pallisadoes, and the top of the hill (which is of an oval figure) by a stone wall. Betwixt the hill and the fort slides along a pretty river. Formerly this was a noted place of retreat for the inhabitants, who used to shelter them selves here. 1659.

The village *Mousala* is built upon a mountain about a league and a half high, being so strong by nature, as to be counted impregnable; notwithstanding which, it has been reduced by the victorious arms of the *Dutch East-India* company, under whose jurisdiction they now live. Mousala.

The following plantations or villages were in 1630, under the jurisdiction of the *Dutch East-India* company.

The district of *Rossenive* which comprehends *Rossenive*, *Amahoesoe* and *Hattoe*. *Rossenive* had in 1630, one *Andrew Rossenive* for their king or captain; *Amahoesoe* one *Domingos Costa Makkake*, *Poeta* and *Hattoe*, one *Lessemesse*. These villages were better inhabited than most of the rest, the inhabitants making profession of the christian religion, yet not without some mixture of *Mahometanism*, except those of *Amahoesoe*, whose captain was a good christian, and lived much better than the rest; which shews that the chief defect lay in their kings; for *Andrew Rossenive* was none of the best livers, tho' he could very artificially play the hypocrite; he had no wife but many concubines; and tho' he was often admonish'd to marry, he continued obstinate in the same course, which gave great scandal as well to the inhabitants as to the other kings and captains. The common people of this town were always more ready for the service of the company than those of the other villages. For the villages *Rossenive*, *Amahoesoe* and *Hattoe* are obliged to supply and manage one half of the governours *Korrakoren*, (or small vessels of war) as the villages of *Kielang*, *Nakko* and *Hattela* are bound to supply the other half. Rossenive.

Kielang was one of the most considerable villages on the south-side of the mountain of *Laytimor*, not far distant from the sea shore, but of no great strength. Near it are very good springs and great store of clove-trees. Under the district of *Kielang* are the villages of *Kielang*, *Nakko* and *Hattela*. In the year 1630, *Manuel de Silva* was king or captain of *Kielang*, but surrendered the government to his eldest son; he was a very good natur'd honest man, and had the second place in the *Dutch* council. *Anthony Pays* was captain of *Nakko*, and *Anthony Lopes* of *Hattela*, they were all three very good christians. Kielang.

Under the district of *Ema* are the villages *Oekorilla*, *Lewary* and *Routon Lasary*; *Manuel* was captain of *Oekorilla*, *Simau* of *Ema*, and one *Anthony Routon* of *Lasary*. These are obliged to furnish a *Karrakore* of four *Nadjos* for the service of the company. Ema.

They

The Isle of
AMBOINA
9

1659. They are very honest and faithful, and profess themselves of the tribe of *Olilymas*, except *Routon Lasary*, which belongs to the tribe of the *Olisivas*.

Soya. To the district of *Soya* belong the villages of *Aboesen*, *Oeritettoe* and *Amantelloe*. These are obliged to find a *Korrakore* of 4 *Nadjos*, are pretty ready in the service, and profess all christianity, and so does the king with all his *Orangkeys*: They are of the tribe of the *Olisivas*. *Laurenzo de Sylva* is king of *Soya*, *Anthony Aboesen* of *Aboesen*, and *Jeronymo Teholopoe* of *Oeritettoe*, and *Amantelloe*.

Hative. Under *Hative* belong the villages *Taviery*, *Hokkonaloe* and *Mardykka*; they furnish *Karrakore* with 4 *Nadjos*. They are good soldiers and christians, and their heads come frequently to the communion. Their chief heads are *Laurenzo Marcus* captain of *Hative*. *Pedro Anthonio* of *Taviery*. *Laurence Mendos*, chieftain of *Hokkonaloe* and *Mardykka*. The inhabitants of *Mardykka* are the remnants of the *Portuguese*, and some other slaves set at liberty: 1630 they consisted of 100, or 120 men fit to bear arms, who did considerable service to the state of *Amboyna*; they were very good christians and faithful, and furnish'd an extraordinary *Korrakore* of 4 *Nadjos*; they accounted themselves to be of the tribe of the *Olisivas*, their chieftain was then *Anthony de Costo*.

Halou. To *Halou* belongs the village *Hative-Kischilect*, they are pretty well peopled, and christians, and furnish a *Karrakore* of 4 *Nadjos*; *Diego Paty* was captain of *Halou*, and *Adam Marano* of *Hative-Kischilect*.

Pouta. *Pouta* has only two small villages belonging to it, *viz.* *Kapa* and *Chery*; their captains were *Stephen Tersera* of *Pouta*; *Manuel Lopes* of *Kapa*, and *Andrew Pardia* of *Chery*.

Oettomary. The inhabitants of *Oettomary* did revolt three times, but were in 1626 reduced to obedience by the then governor Mr. *Gorkum*, they were then under the tuition of *Don Pedro de Oettomary* their captain, who was a very honest person, and ever since that time they have adhered faithfully to the company. They are generally stout soldiers and good christians, for they frequent the christian congregations, and add more children to our schools than the other villages do. They furnish a *Korrakore* with 4 *Nadjos*, and are of the *Olisivas*. The four villages of *Ourien*, *Larik*, *Wakkacsive*, and *Asselou* stand likewise under the jurisdiction of the company; they are all blacks and stout fellows, they belong to the *Olisivas*, and acknowledge *Hittoe* for their captain, yet under the protection of the company. They furnish a *Korrakore* of 4 *Nadjos*. Thus the two villages of *Alang* and *Lillebay* belong to the company: The inhabitants are christians, except 3 or 4 families at *Alang*. Of the last, one *Salvador* was captain, and of *Lillebay*, *Bastiaen Kastango*. The inhabitants are likewise of the tribe of the *Olisivas*. 1659.

These six villages are obliged to furnish the *Dutch East-India* company with a great quantity of cloves; to wit 300 *Bahar per annum*; vast numbers of clove trees having been planted hereabouts, about 1630, which are come to full perfection since, and produce vast store of fruit. Thus 1636, the planting of clove trees was so far encouraged on the south-side of this island, that each family was obliged to plant, at least, ten trees every year, the ground being very fit hereabouts for this purpose; they were also not negligent in planting coco and other fruit trees. *Kamariay*, *Seriwawan* and *Kayrato*, are three villages near the sea-shore; the inhabitants are absolutely devoted to the service of the company, and appear sometimes with an *Orangay* at the head of them at the fort. They adhere to those of *Mardykka*, and belong to the *Olisivas*.

Near the point of the bay are four villages, *Quelipapoety*, *Amassee*, *Marykque*, and *Savoukque*. The first furnishes a *Korrakore* with 3 *Nadjos*, the three last a *Korrakore* of 4 *Nadjos*. In the village of *Amassee* lived at that time two young lads, sons of the *Orangkay*, who formerly had been hostages with the *Dutch* governors for seven years, but now were got into the government of these villages, and seem'd well inclin'd to the company's interest.

Mountains in Amboyna. The isle of *Amboyna* has many high and steep mountains, call'd *Gounen* by the natives, which have several fair villages built on the top, and are irrigated with very clear and fresh-water springs. The vallies serve for walking-places, by reason of the many fine trees that are planted there, as the mountains serve the inhabitants for a shelter against their enemies in time of war, being for the most part inaccessible. There is a certain rock here, call'd the *Elephants Rock*, from its shape and bigness, from whence issues forth a rivulet as clear as crystal, which slides gently thro' the adjacent verdant plain, whence is a very pleasant walk up to the rock.

The air of Amboyna. However the air of *Amboyna* is none of the wholesomest. There rages in this and the rest of the *Molucco* islands, a certain distemper, both among the natives and strangers, which by its symptoms resembles altogether the *French* pox (for which reason the *Dutch* call it the *Pox of Amboyna*) except that this is communicated without any carnal conjunction. In the face, arms and legs, nay all over the body, appear certain crusty boils, which

1659. which either turn ſchirrous, or if they come to a ſuppuration, a ſlimy, tough but ſharp matter iſſues from thence, reſembling in all its circumſtancee the *French* pox, except that they are not ſo painful, neither corrode the bones. This diſeaſe is attributed to a peculiar conſtitution of the climate and the air, and the exceſſive uſe of ſea-fiſhes, and coco nuts called *Zago*, and of the liquor called *Saguweer*. At firſt this diſtemper is eaſy enough to be cured, but if it takes root, not without great difficulty. They commonly apply the ſame remedies as we do in the *French* pox, in the ſpleen and dropſy: to wit, the decoctions of chica, ſarſaparilla, and guajacum, and purge them ſoundly betwixt whiles.

Its conſtitution. The iſle of *Amboyna* is pretty fertile; it produces millet, tobacco, coco-nuts, potatoes, pinang, oranges, lemons, citrons, ſugar, bamboo canes, and ſeveral other fruits. Some places here afford likewiſe nutmegs, but in no great quantity, neither have they ſo good as thoſe in the iſle of *Banda*, neither do they grow wild here, but the trees are planted in orchards. Neither are they deſtitute of divers ſorts of beaſts, eſpecially roe-bucks and hogs, and have great ſtore of fiſhes; but the chief products of *Amboyna* are cloves, which grow wild here; they are called *Nagalen* (nails) by the *Dutch*, from their ſhape, being flat on the top and ſharp at the end: They call them alſo *Geroffel nagelen*, perhaps from the *Greek Karyophyllon*. In the *Molucco* iſlands they call the cloves *Caampe* or *Chanpe*; in the iſle of *Java Sianeke*, and in *Malacca*, *Synken* or *Thinka*; the *Arabians*, *Perſians*, *Turks*, and moſt of the *Indians*, call them *Kalafur*.

The clove-tree. The clove-tree grows up in form of a pyramid, its branches ſprouting forth cloſe together. This tree is of the bigneſs of our cherry-trees, but in the whole reſembling moſt to a large laurel-tree, the leaves being very near of the ſame ſhape; the bark on the ſtem is of a greyiſh colour like that of the olive-tree. In the midſt of each leaf is a large vein which ſends forth many leſſer branches; theſe leaves grow on long ſtalks, ſometimes ſingle, but for the moſt part in cluſters; thoſe that grow near the extremities of the branches are of a purple colour, but the reſt dark green, if they are rubbed betwixt your hands they ſcent as ſtrong as the cloves themſelves, and ſo do the branches. On the extremities of theſe branches grow certain ſprouts which produce certain buds, and thoſe again flowers, ſometimes 10 or 20 in a knot, which at laſt produce the fruit, which are tough whilſt they are growing, but hard when come to maturity. At firſt they are green, then appear of a pale red colour, as if the trees were covered with ſcarlet, affording a very agreeable ſight to the beholders, becauſe there is often more fruit than leaves on the trees. The bloſſom is white at firſt, not unlike our cherry bloſſom, each leaf of the flower having three ſmall ſtreaks, then they turn green, afterwards red, and laſt of all dark yellow inclining to black. They reſemble in ſhape a nail, with a ſmall hollowneſs in the head, in which remains a thin ſkin which falls off as ſoon as it is touched. The cloves are very hard of ſubſtance; when they ſee more bloſſoms than leaves, they foretel great plenty of fruit; the bloſſoms ſmell much finer and ſtronger in dry than in rainy weather, and the firſt is looked upon as the moſt fruitful, it being common in a dry ſeaſon to ſee more bloſſoms than leaves, though even in ſuch a ſeaſon the clove-trees don't hit always alike, for every third or fourth year it is obſerved that they don't bear ſo plentifully as otherwiſe, juſt as if the tree at that time did remit its vigour ſpent the preceding years. The cloves are gathered once a year, *viz.* from the middle of *September* or beginning of *October* till *February*, this being the beſt ſummer ſeaſon here. Some are gathered, the reſt beat down with canes like flails; but this laſt way is not ſo ſafe as the other, for unleſs they be very careful, they bruiſe the tender ſprigs of the tree, which renders it the leſs fruitful the next following year, tho' the ſeaſon be never ſo good. Before they begin to gather, the ground under the tree is cleared of weeds, that they may not loſe part of the fruit. What cloves are left upon the trees grow very large as they ripen, much bigger than the reſt, but are not ſo fit for uſe. The next following year they drop from the tree, and though they are not ſo aromatick as the others, they are uſed for ſeed, and produce new trees, for which reaſon they are called the mother-cloves; for after they are dropt upon the ground they will take root, and in 8 or 9 years time it will come to the perfection of a good tree, and prove as fruitful as the reſt; but if theſe ſprouts be tranſplanted once in two or three years, they will bear more and better fruit. They ſay the clove-tree will hold good 100 years; the fruit immediately after gathering is dark yellow inclining to black, but if dry'd turns quite black, and if they dip them firſt in ſea-water it preſerves them from being worm eaten. Thus prepared they are laid up in ſtore-houſes and are tranſported to other places, where they are picked and the ſtalks taken from them, which are ſold ſeparately. The *Dutch* call theſe ſtalks *Nagelgruis* (the rubbiſh of cloves) and the *Portugueſe Baſton*. Cloves are hot and dry, of a bitteriſh biting taſte, but eſpecially when they are

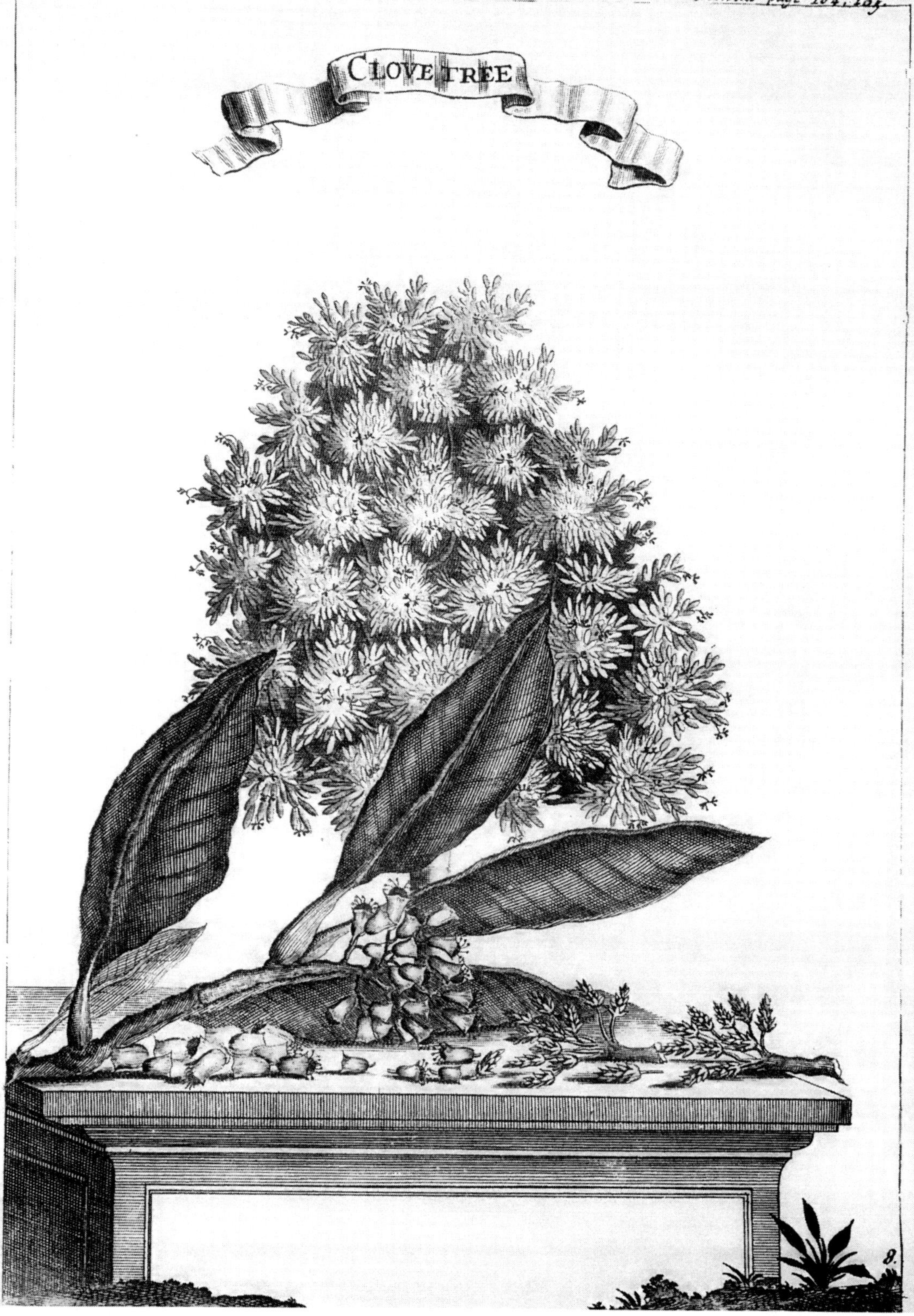

8.

1659. are dry'd. They seem to consist of a gummous sulphurous substance, with a strong drying and attractive quality; as for instance, when the *Indians* are to deliver a certain quantity of cloves, they put in the warehouse, where they are, a tub full of water, which is in a short time attracted by the cloves, to the no small benefit of the seller, it being observable that the cloves weigh as much the heavier as the water that was put there weighed before. The *Dutch* put this likewise often in practice. Some are of opinion that the cloves by their extraordinary drying and attractive quality, draw all the moisture of the ground round about the tree to that degree that no weeds or grass can grow there; but this is a vulgar error, the bareness of these spots of ground being not to be attributed to the cloves, but to the owners themselves who weed and keep them clear, thereby to afford the more nourishment to the trees, and not to lose part of the fruit when they are gathering or beating them from the trees.

'Tis true, the clove-trees are planted for the fruit sake, nevertheless the blossoms, leaves, sprigs, nay the gum itself that issues from the tree, are not destitute of an aromatick virtue, and afford very good medicines; the *Indian* and *Portuguese* women distil out of the green cloves and leaves, a water and a spirit which is very odoriferous and cephalick; and an excellent remedy against the palsy, called by the natives *Beribery*. Against the same distemper they preserve also the cloves with sugar, and draw an oil both of cloves and leaves. Cloves boiled in milk are accounted a great provocative, they are very cordial, and if chewed take away a stinking breath. They make a pickle of the green cloves, which are not so hot as the rest, and provoke the appetite. Persons of quality put green cloves in vinegar, which is a great strengthener of the stomach. The *Indians* call the vinegar *Atzjar*.

Royal clove. There is another kind of cloves but not commonly known, being very scarce and dear. The *Indians* call them *Tvinka Papoha*, or curled cloves, tho' they might rather be called ear-cloves, because they sprout forth like the corn ears. The *Dutch* call them *Royal Cloves*, because they are in such high esteem among the kings of the *Molucco* islands, not so much for their excellent taste and scent (in which they surpass all others) but for their scarcity's sake; for if we may believe them, no more than two such clove-trees are as yet found out, and that in the isle of *Makjan* only: One of these two trees exceeds the other in bigness, but both are like the common clove-trees, except that they are much taller, and the cloves bigger and of a different shape from the common clove, as may be seen by the draught. 1659.

In the island of *Ceylon* are likewise abundance of wild clove trees, but bear no fruit. It is credibly affirmed that in former times the inhabitants of the *Molucco* islands were ignorant as to the use of the cloves, till some *Chinese* coming that way found out their goodness, and from thence transported them to *China*, and so farther to the *Indies*, *Persia*, *Arabia*, and other parts. The islands *Ternate*, *Makjan*, *Mosier* and *Batsjan*, did likewise in former days abound in clove trees, but pursuant to an agreement made with the kings of the islands some years ago, the same have been rooted out.

In the isle of *Amboyna* grows likewise the wild palm, or *Zagou* tree, otherwise called *Papedo*. This tree resembles the other palm or coco trees, the leaves hanging downwards on the branches, the lowermost of which perish commonly: This tree bears but one fruit, which is of no use. The inhabitants make bread of the pith of the young trees; for on the top of the tree grows a certain head like a cabbage, in which is inclosed a certain white flower called *Zagou*, and the bread made of this flower *Zagou manda*. This flower they mix with water, and let it rise a little, then they put it in earthen pots, put burning coals all round about it, and so bake it. This bread, whilst it is new, tastes very sweet, and is of a very agreeable scent, but soon grows dry, and is brittle and shining like glass. They also mix this *Zagou* with water, and boil it like pap, into which they squeeze one or two lemons, and so stir it about with a stick; it is very cooling, and of an agreeable taste. They eat it with a stick, which they put into the pap, and turn it round, till a sufficient quantity of the pap, which is very glutinous, almost like turpentine, adheres to the stick, and so put it into the mouth. Out of these young trees they draw, like out of the coco-trees, a liquor; they cut one of the branches near the top, and in a hole made for that purpose, put a piece of hollow *Bamboo* cane, (which in these parts are used instead of tubs, pails and mugs) thro' which in a short time, issues forth a great quantity of liquor as sweet as honey, call'd by the natives *Zagouweer* or *Zageweer*, but is somewhat harsher than the liquor drawn from the true coco-tree. *Wild palm-tree called Zagou.*

In the isle of *Amboyna* they put a certain bitter root, call'd by a general name *Oubat* into this liquor, which preserves it for some time, for else this *Zagouweer* turns quickly as sour as vinegar, and is then used for such. They distil also a certain liquor of it call'd *Arak*. This *Zagouweer* is the common

1659. common drink, and sold in publick houses for a farthing a glass, but used in great quantity, proves very obnoxious to the nerves, especially whilst you are hot, when it must be taken with great precaution, else it will infallibly cause the gripes in the guts and palsies, call'd by the natives *Beribery*, which leaves a paleness in peoples faces for ever after. Sometimes they can draw 30 quarts of this liquor in 24 hours out of one single tree. In the isle of *Java* there are likewise some of these *Zagou* trees, but the liquor is, as far as I know, not valued at *Batavia*. They draw the liquor out of these trees till they die, and I was told that there was some of these trees in the woods of *Amboyna*, which will give as much liquor in 24 hours, as a man is able to carry away upon his shoulders. Some other islands belong to the isle of *Amboyna*, to wit, the adjacent large country of *Ceram*, the isles of *Manipa*, *Quelang*, and *Amblau*.

The isle of *Amboyna* is divided into two parts; one of which is under the jurisdiction of the *Dutch East-India* company; the other under the king of *Ternate*. Unto the company belongs the country of *Laitimor*, where is the fort of *Victoria*, and the wooden fort *Wantrou*, and on the pass of *Bagoale*, the redoubt call'd *Middleburgh*. The three islands *Homa*, *Honomoa*, and *Nausalaut*, which produce great quantities of cloves: The whole coast of *Hittoe* with the redoubts, the *Amsteldam* at *Hila*, the *Rotterdam* at *Larike*, and the *Leoden* at *Hittoe* and *Lamma*; and several small wooden forts at *Ourien*, *Lebeiehu*, *Ceit*, and *Way*. Under the king's jurisdiction are the country and coast of *Ceram*, the isles *Amblau*, *Manipa*, *Bonoa*, and some others.

Amboyna *under whose jurisdiction.*

The fort *Victoria*, (the staple of the company here) lies five leagues deep in the country, being defended by four bulwarks, a good ditch, and a considerable garrison, with suitable provisions and ammunition. During my stay here, there was a large crocodile in the ditch, which did vast mischief to the wild fowl belonging to Mr. *Hustard* the governor, who took great delight in them. Some soldiers and others were ordered to place themselves whereabouts they supposed the crocodile had his lurking place, but could not meet with it; till at last the crocodile on a sudden leaped towards the secretary of the governor, whom he had certainly devoured, had not the rest that were near at hand, with sticks and half pikes kill'd the beast immediately, which was extraordinary large. Round about the castle live several *Dutch*, *Chinese*, and other nations. Within and without the fort is a church, where divine service is held both in the *Dutch* and *Malacca* tongue.

The fort Victoria.

The men wear large whiskers, but little hair upon their chin; they only cover themselves with a slight piece of stuff round the buttocks and belly. The women tie their hair up in many knots: He that intends to marry a young maid, buys her from her father for money; but if she proves barren, the marriage is null and void: In former ages the natives were a most barbarous people, men-eaters and pagans. Now adays they are for the most part *Mahometans*, the rest are *Christians*, some *Roman Catholicks*, such as were converted by the *Portuguese*, others professing the *Protestant* religion, which was first introduced there in 1647. The *Dutch* have erected schools in all the villages to instruct the youth in reading and writing, and in the fundamentals of the christian religion. The natives are generally brave, but very deceitful and treacherous; they are naturally addicted to laziness, and are so obstinate, that they chuse rather to die than to leave their antient customs. They make use of certain small vessels in time of war. They are very swift in their motion, and managed by *Pagagen* or oars. They call these vessels *Korrakore*, and are shaped like a dragon, the head representing the forecastle, and the tail the stern. They have also some lesser boats call'd *Paros*. Their houses are built of *Bamboe* canes and *Zagou* trees; they sleep likewise in bedsteads made of *Bamboe* canes, or sometimes upon mats only. 1659.

Manners and customs of the Amboynese.

Their weapons are bows and arrows, half pikes, javelins, scimeters, targets and firelocks, all which they manage with great dexterity, as well as the darts. They have also a kind of hollow pipes, out of which they shoot great numbers of small poison'd arrows; the wounds made with them prove commonly mortal, unless the poison be removed immediately by cutting it out.

Their weapons.

The women of *Amboyna* are very lascivious, and extremely desirous of the christians; if they find themselves disappointed in their expectation, or that they are left by their gallants, they have a way of infecting them with a certain poison, the operation of which is so slow, that they die a lingring death, neither can they cohabit with any other woman, unless they receive proper antidotes from the same woman that poisoned them. Many *Chinese* live in *Amboyna*, tho' for the most part among the *Mahometans* at *Hittoe*, *Lochoe*, and in *Ceram*. In the year 1636, at the request of king *Hittoe*, three or four *Chinese* were permitted to settle under him, with this limitation however, that they should pay the usual taxes to the *Dutch* receiver-general of *Amboyna*; afterwards one *Chinese* was allow'd to live in each village, to provide them with distill'd

Their women.

1659. distill'd *Arack.* About the year 1636, the slaves belonging to the *Dutch* had got a custom to run away from their masters, and to shelter themselves among the *Mahometans*, but several being punished with death, pursuant to a proclamation published for that purpose, the rest were so terrified thereat, that no such thing was heard of for a great while after. Certain negro christians dwelt likewise in *Amboyna*, commonly call'd *Mardiikers.*

Courts of justic in Amboyna.

There are three courts or councils belonging to the *Dutch* in *Amboyna*; first the court martial, secondly the civil court of justice, and thirdly the great council or council of state.

The court martial used to meet every *Monday* and *Thursday*, composed of the governor, the head factor, and under factor of the company, a captain, a lieutenant, one of the eldest sergeants, and a secretary; these took cognizance of all matters relating to the soldiers and garrisons.

The civil court of judicature was kept in the town, consisting of four officers of the company, of four of the chiefest inhabitants, and of four or five *Orankays* of the council of state; besides which they had two clerks, one a *Dutchman*, and the other a native of *Amboyna*, and two attendants. The head factor in the castle was president here; they took cognizance of, and gave sentence with the governor's approbation, in all civil and criminal cases, neither had the villages any right of exercising of justice without them.

The council of state, or the *Orangkays* of the chamber, who in conjunction with the governor, and his councellors, were to deliberate concerning all publick affairs, such as the equipping of *Korrakoren*, or the management of a war against an enemy, had their seats appointed thus.

Andrea, king of *Rossenive.*
Manuel, the old king of *Kielang.*
Laurentz de Sylva, king of *Soya.*
Simaon Ema, captain of *Ema.*
Laurenzo Marcus, captain of *Hative.*
Diego Pati Halloe, captain of *Halloe.*
Anthony da Costa, captain of the *Mandiikers.*
Don Pedro, captain of *Vettomoery.*
Salvador Paty Alang, captain of *Alang.*
Simon Baguala, captain of *Baguala.*
John Barkabessier, captain of *Way.*
Stephen Tercera, captain of *Pouta.*
Pedro Anthonio, captain of *Tacieri.*
Fernando Latoehalat, captain of *Rossenive.*

How Amboyna *came under* Ternate.

In former ages the island of *Amboyna* was subject to its own kings, till it was reduced under the obedience of the kings of *Ternate*, which according to the relation of the inhabitants happened thus:

Many years ago reign'd a king in *Ternate* call'd *Babou*, son of *Chieroen Diamelou*, who having been the first that introduced *Mahometism* there, was in great esteem with the *Mahometan* priests, who to this day pay a great veneration to his memory. In the mean while, some differences being arisen betwixt the villages of *Warnalete* and *Makatit*, belonging to the district of *Warnoela*, and the last being unable to cope with those of *Warnalete*, they underhand sought for aid by king *Babou*; who having granted their request, sent a good fleet of *Korrakoren*, under the command of his councellor *Samarou*, to the cape of *Saragi*, betwixt *Erang* and *Lissidy*, where they came to an anchor; the inhabitants of *Cambello*, who as well as those of *Erang* and *Lissidy*, had submitted to king *Babou* against those of *Makatit*, advised the inhabitants of *Warnalete* to go to meet *Samarou*, and to purchase his favour by some presents, which being done accordingly, they all attack'd, in conjunction with *Samarou*, those of *Makatit*, and forced them to submission; but *Samarou*, not thus satisfied, reduced all the circumjacent islands under his king's obedience; so that this island owed the loss of its liberty to the intestine divisions of its inhabitants; *Samarou* returning home victorious, was receiv'd with great demonstrations of affection by king *Babou*, who in reward of his service, honour'd his son *Robobongy* with the title and dignity of *Salabakkum* or Stadtholder of these conquer'd countries, having before been dignified with the title of *Kimelaha*, which his successors in the stadtholdership have retained ever since, tho' it be certain, that not *Kimelaha* but *Salabakkum* signifies a stadtholder in their tongue. After the death of *Robobongy*, his eldest son *Adja* succeeded him in the stadtholdership, who was succeeded by his brother *Bassi Frangi*. After him came *Frangi*, who for his treachery was beheaded by *Sabadiin* of *Loubou* his brother's son. *Leliatte*, son to *Bassi Frangi*, then thrusts himself into the government without consent of the king, and following the footsteps of his predecessor, receiv'd the same reward. He was succeeded in the stadtholdership by *Madira*, son of *Sabadiin*, the seventh in order, our company having made use of all their interest with *Hamsia*, king of *Ternate*, to procure him that dignity, in consideration of the singular kindnesses they had received from his father. But they soon found themselves mistaken in their choice; for this *Madira*, of the antient race of the *Tomogolo*'s, of which *Samarou* was the first, rebell'd 1650, against the king, and with the assistance of the inhabitants, made himself master of several strong holds; to wit, *Amblau*

Madira *rebels against the king of* Ternate.

1659.

blau, *Manipa*, *Lissidy*, *Hatua* the lesser, *Assaboudy*, *Laala* and *Noussatelo*, plunder'd all that oppos'd him, and kill'd about 80 persons belonging to the *Dutch* company. One *John Pays*, captain of *Hatuwe*, *Tawiro* and *Houkonalo*, living near the fort of *Amboyna*, was shrewdly suspected to have had a hand in this conspiracy, which *Simon Kos* (who commanded in the absence of *Arnold Outshorn* at *Amboyna*) having got notice of, secured him in the fort till the arrival of Mr. *Outshorn*, when the war broke out with great violence on both sides.

How the Portuguese *became masters of* Amboyna.

The *Portuguese* made themselves masters of *Amboyna*, 1546, in the following manner: At the time when *Anthony Galvan* was governor of *Ternate*, a great fleet of small vessels belonging to the island of *Java*, *Banda*, *Macassar* and *Amboyna*, was sent to the *Molucco* islands to fetch cloves; *Galvan* being advertis'd thereof, and fearing lest they should by this means spoil the spice trade of the *Portuguese*, armed about 25 *Korrakoren*, with 40 *Portuguese*, and 400 auxiliaries; these, under the command of *Jacob Supi Azevidi*, admiral of the sea *Molukse*, steer'd their course towards *Amboyna*, where meeting with the *Indian* fleet, they attack'd and routed them, taking many of their ships, with good store of great cannon, and a considerable sum of ready money; *Azevedi*, willing to improve this opportunity, landed in *Amboyna*, the inhabitants of which being terrified at their last defeat, did for the most part submit to the *Portuguese*, and receiv'd such laws as they thought fit to prescribe to them; which done, *Azevedi* loaden with glory and spoils, return'd as a conqueror to *Ternate*. After that time, the *Portuguese* used always in their voyages from *Malacca* to the *Molucco* islands, and in their return from thence, to provide themselves with fresh water at *Amboyna*, till 1603, this island was taken by the *Dutch* from the *Portuguese*, who got a vast booty there, tho' the *Dutch* are not very fond of living in *Amboyna*, being a place of no great plenty.

We set sail, as I told you before, the 3d of *May* from *Amboyna*, and with a brisk and prosperous gale arriv'd the 29th before *Batavia*.

No sooner was our ship unloaden, but I received orders to go aboard the ship *Achilles*, *John Vander Werven* master, to *Japan*. Every thing being got in readiness for our intended voyage, I took my leave from the directors of the company, and the 28th of *July* set sail with 15 ships more, Mr. *John Vander Laen* being commadore, with orders to sail to *Teywan*, to attack the city *Makao*, (a populous place, and defended by a garrison of 600 men) and to observe *Koxingas*. But scarce were we come within sight of the isle of *Anyam*, when we were overtaken by so terrible a tempest, that I can safely affirm, I never saw the like in my life, and that it is past my skill to express it; the waves rising sometimes to that height, that the very tops of our masts could not be seen, the winds sometimes falling flat upon our ships, and pressing them down flat under the abyss, so that we expected every moment to be swallow'd up by this merciless element, especially when we saw the yacht *Gorkum* (in which was *Francis Lansman*, formerly my companion in our *China* voyage) in a moment perish before our eyes, without the least possibility of saving one man. At last, however thro' God's infinite mercy the fury of the winds began to allay, when with much ado we got with our ships, which were much damag'd by the storm, into the harbour of *Teywan* the 20th of *September*. The season for our intended voyage to *Japan* being past, as forced against my will to unload my ship here, and the design against *Makao* being laid aside for that time, because *Koxinga* was abroad with a powerful force: We set sail with the whole fleet for the islands call'd *Piskadores*, and came the 3d of *October* to an anchor in the *Church-Bay*: Here I received orders to prepare myself for a voyage into *Persia*, aboard the ship the *Leerdam*, loaden with sugar, which I did accordingly.

1659.

A most violent storm.

The islands of Piskadores *or* Pehu.

The islands call'd *Piskadores* or fisher-islands, and by the *Chinese Pehu*, are situate under 23 and 24 deg. northern latitude, about 12 and 13 leagues from the isle of *Teywan*. They have several good harbours, and two commodious bays, where ships may ride safely at anchor at 8 or 9 fathoms water. At the entrance of this bay are the ruins of two antient stone forts, one built by the *Dutch*, the other by the *Chinese*; and betwixt both is another fort. The country thereabouts is not hilly, abounds in grass, yet pretty strong. It contains many populous villages; these islands being all well stor'd with inhabitants, with fat cattle, especially cows, and birds of all sorts, especially with an incredible number of fine large cocks. During the rainy season they gather fresh water in cisterns or ponds, but in dry weather the water is saltish here. The country produces likewise potatoes and many other fruits in abondance, and here are always to be seen great numbers of *Chinese* vessels, which come some for fishing, some for traffick. At the entrance of the *Church-Bay*, stands to the north-side a *Chinese Pagode*, where is very good anchorage, and a convenient place for shelter to those that are bound to *Teywan*, there being no other safe harbour for great ships hereabouts. The

1659. islands *Piskadores* are many in number; two are the most famous; one call'd the *Piskadore* or *Fisher Island*, the second *Pehou* or *Pehu*.

The south-east side of the *Fisher Island* is so bare, that it produces not a tree; to the west of it is another small island, and the passage betwixt both so shallow, that a yacht is not able to pass that way. To the south of this lies another island, call'd by the *Dutch* the *Troublesome Island*, because there is no anchorage for ships here. About a league from thence to the west is a rocky island, or rather two small rocky islands, divided by so many rocks, that there is no passage or anchorage near them.

Return to Teywan.

After we had dispatch'd our business here, we set sail again for the island of *Teywan*, Mr. *Conject* was at that time governor of this isle, who having not without reason conceiv'd a jealousy at the vast number of ships and men, the *Chinese* had brought together in the river of *Quincheu*, or in the isle of *Ey* and *Queymuy*, on the coast of *China*, I was dispatch'd thither the 31st of *October* with the two yachts the *Graveland* and *Mary*, with express orders, to demand from *Koxinga* whether he was for peace or war, and not to tarry longer than ten days for a categorical answer.

Nieuhoff *sent to* Koxinga.

I tarried aboard the vessels to take care of them, whilst my collegue went to speak with *Koxinga*: Our limited time being near expired, I went ashore in a boat, ordering our vessels to be upon their guard. The banks of the river were so crouded with people, that I had much ado to pass thro' them; by good chance I met with a *Chinese* who understood *Portuguese*, who was so complaisant as to go along with me to the place, where my collegue and his attendants lodg'd; but they being gone abroad to see *Koxinga* muster his forces, I was oblig'd to take the same way; we address'd ourselves to him, desiring a speedy and positive answer, the time of our stay being expired.

Koxinga's *answer*.

He gave us for answer, that being at present busy in mustering his forces, he would give us his resolution to-morrow, in a letter directed to the governor of *Teywan*, which he did accordingly: In this letter he told him, that he had not the least thoughts of any war against the company, but that he would cultivate a good correspondence with them. To remove all occasion of jealousy, he sent several merchant ships to *Teywan*, which however did not remove the suspicion they had conceived of him there, especially after we on the 22d of *December* gave a verbal account of his vast preparations in the fort of *Teywan*. His letter was as follows.

1659.

KOXINGA's letter.

BEING at a great distance from you, I could not but receive your letter with a more than ordinary satisfaction, which I perused more than once, to inform myself the better of your intentions. You mention some false rumours, but at the same time seem to give credit to them. In my father Yquam's *time, the* Dutch *possess'd themselves of a certain place in the isle of* Teywan, *with his consent for the convenience of trade, which I have not in the least interrupted, and therefore judge you to be obliged to me upon that score. I have of late years been so deeply involved in a war with the* Tartars, *that I have had no leisure to trouble my head with an inconsiderable island that produces nothing but grass: It being not my custom to disclose my designs, but rather if I aim at the east to point to the west; how can you suppose to be inform'd of them by rumours? The reason why so few of our ships come to that island, is, because they cannot trade thither with any profit, the customs being so heavy. It was but this year the* Tartars *made a strong invasion into the low lands of* China, *in hopes to put an end to the war with one blow, but they were so bravely received, that they were forced to retreat with the loss of 100 of their commanders, and a great number of their men; we then retired into the islands of* Ey *and* Queymuy, *in hopes to draw them thither, and so to catch them in the trap. Concerning your complaints of having been treated in a hostile manner in the island of* Piskadores, *if it be really so, it has been done without our knowledge. I sent back an immediate answer, together with your presents, to the letter sent to me from* Batavia *four years ago; by which I understand, that you intended us but a very slender satisfaction, for the* Joncken *or ships, and the loading and money aboard them detained by you, notwithstanding which, I did not think fit to urge this business any further, for fear of occasioning a rupture betwixt us; it shall be my endeavour, as soon as the* Tartarian *war is brought to a conclusion, to encourage trade as much as possible may be, and don't question but you will on the other hand contribute to it, as far as lies in your power.*

Given in the 14th year, the 19th day of the 10th month of the reign of king *Indick*.

After the reading of *Koxinga*'s letter, it was resolved by the majority of voices not to engage in a war against *Koxinga*; most being of opinion, that at this juncture he would not undertake any thing against the company, tho' the governor Mr. *Conjet* was of a contrary sentiment, which proved too true afterwards. Thus all the thoughts of war

war being laid aside, the continuation of commerce with him being judged, as indeed it was, to be of more present advantage to the company, all the ships there were ordered to their respective places, and I among the rest, set sail aboard the ship the *Leerdam*, loaden with sugar for *Gamroa* in *Persia*.

The isles of Ey *and* Queymuy.

The before-mentioned islands, *Ey* and *Queymuy*, are high rocky islands; the city of *Eymny* is situate upon a high hill, pretty deep in the countrey, being surrounded with a stone wall, without which you see the ruins of an antient tower, and a *Chinese Pagode* or temple.

The city of *Queymuy* lies upon a river at a pretty distance from the sea, being the capital of the isle from whence it has borrowed its name. It has very large suburbs, which begin on the river side. Not far from thence, deeper into the country, is a strong castle, defended by a very high wall, formerly the residence of *Koxinga*. The country round about is rocky, and not very fertile, except that the valleys afford a little grass for cows; for the rest, the inhabitants feed most upon fish, and some live by traffick.

The Chinese *shelter themselves in these two islands.*

It was not long before the *Chinese*, being forced by the *Tartars* to quit the continent of *China*, and *Koxinga*, strengthned with near 25000 fugitives, and about 500 vessels, they resolved to shelter themselves in the two before-mentioned islands of *Ey* and *Queymuy*, and finding himself in a condition to undertake something against us; he embark'd 20000 of his best men aboard a great number of *Chinese Joncken* or vessels, and the 30th of *May* 1661, appeared within a league of the fort *Zelandia* in the isle of *Teywan*, steering his course directly to the shore, where his countrymen, living in that island, were ready to receive him, with their carts and other necessaries; and soon after, posted a considerable number of his vessels betwixt the fort and the redoubt call'd the *Province*. This put our people under no small consternation, they being not provided either with vessels or forces, to encounter so formidable a power. However captain *Pedel* and *Aldorp*, the first with 240, and the second with 200 men, were sent out to endeavour to prevent the enemies landing, and 4 ships, *viz.* the *Hector*, the *Graveland*, the *Finch*, and the yacht *Mary*, were ordered to fall upon their fleet, which was put in execution immediately. About 60 of the *Chinese Joncken*, each with 2 great guns in the forecastle, came up with our vessels, but were so warmly received, that two of them were sunk, and the rest so much disabled, that they were all glad to retire, except six only, which kept close together, and shot so furiously upon us, that they seem'd all to be on fire; the *Hector* took fire by an accident, and so together with the *Joncken* that lay aboard her, blew up into the air. The other three ships, notwithstanding this fought it out bravely, and killed above a 1000 *Chinese* besides those wounded in the engagement. The yacht *Mary* was also set on fire, but was saved by the indefatigable care and labour of the seamen. On the land-side captain *Pedel*, having divided his forces into two bodies, and exhorted them to stand it out bravely, gave the enemy a very warm salute with his firelocks, which kill'd many of them as they were landing; notwithstanding which, they were so far from giving ground, as we flattered ourselves they would have done, that they sent whole showers of arrows among our people, and at the same time sent a strong detachment to the right, which taking compass round a hill, attack'd us in the flanks, which so terrified our soldiers, that they threw down their arms, and wading thro' the water got into a pilot's boat, and so ashore, leaving the captain with 19 men only, to the mercy of the enemies; upon which, immediate orders were sent to captain *Aldorp* to retire with his forces to the fort; the enemy landed without any farther opposition, and in 4 hours time cut of all communication betwixt the redoubt, the province, and the fort, and betwixt this and the open country; most of the inhabitants afterwards joining with them against us. *Koxinga* being soon informed of our present condition, in very ignominious terms summon'd the fort, threatning to put all to fire and sword if we did not surrender immediately. It was then taken into consideration, whether, considering the enemy had cut off all communication with the redoubt the *Province*, and his great strength, it were not adviseable to treat with *Koxinga*, and to offer the surrender of one of the forts, provided we might preserve a free trade, rather than to lose all; which being agreed upon, and at our request a passport granted for that purpose by *Koxinga*, we sent *Thomas Yperan*, head factor of the fort, and Mr. *Leonardus* the fiscal, as our deputies to him, to salute him in the name of the governor and the council, and to wish him success in all his undertakings, provided they were not intended against the interest of the company. In their letter they told him, that they could have wish'd to have seen him in another posture here, and that they were surprized to find him in arms, without the least declaration of war, that if he had any real cause of being offended, they were ready to give him satisfaction, and to cultivate a good understanding with him. The deputies

Koxinga attacks Teywan.

The Dutch *endeavour to prevent his landing.*

Engagement betwixt the Dutch *and* Chinese.

The Dutch *fly.*

The Chinese *victorious.*

Deputies sent to Koxinga.

1659. ties had express orders, that in case *Koxinga* would not hearken to any accommodation, without the surrender of both the forts, they should treat no farther, and tell him that the company was in a condition to revenge this injury. With these instructions they went the 3d of *May* to *Koxinga*'s camp, which was then about 12000 strong, and busy in the siege of the redoubt *Province*. They were armed with three different sorts of weapons; the first with bows and arrows, which they manage with great dexterity; the second with scimeters and targets only, wherewith they cover themselves, and so break in upon an enemy, when they are seconded by their pikemen, whose arms are backswords and pikes of three or four foot long, with broad and sharp irons at the end.

The deputies received into the camp.

The deputies were at their first entrance into the camp, received by one of their chief commanders, and conducted into a spacious tent, where they stay'd till *Koxinga* was at leisure to admit them to audience. Whilst they stay'd there, several of the enemies troops march'd by their tent, and as far as they could perceive, the same at several times, to make the greater ostentation of their strength. *Koxinga* was in the mean while employed in combing his black shining hair, a great ornament among the *Chinese*, which done, the deputies were introduced into his tent, which was all hung with blue, he himself seated in an elbow chair, behind a four square table; round about him attended all the chief commanders clad in long robes without arms, and in great silence, with a most awful countenance. On both sides towards the door, his lifeguards were placed in very good order. The deputies address'd themselves to him in low *Dutch*, and delivered their letter, which being translated into the *Chinese*, *Koxinga* answered.

KOXINGA's answer.

That he was sensible that the good correspondence the Dutch East-India *company had hitherto cultivated with him, as well as with all the other* Indians *princes, was no longer durable than they found it consistent with their own interest; which always ceased as soon as they found their account in it; that it was contrary to his custom to divulge his thoughts or designs, yet he could not dissemble that it was by reason of the war he was engaged in against the* Tartars, *he had not taken possession of this island, which as it always belonged to the* Chinese, *so it was not injustice that now they stood in need of it themselves, they might retake it from foreigners, who were only settled there by permission. That he was not come there to engage in a war with the* Dutch, *but only to take possession of his own. That he was willing they might take away all that belonged to them, that they might demolish the forts and carry away their cannon; for which purpose he was ready to lend them as many of his ships and men as they wanted, notwithstanding they had so lately attacked him both by sea and land, when he had given them sufficient proofs of his strength.* He told them further, *that they were very proud and haughty in pretending to defend so inconsiderable a fort* (meaning the redoubt the province) *with so small a force against his numerous army, which he threatned to destroy, so as not to leave one stone upon another:* He boasted *that if his forces were united he was able to conquer heaven and earth*; concluding, *that they must take a very short resolution.* 1659.

Our deputies gave for answer, *That since the* Dutch *had left the* Piskadore *islands; this island was surrendred into their hands by contract; but that if he* (Koxinga) *had any pretensions upon the company, they were ready to treat about it, and give him satisfaction.* But after several contests, finding him quite averse to hearken to any accommodation, unless they could surrender all, they departed, protesting that the company would shew their resentments in due time, and so set up the red flag.

The deputies leave the camp. Come into the fort the Province.

Before their departure from the camp they had obtained leave of *Koxinga* to go through the fort the *Province* in their return home; here they found things in a very indifferent posture, and the fort not in a condition to hold out above a week longer, all their powder and ball being spent, there being not enough left to withstand an assault: This, with the weakness of the place, induced the deputies to consent that they might capitulate with the enemy, provided they could get liberty to transfer the garrison into the fort.

Arrive at the great fort.

The deputies arrived the same day in the great fort, where having given an account of their transactions, the governour *Conjet* and the rest of the commanders seeing all the communication betwixt them and the redoubt the *Province*, nay with the whole island entirely cut off by the enemy, were at a great loss what to resolve upon at such a juncture as this: After mature deliberation, the only hopes they had left was, to defend the fort *Zelandia* till such time they could be relieved from *Batavia*, which considering the northern *Monzon*, might perhaps take up a whole twelve months time. However it was resolved to defend this fort to the last extremity, notwithstanding the redoubt the *Province* had been forced to surrender, the garrison with all the cannon being fallen into the enemies hands, who had made them prisoners of war.

Resolved to defend this fort to the last.

To

1659.

They leave the city.

To prepare themselves for a more vigorous defence, all that were able to bear arms were taken into the fort, and the city set on fire, which however could not be executed so speedily, but that the enemy preserved some ware and other houses, by timely quenching the flame, which served them for places of shelter. Soon after they began to batter the fort with 28 pieces of cannon, but their cannon as well as their men being exposed to our shot, we plied them so warmly with cartrages, and other such like materials, that the streets thereabouts were all covered with the dead carcasses of the *Chinese*, and the rest were forced to shelter themselves in the by-lanes, leaving their cannon to our mercy, some of which were rendered unserviceable. On the other side of the fort 6000 *Chinese* advanced boldly under our cannon, and attacked our works hand to hand, but were beaten back with great loss to an adjacent hill; upon which the besieged made a vigorous sally, and nailed up all their cannon. It was then proposed to make a general sally, but considering the disproportion betwixt us and the enemy, who were advanced under our cannon, it was judged too dangerous, for fear, if we should miscarry, the enemy might force their way at the same time into the fort. The next day the besieged made another sally, and carried off a six pounder into the fort. The enemy finding all his attacks unsuccessful, kept the fort close blockt up, and in the mean while made the open countrey feel the effects of his rage; they made all the *Dutch* inhabitants, especially the ministers and schoolmasters, prisoners, because as they pretended, two certain ministers had under hand encouraged their parishioners to kill all the *Chinese* living among them, not questioning but the rest would follow their example; but as it commonly happens in things of this nature where many are privy to a design, this had been discovered by some out of fear, or hopes of reward, for which the ringleaders suffered a most miserable death, being crucified by the *Chinese*, and their crosses erected in their respective villages.

The Chinese *batter the fort.*

The Chinese *repulsed.*

A Dutch *ship taken by the* Chinese.

Some *Dutch* sea-men had no better success, for 13 of them being taken in a *Dutch* ship by a *Chinese* vessel near the *Piskadore* islands, these were put on board a *Chinese* vessel mann'd with 30 men, who were to carry them to *Koxinga*'s camp. So soon as the *Dutch* sea-men came within sight of the *Dutch* fort, they resolved to fall upon the *Chinese* (not above one half of them being above deck at a time) and so to carry off the ship the next following night; but a *Frenchman* belonging to our ships crew, whether out of fear, or hopes to recover his liberty, did betray their design to the *Chinese*, who immediately gave the signal to some other ships near them to come aboard, which being done accordingly, they made them all prisoners, and forthwith sent them to *Koxinga*'s camp, where they had their noses, ears, and hands cut off, and in this miserable condition were sent into the fort for a terror to the rest; they were committed to the surgeon's care, who performed his part so well, that not one of them died.

The Dutch *design to carry off a* Chinese *ship.*

1659.

Miscarry.

Among the rest of the *Dutch* prisoners taken by the *Chinese* in the open countrey, was one Mr. *Hambrocock* a minister; this man was sent by *Koxinga* to the governour of the fort, to persuade him to a surrender, upon condition, *viz.* that they should depart safely with all that belonged to them and the company; but if he refused, he might have a sufficient occasion to repent it at leisure; and that *Koxinga* would revenge himself upon the *Dutch* prisoners: With these instructions Mr. *Hambrocock* came into the castle, being forced to leave his wife and children behind him as hostages; which being a sufficient argument to him that in case he did not succeed in his negotiation, they must expect nothing but death at *Koxinga*'s hands, yet was he so far from persuading the garrison to a surrender, that he encouraged them to a brave defence in hopes of relief; and as a farther encouragement, assured them that *Koxinga* had lost many of his best ships and soldiers, and began to be weary of the siege, fearing lest we should hold it out till we received succours from *Batavia*.

A message sent from Koxinga *to the besieged.*

Mr. *Hambrocock* having made an end of what he had to propose, the council of war left it to his choice, whether he would rather stay with them or return to the camp, where he could expect nothing else but present death, every one entreated him to stay; he had two daughters within the castle, who hung about his neck overwhelmed in grief and tears, to see their father ready to go where they were sensible he must be sacrificed to the rage of a merciless enemy; he represented to them, that having left his wife and two other children as hostages in the camp, nothing but present death could attend them if he returned not; and so untwisting himself from his daughters arms, and exhorting every body to a resolute defence, he returned to the camp, telling them at parting, that he hoped he might prove serviceable to his poor fellow prisoners.

He gave an account to *Koxinga* of his negotiation, and that the besieged were resolved not to treat, unless they were to remain in possession of the castle, which was not at all relishing to *Koxinga*, who now began to be afraid of an uproar; the inhabitants having slain several of the *Chinese*, which

Koxinga's *messenger returns.*

1645. which exasperated him to that degree, that having caused industriously a rumour to be spread abroad that the prisoners did under hand encourage the inhabitants of *Formosa* to rebel, he ordered all the *Dutch* male prisoners to be slain, which was done accordingly; some being beheaded, others killed in a more barbarous manner. The dead carcasses after they were stripped quite naked, were to the number of 500, thus buried 50 and 60 in a hole; of all the rest, only the supervisor of the countrey with 25 others, were saved and carried to *China*, tho' they even did not spare the women and children, many of whom were likewise slain, tho' some of the best were preserved for the use of the commanders, and the rest sold to the common soldiers: Happy was she that happened to fall to the lot of an unmarried man, being thereby freed from the importunities of the *Chinese* women, who are very jealous of their husbands. They were however afterwards, pursuant to the capitulation, sent back to *Batavia*. Among the slain were Mr. *Hambrocock*, Mr. *Mus*, and Mr. *Arnold Winshaim*, three ministers, and many schoolmasters, who were all beheaded.

The Dutch *prisoners killed by* Koxinga.

Whilst these things were transacting here, the *Dutch* in *Batavia* had got notice of this invasion by the *Mary* yacht, which in spite of the contrary season had found means to get thither, and to give them an account how matters stood with us. Ten ships were immediately got ready with 700 soldiers aboard them, which set sail in *June* 1661, under the command of *Jacob Kou*, and not long after arrived at the isle of *Formosa*. This unexpected relief as it put the enemy into no small consternation, so it encouraged our men to make a more vigorous defence than ever; and tho' the wind blew very hard, these ships found means to land some men and ammunition; but the winds increasing more and more, were forced to choose the main, to the no small grief of the besieged, and did not return till about a month after; when the ship called the *Urk* being forced upon a rock on the coast of *Formosa*, was split, and her men saved, from whom the enemy having understood our strength, and some other circumstances, they began to be better satisfied, because they had imagined this succour much more formidable than really it was.

Succours sent to Formosa.

However the besieged took a resolution by making a vigorous sally to dislodge the enemy from the city of *Zelandia*, and to destroy their ships. The 16th of *September* was appointed for this enterprise, but whilst some ships were engaged, the wind beginning to slacken, the rest could not come up; our men endeavoured to attack the *Chinese* in their boats, but being exposed to their shot, without being able to do them much harm, ours had the worst on't some of the boats being overset, others sunk, the rest saving themselves by flight. Two of our ships got upon the sands and were both set on fire. In this sea engagement the *Dutch* lost about 130 men, but the enemy a great many more; however this unfortunate action put a stop to the intended sally, and orders were sent to the garrisons of the two northern forts, to withdraw into the castle, the garrison of which was considerably diminished by the many skirmishes, in which the enemy got but little advantage, and lost many of their best men; which put a check for some time to their design, especially when they understood that we had sent all women, children, and other useless persons to *Batavia*, the better to enable us to make a vigorous defence. 1659.

The besieged make a sally.

The Dutch *worsted.*

Much about the same time the governor received letters from the *Tartarian* stadtholder of *Hocksieu*, who requested some ships and forces, to drive the remaining forces of *Koxinga* out of the countrey, promising to come afterwards with his whole power to the relief of *Formosa*. Hereupon *Jacob Kou* was sent thither with five ships well provided with men and ammunition; but being overtaken by a storm, lost all his anchors near the *Piskadores*, which obliged him to send back three of his ships to the island of *Teywan*: With the other two he returned to *Batavia*, where he met with but an indifferent reception.

The Tartars *promise succours.*

The besieged finding themselves by this disaster bereaved of a considerable number of men and ammunition, began to despair of holding it out much longer; so that many deserted, and among the rest a certain serjeant, who gave *Koxinga* not only an account of our weakness, but also encouraged him not to let slip this opportunity to force us to a surrender. *Koxinga* having well weigh'd the matter, attacked us with his whole force more vigorously than ever, and in *January* 1662 raised three batteries, mounted with 28 great cannon, upon the sandy grounds near the fort; the *Dutch* foresaw the danger that must needs ensue from this near approach of the enemy's batteries, and did all that they could, either with cannon or firelocks, to disturb them in their works, but these not hindring, their men continued to batter the walls till they had made a breach; then they made two several attacks, but were as often repulsed with great loss, the ground being all over covered with dead carcasses. This disaster taught them to be more cautious, and so instead of storming, they continued to fire incessantly their guns with such a fury that they laid a whole redoubt level with the ground, so 1662.

The Chinese *renew the attack against the fort.*

Are repulsed.

1662. so that our men finding it no longer tenible, nailed up the guns, and laid some barrels with gunpowder under it, which blowed up a considerable number of *Chinese* into the air. *Koxinga* himself was in danger of having been among them, had he not been forewarned by the before mentioned serjeant, who told him that it was too dangerous to venture himself in a place so lately left by the enemy. Here *Koxinga* raised a large battery upon a rising ground, from whence he hoped to lay the body of the castle level with the ground. The *Dutch* on their side were not idle to do what possibly could be expected for their defence, with cannon shot, granados and otherwise; they raised their brest-works, and put great packs of linnen and stuffs into the breach; notwithstanding which the enemy played incessantly upon them, and against night had made so large a breach as was judged sufficient to make a general assault. Then it was the besieged began to deliberate what was best to be done in this exigency, whether, since there was no longer abiding in the castle, they should make a sally and force their way to the enemy, or whether they should abide the assault: The most were for a capitulation, there being not the least hopes left of making a sally with any success, and to resist the whole force of the *Chinese* in a place without defence, exposed to the enemies shot, was looked upon no less than to sacrifice themselves to their enemies; these considerations were so prevailing at last, that it was unanimously agreed to capitulate, and to surrender the castle upon articles; this was put in execution immediately, a truce of five days being agreed on for that purpose, at the expiration of which, after great contests it was agreed, *That every thing belonging to the company should be delivered up to* Koxinga. *That all the inhabitants, soldiers and prisoners, should have free liberty to retire to* Batavia *with all their moveables, for which purpose they should be provided with suitable conveniencies.* Thus the besieged after having endured a siege of nine months, with the loss of 1600 men, returned to *Batavia*, where the governour and members of the council of *Formosa*, after all the hazards and incredible fatigues they had been forced to undergo, were put in prison, and their goods confiscated; the governour himself being not long after condemned to a perpetual imprisonment in the isle of *Ey*; but was at the intercession of his highness the prince of *Orange*, and by orders from the directors of the *East-India* company in *Holland* discharged, and returned to his native countrey 1676. Since we have had frequent occasion to speak of the island of *Formosa*, I will give you a short account of it.

The Dutch *defend themselves to the utmost.*

The fort of Zelandia *surrendred.*

The isle of *Formosa* is situated under the 23 deg. 30 min. northern latitude. It is of an oblong figure, being not very broad in proportion to its length, which is 125 leagues. It is full of hills, but intermixed with many fertile vallies; producing great store of grass, and watered by many fine rivers. The countrey produces abundance of rice, but especially sugar, vast quantities of which are exported from thence. Most of the *Indian* fruits are to be seen here, of which more hereafter, as also several sorts of *Dutch* fruits, herbs, and roots, transplanted thither from *Holland*, as peaches, apricots, and such like; cows, oxen, hogs, wild goats, hares, and rabbets, but especially stags are here in great plenty, but the last are somewhat of a lesser size than those of *Europe*, and without horns; the inhabitants catch vast numbers of them meerly for their skins sake, the flesh being not esteem'd here, except their tongues. They have also great store of elks here, which being very strong they use in their carts instead of horses or oxen. One time the master of our ship and I being invited to dinner at his sister's that was married to a native of *Formosa*, they sent us a carr drawn by bufflers; the master of the ship who understood better how to govern the ship than those beasts, would needs supply the carr-mans place, but prickt the bufflers so unmercifully (according to the custom of the countrey) that they run away with us: for some time we kept stedfast in the carr, which overturning at last, threw us at a great distance, but to our great good fortune, without any considerable harm; we walkt the rest of the way on foot, leaving the ordinary carr-man, a native of *Formosa*, to recover the bufflers, which he did at last, and brought them home. Neither do they want partridges, wild pidgeons, and other wild fowl; there are also tygers and bears to be met with, but I never heard of any other ravenous wild beasts here. The mountains are full of brimstone, which questionless occasions so many earthquakes, unto which this isle is much subject. Some are of opinion that these mountains contain likewise gold and silver, some essays of this nature having been made with good success, but it was never attempted to dig for it. This island is destitute of good harbours for great ships, which are forced to ride at anchor in the road of some isles about twelve leagues, from thence. The countrey is very populous, for besides the natives of *Formosa*, above 25000 *Chinese* forced out of *China* by the *Tartars*, have at several times settled themselves here.

1662. *The isle of* Formosa.

The natives of *Formosa*, especially the men, are of an olive colour, fat, strong, well-limbed and nimble, some being able to

Nativ. Formo...

1662. to out-run a wild boar or ſtag; they leap upon the back of them and ſo cut their throats. The mountainers are of a leſſer ſize. The women are not altogether ſo large as the men, but very ſtrong bodied, and are cloathed after the ſame faſhion; they have black ſhining hair, which they tye together in a knot on the top of the head.

Their cloathing. The men throughout the ſummer appear for the moſt part quite naked, but thoſe who do not, eſpecially in the winter, wear a kind of ſilk or callico cloth, which they wrap about their bodies, and button it under the arms; the womens hangs ſomewhat lower down below the knees. Stuffs made of dogs hair are in great eſteem with them. They cut off the dogs hair, like as we do our ſheeps wool, ſpin and weave it afterwards. They are generally very friendly and faithful to the *Europeans*, and don't eaſily break a contract; they are very apprehenſive, and will give a good judgment of matters; many of them were already converted to the chriſtian religion by the induſtry of the miniſters and ſchoolmaſters, which were planted almoſt in every village, there being no ſmall hopes that the whole iſland would in a little time have embraced chriſtianity, had not the conqueſt of *Koxinga* overturned this good deſign.

Their food. Their bread is made of ſeveral roots, but rice is in the greateſt eſteem; tho' they ſow no more than for their own uſe, and that ſcarce ſufficient. Their drink is here, like all over the *Indies*, water, though they prepare likewiſe a ſtrong liquor of rice in the following manner: They juſt parboil the rice and then beat it to a pap, then ſeveral old women chew a certain quantity of rice, which they ſpit out into a veſſel, and mix it with the reſt, to make it ferment. After they have put it into earthen pots, they pour water upon it, and after they have covered it very well, ſet it to ferment for two months, till it is well ſettled and clear, this produces a very ſtrong liquor, which will keep good 20 years, and grow ſtronger every year. When they go abroad into the fields, they take of this liquor along with them to drink, and the ſettlement for their food; moſt of the rice here being conſumed in theſe liquors.

The women manage the ground. Contrary to the cuſtom of moſt other nations, the women cultivate the grounds here, and manage the rice, ſugar, ginger, and other fruits of the earth; the men being employed in nothing but hunting and warlike exploits, unleſs they be very old, when ſometimes they will give a helping hand to the women in the field. At leiſure time the women catch crabs, oyſters, and ſhrimps, which they much admire.

The men are mighty eager in hunting. Whole villages join together, and ſurround a great tract of ground, where they kill all they meet with, and divide it, few of the wild beaſts eſcaping their hands at that time. They alſo catch wild boars and ſtags with ſnares faſtned to canes; which the wild beaſt no ſooner touches but one or other of the legs is entangled in the ſnare, where they kill it immediately. They have alſo certain cane darts of ſix foot long, with ſeveral bent hooks at the one, and a bell at the other end, this they throw at the ſtags or other wild creatures, which being fixed in the body they trace it by the ſound of the bell till it begins to loſe its ſtrength by the loſs of blood, and ſo kill it. 1662. *The men employed in hunting.*

Their houſes are but one ſtory high, but very large, built of cane, with many doors looking to all four corners of the winds, and ſometimes more; they always raiſe their houſes three or four foot high from the ground, looking upon it otherwiſe as unwholeſome. *Their houſes.*

Their houſes are adorn'd with painted callico hangings, with wild boars and ſtags heads; with bows, arrows, clubs, pickaxes, and other warlike inſtruments, but eſpecially with the ſkulls and bones of their enemies, which they look upon as the chiefeſt ornament of their houſes: They eat and drink for the moſt part out of wooden veſſels, or ſuch as are made of bamboo-canes, but have ſome earthen pots to dreſs their victuals in, and for ſome other particular uſes. *Their utenſils.*

This iſle has no king or general governor, each village being a kind of a petty common-wealth; their government conſiſts of twelve perſons, which muſt be at leaſt 40 years of age, and are choſen out of the chiefeſt among them; they continue for life; all their power conſiſts only in conſulting what is moſt expedient for the common good, the reſult of which is propoſed to the aſſembly of the whole village, who receive it with a great deal of ſedateneſs, and after the breaking up of the aſſembly they debate among themſelves what is beſt to be done; if they approve of the propoſition made to them, it has the force of a law, if not, it is of no conſequence. They are alſo much addicted to follow the directions of their propheteſſes or ſhe prieſts; at a certain ſeaſon of the year, they are obliged to go quite naked for three months, otherwiſe (ſay they) we ſhall want rain. At another certain time they are debarr'd from wearing ſilk or other fine cloths, or if they do, their council has power to ſtrip them of them, and to tear them to pieces before their faces, unleſs they redeem them by a certain number of ſtags-ſkins, rice or ſtrong liquor. Corporal puniſhments are unknown *Their government.*

1662. unknown to them; besides this prerogative of consulting and punishing, they are upon the same level with the rest.

Age in high esteem among them. Age is the only thing in extraordinary respect among them; this they shew in giving way, either in the streets or at table, to their elders, who are also first served, and speak before the rest.

Their marriage. The men never marry before they are 50 years of age, but the women as soon as they are marriageable. The natives of *Formosa* don't suffer their hair to grow below their ears, before they come to the state of manhood, when they let it grow as long as it can. If a young man has a mind to marry a certain maid, he sends one of his friends with the ordinary marriage presents, which are commonly a *Chinese* suit of cloths, bracelets of twisted reeds, some broad rings of iron or brass, and such like baubles of an inconsiderable value; if the maid accepts of the presents, the match is made. Whilst they are young they don't dwell together in the same house, which is not allow'd of 'till the husband be 50 years of age. But as soon as the young married man has an inclination to meet with his wife, he comes privately into her hut, which is commonly in the field, and lays himself down in the place where she commonly sleeps, where she comes to him, but is sure to fend him away again early in the morning. All the children begot betwixt them, before both the husband and wife be arrived to the age of 37 years, are kill'd; for after the woman is sure she is with child, one of their she priests lays the big bellied woman upon her back, and squeezes her so long with her hands and feet till she miscarries, not without great hazard and pains, which they willingly undergo, because they reckon it a great sin to keep any children, begot before that time, alive, but preserve them carefully afterwards. The mother keeps the infant close by her till it be two years old, when it is sometimes permitted to see the father. Their marriages are as soon dissolv'd as they are contracted, and that upon very slight occasions; but if the husband parts from his wife without any reason, he loses his marriage presents, but in case of adultery, or that the woman is out-rageous, his marriage presents must be restored unto him; the women enjoy the same prerogative, both parties being afterwards at liberty to marry where they please, which sometimes happens twice or thrice a year. They make no great account of fornication, provided it may be done in private, but are very cautious of committing incest.

Justice. Here are no courts of justice, every one being at liberty to take satisfaction for murther, theft or adultery committed against him. If a man be robb'd, and knows who the thief is, he goes streight to his house and fetches either by fair or foul means as much from thence as he thinks will sufficiently repay his loss, which however occasions great disputes, nay murther. He that has kill'd another flies for it till he has given satisfaction to the deceased's kindred, which consists commonly in some hogs and stags-skins, then he may return unmolested. Adultery, when discovered, is commonly made up with two or three hogs, according to the ability of the cuckold-maker, which done the cuckold lives both with him and his wife in good correspondence. Sometimes one or more villages engage in war against one another, and surprise those that work in the field, whom they kill, and carry their heads and what booty they can get, to their houses; this they often do in the night time; if they have had good success, they rejoyce after their return home, with eating and drinking to great excess. Those who have behaved themselves well in such an expedition, are esteemed before the rest.

Their weapons. Their weapons are long and broad shields, instead of targets, wherewith they cover their bodies, short and broad scymeters which do great execution, darts pointed with iron; they have also bows and arrows, but use no firelocks. As far as ever I could learn, they have no writings or books; their pagan idolatry is transmitted from the parents to their children by word of mouth; they believe the world to have neither beginning nor end, and that the souls of such as have done well, shall be rewarded hereafter. As soon as they are dead, the friends erect a kind of scaffold before the door of the house, where they place the dead carcass surrounded with small standards; near by they set a vessel with water for the soul to bath it self in, and to wash away all its sins; as for instance, to have brought children into the world before 37 years of age; to have worn rich cloaths in the forbidden season; to have catch'd oysters, crabs and such like insignificant things; but murther, man-slaughter, adultery, fornication, theft, and such like horrid crimes, they look upon as small trespasses only, which may be expiated by a certain quantity of rice, stags-skins and strong liquors.

Religion. They have several Gods, but adore two in particular; when it thunders they say the great man is angry with his spouse, and for that reason refuses to send them rain, for which reason they adore his spouse; the other they say, is of a malicious nature, and therefore adore him, for fear he should hurt them. They have no other but female priests, they sacrifice pigs, stags and fruits; during which the she priests cry out, and fall

1662. fall into extasies afterwards, with tremblings all over their bodies, as if they were possess'd by an evil spirit, and then they pretend the idol discovers his secrets to them: The standers by, which are for the most part women, in the mean while get drunk with strong liquors. These female priests ascend to the top of their temples, where they expose themselves quite naked, and wash their bodies in the sight of the people. They pretend to foretel good or ill fortune, to banish the devil, and to purge unhallowed places. It was formerly a custom in some certain villages, that if any of the natives lay sick, past all hopes of recovery, they used to tie a rope about his neck, and so pull him up and let him down again, till they had cured his distemper by a certain death. They dry their dead carcasses over a fire, which occasions a nauseous scent, whilst the kindred, relations and friends pass away the time with eating, drinking and dancing for several days together. The dry'd corps is kept two years after, and then buried in the house. This was the ancient government of the isle of *Formosa*, but since the *Dutch East-India* company has got footing there, they have introduced other laws among them, and instead of their councils, constituted one of their chief men as supervisor in every village, who administered justice, and was accountable to the governor of the island. Thus much of *Formosa*, 'tis time to return to our voyage.

The author goes to Malacca.

After we had left *Teywan*, the 11th of *December*, we arrived the 30th of the same month without any remarkable accident, before the city of *Malacca*, where we dropt anchor, and found Mr. *John Tiis* to be chief director there for our *East-India* company.

The countrey and city of Malaga.

The kingdom of *Malacca*, otherwise *Maleja* or *Maleca*, thus called after its capital city, is situate upon the same tract of ground or demi-island, which comprehends the kingdoms of *Martevan*, *Quedam*, *Pera* and some other countries extending it self as far as *Sumatra*, the streights of which border upon it to the west and south, as the kingdoms of *Pan* and *Johor* do to the east. The kingdom of *Malacca* is by some historians taken for the *Golden Chersonese* of *Ptolemy*, tho' at present it is no demi-island. There are some who affirm, that in former ages *Malacca* was join'd by a streight neck of land to the isle of *Sumatra*, instead of which you see now a branch of the ocean, which divides its self into two navigable channels; the first of which is call'd the streights of *Sinkapura*, because it borders on the east side of the cape of that name; the other is call'd the channel of *Saban*, from an island that lies to the west of it. 1662. This country extends for about 64 leagues in length, all along the sea-coast, beginning at the island of *Cambilan* or *Zabilan* as far as the isle of *Beitan*, its utmost boundary on that side, or rather it ends in the cape of *Sinkapura*, 20 leagues from *Malacca*.

Its capital city.

Its capital city is likewise call'd *Malacca*, being the same, in former time call'd *Takola*; it lies under 2 deg. 30 min. of northern latitude, opposite to *Sumatra*, in a bay at the ascent of a hill, on the west-side of the river *Muar* (otherwise call'd *Gaze* and *Tyga* and *Krosant*, or as the *Dutch* express it *Krüisorant*) which having its rise deep in the countrey, divides the castle from the city, and washing its walls, falls with a rapid current into the sea. Cross this river is a strong bridge built of stone, with several arches: This city is very large in compass, being not many years before surrounded with a wall of square stones and bastions, by the *Dutch*. It is very populous, the houses being built very close, tho' it has some very broad and handsome streets, which are planted on both sides with trees. In the midst of the city is a hill with a very fair church dedicated to *St. Paul*, on the top of it, where divine service is perform'd in *Dutch*: The steeple, church and monasteries founded here by the *Portuguese*, are much decay'd. Most of the houses here are built of strong bamboo canes, which are very durable in dry weather, tho' there are also some stone houses here; they are generally not very large, and low, provided with small appartments and slenderly furnish'd.

Malacca when taken by the Portuguese.

The city of *Malacca* was in 1610 taken by *Albuquerque* the *Portuguese* general, in the following manner: One *Manuel*, an *Aarbian*, or rather *Mahometan*, by birth, being at that time king of *Malacca*, entred into a league with *Albuquerque*, which he soon broke after, putting all the *Portuguese* to the sword. *Albuquerque* soon after appeared before the city, and attack'd it unexpectedly, whilst the king and his courtiers were feasting at the wedding of his daughter; the *Portuguese* set fire to one end of the city, notwithstanding which, the inhabitants defended themselves like desperate men, even the women untiling the houses, and giving what assistance they could for the defence of the place; but at last the *Portuguese* having fought their way thro' the arm'd elephants, they entred the city, forcing the king to fly into the wilderness, where he died. They got a vast booty and above 200000 crowns in money. The *Portuguese* were very careful to fortify the town by a strong castle, and built several fine churches and monasteries; they had

1662. had five parochial churches, and monasteries in great numbers. Among the rest, the jesuits had erected a noble college here, with magnificent appartments; they were very liberal, and received all strangers travelling to those parts. There was a church here dedicated to our lady, where they say *Xaverius* preached often, and performed great miracles. Upon a high hill, within the city, the capuchins had a monastery; whilst the *Roman* catholicks were in possession of it, it was erected into a bishoprick, under the archbishop of *Goa*. Not many years before the *Portuguese* made themselves masters of it, it was no more than a village, but by the *Javanese* made a city.

Malacca *attack'd by the* Dutch. The *Dutch* admiral *Corielius Matclief* 1605, appeared with 11 ships and 1300 soldiers before the city of *Malacca*, where at that time *Don Furtado de Mendoza*, a brave soldier, was commander in chief: The first thing he did was to sieze upon 4 ships that lay in the road; afterwards he set fire to the suburbs, and batter'd the place for two or three months, which occasioned great famine and mortality within the city. But the *Portuguese*, who were sensible of the importance of this place, sent a considerable fleet from *Goa* to their relief, which engaging with ours, a small fight ensued, in which the *Portuguese* and *Dutch* lost two ships each; at last the *Portuguese* finding the *Dutch* resolved to board them, retired under the castle, but were so closely pursued by *Matclief*, that he ruined their whole fleet, consisting of 16 galleots, 14 galeasses, and 14 smaller vessels, with 3000 men on board them.

The Dutch *take* Malacca. The king of *Johor* besieged the city of *Malacca* in 1606, with 60000 men, the *Portuguese* having maintained themselves there till 1640, when the *Dutch* after a siege of six months made themselves masters of it; after the *Portuguese* had been in possession of it 130 years. The *Dutch* found here besides a vast booty, a great cannon which carried a shot of 64 pounds weight, since which time the *Dutch* have left no stone unturn'd to stock this city with all sorts of necessaries as well as with inhabitants, both *Dutch* and *Indians*. The origin and progress of *Malacca* is this, described by *Barros* and some other historians.

The origin of Malacca. The foundation of *Malacca* was laid about 250 years before the arrival of the *Portuguese* in the *Indies*. About that time one *Sangesinga* reign'd in *Sinkapura*, situate under 30 min. of northern latitude, and in the neighbouring countrey of *Java*, one *Paravisa*, who at his death left two sons under the guardianship of his own brother, their uncle; but he having found means to murder the eldest, usurped the throne; at which some of the noble *Javanese* being highly disgusted, did with *Paramisora*, their late king's youngest son, fly to *Sinkapura*, where they met with a kind reception from *Sangesinga*, but it was not long before *Paramisora*, in combination with his *Javanese*, murder'd *Sangesinga*, and put himself in possession of his kingdom. The king of *Siam* being highly exasperated at the treachery committed against *Sangesinga*, his vassal and son-in-law, forced the *Javanese* to quit the countrey, who being now obliged to seek for a new habitation, settled themselves near the river *Muar*, where they built a strong hold, call'd *Pagopago*; besides the *Javanese*, *Paramisora* was follow'd by 2000 others, such as they call *Cellati*, who live upon fishing and robbing; but tho' they had been very instrumental in resettling him in *Sinkapura*, he did not think fit to receive them within the body of his new built city; which made them settle their colony about three or four leagues from the river *Muar*, not far from whence *Malacca* now lies; where they join'd with the inhabitants, who were half savages; since which time their language is call'd the *Malaga* language. But when they began to be streighten'd for room, some of them settled themselves about a quarter of a league from thence, on a hill call'd *Bitan*, surrounded with a large plain: *Paramisora* being taken with the conveniency and pleasant situation of this place, abandon'd *Pagopago*, and transplanted his colony near this place, which afterwards was call'd *Malacca*, *i. e.* a banish'd person, in memory of the exiled *Javanese*; and in process of time, all the traffick of *Sinkapura* was transferr'd to *Malacca*. *Saquan Dorsa*, son of *Paramisora*, succeeded him in the kingdom, and having submitted himself as a vassal to the king of *Siam*, reduced the whole countrey of *Sinkapura* to the east, as far as *Puto* on the isle of *Zambilan*, which lies west of *Malacca*, a tract of land of forty leagues in length. The successors of *Saquan Dorsa* found means to shake off by degrees the yoke of the king of *Siam*, and to make themselves soveraign kings, especially after they were by the *Persians*, and those of *Surat*, brought over to the mahometan religion. The king of *Siam* 1502, about 9 years before the *Portuguese* became masters of *Siam*, did attack the king of *Malacca* with a fleet of 200 sail, aboard of which were 6000 soldiers, under the conduct of *Laosamava Privan*, his admiral and governor of *Ligoor*, but his fleet was miserably scatter'd by a tempest, and many of his ships fell into the hands of the mahometans by treachery.

The harbour of *Malacca* is one of the finest in all the *Indies*, being navigable at all the seasons of the year, a conveniency belong- *Its traffick.*

1662. belonging scarce to any other in the *Indies*. It is most conveniently situated for traffick, for there you may to this day see vast numbers of merchants ships coming from *Bengal*, *Coromandel*, *Banda*, *Java*, *Sumatra*, *Siam*, and in short from all parts of the *Indies*. Whilst the *Portuguese* were in possession of it, this city was very famous for its traffick and riches in gold, precious stones, and all other rarities of the *Indies*; *Malacca* being the key of the *China* and *Japan* trade, and of the *Malacca* islands and *Sunda*. In short *Malacca* was the richest city in the *Indies*, next to *Goa* and *Ormus*. Before the *Dutch* had made themselves masters of *Malacca*, a ship was sent every year thither from *Portugal*, which setting out a month before their *East-India* fleet, and taking its direct course thither, without staying in any place, except in case of necessity, used to freight there, and return with a richer cargo than any other ship ever did.

Great passage thro' the streights of Malacca. All the ships that came from the north, *viz.* of *China*, *Japan*, *Siam*, *Cambodia*, *Tonking* and *Manilha*, and are bound for the west, to wit to the coast of *Coromandel*, *Bengale*, and other places thereabouts, as likewise those coming from the west to the north, must pass thro' the streights of *Malacca* or *Sinkapura*, and consequently by *Malacca*, as I told you before. The *Portuguese* used to take 10 *per cent.* custom of all ships passing that way, whereby they got vast riches, but the *Dutch East-India* company has abolish'd this, looking upon it as an unreasonable imposition, and are contented to traffick there. *Malacca* is a countrey producing but very little it self, but must be look'd upon as the staple of the *Indies*, whither all precious commodities are brought from *China*, the *Molucca* and other neighbouring islands, from *Bengal*, *Coromandel*, *Banda*, *Java*, *Sumatra*, *Siam*, *Pegu* and other places. The island of *Sumatra* furnishes them with gold, pepper and other merchandises; from *Ligoor*, *Pera*, *Queda*, *Outjang* and *Salang* they have vast quantities of tin, which is brought up those places by the factors of the company, and sent to *Malacca*, from whence it is transported to the coast of *Coromandel*, to *Bengal*, *Persia* and *Surat*, and sold for ready money. The *Chinese* bring hither vast stores of silk and porcelain, damasks, brocados, sattins, musk, rhubarb, iron, saltpeter, fine silver, pearls great and small, ivory and *China* fans, which they exchange for pepper, frankincense, stuffs of *Camboya*, coral wrought and unwrought, painted callicoes of *Palakatte*, and white callicoes of *Bengal*, cinnabar, quick-silver, and such other drugs as come from *Camboya*. The island of *Java* supplies them with rice, oxen, sheep, stags-flesh and pork; in short, there is such a vast traffick and concourse of merchants here, that from thence probably it got the name of the *Golden Chersonesus* among the ancients; *Malacca* being certainly the richest harbour that can be seen; for formerly, and even to this day, the merchants were so rich here, that they used to compute by no less than by bars of gold, of which a vast quantity is found near the rivers and in the mountains to the west, to wit, on the famous rivers *Kedan*, and *Peren* or *Peragh*. The mahometans living along the coast, used formerly to trade hither with linen and some other commodities, but not so much of late years, neither is the pepper trade so considerable here now, as in former days, since the *Dutch East-India* company have settled their factories on the eastern coast of *Sumatra*, which produces great quantities of pepper. However, ships are sometimes detained here for a considerable time, by reason of the contrary *Monzon* or season winds.

Formerly they had no other coin but what was made of tin at *Malacca*, being of great weight, but little value; or rather they exchanged their commodities for gold and silver by weight; but now they coin both gold and silver, a piece of eight being worth commonly two gilders 11 stivers. They have two sorts of weights, *viz.* the great and small bar: The great bar consists of 200 *Kattys*, each *Katty* containing 26 *Tayls*, or 38½ ounces *Portuguese* weight, a *Tayl* being a ounce and a half: The small bar comprehends likewise 200 *Kattys*, each *Katty* comprehending 22 *Tayls*. According to the computation of others, a bar of *Malacca* contains 200 *Kattys Aetshyns*, or three *Chinese Pikol* each *Pikol* computed at 122 pound weight, making altogether 366 pound weight. The great bar or weight is made use of when they weigh pepper, cloves, nutmegs, mace, white and red sandals, indigo, allum, eagles-wood and civet; with the lesser weight, quick-silver, copper, leaf-gold, oil of nutmegs, benzoin, camphire and such like commodities. The city of *Malacca* is inhabited by many *Dutch*, but for the most part by *Mestices* and *Kastices*, some *Chinese*, *Pagans* and *Jews*, for the conveniency of traffick. *Coin of* Malacca.

The *Malayars* or natives of *Malacca* are tawny, with long black hair, great eyes and flat noses; they deduce their origin from the *Javanese*, but their eyes are quite different, they are for the most part naked, wearing only a piece of stuff wrapt about the middle, with their arms and legs naged. Their only ornament being gold bracelets and earings set with precious stones. The women *The* Malayars. *Their cloaths.*

women wear ſilk cloaths and ſhort ſkirts, embroidred with gold and precious ſtones, ſome of which are twiſted in their locks, which are very long. The women are extravagantly proud here, expecting more reverence than any other *Indian* women.

Kakerlakken. There is alſo another peculiar ſort of men in *Malacca*, called by the *Dutch Kakerlakken* (from a certain monſtrous creature in the *Indies* of the ſame name) who are blind by day, and can only ſee by night. They can tell money, work, and do any other thing in the dark, which they cannot do by daylight, which they paſs away for the moſt part in ſleeping, and ſeldom riſe 'till ſunſet. In ſhape and proportion of their limbs, as well as by their complexion, they reſemble the *Europeans*, having commonly grey eyes; whereas all the eaſtern nations have black and dark brown eyes. Their hair is inclining to yellow, and of ſuch a length among the women, that it reaches down to their hipps; their feet are bent inward. The ſame kind is likewiſe found in ſome other places of the *Indies*, and in *Africa*.

The Malaya *tongue.* The language uſed at *Malacca* is called the *Malaya* tongue, from the natives of the countrey, being very famous throughout the *Eaſt-Indies*. For the general concourſe of ſo many nations, different in their languages, has put them upon a neceſſity of compiling a certain language, compoſed of the beſt and choiceſt words of all the reſt, which therefore is accounted the neateſt and moſt agreeable of the *Eaſt-Indies*, which is the reaſon that not only the neighbouring, but alſo far diſtant nations that trade with *Malacca*, are deſirous to learn it, and look upon it as a great accompliſhment. For the better encouragement of this language, and the benefit of their officers and factors, the *Dutch Eaſt-India* company has cauſed a dictionary both in the *Malaya* and *Dutch* tongues to be publiſh'd.

Their religion. Moſt of the *Malayers* are either chriſtians or mahometans, tho' there are likewiſe ſome pagans and *Jews* ſettled at *Malacca*, for the conveniency of commerce.

The countrey. The coaſt of *Malacca* is a flat or marſhy countrey, and conſequently not extraordinary wholeſome; but deeper in the countrey are many hills and wilderneſſes, which are plainly diſcovered at ſea. It produces but little for the ſuſtenance of life, except what is brought forth in gardens, and what grows among the mountains, where you meet with ſome rice and peaſe; the defect of which is ſupply'd by vaſt numbers of ſmall veſſels, which come every day from *Bengal* and *Sumatra*, and bring thither rice, and other eatables. However, they are pretty well ſtored with ſuch fruits as commonly grow in the *Indies*. The fruit *Durions* grow here much better and larger than in any other part of the *Indies*: They have likewiſe *Ananas*, *Jambos*, *Mangoes*, *Karambolas* and *Papajas*; they have whole woods of cocotrees. Here grows a certain tree call'd the mourning-tree by the *Portugueſe*, becauſe its flowers cloſe up in the night-time. Here you may meet alſo with cinamon trees, but not very many, neither do they approach in goodneſs to thoſe of *Ceylon*. But of *Kalamback* or *Aloes* wood and *Benzoin* they have great plenty. Here are to be found ſome *Indian* fruits, peculiar only to this place, but no pears, apples, plums, cherries, or any ſuch like *European* fruits. Oxen, cows, ſheep and horſes are likewiſe very ſcarce here, which are brought thither a great way out of the countrey, and are ſeldom very fat. Formerly the countrey hereabouts did abound in wild beaſts of all ſorts, ſuch as tygers, elephants, *&c.* which were ſo ravenous, that they uſed to break in the night-time into the houſes of the inhabitants, who for their better ſecurity, uſed to ſleep upon trees; but ſince it has been ſo well peopled by the *Dutch*, this ſort of wild beaſts are but ſeldom heard of.

Juſt by *Malacca* is the cape or point of land call'd *Rachado*, and the cape of *Barcelai*, being a very high mountain near a point of land. *Cape* Rachado *and* Barcelai. Not far from *Malacca* is a very large mountain call'd *Madian*, which by reaſon of the vaſt quantities of ſalt-petre it contains within its bowels, 1646, did break out with ſuch a terrible noiſe and earthquakes, as if the day of judgment was at hand. *The mountain* Madian.

Sinkapura lies on the moſt ſouthern point of all *Aſia*, about half a degree to the north of the line, and 20 leagues from *Malacca*. Sinkapura. This cape has imparted its name to the ſtreights of *Sinkapura*. The country of *Sinkapura* had before *Malacca* was built its own kings, and was the chiefeſt place of trade on this coaſt, being much frequented by the *Chineſe* merchants, and thoſe of *Camboya*. The mountains near the ſtreights of *Sinkapura* bearing the ſame name, produce moſt excellent diamonds. About *Sinkapura* is a certain nation, which with their whole families live always at ſea in their ſmall veſſels; they are called *Saletes*, live upon fiſhing, and are ſubject to the king of *Jor*. About two leagues beyond the ſtreights of *Sinkapura* is the river *Johor*, at the entrance of which you ſee two mountains, or rather high iſlands ſhaped like ſugar loaves; one is four times bigger than the other, lying N. N. E. as you enter the river, and the other N. E. On the other ſide of the river you diſcover a high hill, tho' the ſouthſide of the river is a champain country.

There

1662. There is 10 fathom water at the mouth of this river.

The isle of Rocks. To the south of *Malacca* is a small isle, of about half a league in compass, by the *Portuguese* call'd *Ilha das Pedras*; or the *Isle of Rocks*, and has very good fresh water.

About half a cannon shot from the city, another small island call'd *Malacca*; and by the *Portuguese Ilha das Naos*, or the *Ship Island*. Two leagues from *Malacca* is a pretty large isle call'd *Sapta*. That vast point or tract of land on which the country of *Malacca* or *Malaya* lies, being the most southern of all the *East-Indies*, comprehends likewise several other kingdoms and cities; to wit, *Patany*, *Pahan*, *Pera*, *Queda*, *Johor* or *Jor*, *Ligoor*; and farther to the north the kingdom and city of *Tanassery*. We will give you a short account of the kingdom of *Johor*, *Putany*, *Ligoor* and *Pahan*.

The kingdom of Jor *or* Johor. The kingdom of *Jor* or *Johor* stands indebted for its name to its capital city, call'd by some *Goer* or *Goera*, and *Joar* or *Goar* or *Gohor*. It is situate at the very streights of *Malacca*, bordering in part upon the kingdom of *Malacca*, and on the other side upon *Pan* or *Pahan*. The antient city of *Johor* or *Jor* (call'd in some maps *Guar*) was very large and magnificently built, but was in 1603 destroyed by the *Portuguese*, who left only a few houses standing, which were immediately inhabited again. The king of *Johor* caused in 1609 another city to be built, somewhat higher up the river above *Johor*; this he call'd *Batusabar*, towards the building of which, the *Dutch* under their admiral *Peter Verkoeven* contributed 3000 pieces of eight, out of the booty they had taken from the *Portuguese* ships coming from *Makao*, near the cape *Rachado*. Most of the chief inhabitants of the old city of *Jor* retired from thence to *Batusabar*; a half day's journey from whence is *Sedalli*, near the sea-side. It is a very fertile country, abounding in lemons, and citrons as big as a man's head, *Bananaes*, *Batataes*, *Ananaes*, and other *Indian* fruits. They have also great store of pepper, cinnamon, bufflers, cows, stags, wild boars, and divers sorts of monkeys and birds, besides some sea-monsters.

The disposition of the inhabitants. The inhabitants are naturally brave, but very lascivious, liers, great dissemblers, and proud beyond measure. Their complection is inclining to a light blue, with broad faces, crooked noses, and very black teeth, which they acquire by chewing the weed *Betel*, black teeth being accounted a great ornament among them.

Their clothing. The common people go quite naked, having only a piece of stuff to cover their members, which hangs down to their toes. The rich and better sort wear a kind of jackets made of blue, green or red callicoe, 1662. or what colour they please; they are shaped like our shirts, with wide sleeves, are open before; and reach only to their knees. They have also two silken strings of the same colour with the jacket; one serves for a girdle, the other for a head-string. They paint their nails yellow, and the greater quality they pretend to the longer they wear their nails. The richer sort commonly wear a poniard on their side; enriched with precious stones. Their king has many other petty kings, his vassals, under his jurisdiction. The king of *Jor* or *Johor* in 1606 attack'd the city of *Malacca* with 60000 men; which shews him to be a potent prince, and in the taking of the city of *Jor*, the *Portuguese* got 1500 brass pieces of cannon; in 1608, *Ratispont* the then king of *Jor*, being about 30 years of age; came aboard *Dutch* fleet with 30 of his wives, he had three gold chains set with precious stones about his neck, and his poinard was likewise enriched with sapphires and diamonds; valued at 50000 gilders. The inhabitants are one half Mahometans, the other Pagans: 1609, one *John de Paratuan* was king of *Jor*, he was styled the *Great King*, being likewise king of *Malacca*, and *Raya Sybrang*, *i. e.* prince of the other side of the river. In 1611, the king of *Azem* sent back the brother of the king of *Jor*, with a fleet of 36 ships; and a convoy of 2000 men, with abundance of cannon and ammunition, in order to assist in the rebuilding of the city of *Jor*. It was generally reported, that the king of *Azem* having given his sister in marriage to him, did intend to set him upon the throne, instead of his brother, who then reigned.

Linga is an island under the jurisdiction of the king of *Johor*, who has a governor there; it produces abundance of *Zagu*, but no rice; in 1606 it had about 3000 inhabitants. *The isle of* Linga.

The kingdom of *Pan* or *Pahan*, is by the *Portuguese* call'd *Paon*, and by others after the *Arabians Phaan*; it being a custom among the mahometan *Arabians* to pronounce *phe* instead of *p*. To the north it borders upon the kingdom of *Patane*, and adjoins to that of *Johor*, as well as to the streights of *Malacca*. The city of *Pahan* is situate about a league from the seashore, being inhabited only by the nobility, the common people dwelling in the suburbs. It is not very large, but surrounded with a wall made of the trunks of trees joined close together, of about four fathoms high, strengthened on each corner with a bastion, but not fill'd with earth. The streets are enclosed on both sides with hedges of reeds, and planted with coco and other trees, resembling rather some gardens adjoining to one another in the suburbs, than a well *The kingdom of* Pan *or* Pahan.

1662. a well regulated city, the houſes being generally of reed and ſtraw, only the king's palace is of wood. The river of *Pahan* is very broad, but not navigable by galleys except at high water: The country round about is very low, and produces about 300 bahars of pepper; as likewiſe *Palo de Aquila* or eagle wood, *Kalamback* wood and camphire, but not ſo good as that of *Bornee*, gold (but very coarſe) nutmegs, mace, *Sapan* wood, diamonds, *Pedro de Porco*, or hogs ſtones, which are accounted a greater antidote than the bezoar ſtone. Deeper into the country are abundance of elephants. The inhabitants are the greateſt impoſtors in the world. The king is tributary to the king of *Siam*, but after *Albuquerque* had conquered *Malacca*, he ſent his deputies to *Pahan*, to oblige that king to promiſe fealty to him. At *Pahan* great quantities of baſkets are made and ſold, they are better than thoſe made in *Java*, but not ſo good as the *Portugueſe*. They alſo caſt great guns here of 3000 pounds weight. The inhabitants are partly mahometans, partly pagans. Their king who reigned in 1612, had married the youngeſt ſiſter of the queen of *Patane*. The two ſiſters having not ſeen one another in 28 years, the queen of *Patane* ſent to the king of *Pahan*, to deſire leave for her ſiſter, his ſpouſe, to come to ſee her, which the king refuſing, ſhe laid an embargo upon all the ſhips loaden with rice, and bound from *Siam*, *Campaja*, *Lugor*, and other places to *Pahan*; and immediately ſent a fleet of 70 ſhips, on board of which were 4000 men, with ſtrict orders to bring along with them the queen of *Pahan*, whether the king were willing or not; but it was not long before the king of *Pahan*, with the queen his ſpouſe, and two young children, being forced by famine and a revolt among his ſubjects to leave the country, came to viſit the queen of *Patane*, where they met at firſt but with a cold reception, not one of all the queen's court giving the king of *Pahan* as much as one viſit, but cauſed all his dogs to be kill'd, he being not able to keep them any longer. Some days after matters began however to look with a better face; for the 1ſt of *Auguſt* the queen of *Patane* invited the king of *Pahan* to a moſt ſumptuous feaſt, where ſhe diverted him with ſeveral *Indian* women dancers. The king of *Pahan* returned not long after with his queen, the ſiſter of the queen of *Patane*, into his country, but carried away with him no preſents to make him amends for the charge he had been at, having ſpent almoſt all he had. The king of *Pahan* who reigned in 1607. was then about 40 years of age, and his ſon had married the daughter of the king of *Queda*.

1662.

The kingdom of Patane.

The kingdom of *Patane* or *Patany*, having derived its name from its capital city, borders to the ſouth upon *Pahan*, being ſituate upon the ſame eaſtern coaſt, to the north upon *Siam* and the kingdom of *Lugor* or *Ligor*; theſe two kingdoms being incorporated into one. The city of *Patane* is ſituate under 7 deg. 56 min. of northern latitude, not far from the ſea, and ſurrounded to the land-ſide by bogs. The harbour is about half a league from the city, which is about half a league in length, and very narrow, fortified with high wooden palliſado's put cloſe together, according to the cuſtom of theſe countries. The houſes are artificially built of wood and canes, and very lightſome. The ſuburbs are likewiſe much longer than broad, and are encompaſs'd on the backſide by a pleaſant rivulet. The royal palace and court where moſt perſons of quality live, are inviron'd with palliſado-work, in the nature of a *Palanck*; the mahometan church is a ſtately edifice of brick-work, gilt very richly within, and adorned with pillars, curiouſly wrought with figures. In the midſt cloſe to the wall is the pulpit, carv'd and gilt all over, unto which the prieſts are only permitted to aſcend by four large ſteps. They have alſo ſeveral temples dedicated to their *Pagan* idols, among which three excel the reſt. When the *Dutch* in 1602 ſettled firſt here, they ſaw in one of thoſe temples belonging to the ſubjects of the king of *Siam*, a gilt ſtatue reſembling a man, but of the bigneſs of a horſe, with one hand down and the other upwards. On each ſide ſtood a very large dragon gilt, with two ſtone ſtatues, to wit, a man on the one, and a woman on the other ſide, with their hands lift up to heaven. The ſame they ſaw in the ſecond, with this difference only, that one half of it was only gilt, the other painted red. In the third was one in the ſame poſture, with a gilt ſtreak croſs the breaſt; and behind the altar of the great idol, was another leſſer ſtatue reſembling a man, with a large horn in the forehead; this idol their prieſts ſay, repreſents the great God.

Temperature of the air.

The climate is very temperate and wholeſome here, notwithſtanding it lies near the line. Their ſummer begins in *February*, and continues nine months, *viz.* till the end of *October*, during which ſeaſon they have two different winds, to wit, by day from the ſea, and by night from the land-ſide. In *November*, *December* and *January* is their winter, when it blows and rains ſo violently from the north-eaſt, that there is no ſtirring for ſhips out of the harbour till *February*, when the wind turning to the eaſt the rains ceaſe, and the fair ſeaſon returns. The countrey

1662. country of *Patane* is very fruitful, abounding in rice and many other fruits, the chiefest of which are the *Durions*, *Mangestans*, *Ananas*, *Lancrats*, *Ramboutans*, *Pisangs*, pomegranates, oranges, lemons, and a peculiar kind of lemons, call'd *Gibol Lemons*, being transplanted hither from *China*. Each month here produces its peculiar fruits, tho' those of certain months are preferable before the rest. The grounds are plowed with bufflers or oxen, which they sow with rice: They also plant good store of pepper, but cannot sell it so cheap here as in some other parts of the *East-Indies*. The woods and wildernesses are stock'd with wild creatures, such as hares, rabbits, (but not so big as ours) stags, wild boars, tigers, bufflers, elephants, apes, monkeys, geese and ducks, (which lay eggs twice every day) and turtle-doves as finely coloured as the best parrots. The wild hogs do incredible mischief among the rice, which obliges the countrymen to watch in the field in the night-time; when they shoot or otherwise kill them, they bury their carcasses under ground; the mahometans (for such those of *Patan* and *Malaya* are) being forbid the use of hogs flesh, neither will they permit any body else to eat it.

How they catch the elephants.

The elephants, as I am credibly inform'd, are catch'd in the following manner: They ride on the back of a tame large elephant into the woods, whom they let loose there; as soon as he meets with a wild elephant he engages him, and whilst their snouts are entangled, some come from behind the wild elephant and twist a rope round his hind legs, and so keep him either to render him useful for the wars, or else kill him for his teeths sake, which are in great esteem in *China*.

The sea hereabouts produces great store of craw fish, oysters and tortoises; and the same drugs, metals, and precious stones, that are found in the kingdom of *Pahan*, are likewise to be met with here.

The constitution of the inhabitants.

The natives of *Patane* are of an ash-coloured complexion and well shaped, but very proud and conceited; the richer sort never appearing abroad without a great train of servants. They are however very affable and civil in conversation, as well among themselves as to strangers; but they are no soldiers, nor inclined to warlike exercises, courage being none of their talent, but more taken with pleasures than the use of arms. Their cloathing is none of the best. The men are extremely addicted to venery, which renders them jealous above measure, their wives and daughters being not permitted to see their nearest and best friends. They have an antient custom since enacted into a law, that to check that enormous vice of sodomy, the men are obliged to wear constantly two or three small bells made of gold, silver or lead, betwixt the prepuce and the glans, or head of the yard. Adultery is a capital crime with them, especially among the great officers and nobles of the kingdom; the father of the person that has committed the crime, or if he be not living, the next of kin is obliged to supply the place of executioner, but the miscreant has the liberty to chuse what kind of death he pleases. Notwithstanding this severe punishment, adultery is very frequent among them, by reason of the extraordinary lasciviousness of the women, who are very desirous, and love to wallow in pleasures. Fornication betwixt two unmarried persons is not look'd upon so much as a trespass. Nothing is more common than if any foreign merchants come to *Patane*, to ask them whether they don't want some women for their conveniency, and there is no want of young handsome women who offer their service, out of whom each may take his choice, and agree with her as he best can, as to what he is to allow her *per* month; which done, she immediately repairs to his lodgings, where in the day time she serves for a chamber-maid, and in the night for a bedfellow; and during this agreement, the man must be as careful to avoid the commerce of other women, as she is on her side, unless he will expose himself to manifest danger. At parting the man pays her her wages, and so they are both free; and if he has a mind to change, he need not look far for one, it being a custom among the nobles here to entertain many female slaves, whom they let out for such a use, and gain great profit by them. For the rest the natives are naturally lazy and idle, living for the most part upon fishing, and some handycraft trades; the best is, that they can be contented with a little, drink scarce any thing but water, and have a natural aversion to strong liquors. Almost all the traffick and other business is in the hands of the *Chinese*, who either themselves or their factors, continually trade betwixt this and the circumjacent countries, such as *Siam*, *Ligor*, *Kamboya*, *Kouchinchina*, *Makassar*, *Pahan*, *Jambi*, *Johor*, *Bantam* and other both inland and maritime places, whither they transport all sorts of *Chinese* commodities from *Patane*, as porcelain pots, pans, kettles, and iron work of all sorts. The chief riches of the natives consist in their lands and slaves, who live upon a small allowance of rice and fish; but the foreign merchants transport thither abundance of rich merchandizes.

1662. Their traffick.

From *Bengale* and *Malacca* they ſend clothes to *Patane*; from *Java* ſandel wood; from *Borneo* camphire, ſlaves, wax and bezoar-ſtones; from *Siam* the inhabitants of *Patane* are furniſhed with gold, rice, ſalt and lead; from *Siampa* and *Camboja* with ſlaves, cotton, *Kalamback*, and the fineſt aloes-wood; from *China* with white and yellow ſilk, gauſes, damaſks, ſattins, porcelain, iron and copper; from *Japan* with ſcimeters, copper, and ſuch like commodities. Many things are alſo tranſported hither that are bought up in other places by foreigners; as from *Amboyna* and *Banda*, nutmegs, mace and cloves; from *Timor* ſandel-wood; from *Jamby* and *Andragny* pepper, which they

1662.

fetch likewiſe from *Champor*, *Lihor*, *Pahan*, *Mordyllion* and *Ligor*: *Pegu* ſupplies *Patane* with abundance of precious ſtones; there are alſo many things exported from thence by the foreign merchants; thoſe of *Lahor* and *Pahan* provide themſelves here with rice, ſalt, oxen, fowls and other eatables; thoſe of *Malacca* tranſport the bezoar ſtones; thoſe of *Borneo* iron, ſteel and copper; the *Siameſe* all ſorts of clothings and pepper; the *Chineſe* pepper, camphire, white and yellow ſandel-wood, ſkins, ivory, bufflers horns, and ſuch like; the *Japaneſe* ſtags ſkins, tin, lead and ſilk.

The country of *Patane* is much more powerful in ſhipping than *Johor*, *Pahan*, or any of the circumjacent kingdoms: They are governed by a king, who as well as the king of *Malaya* is tributary to the king of *Siam*; their uſual yearly tribute conſiſting of a flower wrought with gold, ſome fine cloths, velvets and ſcarlets; the king's chief counſellors are called *Mentary*.

This kingdom was in 1602 under the government of a queen, after the deceaſe of her huſband, ſhe being then but 15 years of age. Her name was *Pratie*, ſhe uſed to keep conſtantly within the court among her ladies of honour, of whom ſhe had a great number; ſhe did not allow them to marry, but connived at their amorous intrigues. Wherever ſhe went abroad to take the air, (which indeed happened but very ſeldom) ſhe was mounted on a very fine elephant, and attended by 2000 nobles and great officers, all clad in her deceaſed royal ſpouſe's liveries, with his coat of arms upon them. Before they returned, ſhe gave them always a ſplendid entertainment, and ſo came with the ſame cavalcade back to her court. The country of *Patane* is ſo populous, as to be able to bring 180000 armed men into the field; the city and ſuburbs of *Patane* alone being able to furniſh 10000 men.

Divers languages are in vogue, *viz.* the *Malayan*, *Siameſe*, *Pataneſe* and the *Chineſe*; Their language.

1662. but the first is most used here, as well as in most other parts of the *Indies*. The king of *Patane* married his daughter to the eldest son of the king of *Johor*, (he having six in all) who with his youngest brother lived at the court of *Patane*; but the youngest being engaged in an illegal commerce with his brother's spouse, he kill'd them both, according to the custom of the country, which punishes adultery with death; notwithstanding which, the king of *Patane*, to revenge his daughter's death, caused his son-in-law, the eldest son of the king of *Johor* to be slain; *John de Paratuan*, and *Regia Sabrang*, two brothers, and both kings of *Johor*, being not without reason, highly exasperated at this proceeding, sent one *Magat Mangsor Hoch* their ambassador, along with admiral *Jacob Heemskerk*, to solicite a powerful aid from the states-general against the king of *Patane*, but the ambassador dying at sea put a stop to that design.

The isle of Ding Ding. Having dispatch'd my business here, we set sail the next day to a certain island call'd *Ding Ding*, abounding in fuel and most excellent fresh water. It lies about 30 leagues to the north of *Malacca*, being covered all over with very tall trees, which grow on the hills. We arrived here the 10th of *January* 1661, and immediately after our landing, fell to the cutting down of trees; among the rest we endeavoured to pick out a certain kind of trees, the wood of which is a pale red, but to our great amazement could meet with none, till at last we discovered our error, to wit, that the pith only was red, but all the other wood round about it of a different colour. This wood is much valued by the *Indians* for its beauty, of which they make many curious pieces. The fresh water which runs down from the rocks, claims the preference before any in the *Indies*; and this isle has likewise the conveniency of a good bay, where ships may ride safely at anchor. On the east-side it has another bay call'd *Cox Bay*, where we used sometimes to catch as much fish at a draught, as our chaloop was able to carry.

Is destitute of inhabitants. It is destitute of inhabitants and all sorts of wild creatures, except wild boars, which swim over thither from the continent to feed upon a certain root that grows there, nevertheless it abounds in water-fowls more than any other place of the *Indies*: Here is a certain kind of birds call'd by the *Dutch Shuies Birds*, being of the bigness of a *Storex*, the head being without feathers. Here are also great quantities of tortoises and oysters, the last of which are often seen fastned to the branches of trees, which hang sometimes above, sometimes under water.

The clearness of the water having invited us to take a turn at swimming, I found something sticking to one of my legs, which when I look'd upon, I found to be a sea-apple, and struck it off; but the sting remaining in the flesh occasioned a great inflammation and pain, which was not appeased till a considerable time after the sting was taken out. 1662.

They leave it. After we had provided ourselves with what this place could afford us, we set sail again the 14th of *January*; as we were sailing the same day along the coast of *Sumatra*, our trumpeter catch'd a stone-bream of about three feet long, which appearing very fine to the eye, we ordered the cook to dress it for the table of the cabin. *A poisonous sea bream.* We were all so greedy, that when it was brought in, we ask'd the cook whether he was sure he had kept none behind, which he took so ill, that he answered us, whether we look'd upon him as a thief? But it was not long after dinner, before all those that had dined in the cabin, were seized with such a giddiness in their heads, that they were not able to sit upright; I was the first who cry'd out, *We have certainly eat a poisonous fish*; but our surgeon having no proper remedies aboard, we sent our chaloop to the ship the *Leerdam*, from whence being furnished with vomits, we were by the frequent use of them, after a sickness of 14 days restored to our former health. During our sickness our best diversion was, that being inform'd how the cook was as sick as any of us, we were convinced, that notwithstanding his great pretence of honesty, our suspicion was not ill grounded, which verified our old proverb, *That the cook is commonly the last who dies for want of victuals:* Two cats that had eaten the bones of this fish died soon after, tho' some tobacco-water had been given them to occasion a vomiting, but none of us died, some few however were troubled with a lingring distemper afterwards.

It is not easy to imagine what could be the reason of this disaster, the sea-bream being otherwise a fish both toothsome and wholesome, unless we supposed this bream to have fed upon some poisonous fish, such as those call'd by the *Dutch Seaquallan*, which are very poisonous in those hot countries; *Reason of the poison of this fish.* for if they touch but your flesh, they cause an immediate inflammation; their flesh is as soft as gelly; they are of the bigness of a trencher, or somewhat lesser, have red and purple spots on their backs, and eight teats below on their bellies: At certain seasons of the year, the seas about *Toutekoriin*, and near other places on the coast of *Malabar*, are so full of them, that they are obliged to desist from fishing. But before we proceed farther in our voyage, it will be requisite to give you a short account of the isle of *Sumatra*.

1662. *The isle of Sumatra's situation.* The large and most potent island of *Sumatra* is by some authors call'd *Somatra, Samatra* and *Zamatra.* Its situation is to the south-west just opposite to *Malacca*, about eight leagues from the continent, the great isle of *Java*, lying to the south of it. Its extent is from the 5th degrees of northern latitude, near the gulph of *Bengala*, to the south south-east, to the 7th degree of southern latitude, as far as the streights of *Sunda*, beyond the coast of *Malacca*, comprehending a vast tract of ground of 12 degrees from the south to the north, amounting to 130 leagues. Its whole length is 195 leagues, its breadth 50, and the whole circumference 360.

This isle was formerly divided by some into four, by others into 10 kingdoms, among which *Pedir, Pazem, Achem, Kampar, Menankabo, Zunda, Andragide* and *Auru* were the chiefest. Some there are who mention *Is divided in many kingdoms.* no less than 30 petty kingdoms, *viz. Daya, Lambry, Achem* or *Achen* or *Achin, Biar, Pedir, Lide, Pirada, Pacem, Bara, Daru, Arkat, Irkan, Rupat, Pury, Gaka, Kamper, Kapokan, Andragvery* or *Andragide, Jamby, Palimbang, Tana, Malayo, Sakampan, Tulumbavan, Andaloz, Piriaman* or *Pryaman, Tiko*, or *Tikouw, Barros, Quinchel*, and *Mankapa*, all which borrowed their names from their respective capital cities; and in antient times were govern'd by their own kings. But in process of time, many of these were swallowed up in the kingdom of *Achin*, the most potent in this island, having under its jurisdiction the kingdoms and cities of *Pedir, Pazem, Daya, Barros, Pastaman, Pryaman* and *Padang*, and consequently the greatest part of the isle of *Sumatra*, besides the kingdoms of *Queda* and *Pera* on the continent. All the other kingdoms and cities of *Sumatra* were conquered by foreign princes. This the southern parts of *Sumatra*, viz. *Sillabar, Dampin, Liampon, Palimbang, Jamby* and some others, acknowledge the king of *Bantam* their sovereign, or else the *Mataram* of *Java* for their protector. Some will have the isle of *Sumatra* to be the same the ancients called *Taprobang*, tho' in my opinion that name belongs more properly to the isle of *Ceylon*.

The inhabitants of Palimbang murther some Dutch. Not many years ago one of the chiefest cities of *Sumatra* was *Palimbang* or *Palembang*, situated near the western coast of *Sumatra*, which on 24 *November* 1659, was laid in ashes by the *Dutch* admiral and general *John van der Laen*, because the inhabitants had about two years before surprized by treachery two of their yachts call'd the *Jakkatra* and the *Watchman*, and miserably murthered the whole ships crew; and in the next following year had cut to pieces two other *Dutchmen* that were sent ashore, from aboard the vessels the *Nieuport* and the *Lee dam* (lately come from the *Texel*) to serve as interpreters, their heads being by special order from the *Orangkay*'s put upon lances, and exposed to the view of their comrades that were in the boats. 1662.

A fleet of Dutch ships sent to Palimbang. To revenge so barbarous a murder, a fleet of eleven ships set sail from *Batavia* the 19th of *October* 1659, under command of *John Vander Lgen* admiral, and *John Truytsman* vice-admiral, *viz.* the *Orange*, admiral, the *Postilion*, the *Molucco*, the *Arms of Batavia*, and the *Charles*; three galleots, to wit, the *Apple-tree*, the *Hour-glass*, and *Hammebiel*; and the chaloops, the *Crab*, the *Tronk*, and the *Flying Dear*, mann'd with 600 seamen and 700 land soldiers. The 30th they arrived without any remarkable accident in their passage before the river of *Palimbang*, where they met with the yachts the *Bloemendahl*, the *Koukerk*, and the *Cat*, and with the chaloops the *Cony*, and the *Koelong*, that were cruising thereabouts. The same day they got sight of a *Chinese* vessel *They arrive before the river of Palimbang.* taking its course towards *Jamby*, which they detained till they had entered the river, and on the 3d of *November* sent her in company of the chaloop the *Tronk* to *Jamby*. They entred the river in the following order. First the *Arms of Batavia*, next the *Postilion*, then the yacht the *Bloemendahl*, aboard of which was the admiral, having left the *Orange* at the entrance of the river; the yacht the *Koukerk* vice-admiral, the yacht the *Cat*, the large chaloop the crab; after these came the three galleots, the *Hour-glass*, the *Apple-tree*, the *Hammebiel*; the ships the *Charles* and the *Molucco*, brought up the rear; the other chaloops were ordered to attack the admiral ship. The 3d and 4th of *November* was spent by the *Dutch* to enter the river, the 9th in the night time they were unexpectedly attacked by some of the inhabitants of *Palimbang*, in which engagement we had four or five wounded, the commanders not being time enough upon their guard. The 10th they were advanced betwixt the isle of *Cambira* and the *Come within sight of the city.* opposite shore, within sight of the city of *Palimbang*, where they discovered three of the enemies forts; the first called *Bamagangan*, situate on the western point of the river of the isle of *Cambara*, the other two upon its east point, opposite to the other, they were called *Mathapoura* and *Menapoura*. At our first appearance the enemy kept close within their works, which gave us the more encouragement to penetrate higher up the river with our ships. But several large floats, upon which houses filled with combustible matter were built, being laid in the stream, captain *Jurian Paulson* was ordered with some boats and the yacht the *Hour-glass*,

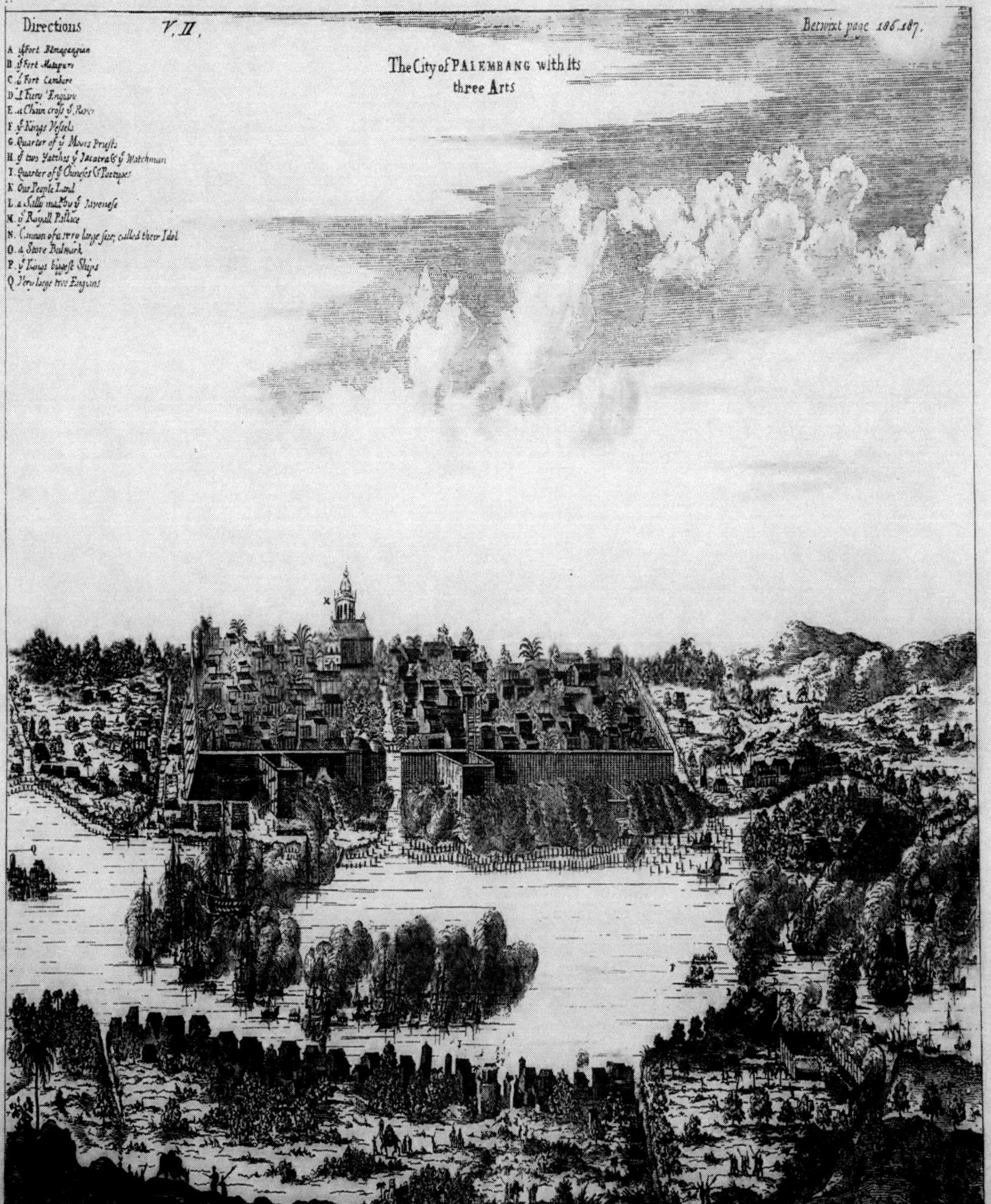
Directions
V. II.
Betwixt page 186.187.
The City of PALEMBANG with its three Arts
E. a Chain cross ye River
F. ye Kings Vessels
G. Quarter of ye Moors Priests
K. Our People Land
M. ye Royall Pallace
O. a Stone Bulwark
P. ye Kings biggest Ships

1662.

But the enemies fire engines.

Hour-glass, to take a view of them, to cut their cables, and set them on fire, which being put in execution accordingly, the whole fleet advanced forward in order to attack the fort of *Bamagangan*. But as soon as we came within cannon shot of the fort, the enemy gave us a very warm salute out of his great cannon, from the forts both on the east and western points, tho' without any considerable loss on our side, which gave us sufficient encouragement to fire most furiously upon the first fort, with such success, that we set their magazine of powder on fire, which blew up with it the greatest part of the fort, and all the circumjacent houses; hereupon the yachts the *Bloemendahl*, the *Koukerk*, and the *Cat*, were ordered to anchor within pistol shot from the shore, from whence we so grievously gall'd the enemy, both with our great and small shot, that at last we landed, and made ourselves masters of the fort, where we found 22 iron and brass cannon, which we immediately turned against the enemy to the land side, and continued in arms all the night long, which proved no unnecessary precaution, for the enemy attacked us most furiously not long after, in hopes of regaining the place, but were repulsed most couragiously, with the loss of only one man on our side.

The fort Bamagangan attacked.

Fire engines of the enemy. Then the enemy sent four or five very large fire engines, being floats of timber with wood on houses filled with combustible matter on the top of them, which took up almost the whole breadth of the river; the yachts the *Bloemendahl*, the *Koukerk*, and the *Cat*, had much ado to escape their fury, being forced to cut their cables; but the *Molucca* yacht had her fore-castle set on fire, and was with much ado saved by the help of many boats that were sent to her assistance, without receiving any considerable damage; so that these fire engines were forced down the river by the current, and soon after vanished into smoak. At the taking of the fort 30 *Javanese* were killed, and among them the old *Quevy*, *Tommagen*, *Nadapen Radia*, with his two sons, who were buried the next day.

The fort Mathapoura taken. The 11th early in the morning we likewise attacked and took the fort *Mathapoura*, where we found only four pieces of cannon, the enemy having thrown four more into the river, which we brought out from thence afterwards; the remaining part of the day was spent in shipping in what artillery and ammunition we had got; eight companies of soldiers were likewise landed the same afternoon in the isle of *Cambara*, to attack the fort there, but to their great amazement found this strong hold left by these cowardly wretches; we found here 12 pieces of cannon, some of which they had likewise thrown into the mud, but were recovered by our people, and carried aboard our vessels, with a small quantity of ammunition. Whilst these things were transacting in sight of the garrison of *Palimbang*, they had found means to set fire to the yacht the *Watchman*, which they burned; and in the evening those that had deserted the fort under favour of a violent rain, did three several times attempt the recovery of it, in which engagement we had two killed and six wounded, and were forced to stand to our arms all the rest of the night. The 12th and 13th were spent in embarking all the cannon and ammunition we had got in the 3 beforementioned forts, which done, it was resolved in a council of war, forthwith to attack the *Chinese* quarter, and so to make ourselves masters of the city before the enemies could recover themselves from the fright they were put in by the loss of their forts: As we were passing by the city we received the same salute we had before from the forts, but without any remarkable harm, or the loss of one of our vessels.

The isle of Cambara taken.

1662.

The fortification of Palimbang. The city of *Palimbang* was fortified with vast trunks of trees put close together, upon which were planted a vast number of great cannon, so that it seemed impossible to be taken by so small a number, being besides this invironed with a deep and miry ditch. We were hard put to it how to find a safe landing place, till at last our admiral having espied at the uttermost point of the fortification a small rivulet, which led up to a place where we perceived very little or none of the enemy's fire, we landed thereabouts with all our forces, and advancing boldly to the very gun-holes of the enemy, they threw their granados through them into the city, which setting the adjacent houses on fire, the enemy were so terrified thereat, that they quitted their post, and thereby gave opportunity to the admiral *Vander Laen*, to Mr. *Truytsman*, and captain *Harman* to break thro' the fortifications into the city by three several ways. Here they met with a brave opposition from the inhabitants, who, according to the custom of these nations, under the sound of their *Amock*, fell couragiously upon these three bodies, of whom they killed 18, among which were a lieutenant, an ensign, and a sergeant, but not without a much greater loss on their side; the violent rains obliged the *Dutch* admiral to reconduct his men on board the vessels that night, but the next morning they landed again, and entred the city in the same place, where a doubtful engagement ensued, till the inhabitants being at last forced to give way, were beat out of the place, and retired into the open

Attacked by the Dutch.

And taken.

1662. countrey. The first thing that was sacrificed to the fury of the flames, was the royal palace, after it had been despoiled of all its riches, and a vast train of artillery, which the king and his cowardly subjects left a prey to the *Dutch*, after they had for some time defended themselves, and fought hand to hand against them; but the admiral *Vander Laen* having laid two of their chief or *Quey Nabeys*, dead at his feet, the rest were so terrified thereat, that they sought for their safety in their heels. It is worth taking notice of that these *Indians* seemed to have paid a peculiar reverence to their great cannon, which we found covered with scarlet cloth lined with ramboutins, and so perfumed with incense that the smell thereof stuck a great while after to our fingers. All the artillery and cannon being taken out of the city and from the ramparts, the admiral ordered likewise the fortifications and adjacent houses to be laid in ashes; we found 15 of 21 of our people that were prisoners among them, in the prison on both sides of the royal palace, miserably murdered and mangled by these barbarous wretches, among which was *Jacob de Groot*; one *Dutch* boy only who was not put in irons, had the good fortune to escape their hands by a timely flight, the remaining six they had carried along with them: To revenge as much as possible this barbarity, all that remained of the city, was after the cannon and all the other booty we got were carried aboard our vessels, set on fire and destroyed, the 16th of the same month.

Fifteen Dutchmen found murthered in the city.

About the same time the enemy sent one of his before-mentioned fire engines, of a vast bigness, down the river; it consisted of 20 wooden houses erected upon floats of timber, which almost extended from one side to the other. But no sooner had the *Dutch* got sight of this engine, but they sent out their long boats well mann'd, who took care to protect our ships against it, and after it was passed by them, set it on fire in sight of the enemy, which consumed both the engines and a good number of houses standing on the banks of the river. The 17th and 18th our people were still busy in embarking the booty, artillery and cannon, and a day of thanksgiving was appointed to be kept throughout the whole fleet for this victory against the 23d. In the mean while we advanced higher up the river, to try whether we could meet with some vessels or plantations that way, but saw nothing of any moment. Mr. *John Vander Laen* and *John Truytsman* also writ a letter to the *Pangerang* or governour of *Palimbang*, which was dispatched thither the 23d by a *Chinese* prisoner and an old woman.

The enemies fire engine unsuccessful.

John Vander Laen general, and captain *John Truytsman*, commanders in chief of the *Dutch* forces now in the river and the countrey of *Palimbang*, send this letter to the *Pangerang* and all the chief councellours of the countrey of *Palimbang*. 1662.

A letter sent to the Pangerang.

Notwithstanding our last success, we could not but put your highness in mind of the most abominable murder committed by your subjects upon so many innocent persons in the service of the Dutch East-India *company: which barbarous act, tho' it was highly resented by the governour, general, and council of the* Indies *residing at* Batavia, *yet to shew their inclinations to continue in peace with your highness, did at that time for the preventing the effusion of human blood, require and actually demand a reasonable satisfaction for these unheard of barbarities: To accomplish which, they caused certain propositions to be made by* John Truytsman *to your highness, with strict orders to insinuate to your highness all such reasons as might conduce towards the accomplishment of that end, which we don't question would have been sufficiently convincing to your highness, had not your evil councellours misguided you, and thwarted your good intentions. But seeing you slighted these conditions, and were very backward in giving due satisfaction, the great God of heaven and earth being highly displeased at your conduct, did so direct the heart of the beforementioned lord governour and his council, as to have recourse to arms, being the only remedy left them, ordained by God almighty to protect the just cause of their subjects. The great God of heaven having been pleased to bless their undertaking, for the due punishment of your malicious subjects, they are however willing to let your highness know, that the hostilities committed against you and your subjects, were undertaken with no other intention, than to revenge the innocent blood of their subjects, and to procure an honourable and reasonable peace; the said governour and his council being always more inclined to peace than war, if your highness is of the same sentiment we expect to hear from you either by your letter in answer to this, or by your deputies, it being our resolution to tarry for that purpose in your highness's territories, and these presents shall be a sufficient passport to those whom your highness shall be pleased to send to treat with us.* Given aboard the *Bloemendahl* the 20th of November 1659.

signed,
John Vander Laen,
John Truytsman.

The 25th our ships went further up the river, and got sometimes sight of three or four lighters, which served for ferry boats; and

The Dutch fleet goes higher up the river.

1662. and some few houses built upon floats of timber; the lighters could not be taken, because they came not within reach of our shot, and afterwards sheltered themselves in the small rivulets among the weeds: The houses were set on fire, and so we returned the 20 before the fort where we lay at anchor till next day. In the mean time *Peter de Goyer* director of the *Dutch* factory of *Jamby*, sent the 11th of *November* from thence by the chaloop the *Tronk*, 75 capons, 100 pullets, and five goats, for the use of Mr. *John Vander Laen*, and the other commanders; this being all he was able to get, all eatables being extreamly scarce thereabouts at that time, because the *Pangerang* of *Adrogory* and the young king of *Jobor*, had lately tarried three months, with an attendance of 2000 persons in these parts; and not long ago abundance of cattle and fowls had been killed for the wedding feast of his highness's daughter, who was married to the young *Patuan*. The admiral and captain *Truytsman* received not long after an answer from the *Pangarang* of *Jamby* to their letter dated the 20th of *November*, which being enclosed in another from Mr. *Peter Goyer* dated the 26th, was translated out of the *Malayan*, and runs thus.

This letter is sent from a sincere heart, by the *Pangarang* of *Jamby* to the commanders in chief *John Vander Laen* and *Daman Sittia Bauwa* (meaning captain *Truytsman*) men famous for their prudence and courage.

The Pangerang *having understood that Mr.* John Maetzuicker *governour general of the* Dutch East-Indies, *has sent 18 ships against those of* Palimbang, *has thought fit to declare, that his sentiments agree with the governour's, and that he is ready to approve all without the least contradiction, what shall be undertaken by the said Mr.* John Maetzuicker, *assuring Mr.* John Vander Laen *and* Daman Sittia Bauwa, *that he will stand firm to this as well as to the other promises made by him the* Pangerang *before. Pursuant to this resolution the* Pangerang *did upon the receipt of the letter, send* Zitta Antacca *with some troops to make war upon those of* Palimbang. *The* Pangerang *also forewarns and commands* John Vander Laen *and* Daman Sittia Bauwa *to be upon their guard, because those of* Palimbang *are near at hand; this being all the* Pangerang *commands at this time to* John Vander Laen *and* Daman Sittia Bauwa.

The 27th all the houses that were yet standing near the fort of *Mansapoura* were together with the fort itself, set on fire by special order from the admiral, and the same day we lifted a great piece of ordnance out of the marshes in the isle of *Cambara*. And being sensible that either out of an obstinate temper or out of despair the *Pangerang* of *Palimbang* would scarce send any deputies or answers to ours of the 20th, we resolved to leave that river; and accordingly with the next tide set sail and returned thro' the branch of the river call'd *Banjarmassum* in order to burn all the houses and plantations we should meet with; but having spent 5 days, *viz.* to the 3[d] of *December* in coming down the said river; we met at its entrance with the ship the *Orange*, which joining with the rest, we continued our voyage the 4th, and arrived with the whole fleet and our forces the 9th in the afternoon, in the road of *Batavia*. Our booty consisted chiefly in 75 pieces of great, and 142 lesser cannon, some of which were of iron. We found no pepper here, but great store of rice and *Padie*, all which was consumed by the fury of the flames, as likewise a vast number of small vessels, among which were the king's pleasure boats, of which there was a vast number; some few were carried away by our people, to be kept in remembrance of this action.

The Dutch *leave the river.*

Arrive at Batavia.

The kingdom of Achin.

The kingdom of *Achin* is situate in the most northern part of the isle of *Sumatra*. Its capital city bears the same name, being situate in a plain upon a pleasant rivulet, about half a league distant from the sea-shore. The royal place, which lies in the very center of the city, is very large, of an oval figure, surrounded with a ditch, and in some places defended by very large pieces of ordnance; the ditch is guarded by pallisadoes, in which are seven gates. On the left side of the river is a fort to defend its entrance, and several other redoubts are erected in the marshes, round about the city of *Achin*, for its defence. The air seems to be much more wholsome here than in the southern parts of the isle. The houses which are covered with reeds are built upon posts, so that you must enter them by several steps, the reason of which is, that at certain seasons the waters rise to such a height, that the whole city is overflown by it. The chiefest riches of the king of *Achin* consist in gold, jewels and elephants; he entertains a great number of concubines which serve both for his bed and his guards in the antichambers; besides which, he maintains a good number of eunuchs, who attend his person. Four *Sabandars* or nobles have the chief management of the government under the king. This kingdom was in 1663 governed by a queen, who, as it was reported, had an inclination to be married to a *Hollander*; but the council of *Batavia*, for weighty reasons would not consent to the match. The inhabitants of *Achin* were always renowned for their courage and conduct beyond all other neighbouring nations, and have not only extended their conquests

1662. quests over the circumjacent countries of *Sumatra*, but also made themselves masters of the kingdoms of *Queda* and *Pera* on the continent of *Malacca*; nay, they frequently have besieged the *Portuguese* in the city of *Malacca*, they having always been declared enemies of that nation.

Sillebar. On the western coast, not above 4 leagues to the south of the line, is within a bay, upon a very large river, a certain place call'd *Sillebar*, being surrounded with craggy mountains and vast woods; tho' the countrey thereabouts is very fertile in pepper; it belongs to the king of *Bantam*. On the same western coast is a very large Bay, the shore of which is all over woody, as the bay of *Sillebar*, is surrounded with mountains; tho' the shore its self is very green and pleasant. Immediately after you come to the bay, you discover a small point of land, behind which lies the town of *Sillebar*.

Tikouw. A few leagues to the south of the line, is likewise the city of *Tikouw*, a place very slightly built, and some leagues from thence Passaman. to the north, is the town of *Passaman*, at the foot of a high mountain.

Barros. *Barros* is also situate on the western coast of *Sumatra*, about a league from the seashore, upon a considerable river, betwixt *Passaman* and *Achin*. The countrey hereabouts produces pepper, camphire and benzoin. Hereabouts are likewise *Sinkel*, *Labo*, and *Daya*.

Pedir. *Pedir* lies ten leagues to the east of *Achin*, with a high mountain betwixt both; the countrey, which was formerly a kingdom, is indifferently fruitful of rice and other fruits. Further to the east, on the inward coast of *Sumatra*, are *Pacem*, *Dely*, *Aru*, *Kampar*, *Andripouro*, *Jamby* and *Palimbang*. *Andripouro* is situate under 3 deg. 30 min.

Padang. *Padang* lies on a very pleasant river, whither a considerable number of *Indian* vessels resort. The *Dutch* divide the coast of *Sumatra* into the outward and inward coast. The inward coast is by the *Javanese* call'd the western coast, as the outward coast is the northern coast, where is the kingdom of *Achin*.

Unwholesomeness of the climate of Sumatra. The climate of *Sumatra*, is, by reason of its situation under the line, extremely unwholsome, especially for strangers, and in the rainy season, when scarce a day passes but they are afflicted with sudden showers, storms, thunder and lightnings, which soon after end in a calm. Besides, that the heat of the sun-beams draws up the nauseous vapours of the standing waters, which infect the air, and produce malignant fevers, and other lingring distempers. This is most visible on the western coast of *Sumatra*, and especially in *Tikouw* and *Pryaman*, where the air is equally obnoxious to the inhabitants and foreigners, which makes the *Dutch* inhabiting there, look bloated and very pale. In the *Devil's-Isle*, and near the river *Indapura* the air is so poisonous, that it kills men and beasts as soon as they set foot on shore; and if they happen to escape by returning immediately, they certainly die soon after. 1662.

The isle of *Sumatra* is full of pleasant woods, craggy high mountains, agreeable valleys, fruitful plains, very fine rivers and large bays affording great store of fish; besides that, the marshes and pools are stock'd with young oak-trees, the bark whereof gives the waters a red tincture. The chief rivers here are, the *Achin*, *Andregiri*, *Jamby*, *Palimbang*, *Manancabo*, *Banjarmassum*, *Sillebar*, *Indapura*, and *Pryaman*, all which have derived their names from their respective adjacent cities, or these from them. The waters of the river *Indapura* are red for two leagues at sea, which proceeds from the great quantity of young oak trees growing in the marshes, the bark of which imparts a red dye to the river; for which reason also the water is very unwholsome to drink. *The nature of the isle.* *Its rivers.*

The soil produces rice in abundance, and all other sorts of *Indian* fruits, such as *Bananas*, potatoes, coco-nuts, oranges, limons, tamarinds, sugar, honey, ginger, but especially pepper, of which a great quantity is transported from thence into foreign countries. Some years ago many plantations of pepper were destroy'd by the soldiers upon the outward coast of *Sumatra*, which were since replanted, yet in many places cotton-trees have been planted in their stead. The same coast also produces camphire, the most durable of all others, which differs from the *Japonese* camphire in this particular quality, that whereas in this, the scent is in the wood; the camphire of *Sumatra* contains it in its own substance, without imparting the least share thereof to the wood. This island affords likewise white benzoin, *Kalamback* or aloes-wood, eagles-wood, and sandels-wood. The forests here feed divers kinds of wild beasts, *viz.* elephants, bufflers, tygers, staggs, rhinoceroses, wild boars, apes, monkeys and serpents; the rivers, lakes, and ports abundance of fishes; in some you meet with crocodiles. The woods are full of wild fowl of all sorts, and the countrey abounds in tame fowl. They have bats here of an exceeding bigness. It is very remarkable, that the island of *Sumatra* is the only one throughout the *East-Indies*, that has bears. The mountains here afford gold, silver, copper, tin, iron and brimstone. The outward coast of *Sumatra* especially, has very *Its soil.*

1662. rich gold mines, but they are neglected for the most part. However the queen of *Achin* drew 1000 pounds weight out of one mine, and the *Dutch East-India* company 300 in the year 1665: They also produce [illegible], hyacinths and other precious stones. On the top of the fiery mountain *Balabam*, is a certain spring of sulphurous liquor like oil; and the like is seen in several other parts of this island, to sweat out of the earth or rocks, not unlike a *Petroleum*:

Earth-oil. The *Indians* call this liquor *Minjah Tunnah*, *e. i.* earth-oil. This is in such esteem among the inhabitants, that the king of *Achin* has prohibited the exportation thereof under pain of death; so that what is carried away by the *English* or *Dutch*, is brought on board by stealth. It has a very strong scent, but not nauseous; its virtue is extraordinary in curing lameness, call'd by the *Indians Beribery*, if the affected parts be only bathed or anointed with it. This island has a certain kind of reed, which grows near 300 fathom high, and twists its self round the trees. They make hops of it.

The language of the inhabitants and their manners. The most general language here is the *Malayan*, tho' they use likewise several others. They maintain certain schools for the young people to be instructed in reading and writing. The inhabitants of *Sumatra* are large of stature, black and brown of complexion like the *Javanese*. The women are well shaped, and of a fairish complexion, with very white teeth; they make no account of chastity, nor look upon it as a disgrace to expose themselves for money. For the rest, this nation is extravagantly proud and ill-natured, which sets so high a value upon itself, as to despise all foreigners; they are very treacherous, and make very little account of their faith, if they find it consistent with their interest. Every body here is like all the mahometans, does marry as many wives as he is able to keep, one however has the precedency before all the rest: Women of any quality are seldom seen to walk along the streets. In the inland countrey lives still the remainder of the ancient men-eaters, call'd *Bataches* or *Batatas*, who not only devour strangers, but likewse kill their own fathers and brothers, if grown very decrepid, and eat them.

Their diet. Both rich and poor are continually chewing the leaves of *Bethel*, mixt with thyme and *Areka* or *Fausel*. Their bread is made of rice, of which they make also a dainty pap, and cakes, and eat them with oil. They feed likewise upon fish, flesh and herbs. Their ordinary drink is water; besides which, they use *Arack* distill'd of rice and coco-nuts, and palm wine. The inhabitants of *Sumatra* are very moderate in their diet, like all the rest of the *Indians*. 1662.

Their cloathing. Most of the inhabitants, especially the poorer sort, go naked to the middle, where they have only a piece of stuff wrapt about them to cover their privities; both sexes go without shoes or stockins. The richer sort wear a kind of coat of silk or callico, after the mahometan fashion; a linnen cloth wrap'd about their heads two or three times, serves them for a cap.

The absoluteness of their kings. They pay a more than slavish submission and obedience to their kings, not so much out of inclination as fear; their princes or governors are stiled *Pangerang*.

Their punishments. They punish the least trespass with great severity, by cutting off their hands and feet. Capital crimes are punish'd after the most dreadful manner that can be invented. In former ages the kings used to surrender the miscreant to the men-eaters, who after they chop'd of their hands, arms and legs, threw pepper upon the trunk of the body and devoured it.

Their Religion. Most of the inhabitants living near the sea-coast are mahometants now, whereas formerly, both those inhabiting the sea-shore and the inland countrey were pagans, of which there are still a great number in the countries remote from the sea.

Traffick of this island. The isle of *Sumatra*, but especially the kingdom of *Achin*, are places of great traffick, whither resort merchants from all parts of the *Indies*, as the *Chinese*, *Malayans*, *Javanese*, christians and mahometans. There are certain places on the western coast of the isle, which are in confederacy, and under the protection of the *Dutch East-India* company, unto whom they are obliged to sell all their pepper and gold at a certain rate. These are *Pryaman*, *Indapoura*, *Padang*, *Tike* and *Barros*. They had also setled a factory in 1665 at *Andragiry*, but the quantity of pepper and gold to be transported from thence was so inconsiderable, that it did not turn to account.

Commodities of Sumatra. The chief commodities of *Sumatra* are, pepper, gold, tin and camphire. The western coast affords *Pedro Porcos*, which are sold at 200 crowns *per* piece. *Jamby* and *Palimbang* are the chiefest places for pepper, where the *English* have likewise their factories, and are much esteemed by that king. The foreigners import commonly pieces of eight, callicoes, *Chinese* gold, iron wire, steel, woollen-cloth, quilts of *Suratte*, silks, salt and such like commodities, which they exchange for those before-mention'd. Thus much of *Sumatra*.

They continue their voyage. We continu'd our voyage without any remarkable accident, 'till the 3d of *February*, when we pass'd by *Punte Gale*, and arriv'd the next day at *Colomba*, both cities belong-

1662. belonging to the island of *Ceylon*. Having soon dispatch'd our business here, we set sail again the 9th, and the 12th came within sight of cape *Comorin* and the city of *Koylang*, steering our course along the coast of *Malabar*, where we met with the ship the *Phœnix*, in the road of that city, to load pepper, which done, it join'd with us, to continue its voyage to *Persia*.

Pass by cape Comoirn *and* Koylang.

Over against the isle of *Baypin* we met with 15 or 16 sail under the command of Mr. *Adrian van der Meyden*, who was sent thither to attack the fortress of *Palipatnam*; we went immediately aboard the *Ulieland*, where we paid our respects to the admiral, who enjoyn'd us, to send all our land and sea men ashore, to assist at the taking of this fortress; which being done accordingly, and the *Dutch* forces marching in good order to the attack, they found, to their great astonishment, that the enemy had deserted the place, and left only one old woman and a boy behind them; thus we became masters of this strong hold, without striking a blow. However our design upon the city of *Cranganor* was laid aside for that time, after we were thoroughly informed concerning its condition, and that we were not sufficiently provided for such an attempt. So we proceeded on our voyage again the next day, and the 5th of *March* pass'd by the bar of *Goa*, where we found several *Dutch* ships under commodore *Roothaes* a crusing, which kept the harbour of *Goa* block'd up. The 6th we came to an anchor in the road of *Wingurla*, where we met several of our men of war, which had been a cruising before *Goa*, and were come hither to refresh themselves: We saw likewise here the *Bantam* yacht, which was sent on purpose hither to carry the queen of *Golconda* to *Mocha*, (a city of *Arabia*, situate on the *Red-Sea*) she being to go from thence to *Medina*, to visit *Mahomet*'s tomb, and to make a present of great value there. Her guards, which had conducted her 80 leagues as far as *Wingurla* consisted of 4000 men, all mounted on fine bright *Persian* horses, well accoutred. They had long coats of mail, on the shoulders of which were imbroider'd serpents-heads in imitation of the ancient *Romans*; they had fine polish'd helmets on their heads, being for the rest arm'd with bows and arrows, and some of them with very long beards. At the head of them rid two trumpeters, who sounded the trumpet by turns. All the persons of quality that attended her, were likewise mounted on very fine horses, with a footman on each side of the horse's head, who held the bridle. The Queen herself and all her ladies, were carried in *Palakins* covered on the top, to keep themselves from being seen by any body; and before them were led several camels cover'd with rich furnitures. On one of these was mounted a kettle-drummer, who with a hammer beat crossways, as we do in *Europe*; the drums, of which one hung on each side of the camel, being somewhat sharp at one end like our bee-hives. The commodore *Roothaes* and M. *Santvliet* (director for the *Dutch East-India* company at *Gamron*) were gone to meet and compliment the queen about two leagues from the town; who, whilst she tarried here, dictated several letters in divers languages to her secretaries; she sent soon after to know whether the ships were ready to sail, and being answered they were, she came immediately aboard the yacht, but finding her much less in bulk than the other ships she saw lying at anchor in the road, she was not very well satisfied, till being told by Mr. *Roothaes* and *Santvliet*, that the yacht was most proper for her purpose, by reason of the shallowness of the shore of the red sea, she seem'd to acquiesce in their judgment. Near the sea-side a tent was set up, and from thence a passage covered all over with callico to the chaloop, in which was likewise a tent, as also in the yacht, to prevent her being seen by the ship's crew. She gave a very fine present of gold and diamonds to the commodore Mr. *Roothaes* and Mr. *Santvliet*. The captain of the yacht who carried her to *Mocha*, did not return from thence, but went along with her, being, as we suppose, turn'd mahometan; because the yacht was reconducted by the boatswain.

Pass by Goa.

Palipatnam.

Come to Wingurla.

The queen of Golconda *goes to visit* Mahomet's *tomb*.

Wingurla.

Wingurla is no more than a large village, situate on the sea-shore of the kingdom of *Golconda*, under the 15 deg. of northern latitude. The *Dutch East-India* company have built a very fine house here of stone and plaister work, because all ships bound for *Persia*, are obliged to come to an anchor here, to provide themselves with fresh water and fuel, which they buy here at a very low rate, the place scarce affording any thing else.

Come to Gamron.

After we had left *Wingurla*, we came the 6th of *April* before that famous city of *Persia* call'd *Gamron*, and anchored at six fathoms water. I went ashore the same day to give notice of our arrival, and to make the necessary preparations for unlading our ship, which being done, I apply'd myself to have it laden again with all possible expedition; and our cargo being for the most part gold and silver coin, we might soon have been ready to sail again, had we not been oblig'd to stay for some other commodities till the 2d of *June*, when we set sail again from thence, and Mr. *James Williamson*, director for the company in *Persia*, took

1662. took this opportunity to go along with us to *Batavia*, the time of his stay in *Persia* being expired.

A description of that city. The famous city of *Gamron*, the only sea-haven of *Persia*, is situate on a flat sea-shore, just at the entrance of the *Persian Gulph*, at the foot of a barren sandy mountain, producing neither grass nor trees; it lies betwixt two castles, under the 27 deg. of northern latitude: This city was built out of the ruins of the castle and city of *Ormus*, the destruction of which proved the rise of *Gamron*. It is to the sea-side defended by three stone bastions, on which are mounted good store of iron cannon. But on the land-side it is only surrounded with a stone wall, which is much decay'd, because they fear as it seems nothing from thence. The *Its houses.* houses here which are built after a very antique manner, like most of the *Persian* houses, stand very close together, having each a square turret, which mounts to a considerable height above the whole structure, having on each side several holes for the free passage of the wind and air; in these turrets they sleep every night during the summer season. The best of their houses are built only of loom, which being form'd in four square pieces, and dry'd with the sun, become as hard as stone, and keep out the rains and winds. They whiten them on the outside with lime made of burnt mussel-shells, but their back and out-houses are covered only with the leaves of palm-trees, and are miserable huts, scarce fit to defend the inhabitants from the injuries of the season.

Streets. The streets here are both narrow and short, with many turnings, and are covered by the houses on both sides, which are almost join'd together on the top; notwithstanding which the heat is so excessive here, that they are scarce passable. They are not paved with stones, but only with earth beaten close together, which being continually watered to allay the heat and dust, becomes by degrees as hard as a stone. Both the *English* and *Dutch* have their factories here near one another, each being distinguish'd by their respective flags; the *Dutch* is built close to the water-side, being a goodly structure, and very convenient for the unlading of vessels.

Scarcity of fresh water. The city of *Gamron* affords no fresh water, which must be fetch'd by the slaves in earthen vessels or sheep skins early in the morning (to keep it the cooler) from the mountains, which are near three leagues distant from thence, which makes the fresh water so scarce here, that most people of fashion will rather present you with a cup of wine than water, there being no pools or basons here where any fresh water is to be met with, but during the rainy season. Neither does the countrey produce any thing 1662. but palm-trees; notwithstanding which there is great plenty here of every thing, wherewith they are supplied from *Persia* and other places. The common drink of the inhabitants is water, tho' they also are provided with good *Persian* wines; they are very strong, and of a high red colour, but as sweet as canary wine: It grows about *Schiras* and *Yezd*, and is transported from thence in large flasks and casks. They have also *Arack* distill'd of coco-nuts and rice. They make likewise a mixture of water, lemons and sugar, but if drunk in too great a quantity occasions the bloody flux.

The air of *Gamron* is from the beginning of *May* till *September* more unwholesome *Unwholesomeness of the air.* than in any place of the *East* or *West-Indies* that ever I saw, so that there is no abiding here for foreigners, except in *December*, *January*, *February* and *March*. The natives of any quality being more used to the air, will continue something longer, *viz.* till *May*, when they retire to their countrey houses, which are for the most part built among the mountains, near some river or other, at 10 or 12 leagues from the city: Here they spend merrily what they have got by traffick in the winter, leaving the management of their city houses to their slaves till *October*, the usual time for ships and foreign merchants to come to *Gamron*. The heat which is most excessive here obliges them to sleep upon leather, or with the lower parts of their bodies in water; or in the turrets, which are on the top of their houses; some cool themselves with pouring rose-water down the neck; such ships as are obliged to stay in the port during the summer season, must be covered all over with sails, otherwise the planks would split asunder, the pitch and tar rising up in bubbles as it were a boiling; so that no body dare walk bare-footed upon the deck. Those who venture to continue during the hot season at *Gamron*, commonly get for their pains an ague of a very malicious nature, which if it does not kill, at least seldom quits them, but leaves such relicks behind, as at last brings them to their graves. The cause of this excessive heat seems to me to be the situation of the place, at the foot of a barren mountain facing the south, so that the sun-beams by their refractions against the mountains are redoubled in their strength, especially if it be considered that the wind here during the summer season blows for the most part from the south, and consequently from the same corner, from whence the sun-beams exert their utmost strength. For immediately after *March* is past, the winds turn commonly to the west and south-west, which are sometimes so stifling that they

1662. they kill men and beasts. The *Arabians* call this wind *Elhamudi*, i. e. fish-winds, and the *Persians Badesambour*, because it choaks on a sudden such as it touches. It is very observable, that the dead carcasses of such as are kill'd by it, if touch'd with the hands, are as unctuous as grease or oil, and appear as if they had been dead a month ago. This wind continues here in *May*, *June*, *July* and *August*, as likewise all about *Muassil* over against the old *Nineve*, and near *Bagdat*, but those who are upon the water, even in boats in the river, never feel the effects of this wind, tho' they are quite naked.

Stifling-winds.

Traffick of the inhabitants of Gamron.

Most of the inhabitants of *Gamron* are merchants, who trade to several cities situate upon the branch of the *Euphrates*, such as *Bassora*, *Schiras*, *Ispahan*, *Tauris* and *Smyrna*. Once every year, to wit, in *October*, the caravans, consisting of several thousands of men and beasts, arrive here from the east, *viz.* from *Babylon*, *Turky* and *Persia*, with all sorts of merchandizes loaden upon camels, dromedaries and asses, which they exchange for *East-India* wares. The staple commodities of *Gamron* are cloth of gold, tapestry and pearls, which they take near the island of *Bahrain*, as likewise fruits of all sorts, plumbs, raisins, currans, nuts, dates, oranges, citrons, pomegranates, peaches, *&c.* They abound likewise in herbs, which are brought thither from other places, especially from the isle of *Kikmis*, not above three leagues from thence. They have also good store of most excellent *Persian* wine, which is brought thither from *Schiras* and *Yezd* in large flasks, pack'd up in casks. They sell also abundance of the best rose-water, which is here in greater plenty than in any other place that ever I saw. There is at certain times such a vast confluence of merchants and ships at *Gamron*, that they want money to buy their commodities; in such cases they write to their correspondents at *Lar*, *Schiras*, *Ispahan* and other *Persian* cities, who if they have ready cash, are sure to buy good bargains at such a juncture. Most of the merchants that resort to *Gamron* are *Persians*, *Armenians* and *Indians*, living in *Persia*. And were it not for the unwholsomeness of the air, abundance more would come from other places, who now stay at home, and rather chuse to buy from the merchants that bring their commodities from *Gamron*.

Disposition of the inhabitants.

The women here, like as in most other eastern countries, are seldom seen abroad, but dwell in separate apartments, where the men live with them for some time, and in the mean while lay aside all other business. The women who expose themselves for money, sit in the evening upon benches at the doors, with lanthorns in their hands, where every man is free to chuse such a one as he likes best. The inhabitants here are generally very brown. The poorer sort go for the most part naked, only with a piece of stuff wrap'd round the middle; in the summer season some appear quite naked, others only in their shirts. The rich clothe themselves very magnificently after the *Persian* fashion, tho' there are yet some few who retain their antient dress with gold, silver, and iron rings on their hands, ears and noses. The common people make use of dates instead of bread or rice; for it is observable, that the ordinary food of the *Indians* all along that coast, from *Basora* to *Sindi* is dates and fish, dry'd in the air. The heads and guts of the fishes they mix with date stones, and boil it altogether with a little salt-water, which they give at night to the cows, after they come out of the field, where they meet with very little herbage. They abound also in hares, sheep, pidgeons and partridges; but as for tame fowl, tho' they have great store of them, they are not much esteem'd, because they have a brackish taste. The sea, especially that of *Solda* and *Sardin*, furnishes them with vast plenty of excellent fishes, and among the rest with very fine oysters, but they are so little regarded by the inhabitants, that if you have a mind to some of them, you must bespeak them of the fishermen on purpose. Preserv'd fruits of all sorts are here in great abundance; the rich merchants, but especially the *Persian* governor, living in great luxury and pomp. 1662.

Their clothing.

Diet.

Sepulchre of an Indian saint.

About a league to the east of the city is a famous sepulchre of a *Banyan* saint, buried there some hundred years ago, under a tree call'd *Arvor das Rais*, i. e. root-tree by the *Portuguese*, or *Lul* by the *Persians*, which he planted here sometime before his death. The inhabitants call this tree the *Tree of the Banyans*, either from its first planter, or because the *Banyans* have founded a *Pagod* or *Pagan* temple under it, and a *Caranvansera* or inn for the conveniency of passengers. This tree has spread its branches at a considerable distance round about, and encreases every year to that degree, that its branches, which indeed all descend from one trunk, but by degrees take root again, encompass a space of 550 feet. Under this tree both inhabitants and foreigners shelter themselves against the heat of the sun when they are walking abroad, and entertain one another. Over the sepulchre itself is built a small *Pagode*, in which you see burning lamps hanging day and night under a canopy of silk. The ground all round about is paved with bricks, and adorned with convenient benches and seats neatly kept, where every body is at liberty to take his

V. II. Betwixt pag. 194. 195.

Goegys of Benjan Saints

8.

1662. *Indian saints.* repose under the agreeable shadow of this tree. Here the *Indians* come in great numbers to offer their sacrifices, especially the *Siogs*, call'd by others *Goegys*, *Gioghi*, and *Joeghi*, and *Fakirs* by the *Arabians* and the moors. There are a certain sort of *Banyan* saints (or at least pretend to be such) belonging to one of the four sects of the *Bramins*, *viz.* the sect of *Cenrawaghi*, of *Samarath*; of *Bisnou*, and the fourth the sect of *Siogs* or *Goegys*. *A sect of Bramins.* You see them sitting on the highways with their legs across, as the *Mahometans* do; they never pare their nails; some have locks of hair hanging down their backs of four or five feet long, others never shave their heads or beards, which makes them appear more like devils than men. They have no dwelling places of their own, but in the night-time they sleep in the porches of their temples, on dunghills and corners of the streets, or perhaps in some cave or other hole. They always appear naked, having only a piece of cloth wrapt about the middle. The *Indian* women resort to them in great numbers out of devotion, to touch the extremities of their fingers, or to kiss their privy members in a most humble posture, which they admit of, without shewing the least sign of sensibility thereat, for if they should do otherwise, they would be look'd upon as unfit for that holy seat. They never cast their eyes upon any body, but draw them in a most frightful manner upwards, as if they were afflicted with convulsions. They lead a most severe and miserable life, constantly mortifying their bodies by some strange and unnatural penances they lay upon themselves. Some retire into caves and cellars, where they continue in their devotions sometimes

The Persian Shepherds about Gamron

9 or 10 days, without eating or drinking. Some walk both day and night for several years together without sitting; and when they intend to sleep, hang themselves with a rope about their middle to the branch of a tree. Others carry both their arms all their life-time strait upright above their heads, so that in process of time they are not able to bend themselves downwards again. In this posture they continue day and night throughout the year quite naked, without the least fear of being scorch'd by the sun, or stung by the gnats, which they won't as much as remove with their hands. Nay they sleep with their arms in the same posture, a thing which needs must be very painful at first, and at last makes their arms thus distorted and bereaved of their usual nourishment to hang down behind their backs. There are innumerable sorts of other penitents,

1662. tents, some always lifting up their eyes against the sun, others fixing them constantly upon the ground, without ever looking upon or speaking a word to any body living. They besmear their nauseous bodies with ashes, and their greasy hair and faces with sandel-wood and saffron, but especially with cowdung mix'd with ashes; during our stay at *Gamron* we went several times to refresh ourselves under the tree; the common custom is to carry some wine and sweetmeats along with one, and as for dates, almonds, nuts, and other fruits, they are to be sold there.

The governor of Gamron. The *Persian* governor residing at *Gamron* lives in great splendor; the king sends every year certain commissioners thither to take an account of the governor's conduct; he commonly meets them at some distance off the city unarm'd, and if they find him to have transgress'd his commission, they cut off his head; otherwise he is regal'd with a present of clothes, and so they enter the city, where they pass their time together in feasting for some days. The governor of the city did in our time meet the commissioners with some armed bands, and thus conducted them into the city.

Persian *posts.* The posts which go from *Gamron* to *Ispaban* are wonderful expeditious in their journeys; they are appointed by the governor of *Gamron*, after he has made sufficient trial of their nimbleness, which is done by running with the rising of the sun, to an appointed place till sun-set; a certain horseman being appointed to ride along with them, and to take care they don't rest by the way: After they have perform'd this trial, the governor presents them with a suit of clothes and with the title of runners. So soon as any stranger of fashion arrives at *Gamron*, some or other of the inhabitants is ready to offer him his service, to attend him in the quality of a porter, or as a servant to show him the way; they are sure to wait at your lodgings every morning, and follow you all day long wherever you go, for a very slender allowance.

Shepherds near Gamron. I had the curiosity to take a view of the shepherds and their huts, with their flocks of sheep and goats; for which purpose, by the help of my guide, I went some leagues deep into the countrey, where I found them feeding their sheep in a very barren ground; these shepherds, who have no other houshold goods but a slight coat, commonly manage a flock of 500 sheep and goats. Their huts they set up at pleasure in the open fields, they having no certain grounds appointed them, but like the *Arabians* change their places according to the best conveniency of pastorage; and tho' the grounds betwixt the city and the mountains are very barren, yet are the sheep and goats here very good, an evident sign that a small matter is sufficient to feed them. These fields extend from the city to the mountains, which surround them at some distance from thence. They have some sheep of an extraordinary bigness, with two horns on east side of the head. Their he-goats have long curl'd hair, of which they make camlets. Some have such long ears that you may tye them together. *Persia* affords great quantities of tann'd goat and sheep skins. Thus much of *Gamron*. 1662.

A little to the right of the harbour of *Gamron*, you may see the isle of *Ormus*, at the very entrance into the *Persian* gulph, as likewise the islands of *Queixome*, *Kesem* and *Lareck*, of which we will give you a short description.

Some put the island of *Ormus* under 25 deg. 30 min. of latitude, and 22 deg. 45 min. of longitude; others under 26 deg. 4 min. and some others under 27 deg. and 30 min. northern latitude. The isle of *Ormus* is by some taken for the same, which by the antient authors, as *Pliny*, *Pomponius* and *Dionysius*, is call'd *Ogyris*, and by *Ptolemy Vorcchta*; it is situate in the *Persian* gulph, about two leagues distant from the continent of *Persia*, having the province of *Caramania* to the east, *Arabia fœlix* to the south and west, being divided from them only by the streights of *Babarem*, and the continent of *Persia* to the north; it is very near triangular; its largest side which faces the N. N. E. extending from S. E. to the N. W. from the chapel of *St. Lucie* to the point of land where the castle of *Ormus* is, being the nearest to the continent, where formerly the *Portuguese* had a fort call'd *Comoran*, built just opposite to the castle of *Ormus*, which thereabouts is not above a league distant. The second side extends from the same chapel, *viz.* from the S. E. to the S. S. W. as far as the cape *Karu*, and so further to the W. S. W. and the W. and makes the basis of the triangle. The third and smallest side begins at *Karu*, and ends at the before-mentioned castle; it faces the country of *Mogostban*, a name commonly given to the *Persian* coast on that side, which is about two leagues from the isle. Its whole circuit is about three leagues. *The isle of* Ormus.

The western part of the island extending along the sea-shore, where the mountains end, is call'd *Karu*, where you see a few houses scattered up and down belonging to the moors: At *Turumbake* are a greater number of these houses, but as wretchedly built as the former, except some few formerly belonging to the *Austin* friars, where they used to divert themselves some times. Near to them is a fine fish-pond surrounded- Karu.

1662. ed with very fine trees, and a large ciſtern for rain-water.

Mountain. The whole iſland is divided by a ridge of mountains, extending from the eaſt to the weſt, behind which there is nothing to be ſeen but white and barren hills, producing nothing except very good white ſalt. Among the reſt there is a mountain here called *Kuykaſtaron*, or *the Mountain of the Dead*; on the top of which the *Portugueſe* had built a chapel call'd *our Lady of the Rock*; which chapel is obſerved to riſe higher and higher, becauſe the ſalt, ſaltpetre, and brimſtone, which are contained in the bowels of this mountain, encreaſe daily in quantity. The inhabitants viſit this chapel with a great deal of devotion, unto which they have made a pretty eaſy aſcent by cutting ſteps out of the rock, which otherwiſe is very ſteep. Near the mountain, where the chapel ſtands, is another, which runs upwards in form of a pyramid. It is compoſed of one entire maſs of the beſt and whiteſt ſalt that can be ſeen, and appears at a diſtance like a mountain covered with ſnow. Not far from hence is a chapel called *St. Lucy*, built behind the ruines of ſome old towers, where formerly the kings of *Ormus* uſed to keep their brothers priſoners, after they had bereaved them of their eyes. About half ways betwixt this and the city, was another chapel dedicated to *St. Lucy*, with ſome houſes about it, whither the inhabitants of *Ormus* uſed to retire during the ſummer ſeaſon, as likewiſe to ſome others built near the ſea-ſhore of reed only, and covered with palm-tree leaves.

Salt-mountain.

From this chapel to the city is a large plain, where the inhabitants uſed to have their ciſterns to gather and keep rain-water in, which were always locked up; for not only hereabouts, but alſo all over the iſland the ground is brackiſh, which makes the rain-water which is kept in theſe ciſterns much better than what is gathered from the pools or ponds; yet does it not come near in goodneſs to the freſh water that is brought from the continent or the iſle of *Queixome*. The remaining part of this plain is taken up with the graves of the mahometans, pagans, and jews, which are buried here promiſcuouſly without any difference; ſome of theſe tombs are covered with a kind of a chapel, but open on all ſides. Hither you ſee great numbers of mahometan, pagan, and jewiſh women, of all ages and degrees, which come to bring their offerings of eatables in flat ſmall diſhes, to the ſouls of the deceaſed. And ſome of theſe are ſo zealous as to pay their conſtant viſits and devotions to the tombs of ſome of their pious men or ſaints, that are in great reverence among them, and their tombs ſumptuouſly adorned. 1662.

Not far from this plain is another extending from the mountains to the city, called by the moors by a peculiar name, *Ardemira*, i. e. *The proſpect over the plain* (in the ſame ſenſe as the *French* ſay *Bellvidere*) where the mahometan courtiers, and other officers of the king uſed to keep their turnaments and running at the ring on horſeback. This plain extends to the weſt as far as the ſea ſhore, the way that leads to *Karu*, from whence the city has the faireſt proſpect. Ardemira

Behind the mountains, being the S. S.W. and the W. S.W. part of the iſland, called *Turumbake*, is the faireſt of all, tho' its compaſs is leſs betwixt the mountains and the ſea than that part beyond the mountains. Here you ſee a countrey ſeat of the old queen of *Ormus*, adorned with walks of palm-trees, and two large ciſterns or baſons, called from the place the *Ponds of Turumbake*, beſides ſeveral leſſer ones. Turumbake.

Their water is the wholeſomeſt and freſheſt of the whole iſland. There is another great baſon belonging to this ſeat, which is continually ſupplied with water out of three adjacent ponds and a ſmall brook; this water is not near ſo ſalt as that which is kept in the ponds more to the E. and N. N. E. where the ſun turns the water into ſolid ſalt. This countrey ſeat was already in a decaying condition 50 or 60 years before my coming here, having only a few apartments left, wherein the king of *Ormus* uſed to lodge during the ſummer ſeaſon; *Turumbake* had at that time not above 15 or 20 huts built of reed cloſe together, like a ſmall village, and covered with palm-tree leaves, after a wretched manner. Moſt of the houſes of this iſland are built after the ſame manner, notwithſtanding which, the inhabitants of *Ormus* retire thither with their families in the ſummer, being taught both by tradition and experience, that the open countrey air is much more wholeſome during the hot ſeaſon, than the city air.

On the north ſide of this iſle lies the city of *Ormus*, which before it was ſubdued by the *Portugueſe* was very populous, foreigners flocking thither daily from *Perſia*, the *Eaſt-Indies* and *Europe* itſelf, for the conveniency of traffick. To be ſhort, the city of *Ormus* was the moſt famous and richeſt trading city of the world, before the *Portugueſe* had found out the paſſage by ſea to the *Eaſt-Indies*, being inhabited and frequented by the *Perſians*, *Arabians*, *Abyſſines*, *Armenians*, *Tartars*, *Turks*, and other mahometans; beſides the *Italians*, *French*, *Dutch*, *Engliſh*, *Poles*, and other *European* nations. It was much inhabited by the *Portugueſe*, but very few *Spaniards*, becauſe the firſt would

1662. would not permit them to go thither by sea, and the *Turks* stop their passage by land, betwixt the *Mediterranean* and the *Persian* gulph; some few dwelt there under the name and protection of some other nations. The natives of *Ormus* are all mahometans, but of different sects, some being called *Kiays*, belonging to the sect of *Hali* son-in-law to *Mahomet*, whose doctrine is followed by the *Persians*; others are called *Suni's*, following the doctrine of *Mahomet*, *Osmar*, and *Osman*, as the *Turks* do; the king himself is of this sect; besides which, divers sorts of pagans, as *Banjans*, *Camboyans*, &c. inhabit here.

The city of Ormus *in the* Portuguese *times.* The city of *Ormus* whilst under the jurisdiction of the *Portuguese*, and before the *Persians* made themselves masters of it 1619, was a very stately, rich, and magnificent place, of which the inhabitants used to boast, *That if the world were a ring*, Ormus *must be considered as the diamond.* For after the *Portuguese* had conquered this city, they were very careful in adorning it from time to time with most magnificent structures, to such a degree, that all the iron belonging to their windows and doors were gilt; and it was the common opinion in those days, that if they had remained masters of it till now, they would have turned them into massy gold. They had built a stately church upon an eminency, dedicated to the virgin *Mary*, with an adjacent hospital called the *Misericordia*. Next to this was the exchange or custom-house, called by the *Persians Beneckfal*, this was a fine edifice, surrounded with galleries on the out side. They had likewise several monasteries, amongst which those of the *Austin* fryars and *Carmelites* were the chiefest. There is yet to be seen a very high steeple, a nost noble piece of architecture, exceeding in magnificence all others of this city; the mahometans call it in the *Arabian* tongue *Alkoran*; on one side of the castle stood formerly a famous *Mosque*, which the *Portuguese* caused to be demolished, as being too near the castle, which proved the occasion of the most inveterate hatred against the *Portuguese*, not only among the moors inhabiting there, but likewise among the *Persians*, their king *Tahamass* or *Tahamas*, grandfather to *Schach Abas*, having been *Under the* Persians. the founder of it. No sooner was this city fallen into the hands of the *Persians*, but she was by them despoiled of her ancient glory, and most of her inhabitants, many of whom were killed in the siege, the rest fled for shelter to some other place. All the churches, houses, and other publick edifices, were laid level with the ground, except some few shops in the *Bazar* or shopkeepers street. The *Dutch* ships which unloaded there, and returned commonly empty from thence, used to make it their practice at that time to ballast their vessels with the finest marble stones, the remnants of the stately structures of this city, and would questionless by degrees have taken all that was left, had not the *Persian* governour there prohibited the exportation of them under a severe penalty. For the *Persians* whose intention was to lay the foundation of the greatness of *Gamron* upon the ruines of *Ormus*, did remove all the best stones from thence, which they made use of in their best buildings at *Gamron*. The fortifications of the city of *Ormus* in the *Portuguese* times, in 1619, were but in a slender posture, the ditch about the castle being filled up with dirt, having scarce 6 foot of water; besides that, it was not spacious enough for the garrison. Their commanders in chief, who were removed from thence every year, had according to the custom of the *Portuguese*, but a slender share of knowledge in martial affairs, the governour at that time being an ancient man, not trained up in the wars, and not provided with experienced engineers and gunners.

The old four-square castle was built on the utmost northern or north-west point of the land of the isle, where it approaches nearest to the *Persian* shore, two sides of it being washed by the sea, the other two facing the city; betwixt which and the castle is a very fair square of about 300 feet long, from whence you have a fine prospect into the sea. This castle, whilst in the possession of the *Portuguese*, was not very large, being defended only by four bastions, which as well as the cortines, were built with a kind of small flint-stones mixt with mortar and sea-water; so that they were not proof against the thunder of the great cannon. The ditch was likewise very shallow, though it might have been made deeper without any great cost, by reason of the nearness of the sea, which waters it on two sides. In this condition was the castle of *Ormus* under the *Portuguese*, of which the *Portuguese* boasted that it was impregnable. After the *Persians* had made themselves masters of it, they were very careful to repair the old fortifications, and to add some new ones, especially on the point of the ditch, they made a half-moon, the cannon of which commanded the plain and a gallery; since which time they keep it always in a good posture of defence, and maintain a considerable garrison there, under the command of the governour of *Ormus*, who residing for the most part at *Gamron*, appoints a deputy for this place, who has his residence in the palace formerly belonging to the kings of *Ormus*. *The castle of* Ormus.

 The

1662. The harbour of this island is a certain bay, made by two points of land that jett out on both sides; upon one of these capes stands the castle, on the other the *Portuguese* had built a church, dedicated to our *Lady of Good-Hope*; but this point turns somewhat nearer towards the city, so that the harbour where the largest vessels, galleys, and smaller vessels used to cast anchor, lies opposite to the north-east part of the city, betwixt the two monasteries built by the *Portuguese*, one of which belonged to the *Carmelites*, the other to the *Austin* fryars. The tide where this bay is deepest rises at high water, near four foot high above the foundations of the houses; notwithstanding which, at low water the shore is dry for above 200 paces; and 150 paces farther the water is not 3 feet high where it is deepest, so that the largest vessels are obliged to cast anchor at 600 paces from the city, and the galleys at 500, which renders this harbour very unsafe, especially if a storm arises from the east, which often forces the ships ashore; nay, this harbour would be much more dangerous, were it not for the nearness of the continent, which covers it on the N. and N. E. side, and the isle of *Queixome*, which lies to the N. N. W. of it, and breaks the violence of the raging waves. Some tell us of two different bays belonging to the isle of *Ormus*, which afford a safe harbour to ships, the one to the east, the other to the west, being divided by a neck of land which jetts out betwixt them a considerable way into the sea.

The harbour.

Scarcity of water.

The whole island is destitute of water, except what some standing pools or ponds afford, which is always brackish, tho' some more than others; some, especially such as are near the sea-side, being tolerably fit for use; for the farther they are from the mountains, the less they participate of the salt. It does sometimes not rain in *Ormus* for three years together; the only springs of fresh water they have being in the royal gardens. *Ferra Gutka* who reigned in 1596 in *Ormus*, found out a spring with fresh water in *Turumbake*. Not far from thence near the sea-side, arises a salt water spring from among the rocks, called by the *Persian* inhabitants *Abdarmon*, i. e. medicinal water, which has a purging quality, and cleanses the bowels from all impurities. Here you see abundance of people drink the waters at a certain season of the year, when they have a mind to be satisfied whether their bowels are thoroughly cleansed, they cut a piece of an orange or citron, and if immediately after they go to stool, they reckon themselves sufficiently purged. 'Tis true, there are three springs here, which all having their rise among the mountains, afford water sufficient for three rivulets, but it is as brackish as the sea water it self. Thus several brooks are to be seen to the S. E. among the mountains which carry a very clear water, but so stockt with salt, that in the summer, when these rivulets are dry'd up, you see vast lumps of salt, which cover the banks on both sides. The vast quantity of salt which is to be met with all over this island, being in some places burnt up and blackned by the violence of the sunbeams, affords a dreadful sight at a distance. They have also a kind of salt clay, out of which they make earthen vessels. 1662.

The whole isle is nothing else but a barren vast lump of salt, which scarce affords either grass or trees, except what is brought forth by force in the royal gardens in the plains, neither does it afford any thing for the sustenance of human life. It has however some few trees in certain places, but bear no fruit except dates, and another small fruit growing on thorn bushes with green leaves; another kind of these thorn bushes they have with a pretty large stem, and small red leaves. In the opening of the rocks you see now and then a large green and well spread tree, notwithstanding several have positively asserted that this isle did produce neither tree, herbs, nor grass. The mountains are full of rock salt, which is very transparent, and contain likewise a considerable quantity of brimstone. In some winters the salt is washed by the rains down from the mountains, which afterwards is again coagulated by the sun, which is the only made use of here, for the rock salt being of too corrosive a nature, does consume the meat instead of preserving it. The *Dutch* transport abundance of salt from hence to the *East-Indies*. The isle also affords a certain kind of white plastering called by the inhabitants *Gueche*, and another that is red of the same kind, but not so good as the white. They have also a certain way of preparing dung for plaister-work, which they perform in the following manner: They take the uppermost part of an old dunghill away, the rest they make up in balls, and let them dry in the sun. This done, they burn them to ashes with fire; the ashes they beat for a considerable time upon an even piece of ground, and immediately after mix it for use, for, if they let the ashes be cold, or keep them only two or three days, they are not fit for their purpose; but this prepared and used keeps the water out of any place for many years. There are scarce any other stones to be met with here but flint-stones, of which the greatest part of the fortifications of the castle are composed. There is also a kind of black

1662. black glistering sand to be found here, which the *Portuguese* used to transport from thence to their factories in the *East-Indies.* No barley or oats is to be seen here. Their cattle they feed with a peculiar sort of pease or beans, which they grind, and afterwards steep in water, being otherwise too hard to digest. Of these they give a certain quantity every night to their horses. But in the morning they give to each horse 2 pounds of black sugar, mixt with a pound of butter and some flour, which they make up into balls; then they wash the horses mouth and teeth, because this mixture sticks very close to their teeth and gums; in the day time they feed them with some herbs which they draw out of the ground with roots and all, and cleanse them very well from all impurities.

Sinking wood. In the bay and all along the coast of the isle of *Ormus*, they fish for wood, of which they find great store in the bottom of the sea, but not very large. This wood is by the violence of the currents of the rivers arising from among the mountains of the continent of *Persia* (which is not above two leagues distant from hence) torn off and carried to the shore of *Ormus*; a thing most surprising, and contrary to what is observed of this kind in other islands lying near the continent, or some other great islands, whither the adjacent rivers force abundance of wood, which however always swims on the surface of the water, and commonly is found rotten, whereas the wood upon the coast sinks to the bottom, and is not quite rotten, but affords the inhabitants great store of fuel, which has induced some to believe that this wood did grow under water.

On the *Persian* coast you meet also with certain kind of light porous stone under water, not unlike our pumice stones; especially near those places where subterraneous fires are; which makes these stones to be always white, in which they differ from the common pumice, which are either blackish or grey; they are found here in such prodigious quantities, that they build their houses of them, because they mix very well with the mortar, by reason of their spongeous substance, and very light; and when well cemented with the mortar, resist the violence of the winds, which blow here exceedingly about the change of the seasons, better than any other stones. Some are of opinion that these stones were cast out by a burning mountain, which seems not improbable, there being on the back side of a neighbouring mountain found vast quantities of these stones, as black as coals. The reason why those on the sea shore are white, seems to be because they have for many years, nay, for many ages past, been scoured by the water of their impurities; the inhabitants call them *Sanchmay*, i. e. *Rock-Fish*, because as many as are taken away grow again in a little time, and furnish them with materials for building. They report that in former ages this island did burn for seven years together, of which they shew the marks to this day; the earth upon the mountains being red, and in the vallies spongeous like ashes or quick lime; besides that the whole island is subject to frequent earthquakes. The mountains are all over covered with salt, and the grounds are full of salt-petre. As often as the wind blows from the south-west, there arises so violent a stink of brimstone from the mountains, as infects the whole air. The heat is more intense at *Ormus* than at *Gamron*, for it continues at least five months, *viz.* from *May* till *September*, and sometimes till the beginning of *December*; in the winter season the heat is somewhat allayed by the dew which falls all the night long, but in the summer the nights are so excessive hot, that it would be impossible for the inhabitants to abide here, if by several ways they did not asswage in some measure its violence. For on the tops of the houses they set certain wooden vessels like bathing tubs, big enough to contain two persons at a time, in these they sit and sleep all night in the open air with the water up to their necks. The cause of this intolerable heat is attributed chiefly to the nature of the soil, which is not only sandy, but full of salt-petre, which occasioning a continual loss of spirits, the inhabitants are forced to repair in some measure this defect, by continually keeping themselves in cold water, notwithstanding it be none of the best here; all the water that is brought hither from *Bandel Kongo*, or the isle of *Queixome*, being taken out of ponds, and consequently not purified from its dregs for want of motion; which is sufficiently demonstrable by its colour which is like milk, and its sediment which is sometimes two or three inches thick at the bottom of the vessel it is kept in. During the violence of the hot season you may see people of both sexes and all ages, flock to the city walls; but the *Europeans* seldom venture at swimming in the sea, the water being so excessive salt that it excoriates their bodies; but they allay the excessive heat of the nights by wetting their quilts and pillows with cold water. It is farther observable, that the winds are so changeable here, that you may in a quarter of an hours time remarkably feel their different effects; some by opening, others by obstructing the pores of your bodies. During the summer season the winds blow for the most part E. and S. E. or W. S. W. but seldom from the

 south,

1662. south, the last of which is not so unwholesome as the rest; and what is more surprising is, that this wind always cools the water contained in any vessels, but not the chambers or rooms where the water is kept.

Their Drink. The drink of the common people is water, those of the better sort drink *Spanish* wine, or *Persian* wines of *Shiras*, but these are very scarce and dear. They distil also a spirit of rice and sugar here, as well as in all other parts of the *Indies*. They have also a certain kind of drink call'd *Tari*, which is drawn from a tree, and as sweet as musk; this is the ordinary liquor sold in publick-houses, who pay a considerable tax for their licenses to the king. This liquor is brought every day to town in casks on horse-back, each horse carrying one on each side.

Origin of the Isle of Ormus. The isle of *Ormus* was in ancient times govern'd by its own kings or princes, descended from the race of these great kings that ruled all over *Arabia*, *Persia* and the adjacent countries. The first famous in their histories, was a certain *Arabian Emir* or prince, call'd *Mahamed Dramku*, of the race of the antient kings that ruled in *Saba*, or *Arabia Fœlix*. This prince being extremely desirous to conquer new dominions, extended his conquests to the *Persian Gulph*, where he landed with a great fleet from *Kalayatta*, a city of *Arabia Fœlix*, and laid the foundation of a city call'd *Ormus* or *Harmus* on the coast of *Persia*. He left for his successor *Solyman* his son, who was succeeded by the following kings. *Isa* the third in rank, son of *Solyman*; the fourth *Lax Kari* son of *Isa*, who left the court and embraced a private life. The fifth was *Katkobad* his son; the sixth *Isa* II. son to *Katkobad*, the 7th *Mamud* son of *Isa* II. who suspecting *Mir Xabadin Molong* his nephew, made him a prisoner in the castle of *Gati*; from whence he escaped to *Seugon*, and married the daughter of the governor of that castle. The 8th *Xaranta* son of *Mamud*, he engaged in a war against *Molong*, but was slain in an engagement with his enemy.

9th, *Mir Xabadin Molong* was declared king in his stead; his daughter *Sed Alkatum* was married to *Emir*, or prince *Seyfadin Aben Azar*, his brother *Aly*'s son, king of the isle of *Keys*, who dying soon after, his son *Seyfadin* obtained the kingdom of *Keys*. *Mir Xabadin* dying likewise not long afer, his *Vizier Xarcar* made himself master of the kingdom of *Ormus*; and those of *Keys* having at the same time deposed *Seyfadin*, he fled to *Ormus*, where being well received by the inhabitants, he besieged the usurper *Xarcar* in the castle of *Karcan*, whom he kill'd, and thereby became master of the whole kingdom. After *Seyfadin* had well settled his affairs here, he undertook an expedition against those of *Keys*, of whom he kill'd many, and made some of their chief men prisoners. From thence he went to the isle of *Gerun*, (since call'd *Ormus*) where he caused all his prisoners to be slain upon a certain mountain, which from thence was call'd *Kay Kastaron*, *i. e.* The mountain of the dead. He returned at last victorious to *Ormus*, where he spent the rest of his days in Peace. The 11th was *Xabadin Mamud*, son of *Isa* II. who suceeeded his uncle in the kingdom. The 12th *Emir Roknadin Mamud*, *Xabadin*'s nephew, son of *Hamud*, who was very victorious, and extended his conquests as far as *Safar*, a province of *Arabia Fœlix*. He reign'd 35 years, and died 1278.

He was succeeded by his son *Emir Sayfadin Nocerat*, but was soon after forced by *Emir Kodbadin Thabantam* and *Emir Moechzadin Fulad*, or *Pulad*, to fly the kingdom, and to seek for shelter, together with his mother, by sultan *Gebaladin Suraget Mex*, governor of *Kernon*, by whose assistance he was restored to his kingdom: But being a second time vanquish'd, by his brother *Emir Kodbadin* was forced to save himself by flight in a small bark, in the isle of *Queixome*. In the mean while, king *Seyfadin*, who had assisted *Kodbadin*, having caused him to be murthered, the soldiers conceived such a hatred, against this *Seyfadin*, that they instantly recall'd *Emir Sayfadin Nocerat*, chased away *Seyfadin*, and restored him to the throne. Notwithstanding which he was not long after murthered, by his two brothers, *Emir Masaud*, and *Emir Turkonxa*, together with his two sisters, *Bibi Banek*, and *Bibi Neyty*, after he had reign'd 12 years, *viz.* 1290.

Masaud the murtherer of his Brother, succeeded him in his throne, being a very couragious but cruel man, which brought upon him the hatred both of the nobility and common people, of whom he caused many to be killed. This made them implore the assistance of *Emir Bahadin Ayas Seyfin*, formerly a slave only of king *Nocerat*, but now governor of *Kalayatte*, a sea-port of *Arabia-Fœlix*; who forced *Masaud* to fly to *Kernon*, and from thence into *Syria*, where he died, after a reign of three years. He was succeeded by *Bahadin Ayas Seyfin*, who caused two brothers of *Masaud* to be beheaded, for endeavouring to restore him to the kingdom.

About that time a great swarm of *Turks*, came out of *Turkestan*, conquered a considerable part of *Persia*, and by their frequent inroads, into the kingdom of *Ormus*, forced the inhabitants to seek for shelter, at

1662. at the command of their king *Azaez*, in the isle of *Queixome*. Whilst they were roving about in the neighbouring seas, to find out a place where to fix their habitations, they happened to light upon a certain island, 2 leagues from *Queixome*, where meeting with a very ancient man, living just on the point of the isle, a fisherman by trade, he advised their king, to settle there. The king approving of his counsel, sent to the king of *Keys*, the proprietor of this, and all the other islands in the *Persian Gulph*, to desire him to sell him the said isle, for a certain sum of money, which being granted, he settled there a colony of his subjects, 1300, and gave it the name of *Ormus*, after his native country. His successors afterwards extended their conquests over a great part of *Arabia* and *Persia*, and over the *Persian* sea, as far as *Basora*; and maintain'd themselves in the possession of it, till this island was conquered by the *Portuguese*. This king died 1312, in the 22 year of his reign.

Some historians give us the following account of this and the succeeding kings of the isle of *Ormus*.

After this king had settled his new colony, he surrendered the government, to *Emir Ayzadin Gordonxa*, son of *Salhor*, and *Bibi Zeineb*, a nephew of the ancient king of *Ormus*, and retiring to *Kalayatte* in *Arabia*, there finish'd his days in peace. *Gordonxa* was engaged in war with the king of *Keys*, because he had intercepted some ships coming from the *East-Indies*, his dominions; *Ormus* he vanquish'd, and forced him to fly his dominions; but the king of *Keys* returning soon after, found means to make *Gordonxa* his prisoner, under pretence of an interview concerning a peace betwixt them; and *Bibi Sultan*, *Gordonxa*'s spouse, committed the administration of the government to *Malek Guaya Hadin Dinar*, son of her husband's brother *Xamxa*; scarce five months were expired, before the king of *Keys* came to *Ormus*, with *Gordonxa* his prisoner, where he was joyfully received by his subjects, except *Dinar*, who being used to rule, would not submit to *Gordonxa*, but forced him to retire to the castle of *Minab*, on the continent of *Persia*. Notwithstanding which, *Dinar* being sensible what affection the people bore to *Gordonxa*, and fearing his return, he thought it his safest way to retreat in time to the kingdom of *Makron*, betwixt *Persia* and the countrey of *Send* or *Ind*. After which *Gordonxa*, once more return'd to his kingdom, where he died 1318.

He was succeeded by his son *Emir Mobaresadin Bararon Xa*, who together with his brother, was by *Emir Xabadin Issuf* his general put in prison; *Issuf* afterwards mounted the throne, but was engaged in a war immediately after, with *Emir Xa Kodbadin*, brother to the imprison'd king: *Dinar* came likewise with a strong flying army, to his assistance, from *Makron*; but finding *Issuf* too strong for them both, he entred into a confederacy with him; and *Issuf* after having caused the imprisoned king, his mother, and one of his brothers to be slain, forced *Kodbadin* to retire to *Kalayatte*, with *Bibi Mariam*, the spouse of *Ayas Ceyfin*. But *Kodbadin* afterwards returned unexpectedly to *Ormus*, with a considerable force, and having made *Issuf* his prisoner, he put the crown upon his head, and caused him, his wife and his two sons, to be killed; after which he likewise made himself master of *Keys*. It happen'd that *Kodbadin* being abroad a hunting on the continent, 1345, *Rid Xur Nosomadin*, in the mean while got himself proclaim'd king of *Gerun* or *Ormus*; but finding most of the inhabitants averse to him, he quitted the countrey. However it was not not long before he return'd with a great power, and having gain'd *Homer Sojadin*, *Kodbadin*'s general, to join with him, he forced *Kodbadin* to fly to *Kalayatte*. He had scarce stay'd here a year, when word was brought him, that *Nosomadin* was dead, and that by his last will, he had enjoined his sons, *Xembe* and *Xady*, to throw themselves at the feet of *Kodbadin*, and to surrender the crown to him; but finding that the two young men, instead of performing their father's will, had seized upon the kingdom; he attack'd them and regained the crown of *Ormus*. He died 1347, in *Nakelstan*, a province of *Mogestan*. 1662.

He was succeeded by *Turonxa* his son, (who writ the lives of the kings his predecessors, both in verse and prose.) He vanquished *Xembe* and *Xady*, and died 1378, after he had reigned 30 years. After him his eldest son *Mazud* obtained the crown of *Ormus*, who was succeeded by *Xabadin*, the second son of *Turonxa*; after whom reign'd *Salgar*, *Turonxa*'s third son. Under his reign, *Sofi Hbalila* conquered all *Persia*, even to the continent, directly opposite to the island of *Gerun*, or *Ormus*, which escaped his hands for want of shipping; but *Salgar* lost all that he was possessed of on the continent. For the rest he reigned in peace, as did his successor *Xauwes*. Him succeeded *Seyfadin*, who reigned 1507, when the *Portuguese*, after they had discovered the passage by sea to the *Indies*, first set footing in the isle of *Ormus*, under the command of *Alfonsus Albuquerque*, the king being then yet in his minority, was under the protection of one *Atar* or *Kogear*, his father's slave, a brave but cunning man,

1662. whose chief aim was to let the young king bear the title of king, but to keep the administration of affairs in his own hands. *Albuquerque* being not ignorant of it, look'd upon this as a favourable opportunity to bring the city of *Ormus*, under the power of *Emanuel*, the then king of *Portugal*, or at least to make it tributary to him, by erecting a fortress near it, by which means he might clear the *Persian* gulph of all the *Turkish* and other Mahometan vessels trading to the *Indies*, and consequently entail that whole trade upon *Portugal*. He was about that time, with six stout men of war well mann'd, cruising in those seas; but thinking it below himself at such a juncture as this to lie privateering at sea, he steer'd his course the 20th of *August* 1507 towards the *Persian* gulph, and passing by the cape *Rosalgat*, came to an anchor before *Kalayatte*, (a noble city, and the first on that coast under the jurisdiction of the kings of *Ormus*) to provide himself with fresh provisions. The inhabitants dreading the name of the *Portuguese*, which was then already become famous throughout the *Indies*, entred into a confederacy with him, upon such conditions as *Albuquerque* was pleased to prescribe them. From thence he set sail for *Kuriatte*, another city belonging to the kings of *Ormus*, on the *Arabian* coast. Here the inhabitants being of a different opinion with those of *Kalayatte* chose rather to defend themselves by force, than to submit to *Albuquerque*, tho' with very ill success. For *Albuquerque* having landing his men, so vigorously attack'd the city, that the garrison after some resistance were forced to leave it to his mercy, which he burnt to the ground, with all their ships he found in the harbour. In the same manner he made himself master of the *Maskate* and *Orfasan*, two strong and well fortified places belonging to the king of *Ormus*; and from thence directly taking his course to *Ormus* it self, the chief aim of this expedition, he sent word to king *Seyfadin* and *Atar* the protector, that *Emanuel* king of *Portugal* having taken a resolution, out of an hereditary hatred to the mahometans, the declared enemies of *Christendom*, to make war against them, which should not end but with the total conquest of either side, he was come to tell them, that if they were ready, according to the example of several other *Asiatick* and *African* kings, to pay his master a certain yearly tribute, he would leave them in the quiet possession of the island, but if they refused to acknowledge the king of *Portugal* for their lord, he was come to denounce them war, which was not to end but with their total total destruction.

The Portuguese *came first into the* Persian *gulph.*

The king being sorely frightned at the last success of the *Portuguese*, and dreading the same fate, thought it his best way to cajole *Albuquerque* with fair words into a belief of his sincere intentions of peace; but at the same time, by the advice of *Atar*, sought to gain time, and to delay his positive answer, till the expected auxiliaries from the continent of *Persia* were arrived. No sooner had he received these supplies but he altered his note, and in plain terms sent word to *Albuquerque*, that the kings of *Ormus* were not used to pay, but to receive tribute from foreigners; that in case the *Portuguese* would be contented with the same privileges of trading other nations enjoy'd there, they should be welcome; but that if they once came to hostilities, they should be convinced to their cost, what difference there was to fight with well appointed *Persians* and *Arabians*, and with an undisciplin'd rabble of *Moors*. By this time *Atar* the protector had got above 20000 men together, part of which he embark'd aboard the merchant vessels then in harbour there, which he posted in a line along the shore, to prevent the enemies landing, whilst he with the men of war put to sea with an intention to attack *Albuquerque* in the rear, so soon as he should be engaged with the merchant men: But *Albuquerque*, instead of attacking the merchant ships, came up with *Atar*'s fleet, and engaged them so furiously, that that in a short time he sunk many of them, and burnt the rest, with a great slaughter of men on the enemies side, whereas the *Portuguese* lost not above ten men during the whole engagement. King *Seyfadin* being sensible that the loss of his fleet must of necessity draw that of the whole island after it, sent immediately his deputies to *Albuquerque* to treat of peace; they were kindly received by the *Portuguese* general, who gave immediate orders, that the fire which had seized by this time upon the merchant ships, should be extinguished immediately, and the next day a peace was concluded betwixt them upon these following conditions. 1662.

That *Seyfadin* king of *Ormus*, and all his successors, submit themselves to, and shall acknowledge the king of *Portugal* their protector, and pay him an annual tribute of 15000 *Serafs*.

That *Albuquerque* shall have liberty to pitch upon a place, such as he judges most convenient for the erecting of a fortress, for which purpose he shall be supply'd with ready money, and other necessaries by the said king.

Accordingly *Albuquerque* apply'd himself with all imaginable speed to the building of the fortress, but many of the gentlemen volunteers,

1662. volunteers and other *Portuguese*, looking upon it as a great hardship to spend their time here in slavish drudgery, whilst they miss'd their opportunity of getting a rich booty at sea from the *Moorish* ships, (the main intent of their voyage) began to murmur, and at last, with the consent of their captains, embark'd themselves aboard two men of war, and in spite of *Albuquerque* return'd to the *Indies*. He was vex'd to to the soul to see himself thus disappointed in this great design, but being forced to comply with necessity he follow'd the rest. But some years after he being sent from the king of *Portugal* in the quality of viceroy of the *Indies*, he did, after the conquest of *Goa* and *Malacca*, bring it to perfection in the following manner.

He caused 1577, 22 men of war, and a good number of merchant ships to be equip'd at *Goa*, and to have it rumour'd abroad, that he intended to go with this fleet to *Aden* (a city at the entrance of the *Redsea*) to prevent those of *Ormus* to conceive any jealousy of this equipment. But no sooner was he come to *Maskate* but he changed his course, and steer'd directly for *Ormus*, where his arrival caused an incredible fear both in the king and people. For *Atar* being dead since, and king *Seyfadin* poison'd by *Noradin*, governor of the city, his brother *Toro* or *Torunxa* had usurp'd the kingdom from his children. *Noradin*, who had both by this act, and before heap'd so many obligations upon this new king, got thereby the sole administration of the government into his own hands, and daily appear'd in publick with a strong guard, consisting most of his own kinsfolks. Those that bore the chiefest rank among these were three brothers, among whom was one *Hamades*, *Noradin*'s chief favourite, a man of about 35 years of age, bold, prudent and very ambitious, and resembling in every respect the late deceas'd protector *Atar*. He took effectual care by placing his creatures in all places of trust, whereby he establish'd himself in the management of the government, so that not only *Noradin*, but also *Toro* himself durst not attempt to act contrary to his sentimens. From hence it was, that tho' the league with *Portugal* had been kept inviolably hitherto, the *Portuguese* had been civilly receiv'd there, and the yearly tribute punctually paid, yet was the power of *Hamades* so prevailing, as to have constrained *Toro* to accept of the *Persian* turbant sent him by *Ismael Sophi*, an evident sign that *Hamades* his inclinations were rather for the *Persians* than *Portuguese*. *Albuquerque* being not ignorant of what pass'd at *Ormus*, resolved, by delivering king *Toro* from the slavish submission imposed upon him by his subjects, to confirm him absolutely in his fidelity and interest to the king of *Portugal*; for which purpose he surrounded the whole island with his fleet, to take away from them all hopes of relief, and immediately sent word to the king, that he was come thither with no other intent than to enter upon a new league betwixt the kings of *Portugal* and *Ormus*. 1662.

King *Toro* being not a little surprized at the unexpected appearance of so great a fleet, dispatch'd immediately his deputies to *Albuquerque*, to treat with him concerning the conditions of is; *Albuquerque* demanded, that besides the annual tribute to be paid to the king of *Portugal*, liberty should be given him to build a fortress, and a factory house to secure the trade of the *Portuguese*; and king *Toro* being willing enough to grant what he desired, the league was confirmed by a solemn oath on both sides. But *Hamades*, who soon foresaw that the building of this fortress would tend to the no small detriment of his authority, left no stone unturn'd to prevent its accomplishment, which *Albuquerque* being soon aware of, he caused this ambitious favourite to be kill'd. After his death, the *Portuguese* meeting with no other obstacle, the fortress was soon after brought to perfection; king *Toro* readily furnishing them with materials and other necessaries. The next care of *Albuquerque* was, how to remove all the opportunities of a future revolt among the inhabitants of *Ormus*; for which purpose, after having taken the oath of fidelity from king *Toro*, he removed all the great cannon out of the city, and sent about 30 persons of the royal family, who had their eyes taken away before, and were maintain'd at the king's charge from thence to *Goa*, where they were to be provided for by certain persons appointed for that purpose by *Emanuel* king of *Portugal*. *Albuquerque* having thus settled the affairs of *Ormus* return'd to *Goa*, where he was no sooner arrived but dy'd. The *Mahometans* call this *Albuquerque Malandy*, because he was born at *Melinde* in *Africa*, call'd by them *Maland*. Albuquerque dies.

It was not long before king *Toro* refused to pay the usual tribute to the *Portuguese*, alledging that they did not defend him against the violences committed by *Mokrin* his vassal prince, of the island of *Baharen*, who hinder'd the ships from coming to *Ormus*. *Sequeira*, then governor of the *Indies* for the king of *Portugal*, sent hereupon seven men of war (aboard of which were 400 *Portuguese* soldiers) to the assistance of king *Toro*, under the command of *Anthony Korrea*, which were join'd by 200 barks of the king's, mann'd with 3000 *Persians*, under the

1662. the conduct of *Xaraf* his admiral. *Mokrin* brought together an army of 12000 men, consisting of three thousand *Arabian* horse, 4000 *Persian* archers, and the rest of *Turkish* firelocks, and some of his own subjects, arm'd only with scimeters and javelins; but being overthrown and slain in battle, the isle of *Baharen* fell into the hands of the king of *Ormus*, who gave it to one *Bardadi*, under condition that he should pay him an annual tribute of 40000 *Serafs*.

By this time *Sequeira* being sufficiently convinced, that the king his master was circumvented in his share of the customs and other taxes, appointed certain *Portuguese* commissioners to have a watchful eye over them, which so exasperated the inhabitants, that king *Toro* in 1521 revolted, and caused all the *Portuguese* at *Ormus*, except such as fled into the fortress, to be kill'd; the same treatment received the *Portuguese* at *Kuriatte*, *Soar*, and in the island of *Baharen*, who were either all slain or imprison'd. Then he attempted the taking of the fortress, but meeting with a brave resistance from the *Portuguese*, and dreading their return with a good fleet, he retired with all his subjects and their effects to the isle of *Queixome*, and set fire to the city of *Ormus*, which burnt four days successively. But not long after *Xaraf*, the chief adviser and promoter of this revolt, having received intelligence of the coming of the *Portuguese* fleet, and fearing to be call'd to a severe account kill'd king *Toro*; and in his stead put *Mamud Scha*, one of the sons of *Seyfadin*, upon the throne. This king being but 13 years of age, made a new league with the *Portuguese*, by virtue of which he was oblig'd to pay an annual tribute of 20000 *Serafs* to the king of *Portugal*: The inhabitants of *Ormus* were to restore to the *Portuguese* all that they had taken from them; in consideration of which, the *Portuguese* were not to intermeddle with their custom-house, or other courts of judicature. In the year 1550, the *Turks* made an inroad into the isle of *Ormus*, and laid it almost desolate. The king who in 1566 reign'd in *Ormus* was call'd *Siasirusia* of *Xasiruxa Gialedin*; and in 1580 reign'd one *Ferraguixa*, who tho' very antient, had a great inclination to marry *Bifatme*, the widow of *Rex Bradadin*, his late governor of *Mogostan*, thereby to be master of her treasure, which was very great; she gave him for answer, *That she would comply with his desires as soon as he had perfected his new gardens at* Tarumbake, *and found out a new spring of fresh water*; both which the king having found means to effect in a short time, he was nevertheless disappointed in his expectation by the crafty widow. He that reign'd in *Ormus* in 1606 was *Xeque*, *i. e.* prince *Ajo*, or as some call him *Ajosia*, *i. e.* king *Ajo*. 1662.

For tho' the *Portuguese* by the conduct of *Albuquerque*, had got into the possession of the island of *Ormus*, ever since 1507, nevertheless the succession of their kings from father to son, was kept inviolable under the protection of the crown of *Portugal*; for no sooner did the king of *Ormus* die, but the inhabitants set another of the royal family, tho' not without the consent of the *Portuguese* governor upon the throne, who was oblig'd to take the oath of fidelity to the king of *Portugal*, after which he was invested with the crown and scepter by the said governor, who conducted him in great pomp to the royal palace, and afterwards gave him all the demonstrations of respect and honour, tho' at the same time he durst not stir from the island without his approbation.

Vast territories belonging to the kings of Ormus.

The antient kings of *Ormus* were masters of vast territories on the continent of *Persia* and *Arabia*; and among the rest of the countries of *Lar* and *Mogostan* in *Persia*, the last of which is commonly call'd the *Persian* coast, and the countrey of *Lar* being a mountainous countrey of very difficult access, serv'd them as a bulwark against the *Persians*. For after these had once taken from the king of *Ormus* the countrey of *Lar*, and what else they were possess'd of on the continent of *Persia*, (whose example was followed by the *Arabians*) the isle of *Ormus* was bereaved of its chief defence, and exposed to the insults of the *Persians*.

How they secur'd the sovereignty.

It was the custom of the antient kings of *Ormus*, in order to secure to themselves the quiet possession of the throne, to confine their next kinsfolks, or such as had any pretensions to the crown, with their wives and children, where they were well entertain'd, and kept till the king thought fit to dispose of them otherwise. They also used to blind their brothers, and others descended of the royal line, because it was a fundamental law amongst them, that no blind man could sway the scepter. It was performed thus; they made a copper bason red hot, which they, immediately after it was taken out of the fire, held frequently close before the eyes of him that was to be bereaved of his eyesight; which without any farther application, had the desired effect, without giving the least blemish to the eyes in outward appearance, which look'd as clear as before. Some will have it to have been done with a red hot iron.

Their riches.

The kings of *Ormus* possessed vast treasures in former ages; the customs they received from all goods exported and imported there, amounting to an immense sum yearly, which empower'd them to extend their conquests on the continent of *Persia* and *Arabia*, which they afterwards lost again by their own neglect. For whilst they themselves were drowned in voluptuousness, they left the sole management of affairs to their favourites, who encreasing in pride as they did in riches, at last left them nothing but the bare royal name, whilst they acted in the government at their own pleasure, disposing of the treasury and all other matters of moment, as it suited best with their own interest, whereby both the power of the kings and the strength of the kingdom being weakned, they were no longer able to cope as before with their enemies, and at last were forced to yield themselves tributaries to the *Portuguese*, who were afterwards, *viz.* in 1622, chased from thence by the *Persians*, with the assistance of the *English*, under the reign of their king *Schach Abbas*, which happened in the following manner.

The *Portuguese* at *Ormus* had no sooner been advertised of the taking of the fort of *Queixome* (situate upon the point of the island of the same name;) but they sent deputies in the name of the king of *Ormus* and of *Goazi* to the *Persian Chan* of *Schiras*, to come with them to an amicable composition, but with such evident marks of fear, that the *Persians*, who had lately received advice of a powerful incursion made by the *Usbeck* and *Nogayan Tartars*, and consequently would have rested satisfied with the conquest of the isle of *Quiexome*, being sensible thereof, resolved not to let slip this opportunity of plundering as it were *en passant* the city of *Ormus*. Accordingly the *Chan* of *Schiras*, without tarrying any longer in the island of *Queixome*, embark'd about 40000 *Persians* and *Arabians*, under the conduct of *Emanculibey* his lieutenant, in some barks, who coming before the city of *Ormus*, found it deserted by the *Portuguese* and most of its other inhabitants, but met with a prodigious quantity of merchandise, which they either could or would not bring into the castle. The *Persians* seeing themselves thus masters of the city without striking a blow, and finding that under the protection of the houses they might open their trenches, without any considerable danger from the cannon of the castle, fell to work without delay, and soon carried them on to the foot of the ditch, which being dry on that side, they pass'd without much opposition. Then they attack'd the bastions of *St. James*, which they undermin'd and made themselves masters of it in a few days; the garrison all this while not making one salley, but were forced to surrender the place the 3[d] of *May*, after a siege

Conquest of Ormus *by the* Persians.

of ten weeks. They consisted of 400 men, regular troops, besides women and children, which were some days before sent to *Maskate*. The *English* had the chief hand in making the conditions for this surrender, which were,

That all the soldiers should have their lives granted them;

And that all such as were willing should be transported to Maskate, *in two* English *ships appointed for that purpose*, which was strictly observed by the *Persians*; they made the king of *Ormus* and *Goazil*, with their families, prisoners, and seized upon their whole treasure, which in pearls and gold amounted to above two millions, besides a vast booty of precious stones, and other riches belonging to the inhabitants, and 300 pieces of cannon, all which fell to the *Persians* share, who lost a great number of men in the siege of this fortress. The *Portuguese*, before they surrendered the fort, took care to make all the cannon useless by nailing of it up. The king of *Ormus*, with some other *Arabians* of note were carried prisoners into *Persia*, together with the beforementioned *Goazil Raia Noradina*. This last was a young lord, a subject of the king of *Spain*, a very handsome person, and well versed in the *Persian* and *Arabian* histories. He had at the beginning of the siege offered 100000 crowns in ducats and *Xerafins*, to the *Persians*, to be transported to *Maskate* or *Goa*; and the unfortunate king of *Ormus*, had likewise made an offer of his whole treasure to the *Portuguese*, to obtain the same favour, which was refused by the *Portuguese*, notwithstanding they were both vassals of the king of *Portugal*, which has given no slender cause of suspicion to some, as if the *Portuguese* had invited the *Persians* thither, when they sued for peace to them in the isle of *Queixome*. The *English*, in consideration of this service, had the moiety of all the customs and other revenues granted them by the *Persians*. The chief reason of the loss of the fortress of *Ormus*, is attributed to the revolt of the garrison in the *Portuguese* fort of *Queixome*, who in spight of *Ruy Freira* their governor, surrendred it to the *Persians*. It was also alledged, that if the Governor of the *Portuguese* fortress of *Ormus*, had, according to the advice of the other commanders, filled the ditch betwixt the city and the fortress with water, by opening the sluices, the *Persians* would have found it a much harder task to have approached so near to the bastion of *St. James*.

Vast traffick of Ormus *in former ages.*

Before the *Portuguese* had discovered the passage by sea to the *Indies*, all the *Indian* commodities were brought into *Europe* by the way of *Ormus*, whither they were first transported

1662. transported out of all parts of the *Indies*, and from thence thro' the *Persian* gulph, and along the river *Euphrates* to *Bassora*, which city lies upon the confluence of the two great rivers the *Euphrates* and *Tigris*. From *Bassora* they were by land carried by camels to *Bagdad*, a city upon the *Tigris*. From hence they travelled with their merchandizes in caravans thro' the desarts of *Syria* to *Aleppo*, being a journey of forty days; and from *Aleppo* to *Tripolis* in *Syria*, bordering upon the mediterranean (only three days journey) from whence they were transported by the mediterranean into all parts of *Europe*. From hence it is evident, that *Ormus* in former ages was the staple of all the *Indian* commodities. But since the discovery of the sea passage to the *East-Indies* by the *Portuguese* by the cape of *Good Hope*, this way of transporting the *Indian* commodities by land is laid aside, tho' even to this day, certain *Indian* merchandizes, but especially *Persian* silks, are brought from *Ormus* by land by the caravans, this island by reason of its situation, at the entrance of the *Persian* gulph, and its two harbours, lying very commodious for traffick and shipping from the eastern parts of the world. After the city of *Ormus* was fallen into the hands of the *Persians*, most of its traffick and the staple of the *Indian* commodities was from thence transferred to *Gamron*, a city upon the *Persian* coast, built upon the ruins of *Ormus*. We will now proceed to a short description of the islands of *Baharen*, *Queixome* and *Kesem*.

The isle of Baharen. Among a great number of other islands in the *Persian* gulph, and under the jurisdiction of *Persia*, one of the chief is the isle of *Baharen*, or *Bahrem*, called by *Strabo* and *Pliny Tilos*, and is by some taken to be the same island, called *Ichara* by *Ptolemy*. It is situate in the streights of *Bassora* or the *Persian* gulph, betwixt *Bassora* and the isle *Gerun*, or *Ormus*, about 60 leagues distant from each, near the *Arabian* coasts, over against the harbour of *Katifa*. This island abounds in water, but is brackish, the best of all being found in certain ponds or pools in *Nanyah*, in the midst of the island; next to which that which is taken out of the sea is in most esteem, which is performed in the following manner.

There are certain springs of fresh water arising in the bottom of the sea, at three fathoms and a half deep. Near the city of *Manama*, certain divers go early in the morning in boats, about three musket shot deep in the sea from the shore, and dive to the bottom of the sea, fill their earthen or leathern vessels with the water that issues from the springs, and so come up again and return to the shore; this they do with a great deal of dexterity and nimbleness. 1662. These springs are supposed to have been formerly on the shore, not far from the sea-side, which since that time have been swallowed up by the inundations of the sea, occasioned by earthquakes. This isle is very fertile, abounding in fruits of all sorts, but especially dates. But all the rice (which together with the dates, is the general food of the inhabitants;) is from the *Indies* transported to *Ormus*, and from thence into this island, which is famous throughout the *Indies*, by reason of the pearl fishery here, *Pearl fishery.* from whence the king of *Persia* draws a vast revenue yearly, as may be gathered from thence, that after this island was fallen into the hands of one *Bardadin*, (who succeeded *Anthony Korrea Mokrin*, a vassal of the king of *Ormus*) he promised to pay a yearly tribute of 40000 *Serafs*. Besides this, the pearl trade here produces yearly at least 500000 ducats in ready money, not to reckon 100000 ducats more, which are shared betwixt the *Persian* governor and the other officers: For there is a great resort of merchants to this place, which come hither from all parts of the world to buy up pearls, and to transport them to the *Indies* and other places, the best and most precious pearls in the world being found near this island of *Baharen*, and the isle of *Gionfar* or *Giolfar*, which both in bigness and roundness, far exceed those found near the other islands of *Latif*, *Lasen*, *Barechator*, *Zezirafilhar*, *Alul*, *Seran*, *Dsiud*, *Daas*, *Emergocenon*, *Ancovi*, *Serecho*, *Delmesialmas*, *Sirbeniast*, *Aldane*, *Festebruatich*, *Cherizorn*, *Dibei*, *Sarba*, *Agiman*, *Ras*; *Emelgovien*, *Rasagiar*, *Daoin*, *Rasaelchimes*, *Sirkorkor*, *Kasab*, *Konzar*, *Mesendenderadi*, *Lima*, *Debe*, *Chorf*, *Chelb*, *Sarar*, *Suet*, *Mestar*, *Garajat*, *Teuji*, *Golaf*, *Furgatile*, *Sam*, *Gameda*, *Bacha* and *Jadi*. All which afford pearls, but they are not exactly round. Near *Maskate*, about 33 or 34 leagues from *Ormus*, are likewise very good pearls to be found.

The pearl fishery near *Baharen* begins sometimes in *June*, but generally in *July*, and continues till the end of *August*. About 200 barks go abroad together, *viz.* 100 belonging to the isle of *Baharen*, 50 to *Pilsar* and 50 to *Nihely*; their rendezvous being commonly near *Katar*, a sea port of *Arabia*, six leagues south of *Baharen*. The pearls taken here exceed all the rest in goodness, beauty, and weight, tho' not in bigness. They catch them by means of a stone, which by its weight is let down 12 or 18 fathom under water. They sell the pearls by *Karats* and *Abas*, three of which make one *Karat*; and by *Matikals*, or *Mitigals*, each of which contains 42 *Karats*; the small pearls are sold by *Mitigals*. Besides this general fishery

1662. fishery near *Katar*, which continues for two months, there are several other particular fisheries, near *Nibely*, *Baharen*, *Julfar*, *Maskate*, *Teude*, and *Rozalgate*, in the *Persian* gulph, which though not of so great consequence as the first, yet are commonly greatly beneficial to the owners. As they take up the oysters they open them, when the pearls drop out. It is generally believed that these pearls are progenerated by the *May* dews, during which month the oysters rise up to the surface of the waters, and opening themselves, receive a small quantity of dew, which being coagulated, afterwards produces these pearls. Certain it is, that if these oysters are opened before *June*, the pearls are soft and pliable like pitch. Most of the inhabitants of the isle of *Baharen* are *Arabians*, but the garrison consists of *Persians*, under the command of a vizier sent thither by the king of *Persia*. Formerly this isle was under the jurisdiction of the kings of *Ormus*, and in 1602 taken from them by the *Portuguese*. But when the *Persian* sultan of *Xiras* had laid siege to the *Portuguese* fortress of *Comoran*, he made himself master of *Baharen*. The king of *Persia* alledging that he had not taken it from the *Portuguese*, but from a vassal of the king of *Ormus*, who was his vassal; so that ever since 1602 the *Persians* have been in possession of it.

The isle of Quiexome Kechmiche.

The isle of *Queixome*, or *Queixume*, or *Quezome*, otherwise called *Kechmiche*, and by the inhabitants *Brokt*, lies close to the continent of *Persia*, being separated from it only by a small branch of the sea: It has about two leagues in circuit, and is three leagues distant from *Ormus*. Its two chief places are *Arbez* and *Homeal*, where the king of *Ormus* at the time when *Albuquerque* first appeared hereabouts, had strong garrisons. The other places of note are *Lapht*, the best harbours of this island, *Darbaga* not far from the *Lapht*, *Chau*, and *Sirmion*, or *Sermion*. It bears plenty of corn, but especially barly, without which the inhabitants of *Ormus*, who are supplied from hence with it for their horses, could scarce subsist there. Here is also a most excellent spring of fresh water; to secure which the *Persians* had erected a fort hard by for fear of the *Portuguese*, who were then as yet masters of *Ormus*. If we may believe some historians, this island was not inhabited in ancient times; partly by reason of the frequent earthquakes that happened there, partly by reason of the vast numbers of serpents and other venomous creatures, which infected both air and some trees, so as to render the island uninhabitable. Among these trees is one called *Baxama* or *Baxana*, the fruit of which is so poisonous, that the least taste of it kills in an instant, and its shadow is so pestiferous, that it kills those who abide there in less than a quarter of an hour. The root of this tree is in several other parts esteemed as the greatest antidote that can be, but here it is mortal, as are its leaves, and fruit called *Rabuzit*. 1662.

The *Portuguese* in 1622 conquered this island from the *Persians*, and on the point opposite to *Ormus* erected a fort, fortified with a wall, and surrounded with a broad and deep ditch, but the wall was very slight, being sustained from behind only by some loose earth. In short it was a place of no defence, without any great cannon, neither in a condition to bear the weight of them. It had three ponds within its precinct, being chiefly built by the *Portuguese*, for that purpose, because the inhabitants of *Ormus*, were from thence supplied with water. Scarce had the *Portuguese* finished this fort, but the *Persians* out of the countrey of *Lara* in 1622, besieged it by land, as the *English* did at sea; the *Portuguese* commander *Ruy Freira de Andreada* defended himself bravely for some time, and killed many of the *Persians*, who would have bought it perhaps at a dear rate, had not the *English* threatned to bring their great cannon against it, which obliged the garrison who were not provided with them, to capitulate, and to surrender the fort upon honourable conditions, which were not performed on the enemies side. There are some others who have given us the following account of the occasion of this siege.

The king of *Persia* had 1612 taken the isles of *Queizome* and *Baharen*, and the fortresses of *Bandel* and *Mogostan* on the continent, from the king of *Ormus*, which he refusing to restore, the king of *Portugal* sent his express orders to *Ruy Freira*, that in case the king of *Persia* would not restore the isle of *Queixome* and the fortress of *Bandel*, he should declare war against him, and erect a fort on the point of the isle of *Queixome*. Accordingly *Ruy Freira de Andreada*, who in the beginning of *June* 1620, came to *Ormus*, caused a fort to be built on the point of the said island, surrounded only with a slender wall made of stone and clay, or loam, being scarce to be compared in strength to some private buildings: The *Persians* with the assistance of the *English* having erected a small battery against it, did play upon the fort with their cannon, which did strike such a terror into the garrison that they refused to stand the brunt any longer, but forced *Ruy Freira* to capitulate. For *Emanchulican* governor of *Schiras* being just then come with 5000 men to *Bandel* or *Gamron*, he sent part of his forces under the command of *Emanculi*-

S bey

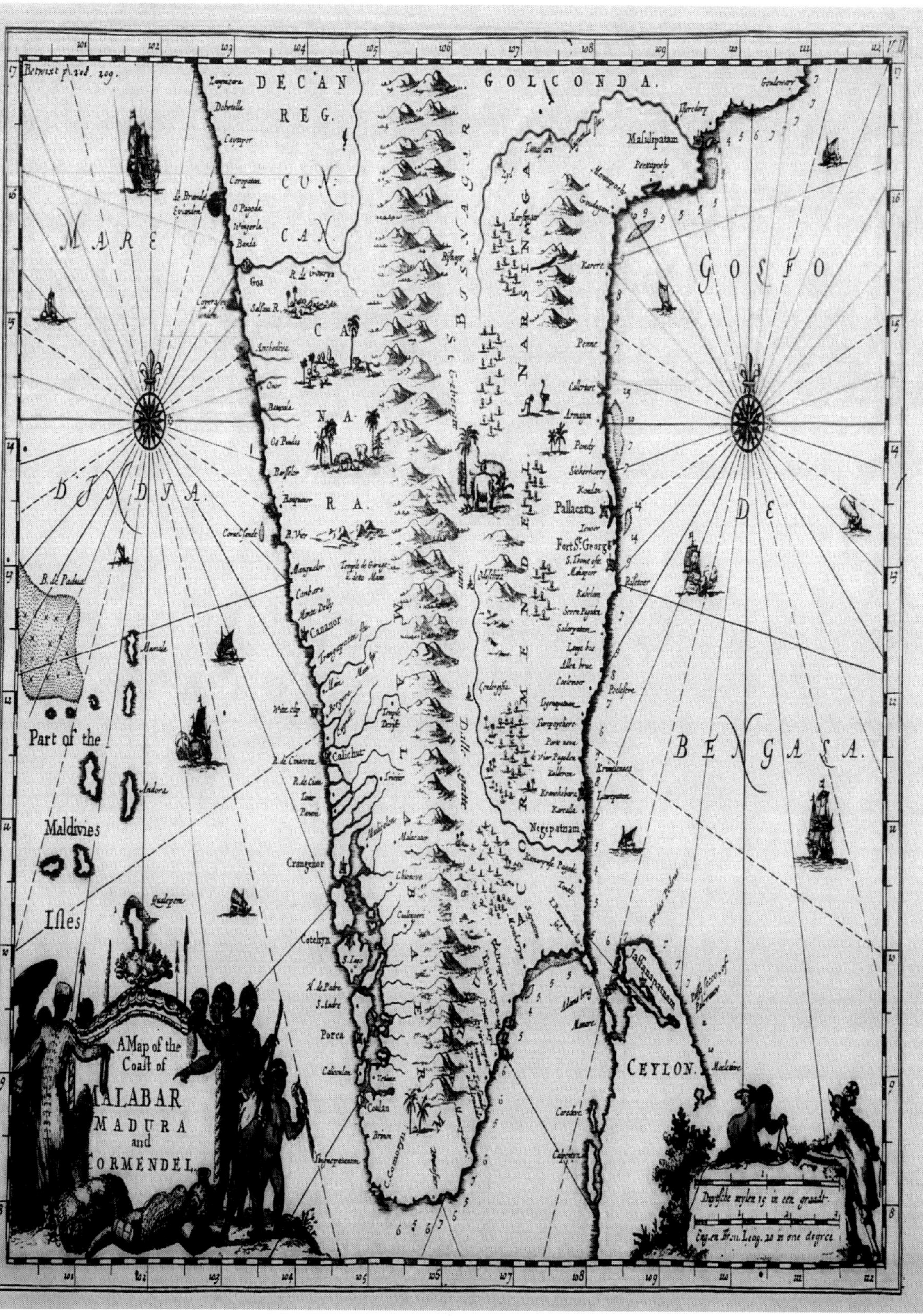

Betwixt p. 208. 209.
VII
A Map of the Coast of
MALABAR
MADURA
and
CORMENDEL
DECAN
REG.
GOLCONDA.
CUN
CAN
MARE
DINDIA
GOLFO
DE
BENGALA.
Part of the
Maldivies
Isles
CEYLON
Masulipatam
Goa
Pallacatta
Fort St. George
Negepatnam
Cananor
Calichur
Cranganor
Porca
Coulan
Jaffanapatnam
Duytsche mylen 15 in een graadt.
Eng. en Fren. Leag. 20 in one degree

St Thomas on y^e Coast of CORMANDEL
1 The City of St Thomas
2 a Wooden Battery
3 y^e French Outgards
4 a Pagan Temple called St Trinlicuri
5 a Stone Battery
6 y^e Outgard at Sea

1662. bey to the siege of the fort of *Queixome*; *Ruy Freira*, as I told you, being forced to surrender, had obtained certain conditions from the *English* for himself and the garrison, among which the chiefest was, that the whole garrison as well *Portuguese* as *Arabians* (the last of which were come thither from *Zulfa* upon the coast of *Arabia*, under the command of *Emir Alikamai Zemur Mahomet*, and had done signal services by sallies and otherwise) should be safely conducted to *Maskate*, a city on the coast of *Arabia* belonging to the *Portuguese*; but this was but ill performed by the *Persian* general, who before the *Portuguese* were embarked, caused all the *Arabians* to be beheaded, in spite of the protestations of *Ruy Freira*, who accused the *English* with breach of faith, but these excused themselves, alledging that these *Arabians* having formerly been subjects of the king of *Persia*, it was not in their power to prevent it: No more than 20 out of 250 *Arabians* escaped with life, who were hid by the *English* seamen. The commander in chief of these *Arabians Emer Genedin* being brought before the *Persian* general, was by his orders stabbed in his presence by *Xarial* his son-in-law, and then governour of *Mogostan*; but the *Portuguese* garrison consisting of 200 men, were by the *English* instead of conveying them to *Maskate*, set on shore in the isle of *Ormus*, from whence they got safe into the *Portuguese* castle.

The isle of Jarek. The isle of *Jarek* is situate three leagues from the coasts of *Arabia*, to the south of the isle of *Ormus*, and to the east of the isle of *Kechmeche*. It is destitute of inhabitants, and very small in compass, the *Dutch* who reside on the behalf of the *East-India* company at *Gamron*, have planted there only a garden near a certain pond, whither the wild boars and stags which are here in great numbers, come to drink; they also keep here some tame fowl for their recreation. It is now time we should leave *Gamron* and *Ormus*, and proceed on our voyage.

After we had taken in our lading at *Gamron*, we set sail from thence the 2d of *June*, and with a favourable gale passed along the coast of *Malabar*, towards the isle of *Ceilon*; for before you come to the coast of *Coromandel*, you are obliged to sail round all that vast tract of land. I had letters by me for the governour of *Punto Gale*, a city of *Ceylon*, which I delived to a certain master of a small vessel, without going ashore myself. After we had provided ourselves with fresh water here, that the rendezvous of the *Dutch* ship was appointed to be at *Punto Pedro*, where Mr. *Rijklof van Goens* commanded a body of troops in order to besiege the city of *St. Thomas*, whither we also directed our course. But whilst the great train of artillery was embarking, and the troops ready to go on board for this expedition, we received intelligence that the *Portuguese* had sold the city of *St. Thomas* to the *Jentyves* or *Pagans*, which made us also alter our measures; and I went to *Jafenepatnam* to dispatch my business.

They came to Punto Gale *in* Ceylon.

The city of St. Thomas. The city of *St. Thomas* is situate under 12 or 13 deg. 30 min. of northern latitude, 26 *German* miles from *Nagapatnam*, one and a half off the river *Ganges* near cape *Komorijn*, and a days journey or five *German* miles to the south of *Paliakatte*, on the coast of *Coromandel*, close to the sea-shore. The city of *St. Thomas* was otherwise called *Kalamina*, and by the natives *Meliapor*, which name the *Portuguese* changed into that of *St. Thomas*, in honour of that apostle, which name it retains to this day, not only among the christians, but also the *Turks* and *Indians*. *Meliapor* signifies in their language as much as a peacock, intimating that as this bird is the most beautiful of all others, so this city did in beauty excel all the rest of the east. Some will have the city of *St. Thomas* or *Meliapor*, to be the same called *Mapura* by *Ptolemy*. This city was quite desolate when the *Portuguese* first came there, who rebuilt it in 1545, since which time it has encreased to that degree, that not many years after she was accounted one of the finest cities in all the *Indies*, both in respect of the magnificence of its building, and the number of rich inhabitants. It is fortified with stone wall, strengthned by several bastions; and had under its jurisdiction above 300 villages and towns. It is one of the richest sea ports of all the *East-Indies*, its situation being in the midst of all the best harbours of those parts, which renders it the more convenient for the *East-India* trade. Whilst this place was in the hands of the *Portuguese*, it was at first incorporated with the diocese of the bishop of *Cochin*, but afterwards erected into a bishopdom, under the jurisdiction of the archbishop of *Goa*. They had a church here dedicated to *St. Francis*, belonging to the *Capuchins*, and two others, one dedicated to *St. John*, the other to the virgin *Mary*, where the *Mahometans* and *Pagans* were instructed and baptized. In the suburbs was the church of *St. Lucy*, and in the city the monastery of *Charity* and *Lazarus*, besides three others. The jesuits, of whom there was a considerable number here, had a goodly college within the city, wherein the children of the *Portuguese* and of the chief *Malabars*, were instructed in the fundamentals of the christian religion. Next to this college was a very large parish inhabited by christians, such as were by the jesuits con- 1662.

1662. verted from paganism and mahometanism, of which 120 were baptized in 1604. Here you see also the famous church of *St. Thomas*, this apostle, as the *Portuguese* pretend, being buried here: his sepulchre is shewn to this day on the top of a mountain near a city, over which they have built a small chappel, which may be discovered at some distance at sea. Close to this college upon a pretty high hill is a chappel, which as they say, was *St. Thomas*'s usual sleeping place. The jesuits to shew their reverence to this place, have adorned that part of the chappel where *St. Thomas* used to say his prayers, with gilt iron steps.

St. Thomas's *chappel.*

Here you see also a stone cross, which they say is the same that in the apostles time did fall from heaven; for which reason they have covered it with an arch, as they have done with the adjacent spring, which arising from a rock is covered by another arch resting upon four columns. The whole chappel is likewise adorned with many ornaments, and the wood of the chappel being looked upon as a precious relick, is frequently set in gold and carried away by the devout pilgrims.

We continued our course along the coast till we came to *Negapatnam*, where we were to unload part of our cargo.

Negapatan.

Negapatan or *Nenapatnam* is composed of *Naga*, which in the *Malabar* tongue signifies a serpent, and *Patnam* or *Patan* a city, because round about this place used to be seen a certain kind of very venomous serpents called *Cobros Capellos*, i. e. *Head-serpents*. It is situate under the 9 deg. 45 min. and the adjacent cape under 11 deg. of northern latitude; beyond the rocks of *Romanankir*, over against the isle of *Manar*, just opposite to *Tripalikorin*, three leagues from the city of *Tranguabar*, and about 39 leagues from the cape *Comorin*, at the beginning of the coast of *Bisnagar* and *Coromandel*. This city as well as its castle call'd *Ragu*, acknowledge the *Portuguese* for its founders, the castle being built for their better security against the attempts of the *Naik* or *Neyk*, lord of the circumjacent countrey. They had several goodly churches here, and a very fine monastery belonging to the *Franciscans*, which was maintained at the charge of the chiefest of the inhabitants. There are to this day remaining divers fine churches and other large structures, with spacious apartments and galleries according to the *Portuguese* fashion. Next to the jesuits college stood the church of *Tranguabar*. The city is pretty well fortified with defensible towers, surrounded with a good mote: It is very populous in proportion to its bigness, but most of the inhabitants are of a tawny complexion, being generally either *Mestices*, i. e. such as are born of a *Portuguese* father, and a she blackamoor; or *Kastices*, i. e. such as their fathers were blackamoors and their mothers *Portuguese* women. It is also inhabited by *Banyans* and *Mahometans*, who are the chiefest traders here. 1662.

This city was the 23[d] of *July* 1658, surrendered to the *Dutch* by composition. For Mr. *John Vander Laen* then commander in chief of the *Dutch* forces in those parts, did pursuant to his orders from Mr *Rijklof van Goens* admiral general of the *Dutch* fleet, set sail from *Jafenepatan* in the isle of *Ceylon*, on friday the 19th of *June*, to *Punto Pedro*, where he cast anchor in the evening, and found the yachts *Workum*, the *Morning-star*, *Manaer*, *Waterpass*, *Narsapour*, the galliot the *Amsterdam*, and the chaloop *Japara*, ready to join him; but the *Pidgeon* yacht was run aground, and the *Workum* was fain to stay behind, having lost 3 of her anchors. He took care to provide the fleet immediately with as much meat and other refreshments as the place would afford; and on the 20th was likewise join'd by the yachts the *Goes*, the *Pidgeon*, and the *Workum*; next day Mr. *Lucas Vander Dussen* took a review of the land forces, which consisted of 500 men, divided into 11 companies, besides the sea-men. Mr. *Vander Laen* having summoned all the captains aboard the admiral's ship, where he gave them the necessary directions how every one should behave himself in his post at their arrival before *Negapatan*.

Surrendered to the Dutch.

The 21st of *July* the fleet set sail from *Punto Pedro*, and arrived the 22[d] early in the morning in the road before the city of *Negapatan*, where he met with the yachts the *Pipelen*, the *Naisepour*, and a *Danish* chaloop. Mr. *Vander Laen* ordered to be set up the white flag in the yacht *Vander Goes*, and sent Mr. *Lucas Vander Dussen*, with 3 captains and an interpreter in a chaloop, and credential letters to *Caspar Alphonso de Karvalho*, the *Portuguese* governour of *Negapatan*, and his council, to summon the said city to a surrender upon honourable conditions. About noon Mr. *Vander Dussen* returned; and gave an account to the admiral, that the *Portuguese* governour and his council, refused to admit any of the company, except himself and the interpreter; that he was very civilly received, and admitted to appear before the council, where he had made use of all the arguments he thought might enduce them to surrender, desiring that they would send aboard the admiral their plenipotentiaries to treat about the conditions. They desired time till the next morning to consider of the matter, and that the admiral would be pleased to send another

The Dutch *come before* Negapatan.

Summon the city.

1662. another chaloop to morrow, because the *Jentyves* or natives did stop the passage of their boats at the mouth of the river. Accordingly the 23^d Mr. *Vander Dussen*, with two ensigns return'd to *Negapatan* in the same chaloop, with a white flag, and brought back from thence *Manuel Karvalho* a jesuit, *Lewis de Quintal Parsire* and *Diego Berisero* two captains, and *Antonio d'Almeyde* a lieutenant, instructed with credentials and full power from the *Portuguese* governor, to treat about the surrender of the city to the *Dutch East-India* company upon reasonable terms. The conditions proposed by them were these; that a church should be allow'd to such *Portuguese* as were willing to remain there, with as many priests as were requisite.

The Portuguese send deputies to treat.

That the inhabitants should have liberty to retire to *Bengal*, and that they might carry along with them all what belong'd to the poor.

Their demands.

After some contests on both sides, it was agreed to surrender the place upon these following conditions.

Conditions agreed upon betwixt them and the Dutch.

That the city of *Negapatan* belonging to his *Portuguese* majesty, should be surrendered on *Wednesday* the 24th of *July*, to the *Dutch East-India* company, with all its territories, cannon, ammunition or arms, as likewise the keys of the magazines and other store-houses thereunto belonging.

That immediately as many soldiers of the *East-India* company shall be admitted into the city, as shall be thought requisite by them and the *Portuguese* governor, for their mutual security; and all merchandizes or what else may belong to the crown of *Portugal*, shall at the same time be delivered without the least fraud.

The *Portuguese* garrison now in the city shall march out with beat of drum, matches lighted and bullets in their mouths, to a certain place to be appointed by the *Dutch* admiral Mr. *Vander Laen*, where they shall be disarm'd, except that the officers even to the ensigns shall have liberty to retain their swords.

All the inhabitants, whether clergy or laymen, married or unmarried, shall be left in the free possession of all their goods, except their arms, as well moveable as unmoveable, houses, gold, silver, merchandizes, slaves of both sexes, till the last day of *October*, of the same year; against which time they shall be provided with convenient shipping, at the charge of the *Dutch East-India* company, in order to carry them to *Goa*, or further to the north, if they please.

The clerymen shall then be at liberty to carry along with them all the church ornaments, or what else belong'd to the exercise of the divine worship, except the bells, as likewise all the moveable goods belonging to them. 1662.

The laymen, soldiers and merchants, may, without the least exception, transport all their moveables, money, gold, silver, jewels, slaves of both sexes, and all their merchandizes, provided the same don't belong to the king of *Portugal*.

The day of their departure being come, the *Portuguese* shall have their swords restored to them.

Gaspar Alfonso de Karvalho the *Portuguese* governor, shall be transported to what place he shall think fit.

Accordingly the 24th about noon, seven companies of *Dutch* soldiers, one of *Bandaneses*, and one of *Laskaryns*, under the *Modlier* of *Negombo*, took possession of the gates of the city, at which time the *Portuguese* drew off from the bastions, and proclamation was made immediately, not to molest, much less rob the inhabitants, under pain of death.

The Dutch *take possession of the City.*

Mr. *Vander Laen* himself was received by the *Portuguese* governor, who was not very well at that time, at the entrance of one of the gates, where he had the keys of all the city gates deliver'd to him. From thence he went to take a view of the bastions, and after having given the necessary orders, he commanded the inhabitants to appear the same afternoon in the court of the *Stadthouse*, in order to be disarmed, pursuant to the last agreement. They were no more than 670 strong, divided into 17 companies, consisting of *Portuguese*, *Mestices* and *Topasses*, being all inhabitants, not in the king of *Portugal*'s pay. Their artillery consisted in 28 brass, and 53 iron pieces of cannon small and great, their ammunition in 8000 pounds of gunpowder, lead, and other things of this nature in proportion; besides which, there were ten large and eight small bells in the town.

Much about the same time the *Dutch* appeared before the city, the *Kapado Negape*, or general of the *Neyk*, or lord of the countrey came to lay siege to it; but understanding that the *Dutch* were got into possession of it, he desired to be admitted into the city to confer with them, concerning the sudden surrender of it. His request being granted, he took a great deal of pains to persuade the *Dutch* that both the city, and all the *Portuguese* ought immediately to be deliver'd to the *Neyk* his master, to make satisfaction for what they stood indebted to him; but this request was civilly refused by Mr. *Vander Laen*, who told him that he was very ready to cultivate a good understanding with the *Neyk* and his subjects, but that both in point of conscience, as he was a christian, and in honour he could not recede

1662. cede from the articles of the surrender. By this time the hour approaching when the inhabitants were to be disarm'd at the stadt-house, he invited the *Kapado* to go along with him, which he courteously accepted of: The inhabitants earnestly intreated Mr. *Vander Laen* to permit them to be transported to *Bengal* instead of *Goa*, unto whom he gave for answer, that he would intercede for them in writing with the *Dutch* admiral general *Vander Goens*. The 25th publication was made by beat of drum, that every one, without any exception of persons or quality, should deliver forthwith all his arms at the stadt-house, unless they would be excluded from the benefit of the capitulation; which was punctually perform'd the next day, which was spent altogether in receiving their arms.

In the mean while the *Neyk*'s army had so inclosed the city, that we began to have some scarcity of provisions; and the *Dutch* living at *Tranguabar*, a *Danish* colony, began to be sorely afraid of being attack'd by *Wardarasje Purmal*, who, as it was given out, was sent for from the countrey of *Tanjaor*, by the *Neyk*, to chastise those of *Tranguabar*; the governor of which, *Esbeck Anderson*, had promised to cruise before the bar of *Negapatan*, with three stout yachts well mann'd, instead of which he had sent only one small chaloop; so that the inhabitants fearing the worst, fled daily with their best moveables into the fort of *Danesburgh*. The 17th the *Kapado Negapa*, sent by the *Neyk* with an *Ola* or letter from *Maniegul*, appeared in the city of *Negapatan*, where he delivered the following letter to Mr. *John Vander Laen*.

A letter from the Neyk *to Mr.* Vander Laen.

THE 16th day of the year Welenby. *I* Assy Para Neyk *send to the* Dutch *commander* Moor *this letter; by which I would have them to understand, that the* Portuguese *inhabitants of* Negapatan *have for these 12 years last past not pay'd their usual taxes, but are run much behind. It is for this reason I sent my army to attack them in the city of* Negapatan, *to demolish its fortifications, and after the inhabitants were reduced under my obedience, to grant them liberty to live as before, under my jurisdiction; having always lived in a good correspondence with the* Dutch East-India *company, I desired their assistance by sea; but now I am credibly informed, that you have made an agreement with the* Portuguese *of* Negapatan, *who have deliver'd the city into your hands, which is very displeasing to us; if you had a mind to maintain a good understanding with us, you ought first to have given us notice of it, and obtained our consent; but now you must surrender the city to us, therefore send one of your deputies to treat with me, and he shall be honourably received, and receive all the satisfaction that may tend to the maintaining a farther good correspondence betwixt us. If you do otherwise, you will have occasion to repent it; but as I know you to be persons of wisdom, I don't question but you will surrender the city to our people; in witness of which I have sent our* Kapado Negapa *with this letter.* 1662.

Unto which Mr. *Vander Laen* sent this answer.

Mr. Vander Laen*'s Answer.*

THE Ola *or letter deliver'd to us by your highness's envoy* Negapa, *I received with all imaginable respect, under the discharge of three pieces of ordnance; out of which having fully understood your highness's intentions, I am obliged to tell your highness, that the* Portuguese *having surrendered to us the strong city of* Negapatan, *without making the least opposition, and under certain conditions, agreed on betwixt both parties; we are bound by our duty, as christians, to observe punctually in all respects the said articles, it being unquestionable that without any injustice to your highness, we have power to annoy the* Portuguese, *our enemies, wherever we can meet with them, which makes us live in hopes that the friendship establish'd betwixt your highness and the* East-India *company will not suffer the least detriment upon this account. What has the undertakings of the said company not long ago against the* Portuguese *in the countrey of the* Neyk *of* Madura *and in other neighbouring countries and kingdoms, which were never interpreted to their prejudice, makes us believe that your highness will not be displeased with the advantages obtained by us against the* Portuguese, *which as they tend to no other end than to increase our trade in your highness's dominions, so they must in time turn to your own advantage. In the mean while we have communicated your highness's sentiments, by two several yachts sent for that purpose, to the directors of* Jafenepatan, *from whence we hourly expect an answer, which we don't question will be to your highness's satisfaction.*

In the mean while *Kamerapanijk* the adviser of this siege was fallen in disgrace with the *Neyk*.

The 30th Mr. *Vander Laen* received letters from *Rijklof Goens*, dated the 29th, with the ratification of the capitulation, with orders to send the *Portuguese*, to the number of 150, according to their request, to *Bengal*, where they were likely to do them the

V. II

1662. the leaſt miſchief, and they might ſooneſt rid their hands of them. As to what concerned the difference with the *Neyk*, he adviſed to endeavour to compoſe the matter by the means of ſome preſents; but if that would not ſucceed, to make his forces to retire deeper into the countrey; in the mean time to give all the courteous entertainment to his deputies, and to aſſure them, that he intended in a few days to be with them in perſon, to adjuſt all matters in queſtion betwixt them and his highneſs; but if he committed any hoſtilities againſt the city, to ſtand upon the defenſive, and to proteſt in writing againſt his proceedings. In the mean while the *Neyk*'s forces continued in their camp, which extended to the very ditch of the city; and as it increaſed daily in number, ſo it occaſion'd great ſcarcity within. The 1ſt of *Auguſt*, Mr. *Vander Laen* was inform'd that the commander in chief of the *Neyk*'s forces before *Negapatan* had received a letter from the *Neyk*, directed to Mr. *Van Goens*; and in the afternoon three perſons were ſent into the city, to give notice of the ſaid letter and ſome preſents, which they deſired might be received with all imaginable demonſtrations of reſpect. In compliance with which Mr. *Vander Laen* commanded immediately captain *Waſh* with his company, and the *Modlier* of *Negombo* with his *Laſkarins*, to poſt themſelves in good order without the gates of the city, in order to receive the preſents with all imaginable reſpect, under the diſcharge of three pieces of cannon. They kept their poſt till evening, without ſeeing any body, when a certain perſon belonging to the *Neyk*'s camp came privately to the *Modlier*, and told him in the *Singaleſe* language (for fear of being underſtood by others) that there was no *Ola* or letter, nor any preſents ſent from the *Neyk*, the whole being only a ſtratagem contriv'd on purpoſe to draw ſome of our forces without the gates into an ambuſh, which they had been diſappointed in, by our forces not ſtirring from the gates, upon which the *Modlier* and captain *Waſh* return'd with their troops into the city, and the *Neyk*'s forces retired back into the countrey. This *Neyk* beſieged *Negapatan* a ſecond time, 1660, in *September*, but the *Dutch* garriſon making a vigorous ſally, in which they kill'd 400 of his men, they came to a compoſition for that time; notwithſtanding which, he appeared before it again in the next following year.

The countrey hereabouts bears ſuch great plenty of rice, that abundance of it is tranſported from hence to other places. But they have great numbers of lewd women and idle fellows here.

Not far from the city is a *Pagode*, with a ſtone ſteeple, call'd *Tzina*, the pinacle of which reaches to the very clouds; the inhabitants believe that it was built by the devil, and that in one night. In the ſuburbs to the north, which are of magnificent houſes, there are likewiſe many *Pagodes* or pagan temples, wherein you ſee many idols of a terrible aſpect, made only of clay. Thus far concerning *Negapatan*. 1662. *The Temple of* Tzina.

From hence we purſued our voyage towards *Paliakatte*, and ſaw the lofty and moſt ancient *Pagode*, call'd *Tyripopeliri*, which ſtands within the precinct of a fort at a little diſtance from the ſea-ſhore, and of which I had the curioſity to take a full view. It is an ancient ſtructure, the front of which is adorned with many ſtatues artificially cut in ſtone. It is ſurrounded by a wall with a gallery on the top of it, over which are placed a great number of large coffins, which reſt upon ſtatues of divers figures, ſome repreſenting a horſe, others ſomewhat elſe. The walls are made of large blue ſtones, which are brought thither a vaſt way out of the countrey, and moſt artfully joined together. The *Indian Pagodes* or temples ſeldom have any light but what comes through a hole in the frontiſpice; notwithſtanding which I ventur'd in, and found ſeveral lamps burning there; by the light of which I aſcended by a pair of ſtairs of wood, to the top of the temple, from thence to take a view of the circumjacent country. But ſcarce was I come to the ſtairs-head, when I ſaw my ſelf in an inſtant ſurrounded by thouſands of bats that were ſtriving to get out thro' the hole in the frontiſpice, ſo that I was glad to get away from this unwelcome company, which, to avoid the brightneſs of the ſun-beams, ſhelter themſelves by day in theſe dark lurking holes. *The temple of* Tyripopeliri.

We ſoon ſet ſail again, and coaſted it along the ſhore, which is flat and ſandy here, till the 15th of *June*, when we arrived at *Paliakatte*, where I delivered our whole cargo of gold and ſilver we had taken in *Perſia*, to the director *Lawrence Pit*. *They come to* Paliakatte.

The *Dutch Eaſt-India* company has a ſtrong fort here, with four baſtions of ſtone work, call'd *Geldria*, of which they have been poſſeſs'd ever ſince the year 1619. Without the caſtle is a plantation or town, which to the land-ſide is defended by an earthen wall, which is but indifferently kept, but the houſes within are very cloſe and well built. It is inhabited partly by *Hollanders*, partly by *Jentives* or pagan natives; the laſt of which live for the moſt part upon trade with painted and white callicoes and linen. The rice which grows in this countrey in great plenty, is as well as all other *The fort of* Geldria.

1662. other sorts of grains brought weekly to market here. The fort is on one side wash'd by a river, which swells very high in the rainy season, when the merchandizes may be unloaden here by the help of lighters. But in the summer season the river being quite dry'd up, the goods are forc'd to be carried ashore on their backs. This river abounds in fish in the winter-time, most of which die in the summer, which makes the inhabitants catch them before that time, and dry them in the sun, and so transport them to other places. The north *Monzon* begins here in *October*, and holds all the *November* and *December*, with such violence, that the ships can scarce ride in the road. In *January* the *Monzon* changes, and the fair season returns.

As to the city of *Paliakatte*, its inhabitants are for the most part *Mestices* and *Kastices*; *Mestices* are such whose parents were married with foreigners; as for instance, when an *Hollander* marries an *Indian* woman, or an *Indian* man a *Dutch* woman; but the children of the *Mestices* are call'd *Kastices*. Thus many of the natives, especially of the *Thioles* have married *Dutch* women, as on the other hand, several *Hollanders* are married to women of the *Thioles*, from whence is come a numerous off-spring of *Mestices* and *Kastices*. Many *Bramans*, *Banyans* and *Panekayers*, or *Thomists* and *Jews* live here, of great traffick; for every month comes hither the *Kaffila* or caravan of *Agra*. The *Banyans* and *Jews* are the chiefest of all the traders here, this city being a place *Golconda*, *Suratte* and *Cambaia* by land; both *Christians* and *Mahometans* bring to this place their merchandizes from the *Red-Sea*, the *Persian Gulph*, from *Suratte*, *Goa*, *Malabar*, *Sumatra* and *Malacca*. There is great plenty of fish at *Paliakatte*, and a neighbouring country furnishes them with all other sorts of provisions.

They leave Paliakatte. After we had dispatch'd our business here, we pursued our voyage towards the great city of *Masulipatnam*, where we were to load wood and other materials for the building of our fort at *Paliakatte*. We set sail the 20th of *July*, and came to an anchor before *Masulipatnam* the 22d, I went ashore the same evening to take care of our loading, which consisted for the most part in timber and other materials for building, besides some callicoes, which took us up till the 14th of *August*, when we were ready to set sail again. In the mean while I had sufficient leisure to take a full view of the city of *Masulipatnam*. It lies near the seashore, upon a branch of the great river *Kisna*, a few leagues from *Negenapatnam*, being surrounded on all sides with water. It is closely built and well peopled, it being the only place of traffick in callicoes, indigo, diamonds, and other precious stones, in the kingdom of *Golconda*. To the land-side, north-west of the city, is a standing pool, over which is built a bridge of 2000 paces long, in the midst of which stands a house for the conveniency of the passengers to repose themselves there. This bridge rests upon very thick posts, which are covered with shells of 12 or 14 feet long, without any leanings on either side. Most of the inhabitants are *Pagans* and merchants. The *Persian Mahometans* have here likewise a mosque built of white stone, after a very antique fashion, in the very center of the city. The houses are all of wood cover'd with pantiles, the king having expresly forbid the building of stone houses, for fear of encouraging his subjects to revolt; who, tho' *Pagans*, wear white callicoe vests and turbants like the *Moors*. They use rice instead of bread, and drink commonly water; they have also great plenty of all sorts of fishes, ducks, geese, and tame and wild fowl. Both the *Dutch* and *English East-India* companies have each a house here, with their respective flags on the top of them. The *Franciscans*, who are all *Portuguese*, have here a Monastery over against the city; on the continent is a village, where the governor has a country-seat, where he diverts himself sometimes.

Arrive at Masulipatnam.

A description of this city.

1662.

Its bridge.

The river Kisna. The river of *Kisna* arises very deep in the countrey, and exonerates itself with one branch about five leagues below the city of *Masulipatnam* into the sea, where it is but shallow, but the other turns to *Masulipatnam*, which is much deeper. This river is not join'd to the city by a bridge, but they pass it in boats; it has plenty of fishes, as likewise crocodiles; it swells sometimes to such a heigth during the rainy season, that you may pass in boats thro' the streets of the city, but in the summer season it is so shallow, that near the city it is scarce four foot deep. About half a league to the west is a champaign countrey, and on the east-side the countrey is planted with palm and syry trees, behind which you may discern the tops of the mountains. We left *Masulipatnam*, and the 29th return'd to *Paliakatte*, where meeting with several sorts of commodities that were wanting at *Batavia*, I made all the haste I could to have the ship loaded; but when we were almost ready to depart, the yacht call'd the *Parroket* arrived in the road, with advice, that the ships *the House of Zwieten*, the *Sea Horse*, the *Exchange*, the *Stadthouse of Amsteldam*, the *Rising Sun*, and the *Encreasing Moon* were at sea, being sent from *Holland* with men and all sorts of ammunition, to assist in the expedition against the coast of *Malabar*.

The Dutch *lay a design against the coast of* Malabar.

2 Misericordia
3 St. Francis
4 St. Thomas

A Mestice Wooman

1662. *labar*. This soon made us alter our measures, every one having received orders to join the said fleet, so that after we had unladen our ships, we set sail the 10th of *September* for *Colombo*, the general rendezvous of our fleet. We stop'd at *Pedro Punto*, where having provided ourselves with fresh water and fuel, we came to an anchor the 7th of *October* before *Colombo*, where we were employed among the rest to take the great train of artillery aboard of us. The commodore *Roodbaes* in the mean while went out before the rest with seven ships only, ordering the rest to follow him to *Manepara*, one of the seven seaport villages on the coast of *Madure*, where all our ships were to meet, which we did accordingly on the 15th of *November*. Mr. *John vander Werf*, Mr. *Symonson*, and myself, were made not only supervisors, but also treasurers of the whole train of artillery: Being provided with every thing requisite for such an expedition, we set sail from thence, and came with the whole fleet the 7th of *December* to an anchor, about two leagues to the south of the city of *Kolang* or *Koulang*. The remaining part of the day was spent in landing our soldiers and other necessaries, and bringing the ships as close as possible could be to the shore. The 8th we march'd in battle array into the country, and the *Negroes* had thrown up a small redoubt within half a league from the city, from whence they fir'd thick upon our yachts, but without any great loss, yet they ply'd us so warmly near the shore, that we were forced to cut our way thro' the woods to attack them from behind. Immediately all our carpenters were set to work to cut down the bushes and trees, whilst the seamen were employed in levelling the grounds to make way for our artillery. After we were advanced a little way into the wood, we came into a small plain, to the left of which, leading to the sea-side, we saw a stone-house, where we halted a little to take breath, because the seamen had been hard put to it, in drawing the cannon thro' the deep sand along the sea-side. The enemy at the same time kept within his strong hold, but as we advanced farther they charged our vanguard, who were order'd to break in upon them; they bravely stood the first brunt, but afterwards retreated again to their fort. In the mean time our cannon having joined us, we prepar'd for a general attack, which was carried on so vigorously, that the *Negroes* deserted the fort, in hopes of saving themselves by flight, but were most of them either kill'd upon the spot or in the flight. A strong party of them happen'd accidentally to fall in with captain *Polmans* company of firelocks, who were sent thro' the woods to attack the fort from behind; here you might have seen them fight like desperate men, the engagement was very terrible considering the number of men on both sides; at last they were overcome with above 100 kill'd and as many wounded on their side; we had no more than three kill'd, but a great many wounded, who were sent aboard the ships to be taken care of. We found two iron pieces of cannon in this fort, which we nail'd up, and beat the carriages in pieces: After we had placed guards in all convenient posts thereabouts, the soldiers reposed themselves under the shadow of trees; but within two hours after we continued our march to the city of *Kolang*, passing all the way by a great many fine plantations, surrounded on all sides with walls, the road betwixt them being very narrow. As we advanc'd to the city, the enemy fired briskly upon us from a small fort near the water-side, where they had set up the *Portuguese* standard, but perceiving us notwithstanding this to march undaunted towards the walls, their hearts began to fail, and betaking themselves to flight, left the city to our mercy, which we took without the least resistance. All the officers and soldiers, each according to their respective qualities, had their quarters and posts assign'd them; we rested the next day, but every one being animated by the last success in taking so considerable a city without opposition, long'd for action, so that before the morning the whole body being put in battle array without the water-gate, the chief minister of the camp, Mr. *Baldeus*, made a short but very fervent speech, and the commanders exhorted them to fight couragiously for the honour of their countrey and religion; which being joyfully accepted by the soldiers, who promised to hazard all for the service of the company, the drums and trumpets began to sound the march. Mr. *Ysbrand Goskeled* commanded the van, and commodore *Roodbaes* the rear, being both persons of known bravery; Mr. *Riiklof van Goens* commanded the main battle; we carried some field pieces along with us to serve us upon occasion. We were forced to march thro' narrow ways, where scarce four could march a-breast, and finding that the enemy gall'd us from an adjacent small fort, some companies wheel'd to the right, and the rest to the left, whilst the seamen undauntedly approach'd with their scaling ladders, and mounting the walls, took the fort with little resistance. We found here no more than two iron pieces of cannon ready charged; notwithstanding all this they skirmish'd briskly with our foremost troops as they were advancing beyond the fort, but gave way by degrees and retreat-

Their fleet meets at Manepara.

Come before Kolang.

Kolang *taken*.

1662. ed to the royal palace, where they made another halt, and engaged our troops a second time, but with no better success; for being once seiz'd with a panick fear, they soon gave ground, and left the place to our mercy, which we plunder'd and destroy'd. They had however in the mean while attack'd our rear several times, because our heavy cannon could not come up soon enough with us, by reason of the narrowness of the way; the enemy making use of this advantage, attack'd us very furiously, but were bravely repuls'd by the help of our field pieces, which being charged with small shot, were discharged among them with such success, that many of them remained dead upon the spot; and by this means we kept them so long in play, till we received a seasonable reinforcement, when they betook themselves to their heels, and left us absolute masters of the field. In the mean while our troops were advanced to the river, where they made themselves masters of another fort, in which they found 2 brass and 10 iron pieces of cannon. In a certain *Pagode* next to the royal palace, call'd *Matta del Reyne*, we found a great chest with gunpowder, which being set on fire, in an instant blew up and destroy'd this antient structure, covered on the top with brass. Then our troops beat the countrey both to the right and left, burning and destroying all they met with. In an instant we saw whole woods in a flame, the *Bambo* canes making a most terrible noise, and burning like brimstone, a miserable spectacle to the enemy, who from the other side of the river, saw the flame consume in an instant, what had cost them many years labour. *John Piccard* my nephew, a captain lieutenant, and *William van Teylingin* were sent with some chaloops up the river *Arwick*, to pursue the flying enemy on that side, but these took another way; most of them wading thro' the river, where they could not come near them with their chaloops. Mr. *Piccard* then landed his company on the other side, where he set 40 houses on fire, which occasion'd a fresh consternation among the flying enemy. After we had thus ravaged the countrey, we return'd to the before-mention'd *Pagode*, where our troops reposed themselves for a while, and the same evening return'd conquerors to the city of *Koulang*. The 12th, all the ships carpenters were sent for ashore to cut down the trees that stood upon the city walls, and orders were given for breaking down part of it, and to bring it into a narrower compass, which was put in execution immediately. About the same time the natives sent some deputies to sue for peace; by what we were inform'd, that at the time of our arrival there were not above 30 true born *Portuguese* in the city, who fled immediately, and that the *Negroes*, who were near 800 strong, having had some notice of our design near 15 days before, had resolved to kill all the *Hollanders* they met with except a few, whom they intended to preserve to send them aboard their gallies, but the scene was altered; in the mean while we continued with breaking down and removing which had almost proved fatal to the ship the *Sea-Horse*, which happened to take fire, and was in great danger of being burnt by the violence of the flame, had not the seamen quenched the fire.

Cruel design of the Negroes.

By this time it being resolv'd to prosecute the career of our victories, the commodore *Roodhaes* with eight ships sail'd towards the city of *Cranganor*, to block up the entrance of that river, the rest being to follow with all convenient speed. The 19th I went on board the commissary *James Borchorst*, with whom I had some earnest business, but scarce was I come thither, but on a sudden there arose such a tempest, that with much ado I could get ashore again, for the wind arose first from the land-side with most violent rains, but soon after chop'd about with such violence, that it tore roots of trees out of the ground, and untiled abundance of houses. By this sudden change of the wind, our whole fleet consisting of thirty ships great and small, were in no small danger of being shipwrack'd. The ship the *Stadthouse* was driven among the rocks, where having lost her rudder, she gave the signal of being in utmost distress, but no body durst venture to bring her off. The ship the *Achilles* was likewise forced from her anchors among the rocks, but by good fortune happened to cast anchor again, not far from the *Stadthouse*. The ship the *Erasmus* was also got adrift, and was in great danger of running upon the shelves; several of our small craft were beaten to pieces by the sea, and many others much endamaged. The ship the *Stadthouse* continued in great distress all that day and night, striking several times against the rocks, but next morning the fury of the tempest being somewhat appeas'd, we sent out some boats to her assistance, which brought both her and the *Achilles* safe from among the rocks into the open sea. So that at last, thro' God's mercy, all our great ships escap'd the danger of this storm without any considerable damage, except what was in their rigging, which however fell most upon the smaller vessels.

The 24th the garrison of the conquered city of *Koulang*, consisting of 663 men, both soldiers and mariners, under the command of captain *Cox*, and *Henry Walling*, being provided

1662. provided with all necessaries, during our intended stay before *Cranganor*, Mr. *Van Goens* set sail the same day with the ships the *Walnut-tree* and the *Ulieland* towards *Cranganor*, commodore *Gotske* being to follow with the rest; we were in the mean while busy with refitting the ship the *Stadthouse*, and I stay'd ashore with Mr. *Gotske* till such time that the gunpowder of the *Stadthouse* and several other ships, which had got wet in the last storm could be dried again; about the same time we were inform'd, that the negroes had receiv'd a good sum of money to fight against us, but when they perceived we were in earnest, they left the *Portuguese* in the lurch, who as we told you before, left the city of *Koulang* the same afternoon, when we landed. The 29th we set sail in the ship the *Exchange* to follow the fleet; by an express sent us from some of the *Malabars*, we were desired to stay till the next day, which we refus'd, it being not our business to tarry here for matters which might well be deferr'd till another time. The next following day we pass'd by *Kalkoulang*, the governor of which came aboard of us, with a present of fresh provisions, which we accepted. The 31 we coasted it along the shore, where we cast our anchor, because one of our yachts approach'd so near to the shore, that we feared she would run herself into danger, which made us detach 20 soldiers in a boat to her relief, if occasion should require. The 1st of *January* 1662, by break of day we found ourselves within a league of the city of *Cochin*, and soon after sail'd so near the shore, that we could hear the centinels speak. We saw five ships lying in the road, the foremost of which carried *English* colours. The same day about noon we came into the road, at the entrance of the river *Palliport*, and the next day having embark'd our men in boats, and our ammunition with two field pieces in another, we landed them without any opposition, except that the enemy discharg'd some of his great cannon against us from *Cranganor*, but without any loss on our side.

The Dutch *land near* Cranganor.

We had posted our forces in three several places, the better to cut off all correspondency betwixt the enemy and the countrey. The next following day we brought two tuns of rice, and two brass guns ashore, and soon after our whole train of artillery, with all other necessaries requisite for such an undertaking. For some time we had kept the place block'd up both on the land and river side, but now we began to open our trenches with such success, that in a short time we carried them on under the cannon of the city, the garrison being all this while not idle on their side, but endeavouring to hinder our approaching by their continual fire out of their cannon and fire-arms, which they did with such dexterity, that they kill'd many of our men in the trenches; among the rest, a certain soldier had his arm and shoulder shot off at once, notwithstanding which, Mr. *Van Goens* order'd him to be dress'd, which the surgeon did accordingly, who told me at the same time, that since he must infallibly die, he would give him something that might ease his pain; I ask'd the poor wretch how he did, he answered me without any alteration in his countenance, *Pretty well, I don't find myself very ill*, tho' he died in a few hours after. Fourteen days after we had carried our trenches to the body of the place, during which we had several smart skirmishes with the enemy, it was resolv'd to venture a general assault; pursuant to this resolution, I was sent with two servants to confer with commodore *Gotske* and Mr. *Roodhaes*, concerning the most convenient place the assault was to be made in. I was sometimes to wade up to the middle in water, and met with captain lieutenant *Piccard*, who had the advanced guards. He forewarn'd me not to approach too near the city, from whence they fir'd without intermission, but I was forc'd to venture at all, being oblig'd to be with the admiral general again the next morning. I went close under the walls of the place, the centinels ask'd me in *Portuguese*, *who was there?* I answered in the same language, *a friend*, and so escap'd the danger. Mr. *Gotske* and *Roodhaes* had been before inform'd concerning the condition of the place by a certain *Negroe*, and where it might be most conveniently assaulted, of which they having given me a circumstantial account, I return'd forthwith, and was with the admiral by next morning, who thereupon resolv'd to assault the city, and as he left me said, *To morrow the city shall be ours*. So soon as every thing was prepar'd for the intended assault, I went on board the fleet to keep a watchful eye over the ships, which were of the utmost consequence to us all.

Consultations about the assaults.

In the mean time our forces mounted the breach, and assaulted the town with great fury under the favour of the smoak of their cannon and fire arms, which by the wind was forced toward the city; I saw from on board the ships the smoak approach nearer and nearer to the place, which I looked upon as a good omen on our side; the enemies defended themselves with a great deal of bravery for a considerable time, but our men pushing on the assault with the utmost vigour, they were at the last forced to give way, and to leave us masters of the city. Mr. *Polman* and *Shuilenburgh*, two of our captains,

1662. captains, were dangerously wounded, 80 common soldiers were killed in the assault, and a great many more wounded. The loss of the enemies side was much greater, 200 *Portuguese* being slain during the action, besides a great number of negroes, who were all thrown into the river, and carried back and forwards several times by the tides, a most terrible spectacle to behold. For we found the taking of this place to be another piece of work than that of *Koulang*, and we were upon the point of sounding the retreat, had not the commanders by their own example animated the soldiers to do their utmost; it being almost surprising how with so small a force we were able to attack and conquer so strong a place as this.

Cranganor *taken by storm.*

Is laid desolate.

After the city was plundered it was laid level with the ground, except one stone tower, which standing upon the river, was preserved entire, and a garrison put into it for the security of the river.

A description of this city.

This city of *Cranganor* (for there is another on the coast of *Malabar*, nearer to the sea shore) lies about four or five leagues to the north of the city of *Cochin*; being the capital city of a kingdom of the same name, bordering to the north upon *Cochin* and to the south upon *Koulang*. It was very famous among the *Indians*, by reason of its antiquity; being situate upon the banks of a river, about a league from the sea shore, defended by a wall of earth, and a stone breast work; which had seven bastions and the wall of earth three more. At the point near the river is remaining to this day a strong stone tower for the defence of the river, which served instead of a bulwark on that side; on the other point was a small fort which commanded the river, and all ships going out or in. Several goodly stone houses were in this city, and among the rest a church, excelling all the rest; on the opposite side of the river, towards the side of *Cochin*, is the redoubt called *Palliport*, built for the better defence of the river; upon a long island called *Baypin* extending to the river of *Gochin*. The royal palace is not far from hence, in a very pleasant countrey; the king then reigning being a prince of great bravery, and well versed in military affairs, in the flower of his age.

The redoubt Palliport.

After the taking of *Cranganor*, it was concluded by the majority of voices to attack likewise the famous city of *Cochin*, not questioning but that the fame of our late victories would open us likewise a way to the conquest of this place, before the enemies of this could recollect themselves from the fear they were in at that juncture. Accordingly we decamped from thence, and set down before *Cochin*, our forces as in the last siege were again posted in three several places, from whence the attacks were to be carried on against the city; Mr. *Isbrand Gotske* had his post assigned him near the sea shore; Mr. *Roodhaes* upon the bank of the river; and the admiral general's quarter was betwixt both. But the garrison of *Cochin* was not so much frightned as we had flattered ourselves, but made a brave resistance. We did all we could to persuade the negroes that we were not come hither with an intention to hurt them, but the *Portuguese*, our enemies; but in vain, for they all appeared in arms against us, and several times attacked us like madmen, throwing themselves in among our ranks, tho' they were sure to die in the attempt, and thrusting themselves upon our swords and pikes, not like men, but rather like wild boars or enraged bears. Not far from the royal palace was a very large *Pagode*, where the negroes had fortified themselves: Our men, notwithstanding their fury, attacked them in this advantageous post with so undaunted a courage, that they chased them from thence with the loss of 400 negroes, and many more wounded. The old queen would fain have hid herself in a corner on the top of the *Pagode*, but was found out, and brought a prisoner by captain *Henry Rēde* into our camp. But after we had spent near two months in the siege, the waters beginning to rise more and more every day, which filled up our trenches to the middle, and our forces by the several losses we had sustained in divers engagements and attacks, and thro' the garrisons we had been obliged to put in the conquered places, being considerably diminished in number, it was thought most expedient to raise the siege for this time, and to return with a greater force against next spring. Accordingly we decamped without any noise, and in one night got all our men, artillery, and ammunition aboard, without being perceived by the enemy, who were not sensible of our departure till next day about noon, as looking upon our motion only as a feint to draw them out of the town into an ambush. But when they found how matters stood, they discharged all their cannon round the walls, unto which we gave no answer for that time, but delayed it till a more convenient opportunity. The next thing the enemy had to do was to slight our works and trenches, which they did immediately, and to cut down all trees and edifices which they had found to be an obstacle to them during the siege, they also took effectual care to have their fortifications repaired and strengthned, as not questioning but that we should give them another visit with the next fair opportunity, in which they found themselves not deceived. 1626.

Cochin *besieged.*

The siege raised.

After

1662. After the raising of the siege of *Cochin*. our land forces and ships were ordered to such places where their presence was judged to be most necessary at the present juncture, Mr. *Ysbrand Gotske* failed with a squadron of ships to *Batavia*, and the rest steered their course to other places thereabouts; I went aboard the ship the *Exchange*, and passed by the city of *Kalkoulang* in my way to *Koulang*, where I was appointed chief director of the company: At the same time it was thought convenient to strengthen the fortifications of *Kalkoulang*, and to put a good garrison into it under captain *Polman* and several other commanders, till we could dispose our forces in more convenient quarters.

The author comes to Koulang.

I arrived at *Koulang* the 7th of *January*, where I gave immediate orders for the repairing the castle, and such houses as belonged to those that were in the company's service; and settling every thing that might tend to the re-establishment of traffick with the queen of *Koulang*, and other neighbouring princes, unto whom I was sent as a deputy, to treat with them concerning the most convenient methods, and to enter into a confederacy with them for that purpose.

Treaty with the queen of Koulang.

The first treaty that was set on foot after the taking of the city *Kalkoulang*, was with the queen of *Koulang*, which was soon concluded upon these conditions; that her palace and great guns should be restored to her, for the rebuilding of which, and other damages sustained, she was to have a certain sum of money to be paid her by the company, whose interest it was, rather to purchase a peace upon reasonable terms, than be at the charge of a war.

A description of Koulang.

The city of *Kolang*, or *Koulang*, or *Koulon* and *Koylang*, the capital of a kingdom bearing the same name, is situate upon the sea shore of the coast of *Malabar*, under 9 deg. of norrhern latitude, about 13 *French* leagues (*Linshot* says 24) to the south of *Cochin*. It is fortified with a stone wall of 18 or 20 foot high, and 8 bastions; its suburbs which are very large and stately, are by the *Portuguese* called *Colang China*. For *Koulang* is separated into two bodies, one of which is called the *Upper* or *Malabar Koulang*, the other the *Lower Koulang*; in the first the king and queen kept their ordinary residences; the last was formerly in the possession of the *Portuguese*, as lying nearer to the sea side; here the fryars of *St. Paul* and the *Franciscans* had each a monastery, adorned with stately chappels and steeples. Besides which there were four other *Portuguese* churches here, dedicated to as many *Romish* saints; they had no less than seven goodly churches, among which was the famous church built many ages ago by the Christians of *St. Thomas*, which was 1662. left standing, after we reduc'd the place into a narrower compass; in this church is the tomb of a certain great *Portuguese* captain, who was governor of *Koulang* 60 years. The houses of the inhabitants were very stately and lofty built of freestone; among which the stadthouse surpass'd all the rest; it was two stories high, and had very curious stone steps on each side. But the castle, the residence of the *Portuguese* governor, surmounted all the rest in magnificence; this I took up for our own lodgings, it lies very near the sea-side, at one end of the city, being cover'd on the top with coco-leaves, as likewise two of its turrets, the third being tiled with pan-tiles. Just upon the sea-shore is another four-square tower, where I set up the company's flag on the top of a mast. In the midst of it is a very lofty edifice, which the *Portuguese* used for a chapel, which I order'd to be made up into divers convenient chambers, and to be fitted for the use of the company's officers. This castle is the strongest the *Portuguese* ever were masters of on the coast of *Malabar*, being built some hundred years ago, by the famous engineer *Hector de la Casa*.

This city, as I told you before, was drawn into a less compass by the *Dutch*, which they fortified on the land-side with two half and one whole bastion. Most of the churches and other publick edifices were pull'd down, except the castle, *St. Thomas's* church, and some monasteries, which remain'd standing within the said precinct. Behind most of the houses here are very pleasant gardens, planted with *Cocoa*, *Mangoes* and other *Indian* fruit trees; and about the city you see very fine basins cut out of the rocks, unto which you ascend by steps. They have also some ponds with fresh water, their water being else for the most part brackish and full of salt-peter. The air is very wholesome in this countrey, which is low and full of rivers, which afford a convenient passage from hence to *Kalkoulang*, *Cochin* and *Cranganor*; and is accounted the best both for fruitfulness and its pleasant situation in all the *Indies*. This part of the countrey affords abundance of pepper, which twists itself round the trees; the fruit is gather'd in *January* and *February*. The harbour is very convenient for small vessels, but not for great ones, because the south wind blows directly upon the shore, and forces the waves with great violence thither; they call it *Coydanel*. Near the sea-side you see great store of stone-like rocks, but they lie loose upon the sand, and are frequently wash'd away by the sea. About a league to the west of *Koulang*, the great river *Eguick* disembogues into the sea.

The

1662.

The *Dutch* were once before masters of the city of *Koulang*, till the *Negroes* took the opportunity of murthering captain *Henry Glunning* their governor there, as he was taking a walk without the gates, and afterwards massacred all the *Dutch*; since which time the *Portuguese* got into possession of it. On the side of *Koulang China*, along the sea-shore, the jesuits had built a great village for the *Parvees*, a poor sort of *Malabars* living upon fishing, where the governor of the king of *Travankor* and Prince *Baryette Poele* kept their residence, which are about a mile in circuit, and surrounded with an earth wall, with some points like bastions, on which are mounted good store of great cannon, which command the roads, without which there is scarce any access to them. If we may believe the *Malabars*, the *Maldive* islands, which lie about 60 leagues deep in the sea, just over-against the palace, were formerly part of the continent and torn from thence by the sea; and as a confirmation of their opinion, shew certain rocks betwixt the shore and these islands, upon which they assure us stood at that time a goodly church. The best houses are built along the river-side, with very good gardens, stock'd with all sorts of trees, fruits, flowers and herbs, but especially with citrons, which grow here not on trees, but shrubs; their houses are seldom above two stories high, their stairs within of stone, their rooms above stairs are pav'd with green and yellow four square stones, the ceiling of which is commonly of *Indian* oak, some being finely carved, others painted. They commonly have an arbour or summer-house belonging to each garden, which is commonly near the river-side, where they spend generally their evenings, and divert themselves with angling.

The river Kalchan.

The mouth of the river *Kalchan* or *Mangal*, or *Mangar*, upon which this place is built, is a very large bay, where yachts of 300 tuns may come close to the shore and unload, being 28 feet deep at high water; but of very difficult entrance, if the winds be not favourable, because they blow the waves directly upon the shore. In the midst of this bay you see three vast rocks laying all together in a ridge. During the rainy season this river frequently overflows the neighbouring countrey, and carries away a great deal of the adjacent grounds; these violent rains are occasion'd by the clouds, which gathering among the tops of the mountains, break out into sudden storms and tempests. The countrey is flat and marshy hereabouts, and the air not altogether so wholesome as at *Koulang*.

By this time the season for action drawing near, and every thing being prepar'd for a vigorous expedition, the siege of *Cochin* was resolv'd upon the second time; for which purpose Mr. *Jacob Hustart*, one of the member's of the great council of *India*, with captain *Peter de Pon* and *Henry Van Rode* set sail the 25th of *October* 1662, with 12 ships from *Batavia*, Mr. *Van Goens* being ordered to follow with three more, with all imaginable speed. No sooner had they landed their men, but they began to form their attacks, notwithstanding they found the place much strengthen'd by some additional fortifications, since the last siege, and put them so to it, that the besieged being enclosed on all sides, and beyond all hopes of relief, were forced to capitulate, and to surrender the city, after a siege of three months; after the *Portuguese* had (with the consent of the king of *Cochin*) been in possession of it above 150 years. The *Portuguese* had not long before forc'd *Momadavil*, the lawful king of *Cochin* to leave the city, in whose stead they had set up an aunt of his of the house of *Godarme*; but whilst our forces lay before *Cochin* the dethron'd king stay'd with me at *Koulang*, in order to his solemn coronation after the taking of the place. I had taken all imaginable care to have his room hung with tapestry, and furnish'd with other moveables, the best the place afford; he came often to visit us, being commonly clad in white callicoe, with his hair tied in a knot on the top of his head, rings on his fingers, and a gold chain hanging down before him. He spoke the *Portuguese* and *Malabar* tongues, and was of a pleasant conversation. But scarce a few days were pass'd, when finding himself not very well, he desired to go to the Queen of of *Koulang* for his diversion; which I was very unwilling to grant, being sensible that his person being committed to my care, I might be call'd to an account by his subjects, who much esteem'd him, if any sinister accident should befal him; but at his reiterated instances, and the earnest request of the queen of *Koulang*, who was an excellent good natur'd person, and engag'd her word to bear me harmless, I conducted him thither; but he found no considerable alteration in his health, for when not long after a yacht was sent to *Koulang* on purpose to fetch this prince to the camp before *Cochin*; he was so very weak, that he would fain have avoided going thither, but there being positive orders given for his coming, I sent him my *Palukin* or letter, and conducted him with some of our officers aboard, but before he could reach *Cochin*, his sickness encreased to that degree, as to put an end to his life. His brother

1662.

Siege of Cochin.

Is surrender'd.

Momadavil *king of* Cochin.

Dies aboard.

Is succeeded by his brother.

Betwixt p. 220. 221. V. II.

1662. ther, who was aboard the same yacht, being the next heir to the crown, was, after, the taking of the city, crowned king of *Cochin*, by the *Dutch*, his crown, which was of gold, having the cypher of the *East-India* company, engraven on one side. He kept his residence not far from *Cochin*, in a place situate in a very pleasant countrey, call'd by the *Dutch Malabar Cochin*, had his guards, musicians, and all other things belonging to a royal court, a cording to the custom of that countrey.

The city of Cochin. The city of *Cochin*, by the *Portuguese* call'd *Cochin*, and generally *Kakochin*, is the capital of a kingdom of the same name, and indeed of the whole coast of *Malabar*. It is situate under 10 deg. of northern latitude, 4 or 5 leagues to the south of *Koulang*, extending along the bank of the great river *Koulang* or *Kolchan*, or *Mangat* or *Mangar*. Some authors make mention of two different *Cochins*, *viz.* the *Old Cochin*, lying about a league and a half from the sea-shore; the *Portuguese* call it *Cochin Dacima*, or *Arabia*, *i. e.* the *Higher Cochin*, because it lies higher up the river; by the *Dutch* it is call'd the *Malabar Cochin*, where the king keeps his residence; being situate upon the banks of a river, and pretty well peopled, and adorn'd with several goodly structures and *Pagodes*, according to the custom of the *Malabars*. The other *Cochin*, call'd commonly the *New Cochin*, is scarce a league distant from the sea, just at the entrance of the same river; it was for many years together in the possession of the *Portuguese*, who had fortified it with a stone wall, and several bulwarks, and beautified it with several fine edifices, churches and monasteries. In the suburbs towards the land-side were several goodly churches, and a little nearer to the sea-shore the monastery of *St. John*. Here the *Austin Fryers*, *Franciscans* and *Jesuits* had likewise their several convents, all magnificently built, with very pleasant gardens and walks, the place being inhabited only by *Portuguese*. But since this city was conquer'd by the *Dutch*, the greatest part of it was laid desolate, and the rest fortified with regular stone, bastions, curtines and a very broad ditch, so that it is now look'd upon as impregnable. Among other steeples, that of *St. Paul* being magnificently built of square stones, exceeded all the rest as well in height as beauty, which is since demolish'd with all the other churches, except one, where divine service is exercised according to the tenets of the reform'd religion. The houses here are cover'd with tiles of about the breadth of a hand, and are fastned to the laths by small hooks. Some make their windows only of a kind of lettice-work, others of canes very artificially twisted together; others make use of large shells in which the pearls grow, these they shave and flatten, and make windows of them, as we do of glass. 1662.

After we thus had made our selves masters of the greatest part of the *Malabar* coast, and had taken all imaginable care, to re-establish the commerce in those parts, it was judg'd necessary for the better obtaining of this end, to enter into strict alliances with the kings and princes of the adjacent countries; for which purpose Mr. *James Hustart*, chief councellor of the *Indies*, of *Ceylon* and the *Malabar* coast, having sent me the necessary instructions and credentials, I provided my self with all things requisite for such a journey, and the 21st of *January* 1664, embark'd aboard a small vessel, with one serjeant, several soldiers, an interpreter, and divers mariners, which carried us up the river, as far as to the city of *Kalkolang*, where we arriv'd safely the next day. So soon as I had provided my self with a convenient lodging, I gave notice of my arrival, by our interpreter to the king, who soon after returned in company of a *Residoor* from the king, to fetch me to court. Accordingly I and Mr. *Willing*, who resided there in the quality of under factor of the *East-India* company, were introduced by the said *Residoor* into the kings presence, whom we found surrounded with a good number of courtiers, that constantly attend his person. After the first ceremonies and compliments, such as are usual in this place, were passed, I surrender'd my credentials to the king, who received them with a great deal of respect and seeming satisfaction. After he had perused them, he gave orders to one of his *Residoors*, one of his chief favourites to treat with me concerning such points as I should propose to him, tending to the maintaining of a good correspondence betwixt us and them, and to make his report to him. This prince had the character of a very sincere person, which appeared both in his countenance and actions; but leaves the chief management of all affairs of moment, to the beforemention'd *Residoor*, who knows how to make his advantage of it. After I had treated with the *Residoor*, as far as my commission would give me leave, I desired to be dismiss'd, under pretence of fetching new instructions, which being granted, I took leave of the king, and with Mr. *Willing* pursu'd my journey to *Porka*, whither I had sent a serjeant with six soldiers before. But at our arrival there, being inform'd that the king of *Porka* was ten days before gone to his palace call'd *Kudda Malair* or *Koramallur*, or *Koromallo*, about ten leagues distance from hence, I resolv'd

The author sent to treat with divers Malabar *Princes.*

His audience of the King of Kalkolang.

Departs from thence to Porka.

1662. resolv'd to go thither. We were forced to go by water through several channels and rivers, the countrey thereabouts being full of both, like the province of *Holland*, which affords scarce any passage by land, but by the dikes, all the rest being rice fields, curiously planted with trees on all sides.

We were forc'd to have our *Mansiool* (vessel) drawn through a narrow sluce, which open'd us the passage into a large lake, which to the north is about two leagues broad; from thence we enter'd into a channel of about a league in length, its entrance is somewhat narrow and so full of flags, that there was scarce room enough to manage our oars. At the end of this channel you see very pleasant rice-fields, which extend to the foot of the mountain, and are stock'd with prodigious quantities of wild and water fouls. The inhabitants hereabouts have a certain way to drain their fields, which makes them bear rice all the year round; so that whilst they are sowing and planting in one field, in another the rice is half ripe, and in another its come to its full maturity, which renders this countrey both very fruitful and populous. The mountains produce some pepper, but in no great quantity. This part betwixt the channel and the mountains is water'd by a very fair and large river, beautified on both sides with many fair houses, gardens and trees, which afford a very agreeable spectacle to those that pass by that way, the houses being all built among small groves. After we had spent several hours in coming up the river, we in the afternoon cast anchor before the court of the king of *Porka*, situate upon the right side of the said river, near a village inhabited by christians of *St. Thomas*, who enjoy great privileges here. As we were passing up the river, not far from the court, we saw a large crocodile sunning himself upon the the sandy bank; I order'd our soldiers to fire at him, which they did, but he escaped under water. This creature was used to set upon the people as they pass'd by that way, and consequently much dreaded by them. The king of *Porka* was at this time rebuilding his palace, in which they say he had already bestow'd 20 years; it was but an odd old fashion'd piece of structure, surrounded with walls of earth and a dry ditch; I sent our interpreter to notify our arrival, and to provide us a lodging, who being return'd, we scarce had set a foot ashore, but the chief *Residoor* of the king came to conduct us to court, where he introduced us into his presence. After the usual compliments I deliver'd him my credentials, which he receiv'd with extraordinary marks of respect, ordering the *Residoor* to entertain me till he had read and consider'd of them. In a little while after he return'd with some of his attendants into the same apartment, where he ask'd me whether I had any other commission to treat with him, and I answering that I had, he declared to me, that his inclications had been always for us, even whilst we appear'd in arms on that coast, though at the same time he was not insensible, that some had endeavour'd to persuade us to the contrary, but that time and opportunity should discover the good sentiments he had for us. He told us farther, that he had caused the flags of the *English* and some other nations to be taken down, and the *Dutch* flag to be set up, for which they threaten'd him with an open war, in his own territories, and refused to quit the countrey, which made them to be look'd upon but with a very indifferent eye by all the neighbouring princes. Having afterwards given him a farther account of the occasion of my coming, he told me that he should be very glad now he was convinc'd of the intentions of the company, which were agreeable to his, to speak with Mr. *Hustart* himself: I return'd for answer, that the company was sensible of his favourable sentiments to them, and had always put a great value upon his person, inviting him at the same time to *Cochin*, to visit Mr. *Hustart*, the last of which he modestly declined, alledging that for several reasons he could not come to *Cochin*, but that if Mr. *Hustart* would come either to *Porka*, or any other place under his jurisdiction, he should be very ready to treat with him concerning such matters as tended to their mutual advantage. The king farther ask'd me, whether I desir'd an account of my negotiation in writing, which I having accepted of, he said it should be sent to my lodgings, and at my departure conducted me in person to the door of his apartment, from whence the *Residoor* carried me to his lodgings, and treated us with all sorts of refreshments, a very welcome entertainment to some of my attendants, who had not met with the like since the beginning of our journey. Towards the evening the *Residoor* brought me the writings, with whom whilst we were taking a view of the court, I had abundance of discourse concerning the intended treaty.

His audience of the king of Porka.

Palace of the king of Porka.

This palace of the king is a four square structure of about 40 paces in the square, in the midst of which is a court, about which the apartments (of which there is a great number) are built; they are all four square, their chief ornaments within being the carving of leaves and other work in all sorts of fine wood; in some of these lodgings you see fine cisterns for the conveniency of bathing; you ascend to them by

1662. by certain broad stone steps, like our grave-stones. In one of these lodgings is a very large bason, surrounded with such stones, which are about 20 feet broad, and a foot and a half thick, which have been brought thither with incredible pains and charges, a great way out of the countrey. The palace it self is cover'd with small tiles of a hand broad, the windows being made either of twisted canes or hells, which transmits the light.

After my return from thence to *Koulang*, I went farther to *Cochin*, to give a verbal account of my transactions to Mr. *Hustart*, who thereupon order'd me to go once more to the court of the king of *Porka*, in order to set matters there upon a sure foundation; accordingly I set out the 3^d^ of *February*, with some of my former attendants from *Cochin* to the king of *Porka*'s court, where within an hour after giving notice of my arrival, one of the king's *Residoors* came to introduce me to the king; whom that time I found in a most magnificent array, (after the *Malabar* fashion) in the midst of his courtiers. After the usual respect paid, I deliver'd to him my credentials, which he having received, he order'd all his attendants and my interpreter among the rest to withdraw, because he had a mind to discourse with me alone in *Portuguese*, which he understood very well. I told him that I was sent on purpose by my masters to his majesty, to assure him of their friendship, and to pay the money stipulated by the last treaty, which sum, though it much exceeded the value of the thing receiv'd, yet notwithstanding all this my masters had thought fit not to recede from what had been promised in their name. The king gave for answer, that it never had been a custom to weigh the pepper at *Cochin*, (which I had desired should be done) and that therefore he hop'd the company would not introduce any novelties in his territories; assuring us withal, that he would be ready to assist the company and their officers upon all occasions, besides several other assurances too tedious to be inserted here. I soon understood his meaning, to wit, that he would not have the pepper trade transferr'd to *Cochin*, which was a matter of no great consequence, so I did not insist any longer upon it, but agreed, that the pepper should be receiv'd and weigh'd at *Porka*; assuring him, that the company had never had the least intention to impair any body's right, as his majesty might easily be convinc'd as well by this as several other transactions and treaties made lately with other kings and princes. The king appeared to be highly satisfied thereat, desiring that a factor might be sent thither forthwith, to buy and receive the pepper; which I having promised to the king, he order'd the *Residoor* to receive the money, and granted me leave to depart.

The author goes a second time to the court of Porka.

Has audience.

Departs from thence.

The next following day, just as I was ready to depart, a *Residoor* come to my lodgings, which was an old chapel, and presented me, from the king, with several refreshments, according to the custom of the countrey, and knowing this *Residoor* to be a person in great esteem with the king, I requested his favour in behalf of the company, which he promised to do.

The king of Porka *and government.*

The king then reigning at *Porka* was a person of 30 years of age, very stately and well made. He was adorn'd with many jewels of diamonds and rubies, which he wore on his hands, arms and ears, according to the *Malabar* fashion. He is a most absolute prince, acknowledging no superior, every foot of the country being his own, and at his disposal. Justice is administred here with extraordinary severity, especially on the account of theft, which makes this crime scarce ever to be heard of here, of which I saw the following instance myself; whilst I was paying the money to the beforemention'd *Residoor*, I was call'd away to the king, and seeing above 50 persons in the same room, I charg'd one of my attendants to take care of the money; the *Residoor* having taken notice of it, laugh'd heartily, and told me, *You need not give yourself that trouble, no body will dare to touch the money, tho' it was untold and unguarded, for we know scarce what thieves are*, which surpriz'd me not a little, knowing that the *Malabars* in general are the errantest thieves in nature.

Theft unknown in Porka.

The kingdom of Porka.

The kingdom of *Porka* or *Porkah*, otherwise *Perkatti*, has borrow'd its name from its capital city; it borders to the north upon the kingdom of *Cochin*, to the south upon that of *Kalkoulang*, it has *Takken Berkenker* to the north-east, and the sea to the west, being about 12 leagues in length; its capital city is *Porka* or *Porkah*. Another of the chief cities is *Koramallur* or *Koromallo*, situate upon the same river with the cities of *Cochin* and *Koulang*. The kings of *Porka* were in antient times great idolaters, who worship'd at least 900 idols, unto each of which daily sacrifices were offer'd, and visits made them about six or seven a clock in the morning till twelve at noon. It was not till the year 1590, that the *Romish* religion was openly profess'd here with consent of the king. Tho' many years before, the Christians call'd of *St. Thomas* liv'd in these parts. This king granted considerable privileges to the jesuites; such as the building of churches with crosses on the top of them, and the necessary bells, near unto which no

Pagodes,

1662. *Pagodes, Jewish* synagogues, or *Mahometan* mosques were to be erected; they had also liberty to baptize as many as were willing to embrace the christian religion, all which was punctually observ'd. The king of *Porka* who reign'd 1599, was call'd *Nambrale* or *Numbrane*, which implies as much as the high priest in the *Malabar* tongue. In the year 1640, one *Siam Baatshery Vaubaar* reigned over *Porka*. They claim a superiority over the king of *Cochin*, against whom they waged heavy wars in former ages; but now adays the kings of *Porka* are under the jurisdiction of the *Dutch East-India* company, being forc'd thereunto by their victorious arms; the chief strength of the king of *Porka* consists in his small frigates, of which he has 500, and are made use of, when the fields are overflown with water; formerly the *Portuguese* were masters of the pepper trade here, with the king's consent; but finding that they intended to fortify themselves in several places, he engaged in a war against them, which lasted three whole years. The *Dutch* never came to *Porka* till 1642, under the reign of *Siam Baatshery Vaubaar*, being then not above 24 years old; they were very kindly receiv'd by him, a treaty being concluded betwixt them at that time, by which the *Dutch* had the pepper trade granted to them. This part of the countrey is very fruitful, but unwholesome, most of the inhabitants being afflicted with thick swell'd legs, occasioned by the drinking of brackish water; blindness is also a common distemper here, which by some is ascrib'd to their feeding so much upon hot rice. Most of the inhabitants live by husbandry, tho' during the rainy season, most of the rice fields hereabouts, as well as all along from the cape *Comarin*, as far as *Pokare Biarbar*, lay under water. This countrey produces also a considerable quantity of pepper yearly, which is for the most part bought up by the *English*, who have had a factory here many years ago. Deeper into the countrey live abundance of christians, who were formerly converted by the *Portuguese*, these buy up the pepper in the countrey, which they are oblig'd to deliver to a certain merchant, appointed for that purpose by the king.

The author goes to Marten.

From hence we went to the king of *Marta* or *Marten*, the capital city of the same name, three leagues to the south of *Cochin* upon the same river. I and Mr. *George Henry Willeng*, under factor of *Koulang*, got on horseback early in the morning, and arriv'd at 10 a clock before noon at *Carnopoly*, where we took up our lodgings in a house near the river side, which the *Dutch East-India* company some years before had purchased from the king. It is pretty large, but not very convenient, being built according to the *Malabar* fashion, with abundance of corners and inlets oddly contriv'd: The gardens are well planted with palm-trees, for the use of the house. I had no sooner given notice of my arrival, but I was sent for to the king. After the usual compliments to be paid to the *Malabar* kings, I deliver'd the following *Ola* (letter) from Mr. *Husta t* to the king. 1662.

James Hustart *councellor of the* Indies, *governor and director of the isle of* Ceylon, *and the* Malabar *coasts, sends his* Ola *to the king of* Marten.

Illustrious prince,

Admiral Hustart's *letter to the king*

Nothing could be more welcome to me, than to understand at my first arrival in these parts, that your majesty had always liv'd in a good correspondency with our company. To shew your majesty what an extraordinary value we set upon your friendship, we have sent Mr. John Nieuhoff *captain of* Koulang, *in order to enter with you into a more strict league and friendship. We hope your majesty will give him entire credit, in what he shall propose to you, which I shall be ready to acknowledge upon the like occasions.*

God preserve and give your majesty a long and a happy life.

Cochin
2 Feb. 1664. James Hustart.

After which I gave the king a more particular account of my commission, unto which he answer'd, that he would consider of it till the next day; accordingly I was sent for at the appointed time, when I found the king surrounded with a great number of his courtiers, and among the rest some mahometan merchants; he order'd immediately two of them, and one of his captains, who was in great esteem with him, to treat with me concerning the propositions made on behalf of the company; but as I was sufficiently inform'd that most of the mahometan merchants here drove considerable traffick to *Cananor*, to the no small prejudice of our company, I did not think fit to treat with them, if possible I could avoid it, which made me to tell the king, that *I had no commission to treat with the mahometan merchants, but with his majesty; that the company at present offer'd peace to the whole coast of* Malabar, *in which, if his majesty was desirous to be included, and to enjoy the benefit of a flourishing trade, he might himself treat with me, but if not, grant me leave to depart.* The king after a little pausing, desired that my propositions might be drawn up in writing, which I did accordingly: Our demands were,

To

1662.

To forbid the importation of amsion, the peeling of the wild cinamome, and the exportation of pepper.

These propositions the king order'd to be read aloud in our presence, which the mahometan merchants endeavour'd to oppose with all their might; and the greatest part of the day being spent in messages betwixt the king and us, by the *Residoors*, who gave an exact account of all what pass'd to the king, he gave leave for us to return to our lodgings, and order'd us to attend him again the next day. But early in the morning a certain person of quality, who bears the second rank in that kingdom, came along with the before-mention'd captain, to tell us, that what we desired, was absolutely to the prejudice of the king and kingdom, which I endeavour'd to put out of their heads, by telling them, that we were come with no other intention, than to establish a free commerce with them, as we had done with most of the other *Malabar* kings and princes before, and which would turn to their great advantage; notwithstanding this they were for making several alterations in each point, and five or six messages pass'd betwixt the court and us; at last they ask'd what quantity of pepper we desired yearly? We answer'd them, that it was no matter about the quantity, since we were for buying all. This point was vigorously opposed by the mahometan merchants, who fain would have persuaded the king to reserve part of it for them; but by degrees we overcame all these difficulties, the king having granted us all we demanded, except the peeling of the wild cinnamome, which we did not so much insist upon, being a thing uncertain whether it would quit the cost to the undertakers or not, because it was in the kings power to set what price he pleased upon it.

The kingdom of Marten

The kingdom of *Marta* or *Marten* is very near as big as that of *Kalkolang*, extending to the north as far as *Porka*; to the south it borders upon the *Indian* sea, and to the east it is surrounded by high mountains, and wash'd by the same river, upon which *Cochin* and *Koulang* lie: The capital city is likewise call'd *Marta* or *Marten*. But to the south near the sea-shore is another city call'd by the inhabitants *Panderatoutte*, and *Pesse* by the *Portuguese*; here we built a house by the king's consent, for the conveniency of the pepper trade, which is always weigh'd here. There is another city belonging to this kingdom call'd *Podiogabo* or *Maulikara*. This king possesses some parts of the countrey in common with the king of *Kalkolang*, a thing not usual on this coast, where are so many petty kingdoms, that it requires no small time, to distinguish and know them from on another. The country is well peopled here, abounding in pepper, pease and beans, and the fields near the river-side in rice and salt-pits. The king is a soveraign prince; he that then reign'd being of about 60 years of age, very large of body and a stern countenance; upon his head he wears a bonnet of scarlet cloth lined with callicoe; he keeps constantly 1200 negroes in pay; his residence is at *Carnapoly*, a place surrounded with an earthen wall of 20 foot high, but appeared much decay'd at that time. This kingdom has long ago been inhabited by christians, which however were forced to live there 12 whole years without a church, *viz.* till the year 1581, when the king then reigning, not only gave them liberty to build a church, but also to cut wood in the adjacent forests dedicated to the pagan idols. He also gave permission to his subjects to turn christians, and the jesuits had full power granted them to exercise the church censure, and to inflict it upon those that were baptiz'd by them. The said church was dedicated to St. *Andrew*, because it was finish'd upon that saints day. 1662.

Upon the banks of the same river, where the kingdom of *Marten* lies, is also the kingdom of *Batyma*, with its city call'd *Katyapery*. It is commonly reported in these parts, that the kings of *Batyma* made a law, by which a man was impower'd to kill any woman that should refuse him a kindness.

By this time our negotiation being brought to an entire conclusion, I offer'd the usual presents to the king, which he order'd to be taken by him who bears the second rank in the kingdom, who as well as several others of his courtiers having been very instrumental in promoting the treaty, we thought fit to engage to our party by some small presents. At last we were appointed to attend before the court in the open air, where the king first, and I afterwards sign'd the treaty with our own hands, in the presence of a great multitude of people, that were flock'd thither on purpose to be spectators of this ceremony. This done I took my leave of the king and his chief courtiers, and the same evening went aboard our vessel, which about a league from thence did ride at anchor in the river. A certain lord commanding over the countrey here, a vassal of the king of *Marten*, came on purpose to meet and compliment us and presented us with some fowls, *Pysang* and other refreshments, of whom I likewise took my leave and return'd to *Koulang*, where I arriv'd the 9th of *February*,

The author leaves Marten.

Returns to Koulang.

Whilst I was negotiating with the king of

1662.

of *Porka*, the king of *Kalkolang* sent for me to his court, where he presented me with a very fine *Brocado* silk gown, made according to the *Indian* fashon, testifying his joy for the good success we had had in our negotiation with his neighbour; I return'd my hearty thanks to the king for this and other favours I had receiv'd at his hands, and went back again to the king of *Porka*.

Is presented by the king of Kalkolang.

But to return to *Koulang*; no sooner was I arrived the 9th of *Feb.* at *Koulang* but the queen of the same name, sent the next day her chief captain to receive the customs and cannon she pretended to be due to her by virtue of the late treaty; I was willing to surrender the cannon, according to our agreement, but could not consent to the other; and in the mean while we were preparing our *Mansio* (vessel) for a voyage to the king of *Travankoor*'s court, the *Residoors* of the king of *Goenree* and *Bariiette Pule* desir'd an interview with me, whom I gave a meeting accordingly in company of Mr. *Cher de Venne*, book-keeper of the *Dutch East-India* company. We saw above 300 negroes all in a body, who with one voice cry'd out for the customs, which made me, after many debates and disputes, tell them, that I would go home, with an intention to return the next day to them, provided they would desist from these things, that were not granted them by the treaty, nor were ever likely to be granted, and so return'd to *Koulang*.

The 12th of *February*, I embark'd at nine a clock in the evening for *Attingen*, where the king of *Travankoor* kept his residence then, being come thither some days before. With break of day we found our selves near the village of *Mappul*, about five leagues to the east of *Koulang*, but not daring to approach the shore with our vessel, we were forced to hire an *Indian* boat, which carried us safely ashore, notwithstanding the violence of the waves that rowled against the shore. We travell'd for about a league along the sea-side, till we came to a large river, which carried us in three hours rowing to the court; here we understood that the king was just then ready to go to *Kalkolang*, I gave immediate notice of my arrival to his majesty, who sent for me by one of his *Residoors*; he met us on the stairs-head, with many of his courtiers; where I presented him with the usual respect, the letter, with some presents, which he receiv'd and caused the letter to be read aloud before all there present, telling me, that he would forthwith let me know his intention, and that in the mean while I might take a walk into the garden of the castle, with some of his *Residoors*; and discourse with them farther in a certain grove, which he pointed at with his fingers. Accordingly I begun to talk more at large, concerning my propositions, with the four *Residoors*, who were for treating with me immediately upon the subject in hand, which I told them I had no orders to do, my business being to treat with the king in person. They having given the king an account of what I said, brought me word, that his majesty, in a matter of such consequence could not take a resolution till next day, desiring me to have patience till then, and presented us with *Pysang* and some other refreshments. On the western-side of the palace is a pleasant house at the foot of a hill, in the midst of a very pleasant grove, from whence there is a prospect into a very fruitful valley full of rice-fields, hedg'd in with palm-trees, this place was assign'd us for our lodgings, our host appearing to be a very honest man, but so mistrustful withal, that when we were going to supper, he refused to let us have dishes or any other utensils; their soldiers being exasperated at this usage, the whole house began to be in an alarum, and I enquiring the reason, could get no other answer from him, than *That the devil and his ill fortune ow'd him a shame, when they brought such lodgers into his house*, desiring us at the same time to look out for another lodging. With much ado I persuaded him, that we were no such fellows as he imagin'd us to be, and so at last with the help of a little money, he let us have what we had occasion for.

Goes to Attingen.

The next day, being the 14th of *Feb.* about eight a clock in the morning the king sent for me to court again by a negro, where we met the before-mention'd four *Residoors* at the gate, ready to receive us, we went together into the garden, where I caused a carpet to be spread under the shadow of some trees, as they did their *Indian* mats; and being seated, the chiefest of the *Residoors* told me, *That his majesty was not a little dissatisfied at our burning the royal palace of* Koulang, *and that he had given him orders to treat of that as well as the other subject with me. That the letter sent to admiral* Hustart *had been written with no other intention, than to treat concerning the pretensions of prince* Gondormo, *and that therefore they would be glad to hear what instructions I had about that matter.* As I thought it not for our purpose to tergiversate in the matter, I told them bluntly, that *Gondormo* might thank himself for his misfortunes; for that when our fleet and forces, about two years ago appear'd near *Cochin*, to attack the *Portuguese* our enemies, the *Dutch* admiral had set up a white flag, to shew his willingness to treat with the queen

Is call'd to court.

P[illegible] made to him.

His answer.

2

1662. queen of *Cochin*, which *Gondormo* had not only prevented, but also attack'd our forces, and opposed and still did oppose all our designs tending to the re-establishment of the government of *Cochin* upon its true foundation. I further told them, that, when about two years ago, I had the honour to see his majesty at *Kalikoli*, I assured his majesty that we had conquer'd *Cochin*, and were engaged in an everlasting alliance with *Monta Davila*, their legal sovereign; and that therefore *Gondormo* need not flatter himself with the least hopes of his re-establishment. Of this they gave an account to the king, who soon sent them back with another proposition, to wit, whether he might not be admitted as a second or third person in the kingdom? To make an end at once of this dispute, I ask'd them whether they did acknowledge *Monta Davila* lawful king? They answer'd they did? I demonstrated to them, how unreasonable it was, to demand that one who had set up against his legal sovereign, should be receiv'd in such a station in the same kingdom, and considering the ill consequences which must needs ensue from thence, I told them it was in vain to say a word more of it. This made them insist no more upon the business of *Gondormo*, they only told us, *That we had best be upon our guard*, Gondormo *and his three brothers being resolved to live, and to be buried in the kingdom of* Cochin. I answer'd him carelesly, that I had travelled thro the greatest part of that kingdom; and that I was sure there was room enough for 100000 of them. I assured them farther, that his majesty of *Travankoor*, had been always in great esteem with our company, that they never doubted of his friendship, notwithstanding he seem'd to bear so great a share in *Gondormo*'s business; that I was sent thither on purpose to enter into a more strict league with him, in the same manner as had been done with several other kings his neighbours. Whilst they were debating this matter, an envoy arriv'd from the queen of *Koulang*, with a letter, in which she complain'd, that she had not receiv'd any share of the customs, nor were the cannon restored to her; the *Residoor* ask'd me what the meaning of it was, and whether we would do less than the *Portuguese* had done? I answer'd him, if we should follow the footsteps of the *Portuguese*, we must be guilty likewise of the same enormities, in murthering, plundering, *&c.* things not customary among us, the intention of our company being to maintain every one in his right, and to establish a free commerce without interruption; and these, said I, are the main contents of my commission, according to which I am to treat with all the kings and princes of the coast of *Malabar*. After several other debates, finding them full of tergiversations, I roundly told them, that I found them very backward in what had been proposed; that for my part, I had done all what I could to procure a peace, but that they seem'd to be rather inclinable to war; and finding them somewhat puzzel'd by their silence, said, that if as yet they could find out any expedient, to compose matters upon reasonable terms, I should be willing to hearken to them, and that, if it was for a yearly present, or a sum of money, once for all, they should have it. The king being inform'd of this resolution, sent me word back, that in a thing of this nature, in which several others besides himself were concerned, he must take some leisure to advise, which done, he would send one of his *Residoors* to *Koulang*, to treat farther of the matter. I insisted upon having all things dispatch'd here, but the *Residoors* telling me, that they durst not urge it any more to the king, for that time, I was fain to acquiesce, and to defer it till our next meeting at *Koulang*, tho' I very well foresaw that this negotiation would meet with no small difficulties, unless something more were granted than had been offer'd hitherto. About the same time the before-mention'd queen, sent me underhand word, that she was very inclinable to a farther treaty, but that it could not be done till the king of *Travankoor* was gone, which as it was no unwelcome news to me, so I desired the *Residoor* whom she sent to me, to use his utmost interest with her majesty to bring it to pass, being sensible that it was the intention of my Masters to live with her in a good correspondence. 1662.

The countrey about *Attingen* has hitherto not been describ'd by any that I know; it abounds in pepper, of which a great quantity is brought thither out of the circumjacent parts. The ancient race of the kings of *Travankoor* owed its origine to *Attingen*, but for want of male heirs, one of the princes of *Cochin* was placed in that throne; the king who then reign'd, being descended from the *Cochin* race of *Rammerankoil*, and elected king of *Travankoor*. The ground where the pepper grows, is hereabouts strong and red, which makes the pepper not full so large here, as in the valleys about *Koulang* and *Cochin*. On the descents of the hills you see very pleasant rice-fields, cut out like steps, and water'd from the top by small rivulets. The king and queen's palace are directly opposite to one another, with some rice-fields betwixt them. Attingen.

The next following day about 10 a clock

1662. clock in the morning, I was call'd to court again, where the king told me in person, that it would be better to reassume the treaty at *Koulang*, which I being fain to be satisfy'd with, I took my leave of his majesty and the *Residoors*, who offer'd me a present from the king, according to the custom of the countrey, which I accepted off, and went directly to the river-side, where we found our boat, and sailing down the river, came just before sun-set to *Maypule*, where I was met by the resident of *Tengepatnam*, whom I had given notice of my coming that way. The next following day, *viz.* the 16th of *February* we reimbark'd our vessels, and steer'd our course by sea to *Koulang*, from whence I immediately dispatch'd our interpreter to *Pule de Margaty*, to inform himself where the queen of *Goenree* at that time kept her court; he return'd the next day with advice, that a month before she was gone deeper into the countrey, to a place call'd *Peretaly*, about four days journey from thence.

Is call'd to court again, and departs from thence.

The kingdom of Travankoor.

The kingdom of *Travankoor* (thus call'd from its capital city) begins at the cape of *Comory* or *Comorin*, and extends all along the sea-coast as far as *Koulang*, comprehending a tract of ground of 20 or 24 leagues in length; the famous village of *Paru*, belonging to the queen of *Singnaty*, being only in the midst. To the east it borders upon the kingdom of *Madure*, and to the west upon the countries of *Peretaly* and *Kotarkery*. It has several considerable villages which are inhabited by the moors, such as *Tengepatnam*, *Kuletture*, *Koritypatnam* and *Allage*. About the year 1544, above 30 villages, inhabited by the *Makaos*, who live for the most part upon fishing, and by the mahometans, were upon this coast. But the chief cities lie deeper in the countrey, which is of a great extent all along the mountains to *Naynar*, near the cape of *Comorin* and toward *Travankoor*, in all 29 great cities and villages. About a league and a half to the north of the cape *Comorin* is the city of *Kotate* or *Kokatti*, a place of great traffick; the populous city of *Simintira* and *Matadavalur*, famous for its bigness, being surrounded by six or seven other towns; *Verrage* is not above a quarter of a league distance from *Kotate* and *Tatikury*, the two most considerable places of the whole countrey. *Kalkolang* is a very large city, being a league and a half long, upon the confines of the *Neyk* of *Madure*. It is situate upon a high hill, 3 leagues from *Tengepatnam*, and 12 from *Koulang*; being on one side strengthen'd by inaccessable mountains, on the other by a wall, the undermost part of which is of stone, the uppermost of brick-work, in all 24 foot high; the royal palace stands at the west end, being surrounded by a stone-wall. On the east-side you see the ruins of an old castle, built on the top of a hill, fortified with a triple wall. The city of *Kalkolang* is the chief residence of the king, who constantly keeps a garrison of 10000 negroes here, to secure it against the *Neyk* of *Madure*, whose power is much dreaded here. It is a very fertile countrey, abounding in pepper, rice and other grains. It also produces wild cinnamome, the best, the whole coast of *Malabar* affords, but it wants several things requisite for the conveniency of life. One of the chiefest rivers which water this countrey, is the river *Mannikorin*, it exonerates itself into the sea; near cape *Comorin*. The king of this countrey is by some stiled the *great king*, because he possesses larger territories than any other of the *Malabar* kings. He is served in great state, and maintains abundance of commanders, whom they call *Mandigals*, and many councellors, call'd *Pullas*. Some ascribe to him a superiority over neighbouring princes, but of this I am convinced to the contrary by my own experience; it is true they reverence him, as a potent king, but pay him no obedience. Others will have him to be a vassal of the king of *Narsinga*. The whole countrey is well stock'd with people, who appear very well cloth'd according to the *Malabar* fashion. 1662.

The author goes to Goenree.

The 18th of *February*, I set out from *Koulang* in company of Mr. *Siewert Baker*, for the kingdom of *Goenree*. But scarce were we come to *Kaligoli*, but one of the *Residoors* told us, that the queen of *Goenree* was a month ago gone into the countrey, and would not return very quickly, by reason of a certain religious ceremony, she was obliged to perform there, before her return; I desired a guide, because I had something of moment to communicate to the queen, but they excused it, telling me that the ways were so rocky and impassable, that it would be impossible for me to go thither, it being five tedious days journey to the countrey of *Peretaly*, bordering upon the territories of the *Neyk* of *Madure*. Being made sensible that this journey could not be undertaken without great difficulty and charge, I thought it most expedient to leave a letter with the *Residoor*, to be deliver'd to the queen, the contents of which were as follows.

His letter to the queen.

THat I was come hither to offer a small present to her majesty, and to enter into a strict and everlasting alliance with her; but tho' I was so unfortunate, as not to meet with

1662. *her majesty, I liv'd however in hopes, that she would not be backward in entering into a general league, which the company had lately concluded with all the* Malabar *princes; to accomplish which as we should be ready to contribute every thing on our side, so we did not question, but that her majesty would be pleased to let us know her sentiments by the bearer of this letter.*

Whilst I tarried here, I understood that the *Residoor* of the king of *Travankoor* was arriv'd the 20th at *Koulang China*, and had notified his arrival by our *Petangatin Thome Bottancho*, desiring to confer with me, concerning certain matters commanded him by the king his master, since my departure from thence. The place appointed for our interview, was the church of the christians of *St. Thomas* in *Koulang China*, where I was present at the appointed hour, but finding them to trifle away the time in altercations and tergiversations; I was ready to mount on horse-back again, in order to return to *Koulang*, which when they perceiv'd, they desired me to stay and give them another meeting, which I agreed to do. At last, after abundance of contests, the following agreement concerning the shares of the customs, the importation of amfion and the exportation of pepper, was made betwixt the *Dutch East-India* company, by their deputy Mr. *John Nieuhoff* on one, and the kings of *Marten*, *Singnaty*, *Goenree*, *Travankoor* and *Barrigetta Pule* on the other side.

Articles of agreement.

I. *NO body shall import, sell or exchange any amfion into these countries, except the* Dutch East-India *company.*

II. *No body, without any exception, shall be permitted to export any pepper or cinamome out of this countrey, or to sell them to any body, except to the said company.*

III. *A certain price was settled, betwixt both parties, and what share each should have in the customs, whereby all former pretensions and exceptions should be annulled.*

February 21, 1664. *Sign'd in the court* Matta del Reyne.

In my return from *Koulang*, in the road leading to *Matta del Reyne*, I found guards posted upon all the cross roads, which made me enquire of *Matta del Pule* chief commander of the negroes, what the meaning of it was, who told me with a sorrowful countenance, that the prince *Barrigetta Pule*, had caused one of the queen's *Residoors* to be slain by his soldiers, who had

Troubles raised by Barrigetta Pule.

also laid about 80 houses in ashes, and cut down many palm-trees. That they had been sent to besiege him in his castle, but that at the intercession of the king of *Travankoor's Residoor*, who had promised that the said prince should be call'd to an account by the king his master, they had delay'd the execution of it for three days; but he much fear'd he should scarce withhold them much longer, from taking a direful revenge of him. He was very inquisitive concerning our late transactions with the king of *Marten*, but I excused the matter, telling him only, that I hoped it would be brought to a conclusion, to both sides satisfaction. 1662.

The 22d I sent a letter by Mr. *Sebastian Ferdinandi*, our interpreter, to the queen of *Singnaty*, in which I gave her an account of what had been transacted betwixt the *Residoor* of the king of *Travankoor* and my self. In the mean while the king's and prince's soldiers were come to blows, several being kill'd and wounded on both sides: Whereupon the prince finding himself besieged in his castle, sent one of his most trusty servants to desire assistance, and some powder and ball for his master, which I thought fit to refuse, for weighty reasons; for whatever may be the opinion of those who think it a maxim of state to fish in troubled waters, I was too well acquainted with the perfidiousness of the *Malabars*, who make not the least account of faith or leagues, unless they are forced to it, than to put the least confidence in them.

In the mean time the beforementioned *Residoor* of the king of *Travankoor* not appearing at the time and place appointed for the removing of some remaining differences, I sent him the following letter, by *Topaes Nicolaes da Costa*.

The captain of *Koulang* sends this letter with his service, to *Narrano Poly*, *Residoor* of *Travankoor*.

The author's letter to the Residoor *of* Travankoor.

PUrsuant to our mutual agreement, I came to Koulang China, *in order to bring the treaty begun before to a happy conclusion: But your highness did not perform your promise, neither had I the least account since, how the queen of* Singnaty *was likely to relish our transactions. And as the nature of the thing would admit of no delay, I saw my self obliged to send my interpreter to the queen of* Singnaty, *and* Topaes Nicholaes da Costa, *to the* Goenree *and* Barrigetta, *to be inform'd concerning that point. They bring me for answer, that the said queen pretends to the customs*

1662. *without the least diminution, which is not in my power to agree to. As I am sensible, that I have left nothing unattempted, which might reasonably and honestly be expected from me, for the terminating of these differences, but all in vain, I have nothing left to do, but to protest once for all, according to the strictest rules of justice, in the name of the whole company, against your* Narrano Poly, *and your transactions, and all others who take part with you, that we will, and hereby declare our selves innocent, and guiltless of all the troubles and miseries of a future war.*

Koulang Feb. 26, 1664. John Nieuhoff.

In the mean while I had given an account of the whole matter to Mr. *Hustart*, desiring him to come in person, and to endeavour by his presence to put a happy conclusion to the negotiations. He sent me an answer dated *Cochin* the 24th of *February*, intimating that he had intended to set out from thence within two days after, of which he order'd me to give notice to the king of *Travankoor*, and queen of *Singnaty*, which I did accordingly by an express sent with letters to both their majesty's. The 27th the residoor of *Travankoor* sent me word by *Topaes Nicolaes de Costa*, that he was willing to treat with me once more about the customs, but that no body except the queen must be privy to the matter; for which reason he could cause a quite different rumour to be raised among the people; but considering with my self that the negroes, who are in great esteem here, might get scent of the matter, and that (as the king had told me himself before) several persons in the first rank were concern'd in the customs, I did not look upon this underhand treaty as advantageous for the company; which made me write to the *Residoor*, that I was willing to contribute all what in me lay, towards the composing of the differences betwixt us, provided it could be done in the same nature as with the other *Malabar* princes, who had not refus'd to read the treaties in the presence of their subjects, to shew that their words were altogether consonant to their deeds. I receiv'd an answer the same evening, in which the *Residoor* desired an interview with me in *St. Thomas*'s church the next day. Accordingly I went thither on horse-back with Mr. *James Cher de Venne*. After many contests on both sides, we agreed at last, and the *Residoor* promised to return to morrow to finish the treaty. About this time I receiv'd a letter from the queen of *Singnaty*, in answer to that I had sent her before; as follows.

Another interview with the Residoor *of* Travankoor

The queen of Singnaty's *letter to the author.* 1662.

I Receiv'd and saw the contents of the letter sent to me from Mr. John Nieuhoff, *captain of* Koulang, *concerning the proposed treaty; I will send word in the Month of* March *to* Kottekkery, *where we will meet together, and I shall be ready to rectify what my plenipotentiaries shall agree to. For which reason I order'd this letter to be written to captain* John Nieuhoff.

The next day the *Residoor* of the king of *Travankoor* came to *Koulang*, who was receiv'd by us with all imaginable respect; he began among other things to renew his former discourse about the prince *Gondormo*, upon which it was agreed to delay the last conclusion of the treaty till the coming of Mr. *Hustart*, who was expected every day at *Koulang*.

The 2[d] of *March* with break of day, the vice-roy of the king of *Travankoor*, call'd by them *Gorepe*, the chief commander of the negroes, call'd *Matta de Pulo*, and my self, set out for the court of the queen of *Koulang*, which was then kept at *Calliere*. We arriv'd there about two a clock in the afternoon, and as soon as notice was given of our arrival, we were sent for to court, where, after I had deliver'd the presents, and laid the money down for pepper, I was introduced into her majesty's presence. She had a guard of above 700 soldiers about her, all clad after the *Malabar* fashion; the Queen's attirement being no more than a piece of callicoe wrapt round her middle, the upper part of her body appearing for the most part naked, with a piece of callicoe hanging carelesly round her shoulders. Her ears, which were very long, her neck and arms were adorn'd with precious stones, gold rings and bracelets, and her head cover'd with a piece of white callicoe. She was past her middle age, of a brown complexion, with black hair tied in a knot behind, but of a majestick mein, she being a princess who shew'd a great deal of good conduct in the management of her affairs. After I had paid the usual compliments, I shew'd her the proposition, I was to make to her in writing; which she order'd to be read twice, the better to understand the meaning of it, which being done, she ask'd me, whether this treaty comprehended all the rest, and whether they were annull'd by it; unto which I having given her a sufficient answer, she agreed to all our propositions, which were accordingly sign'd immediately. This done, I recommended Mr. *James Cher de Venne*, who was to succeed me at *Koulang*, to her majesty, desiring her to acknowledge

The author goes to the queen of Koulang.

Nieuhof's Audience wth ye Queen of Koylang

1662. knowledge him as ſuch, and to continue in a good correſpondency with our company, by whom I was order'd to go to *Toutekorin*, which ſhe promiſed to do. I then deſired leave to depart, becauſe I expected Mr. *Huſtart* every hour at *Koulang*, which ſhe readily granted, and at the ſame time took a golden bracelet from her arms, which ſhe preſented me as a token of her good inclinations to the company. She order'd one of the *Reſidoors* to faſten it to my arm, but it being too ſtreight, ſhe cauſed it to be fitted for me, ſhe having once before, *viz.* when I firſt gave her notice of Mr. *Huſtart's* coming, preſented me with another golden bracelet, for which and all other honours, I had received from her majeſty, ſince my reſidence at *Koulang*, I returned my hearty thanks, deſiring her once more not to withdraw her favour from the company. Thus I return'd to *Koulang*, about two a clock in the night, where I was let in through one of the gates, the admiral *Huſtart* being the day before arriv'd there with two ſhips, the *Eraſmus* and the *Niewenhoven* from *Batavia*. The next morning I paid a viſit to the admiral at his lodgings, where I gave him an ample account of my negotiations, and other matters relating to our factory here, wherewith he was highly ſatisfied, and gave me ſome farther orders about certain matters to be tranſacted before my departure.

Returns to Koulang.

1662.

The viceroy of Travankoor *comes to* Koulang.

About the ſame time the viceroy of the king of *Travankoor* came back to the city of *Koulang*, to compliment the admiral, and to conſummate the treaty. The admiral ſent him aftewards ſeveral preſents, and let him know, that if the king his maſter did give any aſſiſtance of men or arms to prince *Gondormo* againſt *Cochin* and the company, he muſt expect to be treated as an enemy; he return'd for anſwer, that he was ſure his maſter would not do it, but always maintain a good correſpondency with the company, upon which he was diſmiſs'd, and left *Koulang* the ſame night, as did the admiral ſoon after, who ſet ſail for *Cranganor*, leaving the commodore *Bitter* behind him, who with his wife and family was come aboard the ſhip the *Niewenhoven* to load pepper here. His wife being very deſirous to ſee the queen of *Koulang*, I caus'd her to be carried thither in my *Palankin*; the queen receiv'd her very courteouſly, being extremely well pleas'd with the ſight of a *Dutch* woman; and many of the *Malabars* were ſo curious as to peep into the *Palankin* to ſee her; they being no leſs ſurpriz'd at the ſight of the *Europeans* than we were at them. Commodore *Bitter* having by this time got his full cargo, ſet ſail again for *Batavia*,

1662.

The author takes his leave of the court of Gonree *and prince* Baryette Pule.

Batavia, as I did the 11th to the court of *Gonrec*, and so to the prince *Baryette Pule*, where I introduced Mr. *Cherde Venne*, who, as I told you before, was to manage the affairs of the company after my departure; they receiv'd him very civilly, and promis'd to maintain an everlasting correspondence with our company. At parting, prince *Baryette Pule* presented me with a golden bracelet curiously wrought, and the viceroy with a silken suit of cloaths, and so I return'd very well satisfied to *Koulang*, where I prepar'd for *Toutekorin*; for within four days after, *viz.* the 12th of *March*, having first surrendred all my accounts, and what also belong'd to the company, and given the best instructions I could to Mr. *James Cherde Venne*, taken my leave of the chiefest officers belonging to the company, I set out for *Toutekorin*, after a stay of two years at *Koulang*, considering that my appointed time was near expiring, and I had settled our traffick at *Koulang* upon a good foot. I could have been very glad to have stay'd the remainder of my time here, for which purpose I sent a letter to *Colomba*, but the chief director of *Toutekorin* being order'd to *Persia* upon some urgent business, I was forc'd to supply his place. And upon this occasion I think it not amiss to give the reader an account of what I have observ'd most remarkable during my stay on the coast of *Malabar*, together with the products, beasts and inhabitants of this countrey.

Cape Koulang.

Limits of the coast of Malabar.

The coast of *Malabar* is properly called that tract of ground where the *Malabar* tongue is us'd, beginning 50 leagues to the south below *Goa*, and extending to the south to the cape *Comorin*, under 7½ degree of northern latitude, about 80 leagues along that coast. On the west-side it borders upon the *Indian* sea, and to the east it is surrounded by a ridge of high mountains, which divide it from the coast of *Coromandel*. It is commonly divided into five kingdoms, *viz. Cananor*, *Calicut*, *Cranganor*, *Cochin* and *Koulang*, unto which some add the kingdom of *Porka*, *Tanakor* or *Tanor*, *Koulang* and *Travankoor*; not to mention here the petty kingdoms of *Kota*, *Mountingua*, *Badara*, *Chambaya*, *Marta*, *Materte*, and several others among the mountains. It is situate almost in the midst betwixt the line and the tropick of Cancer; which makes the days here excessive hot, notwithstanding which, it is a pleasant, extraordinary fertile and healthful countrey. It is full of very fine springs, pools, rivers and channels, even as far as the mountains, but most towards the sea-side; in which it resembles the province of *Holland*, being scarce passable without boats; tho' most of

Its division.

their rivers are shallow, and consequently unfit for ships of burthen. Here grows great store of the best pepper, exceeding all the rest in goodness; formerly the inhabitants us'd to exchange the pepper with the foreign merchants for silver, gold, amfion and other commodities; but since the *Dutch East-India* company have made themselves masters of the kingdoms of *Cranganor*, *Cochin* and *Koulang*, and forc'd the *Portuguese* from thence, they have by entering into several leagues with the neighbouring princes, got the monopoly of pepper on that coast into their hands, and have so well provided the three before mention'd places with strong fortifications and garrisons, that they are look'd upon as impregnable. Besides this, the countrey of *Malabar* is full of cocoe trees, especially in the marshes, where these trees thrive better than in any other place in the *Indies*, there being some trees here of 95 and more foot high. They drive a considerable trade with the oil and bark of this fruit, neither do they want wood fit for the building of houses and ships. The air is very pure here, and very cold in the night time, during the three months of *January*, *February* and *March*; and when the nights are very foggy, which questionless occasions the cold, the days being excessive hot. The winter begins here in *April*, or at the most in *May*, and ends in *September* or *October*, with thunder, lightnings and storms: This season produces the most fruits, by reason of the warm rains. Then begins the summer season, which continues till *April* or *May* with intolerable heat, and commonly without any rains, which renders the sandy grounds so hot, that they cannot pass over them with their bare feet, but are forced to make use of a certain sort of shoes, call'd by them *Siripous*. Every morning about nine or ten a clock, the land wind blows from the *East*, and immediately after sunset the west wind from the sea, both which contribute much towards the cooling of the air, as well here, as in all other adjacent islands. What is most observable is, that the land wind never reaches above ten leagues in the sea; an observation which has never been known to miss. The seasons here are quite of a different nature from ours, for whilst during the summer months every thing is dried up in the hot climates of *Europe*, here the fruits appear most florid and green, because this is the winter season in *Malabar*, where it rains continually for six months, during which time you not as much as see the least glimpse of the sun, but in the other six months it never rains. During the months of *October*, *November* and *December*, they are much afflicted with dreadful storms. There is another thing which is

1662.

Its products.

Its air.

Seasons of the year.

1662. is most surprizing here, that wher it is summer on the coast of *Malabar*, it s winter on the coast of *Coromandel*. Thi is occasioned by the mountains call'd *Gate*, which stop the passage of the winds; for whilst on the east-side of these mountains, which extend all along the coast of *Malabar*, they have great heats and droughts during their summer season, those on the west-side have their winter with violent rains. Thus on the south-side of the cape *Comorin*, they have their summer during *April*, *May*, *June*, *July*, *August* and *September*, whilst at the same time, those on the north-side have their winter, it being very stormy and rainy or one, and fair and calm on the other side at the same time.

Houses. Their ordinary houses are of bamboe canes, cover'd with leaves of coco-trees; some are plaistered with carving, without any cellars, garrets or windows. They never lock up their houses, because their houshold-stuff is not worth stealing, unless they be persons of an eminent rank; their doors are so low, that you cannot enter without stooping, tho' they have also some houses cover'd with lead, copper and tiles, and built otherwise and well fitted up, according to their fashion; their private buildings don't approach in height to ours, they commonly have two or three apartments within one another; within the compass of the middlemost of these apartments is a small square, with some small galleries round about it, which receive the water from the tops of the houses. At the entrance of all their houses, whether rich or poor, are court-yards surrounded with high walls and ditches, and one of strong pallisadoes. These court-yards are for the reception of travellers, who eat, drink and sleep here, with more conveniency than if they were lodged within, being ready at all times to proceed on their journey when the rest of the company goes. Their royal palaces and pagods are commonly built of stone, surrounded with a mud wall, on which are mounted some great cannon. Most of their princely palaces are erected in large ponds or lakes, some having a league and a half in circumference. They have most excellent carvings in wood, with all sorts of images in their houses; their ceiling is of a plain polish'd wood; among the marshes are to be seen many ruins of old houses, which appear to have been built many ages ago. Some tell us, that *Alexander* the great coming into those parts, after he had order'd his admiral to enter by the way of the river *Ganges* the sea, and from thence by the *Euphrates* to *Babylon*, had laid these countries desolate; others ascribe this devastation to *Tamerlane*.

1662. *How they eat and drink.* The *Malabars* eat and drink sitting upon the ground, after the *Mahometan* fashion, almost like our taylors. Their cups, dishes and spoons are made of coco-nuts; people of quality have them made of metal. Instead of bread they use nothing but rice; besides which, they feed upon flesh, fish, spices, fruits, milk and eggs. They drink abundance of water, as likewise the juice of the coco-trees; some of which give 30 quarts of this liquor in 24 hours, but if they are drain'd too much, the trees perish. They also distil a spirit call'd *Arack* out of this liquor, but it is not near so good nor wholsome as our brandy. When they drink they don't touch their lips with the cup, but pour the liquor from above into the mouth; some eat neither flesh nor fish, but live purely upon the products of the ground.

They use amfion. They use amfion very greedily. They take the quantity or the bigness of a pea, this they either mix with *Arack*, or chew it alone, sometimes till they fall asleep; they pretend that this makes them have very present dreams of the *Elysian* fields and such like. When they are to attack an enemy, they take a good quantity of it, which makes them fall on like enraged wild beasts, and the virtue of the amfion being gone, they don't remember what has past, which shews that it is very obnoxious to the memory. Some have accustomed themselves to use amfion every day, some every two or three days; and before I knew the effects of it, I have been often surpriz'd, that they should be so forgetful in such matters as I had treated with them of before. The queen of *Koulang* asking me once among other things, what was the reason the *Dutch* were more active and perseverant than the *Malabars*, who were generally fickle and unsettled, I laid the fault upon the use of the amfion, telling her withal, that the *Malabars* should imitate the *Dutch*, and drink wines, which used with moderation, did acuate the understanding, made the spirits active, and often discovered the truth.

The Brahmans. Among these several sects of the *Malabars*, that of the *Brahmans* is most reverenced, and maintains a peculiar manner of living. They are generally very wise, ready, active, modest and charitable, and strict observers of their promises. They betake themselves to divers employments at pleasure; some are soldiers like the natives, and wear the same clothes, except that they are distinguish'd from them by the cord they wear round their middle, and abstain from flesh. Others are priests, whose business it is to offer sacrifices to their idols, no other sect being admitted to that service.

1662. Some also encrease traffick, and tho' they grow very rich, yet observe the same rules of living. Some there are among them who addict themselves to natural philosophy and other sciences, but especially to astronomy, others to physick and pharmacy. They eat neither flesh nor fish, nor any other living creature, and drink nothing but water; nor do they ever eat before they have washed and bathed themselves; which done, they only cover their privy parts, and for the rest eat naked. They are forbidden to eat any thing but what is prepared by one of their own sect; which makes them commonly be their own cooks; for they rather chuse to die than eat any thing touch'd by one of another sect; whereas all the others are at liberty to eat what is dress'd by a *Brahman*. They never (no more than all the other *Malabars*) touch the brim of the cup when they drink, but pour it from above into the mouth. They wear a white turbant upon their heads, red shoes, and a callicoe coat, which reaches down to their ankles. Over this they have another large white piece of stuff, which they wrap three times round their bodies, which they draw thro' betwixt their thighs, and tie it together behind upon their buttocks in a knot. They wear about the middle a girdle or scarf of fine white callicoe, as their turbants are, and over the shoulders a piece of colour'd callicoe or silk, as the *Europeans* do their cloaks. They also have long hair, with pendants in their ears. But that which distinguishes them from all the other *Malabars*, is a cord of fine cotton thread, which they wear next to their skin, and is put about them first of all in their temples with a great deal of ceremony, and not without a considerable charge, which is the reason you cannot do a greater injury to a *Brahman* than to tear this cord, which he is obliged to purchase again, if he will pass for a true *Brahman*; and if any of them is to undergo any corporeal punishment, his cord must first be taken from him, which is likewise done if any of them happen to transgress the rules prescribed to their sect. As they pass along the streets in their white callicoe clothes, they tell such as they meet that they are *Brahmans*, because the cord by which they are chiefly distinguish'd is worn next to their skin, and consequently not to be seen; when they are to take an oath, they lay the hand upon it. The *Brahman* women have holes in their noses, in which they hang gold and silver rings, pearls and precious stones, as well as about their legs and in their ears, where they have silver and gold plates set round with precious stones. The wives of the *Negroes*, of the *Moncoris*, and the other *Malabars*, are not permitted to use these ornaments. They also wear bracelets from their wrists up to their elbows, some of gold and silver, others of glass and tortoise-shell curiously engraven and enamell'd. These women are generally handsome and well-featured, some of them being not inferior in complexion to the *Portuguese* or the brown *Dutch* women. They marry very early, sometimes before they are quite 7 or 8 years old; for the boys and girls are permitted to sport together till they come to be in good earnest; but they take great care not to mix themselves with another sect. The men are allow'd to marry twice, tho' no more than one woman at a time. Be they never so poor, they will be sure to keep their rank, and to oblige such as meet them to pass by with making a bow, in token of their reverence. Those among the *Brahmans* who have listed themselves among the *Negroes*, are in the same degree with them, except that they observe more austerity. The *Brahmans* are in great esteem with their kings, who keep some of the chiefest always near their person, to advise with them in all matters of moment. Those of the first rank among the *Brahmans*, as well as other *Indian* persons of quality, have commonly a numerous attendance; some of whom carry their umbrelloes, others a silver bason full of *Bethel*; others one full of water; some are carried in palankins or chairs. 1662.

Feast of the Brahmans.

The *Brahmans* have, under pretence of a religious worship, introduced a feast, which furnishes them with a certain opportunity of being revenged of their enemies. It is a custom among the the *Malabar* kings once every year, *viz.* at the time of the new-moon in *October*, to remember the blessings they suppose they have received from their Idols, by a solemn sacrifice, which is perform'd by setting certain houses on fire, such as are appointed by the *Brahmans*: This is commonly perform'd in the night time, without the least fore-warning given, so that sometimes not only the house, but also the inhabitants, with all their goods are burnt, no body daring to quench the flame. This they call *The sacrifice of fire and blood.*

Several sorts of Brahmans.

There live many of the *Banjans* of *Cambaya* in *Malabar*; these have also *Brahmans*, who are in great esteem among them; the *Brahmans* of *Malabar* are allow'd to frequent their temples. The *Banjans* themselves lead as austere a life as their *Brahmans*, but they are of an inferior degree, nor can they intermarry with them. In the kingdom of *Calicut* is a certain sort of *Brahmans*, who despise all images, and live in chastity after the 20 or 25th year of age. They

1662. They are so averse to the female sex that as often as they stir abroad, some bod cries out aloud before them *Poo, Poo, i. e.* keep back, keep back, to let the women know they must keep out of sight. These don't wear the cord twisted of cotton thread, neither do they abstain (like the other *Brahmans*) from flesh, fish or wine; but to preserve their chastity eat daily a certain quantity of the pulp of the fruit *Karuza*, being taught by experience, that the same has a quality of checking the venereal appetite. Neither do they bury their dead bodies like the other *Brahmans*; some strew themselves all over with ashes, and are enclosed day and night in iron cages, which are so small, that they can scarce sit upright in them. Others burn or scald certain parts of their bodies, whereby they suppose to gain the Affections of the common people. Thus far of the *Brahmans*.

Divers sorts of inhabitants. For the rest it is to be observed, that the inhabitants of the coast of *Malabar* may be divided into foreigners and natives; the foreigners are properly those call'd commonly *Malabars*, being a colony of *Arabians*, who have fix'd their habitations there many ages ago, near the sea-side chiefly. The natives are pagans, divided into *Brahmans* or *Bramenis*, *Bramos* or *Bramen*; into the *Nairos* or *Nayros*, and into the common people call'd *Moncoris* or *Pouleas*, and otherwise *Parvas*. They are also divided into five several degrees; the first are the royal families, among which the house of *Gondormo* is one of the most illustrious; the second is the sect of the *Brahmans*, or of the priests. The third is the military order or nobles, call'd the *Nayros*; the fourth comprehends the merchants, and the fifth the *Parvas* or fishermen.

The Nayros. The *Nayros*, as I told you, are descended of noble families, and brought up to the war. They appear with a shield on their left-arm, which they carry aloft, and with a naked sword in the right-hand. They are very haughty, and at first pretended to dispute the rank with the *Portuguese*, which occasion'd no small disturbance, 'till the difference was agreed to be decided by a single combat betwixt a *Portuguese* and a *Nayros*, in which the last being worsted, the *Nayros* ever since were forced to give way to the *Portuguese*; but all the other *Malabars* must give place to the *Nayros*. They are generally well proportion'd, tho' of a brown or olive colour; they take a singular pride in having long ears, which they perform by art; they bore holes thro' the ears of both boys and girls, which they fill up with palm-tree leaves roll'd together; these rolls they make bigger and bigger by degrees, 'till the holes are extended to the utmost reach the holes can bear, and hang down to their very breasts: This is accounted one of their chiefest pieces of gallantry, and they adorn them with gold, silver and jewels. Tho' the *Nayros* are from their infancy train'd up in arms, and are very bold and brave, they are nevertheless very civil and meek in their conversation, according to the custom of that country; notwithstanding which they are mightily addicted to robbing upon the high-way, and will kill the travellers unawares, unless they be well upon their guard. This is the reason why the mahometan *Malabars* dwelling in this countrey, whenever they are travelling from one place to another, take one of these *Nayros* along with them, who is their conductor for a certain piece of money, to the next place where they take another, and by this means may pass without any danger thro' a thousand of *Nayros*, tho' their conductor should be an old decrepit person, or only a boy. These *Nayros* are strict observers of the times, which are neglected by the common people, for they will not converse with any of the inferior orders, except the *Brahmans*; nay, if any of the vulgar sort happen only to touch a *Nayros*, as he passes by, he will make his servant that carries his meat after him, to throw it down upon the ground; nay, if they do enter their houses, or only touch the doors and walls, they will not eat there for fear of being defiled. However the *Nayros* are not altogether so nice in these points, as the *Brahmans*. For the rest, they are not much inclined to vice, sodomy and incest; nay, the boys and girls, tho' they converse together daily, and that without cloths, you shall seldom observe in them either in word or action, any thing that savours of uncleanness. The *Nayros* scarce ever laugh, and that not but upon extraordinary occasions; and if they see others laugh they will look downward. Those *Nayros* who are watching at the town gates, and serve for conductors to travellers, are the poorest of all, yet will they rather follow this employment than a trade, which they look upon below their quality. They apply themselves from their infancy to the use of arms, and frequently fight together with swords and targets, which renders them infinitely active at that sport. They are the best wrestlers in the world, and are very nimble on foot. They attack their enemies quite naked, their privities being only covered. Their arms are bows, arrows, javelins, swords and shields; these are very large, which they use with the utmost dexterity to cover their bodies. On the hilt of their swords they have small plates of metal, which

1662. which makes a noiſe when they are a fighting, and ſerves to animate them. Since the *Portugueſe* and *Dutch* have got footing there, they have alſo learn'd the uſe of fire-arms to that degree, that they will turn right and left, and give a volley of ſhot with the ſame order as the *Europeans* do.

Their marriages. One *Nayros* is not allow'd more than one Wife at a time, but the women in this point have got the ſtart of the men, they being permitted to have three huſbands at once; except that a woman of the ſect of the *Brahmans* that is married to a *Nryros* is not allow'd more than one. Each of theſe three huſbands contribute their ſhare towards the maintenance of this woman and her children, without the leaſt conteſt or jealouſy. As often as any of them comes to viſit her, he leaves his arms at the door, a ſign that neither of the other two muſt come in, for fear of diſturbing the firſt. From hence the poorer ſort reap this benefit, that they have the uſe of a wiſe, yet contribute only the third part towards the maintaining of the family; tho' on the other hand this carries along with it a great inconveniency concerning the inheritance of their children, which they recompenſe in ſome meaſure, by making the ſiſter's children the heirs of their uncles. The *Nayros* employ the common people in the countrey and other drudgeries, but in their houſes they make uſe of none but *Nayros* (or gentlemen) tho' very poor, who are willing to ſerve them for their bread. The vulgar ſort are all clad after the ſame manner, being quite naked except that they have a ſmall girdle round their waſte, on which they hang a piece of callicoe, or perhaps of the bark of a tree, or a few leaves to cover their privities. The women wear a kind of veſtment of callicoe, which reaches down to their knees, and have very long hair; whereas the men are obliged to cut their hair cloſe, except one truſs which they keep on the crown of their head. All the *Malabars* have black teeth, occaſion'd by the continual chewing of the leaves of *Bethel:* Black teeth are in great eſteem among them, becauſe thoſe that don't chaw *Bethel*, are conſidered here as of a mean extraction. The *Malabars* are ſaid to be much addicted to ſorcery, who are able to kill people as they paſs by or at leaſt throw them into a lingring diſtemper. They are extremely covetous, and will venture at any thing for a ſmall gain. The women are generally unchaſte, the young women about 17 or 18, being obliged by cuſtom to diſpoſe of their maidenheads, for no body cares to marry a maiden here, but ſuch as have been beſt beloved, ſooneſt meet with a huſband. The *Malabars* have great ſtore of great artillery, muſkets and pikes; nay, their arms were in more eſteem than thoſe of the *Portugueſe*, only they did not know the art of hardning their armour: They now make very good and ſtrong gun-barrels and gun-powder. The children of the *Nayros* are from the ſeventh year of their age exerciſed in arms, and train'd up to the wars; but every one betakes himſelf to one peculiar kind of arms, it being their opinion, that they cannot excel in the uſe of all. They anoint the limbs of their young children every day with a certain oil, to make their joints pliable; for when they forced to fly, they put their greateſt confidence in the agility of their bodies, and will in an inſtant turn back upon their enemies, and attack them in the rear; beſides, that in their flight they throw their javelins backward with great dexterity, and as ſoon as they have thrown their darts, they know how to ſhelter themſelves behind their ſhields. 1662.

Tho' the *Nayros* in general are very good ſoldiers, yet there is a certain kind among them call'd *Amokos*, who are eſteemed above all the reſt, being a company of ſtout, bold and deſperate bravadoes. They oblige themſelves by moſt direful imprecations againſt themſelves and their families, calling heaven to witneſs, that they will revenge certain injuries done to their friends or patrons, which they certainly purſue with ſo much intrepidity, that they ſtop neither at fire nor ſword, to take vengeance of the death of their maſter, but like mad men run upon the point of their enemies ſwords, which makes them be generally dreaded by all, and makes them to be in great eſteem with their kings, who are accounted the more potent, the greater number they entertain of thoſe *Amokos*; tho' this their fool-hardineſs is chiefly attributed to the exceſſive uſe of the amſion. You ſee the ſtreets of all the towns on the *Malabar* coaſt full of *Nayros*, with their arms always about them, tho' many of them dwell in the countrey, and a good number are kept near the king's perſon. Moſt perſons of quality here maintain ſome of thoſe they call *Janguys*. If a quarrel happens to ariſe betwixt a *Nayros* and another *Malabar*, the king allows the the latter a guard of another *Nayros*, and as long as he ſtays with him, they dare not fight, the firſt aggreſſor being guilty of high-treaſon; for perſons of the chiefeſt rank, if they will be admitted in the number of the *Nayros*, muſt have the king's peculiar leave for it, and are afterwards diſtinguiſh'd by a gold ring they wear on the right arm, or by a buffler's horn. The *Nayroes* frequently hunt the tigers, ſome apply themſelves to philoſophy, but eſpecially *The Amokos.*

A Malabar Man and Wooman 13

1662. pecially astronomy, but never to traffick or any handicraft trade. They eat all sorts of meat, except cows flesh, and are very fond of pork. They go above half naked, with bare heads and feet, having only a large piece of white callicoe wrapt round their middle; which reaches down to their knees, and is drawn thro' betwixt their thighs, and tied together behind above their buttocks. They wear also a red silken scarf, with a fringe of about half a foot long, being half gold and half silk. They let their hair grow very long, without ever cutting it, by which they are distinguish'd from the common people; they have a way of tying it very neatly together in a puff on the crown of their heads. Their shield they carry on the left arm, and their sword in the right hand; some have also a javelin, musket or pike. The *Nayros* women are clothed after the same manner as the men, so that there is not the least distinction to be seen betwixt boys and the girls, till the breasts begin to appear in the last. They are forbid to marry any other person but of the same rank, and but one at a time; and in case a *Nayros* woman should marry another, except a *Nayros*, she instantly forfeits her head; in the same manner, if a *Nayros* should marry a woman of another tribe but a *Nayros*, he is punished with death. This they have provided against, because they would not have their blood mixt with strangers or those of an inferior rank, of which they are so cautious, that they will not as much as suffer any to approach them; for which reason, when they walk abroad, they cry out aloud to the common people, *Popoire*, keep back; for if any of these should touch a *Nayros*, he would certainly ruin him.

The common people of Malabar.

The common people of *Malabar* call'd *Montois* or *Poulias*, or otherwise *Parvas* or *Parivas*, are a wretched sort of slaves; they are blacker and much uglier than the *Nayros*, neither must their ears hang down above three inches at most. They are again of different kinds, for those inhabiting near the sea-shore, are properly call'd *Moncois*; these are all fishermen, and all along the coast of *Malabar* are employed at sea in rowing and otherwise for certain wages. Their wives and daughters perform all manner of drudgery by land, and expose themselves for money to the first man, without the least distinction of quality or religion, without the least fear from their husbands, who are well enough pleased at it. For it is to be known, that there are no common strumpets here, but the wives and daughters of these *Moncois*, and of the *Tivas*, who are handicrafts men; for the rest are obliged to contain themselves within their own tribes. The common people are often put to a great nonplus when they happen to meet a *Nayros* at the corner of a street, when they are fain to stand aside till they are passed by. There is another kind among the vulgar sort, call'd by some *Tivas*, whose employment is to draw the liquor from the coco-trees: The rest are handicraft and husbandmen. But these intermarry with one another, notwithstanding there is some difference in their rank, for the husbandmen claim the first, and the *Tivas* or handicrafts men the second degree, the *Moncois* or fishermen are the last. 1662.

The Parvas.

Those call'd *Parivas* or *Parvas* live in villages near the sea side; some of these live near the coast, and in the isle of *Makar*, where, as well as near *Toutekorin*, betwixt the cape *Comorin* and the isle of *Ceylon*, they live upon pearl fishing; they are a stubborn generation, more addicted to laziness than labour; they live chiefly upon pearl and oyster fishing, being the best divers in the world, unto which they are accustom'd from their first infancy. Whilst the men are abroad at sea, the women and children are employ'd in gathering of pearl dust near the shore. They are a cowardly and deceitful sort of people, lying and deceit being so customary among them, as not to be look'd upon as a sin. They are great admirers of the ecclesiastical laws, it being a strict custom among them, not to punish a crime, if the transgressor confesses it and promises amendment. The *Parvas* were formerly all *Pagans*, but being sorely oppressed by the *Mahometans*, they rebell'd against them, and with the assistance of the *Portuguese*, shook off the yoke, which proved the opportunity of their conversion to the *Romish* religion.

How they were converted to the Roman faith.

For finding themselves daily more and more oppress'd, by the advice of one *John de Cruis* (a native of *Malabar*) they sent their deputies to *Cochin*, to crave assistance against the mahometans, offering at the same time to be baptized. The *Portuguese* receiv'd these *Pantagitini* (being then their magistrates) very courteously promising them immediate succours against their enemies, which had so powerful an influence upon these deputies, that to shew their gratitude, they receiv'd baptism immediately, and took upon them the surname of *De Cruis*, which name is retain'd by many of the *Parvas* to this day. After the *Parvas* had rid their hands of the *Moors*, with the assistance of the *Portuguese*, and got the pearl fishery again into their hands, many thousands of them, at divers times and places, embraced the christian faith; and under the viceroyship of *Stephen Gamma* the *Portuguese*, *viz.* about 1500, above

1662. 20000 *Parvas* received baptiſm; but for want of good miniſters, who underſtood the *Malabar* tongue (few of the *Portugueſe* clergy being willing to ſettle here) they ſoon return'd to their pagan ſuperſtions, having ſcarce any thing left among them but the name of chriſtians, till *Francis Xaverius* (who arrived in the *Indies* 1540, and went by the name of the great and holy father) being inform'd by *Michael Vas* of the miſerable condition of the *Parvas*, reſolv'd to go thither from *Goa*, to re-eſtabliſh the decay'd ſtate of chriſtianity among the *Parvas*. Accordingly he ſet out from *Goa* (after a ſtay of five months there) in the beginning of *October* 1543, in company of *Francis Manſilla*, who was come along with him out of *Portugal*, and two novices of the college of *Goa*, who underſtood the *Malabar* tongue. After his arrival at the eaſt end of that coaſt, near the cape *Comorin*, finding that his young interpreters ſtood him but in little ſtead, he found out this expedient; he call'd together ſuch of the natives, as he knew to be well verſed in the *Portugueſe* tongue; among thoſe he choſe certain perſons, who join'd with thoſe two he had brought along with him from *Goa*, tranſlated the chief articles of the chriſtian faith, the ten commandmets, with a ſhort explication, a general confeſſion of faith, and ſome other ſuch like neceſſary matters into the *Malabar* tongue. Then he began to preach to them according to the capacity of his auditors, explaining to them the chief duties of a chriſtian, the glory of heaven, and the puniſhment of hell, with the reaſon, why ſome deſerve heaven, and the other hell. He explain'd afterwards to them the ſign of the croſs, and began to unfold to them the myſtery of the holy trinity, of which they had been quite ignorant before, and made ſuch a progreſs among them, that whereas at his coming thither he found not above 2500 demi-chriſtians, at his going away he left near 40000 good chriſtians behind him. *Xaverius* himſelf in his letter dated the 12th of *Jan.* 1554, ſpeaks of the vaſt increaſe of the chriſtians in thoſe parts, ſaying thus:

Return to paganiſm.

Are reconciled to the church by Xaverius.

King, you may gueſs what a great number of theſe poor people were reduced back to the flock of Chriſt from thence, that my arms and hand uſed to be tired with baptizing, ſometimes whole villages at a time. My ſtrength and voice have often failed me, by reaſon of the frequent repetitions of the articles of faith.

The *Romaniſts* tell us, that beſides theſe, *Xaverius* converted ten towns betwixt *Bringen* and *Permanel* (and ſix or ſeven more near *Bengala* and *Remanankoris.*) This they ſay he performed by his miracles, by healing the ſick, caſting out demons, and raiſing the dead from their graves. He raiſed a certaing young man, the ſon of a poor widow, who was choak'd in the mud, from the dead. The ſame he did to another young man, the ſon of a perſon of quality in the city of *Puvicale*, and to a young maid. Another woman in labour, being reduced to the laſt gaſp, he deliver'd without the leaſt pain, as ſoon as ſhe had received baptiſm. By his miracles he converted a whole village at once, near *Toutekorin*; ſo that both chriſtians and pagans uſed to have their laſt recourſe to him in their ſickneſſes, many of which he reſtored by reading the goſpel over them; as may be ſeen more at large in the life of *Xaverius*, of *John de Lucenas*, and other *Roman* authors. 1662.

But whatever ſucceſs *Xaverius* had in converting the *Parvas* and others to the chriſtian religion, certain it is, that he brought no more than one *Brahman* over to the *Romiſh* faith, tho' he beſtow'd much time and pains in ſpeaking to them. And among the *Parvas* themſelves are many to this day, who adhere ſo deeply to their pagan ſuperſtitions, that they make but little account of chriſtianity. However, thoſe that have ever ſince perſevered in the *Romiſh* faith, are from time to time furniſh'd with and inſtructed by the *Portugueſe* prieſts; who ever ſince 1685, when we made ourſelves maſters of *Toutekorin*, lived about a league or two from the town in the countrey, whither they carry their children to be baptized. They are very obſtinate in their religion, which extends no farther than the knowledge of the chriſtian faith, our father, the ten commandments and an *Ave Mary*, but they follow blind-fold the directions of the *Portugueſe* prieſts, carry *Pater Noſters* and a roſary conſtantly about them, and uſe the ſign of the croſs on their foreheads and breaſts, like as the *Roman* catholicks do. The *Dutch* miniſters of the proteſtant religion, have ſeveral times attempted to introduce the reformation into the churches of the *Parvas*, both before and ſince we were maſters of *Toutekorin*, but all in vain; for tho' we cauſed the word of God to be preached in the *Portugueſe* tongue, the *Parvas* durſt not venture to come to church for fear of the *Roman* prieſts living among them. Theſe *Parvas* declared to *Xaverius* and *Michael Jaſſus*, in thoſe days, that whilſt they were yet involv'd in darkneſs of paganiſm, the devil uſed to appear to them in moſt frightful ſhapes, ſo that they durſt not ſtir abroad at night, or go a fiſhing, unleſs in great companies. He us'd to enter into the bodies of the living, and declared he would not leave them, till they had erected

1662. temples for him. But since they had embraced the christian religion, the devil never had appear'd either in their houses or vessels, tho' they freely went abroad a fishing without any company. *Xaverius* having exhorted them to persevere in their religion, set out from thence to *Makarara* and the adjacent places, and so further to the isle of *Ceylon*.

The Mahometan Malabars. All the *Mahometan Malabars* are either merchants or pirates; if any foreigners come into the harbours where their pirates lie, they endeavour to engage them into their service; which if they accept of, they maintain them and their families throughout the whole winter; when they are just a going to engage an enemy, they take some *Bethel*, by which they swear to stand by one another; if they take a prize, they ransack the ship, and all the mariners and passengers before they come ashore; the captain and other officers take the best part for themselves, the rest is divided among the crew. These poor wretches endure incredible fatigues and miseries at sea, and tho' they have no head that has any legal authority over them, they seldom fall out or quarrel, a thing scarce to be believ'd among us. Several of the richer sort of the *Malabars* equip certain vessels, with a good number of soldiers and galley slaves, which always keep at sea, except that now and then the captain comes ashore to dispose of the booty, which the merchants buy without any regard, whether they belong to friends or foes, provided they can have a good bargain; the *Mahometan Malabars* knowing no other preference but riches: the merchants are distinguish'd only by their habits; both these and the corsairs being never to be seen without arms; but the merchants wear their hair short, and have a bonnet of red scarlet cloth upon their heads, sometimes with a handkerchief rowl'd about it like a turbant, which they call *Mondu*, and are commonly embroider'd with gold and colour'd silk. They half shave their beard, but without whiskers, wear a silk or callicoe vest, reaching three inches below the middle, and under that a kind of drawers hanging down to the knees. They commonly carry a silk or callicoe handkerchief flourish'd, in which they tie and hide their purses. The corsairs never shave their heads, but wear their hair very long, like the women, which they like the rest of the *Indians*, tie together in a knot, and wear one of these flourish'd and embroider'd handkerchiefs over it; for the rest they go quite naked, except that they wear a silk vestment down to their knees; both the merchants and corsairs have knives with silver hafts, on which hang all sorts of toys, such as tooth-picks and the like, all curiously wrought. 1662.

The corsairs shave their beards, but leave whiskers, which in time grow excessively, that so one may tie them together behind. These, as well as all the *Malabars* use no shoes. Their women are clad like the men, neither do they wear any other ornament upon their heads but their hair, but have pendants in their ears, and rings on their fingers and toes. They wear a slight callicoe coat, reaching only to the middle, and under it a silk or callicoe vestment, from the middle down to their knees; they walk bare-footed like the men. All the *Malabars* are of a middle size, and very hairy upon the breast and other parts of their bodies. The women are very well featured, but small of stature. Their men undergo incredible fatigues at sea, and tho' they are *Mahometans* they use the *Malabar* tongue, and pay allegiance and taxes to the several kings of the *Nayros*, under whom they live, which is commonly near the sea shore. Their priests never meddle with any thing except marriages, and what relates to their temples. They are clad in white, after the *Arabian* manner; besides which, they have a certain kind of religious men call'd *Abedallen*, or *ministers of God*, who vow poverty, and beg in the countrey: You may see sometimes 30 or 40 of them together, tho' they travel not above two or three at a time, and sometimes one alone.

The countrey of *Malabar* was formerly under the subjection of one potent prince, *Sarama Perimal*, who at the persuasion of some *Arabian* merchants that traded thither, having embraced mahometism, became so great a zealot of that religion, that he resolved to leave his kingdom, and to undertake a pilgrimage to *Meccha* and *Medina*, to visit *Mahomet*'s tomb: And having no children, divided before his departure the whole countrey, betwixt his chief favourites and courtiers, to wit, the countrey of *Cananor* to his Esquire; to his sword-bearer, who was his darling favourite, *Calicut*; to his scepter-bearer *Cochin*; and to another *Koulang*, unto which he annexed the title of kingdoms, and gave several other countries to others of his friends. Upon his sword-bearer, who had *Calicut* for his share, he bestowed the title of *Zamory* or *Zamorin*, or emperor, and to have a preheminency above the rest: For *Zamorin* signifies in the *Indian* tongue as much as an emperor, being otherwise express'd by the word *Tambarana*, i. e. *God*, which is the reason that all the other *Malabar* countries follow the religious ceremonies of those of *Calicut*, as being the chiefest kingdom of *Malabar*. *Government of* Malabar.

1662. *Malabar*. From hence it is, that the *Zamorin* claims the preheminence before all the other *Malabar* kings, he having alone the prerogative of coining. The two next in rank were the kings of *Koulang* and *Cananor*; besides which, many other petty princes on the coast of *Malabar* claim the title of kings, tho' they are not really so, nor enjoy the prerogative of coining. The *Zamorin*, or king of *Calicut* lost a considerable share of his lustre, after the coming of the *Portuguese* into those parts, with whose assistance the king of *Cochin* freed himself from all subjection formerly due to the kings of *Calicut*, and soon after arrived to that pitch of greatness, that they thought themselves not in any wise inferior to the *Zamorins*, and waged continual war against them. Nevertheless most of the petty *Malabar* kings, and the *Nayros* are vassals of the *Zamorin*, and never speak of him but with a great deal of reverence, except the king of *Cochin*; and the king of *Koulang* being the most remote of all, pays the *Zamorin* less respect than any of the rest: However, all the kings of *Malabar* are sovereigns in their own dominions. The *Malabar* kings never marry, but maintain a concubine of a noble family, who lives commonly in the same palace; if they happen to disagree, another is taken in her place, tho' they are so modest as seldom to change their bedfellows.

The sons born from these concubines are not regarded as king's children, neither do they succeed in their territories or estates, but are heirs only to their mothers, except what money the kings are pleased to bestow freely upon them, to make them live with the more lustre among other gentlemen: But the king's sisters sons inherit their dominions. These sisters don't marry no more than the kings, but are at liberty to chuse a gallant, such a one as they like best. If they have three or four sons, and two or three daughters, the eldest son succeeds the king his uncle, and the other brother after him. After their decease, the succession goes to the eldest son of the king's second sister, and to his brothers afterwards. After their decease, the sons of the other sisters are the next heirs to the crown, so that the succession descends from the brothers to their sisters sons. If it happens that the king's sisters bear no sons, the chief men of the kingdom elect a king who is next of kin, but for want of such a one, chuse whom they please. When the king's sisters are arrived to age of maturity, *viz.* to their 13 or 14 years, they pitch upon one of the nobility whom they like best; unto whom, after they have made him considerable presents, they send word that he is chosen to get her maiden-head, and to get her with child. The young noble man accosts her the first time with a great deal of respect and ceremony, and after having tied a very fine jewel about her neck, he diverts himself in private for some days with her, and so returns home: If she proves with child, it is well, if not, she commonly chuses some *Brahman* or other to try his strength whether he can get her with child. When a *Malabar* king dies, the corps is burnt three days after. All his subjects, from the next successor to the meanest child, shave themselves from head to foot, leaving no hair, except what is on the eye-brows and eye-lids. They are also obliged to abstain from the use of *Bethel* for the space of 13 days, and if any one should be found to chew *Bethel* during that time, they cut off his lips. During these 13 days they dare eat neither fish nor flesh, and the fishermen are forbidden to fish upon pain of death. Considerable alms are given to the poor out of the king's coffers, and the *Brahmans* are provided with victuals at the publick charge. After the expiration of these 13 days, every one is at liberty to eat what he pleases, except the new king, who is tied to the same rules for a whole year after; during which time, he must neither have the hair of his head or of his body cut, nor pare his nails: He is obliged to say certain prayers every morning, and must eat but once a day. Some time before dinner he bathes himself, which done, he must forbear to cast his eyes upon any body till after he has taken food. Towards the latter end of this mourning year, his next successor in the kingdom, the other princes of the royal blood, and other persons of the chiefest quality attend the new king, and pay their homage to him, in the presence of many thousands; at which time the new king declares his next successor, and the others each in his degree; which done, he confirms the lords there present in their respective places and offices. He that is declared the next successor to any new king, is oblig'd from that time not to appear at court as long as the king lives; but those princes who are to succeed him may continue there. Before the above-mentioned 13 days are expired, the new king has not the least authority in the kingdom, which they take for a general maxim here, to see whether any body else will lay claim to the succession: But, after the expiration of this time, the great men of the kingdom, and chief officers of state, engage the new king by a solemn oath, to maintain the laws made by his predecessor, to pay his debts, and to endeavour the recovery of the territories lost

Burials of the Malabar *kings.*

under

1662. under the reigns of his predeceſſors. Whilſt he takes the oath he lays his right hand upon an oil caſk, in which are ſet up many lighted wicks, and with a drawn ſword, which he holds in his left, touches a jewel ſet in gold within the caſk. This done, they ſtrew rice upon his head with a great deal of ceremony, and certain forms of prayers, turning their faces to the ſun. In the ſame manner, all the princes of the blood, and other great men ſwear fealty to the new king. During the firſt 13 days after the king's deceaſe, the ſole adminiſtration of the government is lodged in the lord chancellor, who has alſo the management of the treaſury, without whom the king cannot take or diſpoſe of the publick money, unleſs it be in caſe of the greateſt neceſſity. It is alſo the chancellor who puts the king's mandates in execution. The firſt in rank next to the king are thoſe call'd by them *Kaimales*, then the *Brahmans*, who are in great eſteem in thoſe courts, the king of *Calicut* himſelf being of that ſect, and wearing the twiſted cord. After the *Brahmans* come the *Nayros*, or military order, the true off-ſpring of their ancient nobility; then come the vulgar or common people, call'd *Moukois*, or *Poulias*, or *Parvas:* The king is the only judge here, before whom are brought all ſuch as have committed any crime, or refuſe to pay their debts: In his abſence certain great men of the court determine all affairs of any moment; but if a difference ariſes betwixt two or more *Moukois* or any ſtrangers, he that thinks himſelf aggrieved, makes his complaint to the next *Nayros* he meets, who is obliged to do him juſtice immediately, without receiving any reward, unleſs the plaintiff will voluntarily give him a preſent: This holds in matters of ſmall conſequence, for all matters of moment are decided before the king in perſon. Their ordinary puniſhments are impriſonments, or the loſs of a joint of a limb; if the crime be capital the malefactor is thrown to the elephants. They have no other priſons but what are in the royal palaces. In caſe of any difference betwixt two *Pagans*, when the truth is to be verified by a ſolemn oath, they put one hand into boiling oil, or elſe lay hold of a piece of red hot iron; ſometimes they ſwim croſs a river ſwarming with venomous creatures; it being their opinion, that if they have ſpoke the whole truth, they ſhall not receive any hurt; but the trial with the hot iron is moſt generally received. When the *Malabar* kings or their governors intend to inflict a puniſhment upon the inhabitants of a certain place, they ſurround it with wooden ſtakes like an encloſure, out of which they muſt not ſtir, neither may they buy or ſell, or have the leaſt communication with others, till the ſame be removed again under pain of death. This is ſometimes done alſo before the doors of private perſons.

A peculiar way of taking an oath.

Their funerals.

All the *Pagans* here, as well *Brahmans* as the *Nayros* and *Moukois*, burn the carcaſſes of their deceaſed friends; tho' this was more univerſally practis'd before the *Portugueſe* and *Dutch* introduced and ſettled the chriſtian religion here. They take peculiar care to provide in their life-time as much fine ſcented wood and other precious drugs as they think requiſite for the burning of their bodies to aſhes, which is afterwards divided among their relations and friends, who preſerve them, and at their feſtivals mix them with water, and paint their faces with them. When a *Brahman* happens to die, his widow is obliged, as a demonſtration of her affection towards her deceas'd huſband, to burn herſelf; this is commonly done under the noiſe of ſeveral muſical inſtruments, to ſuppreſs the doleful outcries of the dying perſon, and in the preſence of their next kindred. However they may excuſe themſelves as to this point if they pleaſe, but then they are branded with infamy, their hair is cut off cloſe, which they muſt not let grow to any length again; they are excluded from the ſociety of other women, nor are allow'd to marry again. Notwithſtanding which, many chuſe rather to diſpenſe with theſe diſadvantages than to burn themſelves. The wives of the *Nayros* are not obliged to this cuſtom, tho' there are not wanting inſtances, that they have thrown themſelves into the flames which conſum'd their huſband's carcaſs; the men are not engaged to mourn for their wives, except that they are forbidden to marry again.

Their marriages.

The marriages of the richer and better ſort are celebrated here with a great deal of ſolemnity; the firſt thing they do after matters are agreed betwixt them, is to repair to the *Pagode* or temple, where the prieſts perform certain ceremonies; after this, the friends and relations of the new married couple, both men and women, lead the bride for 15 days conſecutively to the bridegroom's houſe, where they are entertain'd at his charge; moſt of the women ſinging and playing upon flutes, ſmall drums, and other muſical inſtruments; the bride and bridegroom are placed together very richly attir'd, eſpecially with jewels, to ſuch an exceſs, that they have been computed to amount ſometimes to 200000 crowns. The room is hung with fine ſilk hangings interwoven with gold; and among other things, a plate with *Bethel* offer'd to every one there preſent; nay, even to thoſe that are ſtrangers; towards 1662

1662. the evening the women reconduct the bride to her house. At the expiration of the 15 days, the bride and bridegroom are mounted on an elephant richly accouter'd, so as to face one another; the elephant is led by a *Nayros*, and surrounded by the friends and relations on foot; thus they are conducted thro' the whole city, and are sure always to stop at the doors of any of their nearest kinfolks, relations or particular friends, who present them with *Bethel*, fruits and sweet meats, and anoint the head of the elephant with sweet scented waters; they are very careful not to miss any of their friends houses, for if any such thing should happen, they would look upon it as a signal affront. When they come to the *Pagode* they dismount, and after they have tarried there for some time, return to the bride's house, where the marriage is consummated, each of the guests being obliged to present the *Nayros* that led the elephant with a coco nut.

They begin their new year in *September*, but have no fix'd day, which they regulate according to the decision of the astrologers and conjurers, who pretend to find out by their art the very hour which is likely to be the most fortunate for the beginning of the year. All those that are above 15 years of age cover their faces that day, for fear of casting their eyes upon any thing; thus they are led by children to the temple, where uncovering themselves, they fix their eyes upon what object they find directly before them; if this happen to be an idol (which their temples are full of) they have a peculiar veneration for it, they look upon it as a good omen that the next year will prove prosperous to them.

Their writing. All over *Malabar* they use a peculiar language call'd by them *Malkama*. Paper they have none, but instead of it write upon the leaves of the wild coco-trees, with an iron pencil or pen; which contain not only their religious ceremonies, but likewise the whole series of their most antient histories. These leaves they cut all in the same shape of the breadth of two inches, and two hands length; of these they lay together as many as they think fit, and put a small stick thro' them on the top; which done, they fasten the stick on both ends to the leaves with a pack-thread, which they loosen as often as they have occasion to peruse them. Each of these leaves is call'd *Ola* by the *Malabars*. They exceed all the *European* writers in swiftness, which they perform with that dexterity, as to turn their faces frequently from the leaves, and to entertain others with talking whilst they are writing. The *Malabar* tongue is very difficult to be learn'd, by reason of its multitude of words, one and the same thing being express'd by different terms; nay, each day throughout the year is distinguish'd by a peculiar name. Several *Portuguese* jesuites have attempted to give us an insight into the *Malabar* tongue, and among the rest father *Gaspar Aquilar*. They have their peculiar letters, which are very ancient, and resembling the *Syriack* characters.

Their religious worship. The inhabitants of *Malabar*, as we told you before, are either natives, or descended from foreigners; the last of which being first come thither out of *Arabia*, are *Mahometans*, as the natives are *Pagans*. Some are of opinion, that all the kings of *Malabar* follow one and the same religion, but that their subjects are divided into 18 several sects; but, as far as ever I could learn by the most exact enquiry I was able to make, all the natives of *Malabar*, as well *Brahmans* as *Nayros* and *Moukois*, perform their religious worship in the same manner; for they adore their idols, and the sun, as they rise in the morning. In their temples you see a golden cow, or some other image, unto which they pay their devotions; which is the reason that neither the *Brahmans*, *Nayros* nor *Moukois* will kill this beast, but pay such reverence to it, that they paint the walls of their houses with its dung mix'd with water; thus, when the king of *Calicut* is to bathe himself, fifteen maids with cow-dung in their silver basons, plaister the rooms with it thro' which he is to pass twice aday. Their chief God they call *Parabramma*, with three sons near him, in remembrance of which the *Brahmans* wear a cord twisted of three threads on their bare skin. They not only worship man, but, as I told you, the beasts also, and erected temples for them, exceeding in magnificence those of the ancient *Romans*. There is one temple dedicated to the ape, the gallery of which is supported by 700 marble columns. Besides the cow they pay likewise a godly veneration to the elephant, it being their opinion, that the souls of men transmigrate into those beasts. They have many books, which contain an account of their religious ceremonies, much resembling the ancient *Greek* and *Roman* fables. The priests and *Brahmans* keep these books from the sight of the vulgar, these being their oracles, unto which they have recourse for their prophecies, to blind these poor wretches, as has been confess'd by some converted *Brahmans*. They make however much more account of religion than the *Nayros*; for they daily provide (at the king's charge) a considerable quantity of boil'd rice in their temples,

A Malabar Shewing tricks with Serpents.

1662. temples, which is distributed among the poor, or given to any body else that will ask for it, this being not look'd upon as ignominious among them. They keep continually burning lamps in their temples; and their prophets are almost cover'd with bells, which when they dance and make other awkard postures make a great noise; the *Moukois* have their own temples, which are nastily kept; they don't frequent them above once a month, *viz.* at the new moon, because they can spare no more time from their daily labour: At the entrance, each of them is presented with some ashes mix'd with water. The *Nayros* go commonly once a day to their temples, where each mutters out a short prayer; these temples are dispos'd throughout the whole countrey, and are most frequented at certain days, when they repair thither with a great deal of devotion; some for 20 or 30 leagues, for they have their appointed feasts, but two or three before all the rest. The chiefest is that of the new-years day, when the *Nayros* come to pay their reverence to the king, who receives them standing at a window, and throws a certain quantity of *Bethel* to each, and some gold and silver among them, as well as the rest of his subjects that appear there.

The *Malabar* kings, *Brahmans* and *Nayros*, pay likewise their devotions to serpents, which they consider as evil spirits made by God to torment mankind for their sins. You meet here with certain vagabonds who carry serpents in a basket, with some bran for their food, hanging on a stick, carried on the shoulders of two fellows; some of these serpents are six, seven or nine foot long, of a grass green colour, and not above an inch thick; some are very large and bulky, with grey spots; so soon as these *Malabar* vagabonds begin to play upon a certain instrument like a bagpike, the serpents set themselves upright upon their tails, twist themselves in a most surprizing manner, and soon after raise their fins or bristles, which are near the head, and fall on with such fury, as if they would tear one another to pieces, to the no small terror of the spectators.

The Malleans. On the tops of the high rocky mountains of *Malabar* (on the foot of which live the christians of *St. Thomas*) dwells a certain nation call'd the *Malleans*, they have a pretty good tillage about 13 or 14 leagues from *Madura* call'd *Priata*. According to the description given us by *Plutarch* and *Curtius*, and the resemblance of their names, these may not unlikely be the same mention'd by them as the most warlike nation of all the *Indians*, *Alexander* the great having receiv'd a mortal wound as he was attacking one of their cities. Now adays they don't inhabit any cities, towns or villages, but only certain enclosures in the valleys betwixt the rocks; their houses are built of canes very low, and plaister'd up with loom or clay. Some of them live in the woods, these make their houses of wood, which they remove from tree to tree, to secure themselves against the elephants and tygers. The first they catch in holes cover'd with the branches of trees, with some earth on the top; they also cultivate the ground, but in a very slender manner, tho' their valleys would be very fruitful if they were duly manag'd. They have but one wife at a time, who goes abroad a hunting with them, or wherever they go, whereas the *Pagan Malabars* marry generally several women. They chiefly differ from the other *Malabars* in their complexion, are just and honest, good natur'd, charitable, without deceit; for the rest, courageous, ingenious and cunning; they pretend to converse with the devils, only out of curiosity to know the event of things; the custom of the other *Malabars* and *Indians*, who hurt others by their sorceries, being unknown to them. They pay a great deal of deference to the sepulchres of their ancestors, and if they happen to be defiled, they look upon it to be an ill omen. Upon their festivals they wear a long gown, with a turbant, as the *Mahometans* do; but at other times they go half naked, like as the other *Malabars* do. They have holes in their ears and noses, in which they hang gold rings and jewels; a custom common also to the *Pagan Malabar* women, who look upon this as their chief ornament, especially to wear such things in one of their nostrils. At their feasts and festivals, the maidens play upon rush-pipes and small flutes and drums; theft is a thing unknown among the *Malabars*, every one living in his house in a profound security, with open doors; sometimes the inhabitants of a whole enclosure transfer their habitations to another. Part of the *Malabars* acknowledge the king of *Turbula*, part the king of *Pugnati Perimal* for their superiors, unto whom they pay some yearly tribute, yet with the entire preservation of their liberty, they being govern'd by their own laws, under captains or judges of their nation, call'd by them *Arley*, each of them has commonly 5000 or 6000 under his district; besides which, each enclosure is govern'd by its own judge, call'd *Pandera*, unto whom they pay strict obedience.

Before 1599, when they began first to be instructed in the *Romish* religion, by the assiduity of the then archbishop of *Goa*, they were all pagans, but since that time, a good

1662. a good number of them have embraced christianity; eight of their best men, among whom were three *Pandaras*, with their whole families, first received baptism, who being follow'd by many others, a church dedicated to St. *Michael* was built in the village of *Priata*. Before their conversion they had no temples erected in honour of their idols, neither did they sacrifice with feasting, dancing and such like ceremonies, but each family had its domestick god, unto whom they paid their devotions. They are much more esteem'd among the *Malabars*, than their common people; neither are they look'd upon as unclean by them, no more than the christians of *St. Thomas*, if they happen to touch a *Nayros*; they keep scarce any commerce with the neighbouring nations, even not with the *Thomists* themselves, who live at the foot of the same mountains. Their weapons are the same as the rest of the *Malabars* use, *viz.* a bow and arrows pointed with a broad iron. They use also scimeters or hangers, and a peculiar sort of fire arms, such as are no where else to be seen among the *Malabars*. On the foot of the mountain inhabited by the *Malabars* call'd *Karatkara*, bordering upon the kingdom of *Karanarata*, stands a church belonging to these *Thomists* or christians of *St. Thomas*, dedicated to St. *Austin*, because the inhabitants owe their conversion to certain fryers of that order.

Products of Malabar. *Malabar*, as I told you before, is a countrey abounding in divers sorts of fruits, such as the *Indies* commonly afford, of the choicest of which we will give you a short description here.

Coco-tree. All along the sea-shore of *Malabar*, and the rivers near the sea-side, the *Indian* palm or coco-tree, grows in sandy and brackish grounds; the *Malabars* call it *Tenga*, the *Brahmans Mado*, and in the *Malabar* tongue it is call'd *Kalappa*. Its trunk, which is of an ash colour, rises sometimes to the height of 95 feet; such I have several times measured my self near the city of *Koulang*; it has commonly 16 inches diameter, tho' sometimes it is so thick, as scarce to be grasped by a man; and is of the same thrickness from the bottom to the top; the wood is spongy, and the pith as white as paper. However the trunk does not grow up strait, but is jointed, without any branches, but only on the top, where commonly sprout forth 16 or 18, and in a very large tree sometimes 28, which bear green large leaves like reeds, being about a finger's length broad, and about two foot long. The root of this tree is very small in proportion of its bigness, and does not reach deep under ground, but creeps just under its surface, so that it seems next to a miracle, how these high trees are able to withstand the fury of the winds. The fruit, call'd commonly coco-nuts, after the *Portuguese*, who call them *Coquo* and *Cocoe*, grow at the ends of the branches, about 6, 8, or 10 in a bunch; a bunch weighing sometimes from 60 to 100 pounds weight; each ripe nut exceeds the bigness of a lusty man's head, being of a triangular figure, and cover'd with a double peel; the first is an inch thick, consisting of many threads, extending length-wise round the fruit; the outside is of an ash colour, but inwardly inclining to red; the next peel is hard and brown, which contains the peel. Before they are ripe, they are of a pale yellow colour, and afterwards turn dark green, having at one end a bush of small leaves, resembling our turnep leaves. The pith is white, inclining to yellow, about an inch thick, and to the second peel, the remaining hollowness being fill'd with liquor, and containing according to the bigness of the unripe nut, a pint of liquor, which in the ripe one diminishes by degrees, and encreases the bulk of the peel. This liquor is good to drink, the pith is sweet, and of no ungrateful taste, only a little flat. The blossom, which is not unlike that of the chesnuts, appears at the ends of the branches which produce the fruit, which ripens in three months time. The pith dried, may be kept and transported like chesnuts; if it be powder'd and mixt with sugar and cinnamon, it tastes very well, augments the seed, and is a strong provocative. When the *Nayros* are to gather the nuts, they climb with most wonderful nimbleness to the tops of these high trees, where they cut off as many branches as are ripe, and let them fall down upon the ground. Besides the fruit, this tree affords also a certain liquor, call'd by them *Sury*, and by the *Europeans* palm-wine: When they are to gather this liquor, they only cut off one of its branches, from whence issues the liquor, which falls into a vessel of bamboe, hung under it for that purpose; if they draw too much liquor at a time, the branches turn brown, and the tree produces no more nuts. These trees being planted in a streight line, the *Nayros* lay sticks reaching from one to other, by which means they get to the branches, where they have fasten'd the vessel that receives the liquor. This liquor, whilst fresh is very good to drink, and will inebriate like wine; but if kept in the sun, turns to vinegar in an hours time. But tho' they take never so much care of it, what is gather'd about noon, will turn by night, taste sourish the next day, and turn quite to vinegar the day after that. The liquor which

A Branch with Cocoa Nuts

1:

1662. which distils from the young trees, is not so strong and spirituous as that gather'd from the old ones, but the first affords a greater quantity. After this liquor has been kept 24 hours, they distil a spirit of it, with the addition of a small quantity of the oil of clove; this is by the *Indians* call'd *Arack*, and by some *Tula* or *Mype*. Out of this liquor they prepare vinegar, thus: They put the vessels in which the liquor has been gather'd, in lime 15 days, during which time it ferments, casting gross sediments to the bottom; the clear is very good vinegar. Out of the same sugar they make a kind of liquor call'd *Jagra*. They put a small quantity of lime in the vessel which contains the liquor, as much as is sufficient to make it turn red; for if you put in too much lime, the liquor turns whiter and whiter, but if you put too little, it does not change its colour. The liquor thus mix'd with a sufficient quantity of lime, must be boil'd and stirred continually with a spoon, till it comes to the consistency of red sugar; where it is to be observed, that if there be not lime enough added, it will produce no sugar, but if too much, part of it will settle to the bottom, which must be taken out before you can boil it into a sugar. If you intend to make white sugar or *Jayra*, you must take care to pour the liquor mix'd with the lime out of one pot into another (to separate the superfluous lime) which you must repeat three times; as for instance, if your liquor be gather'd in the morning, you must pour it into another vessel by noon, and repeat the same a second time about two a clock, and a third time before night, and then boil it. What liquor is gather'd in the night-time keeps longer than that gather'd in the day-time. Whilst it is fresh, its taste is not much unlike our whey, unto which the inhabitants add some raisins, and make it taste like *Spanish* wine. The trunk of the coco-tree is used for timber in the building of houses and ships, the branches and leaves to write upon and to cover houses with, as also by the basket-makers. Out of the hard shell of the nuts (some of which are of a pale, others of a dark brown colour) they make drinking cups and other vessels, which they polish, and sometimes are edg'd with silver. The hairy substance, call'd *Kayer*, is used by the rope-makers; these ropes don't rot easily: They also make matches of them, which burn very fiercely. In the *Maldive* islands (where these trees are found in vast quantities) they sometimes equip whole vessels out of the coco-trees; the body of the vessels being made of the trunk of a tree, without any nails or other iron-work; the sail and ropes of the hairy substance, the provisions consisting of the liquor and kernels of the coco-nuts, their drinking and other vessels being made of the shell, and their hammocks, quilts and other implements of the leaves. In short, this tree furnishes the *Indians* upon occasion, with all that is necessary for their subsistence, being very fruitful in marshy and low grounds, but bears not so great a quantity of fruit, neither so big in the mountainous countries. The coco-tree is in its prime from the 25th to the 30th year, and affords the most fruit and liquor; from the time it begins to bear, the ripe fruits fall off, and others grow continually in their stead, but when it begins to grow old, the fruit grows lesser and lesser. This tree will continue till it is 100 years old; when the small branches and leaves begin to turn yellow, it is an infallible sign of its decay. It is produced out of the kernel of the coco-nut; these the *Indians* put into the ground till they begin to sprout, then they make as many holes as they intend to plant trees, and of such a depth, that the tops of the leaves don't reach beyond the surface of the ground; then they throw a handful or two of sand (unless it be in sandy ground) and half a handful of salt in each hole, upon which they put the kernel, which they cover with the same ground they had taken out of the hole before, and every other day water them, till they are sure the nuts have taken root. They plant them with the point downwards, out of the opposite part of which at first shoot forth two or three broad leaves, after which comes the right leaves, and soon after the small sprouts, which fall off as new ones succeed, till the tree comes to its full growth. The young tree commonly begins to bear in the fifth year after its planting; great care is taken that the horse-flies don't spoil the young trees. This is a kind of worm not unlike our hornets, with two sharp horns, but not so big; this worm gets to the pith of the tree, which he consumes till the tree dies, unless he be taken out in time, at which the *Malabars* are very dextrous, and then the tree will recover. It has been observed that this tree in the third year after its planting, has its branches in their perfection, and from that time the branches begin to fall off. Those branches are at that time about five or six yards long, tho' the stem on which they grow is not above two foot high, and about a foot in circumference. Every month you see commonly a new branch come forth, and then the old ones fall off, but in the summer and dry seasons they fall off more frequently than in rainy weather; these branches come to their full growth in

1662. three months. I cauſed above 4000 coco-trees to be planted near *Koiland*, but moſt of them came to nothing, being not carefully look'd after by my ſucceſſors. There are divers kinds of this tree, which are diſtinguiſh'd by the fruit, but eſpecially by the watery ſubſtance found within the ſhells of the nuts.

Wild cinnamon trees.

Malabar produces prodigious quantities of wild cinnamon trees, but the cinnamon is neither in ſmell nor in goodneſs comparable to that which grows in the iſle of *Ceylon*; this iſland, and that of *Floris* being the only ones where the true cinnamon grows. The *Portugueſe* call this wild cinnamon *Canella de Mato*, *i. e. Wood-Cinamon*, the *Malabars Larva* or *Bahona*, as alſo *Kaunema*, *i. e. Sweet-Wood*, from the word *Kau*, which in their language ſignifies wood, and *Nema i. e.* ſweet, the *Malayans Kais Manis*, the *Zingaleſe* or inhabitants of *Ceylon Kurudo* or *Kurundo*, and the *Arabians Querfaa* and *Querfe*, as alſo *Kerfak*. Before the *Dutch* got into poſſeſſion of *Ceylon*, they uſed to tranſport this cinnamon, but ſince that time they make no account of it. The tree is of the bigneſs of our orange tree, leſs or more, but not large as the cinnamon trees in *Ceylon*. It has abundance of branches, leaves not unlike the laurel leaves, but broader, of a paler colour, with three diſtinct veins. The bloſſom is white, almoſt without any ſcent; the fruit not unlike the wild olives, firſt green, afterwards inclining to red, and when ripe, black ſhining. It has alſo a kernel not unlike the wild olive, which is covered with a pulp like the ſame, out of which iſſues a kind of green oily liquor, of the ſame ſcent as the laurels, biting and bitteriſh upon the tongue. The rind of this tree (or the cinnamon it ſelf) is thick, without any remarkable taſte, tho' the ſmall ſprouts or tacks are ſomewhat bitter, yet don't come near to the cinnamon of the iſle of *Ceylon*.

Oil of cinnamon and volatile ſalt.

Out of the rind of the root they prepare a kind of volatile ſalt, which they call camphire, ſwimming upon the ſurface of the water of a yellow colour, clear, ſtrong and well ſcented, ſharp upon the tongue, and very penetrating, being ſo volatile, that if expoſed to the air, it evacuates immediately. This camphire is exceeding white, excelling the common camphire in its ſcent; the particles of this camphire are inſenſibly mix'd with the oil, whilſt yet warm, immediately after its diſtillation; but as ſoon as the oil begins to cool, they adhere to one another in divers ſhapes, and ſettle to the bottom. This camphire is very volatile, and ſo fiery that it takes fire in an inſtant, and leaves not the leaſt impurity behind, after it is conſumed. The oil approaches very near both in ſmell and taſte to the camphire, and is ſo volatile, that if ſome of it be dropped upon woollen ſtuffs, even of the niceſt colours, it evaporates immediately, without leaving the leaſt ſpot behind. It is alſo very combuſtible, burning with a white and blue flame; if put upon the fire, it evacuates in a inſtant, and turns into a white ſmoak, which is very apt to take fire. This oil mixt with gunpowder, will ſet it on fire by degrees, yet not till a great part of the oily ſubſtance be evacuated. If mix'd with ſulphur or ſalt-peter, or with both, it will take fire immediately and conſume the ſulphur and ſalt-peter, remaining without the leaſt alteration. If you put the oil upon the fire, and receive the flame which evaporates from thence, in a thick cloth, a white kind of ſalt will ſettle in it, which is the camphire itſelf. This oil will alſo in time ſeparate ſome of thoſe camphirous particles, which falling to the bottom, render the oil more clear and pure. The oil drawn out of the *Malabar* cinnamon, is clear, tranſparent, yellowiſh and well ſcented, ſwimming upon the water; whereas out of the common cinnamon of *Ceylon*, beſides that oil which riſes on the top of the water, another is alſo drawn, which ſinks to the bottom. The oil diſtill'd from the leaves is thin at firſt, turns yellowiſh by degrees, and tranſparent, and of a greeniſh colour at laſt, being very ſweet, but ſharp at laſt, having ſomething of cinnamon; it ſinks to the bottom of the water. 1662.

Its virtues.

The oil made out of the rind of the root, with its volatile ſalt (the camphire) is endow'd with greater virtues. It is a ſovereign remedy againſt all lameneſs, if applied outwardly, and gives immediate eaſe in the gout; it may alſo be taken inwardly with very good ſucceſs, being a great remedy againſt malignant fevers, a great ſudorifick, expelling the wind, procuring an appetite in the ſtomach, and conſuming the ſtone both in the kidneys and bladder, and is good in the cough, and many other chronick diſtempers; to be ſhort, it is the moſt univerſal remedy made uſe of there by the *Dutch* in their hoſpitals. The camphire is very proficuous in all diſtempers in the womb, promotes the monthly terms, and is a great ſudorifick, being uſed in all reſpects like the common camphire. The oil diſtill'd out of the bark of the tree, is an excellent remedy in all diſtempers of the ſtomach, and in the cholick, proceeding from a cold cauſe; the water of cinnamon is cordial; the oil of the leaves is good againſt the cholick, if applied outwardly to the belly, and helps lameneſs.

In

1662.

Zua or Zerumbet.

In the woods of *Malabar* about *Kananor*, grows a certain shrub in great plenty, call'd *Zua* by the *Malabars*, at *Surate Dekan*, and *Cachora* by the *Canarins*; by the *Arabians* and *Persians Zerumbet*, and *Zeruba* by the *Turks*. If planted or sow'd, it will grow also in many other places. By some it is reckoned a kind of ginger, and not without reason, its leaves resembling those of the ginger, only that they are somewhat larger, as is also the root, which being cut in pieces and dried, is thus transported into foreign parts.

The tree call'd Macre or Macer.

On the coast of *Malabar*, in the isle of *St. Cruce*, belonging to the kingdom of *Cochin*, near the river *Manatte*, grows a certain tree call'd *Macre* by the *Brahman* physicians, by the christians there *Makuyre*, and by the *Portuguese Arbore de las Canaras* and *Arbore Sancto*, i. e. the *Tree of the Bloody Flux* and *the holy Tree*. The saints of this countrey have this saying of it; *Kura Santea Macre Nistusa garul*: i. e. *Macre was discover'd to mankind for their benefit by the Angels*. *Galen*, *Dioscorides* and *Pliny* call it *Macer*, and *Avicenna Talisfar*; this tree spreads its branches in a large compass, being bigger than our elm-tree. Its leaves are seven foot long, and two broad, the uppermost side of a pale, and the undermost of a dark green colour. It is generally believ'd, that this tree produces no fruit, but only a kind of seed, of the bigness of a farthing, thin, yellowish, resembling in taste the kernel of an almond or peach-stone, cover'd with a white skin. It is enclosed in a kind of a bladder composed of two different peels. This bladder comes forth in the middle of the leaf, resembling that which in *May* sprouts forth on the elm-trees, except that it is somewhat broader and flatter. The leaf of this bladder is of the bigness of other leaves, but not so much pointed at the end, and narrow towards the stalk, of a deep yellow colour, cover'd with a kind of curl'd down from the stalk to the end. The root of this tree is not unlike that of the *Stone*-palm-tree, with large and thick roots spread at a great distance; the rind of those roots is thick, rough, of an ash-colour without, but white within; containing a juice like milk whilst fresh, but turns yellow; when dry it is very astringent. This tree delights in few but sandy grounds, and kills all other trees or shrubs near it. The rind of the root of this tree is in vast esteem among the *Malabars*, as well as among the *Chinese*, *Javanese*, *Malabars* and all *Bengale*; being look'd upon and made use of in their hospitals, as the most sovereign remedy in the world, against looseness and all manner of bloody fluxes. The *Indian* physicians, as well *Brahmans*, *Canarins*, as *Malabars*, cure with this rind whilst fresh, powder'd and mix'd with butter-milk, the bloody flux; some infuse half an ounce of the rind, dried and powder'd in a quartern of whey for 12 hours, which they give the patient twice a day, *viz.* in the morning and evening, immediately after they give the patient rice to eat, boil'd without salt or butter, and after that a chicken boil'd in the decoction of rice flour. If the distemper be very urgent, they add some *Opium* for the strengthening of the stomach; and to stop vomiting, they mix a little mastich with this rind, and give it in mint water. They tell you that a small quantity of this rind, excels much in virtue a considerable number of the *Myrobolan* rinds, or of *Areka*; nay, they prefer it before the *Koru* of *Malabar* itself. The fruit, or rather seed, expels all sorts of worms, and dissolves the stone in the kidneys, being look'd upon likewise as a great preservative both against the stone and cholick. Besides the tree *Macer*, other trees grow here very different in kind, but agree in virtue with the *Macer* tree.

The tree Kurodapala.

The first of these two is by the *Malabars* call'd *Kurodapala*, or *Kuro*, and *Koru* by the *Canariins*, by the *Brahmans Kura*, and by the *Portuguese* the *Malabar* shrub, its use having been first shewn them by the *Malabars*. This tree or shrub is not unlike a small orange tree, especially as to its leaves, except that the vein in the middle of the leaf, out of which come 8 or 9 on both sides, is somewhat thicker. The blossom is yellow, and without the least scent. *Garcias* says this tree is somewhat less than a common crab-tree, its leaves like a peach-tree, with a white blossom. It has a pale green and smooth bark, out of which, if cut with a knife, issues a milk-like juice, more viscous than that which comes forth out of the *Macer* tree, bitterish of taste; the *Malabar* physicians assign it a cooling quality. This tree affords an infallible remedy against all kinds of bloody fluxes, provided the gross ill humours have been purged away before, without which the patient will soon have a relapse. The *Malabars* (according to *Garcias*) prepare a compounded water out of the root, unto which they attribute great virtues against the bloody flux; they take 8 ounces of this root well beaten to powder, and infused in whey, and the liquor of boil'd rice, unto this they add the seeds of pursley, black cummin and coriander, each an ounce and a half; of the *Myrobolan* rind 7 drachms, and fresh butter 2 ounces; this they distil, and mix a quartern of this distill'd water with half a quartern of *Arack*, and give it the patient. They apply this water also in form

1662. form of a clyster in the night time, by reason of the excessive heat of the days in those parts. Inwardly they commonly give it twice a day, *viz.* in the morning about six a clock, and in the afternoon about two. Their diet is rice mix'd with fat, and chickens boil'd in the decoction of rice, which they call *Kaaje* in their language, but the use of wine is absolutely forbidden, unless it be in an inveterate bloody flux, to keep up the spirits. Some give only the juice of the shrub whilst green, of which they give a quartern and a half in the morning, and as much in the evening; and to take away the bitterish taste, allow the patient to drink a little whey after it. In case of necessity they mix some *Opium* with it. It is also a good remedy to strengthen the stomach, and to stop vomiting, if taken in mint water, or mix'd with some mastich powder'd. The root taken inwardly with the decoction of rice, or applied outwardly is very good against the piles. The decoction of the leaves, and those of tamarinds, make an excellent fomentation for swell'd legs, held over the hot steam, and a cloth dip'd in the same decoction is with good success applied in the looseness and dropsy.

Pavate *or* Vasa Veli. The third sort of those vegetables which are us'd here against the bloody flux, is call'd by the *Malabars Pavate*, and *Vasa Veli* by the *Brahmans*, and *Canarins*, and *Arbor contra las erysipelas*, i. e. *the Tree against the St. Anthony*'s *Fire*. It is a shrub not above 8 or 9 foot high, with a few branches and leaves, resembling the small leaves of orange-trees before they come to their full growth, green on both sides; the blossom is white and small, the seed round, in bigness like to that of the mastich-tree; dark green at first, which turns black as it ripens. The stem and tacks are of an ash-colour, the root either without scent or taste, except that it is somewhat bitterish.

Jambos *or* Jambeiro. Among the fruit trees of *Malabar*, that which the inhabitants call *Jambos*, and the *Portuguese Jambeiro*, must not be pass'd by in silence. The *Malabars* and *Canarins* call the fruit *Jambali*, the *Arabians Tufa Indi*, the *Turks Alma*, and the *Persians Tufat*. It is the common opinion, that this was first of all for the pleasantness of its blossom, and excellency of its fruit, transplanted from *Malacca* (where it is found in great plenty) into all the other parts of the *Indies*. There are two kinds, resembling one another in most respects, except in their fruit, which is somewhat different. Both are not unlike, as well in shape as bigness to our *European* apple-trees, and will grow without much cultivating in any ground, and bear fruit within 5 years; they take root very deep, a thing seldom observ'd among the *Indian* trees. These trees are of a pleasant aspect, spreading their branches to the height of a good plumb-tree. The bark, as well of the tree as of the branches, is of an ash-colour and smooth; the wood brittle; the leaves also resemble those of the plumb-tree, but are somewhat more pointed at the end, being a palm in length, and not unlike the iron point of a long pike or lance. The upper side is dark, and the undermost pale green, with a strait vein in the middle, which sends out divers others on both sides. The blossoms are both for scent and colour like our roses, but inclining more to a purple colour; the first is of the bigness of a large pear, or of a goose egg, or rather bigger. They are of two sorts; one of which is a dark red, inclining to black, generally without stones, excelling the other in taste; the other is pale red, has a longish white stone of the bigness of a peach-stone, cover'd with a white rough skin; this, tho' inferior to the former, yet is of a most pleasing taste. Sometimes the first is absolutely red, and these are of a purple colour, and smell like a rose; the fruit is cover'd with so thin a peel, that no knife can separate it from the pulp, which is accounted cold and moist; and so are the blossoms, notwithstanding which they are very well scented, and for that reason in high esteem among the inhabitants. The fruit is commonly eaten before dinner, or at the beginning of a meal; neither are they useless in physick, both the fruit and flowers preserved, being prescribed in violent burning fevers; having besides their cooling quality, a certain virtue of comforting the spirits. This tree may well be accounted among the number of those, which by the excellency of their fruit, and the agreeableness of their flowers, surprizes the beholders; for, whilst you see one side of the tree bare of leaves and blossoms, the other is stor'd with fruit, which last, till the other side begins to renew its leaves; so that in one and the same tree you see a continual spring and autumn at once. Thus you never can cast your eye upon this tree but you meet there either with blossom or fruit; and as the blossom drops underneath on the ground (which is frequently cover'd with those purple colour'd flowers) others come forth in their stead; and whilst some of the fruit are ripening, others are to be gathered. The best way to gather their fruit is to shake the tree, then they fall with ease; but if you endeavour to pull them off, the tacks are apt to break. Karkapuli.

The fruit *Karkapuli*, call'd *Kerkapoli* by the *Canarins*, is in shape and bigness like an orange; they are green at first, af-

2 terwards

1662. terwards turn yellow, and when ripe, white, of ſweet taſte, but a little tartiſh. In the centre of the pulp lies the ſeeds, flat and long, of the bigneſs of a joint of a finger, and are of a dark brown colour.

Koddam Pulli.

The tree which bears this fruit is very tall, call'd *Koddam Pulli* by the *Malabars*, ſometimes *Otta Pulli*, and by the *Brahmans Danubos*, by the inhabitants of the iſle of *Ceylon Choroka*; the fruit is eaten, and uſed in phyſick among the *Indians*, being accounted an excellent remedy againſt looſeneſs, eſpecially if occaſioned by too much venery. Beſides which, the fruit before it is quite ripe, or the juice of it mix'd with butter-milk, or the fruit dried and powder'd mix'd with butter-milk and boil'd rice, is excellent good to acuate the appetite of the ſtomach. This juice alſo, as well as the dry fruit powder'd, is accounted a good remedy againſt the dimneſs, cataracts, and other infirmities of the eyes; they apply the juice, mix'd with ſome other herbs, to the nail of the great toe, on that ſide where the defect of the eye is. The midwives give it to women lately brought to bed, to expel the after-birth, and produce plenty of milk for ſuck. This fruit, when dried, is tranſported to foreign countries. There is another kind of this tree, bearing a round fruit and ſweet, of the bigneſs of a cherry, call'd *Karkapuli* by Mr. *Dinſhoten*; this tree is call'd *Karue Choraka* by thoſe of *Ceylon*, i. e. *ſweet Choraka*; out of the bark of both of theſe trees, if ſlit with a knife, iſſues a gum call'd *Gutta*, but that which comes from the *Kanka Choraka* is the beſt.

The uſe of aloe leaves among the Malabars.

The uſe of aloe leaves is very frequent among the *Malabars*, a purge they boldly give not only to children, but alſo to women with child. They take of the aloe leaves 3 ounces cut very ſmall, theſe they boil with two drachms of black ſalt over an eaſy fire, and after they have ſtrain'd it, add to it an ounce of ſugar, and ſo let it ſtand the whole night in the air. The next morning about ſix a clock they give the patient this decoction cold, ordering him to abſtain from ſleep, and to walk about to promote its operation; three hours after he hath taken it, they give him a little chicken broth, with a few grains of maſtich in it, and an hour after that allow him to eat, and to take a little wine of the ſmalleſt ſort. They either increaſe or diminiſh the doſe of the decoction, according to the conſtitution of the patient.

There grows in *Malabar* a certain fruit of the bigneſs of a hazle nut, but is not quite ſo round and white; it grows on the tacks of a certain ſhrub which they ſow; it has no peculiar uſe in phyſick, tho' *Serapio* aſcribes to it a virtue of augmenting the ſeed, and promoting the birth in women; the ſame the *Malabars* do to this day, who call the fruit *Chevique lenga*, and in ſome places *Kurkas*, and thoſe of *Cambaiak Karpata*. If *Garcias* may be credited, this is the ſame fruit deſcribed by *Serapio* by the broken name of *Habel-culcul*, whereas it ſhould have been *Hab-alcul*, which ſignifies as much as the ſeed of *Culcul*. 1662.

Chevique Lenga.

The tree call'd *Kumbulu* by the *Malabars*, and *Bon-Varo* by the *Brahmans*, grows very tall, with a trunk of that thickneſs, that a man can ſcarce graſp it. The leaves are a ſpan, and two or three inches long, and two palms broad, woolly at the end of the ſtalks, which are round, long and thick; at the extremities of the tacks, which ſprout forth out of the branches, grow certain yellow flowers in cluſters on ſhort ſtalks, conſiſting of five round and thick leaves. After theſe comes a fruit that's like a pear, full of juice, the pulp being of a yellowiſh colour, and a ſweetiſh taſte, but the juice when preſs'd out is deep yellow. They are green at firſt, next of a pale yellow, and turn reddiſh at laſt; in the centre of the fruit is a white ſmooth ſtone, ſhap'd like a pear, with a ſmall kernel in it. The decoction of the root, mix'd with a little rice, is a good remedy againſt the ague, which often follows the gout or rheumatiſm. Taken in butter-milk, or mix'd with the oil of *Sirchelem*, it expels the wind, and eaſes the pain; and the juice of the leaves taken with butter-milk, is good againſt the cholick.

The tree Ganſchi.

The tree call'd *Ganſchi* by the *Malabars*, and *Schivanni* by the *Brahmans*, grows in ſandy grounds a great height and thickneſs, ſo that a man can ſcarce graſp the trunk, which as well as the branches has a bark of an aſh-colour without, but green within. The leaves hang on long, round and green ſtalks, being above a ſpan in length, and two palms broad, of an oblong figure. The bloſſoms faſtened to ſtalks which are pale green, ſweet, round and thin, each flower conſiſting of no more than three, and ſeldom of four leaves. After theſe comes the fruit, which is of a triangular figure, flattiſh, and of a green colour, hanging on long and green ſtalks, the ſeed being triangular, and the pulp very ſubſtantial; the decoction of the root is uſed againſt the gout, and apply'd to the affected part.

The tree Palega-Pajamelr.

Of the tree *Palega* there are two kinds; one is call'd *Palega-Pajaneli* by the *Malabars*, and the other barely *Pajanel*. The *Palega-Pajaneli*, called *Davandiku* by the *Brahmans*, is very tall, with a trunk enough for a man to graſp, having an aſh-coloured bark, as well as the branches, which grow ſtrait upright, of a conſiderable thickneſs.

1662. The leaves hang on stalks, which shoot forth both out of the stem and branches of the tree. On the extremities of the branches grow certain clusters of flowers shap'd like bells, consisting of six thick leaves; whitish or pale yellow within, and streak'd with red on the out-side, the scent of which is offensive to the nostrils. The fruit which follows the flowers is about three spans long, of the breadth of a hand, and an inch thick, with a dark green peel. The pulp juicy and tender at first, but grows hard at last; the seed is very flat. The bark of the tree powder'd and mix'd with wine, applied to a wound, or broken bones, heals them. The decoction of the root is good against the dropsy; and the leaves, whilst yet very young, mix'd with *Malabar* saffron, cures all sorts of ulcers, if apply'd to them outwardly.

The second kind of Pajaneli.

The second kind of the *Pajaneli*, called *Davandiku* by the *Brahmans*, is likewise a very tall tree, whose branches shoot forth upright to a great height; it delights in sandy grounds: The root spreads at a great distance, having a thick ash-coloured rind. The trunk is of that thickness, that a man can scarce grasp it, of a brittle wood, with a dark ash-coloured bark: The flowers are like the former, shap'd like bells, but have no more than five leaves. The fruit is the same: Of the juice of the leaves, and that of the fruit *Kareka*, or *Mirobolans* mix'd together, the *Malabars* make a black dye to dye their mourning cloaths with. The decoction of the rind of the root dispels hard tumours if they be fomented with it.

Of the tree *Pala*, called *Santeru* by the *Brahmans*, there are four kinds; 1. *Pala*; 2. *Kuruta Pala*; 3. *Kadaga Pala*; 4. *Kaikotten Pala*: The first kind, called only *Pala*, is a high tree growing in sandy places, and spreading its branches into a great circumference: The root, which has a dark yellow rind, reaches very deep into the ground, and contains a milky juice: The trunk is two or three fathoms thick, the bark of an ash-colour, as is likewise the bark of the branches. The leaves grow four or five together, on stalks of an oblong figure, and towards the stalks full of a milky substance; the flowers grow in clusters, having five whitish leaves of a strong scent, but offensive to the brains. The fruit which comes immediately after the blossom, do likewise hang in clusters on small tacks, being green husks of about two spans length, but small and flat, full of a milky juice or substance, as is the tree itself, which produces fruit but once a year, *viz.* in *January*.

The second kind of *Pala* is by the *Malabars* called *Kurutu Pala*, by the *Brahmans Kudo*, being a tree from six to twelve foot high, the trunk about the thickness of a foot, with an ash-coloured bark, as well as the branches. The leaves come forth out of the branches with their stalks, being of an oblong figure, and pointed at the end. The flowers grow on the extremities of the small tacks, are white, and bigger than those of the first kind, and have five long leaves. The fruit grows likewise in clusters, being of an oblong figure, dark green at first, and as they ripen turn yellow. The husk contains five, six or seven seeds. The tree bears fruit all the year round, but most in the rainy season. The bark of the tree beaten to powder, and taken in warm water, is good against the loose piles, but if taken in milk stops the bloody flux. 1662.

The third kind of *Pala*, called *Kadaga-Pala* by the *Malabars*, and *Alego-Kugo* by the *Brahmans*, is no higher than the *Kurutu-Pala*, and delights in sandy grounds. The root does not go so deep underground as that of the *Pala*, the bark is of a dark brown colour; the trunk is of a foot circumference like the second kind, but the leaves and blossom being also like the same. It bears long husks like the *Pala*, but are somewhat thicker, of a green colour, a span long, and full of a milky liquor. The bark of the trunk beaten to powder, and taken in butter-milk, stops the looseness; and the rind of the root, taken in the same manner, cures the bloody flux. The decoction of the seeds is given in burning fevers, and kills the worms. The fourth kind, called *Kaikotten-Kala*, is very near the same with the third. Kaikotten-Kala.

There are two kinds of the tree called *Parva* by the *Malabars*; the first they call *Tindaparva*, and the second *Anaparva*, and the *Brahmans Bendarli*. The *Tindaparva* grows to a great height in sandy grounds, having a thick whitish root with a soft rind: The trunk is so thick that a man can scarce grasp it with his arms, having an ash-coloured bark as well as the branches, which underneath the bark are of a dark brown colour. The leaves which are long, and pointed at the end, hang on short stalks, as do likewise the flowers, consisting of four pale green and pointed leaves. The fruits are a kind of round berries, with a very thin peel, green at first, afterwards inclining to white, and turn red as they ripen. In the peel is enclosed a round kernel. The root beaten to powder and taken inwardly, is a sovereign remedy against epileptick fits; and the decoction of the leaves disperses all pain, if the affected parts be well fomented with it.

The tree *Kavalkan*, as the *Malabars* call it, and *Bankar* by the *Brahmans*, grows in stony

1662. ſtony and ſandy grounds; its root, which is very thick, and covered with an aſh-coloured but ſoftiſh rind, ſtretching very deep underground. The trunk is ſo thick that a man can ſcarce graſp it with both his arms, covered with a thick bark, of an aſh-colour without, and pale green within. The wood is alſo white, and may be drawn into thread. The leaves are of an oblong figure, a ſpan and 2 or 3 inches long, pointed at the ends, hanging on long round and green ſtalks: The flowers conſiſting of five ſmall leaves ſprout out in cluſters, with green and hairy ſtalks. The fruit comes forth in bunches, three, four, or five together, being of the ſhape of an egg, with a thick and hard rind, containing nine or ten beans of the length of a finger each, but round and ſmooth, with a double peel: Theſe beans, when roaſted are good food. This tree bears bloſſom but once a year, *viz.* in *May*, and is not uſed in phyſick among the *Malabars*.

The tree Ambalam. Of the tree *Ambalam* there are two kinds in *Malabar*; one is ſimply called *Ambalam*, or *Koduko Ambado*, (i. e. *Sweet Ambado)* by the *Brahmans*; the other, *Kat Ambalam*, or *Pee Ambalam*. The tree *Ambalam* grows to a great height in ſandy grounds, with its branches not ſpreading, but upright. The root which is very large, ſtretching with many twigs under ground. The trunk is of a great circumference, covered with a very thick bark; the wood being very ſoft: The leaves hang on ſmall green ſtalks or ſprouts, in bunches of five together; they are generally as long again as they are broad, ſmooth and ſoft, and of a light green on both ſides. Thoſe leaves which are neareſt to the ſmall twigs, are not ſo large as the reſt, of an agreeable ſcent, and tartiſh, not unlike the rind of the *Indian Mangoes.* The bloſſom or flower do likewiſe come forth out of ſmall and green ſprouts, are of a whitiſh colour, ſhaped like ſtars, having five or ſix leaves. The buds of theſe flowers are round, and green at firſt, but turn white before they open; which when it happens, the leaves fall from the tree, which continues bare as long as it ſtands in bloſſom, but as the fruit grows, new leaves come forth by degrees. The fruit grows in cluſters, being of an oval figure, and pretty hard, not unlike to the *Indian Mangoes:* Before they come to maturity their rind is dark brown, and full of ſour juice, but when they begin to ripen turn light green, and at laſt yellow, of an agreeable tartiſh taſte, and are eaten by the inhabitants. In the midſt of the fruit is a very large ſtone. This tree bears twice every year, *viz.* in *January* and *May.* The root of it thruſt into the matrix ſtops the ſuperfluous monthly times. The bark powder'd and taken in butter-milk is good againſt the looſeneſs, and ſo is the juice mix'd with ice. The decoction of the wood is a good remedy againſt the involuntary emiſſion of the ſeed, and the juice of the leaves mix'd with that of the fruit inſtill'd into the ears, eaſes the pain in thoſe parts. 1662.

The ſecond kind of the *Ambalam*, *Kat Ambulam*, or *Pee Ambalam*, as the *Malabars* call it, and *Kaduko Ambado* by the *Brahmans*, reſembles the firſt in a great many reſpects, except that its leaves are leſs, and ſo are the fruit, being ſomewhat rounder, and the taſte a mixture of ſour and bitter; which is the reaſon they are never eaten. *Kat Ambalam*, or *Pee Ambalam*, ſignifies in the *Malabar* tongue as much as *Wild Ambalam*, and *Kaduko Ambado* among the *Brahmans*, as much as the *Bitter Ambado* from its taſte. *The tree* Katambalam.

The tree called *Agaty* by the *Malabars*, and *Agaſto* by the *Brahmans*, runs up to the height of ten or twelve yards, the branches growing ſtrait upright: The trunk is ſo big in circumference that a man can ſcarce graſp it, having a very ſoft wood, and the pith much tender. If an inciſion be made into the bark, a certain watery ſubſtance diſtils thence, which turns to gum afterward. The leaves come forth out of ſmall and green ſprouts or buds, being near a ſpan and a half long, and growing two and two on long green ſtalks. The flowers conſiſt of five ſmall leaves, and grow in cluſters on ſtalks of a pale green colour. After the bloſſom come thin, ſtrait and green huſks, of about a ſpan in length, and an inch in breadth, having a thick peel, in which are encloſed certain beans, not unlike in taſte to, but ſomewhat ſmaller than, our *French* beans, being white at firſt, but turn pale green by degrees, and are very good food. This tree bears fruit twice or thrice in the rainy ſeaſon, and indeed the whole year round, but not ſo frequently in the ſummer. The juice of the bark of this tree, either by itſelf, or mix'd with honey, is an excellent remedy againſt all the inflammations of the throat and mouth. The juice of the leaves taken into the noſtrils like a liquid ſnuff, cures the quartan ague. *The tree* Agaty.

The tree call'd *Appel* or *Nalla-Appella*, by the *Malabars*, and *Karo-Nervoloe* by the *Brahmans*, has a very thick and hairy root, the rind of which is of a ſaffron colour. The circumference of the ſtem is of five or ſix palms; the branches growing directly upright: Its wood is white, but the peel dark red. The leaves ſprout forth out of the branches in ſmall green and ſquare buds, the ſtalks being round, very ſhort, and of a pale green colour, commonly two and two together. The *The tree* Appel.

1662. leaves are of an oval figure, round near the stalk, and pointed toward the end. The flowers grow in clusters, consisting of four round white and small leaves each. The fruit are round berries, having a round stone in the middle; are pale green at first, but when ripe turn black. The tree bears but once a year. The root of this tree powdered and taken in water, stops the loosenefs, and boiled in sea-water and applied outwardly, appeases the pain of the gout. The decoction of the leaves is a good remedy against the pain of the belly and stomach, occasioned by wind; the same effect has the oil drawn out of the root, if anointed on the painful part; this oil is yellow and transparent, of an agreeable scent, and a picquant bitterish taste.

Schageri-Kottam. The tree call'd *Schageri Kottam* by the *Malabars*, and *Sabali* by the *Brahmans*, seldom exceeds the heighth of six foot, and delights in sandy grounds: Its stem is of the thickness of a man's arm, the root red within, and black on the out-side. The leaves sprout forth out of the twigs and hang on round, and green stalks; they are very large, and pretty long, broad towards the stalk, and pointed at the ends; the upper-side dark green, and the undermost side of a pale green colour. At the very extremities of the small twigs grow the flowers in clusters on small stalks, consisting of four or five great leaves, of a white and pale yellow colour. The fruit is in shape like an *European* pear, dark green at first, and when ripe, turns black; it is of a sweetish taste, and eaten by the *Malabars*. The juice of the leaves boil'd with sugar, and taken inwardly, strengthens the liver, and stops the loosenefs.

Kolinil. The tree call'd *Kolinil* by the *Malabars*, and *Scheara Punka* by the *Brahmans*, does not grow above two or three foot high, its stem being not above three or four inches thick, the branches spreading round about it. The wood of the stem is very hard, and the green bark which covers it of a picquant bitterish taste. The leaves come forth out of small and green sprouts, hanging on very small stalks; they are of an oval figure, round at the ends, and somewhat pointed towards the stalks, of a sharp and bitter taste: The blossom is like our bean blossom, having each four leaves: The fruit is a kind of a small, smooth, and long husk, yet not above two or three inches in length, are green in the beginning, and dark red at last, having within them certain beans, which are green at first, and black at last. This tree produces fruit twice a year, once in the winter, and once in the summer. The root powdered and boiled in milk, or the juice of the coco-tree, is a good remedy against the falling-sicknefs. 1662.

Alu, *or Fig-tree.* There are four kinds of fig-trees in *Malabar*, call'd by one general name *Alu*; the first they call *Atty-Alu*, the second *Itty-Alu*, the third *Arealu*, and the fourth *Peralu*. The fig-tree *Atty-Alu*, call'd *Roembadoe* by the *Brahmans*, grows to a great height, spreading its branches at a good distance. The trunk is of that thickness, that a man cannot well grasp it; the fruit is round, but flat, and lesser towards the stalk, and somewhat hairy and rough, not unlike our figs. Before they are ripe, they are green and full of a milky juice, but turn red when ripe, and are not so juicy. Within the pulp, you see small kernels like those in our figs, and as soon as they are ripe, the pismires get into them. These figs are the only ones that are eaten by the *Malabars*, and eaten raw when ripe are accounted good against the loosenefs. If the inhabitants may be believed, these trees are produced out of the seed of the fruit, after it is eaten by the ravens, and discharged again with their dung. Atty-Alu.

Itty-Alu. The second sort call'd *Itty-Alu*, and *Areka Goli* by the *Brahmans*, is the smallest of all the four kinds, its trunk being to be graspt by any ordinary man. It bears a small and round fruit, which is green, whilst not come to maturity, and full of a milky juice, but when ripe turns yellow. It has also abundance of kernels, like the first kind.

Arealu. The tree of the third kind, call'd *Arealu*, and *Bipaloe* by the *Brahmans*, is as tall as the former, spreading its branches very loftily, at a good distance: The trunk is of such a thickness, that two men can scarce grasp it: The fruit is like that of the *Itty-Alu*, small and round, and not forced, as that of the *Atty-Alu*. These *Pagans* have dedicated this tree to their idol *Vistnu*, who they say was born under this tree, and took of its blossoms: For this reason it is, that they surround it with a stone wall, and worship it. The christians call it the *Devil's-tree*.

Peralu. The fourth sort call'd *Peralu*, and *Vadhoe* by the *Brahmans*, exceeds all the others in height; for which reason the *Brahmans* have given it the name of *Vadhoe*, *i. e.* large. The fruit is much the same with that of the *Atty-Alu*, but very round, and of a very high red colour, being covered with a kind of a *Lanugo* or woolly substance when they are ripe.

Of the tree call'd *Paniti* by the *Malabars*, are likewise four different kinds, *viz.* *Pariti*, *Bupariti*, *Kadupariti* and *Schem-Pariti*. The tree *Bupariti*, call'd *Valli-Kari-Kapoesi* by the *Brahmans*, is a very high tree, with very lofty branches, growing in the

1662.

The tree Buspariti. the ſhape of a crown round the tree, which is never infeſted with any inſects. The leaves reſemble in ſhape a man's heart, of the bigneſs of the palm of a man's hand, ſomewhat pointed at the end, of a lovely green on the upper-ſide, and a pale green on the other. The flowers are of the ſhape of bells conſiſting of ſeveral white leaves; after theſe comes a certain round ſpongeous fruit, which emits a gummous liquor, if an inciſion be made with a knife. For the reſt, the tree produces flowers all the year round.

Pariti. *Pariti*, or the tree of the ſecond kind, call *Karikapreſs* by the *Brahmans*, grows to the height of 18 foot, the trunk being however within the compaſs of a man's graſping. The flowers are like thoſe of the *Bupariti*, only ſomewhat leſſer; and after theſe come certain oval ſponges, covered with a *Lanugo* or hairy ſubſtance. The bloſſom bruiſed and mix'd with womens milk, and infuſed into the ears, cures the head-ach.

Kudupariti. The tree *Kudupariti* of the third ſort, called *Kapuſſi* by the *Brahmans*, runs to the height of 12 foot, tho' its ſtem is not above two palms thick. The flowers are likewiſe like bells, of the ſame ſhape and colour as the precedent, only that they are a little leſſer, and inclining to green. The ſpongeous fruit are three corner'd, pointed at the top, and within diſtinguiſh'd by three ſkins in as many different concavities, each of which contains three or four ſeeds encloſed in a thick white *Lanugo* or woolly ſubſtance: This tree is never without bloſſom throughout the whole year. The leaves bruiſed and mixed with cow's milk, and apply'd outwardly to the head, procures ſleep, and conſequently cures the head-ach. The fruit bruiſed and taken inwardly in water ſtops the bloody flux. The fourth ſort is very near the ſame with the third.

Chavanna Mandaru. Of the tree *Mandaru* are likewiſe four different ſorts, *viz. Chavanna Mandaru*, of which two bear the ſame name; *Velutta Mandaru*, and *Kanſchenapou*. The firſt call'd *Chavanna Mandaru* by the *Malabars*, and *Tambido Mandaru* by the *Brahmans*, grows up to the height of 24 foot, ſpreading its branches far round about. The trunk is not above a foot thick. The leaves hang on very ſhort ſtalks, being even in two at the upper-end, like goats feet, whence the *Portugueſe* have given them the name of *Pee de Capra*. The flowers have five leaves of an oval figure, among which the largeſt and broadeſt is rounder than the reſt, white on the outſide, and of a purple colour within; the other four are more oval, of a pale red colour without, but high red within; two of thoſe four, *viz.* thoſe next to the biggeſt leaf are on the inſide whitiſh towards the bottom, but the other two all over of a roſe-colour within; from which roſe-colour the *Malabars* have given the name of *Chavanna Mandaru* to this tree. In ſome of thoſe leaves you ſee ſtreaks as red as blood, which they ſay are the remnants of the blood of St. *Thomas*, who preach'd the goſpel on the coaſt of *Malabar*, and in the iſle of *Ceylon*. After theſe come certain flat, long and ſmooth huſks, of the length of ſeven or eight inches, in which are encloſed flat and long beans, which at firſt are ripe, but afterwards turn dark red. This tree produces flowers all the year round, but in the rainy ſeaſon in greater plenty. The flowers preſerved with ſugar, are uſed with good ſucceſs for a laxative, as we do with our roſe-ſugar. The ſecond ſort of the *Chavanna Mandaru* is a very tall tree like the firſt, with ſuch like branches, a trunk of the ſame thickneſs, and the ſame leaves, only ſomewhat larger. The flowers have five oval leaves of a purple colour, both in and outſide with white ſtreaks. The huſks of this tree are the largeſt of all the four kinds, being two ſpans long, an inch thick, flat and ſmooth; the beans are the ſame both in ſhape and colour as the firſt; and this tree bloſſoms at the ſame time, and in the ſame manner. The flowers of this tree eaten raw are laxative; the bark, flowers and fruit bruiſed together and mix'd with the liquor of the decoction of rice, is a ſovereign remedy to bring to maturity, and to open all ſorts of tumors. The bark chew'd cures the tooth and head-ach. 1662.

The third ſort, call'd *Velutta Mandaru* by the *Malabars* and *Dove Mandaru* by the *Brahmans*, is not above ſix foot high, and an arm thick; the leaves are cloven like thoſe of the firſt, but the flowers white without the leaſt ſcent, having five round leaves. The huſks are not ſo big as thoſe of the others, *viz.* not above four or five inches long, and an inch thick, for the reſt flattiſh and ſmooth. The beans are long and round, of a yellowiſh colour, neither ſo big nor ſo red as thoſe of the *Chavanna Mandaru*. This tree bloſſoms two or three times every year, but chiefly in the rainy ſeaſon. The flowers bruiſed and mix'd with ſome pepper, and applied outwardly to the head cures the head-ach; and if you waſh yourſelf with the decoction of the root, it lays all ſorts of itching of the ſkin. Velutta Mandaru.

The fourth ſort called *Kanſchenapou* by the *Malabars*, and *Kantſanu* by the *Brachmans*, is a tree which runs up to the height of 12 foot or more, with lofty branches, but the ſtem is not above half a foot thick. Kanſchenapou.

1662. The leaves are cloven like the rest, but not so big, very strong scented if rubb'd betwixt your fingers, especially in the night-time: The flowers consist also of five leaves, of a pale yellow colour, without the least scent. The husks are the same with those of the *Chavanna Mandaru*, very smooth on the outside, but somewhat hairy whilst very young. The beans are small, in shape and colour resembling those of the *Velutta Mandaru*. The tree bears flowers twice or thrice a year, but most plentifully in the rainy season. The decoction of the root taken inwardly, is a good remedy against the worms and inflammations of the liver, and the piles. The bark powder'd disperses tumors, cleanses the wounds, and is an excellent narcotick.

The tree Nilikamaram. The tree call'd *Nilikamaram* by the *Malabars*, and *Anvali* by the *Brahmans*, grows up to the height of 24 foot, tho' its trunk be no bigger than a man's arm, which as well as the branches, are covered with a black bark. The leaves sprout forth out of thin and round twigs, with very short stalks; they grow two and two together, of an oval figure, and very small, being dark green on the upper side, and light green on the other side. Every night the leaves close up like tulips; the flowers grow on small twigs in clusters, consisting of six very small leaves. It bears a round, but flattish fruit, of a pale green colour when ripe, and somewhat transparent; the pulp being likewise green and very juicy, of an agreeable astringent taste: In the midst is a stone, distinguish'd into six different concavities, each of which contains a small triangular seed or small kernel. The fruit is much used by the *Malabars*: The water distill'd from this fruit cools the liver, and dry'd and power'd, and mix'd with four coagulated milk, stops the bloody-flux.

Odollam. The tree call'd *Odollam* by the *Malabars*, and *Uro* by the *Brahmans*, grows to the height of 18 foot, its trunk being so thick as scarce to be encompass'd by a man with both his arms, with crooked branches. The wood of the stem is very soft, and the pith red, the bark of an ash colour, bitter and very hot upon the tongue. The leaves grow scattering upon the twigs and long stalks, are of the shape of a tongue, thick, smooth, dark brown on the upper-side, bitter and biting upon the tongue. The flowers grow in clusters like cornets, on long, thick, and green stalks, having five very white and pointed leaves. It bears a kind of ground-apple, with a green and smooth rind, under which is a white pulp of a waterish taste. The stone which is in the midst, is shap'd like the heart of a man, of a pretty large size, with two kernels within it. Some will have this tree to be the same which the *Indians* call *Mongas*. 1662.

Nurotti. The tree call'd *Nurotti* by the *Malabars*, and *Kaitu* by the *Brahmans*, rises up to a great height, its branches spreading very lofty round about it: The trunk is so big as scarce to be grasped by a man; the wood white, with a thick bark, which is green without and red within. The leaves are scattered here and there on the twigs with short, round and green stalks, of the length of a span, and the breadth of four or five inches, of an oval figure, pointed at the ends, not unlike the laurel leaves. The flowers sprout forth six or seven together out of the extremities of the small twigs, consisting of three rows of small leaves. The first row makes up a star of five small pointed and dark brown hairy leaves. The second row contains five round and small leaves of a rose-colour, and the third or outermost row, five pointed green leaves. The fruit grows on short and thick stalks, being of an oval figure, having a rose colour'd rough peel, and within a large yellowish stone, containing 10 or 12 kernels of an oleaginous substance. This tree produces both flowers and fruit in great plenty all the year round: From the kernels or seeds an oil is drawn, which has an anodyne quality, and applied outwardly, cures all sorts of scurfs and itchings: The same oil, mixed with a certain fruit, the *Malabars* call *Palego*, kills the corns in the feet, if applied to the affected part.

Kaniram. Of the tree call'd *Kaniram* there are four several kinds: One is call'd *Kaniram* only; the second *Karakaniram*, and the third and fourth *Vallikaniram*, The tree call'd *Kaniram*, and by the *Brahmans*, *Karo*, grows up to a great height, with lofty and far spreading branches. The root is very thick, exceeding bitter, and covered with a yellow rind. The trunk is of that thickness as scarce to be grasped by two men, having a dark ash colour'd bark. The leaves, which are of an oval figure, are very broad in the middle, and pointed towards the ends, of a bitterish taste and an odd scent, growing two and two over against the other: The flowers sprout forth in clusters, having each five or six pale green and pointed leaves. No sooner begins the blossom to bud, but the tree loses all its leaves, instead of which new ones come soon after. It bears a kind of round and smooth apple, which is green at first and turns yellow afterwards, two, three, four or more hanging together on short stalks. The pulp, before they are ripe, is white and insipid, but when ripe, bitter with a thick rough peel. It blossoms in the

1662. summer, and brings forth fruit in the winter. In the pulp are round but flattish seeds, which are also very bitter. The juice of the leaves taken in the decoction of the same leaves cures the head-ach, but if used in too great a quantity is mortal, the only antidote against which is man's dung taken inwardly. Two or three of those seeds taken every day for two years successively, is a preservative against the biting of the serpent, called *Cobra de Capelo* by the *Portuguese*.

Manjapumeram. The tree called *Manjapumeram* by the *Malabars*, and *Pariataku* by the *Brahmans*, rises up to the height of 18 or 24 foot, with very thick and lofty branches spreading round about it, but the stem is not above the thickness of an arm, having an ash-coloured bark: The leaves hang crosswise over one another, being pointed at the ends, the uppermost side of a dark green, and the other of a light green colour, of an astringent and bitterish taste; the flowers grow on stalks which stand upright five in a cluster, are very agreeable and sweet scented, having six, seven, and sometimes eight leaves each, of a whitish colour both in and outside. The fruit is of an oval figure, but flat, of a green colour, containing two round and flattish seeds. This tree is of no use among the *Malabar* physicians.

Champakam. This tree *Champakam*, as the *Malabars* call it, and the *Brahmans Champo*, is a very tall tree, with many lofty branches spreading at a good distance: The trunk is of that thickness as scarce to be grasp'd by a man, with a thick bark of an ash-colour without, and soft within, of a bitter astringent taste. The wood is white: The leaves are of an oval figure pointed a good way towards the ends, of the length of a span, and the breadth of four or five inches; the uppermost side dark green and shining, the other side light green, bitter and biting upon the tongue. At the extremities of the small twigs sprout forth pale green flowers, of a quick odoriferous scent, having oval leaves placed in three rows within one another. In the first root are about eight leaves, being as broad again as those of the second row, round but pointed at the ends; but those in the second row are more pointed still, and those in the third more than the second, and pale yellow. The fruit grows in bunches of an oval figure, with a thick rind. Whilst not come to maturity it is green, but turns pale yellow when ripe, being sharp of taste, and of no agreeable scent: Within are three or four seeds, round on one, and flat on the other side; within those seeds, when they are come to their full perfection, is a thin milky substance enclosed in a skin of a purple colour, and within it a black stone. 1662. The tree, if not too old, blossoms twice a year; out of these flowers they distil a good cordial water.

The tree call'd *Elengi* by the *Malabars*, Elengi. and *Vavalli* by the *Brahmans*, grows up very high, with many far-spreading branches: The trunk is of that thickness, that two men can scarce well grasp it, with a dark brown and rough bark, containing a milky liquor within. The wood is full of the same juice, and will keep a great while under water, but not very long in the air. The leaves grow on small round and green stalks; being of an oval figure, but pointed at the ends. The flowers have pale green stalks, growing five or six in a cluster, of a white colour, consisting of 16 leaves of an odoriferous scent. The *Malabars* make nosegays of them. The fruit is shap'd live an olive, green at first, but turns yellow and red by degrees: The pulp is yellow and meally. The *Malabars* eat this fruit, which has two oval but flat and dark brown stones within. This tree bears flowers twice a year, out of which the *Malabars* distil a well-scented water, which is look'd upon as a great cordial, and revives the spirits. The fruit bruised and taken inwardly in warm water, promotes the birth.

Besides these there also grows here *Cassia Fistula*, called *Konna* by the *Malabars*, and *Bajo* by the *Brahmans*; and *Tamarinds* call'd *Balam-Pulli*, or *Maderam-Pulli* by the *Malabars*, and *Sinza* by the *Brachmans*. The coast of *Malabar* produces likewise *Cardamom*, *Berbery* ginger, and some aloes; as also bezoar-stones, salt-petre, honey, lacca, and cotton; to be short, this countrey abounds in all sorts of *Indian* trees and fruits.

The woods afford vast plenty of birds of *Living creatures of* Malabar. all kinds, and among the rest most excellent peacocks, the flesh of which is very white and well tasted. No place in the world abounds more in all sorts of waterfowl, and there are a great many birds here so tame, and so plentiful, that you may kill them with a stick, the reason of which is, that as the *Pagans* adhere to the opinion of *Pythagoras*, concerning the transmigration of the soul; so they won't kill any living creature, which makes all sorts of wild creatures multiply here, almost *in infinitum*. The flesh of their hogs (of which they likewise have great plenty) is also excellent good; but above all, tame fowl is *Plenty of fowl.* so prodigious cheap here, that you may buy a very good pullet for two-pence, and thirty eggs for the same price. I remember I had once bought up 300 pullets against the arrival of our ships, which being put in the old church of *St. Thomas*, we

1662. we found all dead one morning; we could not guess at the cause of this disaster, till a certain *Malabar* told us, that it could not be otherwise, but that a *Cobre Kapel* (a very venomous serpent) must be hidden in the place; whereupon strict search being made we found the serpent under a heap of old wood, which was no sooner removed, but the serpent set herself upright upon the tail, spitting fire and flame, so that no body durst approach her, till one of our soldiers kill'd her with his sword. Of venison there is also great plenty. 1662.

Bats. They have likewise bats of divers kinds; and among the rest a certain sort of that bigness, that their wings when extended are

as long as man can stretch with both his arms together. They have red heads and necks, black bodies, and are shaped like a fox. They are extremely nimble, and having very sharp teeth do a great deal of damage to the fruit. Their wings are bare, like those of our bats, unto which are fastned their legs and tails, so that they can neither walk nor stand; to recompence which defect they have a kind of a hook, of the thickness of a finger on each wing, wherewith they fasten to the branches of the trees: You see here vast multitudes of them in the woods, so that it is no difficult thing to kill them; but whatever you kill, remains hanging among the trees: They are naturally so fierce that they are not to tamed; for if taken alive, they will bite their own wings and flesh as far as they can reach; I once had the curiosity to set two of these creatures a fighting, which they did with such fierceness, that they both remained dead upon the spot. They will drink of the liquor of the coco-tree till they are drunk; they commonly bring forth two young ones at a time, and that generally in the hollow of trees; the *Malabars* eat the flesh, which has no agreeable taste.

Jackall. Here you meet also with *Jackalls*, as our people call them, being not unlike a large fox, of the bigness of an ordinary peasant's dog, of a red grey colour, but thinly covered with hair. They assemble in the night in whole troops, and approaching (especially about the new-moons) to the villages or plantations, make a hideous noise, like the outcries of women or men; they are very greedy after mens flesh, and will scratch the dead carcasses out of the graves, unless they be well covered with stones: They are scarce ever to be tamed. The *Malabars* eat the flesh of these *Jackalls*. And thus much of the coast of *Malabar*.

The author pursues his voyage. After, as I told you, we had set sail the 12th of *March* from *Koulang*, the wind turn'd against us the same evening, but about eleven

ven a clock at night we ſet ſail again with the land wind. The 13th we kept along the ſhore with a gentle breeze and very fair weather; but the wind turning ſoon after to the E. S. E. we were forced to chuſe the main ſea, but made to the ſhore again towards evening, and took the benefit of the land-wind. The 14th there being but little wind we advanced no farther than 12 leagues from *Koulang*; and the 15th finding ourſelves off of the city of *Tengepatnam*, we gave the ſignal by a cannon ſhot for the reſident Mr. *Koek* to come aboard us, which he did accordingly; and after I had diſcourſed with him of what I had in commiſſion to tell him, we continued our voyage, but being towards evening overtaken by a tempeſt, were forced to come to an anchor. The 16th early in the morning the winds being ſomewhat laid we ſet ſail again, but by reaſon of the contrary winds were forced to return towards *Pulon*, near the cape of *Comorin*, where the *Portugueſe* have a ſmall church dedicated to St. *Martin*. The 17th we made this cape, but the winds continuing ſtill againſt us, it was not till the 18th that we could reach *Toutekoriin*, the chief among the ſeaports of the coaſt of *Madure*. Here I tarried for ſome time to obſerve the intereſt of the company, both in reſpect of their traffick hither, and in the government of the inhabitants, who live under their juriſdiction along the ſea-coaſt, in ſeven large villages, the chief of which is *Toutekoriin*, the other ſix are *Manapara*, *Alendale*, *Wiranypatnam*, *Pommekiel*, *Baypaer* or *Vaypaer*, and *Bempaer*. After a ſtay of ſix months here, I received orders from Mr. *Van Goens* to return to *Koulang*, and to take once more upon me the government of this city, being very well known to the queen there; accordingly having ſurrendred my accounts to Mr. *Lawrentz Piil*, in the preſence of captain *Van Reede*, I left this place the 19th of *May* 1665, and went by land to *Koulang*. The number of the inhabitants of the before-mentioned ſeven villages amounted in 1664 to above 20000 ſouls, *viz.* in *Toutekoriin* about 3000, in *Mannapara* 4000, in *Alendale* 800, in *Wiranpatnam* 900, in *Pommekiel* or *Punikael* 2800, in *Baypaer* 700, and in *Bempaer* 800; beſides thoſe inhabiting on the coaſt of *Comorin*, which amounted to a conſiderable number: All theſe villages are adorn'd with ſtately churches, built by the *Portugueſe*, eſpecially thoſe of *Mannapara* and *Bempaer*, but are now in a decaying condition, ſince the *Portugueſe* have been chaſed thence. Some of the *Romiſh* prieſts now and then come to ſay maſs in the neighbouring villages, whither the people flock in great numbers; tho' to ſpeak truth, they are more heathens than chriſtians. *Toutekoriin* conſumes yearly abundance of foreign commodities, by reaſon of the great numbers of inhabitants living along this coaſt, who muſt be provided from abroad with moſt things they ſtand in need of; *Toutekoriin*, otherwiſe *Tutukuriin*, or rather *Tutukury*, or *Tutukuriin*, or *Totokury*, is now, as we told you, the chief of all thoſe ſeaports, being an open place, but beautified with ſtately ſtone buildings. It has three large churches built by the *Portugueſe*, which are to be ſeen at a great diſtance at ſea, the countrey round about being flat and low. In one of theſe the reformed exerciſe their religious worſhip: Beſides which the convent of the *Franciſcans* is lately fitted up for the ſame uſe.

Come over againſt Tengepatnam.

Come to Toutekoriin.

The ſeven ſeaports of Madure.

Their inhabitants.

The village of Toutekoriin.

The *Dutch Eaſt-India* company have a factory here, managed by a merchant as chief governor; by a factor as his deputy; two or three aſſiſtants, and a military officer, under whoſe command are ſome ſoldiers, but the *Nayk* of *Madure* will not allow them to erect any fortifications: During my ſtay here, I begun to erect a brick-wall round the garden, but finding the *Jentives* to look with a jealous eye upon it, I deſiſted; yet I took care to repair the houſe of the company, and ſet their flag on the top of it, which might be ſeen a good way at ſea.

This place was taken by the *Dutch* from the *Portugueſe* 1658, without much reſiſtence. In the road of *Toutekoriin*, is good anchorage at five fathom water in a ſandy bottom.

The village Punikael.

Three ſmall leagues from *Toutekoriin* near the rocks of *Remanekor*, not far from the kingdom of *Narſinga* lies the village of *Punikael*, where the *Portugueſe* formerly had a fort, and a garriſon of 40 men. Two leagues from thence there was a *Pagan* temple of the *Brahmans* call'd *Trichanduri*, againſt which and the prieſts thereof the *Portugueſe* would frequently utter very injurious words, which ſo exaſperated the inhabitants, that they entred into a league with their neighbours, *viz.* the *Badagas* of *Narſinga*, in order to drive the chriſtians thence: Accordingly, having with a great deal of ſecreſy got together a body of 6000 men, and received certain intelligence that the *Portugueſe* in the fort were but ill provided with gunpowder (the chief terror of theſe *Barbarians*) they march'd directly to *Punikael*; the *Portugueſe* being not a little ſurprized at ſo unexpected a ſight, were put to the greateſt nonplus that could be, being in want of ammunition, and no great account being to be made upon the *Parvas* (the chriſtian inhabitants) as being not trained up to military affairs, but living upon

War betwixt the inhabitants and the Portugueſe.

1662. upon fiſhing and ſwimming: Theſe being ſenſible of their inability to reſiſt the enemy, no ſooner heard of his approach, but they began to betake themſelves with their moveables to their boats which lay near the ſhore, which the *Badagas* endeavouring to prevent, ſome retired to unpaſſable places, others to the ſea-ſide, whilſt others were expoſed to the mercy of the enemy, and with moſt dreadful outcries implored the aſſiſtance of the *Portugueſe* in the fort.

Bravery of Anthony Kriminalis. About that time a certain prieſt, named *Anthony Kriminalis*, who was come ſome days before thither to take care of the chriſtians there, ſeeing this miſerable ſpectacle, applied himſelf to *John Ferdinando Korrea*, governor of the fort, remonſtrating to him, that ſince they were not in a condition to oppoſe the enemy, to endeavour to bring things to an accommodation; but the governor anſwer'd, that it was againſt the glory of his king to ſubmit in the leaſt reſpect to thoſe *Barbarians*; *Kriminalis* made what haſte he could to return to his flock, which he met in the church where he had preached the ſame morning, and led them to the ſea-ſhore, endeavouring as much as he could to ſee them embark in their boats, whilſt he refuſed to enter himſelf, being reſolved to ſtay aſhore, and to expect the utmoſt fury of the *Barbarians*, who were advancing apace, and with their arrows had already kill'd ſeveral of the *Portugueſe* and others, among whom was the interpreter of *Kriminalis*, who was ſhot by his ſide, notwithſtanding which he remained immoveable in his reſolution, and wringing his hands up to heaven, fell upon his knees; the firſt troop of the *Bagadas* paſs'd by without doing him the leaſt harm, except that they took his hat, and ſo did the ſecond, but one of the third troops (conſiſting of *Mahometans)* run a lance into his left ſide, whilſt others let fly their arrows at him, and thinking he had been kill'd came to take his cloaths, which he, being yet alive, gave to them, and ſo retreated into the church, with an intention to ſpend the ſmall remainder of his life at the foot of the altar; and being follow'd by the *Bagadas*, he there received a ſecond thruſt, and ſoon after a third, which put a period
Is killed. to his life: They afterwards cut off his head, which together with his bloody cloaths they carried in triumph to their temple of *Trichanduri*; the trunk of the body was afterwards buried by the chriſtians.

Not far from *Punikael* or *Pommekiel*, lieth a great village call'd *Putanam*, and ſo further up the coaſt *Bembar* or *Bempaer*, *Kalekure*, *Beadal*, *Niananko*r, or rather *Romanakoris* and *Kanhameira*; next you ſee *Negapatnam*, the firſt frontier of the coaſt of *Coromandel*, but one of the chiefeſt towns 10[illegible]6.
of this coaſt is *Periapatan*, ſituate near the rocks of *Romanankoris* being the capital city of the *Maravas*, who inhabit the mountains, a barbarous generation, living only upon robbing; the jeſuites that formerly belonged to the church of *Periapatan*, did endeavour to reclaim them in ſome meaſure from their barbarity, but moſt of them ſoon return'd to their old way of living. There is another village ſeated on the other ſide of the rocks of *Romanankoris*, directly oppoſite to *Negapatnam*, the inhabitants of which are all chriſtians. All along the ſea-coaſt are about 30 villages, among which, beſides the before-mention'd, are the chiefeſt, *Trichandar* or *Trekandar*, *Kallegrande* and *Cherakalle*.

Manners and cuſtoms of the inhabitants. The inhabitants of thoſe places are very black and ſtrong; they are deceitful and cunning, make but little account of their wives, but generally keep two or three harlots, by whom they have ſometimes 16 or 18 children. The men wear nothing
Their clothing. but a ſingle piece of callicoe wrap'd about their middle, and another piece about their head, which they call *Romare*. The ordinary women commonly wear painted callicoe, thoſe of faſhion are adorn'd with gold rings and bracelets when they are abroad, but are very naſty at home. They tie their hair up in a truſs behind, like thoſe of *Malabar*, for the reſt they have very good features. They live upon meat
Way of living. and rice, but drink nothing but water, which they are fain to fetch half a league from the ſea-ſhore; they live by pearl fiſhing and catching of fiſh, by weaving and ſhipping, there being ſome who drive a conſiderable trade with the painted callicoes to *Kalpentien*, *Kolomba* and the *Malabar* coaſt. They have abundance of callicoe and linnen weavers here, and great numbers of people are employed in painting of callicoes, which they do very artificially. This trade was in great requeſt whilſt I was here, becauſe I uſed to give all imaginable encouragement to them; the inha-
Government. bitants are govern'd by judges of their own, who are choſen every year by the chief director of the *Dutch* company there, whom they ſtile the *Captain of the ſeven Sea-ports*. Each village has the privilege to propoſe four, out of which the *Captain* chuſes two, who ſwear fealty to the company; all civil cauſes are tranſacted in their reſpective villages, but criminal matters are decided at *Toutekoriin* in the council of nine, whereof the *Captain* is preſident. The remaining *Portugueſe* pay no taxes to the *Dutch* company, but to the *Nayk* of *Madure*; however, this tax is paid with the approbation of the chief director, who al-

1662. lots every one his ſhare according to his ſubſtance; thoſe who are backward in their payment, muſt expect ſpeedy execution, which is done by the ſoldiers of the *Nayk*, and cauſes frequent quarrels betwixt the inhabitants and the ſoldiers, as it happened in my time; when the *Nayk* peremptorily demanded the tax from the *Parvas*, which they were not able to pay, I ſent to him a ſerjeant with ſome ſoldiers, to deſire that he would ſend a commiſſioner with whom they might treat, and obtain ſome time for the payment thereof; upon which the *Nayk* having ſent one of his great officers with a body of horſe, I remonſtrated to him the impoſſibility of the matter, telling him that the ſeven ſeaports were willing to make a preſent of two ſilver diſhes fill'd with ducats to his maſter, which was well accounted of, and the *Nayk*, as a token of his ſatisfaction, ſent me a ſcarf richly embroidered with gold. Theſe ſeven ſeaports were formerly (before the *Portugueſe* fleets appear'd in theſe parts) under the government of the king of *Marten*, a vaſſal of the queen of *Tengauſy*, unto whom they were forc'd to pay many taxes; at which time the *Parvas* lived deeper in the countrey, and uſed to ſerve in the wars to ſuch princes as would pay them beſt.

Wars betwixt the Parvas *and* Moors.

One time a certain *Parvas* happening to fall out with ſome *Moors*, theſe cut off his noſe and ears, which ſo exaſperated the *Parvas*, that they reſolved to take up arms, and to revenge the quarrel of their countreyman. To begin the fray, they took one of the *Mooriſh* merchants priſoners, whoſe noſe and ears they likewiſe cut off, and ſo ſent him home. Hereupon the *Moors* having aſſembled a body of 30000 men, they march'd to, and pitch'd their tents near *Toutekoriin*; on the other hand, the *Parvas* were not above 5000 men, and well arm'd, and truſting more to their bravery than number, fell upon the *Moors* ſo couragiouſly, that they made them quit the field, with the ſlaughter of 7000 of their men; a great number of them being forc'd to the ſea-ſhore, ſaved themſelves in boats, but were ſcarce got to ſea, when by a ſtrong tempeſt from the S. W. they were ſo diſpers'd, that no news was ever heard of them ſince. After this victory the *Parvas* having made themſelves maſters of theſe ſeaports, came to a compoſition with the queen, promiſing to pay her the ſame taxes as the *Moors* had done, which being impoſſible for them to perform, this proved the occaſion of unſpeakable miſeries; ſome of them being impriſoned for want of payment, others ſold for ſlaves to that degree, that at laſt they reſolved to ſhake of the yoke, coſt it what it would: The *Portugueſe* who 1490 appear'd firſt thereabouts with their ſhips from *Cochin*, having at that time traded there for 40 years before, and conſequently their ſtrength at ſea, being not unknown to the *Parvas*, they ſent their deputies to *Cochin* to implore their protection, and to promiſe their obedience, and that they were ready to embrace the chriſtian faith. The *Portugueſe*, willing to improve this opportunity, came with their fleet 1533 on that coaſt, and having made themſelves maſters of the ſeaport towns, the *Parvas* received baptiſm all on one day. However they met with great oppoſition afterwards from thoſe on the coaſts of *Coromandel* and *Malabar*, encouraged underhand by the *Parvas*, till at laſt matters were adjuſted thus, that the *Portugueſe* ſhould remain maſters of the coaſt, that the *Parvas* ſhould pay them a certain annual tribute, according to their ability, and that all the chief men of that coaſt ſhould have their ſhare in the pearl fiſhing, which was to be perform'd on a certain day. After all, the *Nayk* of *Madure* having found means to get into the poſſeſſion of this countrey, left the *Portugueſe* in the full poſſeſſion of their juriſdiction over the *Parvas*, and of the free exerciſe of their religion, in which ſtate it continued till the year 1630, when the king of *Portugal* having ſent thither a governor, to clip the wings of the *Romiſh* clergy, who were grown two powerful there, this occaſion'd new troubles; for the *Parvas* being a zealous kind of people, and for the moſt part at the devotion of the prieſts, they were divided into two factions, during which inteſtine commotions the clergy did not forget to improve their authority, and to enrich themſelves at the expence of their flock, but the *Jentyves* or *Pagans* alſo began to encreaſe to ſuch a degree, that being become formidable to the *Parvas*, they often forc'd them to ſhelter themſelves againſt their forces in the neighbouring iſlands. Since that time the *Parvas* acknowledged the juriſdiction of the *Portugueſe* governor; each village has two judges, who are changed every year, they keep courts twice a week, and in conjunction with the *Petangiins* (who are hereditary officers) decide all controverſies of leſs moment; they raiſe the taxes, and are accountable once a year to the people for all their tranſactions; whilſt the *Portugueſe* were maſters here, the *Jentyves* or *Pagans* durſt not exact more taxes from the *Parvas* than was agreed for, unleſs they would ſee them go with wife and children to the neighbouring iſlands, from whence they did not return till they had obtain'd ſome conſiderable

1662. derable abatement; but of late years the *Parvas* having left off that custom, the *Jentyves* improve it to their advantage, and force them to pay three times as much as they used to do formerly.

The kingdom of the Nayk of Madure.

The kingdom of the *Nayk* of *Madure*, under whose jurisdiction the seven before-mention'd sea-ports are, borders to the west upon the kingdom of *Travankor* to the east upon the sea, and to the north-west upon the countrey of the *Nayk* of *Tanjaor* or *Tanjauwer*, betwixt the coast of *Malabar* near the cape *Comorin* and *Coromandel*; its whole extent being along the whole eastern gulph or coast opposite to *Ceylon* from the cape *Comorin* (where the coast of *Malabar* ends) to the town of *Bempaer* or the river *Ulton*, a tract of 75 leagues in length, and 30 in breadth. The sea-shore, commonly call'd the *Pearl-Coast*, from the many pearl-banks that are hereabouts, extends from south to north in length, and in some places about half a league deep into the countrey. The capital city and ordinary residence of the *Nayk* is *Madure*, five days journey to the north of *Koulang*; being adorn'd with many most magnificent *Pagodes*, or pagan temples, which have very high turrets gilt on the top. Along the coast of *Madure* neither grass or herb, or plant is to be seen, except thistles and house-leek; it having been found by experience, that the coco-trees would not thrive here no more than several other *Indian* trees; notwithstanding which they are sufficiently provided with all manner of necessaries from the circumjacent countrey, as well as from abroad, by the way of *Toutekoriin*; besides that, the sea-shore abounds in hares and partridges, the first of which resemble our rabbits, their flesh being tough, yet in taste like our hares. The flesh of the partridges, which have red legs and round bills here, is of an agreeable taste.

They have here mice as big as cats, which dare not approach them, for if they be pursued, they will settle upon a chair or chest, and sitting upright, fight and bite like dogs: They are in colour and shape like the *European* mice, except that they are without hair, and have a rough skin like an elephant. They will dig underneath the doors, and do considerable mischief to the merchandizes in the warehouses.

There is also here another sort of mice, red and much lesser than the first, but so fierce, that they will make the cats run before them.

This countrey also produces serpents, and divers other sorts of venomous creatures. One morning, as I was rising, I found the skin of a serpent sticking to one of the posts of my bedstead, which she had cast there the night before, without being perceived by me or any body else. In *October*, *November* and *December*, the western winds blow with such violence, the sand from the adjacent mountains to the shore, that you are not able to open your eyes. Much rain falls deeper in the countrey, and near the cape *Comorin*, but never at *Toutekoriin*, instead of which a thaw fall every night, which is very cold, and consequently, by the sudden alteration of the weather, very unwholesome; the winds being sometimes so excessive hot here, as if they did blow out of a fiery furnace; as long as these winds last, the inhabitants dare not go abroad into the fields for fear of being overwhelm'd by the sand. 1662.

The *Nayk* of the kingdom of *Madure* is master of several considerable countries, each of which are govern'd by a peculiar governor; besides which, there is one governor-general, who has the chief management of the whole kingdom, who ruled all our time the countrey, which was called *Boomalapelles*; besides the governors, each village has two judges, who are much respected by the inhabitants. The *Nayk* to secure himself of the fidelity of his governors, detains always their wives and children in a certain castle call'd *Zwela Baddy*, about seven leagues from *Madure*, under the guard of 300 eunuchs; neither are the husbands permitted to see them without peculiar licence from the *Nayk*, and are oblig-ed to depart again in two or three days; some to avoid this inconveniency, content themselves with harlots. Most of the inhabitants of the countrey of *Madure* are *Jentyves* or pagans, (by some they are call'd *Badagas*) tho' some of them have been converted to the *Romish* faith by the *Portuguese*. The *Jentyves* are accounted good soldiers, yet much inferior to the *Malabars*, witness the wars the *Nayk* of *Tanigos*, tho' much inferior in power, wages against them.

There are three *Nayks* in this part of the *Indies*, *viz.* the *Nayk* of *Madure*, the *Nayk* of *Tanjaor*, by the *Dutch* call'd the *Tanjower* and *Tanjouwer*, and sometimes *Teaver*, and the *Nayk* of *Gingi*, otherwise called *Cingie*, or *Chengier*. The word *Nayk*, *Neyk*, or *Najeka*, signifies as much as a governor, vassal or viceroy, their predecessors having in ancient times been only governors of those countries they are now possessed of under the jurisdiction of the kings of *Vidia Najar* or *Bisnagar*, or *Narsinga*; but having revolted against their liege lord, each of them assumed the royal power and title. The *Nayk* of *Madure* had been for a considerable time in war with the *Nayk* of *Tanjaor*, and taken many

5 places

The PEARLE FISHERY near
TOUTE COURYN
1 Toute Couryn
2 Governers house
3 The Church
4 The House thereunto belor
5 St. Paul
6 A Chappel
7 A Heap of Pearle Oysh
8 Marchants of divers l
9 The Pearle ship men
10 Governers Stzat
11 Tents where all sorts of Pro:
visions are Sold while y Pearle
:: Fishery Continues
12 The Mt. called y Bellegaete
or Rasselgate

1662. places from him: At my time the war was renewed with more vigour than ever; and the Nayk of *Tanjaor* having gathered a great army, attack'd the *Nayk* of *Madure* so briskly, that he took from him in a few days all the places he had conquered from him before. The army of the *Nayk* of *Madure* being much disheartened by the victories of their enemies, the *Madure* sent to me, to *Koulang*, his chief governor, desiring assistance from the company; but as it was not our interest to engage on any side, I excused it as handsomely as I could.

The Pearl-Banks. Betwixt the coast of *Madure*, where the seven villages are, and the isle of *Ceylon*, are divers famous pearl banks by the sea, for which reason this tract is called the *Pearl-Fishery*. These pearl-banks are properly rocks of white coral stone, which sometimes are covered with sand; on these rocks, the oyster-shells, containing the pearls, are fastened, but in what manner no body knows. Some of those banks are about 12 or 13 fathoms, and others at 15 fathoms distance from the shore, so that they can scarce be seen from thence: Some of those banks are five, six or seven fathom under water. The oysters live six years, after which time the shells open and the pearls are lost; of which I have seen several that were shown me by the divers. These pearl-banks are search'd every year to see whether the shells are come to their full maturity: This is commonly done in *October*, when the weater is calm, and the sea clear hereabouts. After they are convinced that the said oysters are come to their full perfection, the time of pearl-fishing is appointed and proclaimed throughout the countrey, so that the merchants resort thither from the other part of the *Indies*, nay, from *Arabia* and *Turkey* it self, who set up their tents near the sea-side, to buy the pearls.

Pearl-fishing how perform'd. They fish for pearls, or rather the oyster-shells containing the pearls, in certain boats called *Toniis*, being about 28 foot long, (of these you shall see 3 or 400 at time,) each of which has 7 or 8 stones, which serve instead of anchors, and 5, 6 or 7, nay sometimes 8 divers, who are to dive one after another. These divers are quite naked, being covered only with a kind of thin wastecoat; they have each a net hanging down from the neck, and gloves on their hands, wherewith they are to pick the oysters from the rocks; each of them has also a stone of about a foot in length, and 50 pound weight, to make him dive the swifter: This stone has a hole on the top, wherewith it is fasten'd to a rope; when they are going to dive, they set their foot into a kind of a stirrup, laying hold with their left-hand of the rope, the other end of which is held by one in the boat, stopping their nose with the right-hand to hold in their breath, and so go to the bottom; where they are no sooner come, but they give a signal, by pulling the rope, for those in the boat to pull up the stone. This done, to work they go, and scraping the shells from the rocks, fill their nets, and then pull again the rope, when those in the boat draw up the nets first, and soon after the divers, who are succeeded continually by fresh ones. These divers can hold their breath four times as long as other people; they are obliged to dive from 3 fathoms to 15, being not able to hold their breath any longer. These boats commonly go to sea every morning by break of day, with the land-winds, and return in the afternoon with the sea-winds. Those who equip those boats, hire both the divers and the rest of the boat's crew at a certain price *per diem*, like as we do our day-labourers. All the oyster-shells are brought ashore, and there laid up in a great heap, till the pearl fishery is over, which begins immediately after *October*, and continues all the *November* and *December*, which makes the oysters smell very strong, and sometimes occasions distempers. The pearl-fishing being over, a wooden house is erected for the company and the *Nayk*, where each receives his share, the boats being obliged to fish one day for the *Nayk*, and another for the company; and these take care that they be not disturbed in their fishing, the governor and two judges being every day near the sea-shore, to decide such differences as arise betwixt them. At last the oyster-shells are opened in the before-mention'd house, in the presence of certain commissioners; every oyster-shell does not contain pearls, nay, the most are either without any, or have at least very small ones: On the other hand, some shells contain five, six, seven, nay eight pearls apiece. Some of these pearls are found in the liquor, some in the flesh of the oysters, others, but few, are fasten'd to the shells, of which last I keep several by me. The pearls being all taken out of the shells, are put into sifts of different holes, and according to their different sizes are sold to the fairest bidder: The pearl-dust is bought and sold by the *Dutch*. They stew and eat the flesh of these oysters, but it is somewhat rank and hardy, not comparable in taste to our *English* oysters. They give the pearls a glance by rubbing them with salt and powder'd rice. Out of the shells they make a very fine mortar. *Pearl-dust.*

They have two sorts of pearl-dust, the old and the new: The new pearl dust is search'd

1662. ſearch'd after daily by the women among the dirt and rubbiſh of the oyſters: The old pearl-duſt is dug out upon the very brink of the ſea-ſhore, dirt, ſand and all, ſometimes ſix, ſeven or eight foot deep; this they let dry altogether in the ſun, and by degrees the duſt being blown away by the wind, the black pearl-duſt remains behind, which they bring to thoſe in ſmall parcels, who have given them ſome money beforehand. This pearl-duſt being the worſt of the two, and of no great value, theſe poor wretches can ſcarce get a halfpenny a day for their labour, a wretched gain indeed, but ſufficient to keep them from ſtarving in this countrey.

The horns of Siankos.

Beſides the pearl-oyſter, they alſo catch on this coaſt certain horns call'd *Siankos* by the inhabitants, being in ſhape long, round and thick, and very white; out of theſe they make bracelets and thumb-rings, which they make uſe of in drawing their bows, being valued much beyond Ivory. This product of the ſea is found at 8 or 12 fathom depth, in a tract of the ſea of about 10 leagues in length, from the coaſt of *Vyraamdes Laam* to *Ilha Doce*. They begin to fiſh for it in the middle of *December* till the middle of *May*, when the ſea hereabouts beginning to be unclear, the divers cannot without great danger go to the bottom. Among theſe ſea-horns they now and then, (tho' ſcarce once in 100 years) meet with one they call the *King's-Horn*, being not to be diſtinguiſh'd from the reſt, except by the opening, which is on the contrary ſide, being red within and green without; they are ſaid to ſwim before the reſt, which follow them like their king; for which reaſon it is, that the kings of *Golconda*, and ſeveral other *Indian* kings are accounted out of one of theſe horns, which makes them to be in great eſteem here, eſpecially among the *Jentyves*, who will ſometimes give 800 reals for ſuch a horn. Whilſt I was hereabouts, a certain fiſherman dream'd that he had taken a king's-horn, which he telling to one of his comrades, they agreed, that they would go immediately to try, and divide the booty; accordingly they did, and he who had dreamed the night before, catch'd a king's-horn, but refuſing to give to his comrade his ſhare, they went before the judges, who were obliged to decide in favour of the dreamer, the other having no witneſſes to prove his bargain. I bought the ſame horn afterwards for 170 reals, and was offered 20 reals gain immediately after, by one of the judges. Theſe *Siankos* are ſold at a dear rate at *Bengal*, where they have a way of poliſhing them, that they ſhine with a moſt lovely white, much beyond any ivory: They make bracelets and other ornaments of them. 1662.

As the fiſhing of thoſe horns is one of the main ſubſiſtence of the inhabitants on this coaſt, ſo they muſt be carefully look'd after, that under pretence of fiſhing for them, they don't dive for oyſters, for which reaſon certain people are maintained to watch them. I remember they once brought up a mooriſh boat belonging to *Kalitpatnam*, which under pretence of fiſhing for *Siankos*, had been found among the pearl-banks; when they came before me, I found upon a ſtrict examination, that extreme poverty had inforced them thereunto, and ſo diſmiſſed them for that time. Some are of opinion, that the pearl-duſt dug on the ſea-ſhore, has lain there ever ſince the iſle of *Ceylon* and the *Maldive* iſlands, were torn from the continent, when the pearl-ſhells were caſt up by the floods here, and opening themſelves, were conſumed by degrees, leaving the pearls under ground. The pearl-duſt is gather'd by the men during thoſe intervals, when they can't go a fiſhing, but when they are abroad at ſea their wives and children do it in their ſtead. Abundance of divers are devoured by the ſharks, againſt which they pretend to defend themſelves by certain incantations, notwithſtanding they are chriſtians.

The author retires to Koulang.

After I had ſettled my accounts at *Toutekoriin*, I prepared for my journey to *Koulang* croſs the mountains of *Balligate*; and accordingly as I told you, ſet out the 19th of *May* 1665, under a guard of ſome ſoldiers, and with an attendance of ſome porters to carry my baggage and proviſions, there being no inns by the way, and in many places not the leaſt thing to be got for money. We had ſcarce travell'd a day but were met by a troop of *Malabar* robbers, arm'd with bows and arrows ready to let fly at us: They had already laid hold of two ſlaves, who were carrying ſome *Perſian* wine, but ſeeing the ſoldiers ready to diſcharge their firelocks among them, they thought it their beſt way to retire, and finding us continually upon our guard, quite to leave us at laſt. We paſs'd that dreadful ridge of mountains call'd *Balligate*, extending 120 leagues in length, and is cover'd with a very fine red ſand, which being as light as duſt, is in *October*, *November* and *December* blown by the continual ſtrong weſt winds as far as the iſle of *Ceylon*, a tract of at leaſt 50 leagues; whence it is probable, that theſe mountains are not ſo high now as they were in former ages. When the ſun caſts its rays upon this red land, the reflection thereof appears moſt dreadful to the eyes in the ſky, which ſeems to be all on fire. This high ridge of mountains

The mountains of Balligate.

1662. mountains does likewise occasion most surprizing alterations in the season; so that whilst on the north side of the cape *Comorin*, it is winter during the months of *May*, *June*, *July*, *August*, and *September*; it is summer at the same time on the south-side of that cape; on one side you meet with continual tempests, thunder and lightning, whilst the other enjoys an agreeable and lovely season. About that time black clouds are gathering upon these mountains by the winds, which break out into very hard and sudden rains, occasioning great water floods, by the overflowing of the rivers, which are oftentimes thereby choak'd up with sand to that degree, that they are rendered unnavigable for a considerable time after.

Comes to Koulang. Having at last passed the mountains I arrived the 25th of *May* at *Koulang*, whereabouts I found all the fields under water. Pursuant to the orders I had received, to draw the city of *Koulang* into a narrower compass, and to fortify it on the land-side with one wall and two demibastions, I ordered all the houses, churches, trees, and what else stood in our way to be cut or pull'd down; and 30000 stones, each of two foot long and one broad, to be cut out of the quarries; so that the first foundation of these fortifications being laid the 1st of *July*, the same was continued with all imaginable diligence. In the mean while *Goes to* Cochin. I went in an inland bark to *Cochin*, by the way of *Kalkolang*, to confer with the governor *Kolster* how to regulate the factories of *Koulang*, *Kalkolang* and *Karnopoly*, to the best advantage of the company.

After a stay of three days at *Cochin*, in my return to *Koulang*, we were surprized by so violent a tempest, that we were forced to leave the bark and to get ashore, but the next day the violence of the wind being much abated, we prosecuted our journey to *Koulang*, where I arrived the 4th day after I left *Cochin*.

The war among some of the *Indian* kings continuing as yet, it was generally reported, that the king of *Travankoor* (who was then at *Mansassi*, tho' the queen resided at the same time at *Koulang*) was marching with a considerable force to attack the fort of *Kalkolang*, whereupon I sent our factor with letters from our chief director Mr. *Kolster* to the king, to know the reason of this enterprize: But he was forced to return without any other answer from his courtiers, than that the king being employed in his devotions, no body could be admitted into his presence till that time was expired, which was likely to hold for some time; however the army did remain all the time in its former camp, without committing any hostilities: In the mean while I had taken effectual care to provide for the security of *Koulang*, the walls advancing apace, and being in such forwardness, that we hoped in a little time to bring them to perfection; this being the only thing that stay'd me at *Koulang*; for as the time of my contract with the company began to come near a period, I began to make preparations for my return into *Holland*. But Mr. *Jacob Hustart* being gone to *Batavia*, and Mr. *Goens* put in his place, I happened to have some difference with him concerning the government of *Toutekoriin*, which rose to that height, that he ordered me immediately from *Koulang* to the city of *Kolombo* in the isle of *Ceylon*, leaving captain *Van Reede* governor of *Koulang*. *The author is sent to* Kolombo.

The season for sea-voyages (which must be exactly observed in these parts) being then expired, I was forced to travel for above 60 leagues along the sea-shore, with no small difficulty, there being no such thing as an inn to be met with hereabouts, or any other convenient lodgings, unless you meet with some charitable popish priest or other, who will receive you into his house, most of the inhabitants along this shore being *Roman Catholicks*, who have here and there a small church. However, after some troublesome days journey I came safely to *Toutekoriin*, where I found the *Mary* yacht ready to transport me to *Kolombo*, where I arrived the next day, *viz.* the 18th of *Sept.* 1666, I stay'd here above a whole year; when I resolv'd to go aboard the *Brederoo* yacht bound for *Batavia*, where I landed the 20th of *August* 1667, without meeting with any thing remarkable at sea. I continued for three whole years at *Batavia*, without being engaged in the companies service, and in 1670 return'd thence into *Holland*. During those three years, I had sufficient opportunity to take a full view of the city, both within and without, in which I was so curious, as not only to make draughts of all its publick structures, but also of such plants and trees as grow in and about that city; tho' to confess the truth, the same could oftentimes not be undertaken without great hazard; as well from the wild beasts, as form the barbarous *Javanese*, so that I durst not venture far out of the town without a good guard; but before I proceed to give you a description of the living creatures, trees, fruits and plants, and of the city of *Batavia* itself, in the isle of *Java*, it will be requisite I should give you an account before-hand of the situation of this great island. *Comes to* Kolombo.

The isle of Great Java. The isle known generally by the name of *Great Java*, to distinguish it from the *Lesser Java*, otherwise call'd *Bati*, lies six degrees

1662. degrees to the south of the line, directly opposite to the south-point of the isle of *Sumatra*, from which it is separated only from the streights of *Sunda*, where the same is not above four or five leagues over. To the north lies the isle of *Borneo*, betwixt which and this isle there is a convenient passage for small vessels; to the east it has the isle of *Bati*, or the *Lesser Java*, from which it is divided by the channel of *Balambuam*, and to the south by the main ocean. Its length from the streights of *Sunda* to the channel of *Balambuam*, *viz.* from E. to W. inclining however a little to the S. and N. is about 130 or 140 leagues; its breadth is very different, but the whole circumference is computed at 300 leagues; The north coast of *Java* has abundance of very commodious creeks, bays, harbours, and goodly towns, with many little islands near the shore. In former times the isle of *Java* had as many petty kings as there were cities, but now adays it is divided into two kingdoms only, the one of which is under the jurisdiction of the emperor of *Mataram*, the other under the king of *Bantam*. The first is in the possession of the eastern and greatest part of the isle, the other of the western and lesser part; for since the emperor of *Mataram* (call'd also the emperor of *Great Java* by the *Dutch*) had once found means to subdue his petty neighbours, he soon extended his conquests all over the eastern parts of this isle: The emperor who reign'd all the time of my being there, was a young prince named *Sousouhounan Ingelaga*, the son of *Sulthan Mahomet*.

Java has two kingdoms.

Unto one or other of these two potent princes all the rest are obliged to pay homage, tho' there be also as yet remaining some petty sovereignties along the sea-coasts, besides what belongs to the city of *Batavia*.

Cities of Java.

In the eastern parts of *Batavia* are the cities *Balambuam*, *Panarukan*, *Passarvan*, *Joartan*, *Surabaaya*, *Brandaon*, *Sydayo*, *Tubaon*, *Kajaon*, *Japare*, *Pati*, *Dauma*, *Samarang* and *Mataram*, the residence of the emperor of *Java*. To the west, near the sea are *Taggel*, *Charabaon*, *Dermayaon*, *Manukaon*, *Karavaon* and *Batavia*; of the coast of which we intend to give you a short but exact account. About 10 or 12 leagues from *Batavia* is the famous city of *Bantam*, where the *English* have a factory, and a considerable traffick.

Manners and customs of the Javanese.

The *Javanese* are a barbarous, proud, and fierce nation, of a brown colour, with flat faces, and thin, short, coal black hair, large eye-brows, and large cheeks. They boast themselves to be descended from the ancient *Chinese*, unto whom they resemble in some respects, having very small eyes with large eye-lids. The men are very robust and strong limb'd, and wel fitted for the war; the women are but smal. The men wear a piece of callicoe wrap'd two or three times round their bodies; people of fashion have them with gold flowers or streaks. The women wear it from under their arm-pits down to their knees, all the rest bare. They marry sometimes two or three wives, and perhaps keep divers concubines besides, according to their ability. Lying and cheating is a daily practice with them. Those living near the sea-side are for the most part *Mahometans*, which was introduced there about 150 years ago. In the inland countries they are generally *Pagans*, abstaining from feeding upon any living creatures. When they are to consult about matters of moment it is done in the night time. 1662.

Their clothing.

Religion.

Its fertility.

The isle of *Java* is very fertile, tho' a great part thereof be not known hitherto; it has very high mountains, reaching to the very clouds, witness the pepper mountain on the south-side of the island; it has likewise impassable forests and wildernesses; but to the north, betwixt *Batavia* and *Bantam*, is a very populous countrey, full of rice fields, and all sorts of tame and wild creatures; hereabouts also is salt and pepper to be found, but not so good as that at *Malabar*, besides most other sorts of *Indian* fruits, which are sold in great plenty at *Batavia*. They abound also in fish, are well stor'd with hogs, oxen, sheep and other tame beasts, the flesh whereof is of a very good taste; fowl both wild tame they have in great plenty; but the woods have also large tigers, rhinoceros's and divers other wild beasts; in the rivers you see also often *Crocodiles*, call'd *Kaymans* by the *Indians*.

The air and seasons.

The air or climate of *Batavia* is in my opinion as temperate and healthy as any place whatever in the *Indies*; the east and west winds blowing all the year long along the shore, besides the ordinary land and sea winds. The seasons of the year run here in the same manner as in *Europe*, except that the sun passes twice a year directly over their heads; the most agreeable season begins in *May*, which continues with continual breezes from the east, and a very serene sky till *November*; when the winter season approaching it rains sometimes continually for three or four days without intermission, which sets all the low grounds under water, which however has this convenience, that it kills and washes away all insects, which else would prove very noxious to the fruits. This season ends about *May*, when the dark clouds beginning

to

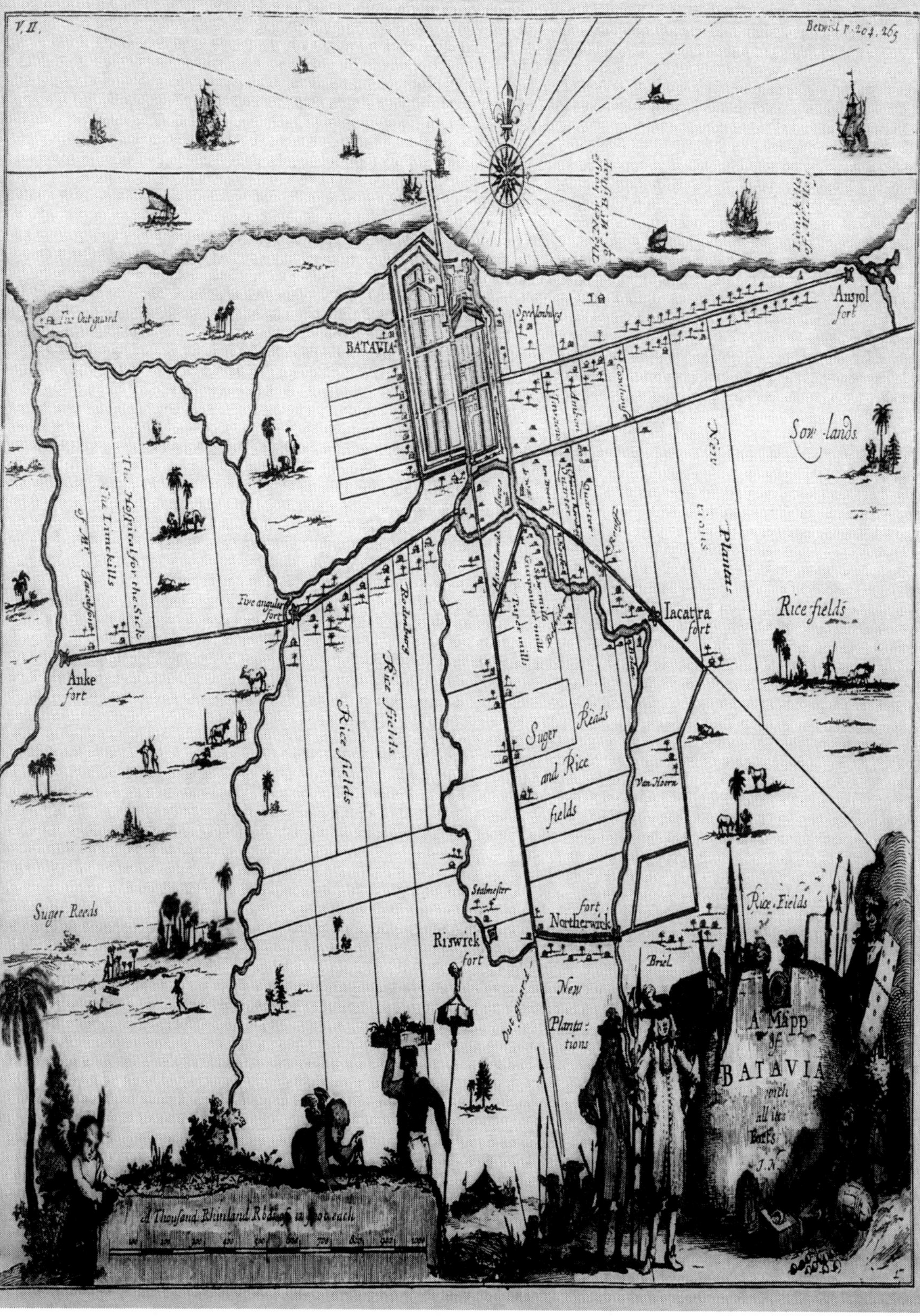
V. II.
Betwixt p. 264, 265
BATAVIA
The Outguard
Anke fort
Five angular fort
Ansjol fort
Iacatra fort
Sow-lands
Rice fields
New Plantations
Rice fields
Rice fields
Suger Reeds and Rice fields
Van Hoorn
Stalmester
Riswick fort
Northerwick fort
Briel
Rice Fields
Suger Reeds
Out guard
New Plantations
A Mapp of BATAVIA with all its Forts
A Thousand Rhinland Rods of 12 foot each

1662. to disperse, the sky assumes its former serenity; in *December* the west winds blow so violently, that there is no going by sea here; in *February* it is changeable weather, intermix'd with sudden storms of thunder and lightning; in *March* they begin to sow, and this month produces some fruit; in *June* is the most agreeable time of the year. In *July* the sugar and rice begins to ripen; in *September* it is the best time, and the *October* affords them plenty of all sorts of fruits.

The happy temperature of the climate produces such plenty of all sorts of necessaries, that there are very few countries that can compare with this island; the pleasant river rising in the mountains divides itself into many branches, and waters the circumjacent countrey, and afterwards recollecting its channels, passes thro' the midst of *Batavia*, (which it divides in two parts) and there exonerates into the sea. 1662.

Batavia. The city of *Batavia*, which got its name many years ago from the *Dutch* after their first establishment in those parts, was first, and is now by the *Javanese* and *Chinese* call'd *Kalakka*; from the fruit of a palm or cocotree, which grows very plentiful hereabouts; the fruit of which the *Javanese* call *Kalakka*. The *Indians* call it *Jacata*, derived likewise from a certain fruit call'd *Jaccas* by the *Indians*, and *Schrookzak* by the *Dutch*. Not long before the *Mahometans* settled in the *Indies*, *Batavia* was no more than an open village, inhabited by *Pagans*; at first it was surrounded only with a row of palladoes of bamboo canes, but as it became more populous, the inhabitants began to wage war against the king of *Bantam*, and some other neighbouring princes, and that with very good success. The city of *Batavia* lies at 5 deg. 50 min. off southern latitude, at the north-side of the isle of *Java*, in a large but fenny plain before it to the south; it is surrounded with abundance of small islands, and to the north or landside with woods and high mountains. It is divided into two parts by a river, is of a quadrangular figure, fortified with a wall of stone, and 22 bastions; the names whereof are *Amsteldam*, *Middelburgh*, *Delft*, *Rotterdam*, *Hoorn*, *Enkahuissen*, *Vienna*, *Gelderland*, *Katzenelbogden*, *Orange*, the *New-gate*, *Hollandia*, *Diest*, *Nassaw*, *Zealand*, *Utrecht*, *Friesland*, *Overysel*, *Groningen*, *Zewburgh*, *Kuilenburgh*, and the *Middlepoint*. The ditch underneath the wall was in the year 1670, surrounded with a quick-set hedge of thorns; it has four great gates, two whereof are very stately and artificially built by the famous *John Listing*, on the south-side; the first 1630, and the other 1657. The third

1662. gate is on the east-side call'd *Rotterdam*, and the fourth call'd *Utrecht* on the west-side. The city of *Batavia* is situate in a bay, extending to the east as far as the cape of *Karovant*, and to the west as far as the cape call'd the *Rough Point*, towards *Bantam*, which lies on the same shore, about twelve leagues from *Batavia*. 1662

The harbour. Both within and without this bay lie about 17 or 18 islands, upon which the violence of the winds and waves being broken and check'd, this renders the road of *Batavia* one of the safest harbours of the whole world, being able to contain above 1000 vessels at once; small vessels and barks lie commonly close under the banks of the river, where they may lie without anchors in a muddy bottom; the river is lined with stones on both sides as far as the boom, which is shut up every night at nine a clock, and guarded by a good number of soldiers. besides which, there is cut a channel out of the main river, for the reception of smaller vessels; no vessel passes the boom without paying a certain custom, every vessel that fetches salt pays a real, and those that carry stones two reals. The ditch without the wall is very broad and deep, and sometimes rises so high, that some of the lowermost streets without the city are laid under water; all the buildings of this city are well contriv'd, most even of the private houses having handsome gardens, well planted with fruit trees and plants and flowers, adorn'd with pearls, springs, pumps, &c.

All the streets of this city run in a streight line, most of them being 30 foot broad; and on both sides near the houses paved with bricks; there are eight streets, which are all well built and inhabited, among which the *Princes-Street* is the chiefest, beginning at the middle point of the castle, and running in a strait line to the town-house, having on each side a cross street. Next to this is the *Lords-street*, beginning on the north-side over-against the castle, reaching in a direct line to the new gate. The first cross street on the east-side has got the name of *John Tirment*, who built abundance of houses in this street. The second is call'd the *Market-Street*, opposite to which lies the third call'd the *Petawins-Street*: The fourth is call'd the *Street of the Hospital*. As you come out of the castle at the first entrance into the *Princes-Street* is the *Princes-Lane* on the left-hand. These are on the east-side of the river; we will now pass over to the western side; the bank of which is planted with pleasant trees, and adorn'd with houses all in a straight line as far as the *Diest-Gate*. The first street on this side is *Its streets.*

Betwixt pag [illegible]

THE NEW GATE

Betwixt page. 266. 267.

20.

V. II. Betwixt pag 200. 207

18

1662. call'd the *Gentlemans-Street*, being divided into two ſtreets by a gracht that comes croſs it: The ſecond ſtreet comes croſs-wiſe thro' this part of the city, beginning at the *Utrecht Baſtion*, from whence it has got the name of the *Utrecht-Street*. But now we muſt look back and take a view of the *Burghwalls* or *Grachts* (being ſtreets with water channels in them) of theſe there are no leſs than 15 among which the *Tygers Gracht* is the moſt ſtately and moſt pleaſant, both for the goodlineſs of its buildings, and the ornament of its ſtreets, which afford a very agreeable ſhadow to thoſe that paſs along the ſtreet; the channel is edged and lined with ſtones from the bottom, over which are four ſtone bridges, ſuſtain'd by as many high ſtone arches; twelve foot broad each; beſide which, there is a wooden bridge at one end. The inward *Gracht* behind the *Carpenters-wharf* (where is alſo the founding-houſe) has three bridges; next to this is the *Kaymans Gracht* with four bridges. The firſt *Gracht* which runs croſſwiſe, is the *city's Inward Burghwall*, having only one bridge: Next to this the *Herb Gracht*, without any bridge at all. The *Seſons Gracht* extending from the *Middle Point* directly to the *Rotterdam-Gate*, with ſix bridges, and the *Inward Gracht* with one bridge only. Theſe are all the *Burghwalls* and *Grachts* on the eaſt-ſide; now we muſt come to thoſe on the weſt-ſide. The firſt is the *Gentlemans Gracht*, with three bridges; the ſecond is call'd the *Rhinoceroſes Gracht*, having likewiſe three bridges; the third is the *City's Inward Gracht*, with three bridges. The firſt *Gracht* running croſſwiſe to the north, is the *City's Inward Gracht*; the ſecond faces the *Carpenters Wharf*, and is called the *Javaneſe Gracht*; and the third is call'd the *Chineſe Gracht*, having only one bridge. The fourth *Gracht* which runs croſſwiſe, begins at the baſtion call'd *Frieſland*, and ends at the new bridge near the *Fiſh-Market*, having three bridges; laſt of all, the *City's Inward Gracht* with one bridge. Theſe are all the *Grachts* and *Burghwalls* within the city, over which are laid 56 bridges, moſt of which are ſuſtain'd by large ſtone arches, not to mention here the wooden draw-bridges which are over the *Gracht* without the walls. At my firſt coming to *Batavia* I lodg'd upon the *Tygers Gracht*, ſo that having ſufficient opportunity to take a draught of it, I thought fit to inſert it here.

The publick buildings of the city. Among the publick buildings of this city, the church call'd the *Croſs-Church* claims the precedency, being built in 1640, of ſolid ſtone: In the midſt of the church ſtands the ſteeple, being exceedingly beautify'd with iron-work. It has but one bell, which is only rung before church-time; the ſtone edgings in the front of the church are artificially carved, and adorned on the top with *Cherubims*. But time which defaces all things, and the air, which is much ſharper here than in *Europe*, has in a few years wrought a conſiderable change in this magnificent ſtructure. The pulpit and ſeats of the chief men here are very finely wrought and adorned with iron-work and ebony-wood. The veſtry is of the ſame workmanſhip. This ſtructure is very lightſome and lofty, within being adorned with five clear branches of braſs brought thither from *Holland*. In the other part of the city, the foundation of the new church was laid during my ſtay there, and before my departure the brick-work was almoſt finiſhed. In the year 1644, there was alſo a church built in the caſtle, of an octagonal figure, being very light within, and flat on the top; the floor covered with well poliſh'd white and blue ſtones neatly done: The glaſs of the lanthorn on the top was of the beſt kind, and the pews of the church carv'd very artificially and made of the beſt kind of wood the *Indies* afford. 1662. *The croſs-church.*

The Town Houſe. The *Town-Houſe* ſtands very near in the centre of the city, in a ſpacious place, being built of brick in 1652. It is two ſtories high, and you aſcend into the ſecond by a pair of winding ſtairs. The great gate is exactly in the middle of the ſtructure, artificially wrought, of the *Corinthian* order, over which is a balcony or gallery of ſtone, unto which you enter out of the upper-hall. When criminals are to be try'd, a ſcaffold is erected before the *Town-Houſe*. The windows of this building are in proportion very high and lofty, finely glazed, and on the out-ſide guarded with iron-work. In this houſe the courts of juſtice are kept; here is the meeting of the *Shepen* or ſenators, as alſo of the maſters of the hoſpitals, and of the overſeers of other places; as alſo of the court for the direction of military affairs within the city. The inward court is encloſed with a high wall, and a double row of ſtone-pillars; here the officers of juſtice have their habitations, and the priſon-keeper with his attendants on the weſt-end of it. It extends from the *Tygers Gracht* to the *Lords-Street*.

The hoſpital for the ſick. The hoſpital for the ſick ſtands upon the bank of the great river, which runs through the city, betwixt the *New-Gate* and the *Dieſt-Gate*. Here ſuch as are ſick, and have not wherewithal to provide for themſelves, are entertained and cured, there being ſometimes 200 or 300 to be ſeen here at a time, who are all provided with neat lodgings, beddings and other conveniencies. In the

The Hospital for the Sick.

1662. the out-houses are the apartments for the overseers and their servants, for the doctor, apothecary, surgeon, minister, cash-keeper, treasurer and others, who are to keep the house clean and look after the sick; all these are plentifully maintain'd by the company. Besides those before-mention'd, three persons of note belonging to the company are constituted overseers, who take their turns every week, and see that every thing be done as it ought to be, and especially whether any of them are recovered so far as to be fit for service. Behind it is a square enclosed with a high wall, and planted with trees, which serves for a walking place for those who are upon their recovery; and a door with a wooden bridge reaching a good way into the river, is also made for the taking of the fresh air of the river. The minister, who is appointed to visit the sick, says prayers every morning and evening, when a bell is rung; every sunday there is a sermon, where all those that are able are obliged to be present.

The Spin-House.

For the encouraging of virtue, and suppressing of debauchery in lewd women, a spin-house has been erected here, having no windows or prospect but only on the east-side towards the *Burghwall*, where certain iron-rails are made in the gate, with wooded shutters within, which are shut and bolted as often as the overseer pleases. Here the women are reclaim'd from their lewdness by keeping them continually at work, under the tuition of a governess, whose business is to look after the House, and to set them their task, which if they miss to perform, they are sure to be scourged. For the rest, there two members of the senate constituted on purpose for the government of this house, whose business is to be present there every sunday at the sermon that is held there, for the reclaiming those lewd creatures from their ill course of life. If they commit any misdemeanor which cannot be corrected by scourge, they are punish'd by the ordinary court of justice. 1662.

Slaughter-houses or flesh-halls.

Upon the very brink of the river are built two slaughter-houses or flesh-halls, sustain'd by wooden piles, by which means they may with conveniency throw the excrements of the kill'd beasts into the river. They kill twice a week, each butcher having his peculiar stall, where he sells his meat at such a price as the magistrates shall think fit to set, tho' most of them find means to sell it as dear as they can. Whilst I was there beef was sold at the rate of four pence *per* pound, and pork at the same rate; but mutton being most esteem'd was sold dearer. All the beasts that are to be kill'd

Betwixt p. 208, 209.

The SLAUGHTER HOUSE
of BATAVIA

1662.

must be taxed by the farmer of the excise upon cattle; according to which the butcher is obliged to pay the tenth-penny excise: But if the farmer should be extravagant in his taxation, the butcher who thinks himself injur'd, may appeal to the general judgment of all the butchers, who if they do not agree to the price set by the farmer, he is obliged to tax it himself at his own set rate.

The hall for the sale of stuffs.

On the west-side of that spacious place which faces the *Town-House*, is a certain structure, in which are sold all sorts of cloaths ready made, as also stuffs and callicoes, white and painted, besides divers other commodities exposed to sail there, by the *Chinese*. These have here their peculiar shops, for each of which they pay 3 crowns *per* month. The whole building is of wood, being divided into 5 walks or galleries, having shops on each side; and as many doors from without, which are kept open day and night, because the shopkeepers don't put up their commodities till very late at night, and lay them out again early in the morning, with a great deal of curiosity, to invite the buyers to give them a good price, at which the *Chinese* are very dextrous and quick, so that unless you be upon guard, you are overreach'd before you are aware of it; however, these little shops have this conveniency, that you may furnish your self here at an easier rate, and that all at once, with abundance of small things, which you can't buy so conveniently at the great shops where they will not be satisfied with a small gain.

The city stables.

On the east-side of the *Town-House* is a goodly structure, fitted up for stables for horses, being all of brick-work without, and provided with racks, mangers, and partitions, and paved with stones, so that the horse-dung may be removed and wash'd away with all imaginable conveniency. The place where they manage their horses is very airy and well situated, having two doors, one whereof leads to the city's *Binne Gracht*, for the conveniency of watering and washing the horses. In this stable are kept, besides the coach and cart-horses, above 100 saddle-horses, that are managed daily by certain persons kept for that purpose. Their best horses are the *Arabian* and *Persian* horses, which they buy here at a high rate, 200 crowns being a common price for an indifferent *Persian* horse, the best being not to be got for money. It is worth observation, that the *Persians* train up and manage their horses without blows, whereas our managers are used to make use of whips and spurs, which makes them unfit for the due management of those horses. Abundance of horses are also brought to *Bata-*

1662. *via* from *Japara* in the isle of *Java*; but these are not comparable to the *Persian* horses: Some of these however are very tractable, if well handled from the beginning, but many of them are broken mouthed before they come to *Batavia*: The natives being used to ride their horses with a light hunting-bridle, they are apt to toss up their heads, when they are rid afterwards with a curb-bridle, to prevent which, our managers fasten a leather string to the girt under their belly, the other end of which being buckled to the bridle, makes them keep their heads steady. 1662.

The Chinese hospital for sick and aged persons.

On the *Rhinoceroses Gracht*, near the spin-house, is the *Chinese* hospital for sick and aged persons, built of brick, and divided into convenient apartments, and a pleasant court to walk in: It was built in the year 1640. In this house such as are sick and superannuated, and have not wherewithal to subsist, are received and maintain'd. For the maintenance of which a certain duty is laid upon marriages and burials; as also upon actors of plays, farces, and such like shews. And as, besides this, many of the rich *Chinese*, either by voluntary contributions or legacies, give great encouragement to this house; it is provided with a considerable revenue. The whole management of this house is committed to two *Hollanders*, and as many *Chinese*, who have a secretary to keep their accounts.

The hospital for children.

At the extremity of the west-end of the *Rhinoceroses Gracht*, you see the hospital wherein poor orphans are maintain'd and educated, being of brick, with convenient lodgings for the servants of the house: It has hitherto no settled revenue, being maintain'd by the voluntary contributions of well-disposed people.

The house of the artisans.

In the east-corner is the house wherein are lodged all the artisans belonging to the company, as carpenters, bricklayers, gun-founders, stone-cutters, glass-makers, turners, ingineers, seal-cutters, pewterers, painters, &c. all which are disposed into their proper quarters, under the direction of three *Hollanders* appointed by the company. Besides the slaves belonging to the house, there is also a chirurgeon and a schoolmaster; the last of which is obliged to say prayers every night; at which all are obliged to be present under a certain forfeiture. In this house the surveyor-general has his lodgings, which are very handsome, and keeps two clerks under him. He oversees the workmen. In this house also are maintained such criminals as have been condemned to the chains, who are kept here

The Hospitall for Chil-
dren of
BATAVIA

1662. here to hard labour, and well guarded. Every night at nine a clock, the doors of the house are shut up, and a guard of slaves is placed to prevent any disorders which might happen among so great a number of people of different callings. I had for some time my lodgings in this house; and here it was that I first made the draught, and afterwards made the description of *Batavia*. The wharf belonging to this house is only fitted for the building of small yachts and boats, such as are used only in the road for the loading or unloading of ships: But ships of bulk are built at the isle of *Ormus*, about a league to the west of *Batavia*, where are considerable magazines for ropes, and other implements belonging to ships, which are defended by certain fortifications. 1662.

The Rope-Alley. The *Rope-Alley*, where they are employed in twisting ropes, is likewise in one corner of the city, opposite to the carpenter's wharf, being planted with large nut-trees, which afford an agreeable shade to the rope-makers. A little beyond it to the west you see the pack-houses of the company; wherein are laid up pepper, cinnamon, nutmegs, cloves, mace, &c. The overseer has a goodly habitation for his own use.

The magazine of rice. Not far from thence, *viz.* near the bastion call'd *Amsterdam*, stands the company's magazine of rice, a large structure, having a door looking to the water-side, where ships may be laden and unladen. It was built in my time 1670, of brick-work. There is a square enclosed with a wall at the inward wharf, where the receivers and other servants of the company have their habitations.

The *Prawenhouse*, so call'd from the word *Praw*, which in the *Malayan* tongue signifies a *boat or small vessel*, stands upon the brink of the river, for conveniency of such small boats as are built or refitted there; here several shipwrights, and a good number of seamen have their quarters, the last being obliged to be ready upon call, wherever they are ordered to row by the deputy governor, under whose tuition they are. On the east-side of the little wharf, the overseer has a small house. Having thus given you an account of the publick structures of this city, with such draughts thereof as time and opportunity would permit us to take, we will now proceed to the four great markets of *Batavia*, and begin with the fish-market.

The fish market. The fish-market is on the western-side of the great river, being sustained by strong wooden

1662. wooden piles, and covered on top with pan-tiles. Opposite to it is the dwelling place of the *Aslager* (or *Outroper*) where the fisher boats are oblig'd to stop, and their cargo is sold immediately by publick sale, to the fairest bidder; the fishmongers are generally *Chinese*, each of which has his own stall, for which he pays two reals *per* month. The *Outroper* pays ready money to the fishermen for what they sell to these *Chinese*, who allow him twopence in the crown, and are obliged to repay it at a set time. Here you may furnish yourself with sea, river, or shell-fish, according to your own pleasure, from 10 a clock in the morning till four in the afternoon; when the fishmongers leave their stalls here, and sell the remnants near the river-side behind the flesh-hall.

The rice or corn market. The rice or corn market is adjoining to the former, or rather opposite to it at the north-end; being built after the same manner, except that it has no stalls or banks; here you meet with grains of all sorts which are sold here, according to the market price, by a certain small measure called *Ganting*, containing about 13 or 14 pounds of rice, which is commonly sold for sixpence. He that has the oversight of the market and measures, has a house at one end; his business among other things is to set the mark upon the measures and weights, which is done twice a year; *viz.* in *January* and *July*, at the town-house, in the presence of two *shepemen* or aldermen. They pay two-pence for each mark. 1662.

The fowl-market. Near the new bridge, as you pass along the river-side to the *Cross-Church*, is the fowl-market, where the *Mardiikers* and *Topassen* (a kind of negroes) sell all sorts of fowl in great plenty, so that you may buy an ordinary pullet for three-pence, but the

best sort are dearer. In this market you see many huts, in which they sell dried fish, eggs and course earthen ware.

The fruit market. The fruit-market begins at the new-bridge, extending by the river-side to the *Middlepoint*. Here you meet with all sorts of fruits and herbs, sold by the *Chinese* and *Negroes*, who pay the 10th penny excise. From four a clock in the afternoon till night, this market is so crowded with people, that there is scarce any passing in it.

The Latin and Greek schools. On the *Tyger's-Gracht* is the *Latin* and *Greek* school, the back-side of it reaching to the *Kaymans-Gracht*, with a lofty stone-gate. It has a very pleasant court, where the schoolboys may divert themselves at

Relates p. 273. 274.

FISH MARKE of BA

1662. certain times. The rector or head school-master has a very handsome house. Besides this school, there are divers other schools at *Batavia* for the instruction of young people in reading and writing; in which some of the natives, and especially the *Topasses* are so ingenious, that they don't give way in that point to any other nation. What books are used here are brought out of *Holland*; but in the year 1667, a printing house was erected, and several books have been printed here with good success.

The castle. The castle is a quadrangle, situate in a level ground, two bastions of which, *viz.* the *Diamond* and the *Rabbet* front the city, one facing the *Tyger's-Gracht*, and the other in a strait line thro' the *Lord-street* to the *Middlepoint* of the new-gate.

On the west-side the river washes the very walls, being enclosed by part of the city, which lies open on that side; the two other bastions call'd the *Pearl* and the *Sapphire* face the sea; the low grounds toward the west are well planted with gardens and orchards; the bastions, as well as the *Courtins* of the castle, are faced with white stone from the bottom to the top, and provided with watch-houses at convenient distances; the ditch is very broad and deep, being inclosed 1669, within a quick-set hedge, serving not only for an ornament, but also as an additional strength to the place, from whence they fire with advantage upon an approaching enemy. 1662.

In this castle the *Dutch* governor general of the *Indies*, and all the members of the council of the *Indies*, residing at *Batavia*, have their places of residence; as likewise the head factors who keep the accounts, and of what is paid to the servants of the company; and the general book-keeper, the secretary of the great council, the captain of the armory, the physician, chirurgeon, and commander of the soldiery; all these I say, besides several others, have their fix'd habitations here. But the house or rather palace of the governor-general surpasses all the rest in magnificence.

It is built of brick, two stories high, yet so lofty, that the top of the roof surpasses in height all the other buildings, and may be seen a great way at sea; especially the lanthorn or turret, which stands in the midst of it, having instead of a weather-cock a ship of iron, very artificially wrought. The door is just in the middle, unto which you ascend several broad stone steps; in this palace is the council-chamber for the great council to meet in, and near it the secretaries office and chamber of accompts. The great hall is hung about with bright and well polish'd armour, ensigns, standards and

1662. and flags, which have been taken by the *Dutch* in ſeveral ſea and land engagements; in this hall prayers are ſaid every night, and here it is that the governor at certain times gives audience to all ſuch as have occaſion to repreſent their grievances to him. Behind it are pleaſant walks planted with trees, among which a *Tamarind* tree of an exceſſive height, and ſtanding in the center of the garden, affords a moſt agreeable ſight. Out of this garden you paſs thro' a little gate of the *Courtin*, by a ſmall bridge to a ſummer-houſe, built upon piles in the midſt of the water, from whence you have a very pleaſing proſpect, not only of the fortifications of the caſtle, but alſo of the rivers mouth, and the road where the great ſhips ride at anchor. At the eaſtern corner of this ſummer-houſe is a door leading thro' a gallery, to the before-mentioned chamber of accompts, which has a flat roof, convenient offices, and pleaſant walks belonging to it; the floor is covered with a kind of grey-ſtone neatly done. In this apartment moſt of the bookkeepers and clerks are boarded at a certain rate by the treaſurer.

The houſes of the members of the great council are on the ſouth-ſide of the caſtle, the land-gate being in the midſt of them.

The armoury is built much after the ſame manner as the chamber of accompts; it extends along the eaſt-ſide of the *Courtin*, having ſeparate apartments for ſword cutlers, gunſmiths, and other artificers of that kind.

The governor of the ſea affairs has his houſe on the north-ſide juſt oppoſite to it, and on the ſame ſide dwell the factors, phyſician, chirurgeon and apothecary. Hereabouts ſtand alſo the magazines of fleſh, bacon, wine, *Brunſwick* mum, *Holland* butter, oil, vinegar, and divers other proviſions; and under ground are made certain vaults for gunpowder and artificial fireworks. The caſtle has four avenues, and as many gates. The firſt and largeſt is call'd the *Landgate*, built 1636, where you ſee a ſtone-bridge, ſupported by 14 arches over the ditch, being 26 rods long, and 10 foot broad, paved with *Dutch* bricks ſet on edge. The *Watergate* faces the north, where is a large watch-houſe for the garriſon, and ſome apartments on both ſides for the overſeers of the magazines and ſtorehouſes.

This was built 1630, according to the inſcription. Beſides theſe, two leſſer gates are in the *Courtins* to the E. and W. which are ſcarce ever made uſe of, unleſs that ſome veſſels laden with ammunition, and ſuch like things, are generally unladen here. There is a ſmall plain before the *Rabbet* baſtion, where the new liſted ſoldiers are exerciſed and taught the uſe of arms, by an officer appointed for that purpoſe. Not many years ago a wooden drawbridge was built near the baſtion call'd the *Sapphire*, by which means you may walk all round the city to the boom, where you muſt be ferried over. 1662.

Before my departure, a project was on foot of building a tower and ſteeple upon the *Rabbet* baſtion, making ſome additions to the *Rotterdam* and *Utrecht* gates, and to enlarge the cit to the E. and N. as far as to the turning of the great river, ſo that the north-ſide of the caſtle ſhould front the baſtion call'd the *Middlepoint*. Thus far of the city of *Batavia* itſelf, we will now take a view of its outſide.

It is eaſy to be gueſs'd at, what moved the regents of this city to ſurround it with forts at ſuch a diſtance, *viz.* to the E. as far as the river *Antjol*, and to the W. as far as the river *Anke*, along the bay of *Batavia*, and on the landſide to the S. by the forts *Northwiik*, *Riſwick* and *Jacatra*; theſe ſerving the inhabitants of the flat countrey, as a defence againſt the incurſions of the neighbouring barbarians, ſo that they may quietly enjoy the fruits of their labour; the countrey all about this city being well cultivated and ſtored with rice and ſugar-reed fields, gardens and orchards, countrey-houſes, brick and tile wharfs and ſugar-mills, which are of great conſequence to the city. To give all poſſible encouragement for the manuring of the ground, the main channel of the great river was ordered to be ſtop'd up 1659, inſtead of which two branches being made, one leading to *Riſwick*, the other to *Jacatra*, theſe ſerve to lay the ground thereabouts under water upon occaſion. One of theſe branches is to the W. brought into another channel, leading directly to the middle of the city, and being ſtop'd near the ſecond bridge of the new gate by a dike and ſluice. Here you ſee ſeven mills, one whereof is a corn-mill, four gunpowder-mills, one ſaw-mill for wood, and one paper-mill, which are driven by the force of the water; near it the millers have their habitations.

Before the dike, juſt at the entrance of the city is the place where they refine the brimſtone; near this place 1658, a very ſtrong ſluice was built for the conveniency of bringing countrey commodities into the cities with leſs charge, but the ſame was ruin'd in a little time after by the force of the water.

Not many years ago, a certain contagious diſtemper began to rage at *Batavia*, which proving mortal to many, it was reſolved, (to ſtop the infection) to build a kind

1662. kind of hospital or pest-house, where such as were seiz'd with this evil, might be provided with lodgings, diet, and suitable remedies. This house, which has with it the *Deist-Gate* near the road to *Arke*, is under the government of several of the richest citizens of *Batavia*.

By the east-side of the dike where the mills are, a house was built in 1609, for the washing and whitening of linen apparel, the latter being carried thither by bamboo canes fastened together. Without the city are besides these many other houses erected partly by the company, and partly by the liberality of some of the inhabitants, which I will pass by in silence here, and say a word or two more of their out-works or forts: All these lie in a flat even countrey, made of earth, surrounded with ditches and quickset-hedges, except the quinquangular fort call'd the *Riswick*, and the fort *Ansjol*, both which are faced with brick-work. They are all well provided with great artillery, and provisions for nine months, or perhaps for a whole year, as well as the garrison of the city of *Batavia* it self. There is a certain officer appointed to keep the cannon and other arms neat and clean, the which being under the over-sight of a captain of the artillery, who commands also the fire-workers, and has his habitation upon the bastion call'd the *Diamond*. The garrison consists chiefly in foot, there being only a troop of horse, which serves as a guard to the governor-general, who are obliged to be upon the guard in their turns: These enjoy great privileges, are commanded by one of the best officers, and are obliged to appear every *Sunday* in their armour well polish'd, and with their pistols, carabines, and broad swords.

Their out-works.

The inhabitants.

The inhabitants of *Batavia* consist either of the citizens, or such as are servants to the company, being of divers nations; among whom the *Dutch* exceed the rest both in riches and dignity, most places of honour and profit being in their hands.

Chinese.

The *Chinese* drive here a considerable traffick, being more industrious than any of the other *Indians*; they deal much in fish, and cultivate most of the rice, reed and corn-fields; some also maintain themselves by fishing, but the chiefest upon merchandizing; they farm the excises and customs; but of late years some of the other nations have found ways to imitate them in their thriftiness and cozenings, at which they are great artists, which I know by my own experience. They live here according to the laws and customs of their own countrey, under the tuition of a *Chinese* governor, who manages all their af-

fairs

1662. fairs with the company. They are dreſs'd after their own faſhion, in a coat with wide ſleeves, either callicoe or ſilk, according to their abilities. They don't ſhave their heads here according to the *Tartarian* faſhion, as they do now in *China*, but wear their hair long and neatly twiſted. Their habitations are ſettled thro' the whole city, but live for the moſt part on the weſt-ſide, near the great river, and many of them on the eaſt-ſide; their houſes are low, with the roof cover'd over the firſt floor.

The Malayans. The *Malayans* as they are not ſo much addicted to trading as the *Chineſe*, live for the moſt part upon fiſhing; their boats are made after the *Indian* faſhion, with large ſails. They have alſo a governor of their own, who lives in the *Rhinoceroſes Gracht*, whereabouts moſt of them have their dwelling-places. They wear light callicoes or ſilks, tho' ſome of their women of faſhion uſe flower'd and ſtrip'd ſilk; their hair, which is very black, they tie behind in a knot, but the men wear a piece of cloath about their heads. Thoſe few merchants that are among them, are next to the *Chineſe*, accounted the cunningeſt traders; the houſes of the *Malayans* are but very indifferently built there, being covered with leaves, and planted round with coco-trees. They have a cuſtom of chewing the *Bethel* leaves continually, and take tobacco through ſugar-canes lackered over with ſtone ball. 1662.

The Moors. The *Moors* or *Mahometans* here maintain themſelves almoſt in the ſame manner, and live near the *Malayans*; ſome however drive a kind of pedling-trade, and ſell coral and glaſs beads in the ſtreets, ſome have ſmall ſtalls in market-towns. A few of them merchandiſe, eſpecially in free-ſtone, which they fetch in their veſſels from the adjacent iſlands. They are clad after the *Mahometan* faſhion.

Amboyneſe. The *Amboyneſe* inhabit a particular part of the ſuburbs, on the left-hand, as you come from *Jacatra* to the city, near the burying place of the *Chineſe*; near it their governor (who has done great ſervice to the company) has built himſelf a ſtately houſe, after the manner of the *Amboyneſe*. They live for the moſt part upon carpenters work, being extremely dextrous in building of houſes of bamboo-canes, and have a peculiar way of ſplitting and twiſting of canes in divers figures for windows, which afford a free paſſage to the air. The *Amboyneſe* are a courageous nation, of a dreadful aſpect, with long black hair, and much inclined to mutiny; their chief weapons are cymeters, and ſhields of an oval figure, where with they know how to ward

a blow

A Melayā Captain.

The habit of a Malayan and his Wife at Batavia .

A Souldier of Amboina

A Negro Pedler with his Wife.

30.

1662. a blow, and to intercept their enemies arrows: The men wear a piece of callicoe wrapt several times about their heads, both ends hanging down, and adorned with flowers and some other ornaments. The women have only a piece of callicoe wrapt about them, and another piece round their shoulders, their arms being left bare; their houses are made of wooden planks, carved with leaves, indifferently high built: Their dress is like that of the *Moors*.

Javanese. The *Javanese* inhabit in houses of bamboo-canes, on the other side of the burying-place of the *Chinese*, some of which are neatly built and cover'd with the twigs of coco-trees. Some maintain themselves with husbandry, and especially with planting of rice, others with building of boats, used by the inhabitants for the carrying of their commodities to the city; they also go abroad a fishing, their boats which are turn'd like horns in the figure of a half-moon, being so nimble, that they call them the *Flying-Boats*. The *Javanese* men go for the most part naked, being only covered from the middle to the knees; some wear a kind of a scarf, whereon they fasten their swords; on the head they wear a cap, but go bare-footed. Their houses excel in neatness those of the rest of the *Indians*.

The *Mardiikers* or *Topassers* are a mixture of divers *Indian* nations, call'd *Topassers*, i. e. *Accommodators*, because they will accommodate themselves easily to the manners, customs and religion of such as they live among; tho' some will have them derive their name from a precious stone call'd a *Topaz*. They live both within and without the city, the chiefest of which being merchants, who traffick in their own vessels with the adjacent isles, live in very stately houses. The rest live upon husbandry, grasing and gardening, and have some artisans among them; they have their own captains, who sit in the council of war, and school-masters who teach their children to read and to write. Their dress approaches near to the *Dutch* fashion, but their breeches reach down to their ankles, and wear a kind of caps on their heads. Their women are clad like other *Indian* women. Their houses are better built than those of the other *Indians*, generally of stone, and cover'd with tiles, stately built and arch'd. Before their houses they plant coco-trees, and all sorts of *Indian* fruits and flowers, but the backside they reserve for the keeping of pigs, pidgeons, fowl and other sorts of poultry, which they bring to sale in the market. 1662. Mardiikers or Topassers.

1662.

The soldiers of Makassar. The chief arms of the soldiers of *Makassar* are certain poison'd arrows of a foot long, pointed at one end with fish teeth, and on the other with a kind of hard wood; when they are to go into the wars, they provide a good number of these arrows dipt a good while before in a poisonous liquor which they let dry upon them. This poison is the juice issuing out of the bark of a certain tree growing in the isle of *Makassar*, and two or three adjacent isles of the *Bougisses*; it is of the height of a clove tree; its leaves resembling also those of that tree; the juice of which, while yet fresh, is mortal, and not to be cured by antidotes. These poison'd arrows the soldiers of *Makassar* don't shoot out of their bows, but thro' trunks, as we let fly at the birds in *Europe* with small earthen balls; with these they will hit any mark within four rods distance. This poison is so pernicious, and penetrates with that swiftness thro' the whole mass of the blood, and seizes upon the spirits, that the *Makassars* themselves know no remedy against it. The most approved remedy against it is man's dung, which taken immediately after the wound is given, causes a vomiting, and hinders the operation of the poison: I have known several of our soldiers cured by this remedy, tho' some others I have seen die not long after they had been wounded, notwithstanding the use of it, and others after two or three days. In the isle of *Makassar* grows a certain root, of a bitterish taste, which is look'd upon as a great antidote against this poison, and is often used as such by the *Dutch*; they chew the root, and lay it about the orifice of the wound.

Timorese *soldiers.* The *Timorese* soldiers or inhabitants of the isle of *Timoor*, use swords of sandel wood, wherewith they can cut a man through the middle at one stroke: For in this isle, and the *Molucca-Islands*, and all along to the S. S. E. beyond the *Lesser-Java*, to the 10th deg. of southern latitude, grow whole woods of white and yellow sandel wood, call'd *Chandava* by the inhabitants. The *Timorese* are very barbarous, but warlike; formerly they were all pagans, but of late years most are turn'd mahometans, and some *Roman* catholicks.

Bougisses. The *Bokjes* or *Bougisses*, who formerly inhabited divers isles near that of *Makassar*, are a warlike people, arm'd with cymeters, arrows, and shields, which they handle with great dexterity. They go for the greatest part naked, having only a piece of stuff about the middle down to the knees. The women are clad like the other *Indians*. After the *Dutch* became engaged in a war with the king of *Makassar*, these *Bougisses* fixt their habitations in and about *Batavia*, till the event of the war; their king having his residence near the out-guard, betwixt the forts of *Riswick* and *Northwick*, the queen being permitted to reside within the city; but after the *Makassars* were conquered by the *Dutch*, under the conduct of *Cornelius Spellman*, and a firm peace was settled with the neighbouring nations, both the king and queen had a house assign'd them in the *Lords-Street*. This house or palace extends to the brink of the river, with very pleasant walks, flower-gardens, and a most delightful vineyard, which in my time, 1676, bore vast branches of grapes. The gate facing the street is very neatly built, of the *Ionick* order, with a gallery on the top of it, and the apartments so spacious and well-contrived, that most of the *Indian* kings and their retinue might live here.

1662.

Number of foreigners at Batavia. Among the foreign nations residing here, there may, according to computation, be raised 6720 fighting men, *viz.* 400 *Topassars* or *Mardüken* under two captains, within the city, besides 710 without the city, under three captains, making in all 1110; of *Regantiins* 70; *Amboynese* 600; *Malayans* 201; *Chinese* 1200; *Moors* 200; of the *Javanese* in their quarter within the *New-Gate* 750; near the burying-place of the *Chinese* 1500; in their quarter beyond the *New-Fort* 800; and of *Brasilians* beyond the fort 300. That this island is sufficiently fruitful, and able to maintain its inhabitants, is evident from the exportations that are made yearly thence to *Amboyna* and other places: It is true no wheat grows here, but supposing the supplies that are brought of that grain from *Suratte* and *Japan* should be stopt, the defect thereof may very well be supplied with rice. The chief artisans here are *Dutch*, most of which live very well, and the *Chinese* have many carpenters and bricklayers among themselves, who will work as journeymen. Their cabinet-makers have a way of joining the wood of their cabinets, so that the jointures are not to be seen. Others get a livelyhood by selling of sugar-beer, cookery, and the sale of *Sury* or coco-liquor, and *Arack* or *Indian* strong-waters, of which they make punch, (as the *English* call it) a liquor that opens both the hearts and purses of the inhabitants. But the chief inns and taverns are kept by the *Dutch*, who pay, as well as all the other nations, two reals *per* month for their license, besides 70 reals excise of every pipe of *Spanish* wine they sell. The distillers of *Arack* are most *Chinese*, who pay 50 reals excise for every chauldron or gosper *per* month.

The

A Marchant of Java.

A Javanese Man and Wooman.

A Makaßer with his Wife as they are habited at Batavia

34.

Tymorian Souldiers.

35.

A Bougis of Bokjes.

Makassar Souldiers who blow poison'd darts out of Trunks. 36

A Topas or Mardick with his Wife 37

1662. The government of the city of *Batavia* is settled upon the same basis as in the *United Provinces*, being administer'd by six peculiar colleges or councils.

The first and chief is composed of the members of the council of the *Indies*, in which the governor-general of the *Indies* presides, whose name was Mr. *Maetzuiper* at that time. In this council all affairs of state are transacted: Their chamber is in the palace of the governor, where audience is given every day to redress the grievances of the people.

The second college or council consists of nine persons, besides the president, who commonly is one of the members of the great council, and is the keeper of the great seal, representing a woman placed in a tower, with a balance in one, and a sword in the other hand, with this inscription; *The seal of the council of justice of the castle of* Batavia; this college being generally called the *Council of Justice*. Here are debated and decided all matters relating to the publick revenue and treasury. They also take cognizance of differences arising about customs. The president in conjunction with the council has a voice in the determination of civil causes, and has a third part of all the fines; but if they exceed 100 reals, he has only a sixth part. His chief business is to take care that no incroachments be made upon the prerogatives of the sovereignty of the *United Provinces*. The secretary is to keep an exact register of all things transacted in this assembly, without any other reward but his salary: He also has in his custody the money which comes from the fines, of which he must give an account. The door-keeper is to attend whilst they are sitting, and to summon such persons as are to appear before them: He wears a stick and a silver-shield on the left-side, with the seal of the council. The goal-keeper keeps three tables for the prisoners; who are to pay half a real for turning the key. This council assembles in the council-chamber of the town-house, twice, and sometimes thrice a week.

The third college or council consists of the aldermen or senators, chosen out of the best citizens. They assemble three times a week, *viz. Mondays, Wednesdays* and *Thursdays*, from 7 till 11 in the forenoon. At their election they are presented with 50 rixdollars, and with 100 more every 6 months. In this council are determin'd all the causes betwixt the citizens, (from whom however lies an appeal to the council of justice;) if any difference arises betwixt a servant of the company and a citizen, the last must be summoned before this court; and no citizen is obliged to appear before the council of justice, but must be summon'd before this assembly first, and there answer for himself. This council issue their orders in relation to the publick structures, bridges and streets, yet not without the approbation of the great council. The president has the custody of the seal, and calls the assembly together when he thinks fit: He may peruse the register, and proposes all matters to the council: He has a double voice, and is commonly one of the members of the great council. The *Landrost* or chief judge, has in this assembly a decisive sentence in criminal causes, and is allowed a third part of all the fines. This council consists of nine persons, among whom are two *Chinese*. They have also a door-keeper, who is called the city messenger, having a shield with the city's arms in it. 1662.

The government of Batavia.

The fourth council consists of the overseers of the hospital of the orphans, being chosen out of the best citizens, except the president, who is generally a member of the great council. It consists of five members only, three whereof are citizens, the other two servants of the company: Their business is to provide for the poor-orphans, and to enquire into their condition, and what is left by their parents.

The fifth is the council appointed for the determination of matters of less moment; the president whereof is a member of the council of justice. They are to give licences for marriages, and not to permit men before they are twenty one, and maids before eighteen years of age, to marry; nor mahometans or pagans to marry with christians, nor any *Hollanders* with the natives that don't understand *Dutch*. They sit twice a week in the town-house, where causes of little moment are pleaded and soon decided.

The sixth council of *Batavia* is the council of war, in which the chief officer of the militia of the city is president. Here are determined all matters relating to the militia of less moment, which are brought before them by the city major; but matters of consequence are referr'd to the determination of the judge and court of the senators. They also meet in the town-house once a week.

All these courts have each their own secretary, clerks and waiters.

The ecclesiastical government.

The ecclesiastical government of *Batavia* is administred by the ministers, church-wardens and overseers of the poor, who assemble in the vestry of the church upon the summons of their president, who is chosen every month. The ministers being chosen in, and sent hither out of *Holland*,

1662.

The original and rise of Batavia.

are confirm'd here, and live in great esteem among the citizens.

Batavia, the capital city of all the *Indies* under the *Dutch* jurisdiction, has been frequently attempted by the natives or *Javanese*; for no sooner had the *Hollanders* in 1618. (after the taking of *Jacatra*, unto which they gave the name of *Batavia*) erected a fortress here, but the natives being encouraged by the *English* of *Bantam*, endeavour'd to drive them from thence. To effect which, the *English* persuaded them to erect a redoubt or great battery, upon which they planted their great guns, from whence they play'd so furiously upon the new bastion of the *Dutch* fort, that they were not able to bring it to perfection. *John Peterson Koen*, the *Dutch* governor, having thereupon call'd together a council of war, it was resolved, that to hinder the further progress of the enemy, they should make a salley the next morning by break of day, in order to attack the redoubt, and the quarters of the *Chinese* and *English* at the same time. Accordingly our men were divided into three troops, commanded by *Peter Van Broek*, (afterwards governor-general of the *Dutch-Indies*) *Peter Van Dirks*, and *Peter Van Rey*, with these they attack'd the before-mentioned posts at once. The *Javanese* fought bravely at first; but seeing the *Hollanders* persisted in the attack, resolved either to die or overcome, they retreated, leaving their strong hold to the enemy, who destroy'd all their work in a few hours. But being sorely gall'd by the fire of the city, they had not the same success at the new redoubt erected by the enemy near the river-side; so, that having endeavoured, but in vain, to make a breach there, they were forced to retire with the loss of 15 men killed and 10 wounded. Besides this redoubt, the *Javanese* had another battery raised in the midst of the city, which being mounted with heavy cannon taken out of the *English* ships, did also considerable mischief to the besieged, who were day and night at work in raising batteries, and putting their fortifications in a state of defence; whereas the enemy being much superior in number, had had time enough to provide themselves with all things for this enterprise. In the mean while the *Hollanders* made a second attempt upon the redoubt near the river-side, but were repulsed with the loss of 7 or 8 of their men, and a lieutenant, whose head the *Javanese* carried in triumph on the top of a launce. The *English* then living at *Bantam*, would fain have revenged themselves upon the *Dutch* inhabitants there, for the damages their countreymen had received at *Batavia*, had they not been prevented therein by the *Pangerang*. Whilst the *Dutch*, who were not above 240 fighting men strong in the fortress, were thus defending themselves against some thousands of the *Javanese*, (besides the *English*) an *English* squadron of 11 ships appeared in the road of *Batavia*, coming from *Bantam*; whereupon the governor of the fort, having recommended the defence thereof to *Peter Van Broek* the deputy governor, he went on board a man of war, with an intention to engage the *English*, but finding himself two weak, left what ammunition he could spare, in the castle, and so set sail for the *Molucca* islands, being pursued for some days by the *English*, but to no purpose; who after their return, came again to an anchor in the road of *Batavia*. Thus the *Dutch* were attack'd both by sea and land, yet did not lose their courage, but defended themselves with so much bravery, that the enemy thought fit to offer a truce, to settle, as they pretended, the preliminaries of a peace.

1662.

Hostages being exchang'd on both sides, the *Dommagon* or prime minister, the king of *Jacatra*'s brother demanded the sum of 4000 crowns from the *Hollanders*, which he said they had forfeited according to agreement, for having attack'd the *English* without the king's leave, and 4000 more for the letting them finish the new bastion, which he said was not comprehended in the said contract; after many debates and contests, certain articles were at last agreed on, which the *Dutch* (who wanted ammunition) were willing to sign; but the *English* finding those conditions against their interest (the *Dutch* being thereby permitted to remain in the possession of their fortress and habitations at *Bantam*) found out the following trick to break off the treaty; they so far prevail'd, first with *Peter vander Broek* the deputy-governor of the fortress, that he came out to meet the king of *Jacatra* at an appointed place, but no sooner appear'd there but he was taken prisoner, with those few that attended him, and laid in irons; being threatned with present death, unless he would prevail with those in the fortress to surrender it immediately; but finding the garrison resolved to defend the place, the *English* brought more of their heavy cannon ashore, in order to batter it with the utmost fury; at the same time they drag'd the deputy-governor, loaden with irons and a rope about his neck, to the walls of the castle, threatning him once more with immediate death upon the spot, unless the garrison would prevent it by an immediate surrender; the deputy-governor was so far from being overcome by the fear of present death, that

Bravery of the Dutch *governor of* Batavia.

1662. that on the contrary, like a brave and faithful commander, he exhorted them to defend the place to the last drop of blood, which so exasperated some of the *Javanese* and *English* that stood near him, that they threw him backwards by the rope, and so drag'd him back to the council, all which he took patiently, and with so undaunted courage, that some of the *English* being asham'd of so barbarous an action, afterwards beg'd his pardon. By this time the *Dutch* having spent all their ammunition, and quite tir'd out with continual labour and watching, without any hopes of present relief, saw themselves under an indispensable necessity to surrender the place under condition, that the garrison and castle with all the artillery should be deliver'd to the *English*, and the merchandizes, money and jewels to the *Javanese*; it was sign'd the first of *February* 1619, by *Wydurk Bama*, king of *Jacatra*, and the *English* chief commander on one side, and by those in the fortress on the other side.

The *Hollanders* being now upon the point of delivering themselves and the fortress up to their enemies, a sudden accident robb'd the *Javanese* and the *English* of all their hopes; for the *Pangerang* of *Bantam* had no sooner notice of this capitulation, in which he had no share, but he order'd his *Dommagon* or chief minister to march with a body of 4000 men to secure the *Dutch* deputy-governor, and the castle with all that was found in it for his use. Accordingly he march'd with all secrecy to *Jacatra*, and meeting with the king in his apartment, put his dagger to his breast with these words: *King, surrender yourself prisoner, or expect no quarter*, which so terrify'd the king, that he comply'd not only with his demands, but soon after retir'd with the queen into the mountains, without ever being heard of since. The *Dommagon* of *Bantam* having taken the deputy-governor into his custody, summon'd the fortress to surrender, which those refus'd to do, except upon the before-mention'd conditions, which the *Bantamese* refusing to agree to, and the *English* in the mean while (seeing they were like to be disappointed in aim) beginning to reimbark their cannon, thro' contrivance of the besieged, these finding their enemies at variance about the booty, began to take fresh courage, and having in several attacks bravely repulsed the *Javanese*, were now so confident of maintaining the fort, that they gave it the name of *Batavia*; thus matters stood, when on the 25th of *March* 1619, their so long look'd for relief, consisting of 17 men of war, under the command of *John Peterson Koen*, came from the *Moluque* islands in the road of *Batavia*: Within a few days after they landed 1100 men, divided into 12 several bodies, and edged on with revenge, attack'd the city of *Jacatra* with incredible fury, the *Javanese* defended themselves with great obstinacy for some time, but no longer able to endure our fire, they left their entrenchments, and look'd for their safety in an open flight, being closely pursued by the *Dutch*, who gave no quarter; this happened the 30th of *March* 1619, which day is yearly celebrated here in memory of this great action. This done, Mr. *Koen* sail'd with the fleet to *Bantam*, demanding the immediate restitution of all the prisoners; the *Pangerang* being at first unwilling to grant his demand, he began to thunder with his cannon into the city, which soon terrify'd him into a compliance. The *English* seeing themselves now quite out of all hopes of accomplishing their design, by the coming of the *Dutch* fleet, made the best of their way thro' the streight of *Sunda*, and those of *Bantam*, finding themselves forsaken by their confederates, thought it most convenient to give over their project. 1662.

The *Hollanders* having now their hands free, and seeing the situation of their new fortress in so fertile a countrey, near a very advantageous bay, capable of containing 1000 ships with safety, resolved and gave immediate orders for the building of the city, under the cannon of the fortress, the adjacent islands furnishing them with sufficient stone and mortar, and what else was requisite for this undertaking, being purchased from the neighbouring confederates. But the *Javanese* not being able to brook the rise and encrease of this new city, the *Mataran* (or *Javanese* emperor) 1629, laid close siege to it with 12000 men, under the conduct of the prince of *Madure*; and being advanc'd with their works within musket shot of the walls, they made several furious attacks in the night-time, but were as often repulsed by the fire of the besieged, who besides this made frequent sallies, and ruin'd their works, without giving them leisure to repair them. The *Javanese* being resolv'd to try all means to reduce the place, stop'd the current of the great river with piles ram'd into the bottom, behind which they threw all the dead carcasses of men and beasts, which not only infected the water, but also the air, which occasion'd distempers among the besieg'd, who were forced to drink salt water for a considerable time, till at last by continual digging having found some springs of tolerable good water, they began to refresh themselves with less danger and more ease. The *Javanese* finding also this design

1662. ſign to prove unſucceſsful, had recourſe again to force, and the 2ᵈ of *October* 1629, made a general aſſault on the ſouth-ſide of the city, relieving their troops continually with freſh men, but were repulſed bravely without any conſiderable loſs of the *Dutch*. At the ſame time they aſſaulted a ſmall outwork or tower call'd *Maaſland-Waerberg*, defended only by 15 men, who defended themſelves courageouſly, as that they were attack'd. At laſt, having ſpent all their powder and ball, they went to work with the tiles and bricks of the caſtle within; the *Javaneſe* being ſenſible of their want, advanced to the very foot of the walls, and having found means to bring a great rope round the building, were endeavouring to pull down the tower; but the beſieged ſeeing themſelves in extremity, made a furious ſally upon the *Javeneſe*, who thought not fit to ſtand the ſhock, but ſoon retreated to their entrenchments, except a few that were ſlain upon the ſpot. The firſt of *November* 1629, about ſix hours after ſunſet, the *Javaneſe* ſet fire to their camp in three ſeveral places, and march'd off with all imaginable ſecrecy, after a ſiege of three months and three days. No booty worth mentioning was found there, but 800 men miſerably murthered all on a ſpot; a miſerable ſpectacle! occaſion'd as we learn'd afterwards by the haughty courage of the prince of *Madure*, which happened thus: During the firſt ſiege of the caſtle of *Batavia*, the emperor of *Mataran* having ſent a body of troops under the command of one of his beſt officers to the king of *Jacatra*, and the ſame returning unſucceſsful, the prince of *Madure* ſpoke ſlightly of the matter, telling openly at court, *That if he had been ſent with ſuch troops, he would have carried the caſtle or died in the attempt.* The *Materan* being inform'd thereof, and reſolv'd to try his fortune againſt *Batavia*, gave the ſupreme command of his army to the ſaid prince, who proving unſucceſsful, juſt as he was ready to march off with his troops, was order'd to be ſlain with all his followers, *to verify his own words* (as he ſaid) *that he would either carry the caſtle or periſh in the attempt.*

Batavia *beſieged by the* Javaneſe.

The *Javaneſe* loſt above 30000 men in this unfortunate ſiege, notwithſtanding which, thoſe of *Bantam* in the year 1655, had a mind to try their fortune againſt the *Dutch*; who meeting them in the open field, this occaſioned many ſkirmiſhes, in which the *Javaneſe* commonly had the worſt, ſo that being pretty well tired with the war, and hearing of the approaching ſuccours from the *Molucca* iſlands, under the command of *Arnold Ulaming*, they thought it their beſt way to come to a compoſition with them, ſince which time they have not thought fit to come to any rupture, but maintain a good correſpondence with thoſe they know are able to cope with them; eſpecially ſince they have ſtrengthned their city with divers conſiderable outworks and forts. 1662.

The fort *Anſjol* on the ſea-ſide, the fort *Aake* to the weſt-ſide, and on the *Quinquangular* fort, the *Riſwick*, *Noothwick* and *Jacatra* on the land-ſide. The fort *Aake* is built 1200 rods from *Batavia* to the eaſt, near the ſea-ſide juſt by the lime-kills, and faced with ſtone. The fort *Aake* lies about 500 rods from the city, more towards the land-ſide, being alſo a free quadrangular figure; hereabouts live abundance of farmers along the river, the grounds being very fertile here. Near it is the *Peſt-houſe*. The fort *Jacatra* ſtands upon the bank of the river, not above 500 paces to the north-eaſt of the city; from whence there is a ſtrait and pleaſant walk thither, planted on both ſides with gardens and orchards. The *Chineſe*, *Amboyneſe*, and ſome other foreigners have their habitations hereabouts. The fort of *Northwick* lies to the north of the city near the river, betwixt that of *Jacatra* and *Riſwick*.

The outworks of Batavia.

Without the city many of the citizens have very pleaſant gardens and houſes. Upon the great river without *Batavia* you ſee a houſe belonging to captain *Burghs*, built flat on the top after the *Indian* faſhion, being ſurrounded with all ſorts of *Indian* trees. Upon the brink of the river is a pleaſant ſummer-houſe. Without the city, near the great river, ſtands another houſe belonging to a rich citizen call'd *Strantwich*, belonging formerly to Mr. *John Maetzuicker*, governor-general of the *Dutch Indies*: It is very airy and pleaſantly built, with a very fine front, the gardens being well ſtored with trees and flowers of moſt ſorts.

Without the new gate, in a grove of pleaſant trees, you ſee the tomb of a *Chineſe* governor, named *Sequa*; being no more than a heap of earth raiſed above the ſurface of the ground, and encloſed with brick-work, plaiſtered white all over: In the midſt you ſee a table, and upon it a cup, into which the *Chineſe* put ſometimes money, ſometimes victuals, to appeaſe the manes of the deceaſed.

A Chineſe tomb.

The grounds about *Batavia*, and indeed of the whole iſle of *Java*, are extremely fertile in all ſorts of fruits the *Indies* afford; but what is moſt ſurprizing is, that divers plants, which in *Europe* grow on ſmall and tender ſtalks, riſe up here very thick, and with hard ſtalks; whereas

Trees, plants and flowers of Java.

7 on

1662. on the other hand, divers sorts of beans and flowers grow in *Java* upon trees. The soil about *Batavia* is so rich, that the seeds brought hither out of *Holland*, *Persia*, and from *Suratte*, thrive extremely, and yield plentiful fruits.

Fruits of the earth. *Holland* cabbages, if sown in due time, and well look'd after, come here to a good perfection, but if neglected they will not cabbage. Provident nature seems to have been careful in abundance of astringent plants for this climate, where the bloody flux and other distempers occasioned by the gall, are so frequent. Of trefoil or clover they have great store here; and in their gardens purslain, asparagus, endive, lettice, bekabung, water-cresses, parsley, radishes, red and white beetes, and such like: The radishes grow longer and better tasted here than in *Europe*, and there is a certain kind of them shorter but thicker than the rest, which are boil'd like our turnips. The *Chinese* pickle radishes, and use them to create an appetite to their victuals. Here also is found a certain kind of *Mandragora*, called *Bella Donna* by the *Italians*, in great request among the *Indians* in burning fevers; they pickle it in vinegar, and eat the fruit roasted in the ashes as a disert.

Vines. Vines are very plenty and good here if well cultivated; whether or by whom the vines have been translated hither is uncertain, there being no mention made of it in the journals of the voyages made into those parts since the year 1595. They grow very lusciously upon the walls of the houses of *Batavia*, which bear fruit in a manner all the year round, provided they be pruned in due time; for 14 days after they are pruned the buds come out, which in 14 days more stand in full blossom, and in two months longer produce ripe grapes; so that every vine brings forth ripe grapes every three months, and consequently four times in the year. But they don't thrive so well without the city; whether the lands be too low, or not sufficiently purged from the salt-petre, I will leave to the enquiry of others; since it is certain, that vineyards would be of prodigious consequence to the inhabitants, there being vines here which bear grapes, each bunch weighing 16 or more ounces; and there are some grapes as big as the *Spanish Muscadine* grape.

Blue beans. All along the roads about *Batavia* grow a certain plant among the woods, with small branches not unlike the hops, which spread very plentifully upon the ground, or will rise up to a good height on stalks like our *French* beans, having leaves like our rose-trees. The flower comes forth out of a bud as large as our ordinary roses, pointed at the end; they are of a lovely sky blue colour, and yellow in the middle, but the fruit being rank is not regarded. 1662.

The *Indian* beets grow in the gardens of *Batavia*, their leaves being not unlike our sorrel leaves, with a pale vein thro' the middle: They bring forth pursley flowers on green stalks; some are white, others a mixture of purple and green. The leaves and stalks when boil'd, are in taste like the *Indian Bajan*: All sorts of garden-herbs are in great request among the *Indians* here, because most of the *Indian* foreigners that come from *Suratte*, and the coast of *Coromandel*, feed for the most part upon fruits of the earth; for believing the transmigration of the soul, they will not eat the flesh of any living creature; for which reason also they abstain from red beans, or herbs of a red colour, as having a resemblance to blood; and for the same reason it is, that the *Indians*, tho' otherwise very ignorant, yet are very well versed in the knowledge of plants and trees. The *Malayans* call all pot-herbs or other eatable herbs *Seir*, but medicinal and poisonous herbs *Oubat*. About *Batavia* are to be found divers sorts of pot and other garden herbs; as red and white beets, parsley, divers sorts of lettices, dill, fennel, asparagus, &c. And of fruits of the earth water-melons, pompions, cucumbers, citruls, &c. And of pulse, all sorts of beans and peas, which grow up to a great height on stalks or trees. *Indian garden-herbs.*

The fruit call'd *Fokky-Fokky* by the *Indians* is shaped like a pear, sometimes near a yard long, and of the thinness of a man's arm: It contains abundance of small seeds, the rind being thin, but so smooth and bright, that you may see your face in them like as in a looking-glass: The leaves are green but rough, and as it were covered with a hairy substance: They grow up to a good height. This fruit is one of the best and most esteem'd of all the *Indies*, being of a delicious taste, and when boil'd with wine and pepper, not unlike our artichoak bottoms. They are frequently eaten both by the *Dutch* and *Indians*, instead of the *European* turnips, being look'd upon as very nourishing and easy to be digested; besides, that by their diuretick quality they are good against the gravel and stone. There is another wild kind of *Fokky-Fokky*, the fruits wereof are round, and when ripe turn yellow, but these are only food for the hogs. *Fokky-Fokky.*

In the plains of *Java* grows a tree, the fruit whereof the *Malayans* call *Jamboes*, and the *Dutch* sloes or small plumbs: This tree resembling in all respects our sloe or wild plumb-tree; the fruits being also of an astringent but not disagreeable taste: The fruit when ripe is yellow, and the juice *Jamboes.*

1662. juice thereof mix'd with *Champana* and rose water, is used against the inflammation of the throat. The juice taken inwardly is good against the bloody flux, and other bileous distempers. Thus this juice of the *Indian* fruit *Jangomas* is equivalent in its virtue to the *Acacia* of the antients, or to our *European* sloes.

Cubebes *or* Kumuk. In the isle of *Java* only, *viz.* in the woods near the shore of the streight of *Sunda*, grows wild a certain fruit called *Cubebes* and *Quabeb* by the *Arabians*, *Kumuk* by the *Javenese*, and by the rest of the *Indians*, except the *Malayans*, *Kubab Sini*, i. e. *Chinese Kubebe*, not because it grows in *China*, but because it is transported thither in great quantities. The tree which bears this fruit is both in leaves and branches not unlike to our apple-tree, but somewhat lesser. The fruit is round, smaller than pepper, of a dark brown colour, and if pinch'd with the nails, will emit a certain liquor like unto the cloves. This fruit is in so high an esteem among the *Javanese*, that they will not permit them to be transported, unless they are boil'd before-hand, to prevent their being transplanted into another place. They gather some of them before they are ripe; these are light, with a rough rind, within which is a small soft and whitish kernel. When they are ripe the rind is smooth, have a bigger kernel, and are much heavier than the others. Before they are quite ripe, they have an aromatick, biting, and bitterish taste, and when chew'd offend the brain: But the ripe ones are neither so sharp nor so bitter, and don't send so much of their offensive vapours up to the head; they are reckoned hot and dry in the third degree; are good to attenuate slime in the stomach and breast, expel wind, and correct the cold symptoms of the womb. Chew'd with mastick, they draw the phlegmatick humours from the head, and strengthen the brains. They are in great request among the *Javanese* and other *Indians*, who steep them in wine, and take them to raise their appetite to venery, and to warm the stomach. Three or four chew'd, disperse the vapours which occasion giddiness in the head, but care must be taken to spit out both the phelgm and *Cubebes*, and to keep the nostrils close while you are a chewing, that so the smell and scent of them may penetrate with the more efficacy, and affect more immediately the head.

Assafetida. The *Javanese*, *Malayans*, and other *Indians*, use very frequently for the relishing of their sauces, a certain drug called *Hin*, by the *Arabians Altit*, and by the *Europeans Assafetida*, by reason of its ill scent. This shrub, out of the root of which this juice is express'd, grows in *Persia*, betwixt *Gamron* and *Lara*. It is of two sorts; 1662. the first is not unlike our *Osier*, out of the leaves and sprigs of which is squeezed the *Hin* by a press, and the juice afterward coagulated in the sun: The second sort is much stronger and worse scented, being the juice express'd out of the root of this shrub. This juice, and that of *Amsion* or *Opium*, are two of the chiefest commodities of the *Dutch* trade in the *Indies*. Our *East-India* ships bound to *Java* and other *Indian* ports, do always carry a considerable quantity of this juice from *Persia*, which they exchange with the *Javanese* for such of their countrey commodities as they have occasion for.

Both great and small *Cardamome*, (as the *Arabians* call it) called *Malignetus* by the *Indians*, grows likewise in the isle of *Java*. Cardamome. The small *Cardamome* grows on a stalk with small joints like reeds, (the leaves being also like theirs, and grow in clusters like them;) but the *Cardamome* seldom grows above two or three foot high, and the leaves rub'd betwixt your fingers, emit a very odoriferous scent. From the root first sprout forth in ears like the *Spicknard*, the flowers being of a pale colour, not unlike the orange-flowers. After these come certain husks, which contains these well-scented seeds, which are green, but in time turn of a dark vermillion colour. The *Cardamome* is a most excellent spice of extraordinary virtues, having an agreeable heat consonant to our nature, without leaving any heat behind it, which is the reason that it is chew'd without any addition. It promotes urine, and the monthly terms of the women; opens the obstructions of the spleen and liver, and procures a sweet breath. The great *Cardamome* grows plentifully in the woods of *Java*; the flowers grow on the stalk like the hyacinth; it differs from the small *Cardamome* in divers respects: It grows to the height of six foot, the leaves are larger, and the stalks not knotty like the reeds. The small *Cardamome* sends forth an ear from the root, and the husks are sometimes a finger long. However, the leaves and flowers are of the same scent in both, but the leaves of the great *Cardamome* are not only much larger, but also covered with a *Lanugo* on the under side. This shrub is very pleasant to behold, of a light green colour, with white flowers tip'd with purple red at the extremities.

The plant called by the *Malayans Moulit Bebek*, i. e. the *Ducks-Beak*, from its Moulit. Bebek. shape, grows in the gardens of *Batavia* on a somewhat longer stalk than the *Cardamome*, being a sempervirent herb; the leaves also differ from those of the *Cardamome*, being carved or edged in the circumference.

 The

1662. The inhabitants use the juice of this herb against pustules and other exulcerations of a bileous nature; and steep'd in vinegar, it is a good remedy against the St. *Anthony's Fire*; the *Malayan* women lay it upon the heads of their children to corroborate the brains.

Indian *Sorrel.* In the isle of *Java*, and adjacent islands, grows an odd kind of sorrel, having no resemblance to the *European* sorrel, growing up to the height of six foot, with a strong, hard, and three corner'd stalk not unlike the hemp; the leaves being also not unlike those of the hemp, beset with sharp small prickles. The flower has but one single leaf of a pale yellow colour, but of a purple colour below. The leaves chew'd have the same taste as our sorrel, but are more oily: The seed is thorny like that of *Carduus*, and of a cooling and drying quality. The *Malayans* eat this herb among their sallads; they also take the leaves, and after they have mix'd them well with the sawdust of sandel-wood upon a marble-stone, and a little coco oil and vinegar, make a cataplasm of it, which they apply to the head to cure the tooth-ach, proceeding from a hot cause.

Benzoin *tree.* In the isle of *Java* grows likewise the tree, out of the bark of which, after an incision made, flows that well scented gum called *Benzoin* or *Benjuin*, being a shrub or tree spread into many branches, of the thickness of a man's arm.

Nardus. About *Batavia* grows a plant in great plenty call'd *Nardus*, most in request among the *Javanese*, who used it in their fish and boil'd meat sauces, to give them a relish. They steep the *Nardus* in vinegar, and make a syrup of it with sugar, which is esteem'd a good remedy against the coldness of the bowels, and opens the obstructions of the spleen and liver. This vinegar and syrup cures also the stings of the serpents and scorpions, if applied outwardly and taken inwardly at the same time.

Amfion, *or* Opium. *Amfioen* or *Amfion*, as it is called by the *Indians*, and *Opium* by the *Europeans*, is nothing else but the juice of poppies, much used by the *Javanese* and other *Indians*, especially when they are upon the point of engaging their enemies. The *Amfion* is a very useful drug to the *Indians*, without which they would be at a stand how to cure many distempers in this hot climate, as the bloody flux, burning fevers, and such like distempers proceeding from the gall. The poorer sort of the *Indians* boil the leaves and sprouts of the *Amfion*, out of which they make a slighter sort of *Opium*, by coagulating the decoction called *Poust*.

Pyzang. The fruit called *Pyzang* or *Indian* figs, as also *Bachovees* from the *Portuguese* word *Bakovia*, are called *Pyzang* or *Banana's* by the *Malayans*, *Gedars* by the *Javanese*, *Thio* by the *Chinese*, by the rest of the *Indians* *Oucelli*, by the inhabitants of the isle of *St. Thomas Oucella*; and by the *Arabians* *Maus* and *Muza*. The stem or trunk of this tree grows up in long oval scollops to the height of 20 or 30 foot in six months time; its circumference being of four foot, but so soft, that you may cut it with a knife like a cabbage stalk. It spreads its branches very loftily, and bears leaves, some of which are a foot and a half broad, and five, six, or seven foot long; green on the uppermost side, but dark on the other side, with a thick vein through the middle. The fruit has an ear, the stalk a yellowish brown, is very pleasing to the sight, and shap'd like a cucumber, turning at the extremities towards one another as they hang on the tree: Before they are ripe they are of a parrot green colour, but when come to full perfection, yellow both in and outside. When the fruit is fit to be gathered the stem is cut down to the ground, and the fruit, which is green as yet, taken and hung up in the house, where it ripens and turns pale yellow in a few days. The rind is so thin, that it may be taken off without a knife. Neither the tree nor fruit produces any seed, but a very handsome flower of the bigness of an ostriches egg, which sprouts forth on the top out of large buds, and opens its leaves by degrees. Whilst the stem has fruit enough to nourish, the leaves fall off one after another: Out of the before-mentioned knot or flower comes forth a branch, on which grows the fruit in a cluster, sometimes 1 or 200 together, so that sometimes one branch is as much as a man can carry, and each stem or trunk brings forth no more than one cluster. There are divers sorts of these figs, distinguish'd by the inhabitants by different names, shapes and tastes; and they put them to various uses; some have a way of drying them in the sun, when they taste as pleasantly as the *Portuguese* figs: Of this kind I tasted at *St. Anthony*, one of the salt islands. 1662.

The *Dutch* fry them with butter and eggs, or with butter alone, and eat it for a dainty; thus dress'd they are accounted cooling, nourishing and opening. The fruit raw is very astringent, and consequently not to be eaten thus, because they are windy, and will create a nauseousness in the stomach; and sometimes will produce the bloody flux. However, they being of so agreeable a scent and taste, they are sometimes eaten raw, provided they are cut off the trees a good while before they come to full maturity; when the rind will remain

1662. green, and the pulp by degrees acquires a very agreeable taste, not unlike our sugar pears: If you cut the fruit thro' the middle, you will see th figure of a cross within: The leaves of this tree are used like as we do our mats, to pack up goods with: And I remember, that in 1660, when I travell'd with Mr. *James Hustart* to the isle of *Buro*, the inhabitants served up their victuals in those leaves instead of dishes, and covered their meats with the same: They also used them instead of napkins to wipe their hands on: When one of our servants offered them a glass with liquor, they refused to take it; but instead thereof brought forth a leaf of a certain tree, which being accommodated for that purpose, they drunk out of it, telling us, that their cup needed no washing: The *Javanese* being of opinion, that the leaves of these fig-trees have a great virtue to extinguish the fire, they plant them near their houses, to make use of them in case of necessity. So soon as the stem or trunk is cut to the root, after the fruit is come to maturity, the root sends forth new ones, round about the old one, which coming to their full growth in a little time, and producing new fruits, the same may be had fresh all the year long. This tree grows without much trouble and in such plenty, that for a penny you may buy a whole bunch; they grow best in a fat and mellow soil. Some will have this fruit the same, which by the spies of *Israel* were brought out of the *Land of Promise* into the camp of the *Israelites:* Others are of opinion, that these were the leaves wherewith *Adam* and *Eve* covered their nakedness: Others again maintain, that *Adam* eat of this fruit, which occasioned his fall, whence they call them *Paradise Apples.*

The Bamboe.

The *Bamboe* grows all over *Batavia*, being strait reeds clove in two at the upper-end, having no root fastened in the ground, but grows without the least portion of earth from the surface of the water, having on the bottom a thick knob, from whence sprout forth small twigs like threads, which being nourished by the air and thaw, bring forth leaves and flowers. Its flowers are very white, having five long leaves somewhat crumpled, not unlike the white lillies; they have also a very odoriferous scent, and a yellow seed within. The leaves sprout forth at the extremity of the twigs bending downwards, which bear long and narrow leaves. It is very surprizing both for its natural growth, and its most agreeable scent.

Button *flower.*

The flower called by the *Malayans*, *Borago Soesan*, by the *Javanese*, *Bunbang Ungo*, and *Licuboa* by the *Chinese*; the *Portuguese* call *Fule de Botano*, i. e. the *Button Flower*, from its resemblance to a button. It grows in great plenty in the gardens, by reason of its pleasing purple colour, (which remains even after it is dried) but has no scent. It grows like our clover, except that the leaves grow closer to one another on thin brown stalks; The flower comes forth with green buds betwixt two leaves.

The white sweet-briar.

The white sweet briar, called *Boenga Dadu* by the *Javanese* and *Malayans*, and *Tyntsou* by the *Chinese*, bears leaves and flowers like our rose-tree, except that the flowers, which are very white, are not altogether so large, and have pointed leaves; they scent like our roses, but not altogether so strong. They say, that this tree was first transplanted from *Persia* near *Batavia* by the *Dutch*, when they first settled here: Out of the leaves of the flowers they distil rose-water, used in the same manner as our rose-water, for which reason they are very industrious to propagate this tree.

Jakkas.

The tree which bears the fruit called *Jakka*, or *Jakkas* by the *Portuguese*, and *Nanka* by the *Javanese*, is one of the largest fruit-trees of the *Indies*, which delights in high and dry grounds, where it will grow up to the height of an oak-tree. The leaves are blue on the underside, but green on the other side, round and less than the leaves of our cherry-trees. It bears no flowers, the fruit growing out of stem and branches, of such a bigness, that one of them weighs sometimes nine or ten pounds, being commonly eight inches thick, and a foot and a half long: They are very pleasing to look upon, not unlike the pompions or large melons, but on the outside like the *Ananas* or pine-apples. The fruit is green at first, but after it is gathered and ripened, yellow: It has a thick rind, covered with a kind of three cornered thorny *Lanugo*, but don't prick. Within this rind you have certain divisions like as in a honey comb, which contain certain kernels or chesnuts larger than dates, enclosed in a yellow pulp, which is eaten. The kernel is generally of the bigness of a joint of a man's thumb, and two of them be sometimes found in one of these fruits if it be of the largest size; some are yellow, others white within; the harder the sweeter they are. The fruit is of an agreeable scent, yet of a rough taste, and if eaten raw create winds, but if roasted like chesnuts are well tasted, and a provocative to venery, for which reason they are frequently eaten by the common people. If you eat too much of this fruit it inflames the blood, produces loosenesses, exulcerations in the bowels and bloody fluxes. In short, this fruit is very unwholesome by reason of its lusciousness, and

1662.

and is commonly evacuated by stool just as it is eaten; the pulp about the kernels being so tough, that it is scarce to be manag'd with the teeth; the kernels are eaten boil'd by the inhabitants with a little salt instead of rice. Of this fruit there are two sorts; one is call'd *Barka*, and is the best, the other *Papa* or *Girasol*, which is softer than the other; as you may perceive by pressing it with your fingers. They grow all over the *Indies*, but those of the isle of *Ceylon*, and the coast of *Malabar* are the best; I remember that the queen of *Signati* presented me with one, which was of so delicious a taste, that I could meet with none afterwards like it.

The flower Siampin.

This flower is called by some the flower of *Camboja*, because it was transplanted from thence to *Batavia*, tho' others look for its original as far as *China*, whence it is call'd *Pakjaboa*. It grows all about *Batavia* in the gardens, on knotty trees, which grow sometimes twelve foot high. It bears no seed, but thick oily leaves, white on the extremities, but a pale yellow towards the stalk; some have red spots on the upper side. The flower sprouts far at the ends of the twigs in a broad knot, which produces several flowers, the scent whereof is like our *May* flowers, but stronger and not so agreeable. The leaves of the stem are long, pointed at the end, green and full of veins; the wood is grey, and near the top where the flower buds out, surrounded with many young sprigs.

The flower Katsiepiri.

The flower call'd *Katsiepiri* by the *Malayans*, *Korban* by the *Javaneses*, and *Micuboa* by the *Chinese*, grows in the gardens of *Batavia*, the tree being not unlike a palm-tree, but somewhat higher, and with larger leaves. The flowers sprout out of pale green buds, are well scented with thick, oily and snow white leaves, with yellow seeds in the middle. This flower is in great request for its pleasing scent, being sold sometimes for two-pence a piece.

Arroz or rice-flower.

The rice-flower is called by the *Portuguese Fulo di Arroz*, by the *Malayans Boingo ritsia Pria*, and by the *Javanese Pella Sidanga*, all in the same sense from its scent, which is like rice when it comes boiling hot out of the pot. It grows on a kind of vine which spreads its branches like our vines, with very fair broad leaves, like those of the quince pear-tree, and are as green as a leek. The branches grow so thick that the sun cannot penetrate them, being supported by bamboo sticks. The flower has single white leaves, streaked with white within, and in the middle a pointed sprout surrounded with small buds.

Jamboa.

The apples called *Pompions* by the *Dutch*, *Jamboa* by the *Portuguese*, and *Yboe* by the *Chinese*, grow scarce any where else in the *Indies* but in the isle of *Great-Java*, especially in the gardens of *Batavia*. This tree is produced by no other ways than either by laying off of the branches, like as we do our vines, or from the seed of the fruit; the first bears fruit the second year, but the tree which comes from the kernel or seed does not bear till the third or fourth year. The apples are of a gold colour without, and some of them red within; their taste being not unlike our cherries. Some are white and somewhat sweeter; they are very like oranges, both in and out side, except that they are five times as big, some weighing 10 or 12 pounds, and being 10 or 12 inches in circumference, so that one apple is sufficient for two or three at a time. They grow in clusters four or five together, on thin twigs supported by bamboo-canes, without which they would either break or hang down to the ground. The tree also grows like the orange-tree, except that the branches are somewhat thicker and closer, and the leaves broader. The blossoms have white leaves, with a yellow seed within, being of the bigness of our apple blossoms: The fruit continues almost all the year round, and after it is gathered will keep four or five months. It delights in a fat soil, and the ground must be kept clear of weeds near the stem.

Mangaes *or* Manges.

Most and the best of the *Indian* fruits continue throughout the whole year, except few, among which that call'd *Mangas* by the *Javanese*, and *Pao Ampelan* by the *Malayans* is one; the trees which bear this fruit are sometimes as tall, thick and well spread as the largest oak trees in *Europe*. The flowers which are white, sprout forth of certain small twigs growing on the branches, which produce such vast plenty of fruit, that when they begin to ripen, they are forced to support them with sticks. Their time of gathering is chiefly in *September* and *October*; tho' less or more they continue throughout the year. And most of the trees bear fruit but every other year. The fruit is something larger than a plumb; green at first, but when ripe of an orange colour; some are spotted, and being of the same colour on the inside are very pleasing to the eye, but somewhat crabbed in taste. The inhabitants make divers relishing pickles of them; they boil them in a certain pickle, and make them as good in taste as the best *Portuguese* olives; others are pickled with vinegar and green pepper, and are used with roasted meats like our pickled cucumbers. They are also preserved with sugar for the use of the women; they have another way of taking off the rind and the kernel, the space of which they

1662. they fill up with ſugar, butter and eggs, and ſo make a delicious diſh of them, very pleaſing both to the palate and ſtomach. The fruit, if eaten in any great quantity after it is ripe, is very unwholſome, but moderately uſed, is good againſt the bloody-flux. The tree is produced out of the kernel, and does not bear till ſome years after, neither does it bear fruits for ſeveral years before it dies.

Mango-ſtan.

The fruit call'd *Mangoſtan* by the *Malayans* and *Manges Tanges* by the *Javaneſe*, carries the bell before all the other *Indian* fruits, for its agreeable taſte. It grows chiefly about *Bantam*, and in ſome places of *Malacca*. The tree which bears this apple, grows no higher than a plumb or mulberry-tree, having a ſtreight ſtem of the bigneſs of a man's calf of his leg; with a rough bark, its branches growing up like thoſe of the clove tree; both the leaves and branches affording a very agreeable ſight. The apples hang at the extremities of the ſmall twigs, each being cover'd with two leaves, of two palms in length, having abundance of veins; they are ſomewhat of a pale green on the outſide, but light green on the inſide. This agreeable fruit comes forth from a pale green bud, which opening produces the bloſſom, and theſe the fruit. On the top of the apple is a kind of a coronet, which opens as ſoon as it begins to ripen. The ſeveral points of this coronet has ſo many marks to direct you how many kernels are contained in the apple; which are ſometimes ſix, ſometimes eight; but thoſe which have the moſt kernels, are generally the beſt. The fruit has a very thick rind, not unlike our granate apples, of a purple colour without and whitiſh on the inſide; Its taſte is ſomewhat crab-like, not unlike the rind of the granate apple, and ſomewhat inclining to bitter; the pulp which is round the inward kernels, is ſometimes white, ſometimes inclining to red, being exceeding pleaſing to the palate, and not unwholſome for the ſtomach, notwithſtanding its cooling quality, it being ſcarce ever known, that any body ſurfeited himſelf by the eating of this fruit, a thing otherwiſe very common to the cooling fruits of the *Indies*. Theſe are accounted very proper even in agues, and have towards the bottom, about the ſtalks, three or four different rinds or ſhells. Theſe are brought in ſuch vaſt quantities from *Bantam* to *Batavia*, that you may buy many of them for ſix-pence, and I have ſeen ſeveral of them in the gardens about *Batavia*, one whereof bore fruit very plentifully, which makes me believe they would thrive very well hereabouts.

Indian *Almond-tree*.

As far as I remember, there is ſcarce any kind of fruit tree in the *Indies* which caſts its leaves ſo as to remain bare except this tree, which as well as the fruit is call'd *Katopper*. The tree grows up very tall, with thick branches and leaves, which afford a very plentiful ſhade; it is in all reſpects like an elm-tree, except that its leaves are above a palm in length and very narrow, with yellow veins. The ſtem of this tree is very ſtrait, out of which come forth the branches one above the other in due order. The fruit grows in cluſters on the extremities of the twigs with the bloſſoms, which are ſmall white flowers with a yellow ſeed, and many green buds not open'd yet near them: The fruit is encloſed in a hairy ſubſtance, which turns yellow, and ſhrinks as it ripens; within which is a hard ſhell, which contains commonly one, and ſometimes two kernels. Theſe are as ſweet as almonds, being not unlike them in ſhape, and are eaten and uſed otherwiſe like almonds; the ſhell is ſo hard that you can ſcarce crack them with your teeth. There are divers ſorts of them; ſome having a pale red ſhell, which are bigger, others a yellow one. 1662.

The Javaneſe Rottangs.

The *Javaneſe Rottangs* grow in thoſe countries wild, and are different in their kind; ſome would have them to be a kind of reed, becauſe they grow ſometimes with knots or joints; whereas otherwiſe they have no reſemblance either in the ſtem or leaves to the cane or reed kind. This grows ſo faſt, and twiſts its ſelf ſometimes ſo cloſely up to the very tops of the higheſt trees, that they die for want of air. They are much uſed in the *Indies*; however the beſt walking canes are brought from *Japan* and *Siam*. They bear alſo a kind of fruit of a brown colour like our earth-nuts, with a very thin rind, containing two kernels, which are white, but of an unpleaſant taſte, and therefore ſcarce ever eaten, except a ſmall portion thereof next to the rinds which is well taſted. The *Chineſe* make divers ſorts of pickles of this fruit, in the nature of the pickled olives, and draw an oil from them, which is very good to heal wounds.

The tree and fruit Anrae.

The tree and fruit call'd by the *Portugueſe* and *Dutch Anrae*, is call'd *Sarboroſia* by the *Malayans*. It grows in divers places of the *Indies*, to the height of an ordinary apple-tree, with rough leaves, which are green at firſt, but turn brown as the fruit begins to ripen, and grow directly oppoſite to one another, like thoſe of the tree *Gojovas*, but are not ſo broad. It bears no bloſſom, the fruit coming forth of buds like the *Portugueſe* figs, which has a rough rind, with pale green knots, not unlike the pine-apple; it comes to full maturity in three months time, when it is gathered, and

1662. kept till it grows soft, that it may be broken with ones hands; within it resembles a rotten medlar, being full of seeds, and the pulp of so agreeable a taste, that one can scarce be satisfied with it. The inhabitants make many incisions in the bark, to make the tree bear the better, as we say of our walnut-trees, when the twigs are well beaten whilst they are gathering the fruit. There is another sort of these figs called *Atanoane* by the inhabitants, which are lesser, as is likewise the tree, which resembles a shrub, with narrow leaves, but above a palm in length. The fruit is of the bigness of a *China* apple, yellow and shadowed with an orange colour, but white within, with brown seeds; they are much more luscious, and when cut open emit a scent like rose-water, being accounted very comfortable to the brains, and therefore held in great esteem. This fruit likewise sprouts forth out of long green buds, which opening, contain another round nut or bud, which produces the fruit.

Date-tree. The date trees grow in great plenty in *Persia* near *Gamron*, and delight much in sandy grounds. Some of these trees have of late years been transplanted to *Batavia*, of which I saw a young one in Mr. *Peter Moleth*'s garden, the draught of which I have inserted, but whether it will bear fruit time will shew. The date trees continue in their full vigour for many years; they have, like the coco-trees, very small roots, and the trunk is thicker near the top, than towards the root. The pith of the three is accounted excellent good to encrease sperm and an appetite to venery, and the *Persians* about *Gamron* are so fond of this fruit, that they eat it at their meals as we do bread, or the *Indian* rice. The dates hang in yellow shells on the trees, being of a delicious taste, especially if eaten green. There is a male and female date-tree, the last of which bears fruit only; they differ also in this, that the female has a thicker and longer stem, but the blossom is the same in both, and shoots forth in a great bunch or cluster on the top of the tree, of the thickness of an arm, which opening after some time produces the flowers, and those the fruit. The *Persians* cut off this knot from the male tree before it opens, which they cut into divers pieces, one of which they put into the knot or cluster of the female tree, (which they have a way to open) pretending thereby to make the tree bear greater plenty of fruit.

They have many stories of the male and female trees, tho' not worth the inserting here.

Water-melons or Patekas. The water-melons, call'd *Batiek* by the *Indians*, as also *Patekas* or *Pateko*, grow almost in all the countries betwixt the two tropicks of *Cancer* and *Capricorn*, yet the nearer to the *Equinoctial* line, the better they are, and continue in vigour all the year round, except in the heighth of the rainy season. Some are white without, as at *Batavia*, but the red ones are the best; they have a thin green rind, which is soft and tender within. The pulp is bright, and so tender as to melt in ones mouth like sugar. The seeds are black, not unlike our pompion seeds: The plant creeps with its stalks and leaves along the ground like the pompions, and at their opening resemble our cucumbers. The fruit is sufficient for four persons to feed upon, and is, among all other fruits that are eaten raw, the most pleasant and harmless, tho' you eat ever so much of it. However, moderately eaten they are best, when they are very refreshing and acuate the stomach; whereas in too great a quantity they are obnoxious, and may occasion the bloody flux: They grow best in sandy grounds. I have seen some of them in the gardens of *Holland*, but the fruit has a watery taste. 1662.

The fruit called *Ananas*, by the *Portuguese* and *Dutch*, is called *Nuna* by the *Malayans* and *Javanese*, and *Unglay* by the *Chinese*. The plant which produces this fruit delights to grow in shady places and a fat soil: First shoots forth a stalk of an inch thick and a foot long, on which near to the ground grows the fruit, not unlike a melon, with a well colour'd rind, being of a pale red colour mixed with orange colour'd streaks, which towards the extremities are green. The fruit looks yellow within. They are sometimes five inches in circumference, and nine long, weighing perhaps five or six pounds. Below and round about the stalk come forth certain sprouts like house-leek or aloes, with 15 or 16 carved leaves of the same colour as the fruit, green in the middle, and of an orange colour about the edges. The *Ananas*, after it is come to its full perfection, is one of the most delicious fruits of all the *Indies*; but before they are well ripe, they contain a corroding poisonous quality, of which the ripe ones even have some remnants, and therefore ought not to be eaten in too great a quantity, unless you cut them into small slices, and by pouring some *Spanish* wine upon them draw out the sharp humour. Some use water instead of wine, notwithstanding which they often create a heat in the throat; but as they are diuretick, so they are accounted good against the gravel: But without being steep'd in wine or water, they would exulcerate the palate of the mouth and the tongue, and cause a mortal bloody-flux. They have a way of preserving them with sugar, *Ananas.*

1662. ſugar, and are thus tranſported frequently from the *Weſt-Indies* into *Europe*. This fruit has ſo fragrant a ſmell, that when it is cut it fills the room with a ſmell like roſe-water: In taſte they approach next to our large ſtrawberries, which being very inviting to the pallate, makes one eat too much, and inflames the bowels, or occaſions burning fevers, for which reaſon they ought to be eaten with caution. Thoſe of the iſle of *Ceylon* exceed the reſt in taſte; thoſe growing near *Batavia*, and in other parts of *Java*, are not ſo fine. The fruits ripen in ſix months; when they are cut from the ſtalks, which remain thus; or elſe they take the ſprouts, and having cut them from the main ſtalk, put them thus without any root in the ground, which afterwards produce new plants. The fruit *Ananas* grows in moſt parts of both the *Indies*, and ſome are of opinion that the firſt plants thereof have been tranſplanted many years ago from *Braſil* unto the *Eaſt-Indies*. 1662.

Among other *Indian* plants, which are beneficial to human kind, is that called *Betel* or *Betele* by the *Indians*, and *Siry* by Betel. the *Malayans*, *Sury* by the *Javaneſe*, and *Lauheu* by the *Chineſe*, which is one of the

moſt inconſiderable ones. It reſembles at a diſtance the black pepper, and runs up with its branches round trees, ſtalks, poſts, or any other thing it meets with, like our hops, to a good height, delighting eſpecially in a well dung'd ſoil, and ſhady places; and growing but ſlowly in the open air: It requires alſo a conſiderable heat, which is the reaſon that it is planted near the ſea-ſide, and after all muſt be defended and covered againſt the cold night blaſts, being ſo tender, that it can't bear the leaſt cold. Both the branches and leaves are in all reſpects like thoſe of the pepper; the leaves being ſometimes ſix inches broad, and as many long, of a dark green colour, having ſeveral veins thro' the length, and 5 or 6 croſſwiſe; the ſtalks are an inch broad. The leaves have a ſpicy taſte, very penetrant and ſomewhat aſtringent. They are ſo generally uſed in the *Indies*, as if the inhabitants could not live without them. They take a ſingle leaf, and a ſmall quantity of lime made of burnt oyſter ſhells, then folding the leaf together, they put into it the lime, and a fourth part of the nut *Areka*, (or *Pinang*) which augments the aſtringent quality of the *Betel*, and draws the ſpittle: After they have chew'd it thus a while, the firſt ſpittle is red, like ſtagnated blood, which being paſs'd, they ſwallow the reſt. The firſt ſpittle taints

1662. the lips with a pleasing red, as soon as it affects the brains, which is chiefly attributed to the *Areka*; and I have seen some, who, tho' used to chew this mixture, were seized with swooning fits: It never fails to create a giddiness in the head to such as are not used to it, which is soon cured by rubbing their gums with a little salt. The juice thereof, which is swallowed down, has an astringent and corroborating quality of the stomach, after the first spittle which contains the lime, is spitted out: It closes the upper orifice of the stomach, disperses the vapours arising from drunkenness, and revives the spirits. It corrects a stinking breath, cures the tooth-ach and scurvy, fastens the teeth and strengthens the gums, but makes the teeth as black as jet, an ornament much affected by the *Indians*; and if you chew too much of this mixture, it will loosen and corrode the teeth. *Betel* chew'd without lime, produces a green spittle, but with lime, makes it red; persons of quality mix some musk, ambergreece or camphire with it: The use of it is so frequent here, that no body pays a visit to another, but a small dish of *Betel* is brought immediately. Nice people spit in pots.

Pynang *tree.* The ancient herbalists have placed the *Pynang* tree among the palm-trees, perhaps because its stem, leaves and branches, are not unlike the coco-tree. It owes its original to the kernel of the nut like the coco-tree, and grows all over the *Indies*, especially in the isle of *Ceylon*, where they drive a great traffick with these nuts, and transport them in prodigious quantities to the coast of *Madura* and other places. In a few years after it is planted it bears nuts. From underneath the leaves sprout forth certain twigs, which grow close together, and are full of small of small white leaves, emitting a most fragrant scent at a considerable distance, especially mornings and evenings. After these flowers come the nuts, called *Fausel* by the *Arabians*, *Areka* by the *Indians*, and *Pynang* by the *Malayans*: They grow very thick together on both sides of very strong stalks, being green at first, but turning yellow by degrees; some are of an orange colour. Some of these nuts grow not so close on tender twigs; others, which are of an orange colour, grow out of certain green husks, in bunches like grapes; they are covered on the out-side with a hairy substance. This tree equals in heighth the coco-tree, but the stem seldom exceeds six or seven inches in thickness, neither has it so long and many branches as the coco-tree, and the leaves are shorter and broader. These trees look very odly at a distance, being so thin of stem and almost without branches, so that they are beat by the wind on all sides, yet never break. The stem is spongy within, but the bark very hard, of which they make laths for the coverings of their houses, for which they are very useful by reason of their straightness. The fruit resembles an acorn, but is four bigger; however, when cleansed from the hairy threads, the nut scarce exceeds the bigness of a nutmeg, and looks like it within. The kernels are astingent, and good for the stomach. They make no other use of them but for chewing with the *Betel* leaves and lime, as we told you before. They cleanse the nuts from the hairy strings with a pair of scissors, and cut the nut if large in four, or else in two pieces; and this put into a leaf of *Betel*, and mix'd with a little lime, they chew so long as it will draw the spittle, and spit out what remains; but the old *Pynang* nuts with the *Betel* leaf will dissolve insensibly in the mouth. Such as are not used to the chewing of *Pynang*, especially if used before it is come to its full maturity, will certainly be seiz'd with giddiness in the head, and will fall down without sense or motion. 1662.

Suryboa is a certain plant which runs up close round the *Pynang* tree to a great heighth, and being planted in rows, afford shady and agreeable walks. The leaves and branches are like those of the *Betel* or of pepper: The fruit is not unlike in shape to the *Bengal* pepper, growing on small and green stalks of two fingers length: It is green and chequer'd, of the length of a palm, but scarce an inch thick, containing a white kernel with small seeds. These kernels are used with the *Areka* instead of *Bethel*, being a pleasant chew. They cut them throught the middle, and taking one half of the *Pinang* kernel likewise cut in the middle, they tie both together wirh a cotton thread, and with the addition of a small quantity of lime made of oyster-shells, use it like as they do the *Bethel*; it has the same effects, and being not so common as the *Betel*, is more esteem'd among persons of quality. Suryboa.

Dap-Daf or *Dap-Dap*, is a very agreeable fruit both raw and dress'd, having a very plesant taste, of a mixture of sweet and sour, and of a cooling quality. It grows out of the bottom of a stem of a tree, having very fine leaves, the flowers or blossom consisting of small red leaves. The fruit is inclining to red, mix'd with black spots of an oval figure, and ragged, bent a little at the end like a cucumber. It contains a white kernel of a delicious taste, being enclosed in a whitish rind. These trees bear fruit all the year long, Dap-Daf *or* Dap-Dap.

1662. long, and grow properly in the *Molucca* islands, from whence they have been transplanted into the gardens of *Batavia*, but do not thrive so well there as in their native soil, being much pester'd with aunts or pismires, which do incredible mischiefs to the fruits there. The tree whereof I took the draught at *Batavia*, was surrounded with rails, within which the ground was paved with stone, and a small cistern in it with water, notwithstanding which the fruit was so covered with pismires as scarce to be discerned.

Takkatak. The fruit call'd *Takkatak*, or *Boa Burun* by the *Malayans*, and *Kannekoeni* by the *Javanese*, are by the *Dutch* called *Red-Currants*, from their resemblance to our currants, tho' in their qualifications they are very different. These berries grow on high trees with large leaves, not unlike the chesnut trees, and sprout forth in large buds in clusters, on the twigs of the trees, being of the same bigness as ours, but are of a sour taste; notwithstanding which they are much coveted, and sold and used in great quantities at *Batavia*, in the same manner as we do our red-currants. They grow in the gardens about *Batavia*, and bear fruit every three months, but most in *September*.

Moringo. The tree call'd *Moringo* by the *Portuguese* and *Dutch*, *Ramongy* by the *Malayans*, and *Kelor* by the *Chinese*, is found not only in all the gardens, but also before the houses: It has a white blossom, which sprouts forth from white buds, having a yellow seed within. The fruits grow several together, being enclosed in hard husks, not unlike our *French* beans, except that the husks are round and longer. So soon as they are ripe, they are gathered, and the twigs on the top being cut off, others sprout forth in their stead, which bear new fruit. The leaves are very smooth and thick, in taste not unlike the coco leaves in *Holland*, but not so biting and penetrant. They stew these leaves with meat, or eat them alone, as we do our spinage, being well tasted and cooling; the same they do with the husks, whilst they are young, but when old are tough; so that both the usefulness and pleasantness of this tree is a sufficient encouragement to the people to afford it a place in their gardens, especially since it wants no great industry to plant it, as growing out of a sprig of the tree planted only in the ground without any root, which in a few months begins to blossom and to bear fruit.

Torre. The tree called *Torre* by the *Malabars*, *Tary* by the *Portuguese*, *Rombang Juri* by the *Javanese*, and *Husk-Tree* by the *Dutch*, does not rise above the heighth of an ordinary apple-tree: It brings forth certain husks hanging strait down on thin stalks of about a quarter of a yard in length, and the thickness of a little finger. The husks contain 8 or o small pease, which are eaten as well as the leaves, which are round and small, growing on small twigs, and the flowers, which are surprising at first sight. They sprout forth out of green buds in the shape of a half-moon, with purple-coloured points, and streaks of the same colour within: From the innermost leaf come forth certain long and thin sprouts like fillets, with yellow hairy points; the stalk is green, but the beginning of the leaves of the flower are white, interspers'd with veins to the extremities, with a parrot-green colour intermix'd with some red, which affords a most agreeable spectacle to the eye: The inhabitants also make use of the leaves as a sovereign remedy against the stings of the serpents, in which case they squeeze them betwixt two stones, and mixing a little salt with them, apply them to the tumor, which give immediate relief. 1662.

The *Portuguese* have given it the name of *Folio di Inverno*, or *Devil's-Leaf*, or *Hellish-Leaf*, because it will over-run all places wherever it lights; the *Malayans* call it *Garrak*, and the *Javanese Klatte*: It has several physical virtues against divers distempers. There are two sorts, distinguish'd by their different colours, one having green leaves, and growing very fast, the other being brown and red, like the leaves of our red-cabbages, and growing up to the heighth of 12 or 14 foot, with carved leaves hanging on very long stalks. On the top sprouts out a bunch of green buds, which opening by degrees, produce yellowish flowers; after which comes the fruit, not unlike a chesnut, containing a bean or kernel, which is very good food. Devil's-Plant.

The plant or herb called the *Broad-Numerado* by the *Portuguese*, and *Bajan Dierdia* by the *Malayans*. The shape of the leaf which grows on the stalk of this plant chequered with various colours like a tulip, is altogether like our beetes, and used in the same manner, but is preserved for the beauty of its leaves, which are on the top, as an ornament of the gardens. There is another sort resembling in colour our red cabbages, and is frequently planted by the *Chinese*, who sell it in great quantities in the market of *Batavia*; it is of an agreeable taste, either boil'd with meat or stew'd by it self. *The broad* Nomerado.

The tree which produces the *Javanese* cotton, is call'd *Kappok* by the *Malayans*, *Jerondo* by the *Javanese*, and *My* by the *Chinese*, grows up to the heighth of a great mast, spreading its branches directly straight- Kappok.

1662. ſtraightways on all ſides. The bark of this tree is white, as far as the lowermoſt branches, but from thence to the top green; the flowers which are white come forth out of certain buds growing out of the branches; then come the fruits of the bigneſs of a hen's egg, pointed at the end, being green at firſt, but turn brown like a dried oak-leaf. Theſe fruits hang on the middle and end of the branches, two and two together, ſeldom one alone. They open at laſt near the ſtalks, and produce the cotton-wool, which covers the ſeed, and extends its ſelf when expoſed to the air. The ſeeds are black, not unlike the brown pepper, but ſomewhat ſmoother. The cotton-wool is gathered in the *Indies* in *October* and *November*, wherewith they drive a conſiderable traffick all over the *Indies*, where they are uſed inſtead of feathers, to ſtuff their cuſhions, bolſters and quilts withal, feather-beds being unknown here, but is not long enough for combing, or for weaving: Great care is to be taken that no fire come near it, for if it takes fire it burns with ſuch violence, that ſcarce any water can quench it. This tree grows whereever it is planted.

Jamboes. The tree *Jamboes*, as the *Indians* and *Javaneſe* call it, the *Portugueſe Roſado*, the *Malayans Jamboe Ramus*, and the *Chineſe Ileapont*, affords a very agreeable entertainment to the eye, while it ſtands in full bloſſom. It grows up very regularly, in the ſhape of a pyramid, the branches growing in good order, neither entangled within one another, neither above one another. It riſes to the heighth of a large pear-tree in *Europe*, and takes deep root. The leaves are long and green, at the extremities of the ſmall twigs ſprout out green buds, which produce flowers with leaves as red as blood, containing certain red fillets within: The fruits are of an oval figure, reſembling in bigneſs and ſhape our ſugar-pears, which grow in cluſters 23, 24 or 25 together: Some are red, others white, but both of the ſame taſte, tho' the white ones are reckoned the beſt. They ſmell very ſweet, but are ſomewhat mellow: The ſtone which lies in the middle has a large but bitter kernel, which is never eaten. Abundance of theſe flowers which produce no fruit, fall from the tree upon the ground, which cover the ground underneath, and afford a pleaſant ſight. The ſtalks of the flowers are red, not unlike the ſea-lion's, but not ſo long. Theſe flowers have ſo pleaſing and ſavory a taſte, that they are uſed and eaten as a delicious ſallad. The fruit has a ſweet, yet reliſhing reſt, and allays the exceſſive heat of the ſtomach; if ſtew'd with ſugar, and a little wine, they eat like ſtew'd pears. The beſt I ever met with were in the iſle of *Ceylon*, where they grow in great plenty. Theſe trees are produced from the ſeed, and bear fruit in the 4th year, and three times in a year, ſo that they never are in want of this fruit throughout all the ſeaſons: 'Tis generally believed that this tree, for his ſweet ſcented flowers and well taſted fruit's ſake, was tranſplanted from *Malacca* into other diſtant countries. There is yet another ſort of *Jamboes*, which grow in the iſle of *Amboyna*, on trees no bigger than our cherry-trees, but they are not ſo well taſted; ſo that this tree is cultivated there rather for its bloſſom, which is red alſo, than the goodneſs of the fruit. 1662.

Among many other fruits, which if eaten raw, are crabbed and ſour upon the tongue, we muſt not paſs by in ſilence what the *Portugueſe* call *Nelyka*, the *Malayans* and *Javaneſe Boa Malakka*, the *Chineſe Soaly*, and the *Dutch Wild-Plumbs*: They grow in vaſt numbers on thin twigs, and are greeniſh of colour; the twigs have ſmall green leaves growing cloſe together. The fruit has a ſouriſh taſte, and is very cooling, for which reaſon it is in requeſt by ſome, tho' generally no great account is made of it. They are in their prime in *Auguſt*, and are then to be ſold in the market in *Batavia*. Boa Molakka.

The tree called *Canary* by the *Malayans*, *Javaneſe* and *Chineſe*, is an *Indian* oak-tree, which grows very high with lofty branches and very ſmooth leaves, interwoven with divers veins. The ſtem grows thick, and extends it ſelf into ſeveral protuberances near the root. The rangers of the foreſts keep a watchful eye over theſe trees at convenient diſtances, when the acorns begin to fall, becauſe the wild-boars appearing in great numbers, they ſhoot them; ſo that during that ſeaſon, the wild-boars fleſh is ſold at a cheap rate in the market of *Batavia*. The fruit is nothing elſe but an acorn or nut, produced out of a yellow bloſſom growing on ſmall twigs. The nut or acorn is encloſed in a green ſhell, and next to that another, which is ſo hard, that you muſt break it with a hammer, if you will come at the kernel, which is as white as an almond, and of as good a taſte, being covered by a thin ſkin. Canary tree.

In and near the city of *Batavia*, grows in the gardens a certain flower, both in ſcent and figure not unlike our camomile-flower, but whether it obtains the ſame virtue, is unknown hitherto. The *Topaſſes* call it after the *Portugueſe*, *Fulo di Madre*, i. e. *Mother-Flower*, becauſe its leaves and the flower are ſomewhat like the *Matricaria*, and perhaps of the ſame kind. It grows Camomil tree or Fulo di Madre.

1662. grows about a foot high, with large carved leaves: The flower which is white, sprouts forth out of green buds, with double leaves carv'd at the ends.

The flower call'd *Four-Lights* comes forth out of small buds, being not unlike a single gilliflower, but of a bright red colour. It consists of four carved leaves, which have certain pleasant curls at the ends. The leaves are dark green on the inside, and pale green without, chequered with streaks which run all along to the point of the leaf, which has the shape of an heart. This flower is kept only for ornaments sake, but is soon faded.

Alli *or water-flower.*

There is scarce a lake or pool in this countrey, but what produces some flower or other; but the flower called *Alli* is found in great plenty all along the ditch or *Gracht* betwixt *Ansjol* and *Jacatra.* It is a pretty sort of a flower, which may be kept a pretty while in water: It comes forth out of long and large buds, is pale green without, and white within with yellow seeds. After it is opened, it is not unlike a tulip or lilly, except that the leaves are green on the out-side. Its virtues are unknown as yet, but is kept for ornament's sake.

White violet or Jarron.

The leaves of this flower growing close within one another like our violets, it has got the name of a white violet, scarce differing from it in any thing but the scent. It grows wild on certain shrubs without *Batavia*; when they are planted in the gardens, the stalks thereof are cut down close to the ground, when new stalks sprout forth, which bring flowers in great plenty. The inhabitants who call this flower *Jarron*, say it was brought hither from the isle of *Baly*. The *Malayans* call it *Benja Susun*, the *Javanese Malati Rompah*, and the *Chinese Beleboa.* It much resembles the *Katsiopiri*, but is not so strong of scent, tho' it has no scent at all, except in the morning, before the sun-beams have dry'd up the dew from its leaves. The leaves are pale green, in shape not unlike peach leaves, but something broader: The flower issues out of a pale green turned bud, of the bigness of a double daffadil, and is snow white.

Cotton of Bengale.

There is a certain sort of cotton which is transplanted from *Bengal* to *Batavia*, called by the *Chinese Algocdan*, but by the *Malayans* and *Javanese Kapas* or *Kappas*; the tree bears flowers and fruit throughout the whole year. So soon as the flowers are gone, there buds out a knot, containing the cotton or wool: The leaves are carved in three places, being not unlike a certain herb the *Dutch* call *Ducksfoot.* The flower is brown red, having within certain pointed fillets. This cotton is fit for weaving. 1662.

Wild Mangas.

The fruit called *Batsjan* by the *Javanese Malayans* and *Chinese*, is a kind of wild *Mangas* of so strong a scent, that you may smell it before all other herbs in the market. The tree which bears this fruit, is very delightful to the eye, and not unlike the *Mangas* tree, but the leaves are somewhat bigger than those of the almond-tree, of a dark green colour. The blossom is also like that of the *Mangas* tree, and yellow. The fruit is green, of the bigness and shape of a limon, within which grow certain almonds, which are much more taking to the eye than toothsom, tho' the smell is much more disagreeable than the taste, which is bitterish, and somewhat nauseous, and not comparable to the true *Mangas*, which is the reason they are not much planted near *Batavia*, but abundance of them are brought to market there from *Bantam*, in *October* and *November.*

Marokko.

About *Batavia* and all over the isle of *Java* grows a certain tree called *Marokko* or *Morukko* by the *Portuguese*, *Dap-Dap* or *Dadap* by the *Javanese*, *Darradap* by the *Malayans*, and *Oysensio* by the *Chinese.* Its leaves are like those of the poplar-tree, but as big again, smell very well, and grow on yellow stalks. These leaves being interspersed with many yellow veins, appear at a distance as if the tree were cover'd with flowers. The inhabitants lay these leaves over their pots, in which they have their boiled rice, the steam of which draws out from thence a very agreeable scent; but have no other use that I know of.

The plant Dutter.

The plant call'd *Ratsiobonk* by the *Malayans* and *Javanese*, *Bantoboa* by the *Chinese*, *Datura* by the *Turks* and *Persians*, *Duroa* by the *Indians*, and in a broken dialect *Dutter* by the *Dutch*, grows wild in the woods, almost all over the *Indies*; it seldom rises above the heighth or thickness of our red cabbages, the stalk being very like the same, but the leaves brown, pale, green and carved. It bears divers flowers, which open every morning, and close up again about noon; they are white within, and pale yellow without, some being near a palm in length, and of the figure of a bell, others carved at the extremities; after these comes the fruit, which has a pale green rind, cover'd with thorny prickles; they seldom exceed the bigness of our yellow palms, and contain yellowish seeds. Whether this plant has the virtue of intoxicating to a degree of madness for a certain time, as some would have it, I am not able to determine; but this I am certain of, that the *Topasses* and other negroes, who keep it in their gardens near

Batavia

1662. *Batavia*, look upon it as a fable. It is properly a kind of nightshade or henbane.

Kananga. The trees call'd *Kananga* by the *Malayans*, *Javanese* and *Chinese*, bear leaves of a parrot green colour, above which comes forth the blossom; they are planted near the *Betel*, which winds about them; and growing to a great heighth, their lofty tops are conspicuous above most of the other fruitful trees in the gardens; as far as I know, they have no other use. Besides that, these trees are easily to be discerned from the rest by their crooked hanging boughs, they commonly set a little wind-mill in the tops to frighten the birds out of the garden, especially the great bats here, which keep their rendezvouses in these trees, and are seen hanging with their claws to the branches thereof with their heads downwards, and that in such numbers, that you see sometimes more batts than leaves on a tree.

Indian oak. The *Indian* oak-tree produces no eatable fruit, yet does its wood make a sufficient amends for this defect, being the most lasting of all, and as good as our *European* oak. This tree grows up to a great heighth, as may be seen by the long pieces of timber in many of the churches, and other lofty buildings of *Batavia*. This tree is sufficiently known by its large branches and broad leaves, which sprout forth out of the boughs and branches, being intermix'd with green veins of a pale brown colour, and somewhat rough, something resembling the fig-leaves, but are not carv'd; at the extremities of the boughs sprout forth certain flowers not unlike the hops, which produce acorns, the seeds from whence this large tree takes its root; the inhabitants use the leaves in the pleurisy: They take a certain quantity of the liquor contain'd in the coco-nuts, in which they boil some of these leaves, to the consumption of half the liquor, and this decoction they give the patient to take inwardly, which appeases the pain. I have seen pieces of this oak-timber as streight as an arrow, no less than forty foot long, and of 2½ foot diameter to the very top in thickness; and nothing more common than to meet with boards of this wood of three and more foot broad. The *Malayans* call this tree *Kyati*, from whence they call this oak-wood, *Kiaten-wood*; which is exceeding hard, and has the same veins as our oak, being very lasting, and not subject to be worm-eaten, being proof, especially against the mice, which sometimes will eat whole pieces of the timber within, tho' the out side appear very sound.

Water-pompions. The fruit call'd water-pompions by the *Dutch* from their shape, are call'd *Katolas* by the *Malayans* and *Javanese*, and with a broken name *Katilas* by the *Portuguese*. It is neither a tree, shrub, herb nor plant, but sprouts forth in the nature of small branches, from a small seed, and spreads to that degree, that it runs over the tops of the houses with its leaves and flowers. The *Indians* frequently lead them over their cisterns in which they bathe, being sustain'd by bamboo-canes to keep off the heat of the sun-beams. They bring fruits the whole years round, but especially in *April* and *August*. The flowers are like those of our pompions, and fade without producing any fruit. The fruit is of two sorts, one grows to the bigness of our ordinary pompions, but the other which is the best, scarce exceeds in bulk our cucumbers or melons. They are used in the same manner for salad. There is another sort of the length of a man's arm. but no thicker than a good walking-cane, the rind being full of spots; that of which I took the draught was 13 inches long and 3½ diameter, weighing 3¼ pounds. When the gardners have a mind to make this grow longer than their ordinary size, they fasten a weight with wire-thread to the extremities of it, which stretches it downwards to a prodigious length. The leaves and branches are like those of the pompions; the fruit green inclining to yellow on the rind without, but white within; as are also the seed. 1662.

Champakka. If we should enter upon giving you an account of all the flowers that grow in the isle of *Java*, it would require an entire volume; among the chiefest and best is that flower call'd *Champakka* of *Siampakka* by the *Malayans* and *Indians*, and *Vinhoa* by the *Chinese*. The tree which produces these flowers, grows up to the heighth of our moderate pear-trees or peach-trees, with large wrinkled leaves, intermix'd with many veins. The branches or boughs grow all in a strait line from the tree, and afterward turn upwards; they are generally so weak that no body can climb up to the tree, so that the flowers which grow on the top, must be taken down with bamboo-canes or reeds. These flowers are in great request among the *Indians*, for their odoriferous scent, and used in garlands: The scent is betwixt a rose and a violet, and so strong, that it may be smell'd in the houses, as the flowers are carried by in the streets; they are of two colours, *viz.* of an orange colour and green, not unlike the blossom of a *Spanish* orange-tree, but resemble in figure the *English* saffron. This flower is one ingredient of that famous ointment made by the *Indian* women call'd *Borbory*; they also adorn their hair among the rest with this flower. This tree also bears fruit, which grows out of the sprigs like bunches of grapes,

1662.

The great creeping-beans.

grapes, and are of the same colour and bigness, but fit for nothing.

The branches which produce the beans, call'd by the *Dutch* the *Large Creeping-Beans*, are call'd *Katsjang Parang* by the *Malayans* and *Javanese*, and run up in many small branches to such a heighth, that their curl d sprigs on the top grow beyond the pinacles of the highest buildings. At the bottom they are of the thickness of a man's arm, and change their leaves and fruits, without any alteration to themselves; they bear fine green and thick leaves, intermix'd with small veins; the blossoms are of a purple colour, and before they open pointed at the end: The husks which contain the beans, are green like ours, having a purple colour'd string all round the husk. They are of divers sorts, among which these following are most in request.

Fabas de Moro.

The *Moors-Bean* call'd *Fabas de Moro* by the inhabitants, are very large, and run up to a great heighth; they commonly plant them near the *Pynang* trees, which serve them for supporters. The husks are about a foot in length, and an inch in breadth; they are chiefly used by the *Chinese* and *Javanese*, but neglected by the *Dutch*, by reason of their unsavoury taste.

Gondola.

The bean call'd *Gondola* runs up likewise to good heighth, affording a very agreeable shade; the leaves boil'd or stew'd are very cooling; the ranks don't hold above one year, tho' the beans will keep green three or four years; I did plant some of the large creeping-beans at *Koulang* about a summer-house, four or five of which yielded me near six bushels of beans.

Kadjang.

Kadjang as the *Javanese* and *Malayans* call it, and the *Chinese Petau*, is a kind of pease known by all the inhabitants of *Batavia*, which grow in vast plenty in the fields about *Batavia*. When they are ripe, they are gather'd and dry'd in the air. These pease are of the bigness of our vetches, which grow among the winter-corn, and grow with green shells at first, but turn black afterwards. Betwixt each two leaves sprouts forth a bud, which produces a flower, and this the pea. These peas are of great advantage to the ships in their return home, and when boil'd with bacon and well butter'd, are very good for the stomach. If you plant them in a pot, with earth and keep them well water'd, they will come in twice 24 hours, and make a good sallad aboard a ship.

Makandou.

The tree, the fruit whereof the *Javanese* call *Makandou*, has very broad, thick and fine leaves, the blossom is long and white, after which comes the fruit *Makandou*, in all respects like a pine-apple, except that it is not pointed at the end, neither so hard, but soft. Before it is ripe, it is green, but afterwards yellow, and almost insipid. The *Malayans* roast it in the ashes, and take it inwardly against the bloody-flux, asthma and pleurisy. In the isle of *Java* grows a certain tree with leaves like those of the ash-tree, and a knotty stem or trunk. It bears a fruit like unto our hazle-nuts, the kernels whereof, after they are taken nut of the shells, are of no ill taste, yet a little astringent. The leaves apply'd to wounds and ulcers, cleanse them and render them fit for healing; a spoonful of the juice of the leaves is a good remedy against the worms. Out of the stem grows a twig, but to no great heighth, which brings forth yellow flowers, like those of the nightshade; after these come the fruits, which before they are ripe are green, but afterwards red, and of a circular figure; if you squeeze them betwixt your hands, they send forth such an ill scent, that no *Assa Fœtida* or *Segapenum* is comparable to it; for which reason the *Indian* women apply to the nostrils of such persons as are afflicted with fits of the mother: The *Indians* look upon them as not fit to be eaten.

In the woods of *Java* grows a certain shrub, call'd *Daulontas*, to the heighth of six foot, spreading its branches at a good distance, like our water-willow in *Holland*; and that in such vast quantities, that the *Chinese* are forced to root them out with fire and steel: The leaves are not unlike those of the *Balsamina*, and cover'd likewise at the ends. It bears clusters of flowers like coronets, not unlike those of the elder-der-tree; after which come certain berries that are very better, both the leaves and flowers smell like the camomile-flowers, and contain the same virtues: its decoction is excellent good against the cough, and nothing provokes the monthly terms of the women beyond this remedy. Daulontas.

The fruit *Mangam* is look'd upon by the *Javanese* as the greatest antidone in the world, even beyond *Bezoar*, *Malaive* nuts, &c. The tree which bears this fruit grows upon the graves of their kings, and the fruit is of the bigness of a coco-nut. Whenever the king of *Bantam* intends to give a mark of his particular favour to any of his particular favour to any of his great men, or some foreign minister, he first puts his drinking-cup upoe this fruit, and then drinks to the person he intends to honour. Mangam.

In the isle of *Java*, on the banks of rivers, but especially about *Bantam* grows a certain plant, the leave, whereof resemble altogether the horn of *Alce*, from whence the

1662. the *Javanese* have given it the name of *Simbar Mangiram*, and the *Malayans* that of *Tanda rousa*; it has no root, but instead thereof a veiny knot or lump, which lies not under ground, but either upon stones, or in hollow trees, sending forth its leaves on all sides. This plant is sempervirent and full of juice, and if some of the leaves happen to rot by the rains, the next sunshine produces others in their stead. The *Javanese* use these leaves like as we do the roots and leaves of the white-lillies, *viz.* to make poultices of to apply to tumors; but they are not proficuous in the St. *Anthony's* fire, which shews that this plant is very hot, which its bitterish and biting taste seems also intimate. Taken inwardly it purges by stool, and applied to the navel kills the worms.

Simbar mangiram.

Water-flower.

The flower called *Tratty*, or *Tongjong Tratty* by the *Malayans* and *Javanese*, *Tienboa* by the *Chinese*, and *Fulo de Tranke*, i. e. *The Flower of the Lake*, by the *Portuguese*, is very large and fair, and grows most commonly in pools and standing waters. The stalk grows to the heighth of a fathom above the surface of the water, and the flower resembling our tulips, except that it has broader leaves, and is at least as big again. Some are of a purple colour near the points of the leaves, which by degrees turns pale yellow or white towards the stalk. Some are quite white, but of the same shape as the former. At the first opening of the buds, these flowers emit a most fragrant scent, and discover to us their beauty, which by reason of its pleasant colour attracts the sight of all that pass by. They sprout forth out of a green bud, which bursts open like those of the peony-flowers: Some of the leaves grow upwards like the flowers, being of the breadth of a brim of a hat, and bright green; some lie flat and close to the surface of the water, being round, out of the midst of which comes forth a stalk with the flower. After the leaves are fallen off come forth round husks or buds of the bigness of a man's hand, of a green colour, containing a pale yellow seed, and many small and yellowish beans, which lying bare in part, resemble the *Faba Ægyptiaca* of *Dioscorides*, *viz.* this husk being flat on one side, is as if it were cut asunder in the middle with a knife, and discovers about 30 beans placed in a circle. As these beans grow to their full bigness, they are enclosed in a peculiar husk, and when ripe, resemble the green husk of a hazel-nut without the shell, and are not unlike it in taste, being very sweet, but somewhat phlegmatick; they are sold daily in the market of *Batavia*: It seems to me to be a kind of water-lilly, having broad and red leaves, and being the same both in the stalk and root, tho' it differs from our *Dutch* water-lillies, which are white or yellow, but are of a purple colour in the *Indies*: It also differs from ours in the fruit and husk. The leaves of this plant are steemed cold in the third degree, like our *European* water-lillies; wherefore also the *Dutch* here, after the example of the *Malayans*, give the decoction thereof in burning fevers, frensies, bloody-fluxes and other hot diseases. There is also another sort, with pale purpled flowers; and a third also worth seeing. There grows also in the rivers and pools abundance of what is commonly called ducks-meat, being a food the ducks are mighty fond of, whereof the *Chinese* keep here great numbers. In the standing pools and rivers grows also the *Potamo Geyton*, or fountain-herb, and water-plantine, which if chew'd causes great burning in the throat and upon the tongue. 1662.

Nothing is more frequent in the *Indies* than to see the trees bear fruit all the year round; but the fruit called *Langzap* by the *Malayans*, *Kakasan* by the *Javanese*, and in a broken dialect *Lansen* by the *Portuguese* and *Dutch*, is gathered but once a year, *viz.* in *February*. The trees which bear these fruits, hanging in bunches like grapes, in vast quantities, spread in a large circumference, with lofty branches, and pale green leaves like the lawrel leave, or those of the chesnut-tree, but are not carved. The fruits have a soft and yellow rind like our peaches, containing a white and sharpish liquor. They resemble most our yellow plumbs, but are inclining to red and white within, the pulp being divided by certain partitions, is of a somewhat astringent taste like our red currants, and so luscious, that one can scarce be satisfied with them; they are in great request here, being accounted very good to allay the heat of burning fevers: Each has commonly two or three kernels, from which you must suck the pulp, the kernels and skin being both bitter. The fruit sprouts out of small yellowish buds or knots, after the blossom. They grow in vast plenty in the isle of *Amboyna*, and especially ar *Gilolo*, where I have seen prodigious quantities of them brought to market. The isle of *Java* produces another sort of this fruit, called *Boa Rampi* by the *Malayans*, and *Kapandung* by the *Javanese*, differing from the former only in the outside, being for the rest the same in taste and virtue; for which reason they might well be call'd the *Javanese Lansen*: These are ripe in *October*, and are brought out of the countrey to *Batavia*. Langzap.

These purple plumbs are so called by the *Dutch* from their colour, but by the *Javanese* *Purple plumbs.*

1662. *Javanese Gapak*, and by the *Malayans Boka Gobok*: They grow in great plenty on trees of a moderate size; they re of purple colour w.thout, but white within, with red stones. They have a sourish taste.

Jambu-ang. The fruit *Jambulang* is the same with our black-cherries, which is the reason the *Dutch* call it by that name here, but the *Javanese Duat*, and the *Malayans Kriango*; tho' they are of an oval figure, and not of so agreeable taste, approaching to our great sloes; they ripen in *Autumn*. The tree which bears these fruits is also much taller than the black-cherry trees, and spread their branches at a great distance. The leaves are dark green, taper towards the stalk, and broader at the ends, being intermix'd with many strings or veins. The flowers have red leaves with small filets within: The fruit is brought to market at *Batavia* by whole large baskets full in the months of *September* and *October*. It is look'd upon among the inhabitants as a very good remedy against the bloody-flux.

Fulo de Sapato, *a single and douple shoe-flower.* The single shoe-flower is call'd by the *Portuguese Fulo de Sapato*, i. e. *Shoe-flower*, because the flower chew'd affords a juice, which is excellently good for blacking and beautifying of shoes. There are two sorts of it, which may be distinguish'd as male and female, like our peony-flowers. Out of the flower, which is darken'd, and not unlike our common roses, sprouts forth on the top a yellow stalk, at the end of which bud out leaves like a coronet, covered with a yellow wool: The leaves are green, and carved at the extremities like our nettles. These produce large buds containing the flower. They are astringent of taste, and consequently cooling: The water distill'd thereof is good in burning-fevers, and applied outwardly to the forehead procures sleep. There is also another kind of these flowers, with single leaves, of an isabella colour, which grow upon small trees like our sweet-briars: They spread their branches at such a distance, that they are frequently used for arbours; they also make baskets of the twigs. The inhabitants wash their heads with the decoction of these leaves, and when steept in vinegar, use it against the looseness; they also apply it to bruises. These bushes or small trees require an excessive heat for their growth, which is the reason they commonly plant them against the east-walls here, as we do in *Europe* against the south-walls, for the exercise of heat. There is likewise a shoe-flower with double leaves not differing from the former, except in its leaves, and the coronet in the middle, which are both of a bright red colour like a ruby.

The flower Dukol. The flower called *Dukol* by the *Javanese*, *Bale Adap* by the *Malayans*, and *Fulo di Poco*, i. e. *Flower of the Bush*, by the *Portuguese*, grows every were in the hedges, to the heighth of 12 or 13 foot; it produces at the top a white leaf growing straight upwards, near unto which the flowers, which are of an orange colour, grow in clusters. The other leaves are dark green, with white veins running through the middle. 1662.

The fruit called *Boenga Tanjong* by the *Malayans*, *Kombang* by the *Javanese*, *Kauky* by the *Chineses*, and *Crab-Plumbs* by the *Dutch*, grows on very high trees with wrinkled leaves. The flowers, which are very small and of an isabella colour, open every morning, and send forth a most fragrant scent, but close up again against sun-set. The fruit is of the bigness and shape of a hazel-nut, green at first, but turns yellow afterwards, and of an orange colour at last: The pulp which is of the same colour, grows about a brown stone, but being of a sour taste, this tree is admired and planted chiefly for its flowers sake. *Crab or wild-plumbs.*

The fruit called *Karembolas*, and likewise *Kamozia*, *Karabelli*, *Chamarah* and *Bolunbach* by the *Indians*, grows in many places of the *Indies* on a tree, with a slender stem, twig and leaves, which is produced from the seed, and growing to the heighth of an ordinary cherry-tree, bears a flower of a pale blue colour, after which comes the fruit, which is green at first, but turns yellow, resembling in shape our pompions. Some of these trees (which is very strange) produce a fruit of so delicious a taste, that nothing can be beyond it; whilst others of the same kind bear a fruit so astringent and sour as can scarce be imagined; when they are cut in the middle, they represent in the inside a star. The leaves of the tree are green, not unlike the rose-tree leaves, but not carved and full of small veins. Karem-bolas.

The tree which produces the fruit called *Boca Bidara* by the *Malayans* and *Javanese*, and *Massam* by the *Chinese* and *Portuguese*, and by the *Dutch Prick-Plumbs* from their thorney prickles, grows up to the heighth of our cherry-trees, with ash coloured leaves, with a triple vein. Its twigs are covered all over with almost invisible thorns or prickles: It produces fruit all the year round, in such plenty, that the twigs bend to the very ground. The fruit is of the bigness of a hazel-nut, of a dark green colour without, but white within, containing a stone of an isabella colour: The flowers are yellow, having no more than five leaves, with as many small stalks betwixt them. This fruit being of an agreeable taste, tho' somewhat astringent, is eaten raw, and very cooling. The tree grows Boca Bidara, or Massam.

1662. grows wild at some distance from *Batavia*, but has been of late years cultivated in their gardens.

Javanese Turnips. The root called *Gadang* by the *Javanese* and *Malayans*, has got the name of a *Javanese* turnip among the *Dutch*, because it grows like our potatoes in the earth, and is of the bigness of our turnips, tho' it differs much from them both in its substance and taste. It bears dark green leaves, with white streaks or veins, betwixt which sprouts forth a twig with flowers of a purple colour. They are accounted very nourishing and wholesome, if not used in too great a quantity.

Mushrooms. Here grow divers sorts of mushrooms or toadstools, called *Kulet* by the *Malayans*, and *Jamor* by the *Javanese*. Some are of a red, others of a pale green colour; they grow without any seed out of the moisture of the earth. Some of them are used here like as in *Europe*, and are eaten with wine and sugar.

Indian Saffron, or Borbori. The plant, the root whereof is called *Borbori* by the *Javanese*, *Saffran di Terra*, i. e. *Saffron under Ground* by the *Portuguese*, *Kurkum* by the *Arabians*, and by the *Latins Radix Curcume* or *Curcumy-root*, has its leaves not unlike those of the white-hellebore, *viz.* thick, long, and broad, smooth and interspersed with many veins. The stalk is thick, and grows up to a considerable heighth: The flower is of a purple colour, and the root resembles the gentian-root. After the flower comes the fruit, like a chesnut, containing a round seed not unlike our peas. The root contains a saffron yellow tincture, whence it has got the name of *Indian* saffron. The *Malayans* boil and eat them both with fish and flesh, and look upon them as the most sovereign remedy in the world, against all the obstructions of the liver, lungs and spleen; again the gravel and stone, the stoppage of the monthly flowers, and other diseases of the womb, but most especially against the yellow jaundice: This root is one of the main ingredients in that oinment, called *Borbori* by the *Javanese*, wherewith they anoint the whole body.

The Indian *tree houseek.* The *Indian* tree housleek, grows in the isle of *Java*, on the *Mango* trees, and a certain *Indian* oak called *Kyati* by the *Malayans*. The shrub has long leaves, in taste not unlike our sorrel, but are more juicy, and much thicker, like our common houseleek. It has long round roots, out of which sprout forth certain threads, which fasten to the trees and stones, and grow thus till they come to their full perfection. It has a small white flower of an aromatick, smell approaching to the smell of citrons, for which reason the *Malayans* look upon it as a great strengthener of the sinews and br[illegible]. The leaves and flowers made up into a co[illegible]serve, are good ag[illegible]inst the cramp, and very cordial, like our borage-flowers. After the flower comes the fruit, of the length of a finger, and an insipid taste, containing seeds as big as our barley. This plant has a certain quality of resisting all putrefactions and poisons; for which reason the *Malayan* physicians prescribe it as an infallable remedy against poison'd wounds occasion'd by the poison'd darts and other weapons of the *Javanese*, which they poison with the blood of a certain serpent called *Gekko* by the *Dutch*. 1662.

The fields and woods of *Java* produce a certain herb called *Veronica* by the *Europeans*, with a white flower; the *Malayans* and *Javanese* call it *Oribat Matta*, i. e. *a Remedy for the eyes*, because its juice allays the inflammations and defluxions in the eye. The same juice or the decoction of the herb, they also use against old coughs and consumptions: By reason of its diuretick quality, they also prescribe it for the gravel and stone, and the *Gonorvirulenta*. The leaves bruised are also apply'd outwardly to ulcers, as having a singular drying quality. Indian Veronica.

The plant call'd *Kolkas* by the *Arabians* and *Moors*, has a very thick root, large broad leaves, and bears a red fruit growing in clusters, not unlike the *Arum*. It contains a slimy poisonous substance, for which reason the *Javanese* cut them in slices, and steep them three or four days in river water; after which they squeeze the remaining juice out by a press, and having laid the roots to dry, make a kind of meal or flour of it, of which they make cakes instead of rice. The *Malayans* and *Chinese* prepare them in the same manner. The bread made of these roots, which the *Javanese* of *Materan* were forced to eat 1629, at the siege of *Batavia*, for want of rice (their magazine of *Tengel* being destroy'd by the *Dutch*) occasioned a pestiferous bloody-flux in their camp; the *Chinese* and *Malayans* also boil these roots, but throw away the the first decoction, and putting on fresh water, boil them again, and afterwards eat them with vinegar, oil of coco and pepper, as we do the red beat-root. Kolkas.

The *Indian Betony* tree has speckled leaves like our *Pulmonaria*. The flowers sprout forth like ears, sometimes a thousand in one ear, of a pale blue colour, like our rosemary-flowers. The decoction of this plant they account a good remedy against spiting of blood, the consumption and coughs, call'd *Sabit Haty*, i. e. *the disease of the heart*, by the *Malayans*, who comprehend the liver, lungs, and even the spleen, under, *The* Indian Betony *tree.*

1662. der the general name of the heart. The *Indian* women uſe the juice thereof as an antidote againſt the ſting of ſerpents, ſcorpions, and ſuch like venomous creatures.

Indian *graſs.* *Java* produces all ſorts of graſs, and among the reſt, a peculiar kind, which has four ears croſwiſe on the top of the ſtalk, the leaves being for the reſt like thoſe of common graſs. There alſo grows here another ſort of graſs, of the ſame kind with ſix or eight ears, which contain ſmall ſeeds. The *Malayan* phyſicians preſcribe the root and the graſs it ſelf for the bloody-flux, ſtoppage of urine, exulcerations and pains of the kidneys, and to promote the monthly times in women. *Java* produces likewiſe another kind of graſs differing from the reſt in the roots, which are three or four ſmall knots, which when chew'd have a flavour like cloves, but are not ſo hot in the mouth.

The Indian *primeprint.* The *Indian* primeprint has got its name from its reſemblance to ours, in its leaves as well as flowers; tho' the leaves thereof have a more odoriferous ſcent than our primeprint, and the flowers, tho' the ſame in ſhape, yet differ in their colour from ours, thoſe of the *Indian* primeprint being inclinable to a blue, whereas ours are as white as ſnow, but the berries of both are black. Like unto this is a certain ſhrub called *Alkanna* and *Henne* by the *Arabians*, and *Chinnets* by the *Perſians*, except that its leaves are ſomewhat leſs. The leaves of *Alkanna* are in great requeſt throughout the *Indies*, to give their teeth, lips, but eſpecially their nails, a red tincture, a thing much eſteemed among the *Moors*. They prepare the tincture, by ſteeping the leaves after they have been rubb'd ſmall upon a marble ſtone, in fair water mixt with a ſmall quantity of lime; with this the *Turks* and *Perſians* alſo die their horſes tails. The leaves chew'd leave a piquant taſte upon the tongue, yet without any ſharpneſs. Both theſe ſhrubs are in high eſteem among the *Indian* women, who uſe the decoction of the leaves in all diſeaſes of the womb, and have an opinion that it keeps them young; and to confeſs the truth, they have a peculiar virtue (if boil'd in water) to cure the *Indian* gout or barrenneſs, called *Beribery*; it grows all over the *Indies*, and the *Malayans* call it *Sagondi*.

The Indian *ſage-tree.* The *Indian*-ſage-tree grows twelve foot high, whole woods of them being to be ſeen about *Batavia*; and if planted in the gardens, ſpreads its roots to that degree, as not to be eaſily rooted out again. The flowers are white, the leaves very long and of an agreeable ſcent. They cultivate the trees in the gardens by pruning and cuting the roots and ſhoots at certain times, and by this means make it as good and as wholeſome as our garden ſage. The *Malayan* women uſe it againſt the diſtempers of the womb, mixt with the *Sagandi* and the *Daulontas*, wherewith they bathe themſelves. The flowers are preſcribed by the phyſicians to correct the cold humours of the brain and ſinews, and by reaſon of their diuretick quality are very proper in the dropſy. Our garden ſage as well as roſemary, are a kind of rarity here, the exceſſive heat of this climate being as unnatural to them, as the cold is with us in winter. 1662.

The *Indian Verbena* grows alſo in *Java*, being altogether like ours, except that the ears are ſomewhat longer and harder. They apply the flowers bruiſed to exulcerated legs, by reaſon of their drying quality, requiſite in the healing of wounds eſpecially at *Batavia*, where the moiſt and hot climate renders the cure thereof very difficult. A ſpoonful of the juice of the leaves taken inwardly, cures the cholick and bloody-flux; and the *Indian* women attribute to this plant a ſecret virtue againſt witchcraft. *The* Indian Verbena.

In the woods of *Java* grows a certain kind of *Eſula*, which ſhoots up to a great heighth, with a three corner'd ſtalk, ſometimes of the thickneſs of a man's leg; it has abundance of thorny knobs, which being however not very hard, don't prick: The leaves grow at ſome diſtance from one another, being not unlike thoſe of our houſleek; out of the ſtalk, (after an inciſion made) iſſues a milky yellow juice, of a ſharp taſte. This juice reduced to the conſiſtency of an extract is adminiſtred in the dropſy, lameneſs and other diſtempers proceeding from cold; it purges both by ſtool and urine. This plant differs not either in ſhape or the manner of growing from that, which affords that yellow juice, call'd corruptly by the apothecaries *Gutta Gemou*, and by the *Indians Lonan Cambodia*, becauſe it is of the product of the kingdom of *Kambodia*. *The* Indian Eſula.

In *Java* alſo grows a certain kind of *Mitium Solis*, reſembling ours in its flowers, leaves and the ſtalk; but the fruit is much larger, and as hard as a ſtone, containing a mealy pulp. The *Portugueſe* have given it the name of *Yerva da Roſarios*, the roſary herb, becauſe the *Malayan* women uſe to make their roſaries of the fruit, and wear it about their neck inſtead of necklaces. Both the berb and fruit is proficuous in the diſtempers of the kidnies and bladder. Mitium Solis.

The fruit called *Boa Kamba* or *Kaman* by the *Javaneſe*, *Boa Binſel* by the *Malayans*, Boa Kamba *or* Indian *ears.*

2

1662. *ans*, and *Letsise* by the *Chinese*, is by the *Dutch* called the *Indian* pear, by reason of its bigness and resemblance to our pears. When ripe they are of a pale yellow with black spots, hollow within, with blue seeds, the pulp adhering close to the peel. They are scarce ever cultivated in the gardens of *Batavia*, by reason of their crabbed taste, tho' very agreeable to the eye; they are brought in great quantities into the market there, especially in *February*. The tree grows up to a great heighth, having a brittle and coarse wood and leaves.

Rambustan *or* Rampostan. *Rambustan* or *Rampostan* as the *Malayans* call it, is one of those fruits, which are produced without flowers, for this comes forth only out of a green bud. They grow in clusters on very small twigs of a tree, of the heighth of our cherry-trees, are of a purple colour, and resemble at a distance our chesnuts, whilst they are hanging on the trees. Within is a slender quantity of a pulp, of an acid agreeable taste, and in this a stone. They come to maturity in *February*. There is another kind of *Rambustan* growing on shorter twigs than the former, and being covered with a hairy substance; but tho' these two fruits are very different in outward appearance, their taste is much the same.

Romani *or* Satarra. The fruit called *Satarra* by the *Malayans*, *Gandaria* by the *Javanese*, and *Romani* by the *Portuguese*, resemble our yellow plumbs, but are somewhat bigger. The inside is not unlike the *Mangas*, and in taste like the *Batsian*, yet not altogether so sour. They are green at first, but turn yellow mixt with an orange colour; the pulp is likewise yellow. The inhabitants pickle and use them like as we do olives; they are of no disagreeable taste, but something more hairy than the *Mangas*.

The Javanese *flower*. The *Javanese* flower called *Fule de Japan* (in the same sense) by the *Portuguese*, *Benga Japan* by the *Malayans*, and *Quiboa* by the *Chinese*, delights in shady places; the stalk is not above a foot high, some of which produce white flowers, others of an isabella and purple colour, sprouting forth with small knobs between the leaves; and no sooner do the leaves of the lowermost flowers fall off, but others come forth on the top in their stead. The stalk, after the leaves have been cast, produces a bud, containing a black seed, as small as tobacco seed, tho' this plant will grow without it, if you put only a twig of it in the ground. These flowers have no other use but to divert the eye.

The tree Patty. The tree called *Patty* by the *Malayans* and *Javanese*, grows in many gardens about *Batavia*, being cherish'd by the inhabitants, by reason of its spacious branches and fine leaves, which afford an agreeable shade; it rises up to the heighth of an apple-tree, with thin branches, on which you see the fruit hanging on the stalks, three and three together, of a crabbed taste, and therefore not regarded; they resemble the pine-apple on the one side, and have a seed within. The leaves are of a lively green colour, and grow very close together. 1662.

The flowers called marygolds by our people, have got their name rather from their colour, than any other resemblance to ours. The leaves are dark green, like those of the apple-tree, but somewhat less: On the tops of the twigs sprout forth certain orange colour'd buds, which opening produce the orange colour'd flowers with four leaves, they have no other use than to please the eye-sight. *Marygolds.*

The huntsman's tree is a kind of wild palm-tree, the stem whereof is covered with a grey rind or bark, twisted about as it were with circles. The leaves which are bright green, grow on long yellowish stalks, the lowermost of which turn yellow by degrees, and hang downwards; being for the rest very agreeable to the eye. The fruit is not near so big as the least coco-nuts, and has no other use, except that the inhabitants draw from it a certain syrup and sugar, which they sell to the neighbouring countries. The wood of the stem is very durable, provided it be kept from the air, and so hard, that they can neither saw nor cut it, but are forced to split it by pieces of wood in it; some of the *Indians* make their bows of the twigs of this tree; and the *Chinese* at *Batavia* make of the leaves and tender sprouts, fans to cool themselves with. The *Malabars* make use of the leaves instead paper, which they know how to order with a great deal of dexterity; for the leaves being about three inches broad, and above a yard long, they make holes at one end of them, and so tie as many of them together with a string, as they have occasion for at a time. They write with an iron pencil, wherewith they know how to imprint and cut their characters on the uppermost surface of these leaves, as that they remain indelible. This they perform for the most part without keeping their eyes so close and earnestly upon them, as we do. These leaves are also very durable and will not easily putrefy, even in water; I have several letters writ to me upon these *Olen* or leaves by persons of great quality among the *Malabars*. This tree also yields a juice like the coco-tree, which if boil'd, tastes very sweet, and is apt to inebriate, but if not boil'd, turns sour immediately. But the chief use they make of *The huntsman's tree.*

1662. of it is, to boil it into sugar. This huntsman's tree is none of the lowest rank among the many kinds of palm-trees of the *Indies*, being much esteem'd and cultivated for its usefulness, especially in the isle of *Ceylon* and in *Javapatnam*, where you see whole woods of this tree.

The tree and fruit Billingbing *or* Blingbing.

About *Batavia* grows a tree of a most delightful aspect, with most pleasant leaves hanging downwards. The stem, which is very thick, and branches send forth small sprouts full of green buds or knobs, which produce red flowers, not unlike a small lilly; after which comes the fruit, growing in clusters, resembling both in bigness and shape our small cucumbers, about the thickness of an inch, and a fingers length. They have a green rind, and within it a seed, not unlike that of the cucumbers, but somewhat more round. The *Malayans* and *Javanese* call this fruit *Billingbing* and *Blinbing*. This tree is among the trees what the sheep are among the beasts, for they not only rob it of its flowers and fruit, but also of its leaves and rind, sometimes to the very root, as having their peculiar use in physick; so that this tree would make but a very slender appearance for the most part, were it not that provident nature did almost cover its stem and branches with odoriferous flowers and well-tasted fruits. The fruit is very juicy and cooling, but somewhat astringent, for which reason it is seldom used alone, but in sauces, to give a good relish: The fruit is also preserved with sugar. Our physicians there prepare a syrup out of the juice, and prescribe it in the excessive heat of the liver and blood; and this syrup is also mixed with the decoction of the rice, before it is peel'd, called *Pady*, and given in fevers. This juice also quenches the thirst, and has one peculiar quality, that notwithstanding its astringency, it takes away that sour taste of divers other fruits which sets the teeth on edge.

The Indian *dog's-tongue.*

The herb call'd hound's or dog's-tongue, from its resemblance to ours, which bears the same name, is by the *Javanese* called *Suroe*, by the *Malayans Sudu-Sudu*, and by the *Chinese Kautsu*. The stalk is thick below, but grows thin towards the top. As you pull off the leaves, you see a milky juice drop out of it; of which two or three drops dropt into the ear, cures the earach; as its use is only in physick, it generally grows wild.

Bitter-green.

The plant called bitter-green by our people, has got its name from its bitter taste: It grows in the gardens of *Batavia*, and creeps up to the next tree or stalk, almost like the branches of the cucumbers, but that it leaves are deeper carved, and more pointed. The fruit is also not unlike a cucumber, yellow with green streaks and a thick rind, yellow within, with a red kernel. When it comes to its full perfection, it is marbled with an orange colour. The *Dutch* make no account of this fruit, by reason of its bitter taste; but the inhabitants use it in their sawce call'd *Karry*, and put the root and leaves in their ordinary drink, which preserves it for two or three days, whereas otherwise it would turn immediately. They cure the bitterness with sugar. 1662.

Durions.

Among all the garden fruits, there is scarce any that exceed the *Durions*; 'tis true the scent of it is not unlike that of rotten figs, and consequently not very inviting to search after the kernel, which makes amends for the smell, being of a luscious taste. The tree which produces this fruit, grows crooked, with abundance of branches, and very harsh leaves pointed at the ends, of a palms length, sometimes grey on the outside, but bright green on the other side. They are not inferior in heighth to the tallest trees of *Europe*. The fruit *Durions* grows in clusters on the thicke stends of the twigs, and sprouts forth out of a green bud, which growing bigger and bigger by degrees, opens at last into an isabella colour'd flower, surrounded on the out-side with hard leaves, like a rind: This flower produces a thorny fruit of the bigness of a melon, covered with a thorny rind, not unlike the fruit *Jaka*; it is green at first, but turns yellow. It has four partitions within, in each of which you see a stone like a peach-stone, of the bigness of a chesnut, containing a delicious sweet and white kernel. Before they take out the kernels they stamp the fruit under foot, to avoid being wounded by the thorney prickles. The *Durions* are always eaten raw, being reckon'd one of the wholesomest fruits in the *Indies*, if used moderately, but if in excess, inflame the blood, and raise pimples in the face. They seem to have an antipathy against the *Bethel*, because they will not grow near it, but die. They come to maturity in three months time, and chiefly in *October* and *November*, tho' I have seen them also in the market of *Batavia* in *August*, for they are to be had all the year round, but not in such plenty. They grow much about *Bantam*, whence they are brought to *Batavia*. The first that I saw was in the grounds of *Christian Chandellour*, near the great river of *Batavia*; and since that I have met with them in divers other places thereabouts; so that this fruit thrives as well here as at *Bantam*, but no where better than near *Malacca*, where the *Durions* are of an excessive bigness.

p. 362
Sagou Tree
Huntsmans Tree
Blimbing
Dogs Tongue
Pepper Tree
Durions
Sagou Fruit
Blimbing Fruit

1662. The pepper, called *Lada* or *Laden* by the *Malayans*, and *Maritsia* by the *Javanese*, grows on tender branches, with abundance of knots, and creeps up along stalks or trees like our hops. Sometimes they will climb beyond the pinnacle of the highest trees, and afterwards hang downwards. On the stalks or twigs of these branches the pepper grows in such thick clusters, that they are scarce to be discern'd from the leaves. These sprout forth out of the buds of the branches, being green and interspersed with veins, not unlike those of the cinnamon-tree, pecked at the extremity, sometimes of the breath of a hand, and long in proportion, of a bitterish taste, and hot upon the tongue: After the leaves come forth certain twigs or stalks not unlike those of the hazel-nut trees, on which hang the berries, like our red-currants, but in larger clusters; these berries turn black as they ripen. The pepper is one of the chiefest commodities in the spice-trade; the best grows along the coast of *Malabar*, near *Koulang*, where I used to buy great quantities for the company's use. The pepper must be planted in a rich soil, and bears fruit within the year. In *Malabar* it ripens chiefly in *January*, but in other places sooner or later, according to the difference of the climate. In the isle of *Java* it ripens in *October*, and is gathered in *November* and *December*, and is then green, but turns black as it is a drying in the sun; after which it is made up into balls of 80 or 90 pounds. The best pepper is white, close and biting within: There is also a sort of long pepper. The *Indians* also make a pickle of green pepper. Of the *Sagon* tree, represented in the next print, we have treated before.

Wild onions. The *Portuguese* have given the name of a wild onion, or *Sabollos de Matte*, to a certain flower, because its root resembles that of an onion, tho' for the rest it has not least congruity with it. The *Javanese* and *Malayans* call it *Hakung*, and the *Chinese* *Taukio*. This flower grows in a bunch on the top of a thin stalk, but near three foot high. They come forth out of red buds, are of a high red colour, with purple colour'd streaks of a palm in length; are very delightful to the eye, and of no disagreeable smell, especially in the morning before the dew is dry'd up by the sun-beams, for which reason they are much cherish'd in the gardens of *Batavia*. The leaves of this plant are above three foot long, and spread all round about, being pointed towards the extremities.

Potatoes. The Roots of potatoes, called *Patattes* by the *Portuguese*, after the *Brasilians*, are called *Ubi Tora* by the *Malayans*, *Ubi* by the *Javanese*, and *Hantsoa* by the *Chinese*. These roots grow in the ground on branches, with leaves not unlike the cucumber leaf; some of these branches bearing white, others blue flowers, shaped like bells. The *Chinese* cultivate these roots in the fields near *Batavia*, which must be well dung'd beforehand: They cut the ranks near the extremity, which they put into the ground, and let them grow for some time. Then they cover these ranks with rich earth, at a foot distance perhaps, into which the ranks send forth their roots, which come to maturity in a short time, and sometimes grow to the thickness of a man's arm, and a foot long. Some are red on the outside, and these are in greatest esteem at *Batavia*, but don't approach in goodness to those of *Brasil*, especially near *Rio St. Francisco*, where these roots are red both within and without. This root is frequently boil'd by the *Dutch* both with fish and flesh, excelling in taste and sweetness much our parsnip-roots or artichokes; they are also eaten raw with salt, oil and vinegar, like a salad, but are not so easy a digestion then: The best way is to roast them in the ashes, which makes them taste like chesnuts, and are good to stop the looseness, a symptom very frequent to those that inhabit near the line; for which reason this root is in great request here, and cultivated with a great deal of care, which makes them very cheap here; for you may buy as much for a half-penny as will suffice for a whole meal. In the isle of *St. Thomas* they use them instead of bread. They also make a kind of drink of them. They boil a considerable quantity of these roots in a kettle well cover'd, till they are soft or tender; then they stamp them well, and put them in a vessel with water, where they begin to ferment in twice 24 hours, when the vessel must be stopp'd up; which done, it turns clear, and as strong as good beer.

Besides the potatoes, there grows another root about *Batavia* called *Injames* by the *Portuguese*, after the *Brasilians*, by the *Javanese* and *Malayans* *Byra*, and *Siatsini* by the *Chinese*. It has a very fine green leaf, and interspersed with veins: The root has commonly five or six inches diameter, and is one foot and a half long, having a brown rind, but is white within. The flower is of a greenish colour. These roots are sold in the market of *Batavia* by the piece, weighing each 15 *Katty*, or thereabouts, a *Katty* being a pound and a quarter, according to our weight, so that 30 persons may dine upon one root. Its taste is however not near so good as the potatoes, and being of a hard digestion and very dry, they are not much look'd after by the *Injames or Byra.*

1662. the *Dutch*, but the natives are very fond of them.

Blue plumbs. The tree which bears a kind of blue plumbs, spreads its branches very loftily, not unlike the mulberry-tree, except that its leaves are of a different shape. You see this tree frequently at one and the same time laden with flowers and fruit, both ripe and unripe: The wood is very tough, so that you may venture to climb up by the smallest branches. The flowers are of an agreeable scent, especially in the morning before the dew is gone. This fruit is not regarded at *Batavia*, because the markets are over-stock'd with them by the country people, who bring them in vast quantities thither out of the mountains; tho' for the rest it is of an agreeble taste, somewhat like the dates. They are rarely to be met with here in the gardens. This plumb comes forth out of certain buds, consisting of five white leaves each, and grows on the twigs like our oval plumbs. It is green at first, but turns to a dark red, but the pulp is white, within which are three stones. The *Malayans* and *Javanese* call these plumbs *Boa Soa*, or *Sau*, the *Chinese Theely*, and the *Portuguese Fruite de Manilha*, i. e. *Fruit of Manilha*. At *Batavia* I never saw but one tree, bearing at the same time flowers and ripe plumbs.

Oranges. *Java* produces divers sorts of oranges, among which threee are prefer'd before the rest, *viz.* the common ones, and those of *Japan* and *China*. The trees are much of the same heighth, but different in their leaves; those of *Japan* have broader leaves than the ordinary ones, and these again broader than those of *China*. They all are of a different taste, yet very agreeable. The *Javanese* oranges are the biggest and most juicy, but somewhat inclining to a four taste; among the ordinary ones, some are exceeding sweet, others quite crab-like. The *China* oranges have a pleasant taste, betwixt sweet and four, being prefer'd here before the rest, having a very thin rind: They are preserved with sugar, like the *Portuguese* figs, and thus transported all over the *Indies*.

Wild Jamboes. Tho' this fruit called the wild *Jamboe* by our people, and *Jamboe* by the *Malayans* and *Javanese*, has not the least resemblance to the *Jamboe* we have given a description of before, in outward appearance, because that grows upon high trees, with a most delightful blossom; whereas this grows upon a low tree not unlike our mulberries, without any blossom, but is produced out of certain green buds, not unlike the figs; yet are they the same in taste, and divers other qualities. Some of them are extremely well tasted, and quench the thirst. Some are dark red, others white, mix'd with red, and that on the same tree, where they grow in clusters in such prodigious quantities, that they cover the very leaves and twigs, as if they had been spread over with a scarlet cloth. They are of the bigness of a sugar-pear. In *Amboyna* they grow in such plenty, that you may see the ground under the trees covered with them, every one being free to gather them; one reason whereof is, that they being used there as we do our acorns, for the fattening of hogs, which the *Moors* and *Mahometans* abominate, they are not much regarded.

1662.

The weed call'd *Tobako* by the *Malayans* and *Javanese*, after the *Portuguese*, grows in all parts of the *Indies*; the *Chinese* call it *Hun*. Tobacco being frequently used by the inhabitants, is consequently in great request, and carefully look'd after: that of *Ternate* being esteem'd the best, is most generally made use of at *Batavia*. They have a way of tying several leaves, weighing about two pounds together, with small twisted canes, each parcel of the best being commonly sold for six-pence; but you may buy also very good tobacco at *Batavia*, for two pence. In *Amboyna* each family commonly plants as much tobacco in their garden as they have occasion for, not troubling themselves with any other plantations. About *Batavia* the plantations of tobacco are chiefly managed by the *Chinese* and *Javanese*, and this weed grows here and thrives extremely well, provided it be planted in a rich soil, when it will grow up to the heighth of eight foot, with leaves of 18 inches long and eight broad. The *Indians* don't take tobacco through pipes, but have a way of rowling one or more leaves (according as they are big) together, and lighting the same at one end, suck in the smoke as we do with our pipes. The women commonly take of the worst sort, and rowl up their leaves in a piece of dry'd *Pysang*. *Tobacco.*

Among all the flowers of the *Indies*, that call'd *Fula Mogori* or *Mugri*, i. e. *the Flower Mogori*, by the *Portuguese*, *Kombans Malati* by the *Javanese*, and *Badihoa* by the *Chinese*, is more esteemed by the inhabitants, which they plant with singular care upon long and well dunged beds, with little walks betwixt them: The stalk on which this flower grows, seldom exceeds two foot in heighth, and grows like briars: The leaves are smooth like the quince-pear tree leaves, the flowers exceeding white, consisting of four leaves, which seldom open, and imitate in their odoriferous scent our white-lillies, but are no bigger than the blossom of an apple-tree. The *Javanese* of both sexes wear these flowers upon strings on their Fula Mogori.

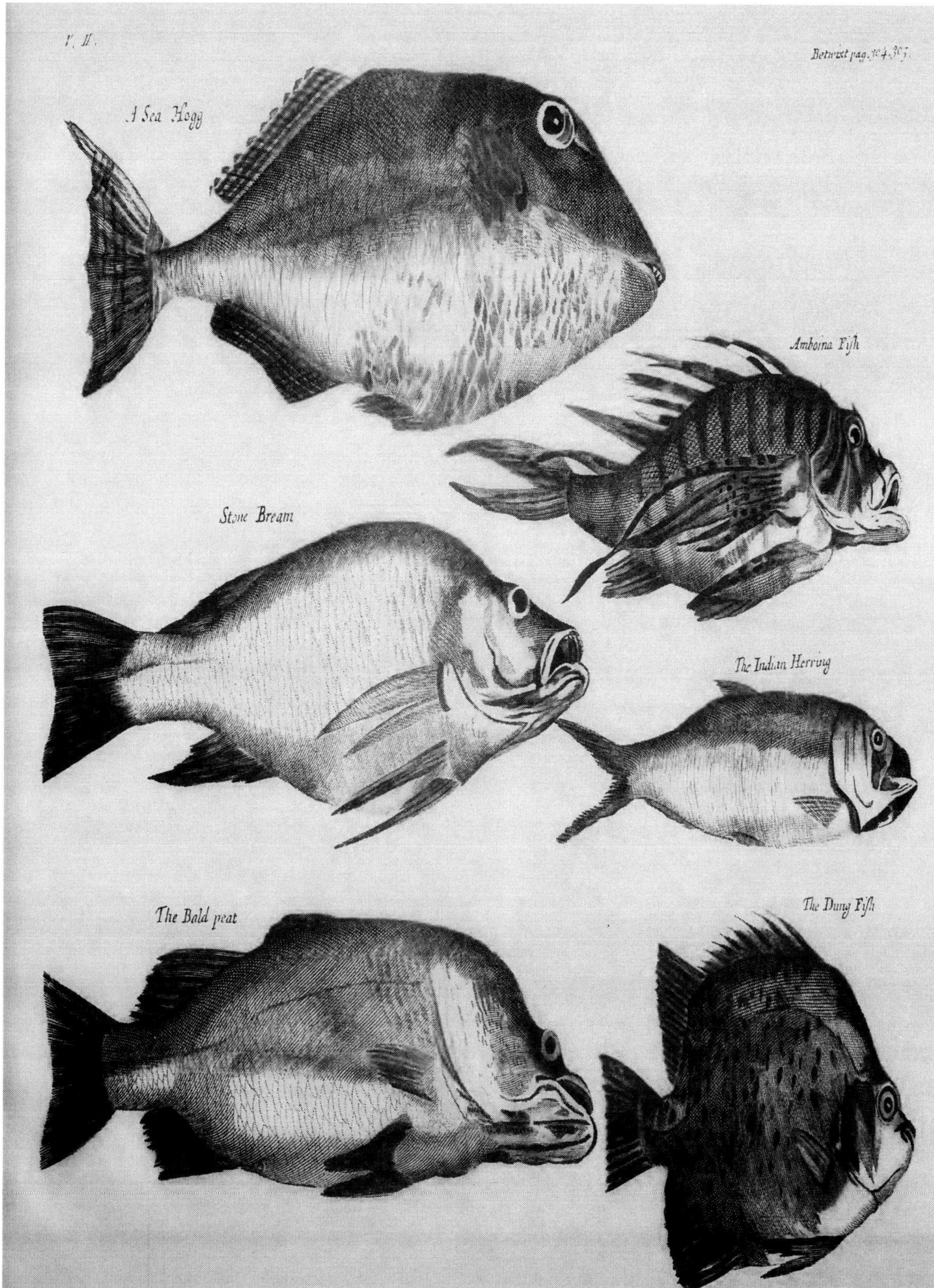
V. II.
Betwixt pag. 304, 305.
A Sea Hogg
Amboina Fish
Stone Bream
The Indian Herring
The Bald peat
The Dung Fish

1662. their festival days. I remember that at a certain turnament on horseback at *Japara*, I saw the *Javanese* thus adorn'd with these flowers, some of which had these strings tied several times round above their ears, with the two ends hanging down before upon their breasts. They also distil a water out of these flowers, which they esteem a great cordial in fainting-fits especially, much beyond our rose-water, it being reckoned equal with orange-flower water. They prescribe it in burning-fevers, and head-achs, proceeding from a hot cause. The *Javanese* also wash their faces with this water, to make them smooth. The leaves bruised are a good remedy against the rheum or defluxions of the eyes: These flowers grow in vast plenty all the year round, and are sold in the streets by the slaves.

The tree called the melancholy-tree, has got its denomination from its opening its flowers not till after sun-set, which continues no longer than the night time. Hence the *Portuguese* have given it the name of *Arvore da Noyte*, i. e. *the Night-tree*; at *Goa* they call it *Pareavtako*, at *Malacca Singadi*, in the kingdom of *Dekan Pul*, the *Arabians Guart*, the *Persians* and *Turks Gul*, and the *Malabars Mogli*, i. e. *trees*, for its excellency's sake; for which reason the same *Malabars* call the water distill'd from the flowers *Mogli-water*: There is another kind of this tree, which begins to blossom in the morning, and is bereaved of its leaves by night: These trees grow for the most part about *Cochin* and *Malacca*.

Arvore da Noyte *or the melancholy-tree.*

Boenga Mera.

The plant called *Boenga Mera* by the *Malayans*, *Kombang Merak* by the *Javanese*, and *Konkusiou* by the *Chinese*, has very fine green leaves, growing on small stalks, close together. The flowers, which are not unlike our gilliflowers, are high red, but yellowish at the extremities; they no sooner open, but drop of, leaving small husks behind them, which contain a kind of pease, but are not eatable.

Katsian.

Among several other sorts of beans which grow and are eaten at *Batavia*, those called *Katsian Goedi* by the *Malayans*, and *Katsian* only by the *Javanese*, but by the *Chinese Lak Goetuin*, exceed the rest. They grow in the fields all about *Batavia*, especially in those belonging to the *Chinese*: The stalks and husks of these beans are pale green, and somewhat woolly, but the leaves are smooth, and resemble those of our *French* beans, being interspersed with many veins. The blossoms are white, and sprout forth out of green knobs or buds. These beans grow almost all the year round, and consequently are no small advantage to the inhabitants of *Batavia*, affording very good food to the labouring men; as likewise for our ships, because they will keep a great while at sea.

Turkey wheat or Maiz.

The *Turkey* wheat, called *Maiz* by a general name among the *Indians*, and *Jangon* by the *Malayans*, *Javanese* and *Chinese*, grows in many places in the *Indies*, and in good plenty about *Batavia*; for they take the corn fresh out of the ears, and put it into the ground, which produces fresh corn in three months time. It is boiled and roasted with the chaff, and look'd upon as a great dainty; some of this corn is white, some red. The *Indies* produce also rice, ginger, cotton, and sugar in many places, figs, quince-pears, apples, lemons, besides many other fruits.

Thus much concerning the trees, fruits and plants of the *Indies*, and of *Java* and *Batavia* in particular; we will now proceed to give some account of the living creatures of the *Indies*, and begin with the fishes.

The sea-porpoise or hog-fish, sea-hog.

The sea-porpoise or hog-fish is about 15 or 16 inches long, and and about seven in breadth. It has a very thick skin, and such close and hard scales, that scarce any instrument will pierce them, but when boil'd the scales come off with ease, and the skin is very soft. Their flesh is very white resembling the breast of a boiled capon; the mouth is but small in proportion of the rest of the body, but is armed with two rows of white glistering teeth, one above, the other below. Upon the back, which is brown, you see a sharp fin of half a finger's length, which the fish can erect at pleasure, and such another is below near the navel; the other fins are not so strong, of a pale blue colour. The belly is white, and glistering like silver, but the sides are mix'd with yellow, which by degrees, towards the back, turns into an ash colour. It has large brown shining eyes, and when boil'd is of a very pleasant taste.

Amboynese *fish.*

The *Amboynese* fish has got its name because it is found chiefly in the rivers of *Amboyna*, but being very scarce, and of a very good taste, is look'd upon as a dainty here. It is about a span in length, something like our perch both in shape and taste. Its colour is inclining to brown, with blue streaks under the head, the fins below the mouth are likewise blue, but those on the sides are green and speckled. It is both a very wholesome and toothsome fish, especially with good sauce.

The stone-bream.

The stone-bream is a most excellent fish, some of which are four foot long; they resemble our breams, (which has begot them their name) but are much bigger.

1662. ger. Their eyes are very large, with a large red mouth, as are also the fins and extremity of the tail. They are catched at sea with a hook, being not easily to be taken with the net, and are eaten either broil'd or boil'd. There is another kind, but not so good as the former, the flesh of which shrinks when they are cut, from whence some call them shrinkers.

The baldpate. The fish called baldpate has got its name from its head and neck, being without scales, whereas the rest of the body is covered with them. It is of a greyish colour, its mouth, which is very wide, being spotted with red. The eyes are large, yellow and starting out of the head: It is one of the best sorts of fish that can be eaten, of a very agreeable taste: It is taken both in the sea and rivers.

Among the great variety of fish found in the *Indies*, most of which turn immediately after they are catch'd; there are however a few that will take salt like our herrings; such is the sea-bleak, a fish much of the bigness of a herring, but not so long and something broader: It is green on the back, but white on the belly, with a forked tail: The head is of a very odd shape, with a wide mouth and large eyes. They are catch'd in prodigious quantities, because they swim in vast shoals like the herrings, especially on the coast of *Malabar*, where they dung their rice-fields with them. They are of a tolerable good taste, but not so good as our herrings.

The sea-bleak.

The thurd fish. This fish is called thurd fish, because it delights in nasty places, tho' otherwise it is of no ill taste, but is not regarded. It is very flat, about a span in length, and near of the same breadth. The belly is blue, and the body is full of brown spots.

The yellow-tail. The fish called yellow-tail is in shape and bigness like a bream, with very sharp prominent teeth in the fore part of the mouth. The back all along to the tail is inclining to a yellow, and the tail very yellow, whence it has got its name. The belly is blue, inclining to a brown towards the forepart. It has red fins, and is catch'd with hooks at sea near the rocks: It is both a wholsome and toothsome fish.

The Kaelt *fish.* The *Kaelt* fish, as our people call it, is a kind of pike with a large piked mouth full of teeth, and large bright eyes. The belly and tail is of a purple colour, but the back brown: It is very thick and plump, about a foot and a half long, swims very swiftly, and of a good taste, but somewhat hard.

Ravens fish. The raven fish, has got its name from its mouth, like a bill under the head. It is about a span in length, red on the back and tail, but inclining to yellow on the belly, and has two yellow streaks on each side, which vanish by degrees. It is a very firm fish, and very wholesome to eat, and is taken in salt waters. 1662.

The king's fish. The king's-fish has obtain'd his title from its excellent taste, being one of the best and most wholesome fishes of the *Indies*. Some are five foot long, and have long forked tails. The back and sides are full of brown spots, but the belly is white. They can open their mouths very wide, and are very greedy after carrion.

Eels. The rivers and standing pools afford also abundance of eels; they are generally black on the back, which turns pale towards the belly, and are full of blackish spots. It is the general opinion here, that they are a kind of water-serpents. There is another sort of a ruddy colour with yellow streaks, having a sharp head with very small eyes; some of them are a foot and a half long. They are eaten by none but the natives.

The sea-eel. There is another kind of sea-eels, or rather water-serpents in the *Indies*, of about three foot long, of a brown colour, chequered with black spots like the skin of a serpent. The forepart of the body is slender, but is as thick again towards the tail. It has a long head and mouth with sharp teeth, but so small as scarce to be discerned. It delights in rocky places, and serves the natives for a dainty. This fish has one peculiar quality, *viz.* That those who kill or exenterate it, are commonly seized with a trembling, and sometimes with fainting, which however continues not long, which seems to intimate that this creature contains something of poison, which exerts its vigour at the time of its expiration.

The sea-cock. The sea-cock is a fish of a very odd shape, more like a sea-monster than a fish. Some are about two foot long, very broad and thick; a great part whereof is nothing but head. On the back it has two long fins, but one longer than the other, and below three other very long fins; a forked tail of a brown colour, but is yellow on the belly. The skin is glistering like silver, and the fins on both sides are red: It is catch'd in salt-water.

The white fish. The white-fish has a thick short head, a brown back, and blue belly inclining to yellow; it is of a tolerable good taste, and catch'd in prodigious quantities in the sea near the shoar with nets, but is generally not much regarded.

The grunting fish. The grunting fish has got its name from a certain grumbing noise it makes when it is taken; cross the back run along both sides two brown and one yellow streak; it is very plump, with little scales, not a-

above

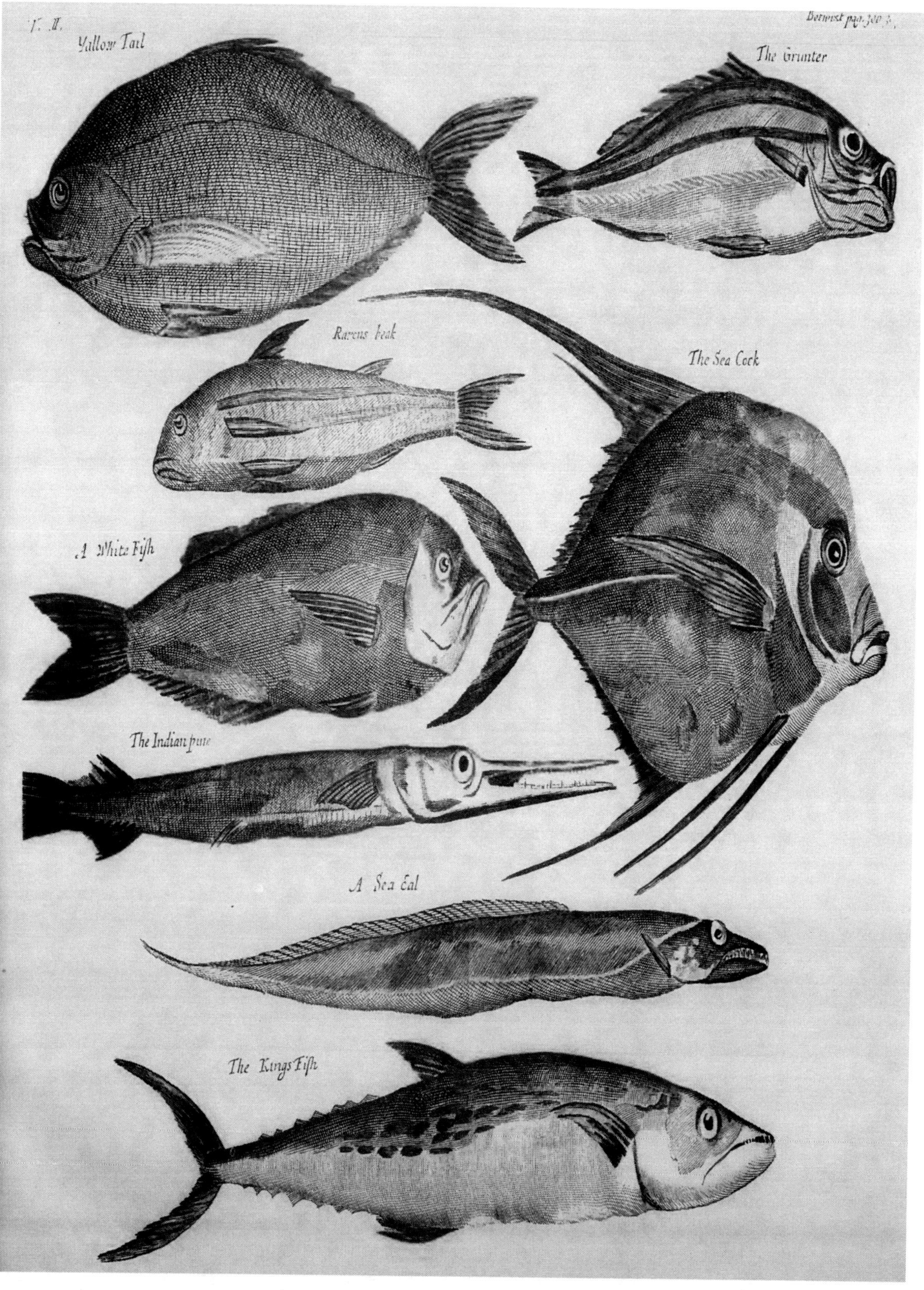
T. II.
Betwixt pag. 300 3,
Yallow Tail
The Grunter
Ravens beak
The Sea Cock
A White Fish
The Indian pike
A Sea Eal
The Kings Fish

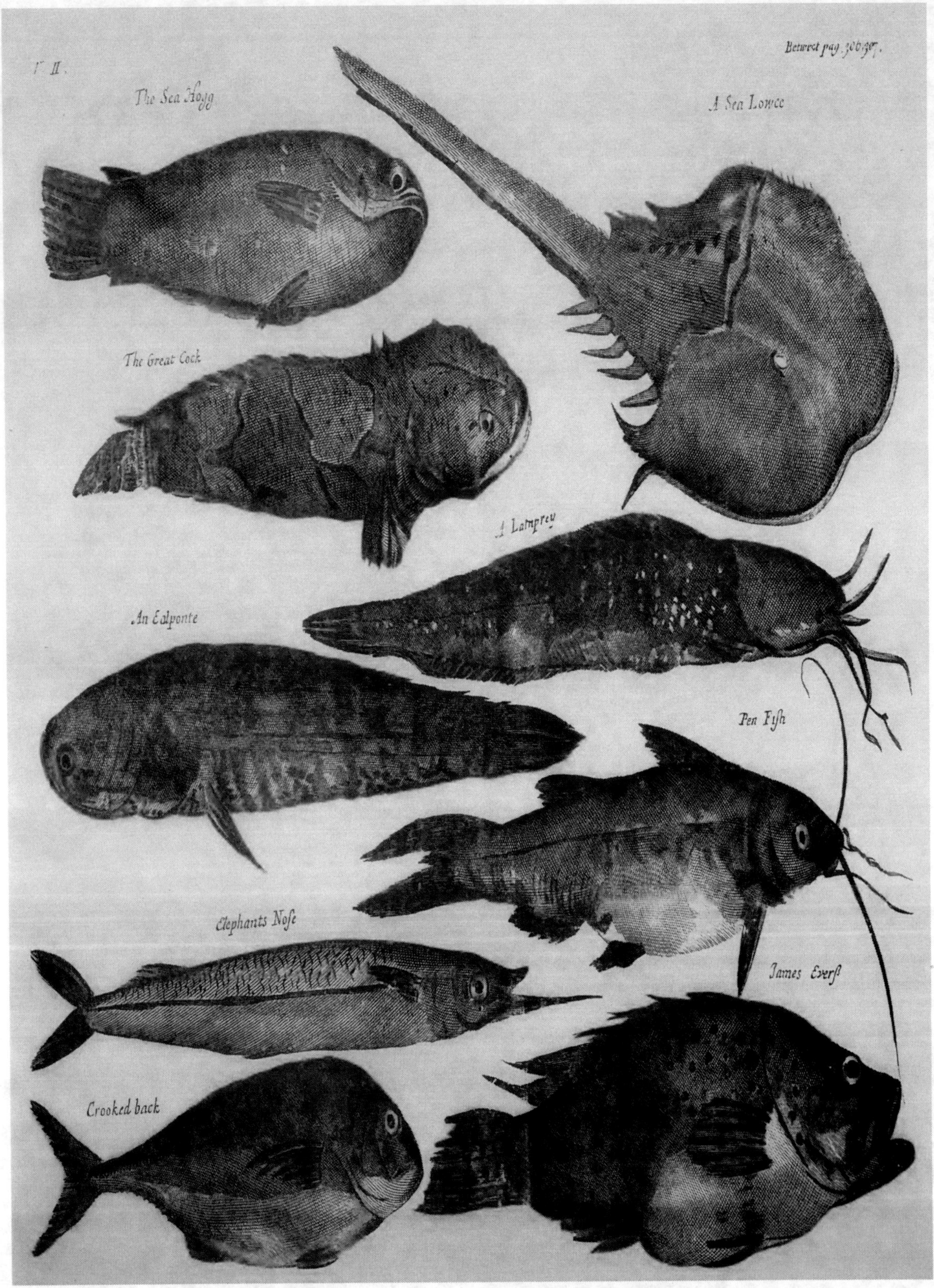
V. II.
Betwixt pag. 306.307.
The Sea Hogg
A Sea Lowce
The Great Cock
A Lamprey
An Ealponte
Pen Fish
Elephants Nose
James Everst
Crooked back

1662. bove a ſpan in length; the head not unlike a pope. It is of an agreeable taſte, and eaten like as we do our popes or ſmall perches.

The ſea-hog. The ſea-hog or ſea-porpoiſe called *Pixoporkas*, in the ſame ſenſe by the *Portugueſe*, is of a different kind from the former, this being not above a ſpan in length, inclining to a green with blackiſh ſcales, the fins and tail of the ſame colour, but the eyes are yellow: It is a freſh-water fiſh, very plump and fat and well taſted.

Another kind of grunting fiſh. There is alſo another kind of grunting-fiſh, ſo call'd for the ſame reaſon with the former; it is almoſt round, with a ſmooth ſkin, but full of knobs and ſpots; it is of a browniſh colour ſtreaked with black. The head is very thick, ſhort, and full of knobs, with a large mouth and red eyes. The tail is alſo very round and ſhort; on each ſide of the body is a red fin, and the fiſh is of a tolerable good taſte.

The ſea-louſe. The ſea-louſe is a ſtrange kind of ſhell-fiſh, of above a foot in length. It appears like a round lump, with a large tail, with many legs on both ſides. Its colour is gray inclining to green. It is catched near *Batavia*, but is ſeldom eaten, unleſs it be by the *Javaneſe* and *Chineſe*.

The lamprey. The *Lamprey* is a kind of an eelpoute, above a foot long, with a ſmooth ſkin, and fat like an eel, but of a different ſhape. It is brown on the belly, with yellow ſpots on the back, and has purple coloured fins under the belly. The head is not unlike that of a ſnail, with horns, and its fins are venomous. It is catch'd in ponds and pools, and eats beſt ſtew'd.

Kabos. *Kabos* is a kind of an eelpoute, but bigger than the laſt; theſe being above two foot long and very fat. The ſkin is likewiſe ſmooth, without ſcales, of a browniſh colour, but the belly is ſomewhat paler, with black ſpots. The head is thick and ſhort, with the eyes in the forehead; they are well taſted.

The pen fiſh. The pen fiſh is alſo a kind of eelpoute, with a ſmooth ſkin without ſcales; of the length of a foot, the back brown, and the belly of a pale blue colour. The fins are brown, very ſharp and venomous, ſo that if the leaſt part of it remains in a wound, it will ſcarce heal; the fiſh is of a good taſte, but unwholeſome if eaten in any quantity. It is likewiſe a freſh-water fiſh, and taken in pools and ponds.

The elephant's-noſe. The fiſh called the elephant's-noſe is of an odd ſhape, its undermoſt jaw being as ſharp as a pin. The body is prettily ſpotted, with a broad ſtreak running croſs the middle. It is a very thick fiſh, which is taken in the ſea, and in bigneſs and taſte is not unlike our large ſmelts.

The fiſh called *Jacob Evertſon*, is above ten foot long, weighing ſometimes 400 pound. It is blue on the belly, and brown on the body, with many dark red ſpots near the head and tail. It has a large white mouth, with a ſhort brown tail, and many fins turning up towards the back. 1662. Jacob Evertſon

The fiſh crooked-back has got its name from its ſhape: It has a ſmooth ſkin without ſcales, a white belly, and yellow tail and fins. It is in great requeſt all over the *Indies*, by reaſon of its agreeable taſte; ſome are four foot long. *The crooked-back.*

The horn fiſh is about a ſpan in length or ſomething more, with a large head, but a little mouth; half of the body being taken up with the head. The ſkin is very bright, the back bluiſh, the belly white, but the fins and tail yellow. The body repreſents it ſelf in various colours, according to its ſeveral turnings. *The horn fiſh.*

The fiſh called *Kneſſen*, is a baſtard carp, about a ſpan long, and pretty broad with thick ſcales. It is a well taſted freſh-water fiſh. Kneſſen.

Their flounders are in ſhape and bigneſs like ours, except that they have teeth, wherewith they take hold of all they light on; they alſo are as well taſted as the *Dutch* flounders; they have here alſo turbuts and ſoals, little different from ours both in ſhape and taſte. *The flounder.*

The *Klip* fiſh is a kind of fiſh with a ſmooth ſkin without ſcales, flat, broad, and of the bigneſs of our plaiſe: It is brown on the back, ſpotted with white, but very white towards the belly, with many ſtreaks of various colours. The mouth and eyes are like thoſe of the bream, and it is a well taſted fiſh. *The* Klip *fiſh.*

The cod fiſh here is of the ſame ſize and colour with ours, except that it has very ſharp fins on the back and the under part of the mouth jets out beyond the uppermoſt. *The cod fiſh.*

The horn fiſh has got its name from the horn upon his head, and two more underneath, which being very brittle are alſo very poiſonous, and if part thereof remain in a wound, will ſcarce admit of a cure; and if you happen only to be wounded by it, it will exulcerate immediately. *The horn fiſh.*

The flat fiſh is about a foot long, with a ſmooth ſkin without ſcales, and a white mouth: It gliſters all over like ſilver; on the back it has a ſmall fin, and one more on each ſide. Underneath the belly, it has only one fin which is inſtead of the tail. It is a freſh-water fiſh, of a very good taſte, but full of ſmall bones, and therefore not much regarded. *The flat fiſh.*

The

1662.

The red fish.

The red-fish is a kind of a bream, of a dark red colour, as are likewise the fins; however the belly is blue, and has two yellow fins; it is very thick of body, and the head is sharp at the end, with a large mouth and yellow eyes, some are four foot long.

The bitter fish.

The bitter fish is of the shape and bigness of a carp, with large scales and red fins, and two black streaks round the tail. It is a fine well tasted fish, but being full of small bones, is not much in request.

The parrot fish.

The parrot fish has got its name from its mouth, which turns like the bill of a parrot. It is a foot long, and sometimes bigger. It is of a greenish colour, marbled or chequered towards the head with yellow. Both the fins and eyes are of a blue colour; the last very large and sprightly, and surrounded with a yellow circle. It has very large scales, and two rows of very hard teeth, wherewith they often bite off the hooks. This fish is very greedy after muscles and oysters, which it cracks to pieces to come at the fish. It is a very firm fish, and of a good taste.

Short nose.

The short nose is a fish like our haddock, having a round body; it is yellow on the belly, and the fins are of the same colour. The mouth is just under the nose, which is very short; it is a well tasted fish.

The bone fish.

The bone fish is of the bigness and shape of our carps, but flatter, and has another head: It has large scales, and a forked tail; its taste is very good, but being full of small bones, is not much regarded.

The sand smelt.

The sand smelt resembles in colour and bigness a small whiting, and is round of body, and inclining to a yellow on the belly: It is a sea fish, and of an excellent taste.

The pock fish.

The pock fish is generally above a foot long, with a smooth skin, without scales; but being very bright, it varies in colour according to the various position of its body, appearing sometimes blue, then green, and soon after of a purple, or some other colour. It is a long fish, but not broad, not unlike a great smelt, with a forked tail, and teeth in its mouth. Tho' it is a well tasted fish, yet being full of small bones, is not eaten, except by the natives.

The Chinese fish.

The *Chinese* fish is round, and about a span long; the head is like an eel, with small eyes, and a long tail. It is green on the back, but white on the belly. It is a fresh water fish, and well tasted, but those catch'd in ponds are accounted unwholesome.

The pit fish.

The pit fish is no bigger than a large smelt, with a round body, full of green and yellow spots, and without scales. The eyes, which they can draw in or out, are starting out of the head. On the back they have sharp pointed fins; they delight in muddy places, notwithstanding which they are well tasted; they are very nimble, and will leap a great way.

1662.

The mullet.

The mullet is a very fine fish, which being catch'd in particular places only, is dry'd in the sun, and transported all over the *Indies.* It is white of colour, chequered with blue and purple; it swims with great swiftness, and is so nimble, that it will not only leap over the net, but even over the fisher-boat. These fishes are of a dainty taste whilst in season, but at certain times they are pestered with worms, at which time they are neither toothsome nor wholesome.

The sea snipe.

Nothing more common than to give names to fishes in foreign countries from what they most resemble; whence it is, that the sea snipe has got its name from tis mouth, which is like the bill of a snipe. Some of them are five foot long, with a head like that of a hog, and large bright eyes: On the back are large and sharp fins, reaching from the head to the tail, and full of spots.

The korets.

Some korets are six or seven foot long, have large yellowish eyes, and a forked yellow and greyish tail, with yellow fins; under the belly, which is blue, inclining to green, and under the tail, are divers fins. They are very bright, and shine like silver, when they are catch'd at sea with hooks: They are very well tasted and not unwholesome, being sometimes a great refreshment to those ships that come to these parts.

The sea devil.

This kind of fish has deservedly got the name of sea devil, by reason of its ugly shape; having the eyes on one side, and the mouth in the concavity below the head. Its tail is like that of a roach, with two teats on each side, pointed towards the end. The skin on the head is full of brown spots; some are near seven or eight foot long, but afford very course food.

The stip fish.

The stip fish has a skin full of spots, is well tasted, and taken generally with hooks near the isle of St. *Vincent.*

The sea pidgeon.

The sea pidgeon has got its name from the resemblance of its head to that of a pidgeon; and of its breasts protuberating like those creatures. This fish is without scales, but not without divers spots. It is but rarely catch'd, and none of the best tasted.

The sea hedge-hog.

The sea hedge-hog is justly so called from its sharp fins about the head and mouth, which is round, and has very large eyes. They can't swim very swiftly, and consequently would soon fall a prey to other fish, were it not that nature has arm'd them with these pointed fins against any attempt.

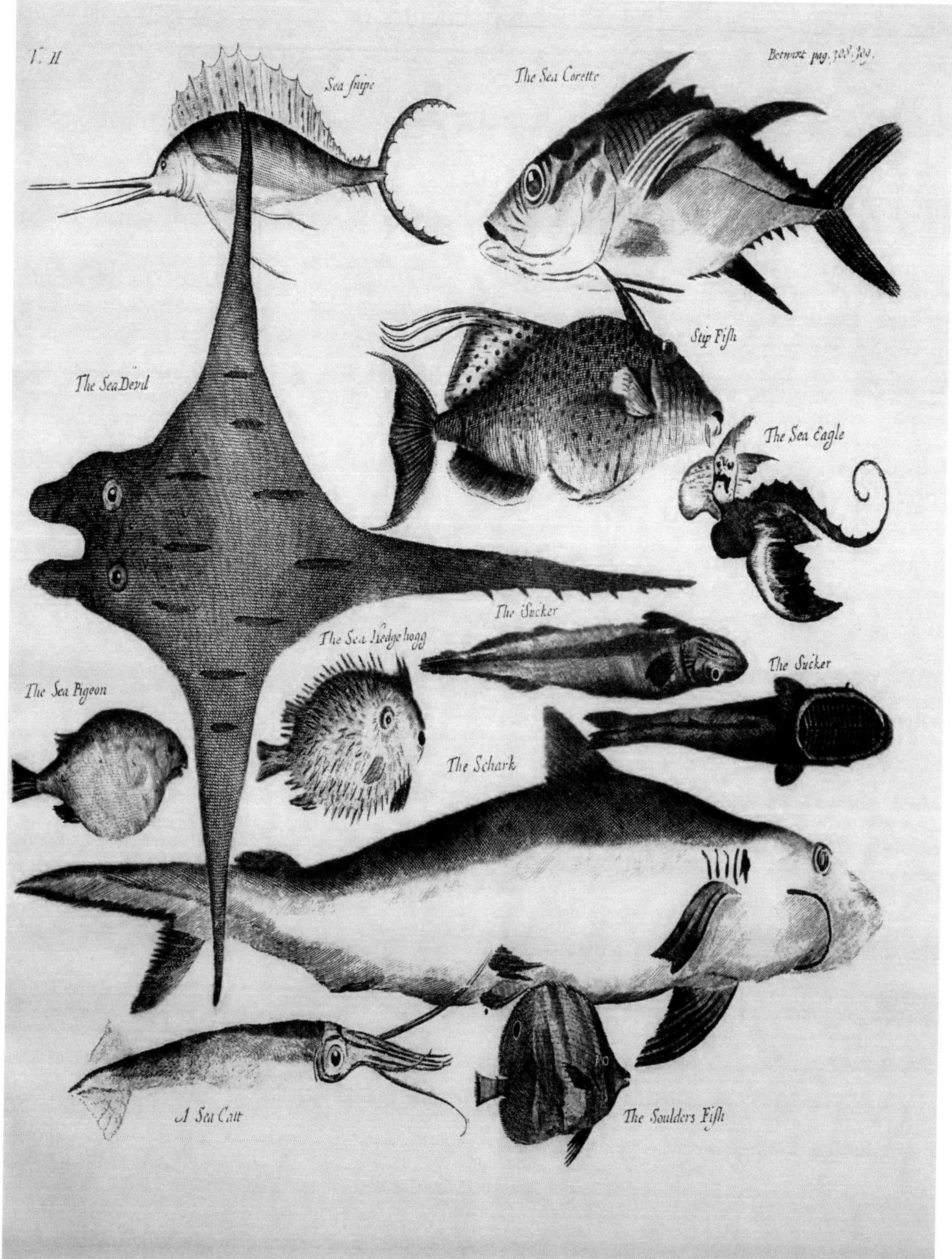
V. II
Betwixt pag. 308, 309.
Sea Snipe
The Sea Corette
Stip Fish
The Sea Devil
The Sea Eagle
The Sucker
The Sea Hedge hogg
The Sucker
The Sea Pigeon
The Schark
A Sea Catt
The Soulders Fish

1662.

The suckers. The suckers are represented at length in the cut, tho' there are some much bigger. They are blue, with bright yellow eyes, a smooth skin without scales: They have no teeth, but broad lips, wherewith they will suck, and adhere so close to other fish, that they will rather be kill'd than let go their hold. They will stick so close to the shark, that they are often catch'd with them. They are eaten sometimes for want of better food, but are but of an indifferent taste.

The shark. Some sharks are eight, ten, or fourteen foot long: Their skin is rough and sharp, and they have a double row of teeth, and some three or four rows, which are covered with the gums. Their eyes lie forward near the mouth. It is a very pernicious fish, which oftentimes bites off an arm or a leg of those that divert themselves with swimming. The sharks bring forth their young ones alive, which follow the she-shark wherever she goes, and in bad weather creep into her belly, and come out again after the storm is over. It is observable that certain fishes of a foot long always swim after the shark, which are plainly to be seen in still weather.

The sea cat, (the draught whereof you see in the cut) is a very odd creature, both for its colour and shape. *The sea cat.* The eyes are exceeding large in proportion to the body, the back is of a purple colour, and the belly blue, with divers purple spots. The tail is in comparison of the rest of the body, vastly large, and pale red, wherewith it swims, it being destitute of fins. However, just on the front of the head, it has seven fins, which stand out strait forward like those of the shrimps. It affords very good food, especially if dry'd in the sun.

Souldier-fish. The klip-fish, or soldier-fish, is a kind of bream, but sometimes grows not above to the length of a span: It is flat and of a pale colour: On the back it has sharp fins like a perch; a sharp tail, and yellow eyes. It is one of the best fish in the *Indies*, of a very delicious taste.

The sea eagle. The sea eagle is an odd kind of fish: It has a tail like a roach, with large fins like wings, a thick head, and tastes like a roach.

The sea cat. The sea cat is a round fish of a span in length, of a very odd shape; the hindermost part of the body being an oval lump, on which hangs the head. It has long and large eyes, a smooth skin, inclining to blue, but brown upon the belly. The entrails of this fish contain a certain gum, out of which the *Chinese* make their ink. They dry this fish in the sun, as the *Dutch* do the plaise; and they are in great request among the *Indians*, tho' they are of no easy digestion.

1662.

The leaping fish. The leaping fish is so called, because they leap and play continually upon the surface of the water. They are of the bigness of a herring, and are without fins on the back, from the head to the tail. They have a knotty head, and the body of a greyish colour, with black spots; but toward the belly they begin to be white. They look very fiercely before they begin to leap. They are sea fishes, and of a very good taste, especially broiled.

Pampus. The fish *Pampus* is above a foot long, and about a span in breadth; for the rest in colour and shape, not unlike our plaise, with a smooth skin: The eyes stand on both sides, and the mouth strait forward. It is a well tasted fish, especially if dry'd and eaten as the *Dutch* do their plaise.

Peyxe Kok. *Peyxe Kok*, i. e. the *Fish Kok*, so called by the *Portuguese*, because when taken it makes a noise or sound like *Kok*. It is taken near the isle of *St. Vincent*, and is but an indifferent fish.

The blower. The blowers are huge fishes which appear now and then in the open sea. They have got this name from their drawing in of the water, and spouting it out again with great force into the air.

The white fish. The white fish is about the bigness of a whiting, with a round hanging belly, a strait back, and turn'd up mouth: Its tail is forked, it has one large fin upon the back, and abundance of small ones betwixt the belly and the tail. It is full of streaks all over the body, and on the mouth it has two long teats: It is of a very good taste.

Five-finger-fish. The five-finger-fish has got its name from five black spots on each side, resembling the prints of fingers. Its length is about a foot and a half, with a small head, large mouth, and brown pointed fins towards the tail. It is of a shining blue colour mix'd with purple, without scales. It is of a pretty good taste, and taken in the sea all over the *Indies*.

Karappa, or round fish. Karappa, or round-fish, is not unlike a whiting, of a very good taste: It has but a small head and tail, but a pretty bulky belly. Below it has some some fins not unlike those of an eel.

Flying-fish. Some of the flying-fish are near as big as corette, of a blueish colour on the back, but inclining to a brown towards the tail. They have large eyes, and large yellowish fins, and resemble in shape our smelts: They are of an agreeable taste, but not easy to be catch'd, except when they fly against the sails, which they frequently do, and so fall upon the ships deck.

The fork-tail. The fork-tail is a long and round fish, with a very long forked tail, whence it has got its name. Its head is not unlike that

1662. that of a herring, with a long teat on the top of it, and two more below near the mouth, like those of the shrimps, but larger; they keep them close to the body when they are swimming. They are of the bigness of a mackrel, but of no extraordinary good taste.

Soals. Some soals here are a foot long, of the same colour as ours, and as well-tasted; but their heads are strangely shaped, the mouth turning quite to one side, as well as their eyes.

Bonites. The bonites are not unlike the corettes, but with lesser fins and blue streaks, which vanish by degrees towards the tail. The back is of a dark brown, and the belly white, the eyes blue, surrounded with a yellow circle. Some are a foot and a half long, and very bright when first taken, which is done without much difficulty, because they follow the ships, and are very greedy after a bait. They eat best if they are salted a little before they are broil'd.

The sword-fish. The sword-fish has a very odd head, not unlike that of an owl, with a very wide mouth: The skin is hard, the back grey, the belly white without any scales. On each side of the sword, which is above five foot long, are 27 teeth: Their whole length, including the sword, is generally 25 foot long, and so thick, that scarce two men can grasp them. Near the eyes they have two nostrils, through which they draw the water in and out.

Siap Siap. The fish called *Siap Siap* by the *Javanese*, is a river fish in great request among the *Javanese*, and is taken in considerable quantity near *Batavia*.

The pyed-fish. The pyed-fish has got its name from its colour; its tail and fins being brown, spotted with pale blue spots: It is about a foot long, and pretty thick, without scales. The eyes, which are yellow, are surrounded by a blue circle; underneath the throat hangs a crop extending it self to the tail: It has a little mouth, and on each side a yellow fin. It is in great esteem among the inhabitants, and well tasted, but contains a certain venomous matter, which must be carefully taken out when it is gutted.

Five-eyes. The five-eyes have got their name from five black eyes, enclosed in yellow circles, which are in the fins near the tail. They are smooth and yellow without scales, pretty thick with a small head and sharp nose, which turns over the mouth, near which they have two red fins; they are catch'd in the rivers and are well-tasted.

Sea-bats. The sea-bat has got its name from its resemblance to a bat: It has two yellowish wings streak'd with three blue streaks; a long tail, thick head and large mouth. By its taste it seems to be a kind of thornback.

The gudgeons of *Java* are of the length of a finger, but scarce an inch thick. They are speckled with pale blue, and other colours without scales; they have small forked tails, are catch'd in the rivers and are exceeding well tasted. There is another kind of them taken in the sea, in such prodigious quantities, that they sell a whole canoe full for eight or ten pence, and fatten their ducks and geese with them. 1662. *The gudgeon.*

The *Indian* carps are taken in the rivers, being not in the least different from ours either in shape or taste. *Carps.*

The sea-monster is an odd kind of fish, having a knobby star of eight tacks upon the head, and upon that a certain excrescence resembling a bishop's mitre: From the sides of the head issue two fins of the same length with the body of the monster. It has a very dreadful wide mouth, and very broad tail, wherewith it guides it self in swimming. *The sea-monster*

They have divers sorts of shrimps and creafishes in the *Indies*; and of the latter sort, a certain kind which have teeth like a saw on the back; some of them are of that bigness as to weigh six pounds, of a delicious taste, and very wholsome, being accounted good for such as are troubled with the asthma, or spit-blood. The sea-shrimps are a salt-water fish, the biggest of which are near a span in length, and have shells like ours, of a sallow colour with a red fork'd tail. Out of the head come forth divers fins, on which hang two small thin horns. They are very well tasted, and five or six are sufficient for one man's meal. The river-shrimps are about the bigness of our sea-shrimps, of a blue colour, with a small head and thick body. Out of the head come two long fins, as fine as a thread. Their shell is not so hard as the former, neither are they so well-tasted. The rivers here afford also abundance of creafishes, which are taken in holes among the oysters. They are better tasted than our lobsters. *Shrimps and creafishes.*

The sea-star is an odd shaped fish with five branches or tacks like a star: They are of a pale red colour, an inch thick, covered with a knobby skin, underneath which are many small bones: They have a hole in the middle, through which they draw their sustenance: They are never to be seen at sea, except in calm weather, and are taken and kept rather for curiosity's sake than any other use. *The sea-star.*

The sea-crabs are of about the bigness of a span, of a most curious colour, the shell being specked with yellow spots; besides which they have three purple spots enclosed within white rings. Their claws are yellowish towards the body, afterwards white, *Sea-crabs or lobsters.*

V.II.
The Fire Eyes
The Sea Shrimp
Klip Gernael
A Sea Batt
Land Crabb
Horn Fish
The Pide Fish
The Sea Catt.
Pitt Fish
The Soft Fish
River Shrimp
The Sea Crabb
44.

1662. white, and at the extremities of a high purple colour; their eyes are fixt upon certain small tacks an inch breadth without the head. There is also a kind of blue-crabs, some of which are a foot and a half long: They are of a purple colour spotted with white; the claws are blue, and of a purple colour towards the body; their eyes are fixt upon small tacks like the former, and stand a fingers length without the head. They are a salt-water fish, and very well-tasted.

Lobsters. There is another kind of lobsters not quite so big as the former, which run very swiftly: Their eyes stand likewise about two inches breadth without the head, especially whilst they are running, but otherwise can draw them back, and lay them close under two fins. Their bodies are marbled with divers colours, the claws of a purple colour; behind they have two small round and blue shells edged with yellow. Some are of a considerable bigness, and of a very good taste. There is another sort of sea-crabs, of the same bigness as the blue-lobsters, but easily to be distinguished from them by their colour, which is inclining to green, with red claws, and by their taste, which is exceeding delicious, these being the best sort throughout the *Indies*. Their eyes stand likewise an inch's breadth without the head. Some sea-crabs here are of a prodigious bigness, and are, as well as all other shell-fish, best in the encrease of the moon. Some crabs here cast their shells, and during a certain season of the year abide under ground till they grow again. The *Indian* oysters are prefer'd before those of *Europe*.

Muscles and oysters. The muscles of the *Indies* are like ours, but somewhat bigger; the shell is brown both in and outside. There is another sort of muscles called tail muscles by our people; these are of a greenish colour; they have on that end where they open, two sharp horns, and on the other end, a pale yellow tail, wherewith they can fasten themselves in the mud. They are of the same taste, and used like ours, as well as those we commonly call St. *James's* muscles. Of oysters they have also several sorts, the biggest adhere to the rocks, some to the roots and tacks of the trees; they are all of a very good taste; and are either stew'd with spices, or eaten raw with lemon-juice and pepper.

Purple-snails. Abundance of purple-snails are found in the islands over against *Batavia*: The scallop or shell is of a yellow colour, of the bigness of a good citron, with curious windings at one end. Within this shell is the *snail*, which is round, plump and yellow, streak'd with black. They are boil'd and eaten by the *Chinese*, who have a way 1662. of polishing the shells, and pick out of the middle of the snail a certain purple colour'd substance, which they use in colouring and making of red ink. There is also another kind with green shells, streak'd with black, white within, and of the bigness of a child's head: The snail is of the same colour, and is not ill tasted. Another sort has a shell pale-red, marbled with white, and curiously twisted, of the bigness of an orange: The snail is of the same colour, and is eaten as we do our perewinkles, but is of a hard digestion.

The *Quallen* are a certain product of the *Quallen.* sea, of a mucilaginous substance, without head or tail, or entrails; they commonly are of the bigness of a trencher, and sometimes less. They have purple edges all round them, wherewith they swim. In the midst is a certain white spot, (which is sometimes blueish) wherein perhaps their victuals are contained. If they are forced ashore, they are dissolved. The *Chinese* have a way of distilling a certain *Arack* or strong-water out of them, which is excessive hot, sharp and unwholesome, causing exulcerations in the body. For if this substance happen to adhere to the bare skin of a man in swimming or otherwise, it burns with violence, and raises blisters immediately.

The *Dorades*, by some called sea-breams, *The Dorades.* are a kind of dolphins. They have long and sharp fins on the back, and a very long tail; underneath the belly they have three fins, the last of which extends as far as the tail. Some are 4 or 5 foot long, and rather broad than thick. They eat tolerably well, if salted before they are dress'd, but are of a hard digestion: They are sometimes taken with the hook, being not easily catched with the harpiron, by reason of their nimbleness, which is such, that they will leap sometimes five or six foot high above the water, after the flying-fish.

The *Indies* afford excessive large thorn- *Scates or thornbacks.* backs, some of which are as big in circumference as a moderate table, and will suffice to dine forty people. They have vast long tails, but are of the same colour with ours, and of the same taste, but are hard of digestion, but the young ones are much better. Their fins, which are very large, are of a purple colour. All fish with scales cast their spawn; but those without scales bring forth their young ones alive.

Indian *and* Javanese *birds and four leg'd beasts.*

In the isles of *Sumatra*, *Banda*, and the *The bird Emeu.* other adjacent *Molucca* islands, is to be found

1662. found a certain bird, called *Emeu* or *Eme* by the inhabitants, and *Casuaris* by the *Dutch*. He walks constantly with his head straight upright, when he is above five foot high, and about three in length from the breast to the tail. The head is in proportion of the body, but small, very smooth, and of a dark blue colour. Before, on the neck, hang two red teats or bags. The eyes are large and fierce, behind which are the ear-holes, and almost at the extremities of the bill two nostrils; and from the midst of the bill to the crown of the head, grows a hard yellow substance, like a cockle-shell, especially in the males. They have very long and grofs legs, covered with a yellowish rind, their feet are thick, knobby, and without spurs, instead of which, they have on the forepart three long horny claws, in which they differ from the ostriches, whose feet are cloven both before and behind. They are covered all over with feathers, or rather with plumes of a dark red mix'd with black. Those upon the breast and thighs, grow two and two together, but those on the tail are much longer and stronger. Underneath the feathers, which grow on both sides, are hidden certain pens, which serve them in running, for these birds are scarce able to raise themselves from the ground. They are exceeding greedy, devouring every thing 1662.

they meet with, even to iron and burning coals, all which they evacuate backwards without any alteration; nay, they sometimes throw out what they have eat, not till a year after, without the least sign of any digestion: For the rest they live upon herbage. Their strength consists in their legs and feet; and run so fast that no man can overtake them, and when exasperated, kick with their feet backwards and sideways like a horse. They lay greenish eggs upon the ground among the shrubs, scarce so big as our hen-eggs, speckled with dark green spots; the yolks thereof are eaten by the inhabitants. They have neither tongue nor tail.

Flying-cat. Among the several sorts of flitter-mice or bats, that which by some is called a flying-cat, may well challenge a place; its head, tail, nay the whole body and bulk resembing to a cat. It differs from the bats in this, that whereas they hang on certain tacks, this hangs on its claws, and hides its self within its wings: The hair brown red, except on the back, where it is black, Betwixt the fore and hindermost legs grows two skins, a little hairy on the outside, which serves them for wings. There is also a sort of flying-apes, these have very sharp teeth and claws, and very lively eyes.

In

1662. In ſome parts of the *Indies* you meet with a certain bird call'd the hunter's-bird. The breaſt and whole body is black, but the tail grayiſh; the head is dark yellow, but without feathers; below the neck hangs a bag, not unlike thoſe of our turkeys: The bill is diſtinguiſh'd by certain twiſted rings, by which they diſcern their age, every year producing one like our oxes horns. On the top of the bill grows a horny ſubſtance; they are look'd upon as a rarity, and ſold at a dear rate.

The hunter's bird.

Dronte or Dodaers. In the iſle of *Mauritius* you meet with a certain bird call'd *Dronte* by the inhabitants, and *Dodaers* by the *Dutch*. In bigneſs it is betwixt an oſtrich and a large turkey, and has alſo ſome reſemblance to them in his feathers and tail. His head is very large, not unlike that of a cuckow, but covered all over with a ſkin. The eyes are large and black, the neck crooked and very thick: The bill is very long, thick and pale blue, except towards the extremities, the uppermoſt whereof is blackiſh, and the undermoſt yellowiſh, but both ſharp and bent. He is very thick and round of body, covered with ſoft grey feathers, like thoſe of the oſtrich; the belly and hindermoſt part are ſo thick as to touch almoſt the ground, which is the reaſon he is eaſily catch'd. On both ſides he has certain pens inſtead of wings, of a pale yellow colour, and inſtead of the tail five curl'd plumes of the ſame colour: His legs are ſhort and thick, with four large claws. The meat, eſpecially that of the breaſt, is fat and toothſome enough, and three or four of theſe creatures afford a meal for 100 perſons. In his ſtomach is ſometimes found a certain porous hard ſtone. 1662.

Parraquets. The parraquets are of a green colour, of the bigneſs of a ſterling; their bills are yellow, the neck red mix'd with green, and the wings yellow at the extremities: They are found in vaſt numbers in the woods, and are eaſily tamed and taught to ſpeak. There are divers ſorts of them of different colours.

The martins. The martins here are as big as our magpies, of a black colour with a yellow bill, and a yellow tuft upon the head. The midſt of the wings is white, the feet yellow, with large crooked claws. The *Javaneſe* are great admirers of this bird, and teach him to whiſtle and ſpeak, which he does as diſtinctly as a man, but with ſomewhat a rough voice. There is another ſort of them not ſo big as theſe; they are found all

all over the *Indies*, and feed upon rice and other fruits of the earth.

Crows. The *Indian* crows are pale blue, in ſhape betwixt a heron and ſtork. The head and neck is ſomewhat of a darker colour, with a curl'd tail and ſharp bill. They live moſt in wilderneſſes, and fly (as they ſay) ſometimes as far as *Europe*, under a certain leader, who flies ſometimes before and ſometimes behind.

The bird Rubus. The bird *Rubus* is of the bigneſs of a ſtarling, with a blue bill and legs, the back and tail red, and white and black wings. The head is green, and in his tail he has two large feathers, like the *Paradiſe* bird.

Bats. In divers parts of the *Indies* are very large *bats*, exceeding in bigneſs our cats. In the iſle of *Java* are ſome of the ordinary ſort, no bigger than a pidgeon; they live in the woods, and are accounted a dainty by the *Javaneſe*. In the night-time they will get ſometimes into the chambers, if the windows be left open, and draw blood from ſuch as are aſleep there.

Gwira. There are two ſorts of the bird called *Gwira*, they are both white, mix'd with ſome brown feathers. One ſort has a red belly, and the other a blue tail, with one very long feather in it.

Poreo. The *Poero* is a long, but ſlender bird, of a ſpan in length, including the bill and tail. The bill is ſomewhat crooked, and the tail like that of the bird *Gwira*. His feathers are blueiſh, mixt with yellow, and his feet very ſmall. He feeds upon piſmires.

Cormorants. In *Java* you meet often with cormorants, not unlike our geeſe, except that they are much bigger; underneath the bill hangs a large bag, which they can extend and draw together at pleaſure, and in it keep ſuch fiſh as they have ſwallow'd. Their feet are like thoſe of the ſwan, and their bills are crooked towards the extremities. They are ſo greedy after prey, that they ruſh out from among the flags with ſuch violence, that they are eaſily taken by that means. They ſwallow oyſters with the ſhells, and keep them in their bags till they open, when they ſpew them out again and pick out the oyſter. They are frequently found in the iſle of *Din Ding*, and ſoon diſcovered by their noiſe.

Ducks. All over the *Indies* you meet with ducks in great numbers, reſembling ours both in bigneſs and taſte. They are generally dark yellow, with a black bill and legs, large bellies, and tufts on their heads. But whereas the *Weſt-India* ducks have hanging bellies, theſe carry them more upright. By reaſon of the exceſſive heat they are not eaſily brought to ſit upon their eggs, which are generally laid under hens, or fomented in horſedung or ovens. Their meat is very wholeſome, provided they are well fed.

Wide-bill. The wide-bill has got his name from his bill, which reaches up on both ſides to the eyes: He is ſcarce of the bigneſs of a pidgeon, of a pale black colour, with black wings, and underneath the eyes and bill white. They are brought to market in great quantities at *Batavia*, their meat being well taſted.

The ſtrand bird or ox-eye. The ſtrand bird is a kind of ſnipe of the bigneſs of our wood-cocks. Their feathers are green mixed with black, they are ſold in great numbers at *Batavia*, and in taſte are not unlike our wood-ſnipes.

Turtles. The *Indian* turtles are not altogether ſo big as ours, and of a yellowiſh colour mix'd with grey: They have a black feather in each wing, and the tail is black and white; under the neck they are ſomewhat brighter, and the breaſt almoſt red. They are taken in great quantities in the rice-fields, and are fat and well-taſted.

Geeſe. The *Indian* geeſe are much finer and larger than the *European* geeſe, reſembling rather our ſwans, their necks being exceſſive long, of a yellowiſh colour, but their bills black. Along the back, upon the wings and tail they have dark grey feathers mix'd with ſome light ones, but on the belly they are white. They have not ſo ſhrill a voice as our geeſe, but differ not in the leaſt from them either in ſhape or taſte, their feet being likewiſe red. They have both wild and tame ones.

Birds of prey. In divers places of the *Indies* are great quantities of birds of prey, as eagles, hawks, kites, and ſuch like, which do prodigious miſchief both among the wild and tame fowl, and are of ſuch ſtrength, that they carry ſometimes a young pig away and devour it in the woods or among the rocks. There is a certain bird of prey here, which you ſee moving in the air without moving its wings; and another called *Jin* by the *Chineſe*, exceeding all the reſt in nimbleneſs: It is greeniſh on the back, but white on the belly. The eyes are quick and red, and the bill yellow, bent like a hook at the end. Their feet are likewiſe yellow, arm'd with long and very ſharp claws.

Kokoy. The *Kokoy* is a kind of a heron, but much exceeding ours in beauty, being yellow before and green in the hindermoſt part. On the head he has a delicious plume, ſpreading all over the neck. The young ones eat tolerably well, but the old ones are tough and taſte much after fiſh.

Kolibry *Kolibry* is the leaſt of all the birds, being no bigger than a horſe-fly; it has a very ſharp bill, wherewith it ſucks its ſuſtenance out of the flowers, though ſome are

1662. of opinion it feeds upon the dew. It has all the colours of the rain-bow, and its wings are not unlike those of the pidgeons or ducks: It builds a nest to the south under the branches of orange, limon, or cotton-trees, to defend itself against the injuries of the north winds: Its eggs are no bigger than peas. There is another which sings exceeding fine, but is not so well colour'd; it weighs not above 24 grains, and is catch'd by throwing hot any thing else upon it.

Birds like quails or throstles. In the woods of *Java* you see vast numbers of birds not unlike our quails or throstles, but of the bigness of our wild pidgeons; their bills are however somewhat longer than those of our quails, and their noise is very different. They are of so cold a constitution, that if exposed on the cold ground, they are in danger of perishing by cold; for which reason they hide themselves, cover'd with their wings in the hollowness of trees, immediately after sunset, and at sun-rising come forth again and begin to chirp with a great deal of chearfulness.

Quails. The *Indian* quails resemble those of *Europe*, are brown on the back and blue on the belly: they have a yellow bill and four claws, *viz.* three before, and one behind; they don't make any noise, but are very good meat.

Rice-birds. The rice-bird is of the bigness of one of our pullets, but something longer leg'd, with brown feathers on the body, a red head, and very large claws; they live among the rice, whence they have got their name, and eat very deliciously roasted.

Pheasants. In many parts of the *Indies* are also pheasants with long and pointed tails; some are white on the breast and about the eyes.

Butterflies. They have prodigious numbers of butterflies of various colours; they have long bills, which they can stretch out when they suck the juice of the flowers, or draw back at pleasure. Some are of a most delicious colour, intermix'd with blue, white and red, beyond what can be express'd. They are generally of the bigness of the palm of the hand, when their wings are spread; some have larger wings than others, and have two small feathers on their heads.

Wood-pidgeons. The *Indian* wood-pidgeons are of the bigness of our tame pidgeons, with brown spots on their backs; a white belly, purple colour'd breast, and red feet; they resemble entirely our turtle-doves, or common pidgeons; live generally in the woods or in the rice-fields, and are a most delicious food; when they are tamed they will breed in our houses.

The Lory. The *Lory* bird is a bird as big as a parrot, but of a much finer colour, with a lofty round breast, cover'd with yellow feathers. The wings are green, the head black and shining, with a yellow bill. The *Indians* give sometimes 30 crowns for such a bird, because they will learn and speak several languages, and are very tame: There is another with large and long tails, sometimes three quarters of a yard long, these are blue on the back, and yellow under the belly, and commonly call'd *Kakkataws* or *Indian* ravens. Another kind there is, which is white all over, except a yellow tuft on the head, which they set upright, when they are vexed. They have also some resemblance both in shape and bigness to our magpies or blackbirds; these imitate a man's voice much more distinctly than the parrots: They are of a blueish colour, mix'd with dark blue spots and streaks, they have a yellow tuft on the head, which is black, and as smooth as velvet. 1662.

The *Yelambers* are as big as our larks, with a thick bill and red feet; their feathers are yellow, chequered with grey, they are catch'd in prodigious numbers, and sold in the markets of *Batavia*, being look'd upon as a dainty. *The Yelamber.*

The rice-sparrows are no bigger than our ordinary sparrows, and of the same colour, except that their bills are somewhat thick, with a few black feathers near the tail, and some white ones underneath on the belly; their feet are blue. They are found in such prodigious quantities, that the inhabitants are scarce able to preserve the rice from being devour'd by them. *Rice-sparrows.*

These birds properly called parrokets, are no bigger than our larks, but have a very fine green head and wings; the back underneath the wings is of a high red colour, the breast light green, and the tail of a most agreeable colour: They are found in the woods in great numbers, feed upon rice and fruits, but will not speak, being kept only for their feather's sake. *Parrokets.*

The *Indian* pullets are generally white, with long red tails, and their feet almost cover'd with feathers, and a bright red comb on the head. They are not much bigger than our largest tame pidgeons, but very well tasted. They were first transported to *Batavia* from *Siam*. They have also a kind of tame fowl with black feathers, legs and flesh, which however is not ill tasted, and accounted very wholsome: Another kind there is that have hair instead of feathers, others have their feathers turn'd towards the head, in lieu of declining backwards. *Pullets.*

About *Batavia* and many other parts of the *Indies* abundance of herons are to be seen in the low grounds; they are in bigness *Herons.*

1662. nefs the fame with our herons, with long gray feathers and black wings; they are generally feen near the water-fide, where they are looking for their prey, but build their nefts in trees; the meat is tough, and taftes much after fifh.

The jumpers. The jumpers have got their name from their continual motion from branch to branch: They are of the fame bignefs with our blackbirds, and will whiftle like them; they have a black head, wings and tail, but are white on the breaft and belly; I have feen them kept at *Batavia* with a chain to one leg for diverfion fake, and they feed them with boil'd rice. They are eafy to be tamed.

Stock doves. The ftock-doves are in fhape and bignefs like our pidgeons, but of a much finer colour; the neck and breaft is green, the reft of the body purple colour'd, and the tail and wings blue with a white edge. They are catch'd in great numbers in the woods near *Batavia*, and eat very well roafted.

The goldfinch or linnet. The goldfinches here are very agreeable for their fine colour'd feathers, being for the reft no longer than our linnets or goldfinches; their bill is pale red, the head white, the back and wings blue, the belly red, and the tail dark blue. They are taken in prodigious quantities near *Batavia*, and fometimes kept in cages: They feed upon rice.

Scorpions. At *Batavia* you fee often large fcorpions of a quarter of a yard long; but thofe of a leffer fize are fo frequent, that you can fcarce move a ftool, bench, cheft, lookinglafs or picture, without being in danger of being ftung by them, unlefs you be very careful to avoid them. The fmall ones are about a fingers length, compofed of many joints, of the thicknefs of a goofe-quill. They are yellow, fpeckled with brown ftreaks; before they have two claws, with two fharp pinchers; their tail is long, and lies turn'd upon the back, at the end of which is the fting, wherewith they poifon fuch as they touch. They have eight long legs, not unlike thofe of a creafifh. The fting of a fcorpion is accounted mortal, unlefs prevented in a little time; tho' fome are of opinion that the fcorpions in the *Indies* are not fo venomous as thofe of *Italy* and *Spain*. A fcorpion bruifed to death, or ftifled in oil, and apply'd to the wound, draws out the poifon. They fay that a radifh fliced and laid upon a fcorpion, kills him in a minute: They have alfo another ftory, *viz.* that the fcorpion is fometimes fo pefter'd with the pifmires, that he ftings himfelf to death in the head with his tail, and fo becomes a prey to the pifmires.

The thoufand-legs are about five or fix inches long, of the thicknefs of a man's finger, of a ruddy colour, and compofed of many joints and bones. They have two claws or pinchers, wherewith they wound as dangeroufly as the fcorpions; occafioning fuch violent pain, as is almoft unfpeakable: The cure is perform'd by ftifling them in oils like as with the fcorpions, and they are generally found like them, in holes, and behind old chefts or benches. 1662. *Thoufand-legs.*

Both the *Eaft* and *Weft-Indies* produce fnakes of divers fizes and colours: Among others they have a certain fort in the ifle of *Java*, not exceeding a foot in length, which are frequently met with in the fields among the grafs: They have others with large fhining fcales on the back, and their eyes fo bright, that in a fun-fhiny day you fee them at a great diftance; others are fo full of fpots, that they are terrible to behold. Befides thefe, they have another kind of fnakes much leffer than the field fnakes; thefe dwell in houfes, and feed upon flies, ants and other infects. They will ftick fo clofe to a wall or roof, as if they were immoveable, but no fooner perceive their prey, but they fhoot down all on a fudden to catch it. The tail of a fnake feparated from the body, will grow to it again. Thefe fnakes are not in the leaft pernicious, and will pafs over the bare faces of perfons fleeping in their chambers, without doing the leaft harm.

In the woods of *Java*, as likewife in the the fens and pools is found a certain fort of fnakes, or rather a kind of crocodile call'd *Legoaen* by the *Indians*; it refembles altogether a crocodile, except that it is lefs, being not above five or fix foot long, whereas the crocodiles are from 15 to 20 foot: The *Javanefe* however affirm, that thofe in the mountains are much larger. They have a knobby green fkin, but the meat is white, like that of our rabbets, and very well tafted. They have a long head, wide mouth, and a tail as long as the whole body; each leg has four paws arm'd with fharp and long claws. *Snakes.*

In the woods of *Java* are certain flying-fnakes, or rather drakes, they have four legs, a long tail, and their fkin fpeckled with many fpots; their wings are not unlike thofe of the bat, which they move in flying, but otherwife keep them almoft unperceived clofe to the body. They fly nimbly, but can't hold it long, fo that they fly from tree to tree at about 20 or 30 paces diftance. On the outfide of the throat are two bladders, which being extended when they fly, ferve them inftead of a fail; they feed upon flies and other infects: The *Javanefe* don't in the leaft account *The flying-fnake or drake.*

1662. count them poisonous, but handle them just like the common snakes, without the least danger.

Frogs. The frogs here are about the same bigness with ours; of a dark yellow colour, with brown spots: They are sold daily in the markets of *Batavia*, the *Chinese* accounting them a dainty, but eat only the hindermost parts. There is another sort of frogs in *Java* near as big as a rabbet, but are not eaten. They make a noise like the bellowing of an ox.

Fireflies. The fire-flies have got their name, because they appear in the dark shining like a light, and are catch'd by means of a fire or candle, through which they will fly till they are taken. They are about an inch broad and long, and sometimes bigger: The head, which is brown, has two small horns; the neck is red, but their hard wings brown, underneath which they have two softer wings, which they make use of in flying, and then it is you discover that shining substance, which is contained in a black bladder or their backs, which they hide with their wings whilst they are not a flying. In the rainy season they dwell in prodigious numbers among the trees, and draw their chief sustenance from the blossom. There are divers sorts of them.

Horse-flies. The horse-flies here are a most pernicious insect, which sting most furiously. They are about two inches broad and long, of a brown colour, with a yellow streak along the body. They build their nests very curiously on the roof or rafters, as the wasps do on the sprigs of trees: In these they lay their eggs and hatch their young ones. They feed upon fruits, and emit a most nauseous scent after they are kill'd.

Kakkerlakken, or Kakalakkas. The *Kakkerlakken* are so called by a corrupted name from the *Portuguese* word *Kakalakkas*, because their eggs are both in colour and smoothness like to the *Lacca*. They are much of the same bigness with the horse-flies, of a brown colour, with two long horns on the head. They both run and fly very nimbly, and are very pernicious, there being no chest or trunk so strong, but they will gnaw through it. They are also to be found in ships, tho' newly built, in their way from *Europe*, especially at the time of their passing under the line; when the lice die, these begin to appear; and in their return, as soon as they are pass'd the line again, and the lice appear, these begin to vanish by degrees. They are very pernicious to paper, linen, and woollen cloaths.

Jakalat. The *Jakalat* is a mischievous insect, but only in the lower parts of the houses, its delight being in moist grounds.

About *Batavia* you find a kind of locusts of a finger's length, but no thicker than a pen or goose-quill, distinguish'd by divers joints. They walk upon six feet, and have two small horns. The locusts here are however of divers kinds; some are yellow on the belly, with brown wings, and two horns on the head; they can leap a great way, and fly together in great numbers. There is another sort of the same shape, but green, and of a finger's length. These come sometimes in such prodigious swarms, that they darken the sky as they pass by, and devour all in those parts where they settle, so that the inhabitants are often obliged to change their habitations for want of sustenance, as it has happened frequently in *China* and the isle of *Tajowak*. 1662. *Locusts.*

The blister-drawers are so called, because when they sting they raise blisters. They are of divers sorts, different both in colour and bigness, but commonly of the length and breadth of a finger. They have very large eyes, and delight in marshy places. They are most frequent at *Batavia* in *October* and *November*. *A kind of* Spanish *flies.*

There is here a kind of hornets that have a certain claw like a pincher on the head, wherewith they pinch to that degree, that they will not let go their hold unless you cut off their heads. They are of divers sorts, bigness and shape, some being above five inches long, of a dark brown colour; they have double wings, the uppermost are hard, the undermost soft; the last they make use of in flying, the others being only for the defence of the undermost ones. They feed upon herbs, and the fruits of certain trees, which they know how to choose among all the rest. *Hornets.*

Of ants or pismires there are in *Java* and throughout all the *Indies* prodigious quantities of divers sorts; some of them are above a finger in length, of a ruddy colour, inclining to black, some with, others without wings. They are very pernicious to the fruits of the earth; and even in the houses scarce any thing can be preserved against them without a great deal of care. It is observable, that an ant meeting another with something in her mouth, will give way to her, if she be not loaden her self. *Ants or pismires.*

The gardens about *Batavia* are extremely pestered with catterpillars; they are about 5 Inches long, with long brown horns standing upright on their heads. The head and whole body is yellowish, but the wings inclining to a green spotted with yellow. They feed upon herbs and leaves like the locusts. *Catterpillars.*

This insect has got its name from the knotty composition of its body, which, as well as *Schrankels or Knobs.*

1662. as the feet is of a pale-green colour. It has two fore legs covered with a hard shell like a crab or creafish. It seems to be a kind of locust, and feeds upon greens, but can neither fly nor run very fast. There is another kind with a monstrous head and neck, and a thick body, on the hindermost part of which are two small pins like thorns. The two fore-feet are enclosed in a hard shell and of a very odd shape; it has two wings, but can scarce fly, by reason of the weight of its body. 1662.

Spiders. There are many sorts of spiders in the *Indies*, and of a very different bigness; some are above four inches long, and have very thick legs; others have eight feet, a thick speckled body, and round head with brown eyes. These have two teeth bent like hooks, wherewith they bite fiercely. I have seen toothpicks made of these teeth.

The lynx. The lynx is a fierce creature, of the bigness of a large dog, and in shape seems to participate both of that and a cat. He is of a brown colour chequer'd with red, with black streaks; his tail is very short, and the ears very black; he lives upon prey, and is extremely nimble.

Sucotyro *or* Sucotario. The *Sukotyro*, as the *Chinese* call it, is a very odd shaped beast; it is of the bigness of a large ox, with a snout like a hog, two long rough ears, and a thick bushy tail. The eyes are placed upright in the head, quite different from other beasts: On the side of the head, next to the eyes stand two long horns, or rather teeth, not quite so thick as those of the elephant: It feeds upon herbage, and is but seldom taken. Of the jackal we have given a description before.

Oxen with bunches. On the *Cape of Good-Hope*, but especially in the isle of *Madagascar*, are certain oxen with bunches upon their necks and shoulders, which being nothing but fat, is melted and used by the inhabitants like butter; but these oxen have not so great a quantity of suet about their kidneys as ours. The cows of this kind frequently bear two or three calves at a time.

The Macassar-fox. The macassar-fox has got his name from the isle of *Macassar*, where he is most found. He has an excessive long bushy tail, which stands upright, flat feet, long claws, and short ears, just as he is represented in the cut.

Apes and monkeys. There are divers sorts of apes and monkeys distinguish'd by peculiar names. Some are very small, others middle sized, and others as big as a boy of eight years of age; such a one I saw my self once at *Batavia*. In many parts of the *Indies*, where the inhabitants think it a crime to kill any living creature, they multiply to a prodigious degree, and are very tame: They

1662. They live for the moſt part in woods, and feed upon fruits. Some are green with a long beard and large eye-brow, like an ancient man: Some, call'd *Cicatic* by the *Indians*, have long buſhy tails, for which reaſon they are reckon'd by ſome among the fox kind. There is another ſort call'd *Saragoſe*, with long tails, which they carry ſtraight upright. Another ſort are called death's heads by the *Dutch*, from their pale faces. The *Suri* monkeys are in bigneſs and ſhape not unlike a ſquirrel, but of a yellow colour; they have ſhort and round ears, large eyes, and a large buſhy tail, wherewith they can cover the whole body: They can leap at a great diſtance from tree to tree, and guide themſelves with the tail ſo exactly, that they ſeem to fly.

There is a certain ſort of monkeys or apes that are not in the leaſt miſchievous; they are no bigger than a rat, but have a long tail, which they carry upright. They have a green, ſoft and woolly hair, ſomewhat inclining to a grey about the eyes, and a little white on the feet. They have ſhort ears, a ſharp mouth and brown noſe, the feet being like thoſe of an ape; but theſe are very ſcarce. Thoſe call'd *Sangwyns* are likewiſe of the bigneſs of a rat, and very nimble; their face, hands and ears are black, and the reſt of the body of a cheſnut colour, except that they have ſome dark yellow hair along the back; they have very long tails, feed upon fruits, and are very diverting. 1662.

The piſmire-eater or ants-bear. The piſmire-eater or ants-bear, is ſo call'd, becauſe he feeds chiefly upon ants: There are three ſeveral ſorts of them; the firſt is of the bigneſs of a young hog, the ſecond ſomewhat leſſer, and the third like a cat, but longer. They are all of a ruddy colour like a fox, with a long ſharp mouth, ſmall ears, and a head like that of a pig.

Stags. Abundance of deer or ſtags are found in the foreſts of the *Indies*, they are eaſily to be tamed here, ſo that they will feed among the cattle. They are generally red, ſpeckled with white, and much of the ſame bigneſs as ours. They have large ears, long legs, and are white underneath the belly. The horns of the male are wrought towards the head, and brown and very hard towards the extremities. Their fleſh is very well taſted. With the deer-ſkins a great traffick uſed to be carried on in the iſle of *Tayowan*, whilſt the *Dutch* were maſters of it; for they uſed to take many thouſands of them only for the ſkin's ſake, which were ſold to the *Japoneſe*; and ſcarce to preſerve any part of their

1662. their flesh, except the tongue, which is accounted a dainty here.

The iron-pig or porcupine. About *Batavia*, and in the woods of *Java* are abundance of iron-pigs or porcupines. They grunt like hogs, and are covered with certain painted pens or pegs like iron, whence they got their name: They are of different sizes, some of the bigness of a good large dog, but somewhat longer, and more short leg'd. They are generally brown, with a grey tuft on the head, and a mouth like a hare, with two great teeth both below and above, like a horse, the two fore-feet like those of a deer, and the hindmost like a bear. The pens or pegs are very sharp, a foot long, and checquered with black and white. When they are at rest, they lay them close to the body, but if they are vexed, they can, by contracting themselves, cast them forth with such strength, that they kill man or beast: Thus some years ago, a dead lion was found at the *Cape of Good-Hope* with a porcupine's pen sticking in his body, wherewith he had doubtless been killed. In the winter they retire into holes, where they remain without either eating or drinking. They feed upon herbs and roots, and cast their pens as other creatures do their hair. In the stomachs of some of these animals grows a certain stone, which by reason of its sudorifick quality is accounted very good in pestilential fevers; just as the stone found in the *Vesica Bilearis* or gall-bladder of the wild boars, is reputed the most sovereign remedy in that distemper called *Morderi* by the *Javanese*, and as much dreaded among them as the plague in *Europe*, because it commonly kills in a few hours time.

Tame and wild boars. There are several sorts of hogs in the *Indies*, some with, but the most without any hair; hogs flesh is accounted wholsomer and better than beef or mutton, and is by the *Chinese* prescribed even for sick persons. The wild boars feed upon what roots or fruits they can meet with; and I remember that I saw a considerable number of them swim cross the water in the isle of *Dingding* near *Malacca*, to look after provisions. In the gall-bladder of the *Indian* wild boars, grows a certain porous stone, called thence *Piedra da Puerco*, i. e. hog's stone by the *Portuguese*; it is sudorifick, and expedient in malignant distempers; they steep it in wine for twelve hours, and give the infusion to the patients; or they give the quantity of 25 grains poudered in wine. Women with child must be cautious of it, because it makes them miscarry, it being a general opinion among the *Malayan* women, that they can procure their monthly times, with only holding this stone in their hands. 1662.

Sheep. The *Javanese* sheep are much of the same bigness as ours, some being white, others pyed white and red, with short legs and little or no wool. Their meat is not so good as the *European* mutton, pork being much prefer'd before it here. The sheep have sometimes teats hanging below their throats like some of our hogs, others have such long ears that you may tie them together underneath the throat. Others have tails of 20, 30 or 40 pounds, being one lump of fat, which eats best boil'd. Some have a plain hair like our goats, others a curled wool like our sheep, and are milked like cows.

He and she goats. The goats here are not near so big as the sheep, nor is their flesh so well tasted, tho' the kids in some parts of the *Indies* afford excellent good meat. Some are white, some pyed, and have generally long hair. Others have very long ears, and horns standing upright on the head. In some places they bear three or four young ones at a time: They make cheese of their milk.

Bouffles. The Bouffles are bulkier and stronger than an ordinary ox; they have no hair, their flesh is very good, but not so juicy nor so digestible as beef, for which reason it is most used among the slaves, and other labouring people. Their horns lie close to the head; some of them are black, and, when polish'd, are very useful for several things to be made out of them. The tame bouffles are used in the sugar-mills, plough and cart: They guide them by means of a chain drawn through their nostrils: Their milk is accounted very wholsome. The wild bouffles that live in the forests are very fierce, and not easy to be taken.

Oxen and cows. Many places of the *Indies* afford oxen and cows, the flesh whereof, as well as the milk and butter, are very good; some are red, others white, others pyed, and of several other colours. Some have horns standing upright on the head, others crooked horns like ours; and others long ears hanging downwards: However, the beef is much better in some places than in others. It is generally eaten fresh, because it will scarce take salt well in this hot climate, and is not to be kept above three or four days. They bring a certain kind of oxen from *Suratte* to *Batavia*, not much bigger than a large dog; they look very fierce, notwithstanding which they are used in small carts to draw children, or any other odd thing.

Horses. The horses here are of different sorts and colours, some black, others of a chesnut

5

1662. nut colour, and others white and grey. The *Javanese* horses are not very tall, but thick and well-set, like the *Norwegian* or *Westphalian* horses, very strong and hardy, but are not near so high-spirited as the *Persian* horses that are transported from *Suratte* to *Batavia*, and excel all the rest in swiftness, courage and beauty. The *Indians* carry on their wars for the most part with foot soldiers, and preserve their horses for the draught and travelling. 1662.

Thus much of the isle of *Java* and the city of *Batavia*: We will now proceed to give an account of our return into *Holland.*

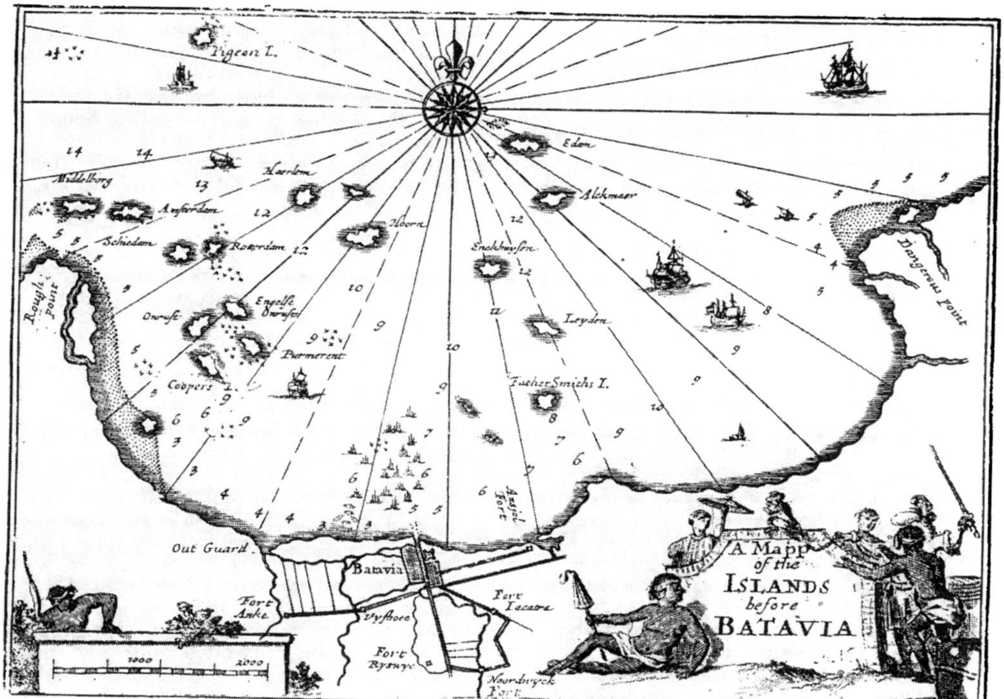

The author's return into Holland.

Every thing being got ready for our voyage, we weigh'd anchor in the road of *Batavia*, the 17th of *December* 1670, and with the land-wind, pass'd betwixt the isles to the south of *Batavia*, situate betwixt the *Ruigenhoeck* or *Rough-Point*, and *Karowan*, most of which have borrow'd their names from some places or other in the *United Provinces*; as the *Coopers-Isle*, the *Schiedam*, *Amsterdam*, *Middleburgh*, *Purmerent*, *Rotterdam*, the *Pigeon-Island*, the *Harlem*, *Hoorn*, *Enckhuysen*, *Edam*, *Alcmar*, &c. we came the same evening to an anchor near the isle call'd the *Men-eaters Island*, near which the ship called the *South-Pole* struck upon the sands, but got off again. Here a general review being taken of all the persons on board the ships, such as were found to be indebted to the company, were sent back to continue in the service 'till they had discharged their debts.

Then we set sail again, and had the 19th the point of *Bantam* to the west of us, and *Pulo Paly* to the north; but being becalm'd were forced to come to an anchor at 15 fathom water. The 20th, having received some refreshments by the *Golden-Lion* from *Bantam*, we set sail again, but the calm obliged us to come to an anchor again at 15 fathom. The 21st we continued our voyage, and had the 23d the point of *Java*, called *Krakketou* to the east-south-east, at 23 fathom water. The commodore having, by the usual signal of the white flag, summon'd all the commanders of ships aboard him, to know whether they were provided with what was necessary for so long a voyage; the *Golden-Lion* was sent back, and we had the north point of the *Princes Isle*, west to the north; and the 25th the south-point about four leagues from us.

1662. About noon the commodore went aboard and took a view of all the ships under his command, and in the afternoon set sail again: We met with several fierce but short travadoes or storms, at 7 deg. and 41 min. southern latitude. The 31st we had another most violent travado at 9 deg. 54 min. but continued not long.

Isle of Mony. The first of *January* one of our ships crew died, and we got sight of land to the south-east, which we found to be the isle of *Mony*, and that we were 64 leagues to the south-south-west of the *Princes Isle*, being forced thus far to the east by the tide; we were at the latitude of 10 deg. 29 min. The 2d we had the said isle to the south-east, and found its situation to be 52 min. more to the north than it is placed in the maps. The 3d, we were within four leagues of the said island, at 11 deg. 15 min. Hereabouts one of our ships crew was found dead in his cabin. The 6th we were at 13 deg. 40 min. and the 9th at 14 deg. 17 min. The same day Mr. *Dirk Indiik* died of a long and lingering distemper: As he had been factor and fiscal at *Suratte*, and was accounted very rich, his goods were all sealed up in the presence of the commodore and the other commanders. The next following day we made 32 leagues, and so continued our voyage with a prosperous gale till the 19th, when we found our selves at 20 deg. 54 min. of latitude, and at 105 deg. 14 min. longitude. The 26th the commodore having by the usual signal summon'd the chief officers aboard him, to adjust the difference in the compasses, and the same being found only 1 degree 33 minutes, no alteration was made therein.

The 2d of *February* we were at the heighth of 29 deg. overtaken by a most furious tempest, with thunder and lightening from the west, and had frequent travadoes till the 4th, and for many days after had very changeable weather, sometimes good, sometimes bad. The 26th with break of day we found 112 fathom depth, but saw no land: About noon we found our selves at 35 deg. 17 min. steering our course westward, the weather being very fair, we saw divers whale-fish sporting in the water, and some sea-birds, which together with the colour of the water, was a sufficient sign that we were not very far from land. The next day we found seven fathom water without seeing the land.

They discover land. The 28th very early in the morning we discovered land to the north-north-west of us, at 45 fathom depth, and the next day after sun-rising at 38, being then within three leagues of the shore, which appeared hilly and white. About noon we were at 34 deg. 36 min. the weather cold and fair. The first of *March* we found our selves at 35 deg. and steering our course to the south-east in sight of the land, which was very hilly to the north-east, found 65 fathom depth at night, in sight of a mountainous shore. The 4th we still saw land at 48 fathom water, and in the evening at 20. 1662.

Arrive at the Cape of Good-Hope. The 6th before sun-set, we saw the famous point of the *Table-Bay* of the *Cape of Good-Hope*, where we cast anchor before the fort, at eight fathom water. Here we met with three ships, *viz.* the *Crown'd-Peace*, the *Damiata*, and a yacht bound for the *Indies*; and heard the good news that the commodore *Ysbrand Gotske* did come to the cape, the last 2d of *February*, and thence continued his voyage with three ships the 24th for *Holland*. Our commodore being then sick, he sent one to the commander in chief of the cape, named Mr. *Hakkius*, to notify his arrival, and the next day went ashore himself.

The marquis de Mondeverguin arrives at the Cape. The 8th the *Mary Yacht* arrived at the cape from the isle of *Madagascar*, having on board the marquis *de Mondeverguin*, a *French* governor of *Madagascar*, and the other adjacent places under the *French* jurisdiction. He was a person of 70 years of age, and of a goodly aspect. He sent word to Mr. *Hakkius*, commander in chief of the cape, that he should be glad to come ashore, provided he might be sure of a reception suitable to his quality: However, he set sail again on a sudden, without coming ashore, perhaps by reason of the rumour that was then already spread abroad of a war betwixt *France* and the *Dutch*.

The same evening the ship called the *Spanbroeck* came into that road from *Ceylon*, with advice, that the *Cingalese* had taken up arms under their king *Radya*, and we were in the mean while not idle to provide our selves with what necessaries we could get for the prosecution of our voyage, till the 17th of *March*, when the commodore summoning all the officers aboard him, told them, that he intended to set sail the next sunday, *viz.* the 22d of *March*, without staying for the two ships we left behind, and a war betwixt us and the *French* being then much talk'd of, he ordered every body to be upon his guard, and to prepare for a vigorous defence in case of an atrack.

The 20th was spent in letting the seamen go ashore in their turn.

The 21st the goods of the before-mention'd Mr. *Indyck*, deceased were exposed to publick sale, and 13 diamonds, besides four more of an extraordinary bigness, with

3

1662. with ſome bezoar-ſtones, being found concealed in a private pocket in his breeches, the ſame were ſealed up, ſeized by the commodore as contraband goods, for the uſe of the company.

They leave the Cape of Good Hope. The 22ᵈ after dinner, the commodore having given the ſignal to ſail, to the five ſhips, the *Peace*, the *Arms of Veer*, the *Count of Breda*, *South-Pole* and *Spanbroeck*, they weighed their anchors, and after ſunſet were about two leagues and an half from the *Table-Bay*.

The 23ᵈ, a conſultation being held aboard the commodore about regulating the compaſs, and the ſame being fix'd to 3 deg. to the weſt we found our ſelves that evening at 33 deg. and about 18 leagues to the ſouth-eaſt of the *Table-Mountain*.

Sail to St. Helens *iſle.* From hence we ſteer'd our courſe to the iſle of St. *Helens*, of which we got ſight the 12ᵗʰ of *April*, at 16 deg. 44 min. without any remarkable accident.

The 13ᵗʰ with ſun-riſing we were within five or ſix leagues of the ſaid iſle, when the commodore ſummoned again all the officers aboard him, in order to conſult what courſe they ſhould take towards the *Aſcenſion* iſland.

The 24ᵗʰ we were at 4 deg. 32 min. and the 27ᵗʰ at 16 min. of ſouthern latitude, ſteering our courſe north-weſt to the weſt with an eaſterly wind and briſk gale.

They paſs the line. The next following day we were at 15 min. of northern latitude; and the 29ᵗʰ at 2 deg. 38 min. having been much peſtered with ſudden ſtorms and travadoes.

The 14ᵗʰ of *May* the *Breda* gave a ſignal as if they had ſeen land, but it proved only a refraction of the ſun-beams through the clouds. The ſea hereabouts ſeem'd in the night-time all on fire, a thing uſual in hot weather.

Se. the Braſil *voyage.* The 24ᵗʰ, at 25 deg. 29 min. we found our ſelves in the *Kroos* or *Croſs-Sea*, (ſo called from a kind of water-creſſes or ducksmeat that floats in prodigious quantity upon the ſurface of the water) and the 25ᵗʰ finding theſe ſort of herbage encreaſe, we judged our ſelves to be more eaſtward than we intended.

The 30ᵗʰ at 26 deg. 15 min. our conſtable *Mans Timmer* died, and we were ſtill much peſtered with theſe *Creſſes*, which continued the 1ˢᵗ and 2ᵈ of *June*.

We continued the ſame courſe till the 13ᵗʰ, when it being agreed to fix the compaſs 4 deg. more to the weſt, we took our courſe north to the eaſt, towards the *Dutch* coaſt.

The 15ᵗʰ being a foggy day, we diſcharged every hour a muſquet, as a ſignal to the ſhips to prevent their being ſeparated from one another.

About midnight the commodore ſent for me, and in the preſence of the maſter of the ſhip, *Henry Span*, the firſt chirurgeon, and the miniſter, told me, that finding himſelf very ill, he was reſolved to make his laſt will, which he did accordingly, recommending his affairs, and what he had of the companies in his hands, to our care. 1662.

About ſix in the morning he ſent for me again, with an intention to make ſome alterations in his teſtament, but before the clerk could finiſh it, he expired, without ſigning of it. We took care to ſummon immediately the council of war, where every thing being ſettled for the proſecution of our voyage, we diſcovered land the 29ᵗʰ to the north-eaſt at 115 fathom water. *The commodore dies.*

The 30ᵗʰ we found our ſelves over againſt the iſle of *Fulo*, and underſtood by one of their fiſher-boats, that the peace continued betwixt *France*, *England* and *Holland*, and that 14 days before, 11 ſtout ſhips paſs'd that way. *The iſle of* Fulo.

Having provided our ſelves with ſome cods, which we bought or exchanged at the rate of two pence a piece, we gave the ſignal by a cannon ſhot, to our convoy, which we expected to meet us hereabouts.

The firſt of *July* meeting a boat betwixt *Fulo* and *Hitland*, we charged the maſter thereof with the body of our deceaſed commodore, in order to his burial in *Hitland*: He had ſix crowns given him for his pains and charges, with a promiſe of ſix more, after we had received certain advice, that he had well diſcharged his truſt. About noon our two convoys, the *Middleburgh* and *Leyden* came up with us, and after the uſual ſalute, brought us freſh orders from the company.

The 2ᵈ and 3ᵈ of *July*, ſeveral of our ſeamen, and among the reſt, the quartermaſter died of the dropſy, an uſual diſtemper to thoſe that return from the *Eaſt-Indies*, and many more falling ſick daily for want of proviſions; the reſt were hardly put to it, eſpecially in our ſhip, which being leaky, four men were continually employed at the pump.

The 5ᵗʰ we advanced bravely with a very cold wind and air.

The 6ᵗʰ it was fair weather, and we had 18 fathom water.

The 7ᵗʰ it proved cold and rainy, at 16 fathom: The ſame evening the ſhip called the *Arms Vanter Veer* left us, and ſoon got out of ſight.

The 8ᵗʰ of *July* we got ſight of the *Dutch* coaſt, and the ſhip *Spanbroeck* having taken its courſe towards the *Spaniards-Gate*, we were forced to lie by till four in the

1662. the afternoon, when with turning of the tide, we made the *Texel*, where we came to an anchor the same night.

They arrive in the Texel.

The 9th Mr. *Silvius*, Mr. *Bekker*, and Mr. *Schagen* came aboard us, three directors of the company; who having given the necessary orders for the unloading of our vessels, and taken the diamonds belonging to the company into their custody, discharged the ships crew from their service; and I embark'd in a boat for *Enkhuysen*, and arrived at *Amsterdam* the 11th. Count *Maurice* of *Nassau* happening to pass at the same time through *Amsterdam* in his way over *Zealand* to *Cleves*, he sent for me; and I having shew'd him my observations and draughts of *Brasil* and the *East-Indies*, he engaged me to meet him the next day again at dinner, at the house of Dr. *William Piso*, where I took my leave of the said earl, he being just upon his departure. 1662.

Some days after I appeared in the assembly of the directors of the company, unto whom having given a satisfactory account of all my transactions, they return'd me thanks; and as a mark of their satisfaction, bestow'd upon me another factor's place; so that accordingly I undertook my third voyage to the *East-Indies*, in the ship called the *Arrow*, before the expiration of the year.

Nieuhoff *gives an account to the company.*

The third sea and land voyage of Mr. JOHN NIEUHOFF *aboard the* Arrow *to the isles of* Majotte, *upon the* African *coast of* Mosambique, *extracted from his own journals, and brought over and deliver'd by capt.* Reiner Klacson *to his brother* Henry Nieuhoff.

MR. *John Nieuhoff* having embarked aboard the *Arrow*, they pass'd by the *French* coast the 18th of *December*, and the 1st of *Jan.* 1672, at 29 deg. by the *Canary* isles, about three leagues off of *Teneriff*, where they met with the *Lion* bound for the *East-Indies*. They continued their voyage with a prosperous gale, without any remarkable accident, and passing the 4th of *Feb.* the line, and the 16th the high islands of *John Christian de Akonga* at 36 deg. 36 min. southern lat. arriv'd the 8th of *April* within sight of the *Cape of Good-Hope*, at 33 deg. 30 min. lat. and cast anchor in the *Table-Bay* the same night. Here they met with seventeen vessels, thirteen of which were bound from the *East-Indies* for *Holland*, and accordingly set sail the twenty forth. The ship the *Arrow* had aboard her a large chaloop or boat, which being taken to pieces before they left *Amsterdam*, was now set together again, for its more convenient passage along the shore of *Sofala*, *Mosambique* and the island of *Majotte*.

They come to the Cape *of* Good-Hope.

In this chaloop (unto which they gave the name of the *Bow*) they embark'd, and in company of the *Arrow* and another small vessel called the *Goldfinch*, bound for the isle of *St. Maurice*, having aboard Mr. *Huigens*, governor of that isle, set sail the 30th of *April*. The 6th of *June* being at 36 deg. 3 min. latitude, the *Goldfinch* steer'd her course towards *St. Maurice*, leaving the *Bow* and *Arrow* to prosecute their voyage towards the isle of *Madagascar*, which they got first sight of the 20th. They kept along the coast which was high and rocky, and near a large point of land found 20 fathom water at a league distance from the shore, and near it a long sand-bank. They were then at 24 deg. and being, by reason of the land wind, obliged to advance sometimes nearer the shore, sometimes to keep off at sea; they at last cast anchor at 30 fathom, whereas three leagues from the shore, they could find no bottom. The *Bow* afterwards follow'd the *Arrow*, but kept closer to the shore.

They leave the Cape *of* Good-Hope.

The twenty second they discover'd a small isle not above half a league from the shore, where the *Arrow* cast her anchor at 17 fathom; they went a fishing, and brought back along with them two canoes belonging to the inhabitants, loaden with coco-nuts and water-limons. The *Bow* being sailed before, and come to an anchor in the bay of *St. Austin* near a small isle, the *Arrow* followed her thither, and found at the mouth of the river two white points of land jetting out into the sea.

The

1672. The inhabitants brought some fruits aboard us, and Mr. *Hugo* and Mr. *Nieuhoff* went ashore the next day, to see whether they could traffick with them, but could only exchange a few slaves with them; however Mr. *Nieuhoff* catch'd abundance of fish at the mouth of the river.

They land at Madagascar.

The second of *July* the *Bow* sail'd within the mouth of the river to refit, having received some damage; they endeavour'd to catch some *Tortoises* but could not take any: About noon the captain of the *Madagascarians* came aboard us to exchange some slaves; and the seventh the *Bow* in which was Mr. *Nieuhoff*, and the *Arrow* separated, the first some leagues to the north, but were to meet again at the island of *Majotte*.

The 14th the *Bow* after 17 leagues sail was at 16 deg. 56 min. latitude within sight of the continent of *Mosambique*, and at 3 leagues distance from the shore, found 100 fathom water near a sand-bank: The next day they came within 1½ league off of the isle of *Paimibris*.

The 18th at 16 deg. 15 min. they saw white downs, and in the evening cast anchor near a sand-bank at 18 fathom, whereas at the stern of the ship there were at least 60 fathoms. The 20th they passed by a large bay, cover'd with a great sand-bank, which at low water has six fathom water. The 22[d] they pass'd betwixt the southern islands of *Mosambique*, named *St. James* and *St. Joris*, where coming to an anchor at nine fathom, they met here with a stout *Portuguese* ship at anchor behind the fort, having aboard the governor of *Goa* lately come from *Portugal* with three lesser vessels. The *Arrow* coming likewise afterwards to an anchor here, divers *Portuguese* officers came aboard us, to buy certain commodities, and about the same time three other *Portuguese* ships, one of which had the governor of *Mosambique* aboard her, arrived here from *Sofala*. It prov'd a very tempestuous day.

The first of *August* the *Bow* and *Arrow* set sail again, steering their course eastward to the isles of *Madagascar* and *Masyeleyn*. The 10th they got sight of the shore of *Madagascar* at 15 deg. 53 min. and about half a league from a round mountain cast anchor at ten fathom water. The *Bow* entred the river, and discovered two boats with masts, and divers canoes, but could not come up with them. As the wind hereabout turns every 24 hours thro' all the points of the compass, so it is easy sailing along this coast. The 12th Mr. *Nieuhoff* in the *Bow* sail'd towards the isles of *Makandari* and *Magelagie*, taking a *Madagascarian* slave along with him.

The 15th the *Bow* and *Arrow* met again, but had not been able to traffick much: They saw nine boats with four square sails pass in sight of them, and in a small river met with another boat, that furnish'd them with eight pullets, and told them, that farther to the north they might meet with fresh provisions enough. So they set sail again, and after five days came to a large bay, where they cast anchor at seven fathom. Here they were told, that it was a plentiful coast, and that *Magelagie* and the islands of *Makandari* were farther to the east. The 22[d] they came within a league of an Island, where they cast anchor at 11 fathom. The 24th Mr. *Nieuhoff* sail'd in the *Bow* up the river *Magelagie* and returning the 26th reported, that this was the river upon which *Magelagie* stood, a populous and plentiful place; that he had seen there an *English* ship, that had bought slaves there to be carried to *Barbadoes*, besides several other *Moorish* vessels trading in slaves. Hereupon Mr. *Hugo* and Mr. *Nieuhoff* went thither, and return'd the 30th. About two leagues into the country you see a high ridge of land. The 31st Mr. *Nieuhoff* carried certain commodities ashore, but could not agree about the exchange, the inhabitants offering very little, and holding their slaves at sixteen crowns a piece: however the second of *September* Mr. *Hugo* and Mr. *Nieuhoff* went ashore with some cloves, for which the king had offered some money before, but return'd unsuccessful; and the *Madagascarians* (a very malicious generation) having besides this spoil'd the ponds where we used to fetch our fresh water, they set sail again for the river *Marigando*; where they cast anchor the ninth on the east-side of the cape, and met with good fresh water on the west-side of the bay. Mr. *Hugo* and Mr. *Nieuhoff* had the good fortune to exchange some of their commodities with the king of the place, and brought back 22 slaves, 13 cows, some sheep and other provisions, of which they stood in great want. The 22[d] it being resolved to sail 36 or 40 leagues farther to the *North*; Mr. *Nieuhoff* sail'd before with the *Bow* to discover the lands and rocks, and came into the *Young Man's Bay*, where there is 10, 12 and 15 fathom water. Hence continuing their voyage, they came the 27th about noon to the point or cape of *Parmira* near one of the five islands at 13 deg. 13 min. The 29th they were near the cape of *Konquiso*, where they saw some fisher boats. The middlemost of these islands is a high, steep and unaccessible rock, which may be discovered a great way at sea. Some of the fishermen having shew'd them where their king kept his court, Mr. *Nieuhoff* set sail thither in the *Bow*, leaving the 1672.

Arrow

1672. *Arrow* in the bay, and in company with the ſhips mate, and ſome few ſeamen went aſhore, in hopes to exchange ſome of his commodities; but on the 7th the *Arrow* was much ſurprized to ſee the *Bow* making towards them, and with two cannon ſhot to give the ſignal of diſtreſs. They ſent out their boat to meet them, which returning with the maſter of the *Bow*, gave an account, that Mr. *Nieuhoff* being gone aſhore with ſome of the company in the bay of *Antegoa*, or *Ant Oſy Sambo*, by ſome ſtyled the *Murtherers Bay*, to traffick, was not returned, and that therefore the *Bow*, after a ſtay of three whole days, had weighed her anchors, and ſet ſail again without them. It was concluded on all hands, that the *Bow* ought to return thither, but Mr. *Hugo* alledging that having at firſt no more than ſix months proviſions, they would be in great danger of being ſtarved, if they tarried any longer here, he inſiſted upon returning to the cape firſt, which they did accordingly, and ſet ſail the ſame afternoon at 25 and 30, and again at 20 and 25 fathom water. In the evening they paſs'd near a great ſand-bank ſouth to the weſt, and north to the eaſt, of the biggeſt of the three iſlands near the cape of *Koaquiſo*, about three leagues from the ſaid iſle, and the northern point and the great iſle of *Nauſby*.

This was the end of Mr. *John Nieuhoff*, who had ſpent ſo many years in viewing the *Weſt* and *Eaſt-Indies*, and conſequently deſerved a better fortune. What *Hugo* alledged, concerning their ſcarcity of proviſions, was indeed true enough; but on the other hand, it is unqueſtionable, they needed not to have beſtow'd much time in looking after him. The *Bow* and *Arrow* proſecuted their voyage, and on the 8th found themſelves at 12 deg. 40 min. latitude, having the weſt cape of *St. Sebaſtian* ſix leagues to the north-eaſt. The next 1672. following day they came in ſight of a ſmall iſle full of trees, about three leagues from the cape of *St. Sebaſtian*, near which place being toſs'd to and fro by tempeſts and contrary winds, they were reduced to that extremity, that they were forced to live upon a ſpoonful of rice 24 hours: So that after having endured a great deal of miſery, and loſt many of their men, both the *Bow* and *Arrow* return'd to the *Cape of Good-Hope* the 17th of *December*, where Mr. *Hugo* met but with an indifferent reception, and the maſter of the *Bow* was caſhier'd for having not tarried longer near the place where Mr. *Nieuhoff* went aſhore. The firſt of *Jan.* 1673, the *Bow* and *Arrow* being provided with ſufficient proviſions, ſet ſail again, the firſt for the bay where they had left Mr. *Nieuhoff*, the ſecond for the iſle of *St. Maurice*, whither ſhe was to carry Mr. *Hugo*. After their parting at ſea, no news was heard of the *Bow* for a long time after, till at laſt it was diſcovered that the ſhips crew mutinied and ſold the veſſel to the *French* at *Moſambique*; ſo that it remains uncertain, whether any of them had any intelligence concerning Mr. *Nieuhoff*. At the requeſt of his brother, Mr. *Henry Nieuhoff*, the directors of the chamber of *Amſterdam* diſpatch'd, the 2[d] of *May* 1676, the yacht called the *Voerhout* from the *Cape of Good-Hope* to the place where Mr. *Nieuhoff* went aſhore; which returning to the ſaid cape the 20th of *September* with 250 ſlaves, brought no farther account than that they had ſeen the king of the place, and that he had declared to them, that he knew nothing of the matter; ſo that it is very probable that Mr. *Nieuhoff* and his company were at their firſt landing maſſacred by the barbarous inhabitants.

THE